Atlas of Ancient Archaeology

MAPS AND PLANS BY
John Flower
DRAWINGS BY
Dr Vincenzo Di Grazia

CONTRIBUTORS

Africa	Sonia Cole
England	Gale de G. Sieveking
British Isles other than England	Dr George Eogan
France	Ann de G. Sieveking
Germany and the Netherlands	Dr Raymond Newell
Scandinavia	David Liversage
Eastern Europe	Doc. dr Bogdan Rutkowski
Iberia	Dr H. N. Savory
Central Mediterranean	David Trump
Greece and the Aegean	Dr Frank Stubbings
Crete	Jacquetta Hawkes
Anatolia and Soviet Armenia	Professor Seton Lloyd
Egypt	Barry Kemp
Mesopotamia	Professor David Oates
Bahrain and the Arabian Gulf	Geoffrey Bibby
Iran	Michael Roaf
Syria, Lebanon and Palestine	Dr K. Prag
India	Professor Stuart Piggott
South East Asia	Professor William Watson
North America	Dr J. D. Jennings
Mesoamerica	Dr Warwick Bray
South America	Dr Norman Hammond

EDITED BY
JACQUETTA HAWKES

Atlas of Ancient Archaeology

HEINEMANN · LONDON

© Rainbird Reference Books Limited 1974

Designed and produced by
Rainbird Reference Books Limited
Marble Arch House, 44 Edgware Road, London W2
and published by
William Heinemann Ltd
15 Queen St, Mayfair, London W1X 8BE
London · Melbourne · Toronto ·
Johannesburg · Auckland

First published 1974

House Editor: Peter Faure
Designer: George Sharp
Indexer: F. T. Dunn

Text setting, origination, printing and
binding by Butler & Tanner Limited, Frome, England

SBN 0 434 31405-6

Contents

Acknowledgments

I should like to thank the Society of Antiquaries of London and particularly its Librarian and also the London University Institute of Archaeology for the patient help they gave in the work on the illustrations.

Note. The names of sites which have their own entries are set in SMALL CAPITALS when they first occur in the Introduction or in other entries.

INTRODUCTION

Now that we have all shared in a moon's eye view of our little Earth it has become more nearly inevitable to treat its history as a whole. Looking at that blue and white ball, that prettily marbled bubble, it seems easy to imagine its continents and islands drifting gently and freely through the seas. Then it is not too difficult to envisage that last moment of astronomical time, that mere twinkle of a star, during which men spread about those continents, sailed to those islands, carrying the irresistible forces of mind into every part.

Ideally one would like a world atlas to follow this human epic with all its marvellous episodes as the continuous, interrelated whole which in fact it was. Even if it could be the life's work of a genius, or the creation of an editor and contributors of extraordinary capacities and virtues, such an ideal volume would still be an impossibility. Our knowledge is both insufficient and too much fragmented.

It might even be said that in this actual volume we have turned right away from the ideal of continuity and coherence. I thought it best (and the publishers agreed) to allow the individual contributors as much freedom as possible in deciding how to present their regions. It will be found that there is considerable variety of treatment in texts, maps and drawings alike. This may be partly due to the individual methods and outlook of the contributors, but it has also been caused by the diversity of the archaeological material in different regions and periods. For example where large numbers of relatively simple monuments are involved – such as megalithic tombs or rock engravings – it may be best to present them as a group. Where great buildings, cities, ceremonial centres and other famous sites are the subject, then each will have its own description.

Again, there is a vast difference in size between the regions, and in particular it might appear that relative to other continents, Europe has so much more space in the Atlas than on the globe that a strong bias of interest must be manifest. No doubt there would be some shift in balance if the Atlas were being prepared in another place, but I find this more nearly inevitable than it is objectionable. The solid justification is that western and southern Europe is very rich in ancient monuments and has enjoyed generations of men eager to explore, record and conserve them. In other equally favoured regions, such as the Nile and Tigris–Euphrates valleys, Mesoamerica and Peru the space allowance is comparably generous.

The fact that wealth of ancient monuments is a necessary qualification for generous treatment in the Atlas leads on to a final editorial point. This volume has been compiled partly, perhaps primarily, for students of archaeology and ancient history, but it is also intended for use by travellers. For this reason the monuments chosen for individual description and illustration are all sufficiently substantial and visually interesting to be worth a visit. Some, perhaps, would not appeal to hurrying tourists, but to the interested traveller, yes.

While it is true that there is some diversity in the method of presenting the seventeen regions into which the continents have been divided, it is not true that the ideal of coherence, the attempt to see the ancient human world as a whole, has been evaded. The regional maps, and still more the general Introductions that go with them, provide the wider cultural background for the selected sites. Here the authors can indroduce elements in the cultural history of their regions that may be important but have left no conspicuous monuments behind them. Moreover taken all together the general Introductions do provide at least a jigsaw picture of the ancient world. It is the editor's present duty to try to give the outline sketch that will serve as a key for fitting the pieces together.

No one who reads newspapers can fail to know that there is now convincing evidence that the first steps in human evolution (the emergence of the hominid family) took place in Africa south of the Sahara. It seems that between four and three million years ago when the warm climate of the Pliocene Age was giving way to the much colder Pleistocene, primates in sub-Saharan Africa were evolving into the earliest 'men' or hominids, represented by several species all classified under the genus of *Australopithecus*. During the earlier part of the Pleistocene a progressive hominid strain had evolved to a species considered to be worthy of the genetic label of *Homo*. This *Homo habilis* may well have been the first stone tool *maker*, the earlier Australopithecines having been content to use natural objects, particularly bone and teeth. He was a little fellow, averaging about four feet (1·2 m) in height, but had a relatively large brain of about 700 cc, and is thought to have dominated, perhaps hunted and eaten, the surviving Australopithecines. It also appears probable that *Homo habilis* provided the ancestral stock of *Homo erectus*, the human type (formerly called *Pithecanthropus*) that became dominant during the middle phase of the Pleistocene between about half and quarter of a million years ago. This was also the period that saw the development of the culture known as Acheulean, in which tool making reached a far higher standard, the hand axe with its carefully formed point and cutting edge being the most characteristic among a number of more or less standardized implements.

Although the evidence for the direct evolution of the Acheulean from the roughly sharpened pebbles associated with *Homo habilis* no longer seems as clear as once it did, it is still thought most likely that this important advance in skill was made in east Africa, probably by men of *Homo erectus* breed. It is therefore appropriate that such crucial opening stages in human history should be represented in this Atlas principally by the African region. At OLDUVAI GORGE (p. 17) almost the whole story can be followed in the successive strata, and at OLORGESAILIE (p. 18) is an Acheulean encampment uniquely preserved and displayed. KALAMBO FALLS (p. 19) carries us on through later phases of the Stone Age.

In fact, of course, early hominids did not remain confined to Africa. *Homo erectus* was indeed first recognized in Asia in the long-famous skulls of Java and Peking man, and in Europe in the Mauer jaw of Germany. The caves of Chou-k'ou-tien where Peking man lived, hunted deer and other game, and used fire even while his tools were still primitive, would certainly have found a place in the Atlas had they not been largely quarried away.

Before long the Acheulean culture, which had been developing further south, was carried throughout north Africa and then north-westward through Europe where it reached as far as south-eastern England, and north-eastward into Palestine and on to Mesopotamia and southern India. The hand-axe people never penetrated northern India or further east where the rough flake type of implement survived in use for an immensely long time.

What is so remarkable about the Acheulean hand-axe makers for the cultural-cum-geographical concern of this Atlas is the immensity of the area they came to occupy. Although there were, of course, many regional differences in the range of tools, and probably also in other cultural traits and ways of life of which we can have no knowledge, the fact remains that the hand axe itself, which was for such an immense stretch of time man's highest achievement in tool making, was made and developed into more and more elegant and efficient shapes, over almost the entire African continent and from southern India across the whole of southern Asia and Europe to southern England.

There are no Acheulean sites in the whole of this great Eurasian territory worthy to set beside African Olorgesailie, but we shall come across very late elements of the Acheulean tradition in the caves of MOUNT CARMEL (p. 197).

Acheulean implements have seldom been found with human fossils, but at Olduvai they had evidently been made by *Homo erectus* and probably much of their diffusion and development was in the hands of men of this type. However, in a gravel pit at Swanscombe in the Thames valley (map p. 25) the skull of a man much further evolved towards our own species in brain size and skull form was found in an Acheulean context. Another similar 'progressive' contemporary is known from Germany (Steinheim).

These human events of the Old Stone Age have to be seen against the great climatic fluctuations of the Pleistocene Age, which in the northern hemisphere were manifest by the four glacial phases when, at its greatest extent, ice covered a third of the land area and the sea level fell sharply. The Swanscombe and Steinheim men had lived in the long warm period between the second and third of these glacials: by the time the last glaciation was building up about 70,000–100,000 years ago human evolution had produced some races already acceptable as *Homo sapiens*, but others under the bitter, harsh conditions prevailing gave rise to the true Neanderthal men, apparent 'throwbacks' in that they had heavy brow ridges, massive and chinless jaws, clumsy limbs. Nevertheless, these Neanderthalers, (whom we shall encounter on Mount Carmel and in England, France and Germany) had large brains and are in fact the earliest known human beings to have thoughts that led them to bury their dead in graves provided with food and implements.

While large numbers of Neanderthalers and their distinctive Mousterian culture have come to light all round the Mediterranean, throughout much of Europe and eastward as far as Uzbekistan, the contemporary history of *Homo sapiens* remains bafflingly obscure. What is certain is that from about 35,000 years ago Neanderthal man as a recognizable breed disappeared while men of our own species, fully evolved *Homo sapiens*, appeared in many parts of south-west Asia, north Africa and Europe, using skilfully made specialist tools and weapons. During the second part of the last glaciation (which itself was marked by considerable climatic fluctuations) these hunters created the magnificent painting and sculpture of the French and Spanish caves. But where did our sapient ancestors develop their high hunting cultures? It seems that in this late Pleistocene period the centres of human progress had shifted from Africa into Eurasia. There are signs of such cultures emerging in south-west Asia (once again see Mount Carmel) and at present it is thought most likely that this was the formative area. Yet so uncertain is the evidence that a good authority has only been able to say that it lay 'somewhere between Atlantic Europe and Inner Asia'. So little do we know about the approach to one of the great turning points of our global history – for this the achievements of the advanced Upper Palaeolithic hunters undoubtedly were. Not only were these the first men of the highest mental capacities, able to express their new imaginative powers in art, in the dance and no doubt also in oral literature and the use of musical sound (bone pipes), but they were also dynamic. Culture change was immensely accelerated and diversified, with many groups developing their own specialized forms. Undoubtedly the various cave dwellers of western Europe from the Aurignacians to the Magdelenians had the supreme achievements both in art and ingenious tool-making, but there was also great dynamism in the Gravettians who seem to have created their culture in southern Russia and eastern and central Europe, but who extended as far east as Siberia. Theirs are some of the earliest known substantial man-made dwellings, they were successful mammoth hunters (MEZHIRICH p. 78), and their famous 'mother goddess' figurines probably represent an advanced religious cult.

Energy and adaptability also made this age between about 35,000 and 10,000 BC one of the great periods of human expansion. In Europe hunters were able to push northward into Scandinavia as the ice sheets retreated. Meanwhile the earliest settlement of the Americas was taking place – by 20,000 BC if not before (p. 224 and 236), immigrants being able to cross by the landbridge that then linked Siberia with Alaska. The settlement of Australia, which had probably begun by 20,000 BC, was more remarkable still, for although at that time of low sea levels the sea passages were much shorter than today, migrants had to make crossings between Indonesia and New Guinea. In Australia, their descendants were to maintain the hunting way of life until the arrival of Europeans – and have not altogether abandoned it yet.

About 10,000 years ago the rapid onset of warmer climatic conditions was having a drastic effect on the human environment throughout much of the northern hemisphere. In Europe north of the Alps and Pyrenees, country which in glacial conditions had been open steppe and tundra became forested, and the huge game herds on which the advanced Palaeolithic hunters had lived dwindled away, or, like the reindeer, retreated northward. In north Africa, including the Sahara and some parts of south-west Asia, on the other hand, what had been grasslands became desiccated.

This period after the last glaciation, when the various nunting peoples were adjusting to new conditions, is widely referred to as the Mesolithic, that is to say the Middle Stone phase between the Palaeolithic age of the hunters and the Neolithic of the first stone-equipped farmers. In Africa, however, we shall find that a different nomenclature is used.

Western Europe had undoubtedly seen the highest attainments of hunting man, and even in the new, more difficult forest condition the Mesolithic hunters showed great ingenuity in adapting their way of life by increased fishing and food gathering and a very much greater use of wood. However it was hardly possible for them to take the next big step in human history, partly owing to the forest environment, more because western Europe lacked the wild grasses and the wild sheep and goats most suitable for domestication.

Ideal conditions for the development of mixed farming and the large settlements and more complex societies that went with it existed among Mesolithic peoples in the Near and Middle East. Their territories largely coincided with those of the wild ancestors of emmer wheat and barley and of sheep and goats. It was in just these regions that the world's first farming communities were established, that is to say at the eastern end of the Mediterranean and from Anatolia (Turkey) through northern Iraq to Iran and Turkestan. In the hill and piedmont country of this wide zone there was adequate rainfall and light soils suited to the digging stick and hoe. There, something like 11,000 years ago, the pioneers seized the opportunities nature offered. With the Natufians of Mount Carmel (still essentially in a Mesolithic state of culture) we shall meet the initial enterprise of reaping and grinding wild grain on a large scale and at Jericho their descendants living in a small fortified town by the 7th millennium BC. At ÇATAL HÜYÜK in Anatolia (p. 139) we come to a far larger town where by 6000 BC the inhabitants were building good houses and elaborate public shrines. We shall also see the rise of agricultural settlements on the foothills round the head of the Tigris–Euphrates valley and in western Iran where they were flourishing by 7000 BC. Houses were usually built of mudbrick, and with their frequent decay and replacement, villages and towns formed mounds or 'tells', their accumulated layers sometimes representing thousands of years of occupation. The craft of potting, unknown in the very earliest settlements, was spreading by the 6th millennium BC.

From this wide territory where men first settled down to a farming life, the Neolithic economy spread eastward and westward. There were certainly agricultural villages in India by the 5th millennium and possibly before (p. 206) and already by the 4th millennium a highly developed Neolithic culture existed in northern China. In the south of China and Japan, however, although families were living in large settled communities and had practised the craft of potting from as early as the 7th millennium, they did not adopt farming but lived on for thousands of years as fishermen and hunters (p. 66).

It was inevitable that farming economy should also spread to the west. The shores of the Aegean and the Balkans were easily accessible from Anatolia; north of the Black Sea, steppe country offered no obstacles to the spread of agriculture up the Danube valley into the vast plain of Hungary and on into western Europe. In the Balkans the way of life of farming communities could be similar to that of Near Eastern cradle lands as is shown in numbers of small tells. Further to the north and west farming had to be adapted to the very different climate and to local traditions. Dating is at present uncertain, but mixed farming had been adopted in eastern Europe by the 6th millennium BC and had reached the west by the end of the 5th. In Britain, by then an island, the earliest Neolithic settlements appear to date from the middle of the 4th millennium.

Parallel with these transcontinental routes were the coastal seaways of the Mediterranean. Mixed farming was being introduced to Italy by about 6000 BC and the Iberian peninsula during the following millennium (p. 85). The diffusion of the massive megalithic tombs on which Neolithic communities from Iberia to Scandinavia were to lavish so much labour probably owed much to these Mediterranean seaways and their extensions along the Atlantic coasts. Megalithic architecture, seen at its best first in the great passage graves of Brittany, Ireland and Shetland, and rather later in STONEHENGE, AVEBURY and other stone circles, has left us the most striking monuments of the earlier prehistoric past of western and northern Europe. There is nothing to compare with them before the hillforts, oppida and other military works of the Iron Age.

Meanwhile, in the arc of upland country where farming had begun, villagers developed their cultural life, making exquisite painted pottery and beginning to use the copper that was present in their native hills. Yet this terrain was not suitable for the next momentous change in human life, the growth of cities. Instead this was to be initiated in Mesopotamia, the great tract of valley and flood plain formed by the Tigris and Euphrates. Peoples from the adjacent uplands moved down into the upper valley, where rainfall was sufficient for grain cultivation, and formed flourishing villages, but it was in the wide, potentially fertile plain of Sumer that settlers, apparently coming from the Iranian uplands to the north, created the world's first truly urban civilization. Struggling to clear and drain reedbeds and swamps, and gradually to establish irrigation in an arid land, they were able to raise so much wheat and barley, pasture such large flocks and herds, that their numbers could multiply.

Settlements such as ERIDU, URUK and UR (pp. 171, 172, 173) grew into townships and then, by the middle of the 4th millennium, into populous cities dignified by monumental temples. In another 500 years Sumeria was divided into city states with powerful royal courts and priesthoods. These rulers employed a variety of skilled craftsmen, importing metals and precious stones from the hill country. They also invented writing to cope with the administration of so much wealth. Bronze Age civilization had taken wing.

The subsequent history of how the centres of civilized power gradually shifted northward and passed from Sumerians to Semites, until at last the Assyrians became the most powerful people of the ancient world is told in its place (p. 170). Meanwhile Bronze Age civilization was having a parallel but different evolution in Egypt where small farming villages had been established by 5000 BC. The swift rise of Egyptian civilization was furthered by contacts with Mesopotamia, but it immediately created its own distinctive form. In about 3100 BC Lower and Upper Egypt, the Delta lands and the Valley, had been united, and some four to five centuries later this Early Dynastic or Archaic period was followed by the amazingly creative age of the Old Kingdom with its noble art and its pyramid building. While Mesopotamia was constantly harassed by mountain folk coming down from the north east and Semites drifting in from the Arabian deserts, the Nile valley was relatively secure, enabling its people to maintain their ideal of changelessness for well over two thousand years. Asiatics did, however, arrive in sufficient numbers to add to the social upheavals that ended the Old Kingdom, while others, the Hyksos, made a more definite conquest at the end of the Middle Kingdom. When the Hyksos were expelled, the powerful Egyptian Pharaohs of the New Kingdom adopted an imperial policy, seeking to prevent further incursions by controlling the small states that had been established in Palestine and Syria. Asia may be said to have counter-attacked when the Assyrians conquered and briefly ruled Egypt in the 7th century BC.

Rather as the swift rise of Egyptian civilization was stimulated by Asian contacts, the Minoan civilization of Crete owed much to a maritime trade that brought technical skills and other cultural influences from Anatolia, Syria and Palestine and directly from Egypt itself. The Cretans digested them and produced their own brilliantly individual culture. In the high days of the Old Kingdom the whole eastern Mediterranean and the Aegean flourished in what might today be called a co-prosperity sphere. This led on to the full Minoan civilization in Crete with its elaborate palaces and exquisite art, which in turn was to have a dominating influence on the Mycenaean culture of the mainland.

Although many cultural advances, such as the efficient manufacture of bronze and the ability to feed more people living in larger settlements, were to develop among other European peoples, particularly along the Mediterranean (pp. 85, 96) and in the Balkans, they did not succeed in making the next advance to urban society, literacy and other attainments proper to fully civilized living. This was to be left to the colonizing and imperial enterprises of classical Greece and Rome.

Meanwhile far to the east of the Mesopotamian cradle of civilization a third great river valley followed the Trigris–Euphrates and Nile as the seat of an urban civilization founded on irrigation farming. This was the Indus valley of north-west India. At present no true formative stage of the Indus civilization, such as is known for the Egyptian and Sumerian, has come to light: it appears fully mature round about the middle of the 3rd millennium BC. Except for the fact that the villagers and small-town folk of Baluchistan and the hill country to the north were like the Indus citizens in growing wheat and breeding zebu cattle, it has not been possible to prove much connection between them; nor is the nature of the relationship with Sumeria well understood. At the present time it is the fashion to lay emphasis on independent development at the expense of diffusion, but it cannot reasonably be doubted that the Indus civilization was not in some way related to the Sumerian that had already been flourishing for so many centuries. The Persian Gulf made an easy seaway between the two valleys that was certainly used by traders in the later 3rd and earlier 2nd millennia BC. We shall find the great entrepôt and watering place on this route at BAHRAIN (p. 186). There were also overland routes by way of Iran, which must have maintained at least indirect contacts between these two great river-valley civilizations of the Bronze Age.

The Indus civilization was in decline by about 1700 BC, perhaps due to flooding and other local conditions. Yet it still appears probable, in spite of chronological difficulties, that its final destruction was due to the invasion of the north west of the subcontinent by the Indo-European ('Aryan') warrior peoples who were to play so great a part in subsequent Indian history. The earliest record of their language (and of their history) is in the *Rigveda*, composed after 1500 BC, from which classical Sanskrit was to emerge. We shall find archaeology trying to track these colourful Aryans by means of a sober Grey Ware culture (p. 208).

The obscure question of the expansion of Indo-European languages and of the various groups of peoples who spoke them must be discussed before closing this attempt at a unified view of the prehistory and early history of the Old World. It is now widely agreed that peoples speaking related languages, much concerned with cattle raising and using horse-drawn wagons and chariots to give them mobility in peace and war, radiated out from home lands lying in steppe country north of the Black Sea between the Carpathians and the Caucasus. They had some knowledge of metallurgy and, when settled, raised cereal crops.

What caused their migrations southwards, eastwards and to the west is uncertain, but the fact that in the centuries on either side of 2000 BC they caused upheavals across the Old World from Europe to India is well enough established. We shall meet with Indo-European peoples, or at least peoples on the move under Indo-European leaders, in the Hittites of Anatolia, the Hurrians who disturbed Mesopotamia and the Aryans already seen sweeping across Iran to India. We shall find the Greeks thrusting down among the old Mediterranean stock in Greece (particularly at LERNA p. 117) and Italic speaking peoples in Italy, while in the remoter parts of Europe the spread of horse-driving, battle-axe wielding warriors similarly came to upset the old order and dominate its farming communities. Complex and uncertain though the evidence is, these and later movements must be connected with the development of the Celtic, Germanic and Slav peoples and their languages. The Romance tongues of French and Spanish were, of course, second-stage Indo-European, deriving from the Latin of the Roman Empire.

It must be remembered that while the scanning eye of history inevitably focuses on regions where high cultures rose and fell or where important historical movements took place, there were always other regions where men continued with simple farming essentially little changed from that of Neolithic times, or with the still more primitive hunting, fishing or food-gathering economies. These quietly efficient but non-developing cultures were most conspicuous in the Arctic zone of the far north of Eurasia and in Africa. Unambitious folk such as maintained these cultures do not normally leave conspicuous monuments behind them, but some were admirable artists. It is through this talent that we shall meet them – in the rock carvings of Scandinavia (p. 69) and in the Bushman art of southern Africa (p. 23).

This same extreme unevenness in the rate of cultural advance is perhaps even more striking in the New World. There the areas where high civilization arose were relatively more limited, while in vast territories simple ways of life remained little changed through the millennia. It is to the Americas, last seen receiving their first human settlement during the final Ice Age (p. 224), that we must now turn. Because their historical pattern was less complex than those of the Old World they need only brief discussion here; the whole story is clearly told in the three Introductions to North America, Mesoamerica and South America.

The first human immigrants having entered America by the Bering Strait route (p. 224) their successors extended gradually over the vast new land. They had reached South America by 10,000 BC and the extreme south within another millennium. Meanwhile a life dependent on hunting big game, including mammoth in North and Mesoamerica, had come to prevail over most of the continent. In many ways it can be likened to that of the late Palaeolithic hunters of Eurasia, though so far as we know no one had time for the visual arts. The first tentative steps towards agriculture seem to have been taken in Mexico during the 7th millennium BC, but for a very long time wild plants remained more important than cultivated. By the 3rd millennium, however, what was to be the standard form of New World cultivation, based on maize, beans and squash, had been developed.

In the southern subcontinent it was in the fertile coastal valleys watered by rivers coming down from the Andes that horticulture first flourished, with beans, squash and various tropical plants preceding the growing of maize – which was probably introduced from Mexico. Sedentary cultivation was well established here by about 2500 BC and soon extended throughout the highlands of Columbia, Ecuador, Peru and Bolivia as well as the coasts of Ecuador, Peru and Chile.

So by the last millennium BC when the great Bronze Age civilization of Egypt and Mesopotamia were in decline and the Assyrians were to dominate a much-changed, iron-using Old World, the various peoples of South and Mesoamerica were still only advancing (with the Olmecs in the lead) towards their own age of high civilization which came with the early centuries of our era. The various cultures and art styles that flowered in South America before the Inca Empire established its rule over almost all the highland and coastal areas of sedentary cultivation named above, will be found in their proper place (p. 256). So will the history of Olmecs, Toltecs, Maya, Aztecs and others in Mesoamerica. Here it is appropriate to compare the highest achievement of the New World with the Bronze Age civilizations of the Old – with which they are partly analogous. Although the farming base was very different owing to the lack of cattle, sheep and pigs (for which llama and guinea pigs were a poor substitute) the all-powerful ruling theocracies, their temples, palaces, huge temple mounds and ceremonial centres, their love of gold, all find much earlier parallels in Egypt and Mesopotamia. Among the civilized peoples, the Maya certainly came nearest with their hieroglyphic writing (while the Inca remained illiterate) and their passion for mathematics and astronomy. On the other hand, as is well known, there were large gaps in the technology of the New World peoples: they never invented the plough, nor the wheel for transport or potting. Above all they were so backward in metallurgy that the soldiers who confronted the Spaniards were still armed with stone weapons.

In North America, meanwhile, the step to full civilization was never taken. In the Archaic period efficient food-gathering and hunting economies prevailed throughout the subcontinent. Then after about 1000 BC influences from Mexico, perhaps accompanied by small-scale immigration, introduced maize growing and settled cultivation to both the south east and the south west. By the 1st millennium AD there were sizeable townships with modest ceremonial buildings in both regions. But from that point the tribal societies failed to advance, for what reasons it is difficult to judge. In the south west they were past their peak before the European conquest. Yet anyone looking at those wonderful little towns built into the cliffs (p. 231), or at such a highly Mexicanized settlement as SNAKETOWN, can see how near the Hohokam and Pueblo peoples came to sharing the civilized urban life of their southern neighbours.

The archaeological history of the New World has one great advantage for the editor of this atlas: it can be ended fairly precisely with the Spanish and other European conquests. For the Old World it has been so difficult to fix terminal points for the many regions that inconsistencies are inevitable. In general the policy has been to stop short of monuments that can be said to belong substantially to the present world. Thus no Buddhist, no Christian, no Islamic monuments are included. No classical Greek or Roman sites have been admitted either, partly for the same reason, partly for the more practical one that several good classical atlases already exist.

A very few purely archaeological sites of outstanding interest have been included although in actual date they fall beyond the general terminus of their region. Thus, for example, the late 10th-century AD Viking settlement of Trelleborg has been allowed a place. Critics may well question these omissions and selections. An editor can only ask for tolerant recognition of the fact that it is unwise to divide the monuments of human history by straight chronological fences.

AFRICA

The vast expanses of grasslands and open woodlands in tropical Africa provided an ideal environment for the first hominids when they emerged from the forests. These same areas, with their huge populations of herbivores, were exploited by hunter-gatherers throughout the Stone Age.

The first undoubted hominids, the Australopithecines, lived in the Transvaal and Botswana in South Africa and also in East Africa during the late Pliocene and early Pleistocene. Fossil hominids have been found at more than 70 sites in East Africa (see p. 16), stretching from the Omo valley north of Lake Rudolf to the Serengeti plains in Tanzania. The Rift Valley with its chain of lakes was associated with volcanic eruptions. Australopithecines, and later men, camped near the lakes, and lake sediments and volcanic tuffs preserved their bones and enabled them to be dated. The oldest is a jaw five million years old from Lothagam in northern Kenya. Numerous specimens from Omo fall into the three to two and a half million years range; while those from Koobi Fora east of Lake Rudolf, as well as stone artifacts, are more than two million years old.

In Africa, the Palaeolithic and Mesolithic are divided into the Earlier, Middle and Later Stone Age (E.S.A., M.S.A. and L.S.A.). During the E.S.A., the Australopithecines were succeeded by *Homo habilis* (p. 17) and by *Homo erectus*, whose remains have been found at OLDUVAI GORGE (Tanzania), Ternifine (Algeria) and Sidi Abderrahman (Morocco). The first human culture, the Oldowan, was followed by the Acheulean which, according to potassium-argon dates from Olduvai and Peninj (Lake Natron), began about 1.4 million years ago. The hand axes and cleavers so characteristic of this culture must have been efficient for cutting up the carcases of large animals and their profusion at Olduvai and OLORGESAILIE is unrivalled anywhere in the world.

The E.S.A. was a period of cultural uniformity all over the continent. Regional specialization began with the M.S.A., perhaps 70,000 years ago. Hunters who followed the Acheuleans in the more open country of southern and eastern Africa adopted one kind of tool kit (Fauresmith, followed by Stillbay); those who for the first time penetrated the forest fringes developed others (Sangoan and Lupemban), with many wood-working tools. In the Sahara, which was well watered throughout much of the Stone Age, there was another local culture (the Aterian) which included tanged spearheads.

Homo sapiens may have appeared 130,000 years ago, judging by a thorium–uranium date for two skulls from the Omo valley. More modern-looking skulls from Kanjera in western Kenya are undated but were probably contemporary with an Acheulean industry there. The makers of the early M.S.A. cultures in sub-Saharan Africa were the heavy-browed 'Rhodesian man' (*Homo sapiens rhodesiensis*), whose remains are known from Broken Hill (Zambia), Lake Eyasi (Tanzania) and Hopefield, Saldanha Bay (Cape Province).

North Africa has always belonged more to the Mediterranean than to Africa, and here the contemporary of Rhodesian man was Neanderthal man. His bones have been found at Jebel Ighoud (Morocco) and other sites and his typical Mousterian industries are especially well represented in the long stratified sequence at the cave of Haua Fteah in Cyrenaica.

Several sites in sub-Saharan Africa also have a long sequence of occupation floors, such as the Cave of Hearths (Transvaal), Montagu Cave (Cape) and KALAMBO FALLS in Zambia. At such sites it is possible to see how M.S.A. cultures evolved and were replaced by regional variants of the L.S.A. This began more than 20,000 years ago, according to recent radiocarbon dates from Rose Cottage Cave (Orange Free State) and Border Cave (Ingwavuma) (Natal). The tempo of innovation now speeded up: the bow and arrow was invented and microlithic tools, often hafted, were widely used.

L.S.A. skeletons in South Africa are Bushman-like, but larger and with bigger skulls. In other parts of Africa, forerunners of modern peoples can be recognized somewhat later, from about 10,000 BC onwards. The first known Negro skeleton comes from Iwo

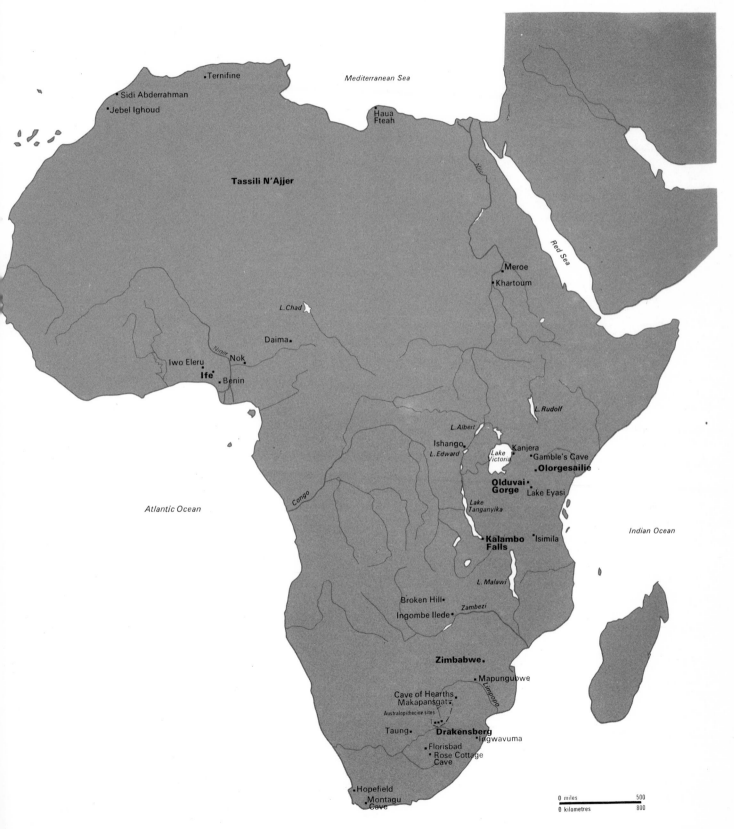

Ternifine

Sidi Abderrahman

Jebel Ighoud

Mediterranean Sea

Haua
Fteah

Tassili N'Ajjer

Nile

Red Sea

Meroe

Khartoum

L.Chad

Daima

Niger

Iwo Eleru Nok

Ife

Benin

Congo

Atlantic Ocean

L.Rudolf

L.Albert

Ishango

L.Edward

Lake
Victoria

Kanjera

Gamble's Cave

Olorgesailie

Olduvai
Gorge

Lake Eyasi

Lake
Tanganyika

Kalambo
Falls

Isimila

Indian Ocean

L. Malawi

Broken Hill

Ingombe Ilede

Zambezi

Zimbabwe

Mapungubwe

Cave of Hearths

Makapansgat

Limpopo

Australopithecine sites

Taung

Drakensberg

Ingwavuma

Florisbad

Rose Cottage
Cave

Hopefield

Montagu
Cave

0 miles   500

0 kilometres   800

15

U . . . Usno, S . . . Shungura Lower Omo Basin.
I . . . Ileret. KF . . . Koobi Fora, East Rudolf.
L . . . Lothagam. Ka . . . Kanapoi Kerio R.
C . . . Chemeron, Ch . . . Chesowanja. Baringo basin.
K . . . Kanam Kavirondo Gulf.
P . . . Peninj, Natron basin.
OG . . . Olduvai Gorge,
La . . . Laetolil Serengeti Plains.

Vegetation

- Montane Forest
- Lowland Forest
- Moist Woodlands, savanna etc.
- Dry Woodlands, steppe etc.
- Desert and subdesert
- Macchia (Mediterranean and Cape)

Eleru in Nigeria and dates from about 9000 BC. In Algeria and Morocco, rugged skeletons like those of the earlier Cromagnons of western Europe are followed by a more lightly built Mediterranean type, probably ancestral to the Berbers. In East Africa, the long, narrow skulls of people from Gamble's Cave in the Kenya Rift Valley resemble those of the Tutsi of Rwanda and Burundi.

From about 6000 BC, some groups living beside lakes and rivers adopted a more settled way of life based on fishing, for which they used bone harpoons. Examples are the people from Gamble's Cave, from Khartoum, from Ishango on Lake Edward, and from Daima south of Lake Chad. Elsewhere, L.S.A. hunters continued their old way of life until – and sometimes long after – the introduction of iron working. In certain areas, notably the Sahara, Neolithic pastoralists preceded iron workers, but this was exceptional in Africa.

The earliest centres of iron working in sub-Saharan Africa, beginning about 400 BC, were at Nok in Nigeria and Meroe on the Nile. The new technology had reached as far south as Rhodesia before AD 100 and was associated with distinctive pottery decorated with grooves or 'channeling'.

The later prehistory of Africa south of the Sahara is linked with the tremendous expansion of these iron-using agriculturalists, believed to be the ancestors of the Bantu-speakers. Some linguists consider they originated in west Africa, others in the Katanga area. Evidence of their prosperity can be seen in the gold ornaments accompanying their burials in the Zambezi and Limpopo valleys (at Ingombe Ilede and Mapungubwe) and in the complex stone enclosures they built in Rhodesia (p. 21). Stone Age hunters like the Bushmen, and pastoralists like the Hottentots, were either absorbed or ousted.

Olduvai Gorge TANZANIA

Important Early Stone Age site
From c. 1·8 million years ago onwards

BIBLIOGRAPHY
[1] Leakey, M. D., *Olduvai Gorge*, vol. 3, 'Excavations in Beds I and II 1960–3', Cambridge University Press, 1971

Olduvai Gorge, in northern Tanzania, slices through the south-eastern corner of the Serengeti Plains and through nearly two million years of human history. Serengeti is famed for its seasonal migrations of wildebeeste and zebra, and about 25 miles (40 km) east of Olduvai is Ngorongoro Crater, also teeming with game. This dry steppe country is perfect for herbivores and their hunters, which is why Olduvai has been occupied for such a long time.

The gorge cuts through up to 300 feet (91 m) of sedimentary deposits. The four Pleistocene beds (in geological terms, 'formations') contain various layers of volcanic tuffs which are excellent for the preservation of bone and invaluable for correlation and dating. Results from potassium-argon show that the earliest bed, Bed I, formed about 1·8 million years ago.

Dr Louis Leakey found the first stone tools at Olduvai in 1931 and subsequently recovered enormous quantities of fossil mammals, including many new genera and species. But work on a really intensive scale has been done only since 1959, when his wife, Dr Mary Leakey, discovered the skull of *Australopithecus* (*Zinjanthropus*) *boisei* in Bed I. Since then, her meticulous excavations have revolutionized our knowledge of the way of life of the early hominids. By 1971, when her book [1] was published, 72 archaeological sites and the remains of 34 hominids had been discovered in the gorge.

The importance of many of these sites is that they are occupation floors. At FLK, near the junction of the main and side gorges, more than 3,000 square feet (279 sq m) of the 'Zinjanthropus' floor was exposed by excavation. Stone tools and smashed bones lay everywhere, but were concentrated particularly within an oval 21 feet by 15 feet (6·4 × 4·6 m).

Subsequent finds of a less robust and bigger-brained hominid, named *Homo habilis*, at this and other sites in Bed I and Bed II suggest that he was the tool maker. Remains of at least 11 individuals of this type, including hand and foot bones, have now been found; they seem to be similar to fossils from the Lake Rudolf area, the Transvaal, and Lake Chad in the Sahara.

The artifacts of Bed I are no longer the earliest known – even older ones have been found north and east of Lake Rudolf – but they are still unique in showing the extraordinary range of tools in use 1·8 million years ago. Oldowan tools include choppers, polyhedral pounders, scrapers and flake knives; bone was also shaped for use as tools. At one of the earliest sites at Olduvai is a circle of piled stones which may have supported branches to form a windbreak. Although the main diet of these hominids must have consisted of vegetable food, there is evidence that already they were successful hunters: antelope skulls have fractures above the eye sockets which must be the result of blows at close range.

A wind-blown tuff in Bed II marks the boundary between Lower and Middle Pleistocene. During this dry period, hominids and other animals probably left the area and afterwards the Oldowan was succeeded by the developed Oldowan, in which there is a gradual increase in small flake tools and stone balls. Dr Mary Leakey believes that the contemporaneous lower Acheulean culture, in which at least 40 per cent of the artifacts are hand axes, was intrusive to the area. Probably it was made by *Homo erectus*, represented by a massive-browed skull from the upper part of Bed II.

This period saw the arrival of gigantic herbivores, including buffalo-like creatures with enormous horns and an incredible variety of pigs, some as big as a rhino. Acheulean hunters evidently drove these animals into swamps, where they killed them and cut them up on the spot with hand axes, cleavers and flake tools.

Bed III, conspicuous by its red colour, has relatively little archaeological material. By the time of Bed IV, the culture was a fully evolved Acheulean, similar to but probably earlier than that of OLORGESAILIE. Something new is always turning up at Olduvai: in 1972, Dr Mary Leakey reported hydraulic engineering by *Homo erectus* (?). A complex of pits and connecting channels in Bed IV was perhaps made to collect salt and store water.

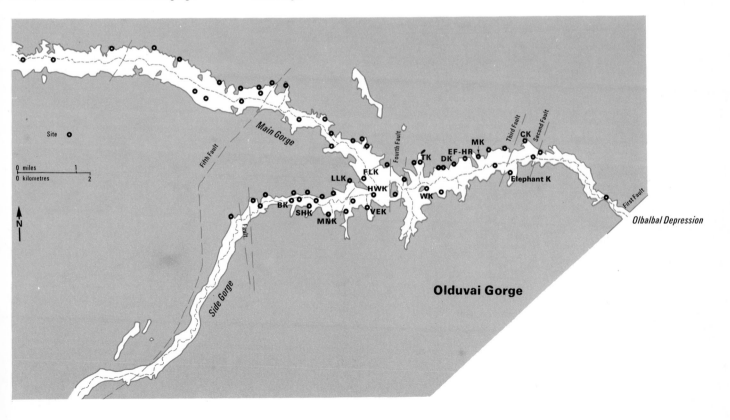

Olduvai Gorge

Olorgesailie KENYA

Hand-axe site
c. 400,000 years ago

BIBLIOGRAPHY
[1] Miller, J. A., in *Background to evolution in Africa*, ed. W. W. Bishop and J. D. Clark, Chicago, 1967, p. 367
[2] Howell, F. C. et al., 'Uranium-series dating of bone from the Isimila prehistoric site, Tanzania', *Nature* 237, 1972, p. 51

The road from Nairobi to Lake Magadi skirts the Nairobi National Park, descending steeply from the Ngong Hills to the floor of the Rift Valley. After about 40 miles (64 km), an expanse of white contrasts sharply with the surrounding country and a number of thatched huts show the visitor that he has arrived at Olorgesailie National Park.

In Middle Pleistocene times there was a lake in this hot, dry area and the white sediments consist of silts, diatomite, sands with pumice, and volcanic tuffs. Acheulean hunters camped along streams and beside a rocky peninsula running through swamps bordering the lake. The whole area has since been tilted and faulted, and the various occupation levels, once deeply buried, have been exposed by erosion.

The main site area was excavated by Dr Louis and Dr Mary Leakey in 1942–5 and in some cases the artifacts and bones have been left in the position in which they were found, shaded by grass roofs. The most impressive concentration of hand axes, cleavers and other tools is viewed from a raised 'cat walk'. Most are made of lava and some are very

large: one hand axe is 13 inches (33 cm) long and weighs six pounds (2·7 kg). Such implements would have been useful for cutting up meat from the gigantic fauna characteristic of the period. In one small excavation were the remains of more than 80 giant baboons (*Simopithecus*), their bones smashed to obtain the marrow. Other animals hunted by the Acheuleans were large extinct horses and pigs, hippos and elephants. About a quarter of a mile (400 m) away from the baboon site, the humerus of an extinct *Elephas recki* makes a similar bone from a modern elephant, placed there for comparison, look quite puny.

Potassium-argon dates of around 400,000 years have been obtained[1] for the Upper Acheulean occupation at Olorgesailie, much older than previous estimates based on guesswork. Uranium-series dates obtained for comparable industries at Isimila, Tanzania, are more than 260,000 years[2], supporting the evidence for the great antiquity of the Acheulean.

Hundreds of hand axes and other Acheulean tools can be seen from the 'cat walk' at Olorgesailie

Kalambo Falls ZAMBIA

Stone Age and Iron Age site
From more than 60,000 years to AD 1000

BIBLIOGRAPHY
Clark, J. D., *Kalambo Falls Prehistoric Site*, vol. 1, Cambridge University Press, 1969; vol. 2, 1973

Twenty-one miles (34 km) from Abercorn on the Zambia–Tanzania border, the Kalambo River plunges 726 feet (221 m) – twice the height of the Victoria Falls – into a spectacular gorge. Marabou storks nest on ledges in the quartzite, this being one of the few places in Africa where they are known to breed. After a short scramble through the narrow spillway gorge above the falls, the visitor emerges into a small basin through which the river meanders. The sands, clays and gravels which once filled this basin, and which have been exposed by erosion, contain a series of artifacts dating from the later part of the E.S.A. (see Introduction) to the present time. They were excavated by Professor J. Desmond Clark in 1956–66.

At the most westerly site, A, the stratigraphic sequence is exposed in the steep left bank, which is kept vertical by seasonal flooding. The annual rainfall is 45 inches (114 cm) per annum and the bank retreats some five feet (1·5 m) each year. Rapid regeneration of the vegetation has destroyed the excavations near the river, but in the deep trench upslope the thick red rubble horizon containing M.S.A. artifacts can be seen clearly. At the end of the dry season in September and October, lower horizons containing Sangoan and Acheulean industries are exposed near the centre of the basin at sites B and C. At site C also the early Iron Age settlement and underlying L.S.A. camping site can be seen.

The deposits have been permanently waterlogged, thus preserving wood and other vegetable matter, pollens and charcoal (though unfortunately not bone). These have provided a series of radiocarbon dates, as well as a means of reconstructing the fluctuating past climates and vegetation.

The *minimum* age for late Acheulean industries just above the present level of the river is 60,000 years: but this is the maximum age obtainable by carbon 14 dating and the industries may well have been much earlier. (See pp. 17 and 18 for much older dates obtained for the Acheulean.) Soundings made below the river in a coffer dam show that there are more Acheulean horizons below water level. The floors are 'one stone thick, and every stone is an artifact'. These were seasonal camps, occupied during the dry season and sealed over by sediments when the river rose again.

Apart from the usual Acheulean stone tools, wooden implements were found. Sticks pointed with the aid of fire would have been suitable for digging out vegetable foods and there was also a club for throwing at small game. Carbonized fruits are the same kinds as those still eaten today round Kalambo; and slight hollows filled with carbonized grasses were probably sleeping places.

In Sangoan times, the large cutting tools (hand axes and cleavers) of the Acheulean were replaced by heavy duty picks, choppers and core axes. There was also a great increase in light duty tools, particularly scrapers for preparing hides and woodworking. As in the forested areas of central Africa generally, the Sangoan was followed by the Lupemban about 30,000 years ago.

A microlithic L.S.A. industry appearing about 1900 BC includes axes, adzes and bored stones (weights for digging sticks). The early Iron Age Kalambo industry, lasting from about AD 360 till at least the end of the 10th century, is one of the few settlement sites of this period known in Africa. The channel-decorated pottery characteristic of this Kalambo industry was replaced by plain pottery, made by ancestors of the present Lungu people.

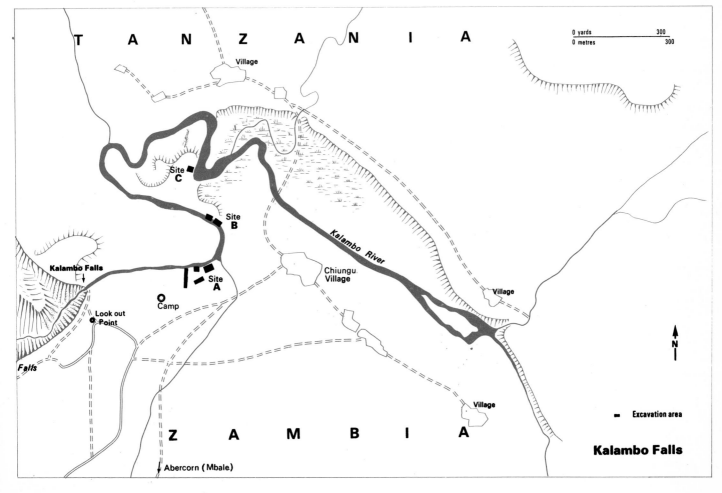

Ife NIGERIA

Holy city and its sculpture
c. AD 1200–1400

BIBLIOGRAPHY
Willett, F., *Ife in the history of West African sculpture*, London, 1967
Shaw, Thurstan, 'Archaeology in Nigeria', *Antiquity* 43, 1969, pp. 187–97

The tradition of West African sculpture begins with the curious terracottas from Nok, northern Nigeria, about 400 BC. The best of the famous ivories and bronzes of Benin date from the 16th–18th centuries AD. In between, influenced by Nok and influencing Benin, are the superb heads from Ife, which reached their peak in the 13th–14th centuries AD. Ife is the holy city of the Yoruba and home of its priest-king, the Oni, and some of the heads are believed to represent former Onis. Many of them can be seen in the museum in the grounds of the Afin, or palace, in the centre of the town.

Both terracotta and 'bronze' (actually brass) were used. The technique of bronze casting by the lost-wax process was probably introduced from the Mediterranean. (The earliest known West African bronzes are 9th century, from Igbo Ukwa, east of Benin.) The finest Ife heads, many of them life-sized, may have been mounted on wooden effigies and carried at the Onis' funeral ceremonies. Some have crowns, more often there are holes round the hair line to which real crowns may have been attached. Holes round the lips and jaw may have held a bead-work veil, and the faces are often covered with striations. Terracottas are far more numerous than bronzes and the subjects are more varied.

The first major (accidental) discovery was of 18 bronzes in 1938–9 in Wunmonije Compound, near the Afin. Others were found by builders at Ita Yemoo, but excavations there produced only terracottas. At Lafogido, named after one of the early Onis, a potsherd pavement surrounded by water-pots with lids in the form of terracotta animals' heads was uncovered in 1969. A depression in the pavement may mark the grave of Lafogido. Potsherd pavements are a notable feature of Ife and many houses had floors of pottery arranged in decorative patterns.

Complex town walls, some medieval, enclose most of the area in which sculptures have been found. Most of the terracottas came from shrines in sacred groves, or igbos, still in use today; particularly large collections were found at Igbo Obameri and Igbo Iwinrin. Standing in its grove of palms on the Ondo Road is the shrine of Oronmiyon, a legendary warrior; it contains his so-called staff, an impressive carved granite column 17 feet (5·2 m) high.

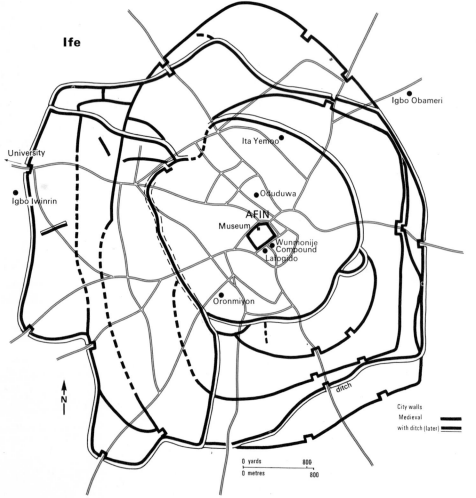

Ife

University

Igbo Obameri

Ita Yemoo

Oduduwa

AFIN
Museum
Wunmonije Compound
Lafogido

Igbo Iwinrin

Oronmiyon

ditch

N

City walls
Medieval
with ditch (later)

0 yards 800
0 metres 800

The conical tower in the elliptical building at Zimbabwe, 34 feet (10.4 m) high

20

Zimbabwe RHODESIA

Medieval stone ruins
AD 1300–1450

BIBLIOGRAPHY
[1] Summers, R., Robinson, K. R. and Whitty, A., *Zimbabwe excavations 1958*, The National Museums of Southern Rhodesia Occasional Papers, vol. 3, no. 23A, 1961, pp. 157–330
[2] Garlake, P. S., 'Rhodesian ruins – a preliminary assessment of their styles and chronology', *The Journal of African History*, XI, no. 4, 1970, pp. 495–513

Of the many stone ruins in Rhodesia, Zimbabwe, 17 miles (27 km) south east of Fort Victoria, is by far the most impressive. It consists of three complexes: the 'acropolis' or hill ruins, a fortification on top of a granite kopje; the elliptical building or great enclosure, about a quarter of a mile (400 m) away; and, between them, the scattered valley ruins.

Zimbabwe was a very important religious, political and trading centre of Bantu-speaking peoples, which eventually became a royal capital. Excavations in 1958[1] established a chronological sequence of building and pottery styles, supported by radiocarbon dates. More recent work[2] has shown that the building reached its peak not in the 17th–18th centuries AD as was believed at that time, but in the 14th–15th centuries (the evidence is based on imported ceramics).

The first site to be occupied, and always the most sacred spot, was the acropolis. Iron Age people, who were expert potters, lived there in clay-walled thatched huts about 330 AD. In about the 10th century a new group arrived; they made plain pottery and clay figurines of long-horned cattle. Soon after, the first building in stone began. Quarrying the local granite, these people erected a maze of walls connecting the huge boulders of the acropolis to surround their huts. At about the same time, the first enclosures were erected in the valley and a prototype of the elliptical building was made.

The culmination of power, prosperity and technical skills was achieved in the 14th–15th centuries. The stone walling improved, with the rectangular blocks laid in regular courses. The tremendously impressive outer wall of the elliptical building, which must have screened the huts of the king and his entourage, is more than 800 feet (244 m) long and has a maximum height of 32 feet (9·8 m). An attractive chevron pattern runs part of the way along the top of the wall. Within the elliptical building is the conical tower, 34 feet (10·4 m) high, whose purpose is unknown.

The wealth of Zimbabwe can be judged by the fine gold and copper ornaments made there, as well as by the imports. Swahili traders must have brought the Chinese ceramics and glass beads from the Indian Ocean, and iron gongs and copper ingots came from the Zambezi area to the north. The most famous objects from Zimbabwe are the soapstone birds standing on pillars. Now scattered among various museums, mostly in Cape Town, they came from the eastern enclosure of the acropolis and may have been the symbols of chiefs.

The splendour of Zimbabwe came to an end around 1450 AD, about the time when the Mwene Mutapa ('Monomotapa') confederacy migrated northwards. Its religious significance, however, continued after its economic decline. Eventually the elliptical building became a cattle kraal and the site was abandoned shortly before it was first seen by a European, Adam Render, in 1867.

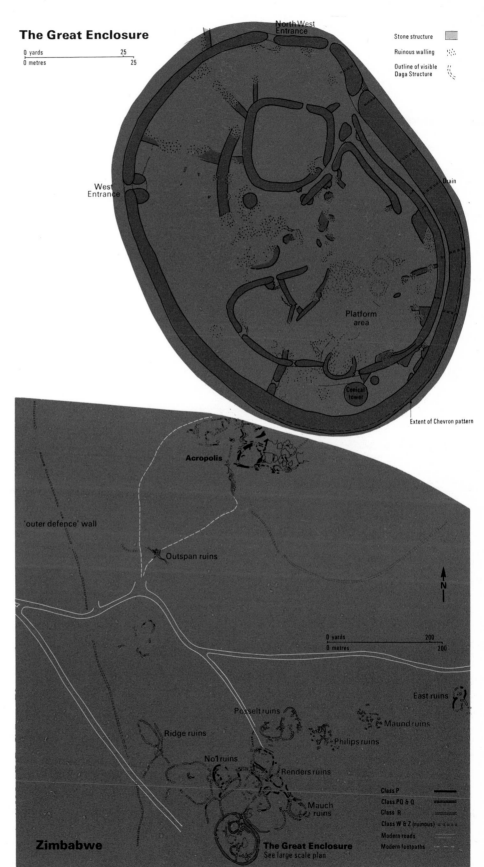

The Great Enclosure

0 yards 25
0 metres 25

Stone structure

Ruinous walling

Outline of visible Daga Structure

North West Entrance

West Entrance

Drain

Platform area

Conical tower

Extent of Chevron pattern

Acropolis

'outer defence' wall

Outspan ruins

0 yards 200
0 metres 200

N

East ruins

Posselt ruins

Maund ruins

Ridge ruins

Philips ruins

No1 ruins

Renders ruins

Mauch ruins

Class P
Class PQ & Q
Class R
Class W & Z (ruinous)
Modern roads
Modern footpaths

Zimbabwe

The Great Enclosure
See large scale plan

Tassili N'Ajjer SAHARA

Neolithic rock paintings and engravings
From 3000 BC

BIBLIOGRAPHY
[1] Lhote, H., *The search for the Tassili frescoes*, tr. A. Houghton Brodrick, London, 1959
[2] Lajoux, J.-D., *The rock paintings of Tassili*, tr. G. D. Liversage, London, 1963

Rock engravings, common all over the Sahara, have been known for a long time; but the amazing wealth of paintings has been discovered only quite recently. The huge sandstone plateau of Tassili n'Ajjer in eastern Algeria, some 500 miles (805 km) long and averaging 35 miles (56 km) wide, contains more rock paintings than any other known area of comparable size. Tens of thousands have been recorded, perhaps as many remain to be discovered.

The first Tassili paintings were seen by a camel corps officer in 1933, but it was Henri Lhote who brought them to the attention of the world.[1] His 1956–7 expedition copied an enormous number of paintings, some of which have also been beautifully photographed.[2] Lhote's book describes vividly the extreme difficulties of the terrain and the awe-inspiring majesty of canyons and pinnacles. Incredibly, they were eroded by water: Tassili, in Tuareg language, means 'plateau of the rivers'.

At the time when Neolithic pastoralists painted the Tassili shelters, a Mediterranean climate extended far south into what is now desert. This is proved by fossil pollen grains and by the bones and paintings of animals now typical of the grasslands of sub-Saharan Africa. The rock art reached its peak from about 3000–2500 BC, after which it gradually deteriorated as aridity forced the pastoralists to move away.

Four main 'schools' of art have been distinguished: archaic, naturalistic, the era of the horse, and the era of the camel. 'Archaic' human figures have large, round heads and are sometimes gigantic: one mythological figure is over 18 feet (5·5 m) high. Most typical of the naturalistic school are cattle and their herdsmen; but there are also superb pictures of wild animals, particularly sable antelopes and mouflon. Hunters with bows and arrows are common, as well as leaping dancers and domestic scenes with women and children.

In historical times, the art became schematic and there were various conventions for showing the human figure, such as headless 'diabolos' with the body sketched as two triangles. Chariots pulled by galloping horses, with the driver standing precariously, are common all over the Sahara, particularly in engravings but also in paintings.

The most remarkable engravings at Tassili are those of the Wadi Djerat, where there are more than 4,000 in a distance of 18 miles (29 km), including elephants, rhinos and giraffes. The largest collection of archaic paintings is centred on Sefar. Some of the finest of the naturalistic school are in the deep shelters of Jabbaren, where at least 5,000 figures have been recorded. They include a huge herd of cattle; a hunting scene with over 100 figures; and a beautiful kneeling woman, nearly six feet (1·8 m) high, with a curious headdress. On the other side of the wadi, at Aouanrhet, is perhaps the most famous of all the Tassili paintings: the so-called horned goddess, a running woman with a dotted area above her horns which has been likened to a cornfield. This painting, and the masked men and godlike figures of Sefar, symbolize the mystery of the Tassili paintings, so much of whose meaning we can never hope to discover.

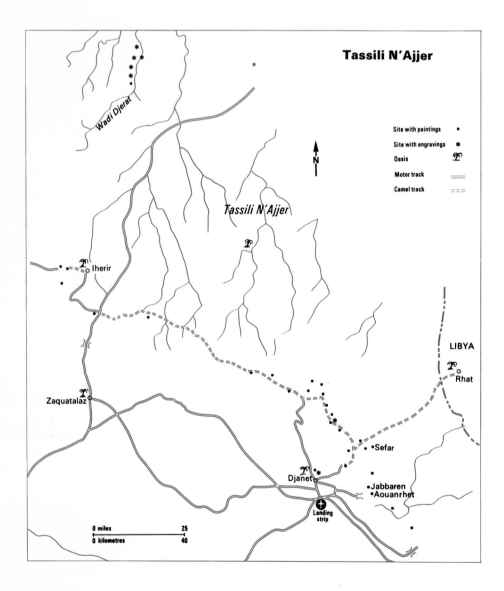

The Drakensberg SOUTH AFRICA

Bushman rock paintings
From *c.* AD 1500 to 19th century

BIBLIOGRAPHY
[1] Willcox, A. R., *Rock paintings of the Drakensberg*, London, 1956
Willcox, A. R., *The rock art of South Africa*, London, 1963

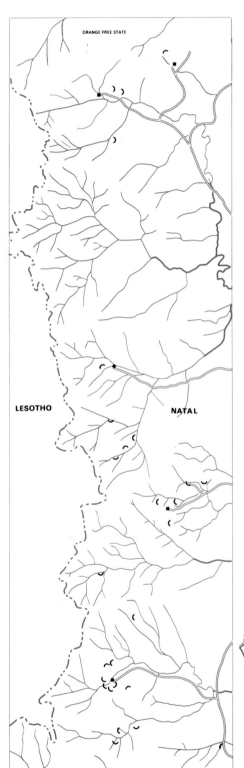

The Bushman rock paintings and engravings of southern Africa are particularly interesting as a continuation of Stone Age art surviving into the last century. There is no question of degeneracy: some of the finest polychrome animals, which compare favourably with the much earlier ones of the Sahara and even western Europe, were painted between AD 1650 and 1850.

The engravings are out in the open, on the plateaus; the paintings are in shelters in the mountains. Some of the best paintings are in the Drakensberg – Dragon Mountains – in Lesotho, Natal and Griqualand East, where the scenery is magnificent. Towards Natal, the 'Berg' descends in a precipitous scarp; parallel to it to the east is the 'Little Berg', and between them are game and forest reserves which, up till the middle of the 19th century, were a Bushman paradise. These hunters decorated the numerous shelters weathered out of the yellow sandstone of the Little Berg.

The chronological sequence of the paintings is thought to be monochromes, bichromes, unshaded polychromes and, finally, shaded polychromes. This evolution was accompanied by increasing skill in the depiction of movement and foreshortening in naturalistic animals, particularly eland and other antelopes. Human figures are often elongated and conventionalized, but there is plenty of movement and scenes showing leaping dancers and bowmen are very similar to those in the rock art of eastern Spain and the Sahara.

Stone industries in the shelters of the Smithfield–Wilton complex are dated to less than 10,000 years, but probably most of the surviving art is not more than about 500 years old.

Paintings showing soldiers in uniform and horses bear witness to the conflict which inevitably arose after the arrival of Europeans in 1840. To quote Mr A. R. Willcox,[1] who discovered and photographed so many of the paintings, the Bushmen of the Drakensberg 'held on until about 1890 and at last perished, regretted then by none but regretted now by every serious student of anthropology, psychology and art, for they were the last of the Palaeolithic artists'.

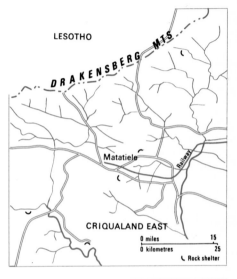

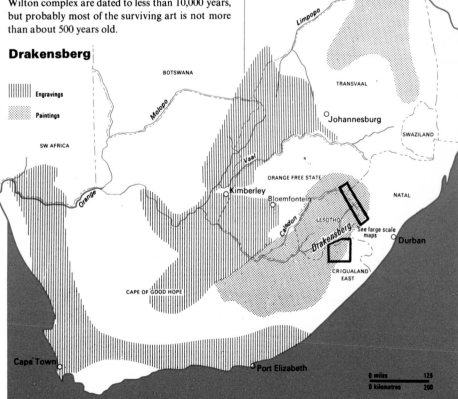

Drakensberg

|||||| Engravings

.... Paintings

BRITISH ISLES

For much of the Pleistocene Ice Age, Britain and Ireland were joined to the continent of Europe, but conditions on the ice margin were generally too extreme for permanent human habitation and no traces of the Palaeolithic hunters have been found except in southern Britain. The earliest known habitation sites, dating from the Upper Palaeolithic period some 15,000–20,000 years ago, are well represented by the caves of CHEDDAR GORGE and CRESWELL CRAGS. Some of these were perhaps the summer camps of hunters who had more permanent homes further south.

When by about 5000 BC rising sea levels made Britain an island, certain geographical features came to play an important part in the settlement and history of the country. The greater part of England, low-lying, fertile and penetrated by navigable rivers, was open to immigration from the adjacent parts of the continent. The east coast naturally invited settlement and contacts across the North Sea, while the south coast was readily accessible from France. In contrast the south-western peninsula, Wales and Scotland were generally rocky and mountainous, settlement patterns were much divided and communication largely by water. This highland country, together with Ireland, tended to have connections by Atlantic coast routes with Brittany, Iberia and the Mediterranean.

The descendants of the old Palaeolithic hunters must have played their part in the development of a pastoral economy and finally, between 4000–3000 BC of a full Neolithic type of economy based on mixed farming. They were, however, reinforced by the arrival of other Neolithic peoples coming by sea. Small boats were already in use for coastal transport by 5000 BC, and the first domestic cattle must have been shipped from the continent.

Beaker peoples made the short sea crossing from Holland and Germany, but the builders of the great megalithic tombs in the Cotswolds, west of England, Anglesey and the Boyne Valley in Ireland, came from Brittany and ultimately from Spain or Portugal, and these travellers can be followed up the Irish Sea as far as the MAES HOWE tomb in Orkney and out into the Atlantic Ocean to the CARROWKEEL cemetery near Sligo.

Many other distinctive types of monument, such as the long barrow, the henge, the causewayed camp and earthworks such as cursus, are associated with the development of the Neolithic economy (3500–1800 BC). At a later stage ploughing and fixed field farming succeeded a more sporadic form of such agriculture. Small farms associated with field systems are among the most easily recognized structures of the next thousand years or more. This period (1800–500 BC) sees also the widespread use of metal for tools and weapons; the development of various kinds of bronze and the introduction of iron. Changes in burial practice occur. Single-grave burials beneath round barrows, introduced perhaps by the Beaker people from the continent in 1900–1800 BC replace various types of collective burial under megaliths and long barrows and individual cremation in henges. Cremation beneath barrows is substituted for the simple curled-up burials of the Beaker peoples, and at a later date large cremation cemeteries under barrows and in flat graves illustrate the increase in population. In the simple manufactures there is strong evidence of continuity. The pottery for much of the Bronze Age is developed directly from Neolithic models, the flint mines and axe factories are in operation until around 1200 BC, the round barrows continue to cluster round the ancient sacred monuments, such as STONEHENGE and TARA, which remain in use for many centuries, and some smaller stone circles continue to be built. Later sacred monuments may be largely of timber, like their domestic counterparts and are consequently difficult to identify. After a gap of some centuries, which is more apparent than real, a new class of structure appears: the first undoubted defensive or military fortifications. These are the colossal structures known as hill forts, whose massive ditches and ramparts sometimes enclose areas of more than 100 acres (40 hectares). Some hundreds of these fortifications were built in Britain, and the brochs in north-west Scotland and Orkney

See p. 49 for generalized distribution of megalithic chambered tombs in British Isles.

(MOUSA) are another response to the unsettled conditions of this period. The more highly developed hill forts, with complex entrances and multiple ramparts (such as MAIDEN CASTLE), were the results of improvements in warfare, such as the use of the sling. Hill forts and running earth walls continued to be used sporadically in the Roman and Anglo Saxon periods, particularly in unsettled parts of Britain, but those in southern England seem to have been reduced and dismantled shortly after the Roman conquest.

There is good evidence that some of the Celtic and Belgic tribes who were responsible for the construction of the more highly developed hill forts were actual colonists or invaders from France and the Low Countries. But the construction of hill forts may have commenced on a small scale in the Bronze Age and in the disturbed years after 500 BC was a common response to population pressure on resources in Britain, as elsewhere in western Europe, when the effects of classical and Celtic conquests were becoming apparent.

SHETLAND

Mousa

Mid Howe
Skara Brae • Maes Howe ORKNEY

Cairnpapple

North Sea

Carrowkeel •

ISLE OF MAN

Knowth • • Dowth
• Newgrange
Tara • Irish Sea

Boyne

ANGLESEY

Barclodiad Y Gawres • Bryn Celli Dhu
Bryn Yr Hen Bobl

Creswell Crags

Grime's Graves

Hetty Pegler's Tump •

Severn

Waylands Smithy
Windmill Hill
Silbury Hill • Avebury
Stoney Littleton • The Sanctuary
Cheddar • West Kennet • Knap Hill
Stonehenge • Durrington Walls
Woodhenge

Thames
Thames Estuary
• Swanscombe

Straits of Dover

Maiden Castle

Bristol Channel

English Channel

0 miles 62
0 kilometres 100

Atlantic Ocean

Creswell Crags ENGLAND

Prehistoric cave dwellings
c. 40,000–8000 BC

BIBLIOGRAPHY
Garrod, D. A. E., *The Upper Palaeolithic Age in Britain*, 1925
'Excavations at Pin Hole Cave', *Proceedings of the Prehistoric Society of East Anglia*, 1931
Armstrong, A. L., 'Excavations at Mother Grundy's Parlour', *Journal of the Royal Anthropological Institute*, 1926

Four miles (6·5 km) south west of Worksop in Derbyshire is the gorge of Creswell Crags. It contains some of the most important prehistoric cave dwellings and rock shelters in England. An eastward-flowing stream has cut through a narrow Permian limestone ridge to form the Gorge. The Crags on either side are much fissured, and contain a number of caves, four of which were inhabited by prehistoric hunters. Though it was close to the glaciated region during the colder period at the end of the last glaciation, Creswell Crags seems to have been free of ice, and formed a particularly favoured base for the hunters, perhaps at the edge of an ice-dammed lake. Some of the caves are now only 10 feet (3 m) above the floor of the gorge but would have been 30–40 feet (9–12 m) above the stream in Pleistocene times, and commanded extensive views to the east and west.

The sketch map shows the position of the caves. The three most important – the Pin Hole (a narrow fissure), Robin Hood's Cave (which is the biggest) and Mother Grundy's Parlour (a shallow semicircular room) – are all north of the road, and a less important fissure, Church Hole, is on the south side of the gorge. These were excavated in the 19th century (1875–8) and later excavation took place in the occupation deposits which accumulated on the 'platforms' outside the cave entrances. In the case of Mother Grundy's Parlour the platform is protected by an overhanging rock shelf, forming an ideal rock shelter.

The deposits in all four caves tell basically the same story. The caves themselves must have been cut during the last (Eemian) interglacial period, and this warmer climate was still prevalent when hippopotamus bones were washed into Mother Grundy's Parlour. After the onset of the last glaciation the earliest occupation deposits indicate that the caves were used by Neanderthal man, for they contained roughly chipped quartzite implements of Mousterian type. Later again they were at least visited by various Upper Palaeolithic hunting groups.

These were minor, though important, episodes in the history of Creswell Crags. The number of implements left was small, and may represent no more than brief camping by summer hunting parties. The final, and most significant, episode opened about 12,000 BC, late in the last glacial period. The hunters who now made more permanent homes in the caves represent the earliest known distinctively British culture – named after this place of its first discovery. The evolution of the Creswellian over a period of several thousand years can be observed both here and at CHEDDAR; it survived to make an important contribution to the cultures of the Mesolithic age.

This Creswellian shows a highly individual tradition of flint working affected by influences and actual imports from what was to become continental Europe.

The Creswell caves are further distinguished by having yielded the only pieces of Palaeolithic representational art to have been found in England. These are two engraved rib bones, one from Robin Hood's Cave with a horse's head, and one from the Pin Hole showing a masked man. Both resemble the Magdalenian art of France, yet seem to possess some elements of a local style. Other bone work, such as an ivory javelin head from the Pin Hole, are claimed to be imports from the French area.

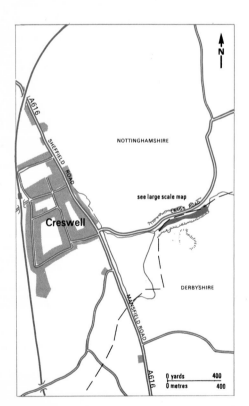

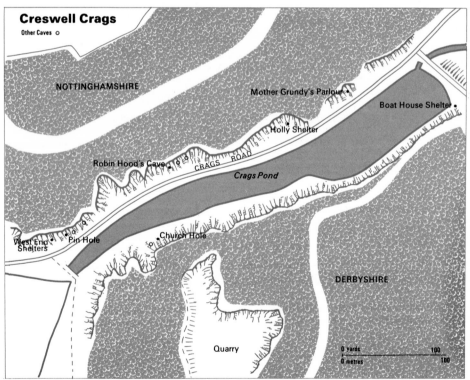

Cheddar Gorge ENGLAND

Prehistoric cave dwellings
c. 20,000–10,000 BC

BIBLIOGRAPHY
Garrod, D. A. E., *The Upper Palaeolithic Age in Britain*, 1925
Donovan, Desmond, 'Gough's Cave, Cheddar', *Proceedings of the British Speleological Society*, 1956

Cheddar Gorge is a picturesque ravine cutting through the limestone at the edge of the Mendip hills of Somerset in the south west of England. The river that cut it is now shrunken to a stream. It contains several caves, some of them famous for their stalactites; those occupied by prehistoric man are at the mouth of the gorge, where it opens on to the Somerset Level.

The most important of these, known as Gough's Cave, is slightly above the road on the south side of the ravine. A very rough clearance was started, for the benefit of visitors in 1891, before which it had been 'a recess where roof and floor met . . . with a low creep penetrating to a distance of 43 yards (39 m).' As a result of this and several subsequent diggings, all of an amateurish kind, some spectacular discoveries have been made. A large collection of flint tools shows that the principal occupation was by hunters of Creswellian culture (CRESWELL CRAGS). They also left bone and antler implements, including fine needles and cut-marked bones that may be some kind of calendrical tallies. Another find was a piece of Baltic amber, the earliest known import from that region.

By far the most interesting discovery is, however, the bones of Cheddar man unearthed in 1903 at a point some 90 feet (27 m) in from the entrance. This is the only complete Upper Palaeolithic skeleton to have been found in England. The body had been ceremonially buried 'with the legs drawn up under the chin and the arms bent so as to bring the hands to the back of the head'. This is the 'contracted' burial common to many hunting cultures, plausibly supposed to imitate the position of the foetus in the womb. The skeleton has been radiocarbon dated to about 10,000 BC.

A perforated baton made from a human femur and decorated round the shaft with a spiral of incised lines appears to have been buried with

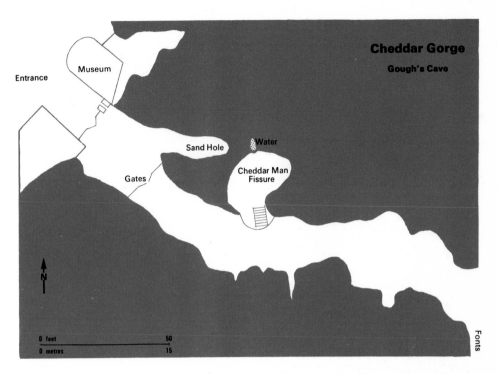

Cheddar man. A second baton, similarly decorated but made of reindeer antler, was found much later in another part of the cave. These are the only known British examples of a class of objects relatively common in contemporary European cultures.

The finds from Gough's Cave, certainly the most important collection from any Palaeolithic living site in England, are to be seen in a museum of a commercial kind, run in conjunction with the cave and a restaurant.

Two other Cheddar caves were occupied in prehistoric times: Soldier's Hole, high in the cliffs above

Gough's, and the Sun Hole, at the top of the slope on the north side of the gorge. To judge from leaf-shaped, bifacially flaked spearheads found there, Soldier's Hole was inhabited at a time transitional between the Mousterian and Upper Palaeolithic periods – when Gough's Cave was still flooded and uninhabitable. Sun Hole was occupied by Creswellian hunters, and also by Neolithic people, who left behind among other remains one of their rare pottery spoons. This was almost the only object from the Sun Hole to survive the wartime bombing of Bristol Speleological Museum.

Grime's Graves ENGLAND

Flint mines
c. 2500–1400 BC

BIBLIOGRAPHY
Rainbird Clarke, R., *Grimes Graves*, 1964

Grime's Graves is the name given to the prehistoric flint mines near Thetford on the Norfolk–Suffolk border. These are a series of shafts dug in the chalk to extract good-quality flint for making axes. The mines appear in England after the beginning of the Neolithic period but are undoubtedly a response to the need for axes to clear land for farming. There are 15–20 of these flint-mining sites in Britain, those in Sussex and outside Salisbury Plain being the earliest (3200–2700 BC), while Grime's Graves is dated between 2500 and 1400 BC. This site is the biggest in England and the best explored. A total of 366 mine shafts has been plotted from surface indications, and there are no doubt many more, since the area west and north of the main visible concentration has been ploughed flat. To judge from the excavated examples on the crown of the hill the vertical shafts vary from 20 to 42 feet (6–12·8 m) in depth. The flint was mined from the shaft itself and from horizontal galleries radiating from its foot. The galleries from one mine interconnect with those of other mines. An estimate for flint taken from one shaft is approximately 7 tons (approx. 7100 kg). This could have been extracted in six months of continuous work by a group of seven labourers – the most that could be employed in the confined space at the foot of the shaft – with five men carrying the flint nodules to the surface. These porters probably used ladders set at an angle of 45°, reaching from the base of the shaft to a ledge half-

way up (traces of which have been found in recent excavations) and thence to the surface.

There is evidence that mined flint had particularly good properties for making axes. At Grime's Graves there are two upper bands of inferior quality flint, but these were ignored by the miners, who dug their shafts some 10–15 feet (3–4·5 m) deeper to reach the superior bands that lay below. It seems likely that this flint was first found where it outcrops in the dry valley, and that the small prehistoric pits and surface workings called primitive pits found on this part of the site were the first to be worked.

If one allows that there are approximately 500 shafts at Grime's Graves, and that flint extraction may have lasted 1,000–1,200 years, one shaft could have been excavated every 2–3 years. Even so the amount of flint extracted seems excessive for use in the immediate locality, and it is likely that it was traded to more distant parts of England, as is the case with similar axes made of hard rock in Wales, Cornwall and the Lake District. Groups of unfinished axes are sometimes found buried in the ground far from the mines and these support the argument for long-distance trade.

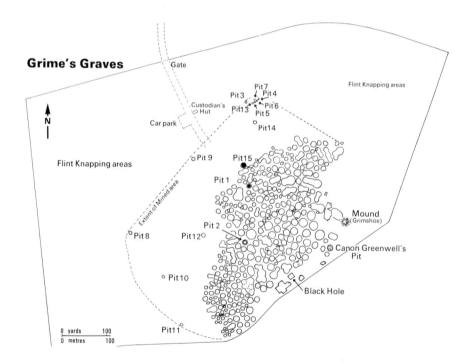

28

Hetty Pegler's Tump ENGLAND

Gallery grave

c. 3000 BC

BIBLIOGRAPHY

Crawford, O. G. S., *The Long Barrows of the Cotswolds*, 1925

Clifford, E. M., 'Hetty Pegler's Tump', *Antiquity* XL, 1965, pp. 129–32

Hetty Pegler's Tump, near Uley on the Cotswold hills in Gloucestershire, is one of the best preserved of the very numerous Cotswold–Severn group of long barrows with megalithic chambers that is distributed on both sides of the river Severn and its estuary. This tomb, like its near neighbour of Nympsfield, stands in a fine position on the edge of the escarpment overlooking the Severn valley.

The burial chamber is set in the larger end of a mound some 120 feet (37 m) long, originally contained within a trapezoidal drystone reveting wall. As is usual with these long barrows, the larger end faces eastward. Here the chamber was probably approached through a splayed entrance way narrowing toward the actual portal. Inside, a pair of projecting upright slabs form an inner doorway, beyond which the roughly parallel-sided gallery extends about another 20 feet (6 m). When complete, there were two pairs of opposing side chambers, but those on the north side, still in existence as late as 1821, have been destroyed. Gallery and side chambers are built of large standing stones, the spaces between them filled with drystone work. They are roofed with large flat slabs.

As is usual for all forms of megalithic tomb with visible entrance passages, Hetty Pegler's Tump had been periodically reopened to receive further burials. The introduction of new corpses disturbed the ancient bones. Of the remains of 23 interments in this tomb, only the latest (near the entrance) was found with the skeleton fully articulated.

The chamber is classified as a transepted gallery grave in megalithic typology, while in the special terminology of the Cotswold–Severn group, Hetty Pegler's is a 'terminally chambered' tomb. (Notgrove and Nympsfield are other notable examples in the area.) The 'terminally chambered' label is used to distinguish this class from a second, which is architecturally poorer and generally (though not universally) held to be a later derivative. This is the laterally chambered type, well represented by Belas Knap, near Winchcombe and Rodmarton near Cirencester. These have two or more much smaller chambered tombs set in the long sides of the mound and entered through them.

The theory that the small side-chambered form derived from the large end-chambered is supported by the fact that they commonly retain the imposing recessed entrance at the east end, probably always used as a ceremonial meeting place, but now only as a blocked false portal leading nowhere.

Also in favour of this is the fact that the theoretically earlier type is the more widespread, both in England and Wales, fine examples being seen at Uffington on the Berkshire downs (Wayland's Smithy) and at AVEBURY (West Kennet), and at Stoney Littleton, at Wellow, south of Bath, in Wiltshire. These facts are of interest in relation to the supposed origin of the people who built the barrows. Research has been notably unsuccessful at finding the settlements of the barrow users, and as all the tombs were robbed before the development of modern excavation techniques, there are few facts to go on. What there is indicates that they were constructed in Neolithic times between 3200 and 2500 BC. The tomb builders probably first introduced agriculture to the Cotswolds; the distribution pattern of their tombs on either side of the Severn suggests that they came by boat up the river. Theoretical studies based on the plans of the tombs themselves show that they could be derived from others on the coast of France in the neighbourhood of Nantes.

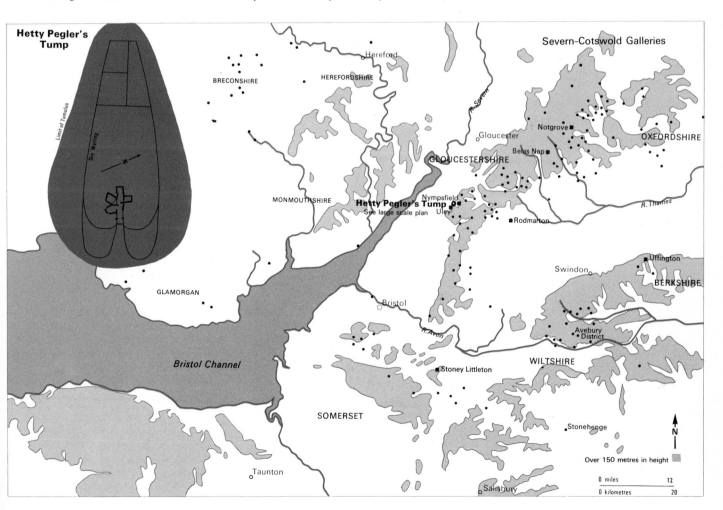

Hetty Pegler's Tump

Limit of Tumulus

Dry Walling

Severn-Cotswold Galleries

Hereford

BRECONSHIRE

HEREFORDSHIRE

R. Severn

Gloucester

Notgrove

OXFORDSHIRE

Belas Nap

GLOUCESTERSHIRE

MONMOUTHSHIRE

Nympsfield
Hetty Pegler's Tump
See large scale plan
Uley

R. Thames

Rodmarton

Uffington

Swindon

BERKSHIRE

GLAMORGAN

Bristol

R. Avon

Avebury
District

WILTSHIRE

Bristol Channel

Stoney Littleton

SOMERSET

Stonehenge

N

Over 150 metres in height

Taunton

Salisbury

0 miles 12
0 kilometres 20

The Avebury District ENGLAND

Sacred stone circles, causewayed camp, gallery graves, mound
c. 3000–1800 BC

BIBLIOGRAPHY
Smith, I. F., *Windmill Hill and Avebury Excavations by
Alexander Keiller 1925–39*, 1965
Piggott, Stuart, *The West Kennet Long Barrow: Excava-
tions 1955–6*, London, 1962

Avebury, on the Marlborough downs, Wiltshire, lies west of the major groups of round barrows and later earthworks and field systems which are strung out along the ancient track called the Ridgeway. Its immediate neighbourhood contains some of the most spectacular prehistoric sites. The modern village of Avebury lies inside the finest, the Avebury Circle. This, like Stonehenge and many prehistoric monuments, is of composite construction, and was added to or altered at different periods. As we know it, the circle consists of a 20-foot (6 m) high grass-covered chalk bank and an inner ditch (clearly not defensive) with four entrances at cardinal points of the compass. Just inside the ditch is a circle of massive irregular sarsen stones enclosing about 28 acres (11 hectares) of ground. There were originally 100 of these, but many were broken up to build houses in the village, or thrown to the ground and buried. Some stones have been re-erected and concrete markers show where the stoneholes of the missing sarsens have been discovered. Leading south from the circle is a ceremonial avenue (the West Kennet avenue) consisting of lines of tall stones, nearly one

and a half miles (2·4 km) long and originally much longer, leading to another monument (the Sanctuary) on Overton Hill. (A similar avenue probably once ran from the west entrance to Beckhampton.) The stones in the avenue are in pairs, one broad and short, the other long and thin, and are thought to represent men and women.

Inside the Avebury circle itself are parts of what were once two further small rings of standing stones, each with internal 'constructions'. These two small circles may have been the earliest Avebury monument or may, like the similarly placed wooden structure at Durrington Walls (STONEHENGE DISTRICT), represent houses contemporary with the main circle. Two Beaker Culture burials (1800–1600 BC) and a single Grooved Ware Neolithic interment have been found at the foot of different stones in the West Kennet avenue and may date from its construction. The main ditch and bank at Avebury appear to be of Henge monument type: Grooved Ware and decorated Neolithic pottery have been found beneath the bank and perhaps date from before 2000 BC. The sarsen circle may be a later

construction, associated with long-necked Beaker pottery found in the upper silting of the ditch.

The use of such monuments as these is usually considered by prehistorians exclusively in religious terms; recent astronomical archaeology confirms earlier suggestions that this religion was based partly on observing events in the Heavens.

The Sanctuary, a much smaller circle, was probably roofed, but seems also to be a sacred building rather than a human habitation. Its principal elements were two concentric stone circles; within them were four concentric circles of wooden post holes now represented at the site by concrete markers. These are said to represent four reconstructions of the same sacred building: the earliest a wooden house contemporary with Windmill Hill camp; next two wooden circular houses with Grooved Ware and other decorated Neolithic pottery; and, lastly, a stone building, including the two stone circles and a sacrificial burial of a child in the centre, erected by the Beaker people.

Windmill Hill, north west of Avebury, the best-known Neolithic causewayed camp in England, is another enclosure, of about 20 acres (8 hectares), encircled by three concentric lines of shallow ditches, with low, almost invisible banks on their inner sides. The lines of the ditches are discontinuous, giving the causewayed appearance, so noticeable from the air. The purpose of this sort of enclosure is unknown, though many have been examined. There are no traces of occupation inside the enclosure, only a single (much later) round barrow; but the ditches are full of pottery and animal remains. Whole cattle were buried, their bones being found fully articulated. The masses of bones collected and thrown into the ditches seem to have been deliberately and rapidly covered by chalk from the banks, as none of the bones has been gnawed by dogs. This has all the appearance of large-scale feasting. It is suggested that these camps may be connected with cattle ranching, used for some function such as an annual round-up and tribal gathering. One recalls the large quantities of meat eaten by the Gauchos of Argentina at similar gatherings. Some of the pottery seems to have come from near Bristol, to judge from the type of stone grit used to temper the clay; and this also suggests long-distance travel and seasonal occupation of the camp. The Windmill Hill site relates to the earliest farming cultures (3100–2700 BC) on the Marlborough downs. Finds from the camp and the Avebury circle are in the excellent little Avebury Museum.

A similar camp, Knap Hill, is found south of Avebury, as are two fine chambered long barrows of Cotswold–Severn type (see HETTY PEGLER'S TUMP) at East and West Kennet. The West Kennet long barrow is the finest in Wiltshire. The mound is altogether 340 feet long by 75 feet (104 × 23 m), and has deep ditches on either side. It was carefully re-excavated and restored 20 years age, and found to be a transepted galley grave with two pairs of side chambers, still untouched when they were discovered in 1955. Finds within the chambers in-

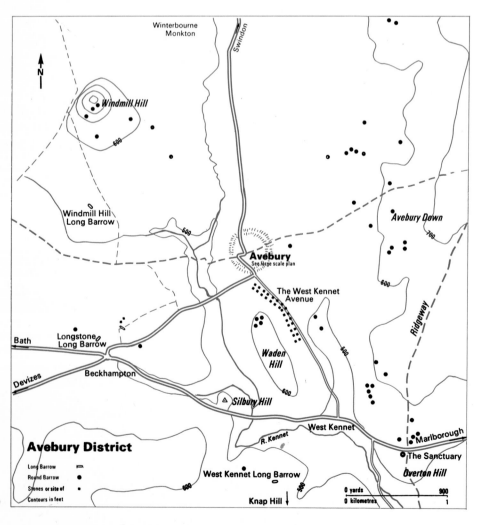

Avebury District

Long Barrow
Round Barrow
Stones or site of
Contours in feet

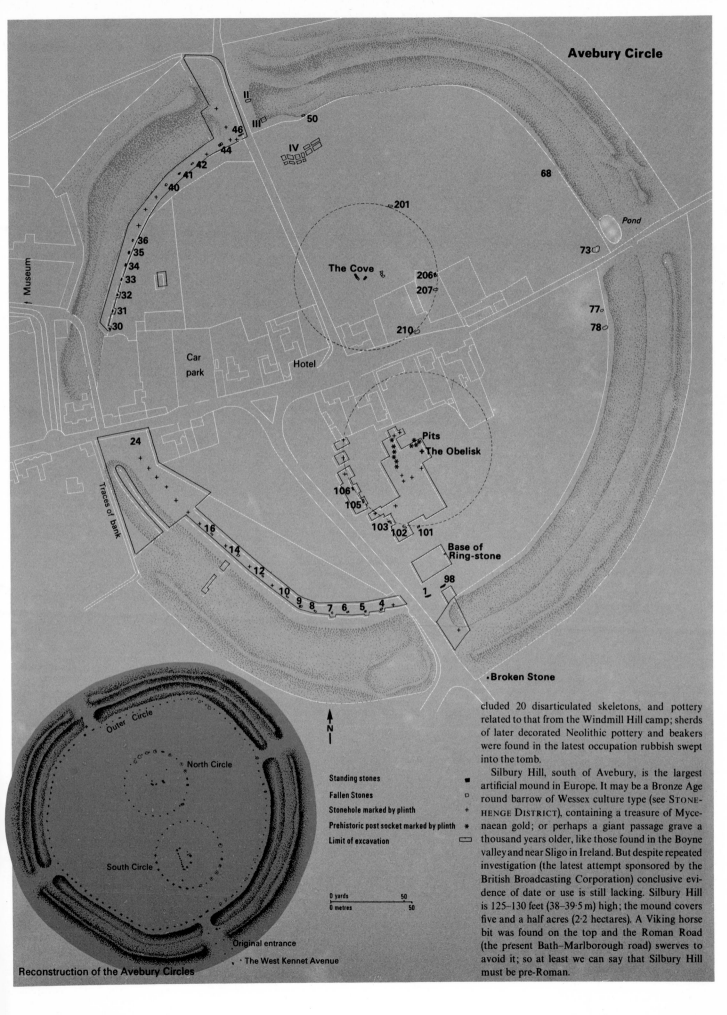

II

50

III

46

44

IV

42

41

40

68

201

Pond

36

35

34

73

The Cove

206

207

33

32

77

31

78

30

210

Museum

Car
park

Hotel

24

Pits

The Obelisk

Traces of bank

106

105

16

103

14

102   101

12

Base of
Ring-stone

10

9   8

1   98

7   6   5   4

• Broken Stone

Outer Circle

N

North Circle

South Circle

Standing stones

Fallen Stones

Stonehole marked by plinth

Prehistoric post socket marked by plinth

Limit of excavation

Original entrance

• The West Kennet Avenue

0 yards   50
0 metres   50

Reconstruction of the Avebury Circles

cluded 20 disarticulated skeletons, and pottery
related to that from the Windmill Hill camp; sherds
of later decorated Neolithic pottery and beakers
were found in the latest occupation rubbish swept
into the tomb.

Silbury Hill, south of Avebury, is the largest
artificial mound in Europe. It may be a Bronze Age
round barrow of Wessex culture type (see STONE-
HENGE DISTRICT), containing a treasure of Mycenaean gold; or perhaps a giant passage grave a
thousand years older, like those found in the Boyne
valley and near Sligo in Ireland. But despite repeated
investigation (the latest attempt sponsored by the
British Broadcasting Corporation) conclusive evidence of date or use is still lacking. Silbury Hill
is 125–130 feet (38–39.5 m) high; the mound covers
five and a half acres (2.2 hectares). A Viking horse
bit was found on the top and the Roman Road
(the present Bath–Marlborough road) swerves to
avoid it; so at least we can say that Silbury Hill
must be pre-Roman.

The Stonehenge District ENGLAND

Sacred circle, and associated barrow cemeteries and earthworks
c. 3000–1200 BC

BIBLIOGRAPHY
Atkinson, R. J. C., *Stonehenge*, 1956
Robinson, J. H., 'Sunrise and Moonrise at Stonehenge',
   Nature 225, 1970, pp. 1236–7
Wainwright, G. J. and Longworth, I. H., *Durrington Walls*,
   Society of Antiquaries Research Report, 1970

The central structure of Stonehenge today, the tall
lintelled circle of sarsens surrounding the horseshoe
setting of trilithons, is justly the most celebrated
prehistoric monument in Europe. But Stonehenge
has been reconstructed a number of times. The
earliest ceremonial structure, Stonehenge I (radiocarbon dated 2180 BC), was a circular Henge monument 350 feet (107 m) in diameter: a low encircling
internal bank and ditch system broken by a single
entrance, with a wooden building in the centre. Just
inside the ditch and low bank, which can still be
seen, is a circle of 56 holes (now marked in concrete) which contained human cremations. These
are called the Aubrey Holes after John Aubrey, the
17th-century antiquary who first noticed them.

In about 1800 BC Stonehenge was altered. Two
circles of small bluestones were put up, surrounding
the central area, and the entrance was altered to
align with the Avenue (two parallel ditches and
banks two and a half miles – 4 km – long) which
ran from Stonehenge to the skyline and then down
to the river Avon. The bluestones, which are made
of rocks not found in the district, and native to
Pembrokeshire (South Wales), are supposed to have
been brought from Wales by water and up the
Avenue from the river; an overland route has been
proposed, and a geologist has also suggested the
stones could be glacial erratics, carried there by the
ice, though this is by no means proved.

In Stonehenge's latest phase the bluestone circles
were demolished to make room for the sarsen
lintelled circle and trilithons, the major monument
of Stonehenge today (radiocarbon dated to about
1550 BC). Finally, the bluestones were put back in
their present positions, as another central horseshoe, and a smaller circle between the two sarsen
constructions. The tall lintelled circle and the trilithon horseshoe are unique in western Europe, both
in plan and elevation, and in the sophisticated way
in which they are treated. The large stones are
carefully dressed to a rectangular form. Each sarsen
tapers towards the top, the taper in a number of
cases being convexly curved to counteract the effect
of perspective: an architectural technique found on
the columns of classical Greek Temples. The lintel
stones are curved to fit the circumference. It has
been suggested that the lintelled circle is a skeuomorph of the wooden columns and lintels surrounding the open central courtyards of houses such as
those at Durrington Walls and Woodhenge (see
below). Carvings of axes and daggers have been
found on several of the sarsens, one or two of
which are thought to represent Bronze Age weapons
from the east Mediterranean.

In its most developed form, Stonehenge seems to
have been laid out so that Midsummer sunrise and
Midwinter moonrise could be observed within the
horseshoe. Four sarsens known as the Station
Stones were erected within the Aubrey Hole Circle
at the same time as the main structure. These, together with the Heel Stone in the Avenue, and
certain other stones, can be seen to mark the positions of these events.

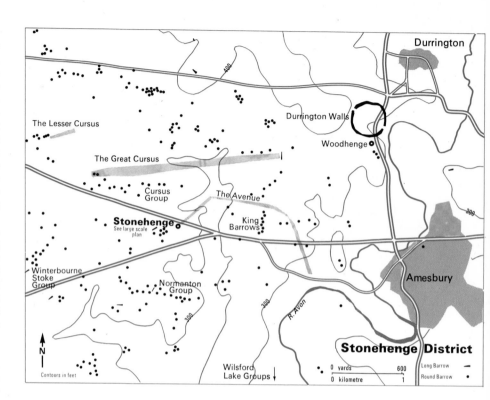

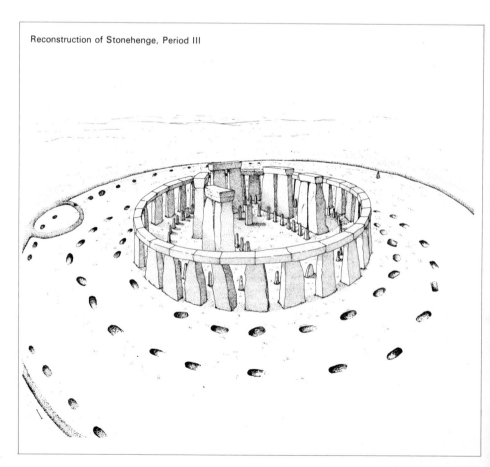

Reconstruction of Stonehenge, Period III

No stage of the building of Stonehenge is later than about 1200 BC, and any connection with the Druids, who flourished a thousand years later, is purely conjectural. All round the structure are other monuments and burial mounds which belong to the same period and are likely to be connected with its use. Most prominent are the barrow cemeteries which appear to be deliberately sited round Stonehenge. These are groups of round barrows including some very large bell and bowl barrows of the type used by the group of wealthy priests or chieftains, creators of the Wessex Culture, to whom the unique structures at Stonehenge are attributed. The main cemeteries are the Winterbourne Stoke crossroads group, the Normanton crossroads and Lake groups, the Wilsford group, the Cursus group and King Barrows. Bush Barrow in the Normanton cemetery contained the sort of princely burial held to be typical of the Wessex Culture, including fine metal weapons, a breastplate and gold, a fine stone mace and a bone-inlaid wooden staff. In several of the barrow cemeteries (Winterbourne, Stoke, Normanton) are single examples of the unchambered long barrow, structures that may predate the construction of Stonehenge I. These are wedge-shaped mounds, with burials, usually 20 or more, lying on the surface of the ground under the broad end. In the ground surrounding the burials are rectangular settings of deep post holes, which once held heavy upright timbers, and it is thought that the corpses were accumulated in so-called mortuary houses or roofless enclosures, until there were sufficient burials to warrant building a communal barrow. In addition to such tombs, which replace the chambered long barrow (see HETTY PEGLER'S TUMP) as the earliest tombs south of the AVEBURY DISTRICT, there are other notable structures in the immediate vicinity of Stonehenge.

Two very low rectangular earthworks of unknown purpose, The Great Cursus and The Lesser Cursus can be seen near the Avenue between half a mile and a mile (800–1600 m) to the north. The Great Cursus is an embanked strip one and a half miles 2·4 km) long and more than 300 feet (91 m) wide, with squared ends defined by two parallel banks and ditches. The Lesser Cursus is another smaller example. These two are of the same date as Stonehenge I. They were named by Stukeley, the 18th-century antiquary, after the examples of the Circus Maximus in Rome, as he recognized their relationship to the barrows and to the Stonehenge Temple, and thought that they were intended for the performance of funerary games. There are also two further Henge Monument enclosures, Woodhenge and Durrington Walls, beside the river Avon, two miles (3·2 km) north east of Stonehenge. Durrington Walls is a very large ceremonial enclosure of an unusual type (similar to, but larger than Avebury) surrounding a dry valley which runs down to the river, and enclosed by a broad bank that could have commanded a view of ceremonies in the enclosure. The bank has been mostly ploughed away, but the deeper soil in the interior has preserved traces in the

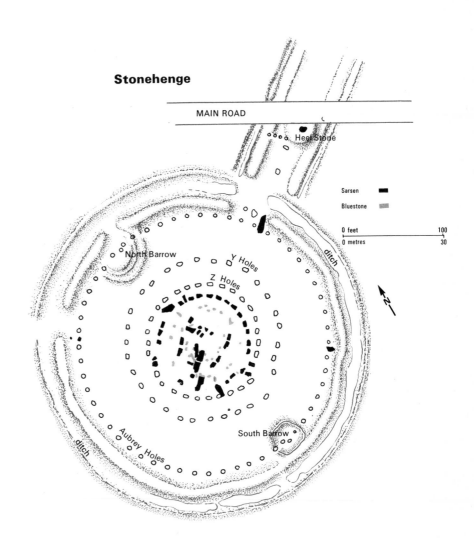

Stonehenge

MAIN ROAD

Heel Stone

Sarsen
Bluestone

0 feet 100
0 metres 30

North Barrow

Y Holes
Z Holes

Aubrey Holes

South Barrow

ditch

ditch

N

form of post holes of at least two structures of wood (found on the line of the new main road, which runs through the enclosure), a small round house with an avenue of wooden posts leading to it, and a larger building defined by six concentric circles of wooden posts, with an open central court. Woodhenge, another ceremonial building with a central courtyard, surrounded in this case by its own ditch and bank, is just outside Durrington Walls and must have been part of the same ceremonial complex. Both sites belong to the same Late Neolithic cultural group, defined by a pottery called Grooved Ware, dated from radiocarbon samples at Durrington Walls to 2050–1950 BC.

Large quantities of food remains are found in the ditches at Durrington Walls adjacent to the buildings, and in this case as at Windmill Hill (AVEBURY DISTRICT) these are interpreted as the remains of ritual feasts. The Durrington Walls feasts seem to have consisted largely of pork, and as pig breeding is a sedentary occupation, those taking part are likely to have lived nearby, though not within the enclosure itself.

Maiden Castle ENGLAND

Hill Fort
c. 400 BC–AD 100

BIBLIOGRAPHY
Wheeler, R. E. M., *Maiden Castle*, Society of Antiquaries
Research Report No. XII, London, 1941

Maiden Castle in its present guise is a Celtic hillfort of the last century BC – when it became the principal oppidum of the Durotriges tribe. It is not exceptional in size (56 acres – 23 hectares) but in the complexity, strength and beauty of its defences. The immense chalk ramparts running round the low, slightly waisted, hill have been described by Thomas Hardy as 'an enormous many-limbed organism of an ante-diluvian time . . . lying lifeless and covered by a green cloth, which hides its substance while revealing its contour'. Seen from the air this and one or two of the other Dorset hillforts (Badbury Rings and Hambledon Hill near Blandford) resemble the abstract curvilinear decoration on Celtic metalwork of this period.

These exceptionally strong defences were required for slingstone warfare. With a sling, a defender inside the hillfort could hurl his stones further downhill than an attacker could hurl his uphill. With several ramparts, the occupying force could drive off the attack, while remaining themselves still out of range. The use of these weapons at Maiden Castle has been proved by the discovery of two arsenals of slingstones, containing respectively,

22,000 and 16,000 slingstones, collected from Chesil Beach, near the place where the invaders landed. The present fort at Maiden Castle succeeds earlier structures on the eastern part of the hill. A causewayed Neolithic enclosure like that at Windmill Hill (AVEBURY DISTRICT) represents the earliest inhabitants and this structure is overlaid by a later Neolithic monument, a mound, 597 yards (546 m) long, running across the top of the hill. Today these features are mostly concealed beneath the later, Iron Age, earthworks. An early hillfort with a single rampart revetted with timber was built shortly after 400 BC at this east end of the hill. Hillforts of this early date formed part of a pastoral and agricultural economy, and were used as refuges or centres of tribal gathering, rather than as permanently occupied settlements. Each block of downland between the rivers had one or two hillforts. Poundbury Fort, near Dorchester, would appear to be a pastoral enclosure belonging to the same tribal unit as Maiden Castle. Such districts were self-sufficient.

Maiden Castle's first fort shares this peaceful appearance. It has a single entrance to the east, with a paved 'market-place' and cattle pens outside. The

main period of hillfort warfare does not begin until after 250 BC, some hundred years later. At this time Maiden Castle was increased in size from 15 to 45 acres (6–18 hectares) and given another, double, entrance, at the western end of the hill. Huts and grain-storage pits found inside show that the fort was at least semi-permanently inhabited. Thereafter the ramparts were twice strengthened, but whether this was the work of invaders from France is uncertain. Final small additions were made before 50 BC by the Belgic (p. 25) rulers of the Durotriges. In AD 43 the Roman 2nd legion under the command of Vespasian, attacked and overcame the Durotriges. In the war cemetery outside the east entrance, most of the burials had wound marks, showing that they had died in battle. In some cases the missile is still in place: a skull is pierced by a quadrangular Roman ballister bolt; an iron arrowhead is stuck in a vertebra, or between the ribs. The dead had been carefully buried and were accompanied by the offerings of the last native inhabitants of Maiden Castle. After the Conquest a new tribal capital was founded by the Romans at Dorchester, two miles (3·2 km) north east of Maiden Castle, in a less defensible position.

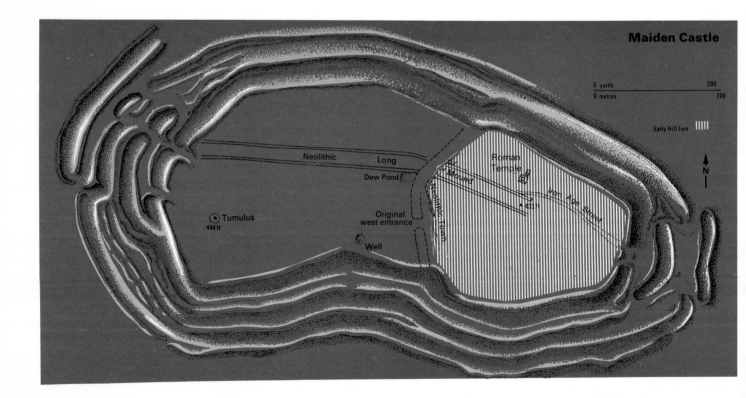

Dowth IRISH REPUBLIC

Passage grave
3rd millennium BC

BIBLIOGRAPHY
Coffey, George, *Newgrange and Other Incised Tumuli in Ireland*, Dublin, 1912
Leask, H. J., 'Inscribed Stones recently discovered at Dowth Tumulus, Co. Meath', *PRIA* C., XL, 1932–4, p. 162
Wilde, William, *The Beauties of the Boyne and its Tributary the Blackwater*, Dublin, 1849

During the 3rd millennium BC a sophisticated culture flourished mainly in the northern part of Ireland. This culture was established as a result of the arrival in east Ireland, and principally about the estuaries of the rivers Boyne and Delvin, of people of Breton and ultimately Iberian stock. The passage-grave builders initially colonized the fertile agricultural lands of Meath but apart from being skilled farmers they also paid considerable attention to spiritual matters and in particular a cult of the dead played a big part in their lives. So that they could display full reverence to their departed relatives and friends they set aside areas for cemeteries. One of the most important cemeteries of passage graves not only in Ireland, but in western Europe, is situated a few miles upstream from the mouth of the Boyne. This cemetery, Brugh na Bóinne, contains a number of passage graves and among these are the internationally known sites of Dowth, NEWGRANGE and KNOWTH. These are the largest passage graves on record and they are probably the greatest architectural achievements of Neolithic man in Europe.

Passage graves were used for communal burial, cremation being the predominant rite in Ireland. Apart from concentrating in cemeteries, passage graves have other characteristic features such as a round mound and a hilltop setting.

The circular mound at Dowth covers about an acre (approx. 4,000 sq m). It is 280 feet (85 m) in diameter and its present maximum height is 50 feet (15 m). The base of the mound is surrounded by kerbstones. These occur end-to-end. About 50 can be detected at present but the total is probably double that. Several of the kerbstones are 'decorated' with pocked designs. This 'megalithic art' is a feature of passage graves and it was probably religious symbolism that was associated with the cult of the dead.

The mound covers two chambers. Both are on the western side. The larger of the two has a passage that is almost 27 feet (8 m) long. The passage averages three feet (approx. 1 m) in width. It is formed from orthostats, probably nine on each side originally. The roof consists of seven transverse slabs which rest on the orthostats. There are three sillstones across the floor of the passage and another at the junction between passage and chamber. The central part of the chamber is almost circular and it is formed by four tall stones. Three recesses open off it so that the whole has a cruciform ground plan. There is a stone basin in the centre of the chamber. The corbelled roof of the chamber is 10 feet (3 m) in maximum height. An unusual feature of this tomb is an extension of the southern recess. This consists of two chambers each of which is at right angles to the other. A sillstone subdivides each chamber into two.

The other chamber, situated some 60 feet (18 m) to the south, is less elaborate. A short passage 10 feet (3 m) long and consisting of three orthostats on either side leads into a circular chamber 14 feet 6 inches (4·4 m) in diameter. It is formed from 12 orthostats. The original roof collapsed and this has been replaced by a modern reinforced concrete roof. A recess opens off from the chamber on the southern side.

Some of the orthostats in both tombs are decorated.

A souterrain on the western side shows that activity, likely occupation, took place on the site during the Early Christian period.

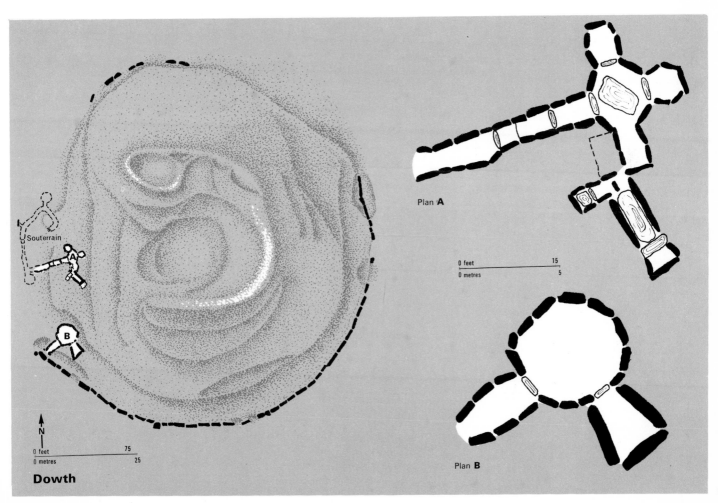

Souterrain

Plan A

Plan B

0 feet 75
0 metres 25

0 feet 15
0 metres 5

Dowth

Newgrange IRISH REPUBLIC

Passage grave
3rd millennium BC

BIBLIOGRAPHY

Coffey, George, *Newgrange and other Incised Tumuli in Ireland*, Dublin, 1912

O'Kelly, Claire, *Illustrated Guide to Newgrange*, Wexford, 1967

O'Riordain, Sean P. and Daniel, Glyn, *Newgrange and the Bend of the Boyne*, London, 1964

Pownall, T., 'A Description of the Sepulchral Monuments at Newgrange, near Drogheda', *Archaeologia* II, 1773, pp. 236–75

With DOWTH and KNOWTH this celebrated passage grave is a further confirmation of the architectural and engineering concepts and the skill of the passage-grave builders. Nobody who looks at its great corbelled roof can fail to marvel at the accomplishments of the unknown builders of four and a half thousand years ago.

The heart-shaped mound measures 260 feet (79 m) north west–south east by 280 feet (85 m) north east–south west. It covers slightly over an acre (approx. 4,000 sq m) of ground and it is about 36 feet (11 m) in height. The mound is made from stones but at some places layers of turves were incorporated. Ninety-seven kerbstones delimit the base of the mound. These vary in size. The smallest is about five feet six inches (1·7 m); the largest almost 15 feet (4·6 m).

The entrance to the tomb is on the south east. The passage is 62 feet (19 m) long and almost 3 feet (approx. 1 m) in width. Its structure is similar to that of the Knowth and Dowth passages. There are 22 orthostats on the left-hand side (as one enters the tomb) and 21 on the right-hand side. The orthostats average five feet (1·5 m) in height but the tallest stones occur close to the chamber where they are six feet (1·8 m) in height. The passage is roofed by 17 capstones. Two of these (the first and third as one enters) are huge and weigh between six and eight tons (6,100–8,120 kg). From the entrance the passage gradually increases in height.

The chamber is cruciform in plan. It is 17 feet (5·2 m) long and 21 feet 6 inches (6·6 m) wide. The left-hand recess is the smallest of the three. Its sides and back are formed from single stones. The end and right-hand recesses are formed from two stones on each side and a single stone at the back. Stone basins occur in the recesses. The beehive-shaped roof of the chamber rises to a height of 20 feet (6 m). From the tops of the orthostats the roof is constructed from courses of slabs which were used to form corbels. In this way the roof is narrowed so that it could be spanned at the top by a single slab.

A large number of the kerbstones and the chamber stones are decorated.

The mound is surrounded by a free-standing stone circle. This is 340 feet (104 m) in diameter and it encloses an area of about two acres (approx. 8,000 sq m). Originally the circle may have consisted of 35 stones but only 12 survive. The largest of these stones stands to a height of about eight feet (2·4 m) above the surface. In the neighbourhood of the tomb entrance there was a settlement by Beaker Folk. It may have been the Beaker Folk who erected the circle.

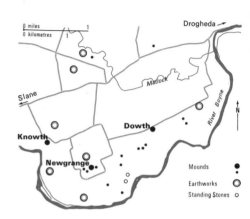

Newgrange

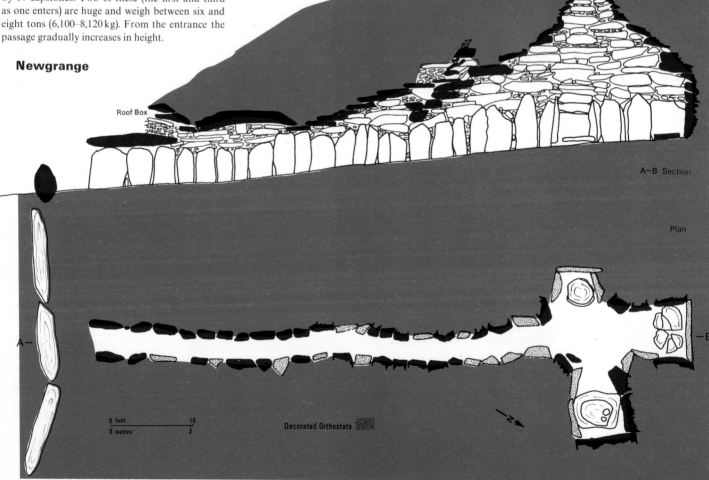

Roof Box

A–B Section

Plan

A—

—B

0 feet 10
0 metres 3

Decorated Orthostats

Knowth IRISH REPUBLIC

Passage grave cemetery and Iron Age – Norman settlement
3rd millennium BC

BIBLIOGRAPHY
Eogan, George, 'Knowth (Co. Meath) Excavations', *Antiquity* 41, 1967, pp. 302–4 and 43, 1969, pp. 8–14
Eogan, George, 'Excavations at Knowth, Co. Meath with historical note by F. J. Byrne', *PRIA* 660, 1968, pp. 299–400
MacAlister, R. A. S., 'Preliminary Report on the Excavations of Knowth', *PRIA* 490, 1943, pp. 131–66

The Knowth passage-grave cemetery is part of the larger Brugh na Bóinne cemetery (see DOWTH).

Excavation has proved that the summit of the low hill of Knowth was utilized on various occasions during the prehistoric and historic periods. The area first came into prominence during the 3rd millennium BC when the cemetery of passage graves was created. This cemetery consisted of a vast mound and several smaller ones.

The principal mound covers two large tombs. These tombs were placed back-to-back. The entrance to one faced west; the entrance to the other to the east. The Western Tomb is 114 feet (35 m) long. The passage and the chamber are constructed with orthostats and capstones. The parallel-sided passage averages two feet (60 cm) in width. It is straight for nearly three-quarters of its length. It then turns slightly to the right and finally widens into a single chamber. The Eastern Tomb is a much more impressive structure 130 feet (40 m) long. The passage is straight and is of similar construction to the passage of the Western Tomb. The chamber is a massive cruciform-shaped structure that measures

27 feet (8·2 m) across. At the bottom it is constructed from orthostats but from the tops of these the height of the chamber is carried upwards by the skilful use of the corbelling technique so as to form a beehive-shaped chamber that is up to 18 feet (5·5 m) in height. A number of orthostats and capstones in the passages and chambers of both tombs have been decorated. Neither tomb has as yet been excavated, but it may be pointed out that in the northern (right-hand) recess of the Eastern Tomb there is a very fine carved stone basin that measures four feet (1·2 m) in diameter at the mouth. The mound covers about an acre and a half (approx. 6,000 sq m). It is up to 33 feet (10 m) in height and it was constructed in an ordered fashion by laying down layers of different materials, such as turves, shale, boulder clay and stones. It has a kerb of large blocks of stone laid end-to-end. These average six feet six inches (2 m) in length and nearly all are decorated.

A number of smaller passage graves were erected close to the large mound. To date 16 have been discovered.

The second main phase of activity started during the Iron Age. At that time the large passage-grave mound was taken over for occupation purposes. In order to protect the settlement this site was transformed into a 'citadel' by the digging of two deep concentric ditches around it. Houses were constructed and at least nine souterrains were built. Both from the structures and finds it is clear that during the 1st millennium AD Knowth became a site of considerable importance and from the early historic accounts it appears that it was the royal residence of the kings of Northern Brega. Gaelic occupation lasted down to the 12th century AD. At that time it was taken over by the Normans who refurbished it and built a substantial mortared stone structure on the top. It seems that Norman control lasted for about a century. Thereafter Knowth ceased to be a place of importance but mention of it in Irish medieval mythology no doubt harks back to the time of its former greatness. For instance, it was considered to be the entrance to the *sid* or underworld and it was also as one of the *trí lorcha Hérenn* (three dark places of Ireland).

Knowth

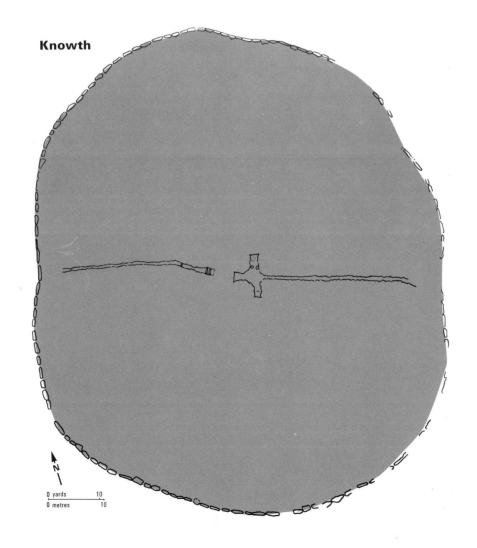

0 yards 10
0 metres 10

Tara IRISH REPUBLIC

Royal residence
c. 300 BC–AD 500

BIBLIOGRAPHY

Gwynn, E. J., 'The Metrical Dindsenchas', part 1, *Royal Irish Academy Todd Lecture Series*, vol. VIII, 1903, pp. 2–45, 57–79

MacAlister, R. A. S., *Tara: A Pagan Sanctuary of Ancient Ireland*, London, 1931

O'Riordain, Sean P., *Tara: The Monuments on the Hill*, Dundalk, 1954

Petrie, George, 'On the History and Antiquities of Tara Hill', *TRIA* XVIII, 1837, pp. 25–232

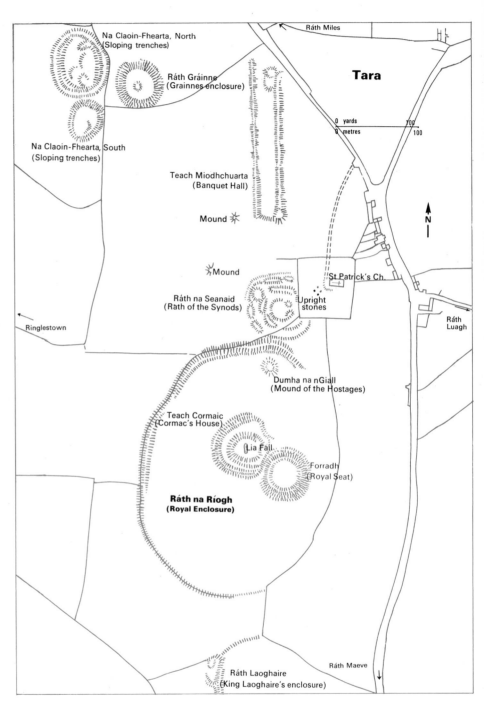

Although a low hill, 512 feet (156 m) above sea level, Tara commands an extensive view of a large part of eastern and central Ireland. Teamhair na Riogh, Tara of the Kings, is one of the most notable sites in Ireland. It is considered to have been the place of residence of the High Kings of Ireland and a centre of pagan pomp and ceremony in the centuries preceding the dawn of the Christian era. Tara is frequently mentioned in the early Irish literary sources but apart from that, the variety of monuments that still survive on the hilltop – barrows, standing stones, ring forts and a hill fort – provide striking evidence for the former greatness of the site especially during the Iron Age (last centuries BC–early centuries AD).

While it is as a Celtic centre that Tara is famous, people utilized the hill well before the Iron Age. Indeed, there was considerable activity on the hilltop during the Neolithic period. At that time at least one monument was built. This is Dumha na nGiall (Mound of the Hostages), a simple passage grave, 17 feet (5·2 m) long under a round mound 72 feet (22 m) in diameter. The chamber contained a mass of cremated bone and the finds (pottery, stone pendants, stone balls, bone pins, and beads) are the most comprehensive collection of grave goods known from any Irish passage grave.

Activity on the hill continued during the Early Bronze Age. During that period, firstly by the Food Vessel people and later by the Urn people, about 50 single-grave burials took place on Dumha na nGiall. These were in pits and some were lined with stones (cists). The burial rite was usually by cremation although there were two inhumation burials. One of these, that of a youth, was adorned with a necklace of beads of copper, jet, amber and faience.

Three gold-bar torcs, the largest on record, which were found in 1810 on the northern edge of Ráth na Seanaid show that the hill was being visited, even if it was for ritual purposes, in about 1000 BC.

It was, however, during the Iron Age that Tara became an outstandingly important settlement and possibly also assembly site. It was probably at this time that most of the surviving monuments were erected. These include the largest building on the hill, the great hill fort, Ráth na Ríogh or the Royal Enclosure. This consists of an oval area about 950 feet by 800 feet (290 × 244 m) surrounded by a wide ditch with a bank, now much denuded, on the outside. The ditch was dug into the underlying rock for a depth of over 11 feet (3·4 m) and there was a wooden palisade on the inside of the bank. The Forradh, Ráth na Seanaid (Rath of the Synods), Ráth Grainne and possibly Teach Cormaic are ring forts (protected settlement sites) and Ráth Laoghaire may be a large ring fort. In addition to Dumha na nGiall there were at least five other barrows (it has only been conclusively established that one of these is of Iron Age date), and Na Claoin-Fhearta (The Sloping Trenches) may also be burial mounds of an unusual form. The most enigmatic site at Tara is Teach Miodhchuarta (the Banquet Hall). This is a sunken area, about 750 feet (229 m) long, between two parallel banks. Despite the name it is not known if this was used for feasting. Finally, there are three standing stones. The best known of these is the Lia Fáil on Teach Cormaic. Supposedly it was on this stone that the king sat during his inauguration.

Close to the hill itself there are a number of prominent settlement sites. Of the large ring-fort, or hill-fort, class are Ráth Maeve, Ráth Miles, Ringlestown and Ráth Luagh. Ráth Maeve, to the south, resembles a hill fort. A bank encloses a circular area that is about 750 feet (229 m) in diameter.

Carrowkeel IRISH REPUBLIC

Passage grave cemetery
c. 2500–2000 BC

BIBLIOGRAPHY
Evans, Estyn, *Prehistoric and Early Christian Ireland: A Guide*, London, 1966, pp. 185–6
Killanin, Lord and Duignan, M., *Shell Guide to Ireland*, 2nd edition, London, 1967
Piggott, Stuart, *The Neolithic Cultures of the British Isles*, Cambridge, 1954, pp. 193–222

From their area of primary settlement in the east of Ireland the passage-grave builders spread to other parts. An area that particularly appealed to them was a portion of the north west, the modern county of Sligo. In that county there is a number of isolated passage graves and also cemeteries at Knocknaree, Carrowmore and Carrowkeel.

The Carrowkeel cemetery is situated on the Bricklieve mountains, from which extensive views can be obtained in all directions. These mountains, of carboniferous limestone, have a maximum elevation of 1,029 feet (314 m). The summit is an extensive plateau but its continuity is broken by a series of rifts which cut across it north north west–south south east. These rifts have steep sides: they measure about 300 to 600 feet (approx. 90–180 m) across and they are 100 to 200 feet (30–60 m) deep. Today most of the surface is covered with peat but at the time that the cairns were constructed the major part of the surface was bare limestone. The surface would have been strewn with blocks of different-sized stones and these provided a ready supply of material for the cairn builders. It can be assumed that the passage-grave people cultivated the better low-lying lands, but at the time that the tombs were built large tracts of this were forested and the wild animals included red deer and boar.

This cemetery consists of 14 cairns, a number of which were partly investigated in 1911. The cairns were numbered from A to P (excluding the letters I and J) by the excavators. Due to the incompleteness of the excavations many features of the monuments have not been revealed. The mounds were built from stone and except for site E, which is long, they are circular in ground plan. Evidence for a kerb exists at a number of sites. Site H had a double kerb and at site B there was a drystone revetting a short distance in from the kerb. The round cairns vary in diameter from 20 to 100 feet (6–31 m). The long cairn, site E, is 120 feet long by 35 feet in maximum width (37 × 11 m). This site was also delimited by a kerb. At the southern (broader) end there was a court with a blind entrance in the centre. At the opposite end of the cairn there was a passage grave of the transeptal variety.

The nature of the chamber has not been determined in sites A, L, O and P. Sites C, F, G, K, M and N have transeptal chambers. In sites C, G, K, M and N there is a single transept on each side of the chamber (i.e., a straightforward cruciform passage grave) but site F has double transepts. Sites B, D and H have chambers of simple, or undifferentiated, plan.

Although Carrowkeel does not possess massive tombs, nevertheless there is evidence that the builders possessed architectural skills and organizational abilities. This is clearly shown in the three large transeptal sites, F, G and K.

The burial rite was cremation and the grave goods included different varieties of bone and antler pins, stone pendants, beads and balls, and pottery.

On a bare rocky platform below sites O and P there is a group, up to 50, of circular stone structures. Their diameters vary from 20 to 42 feet (6–13 m). These look like the remains of hut or house sites, but their exact nature and date are not known.

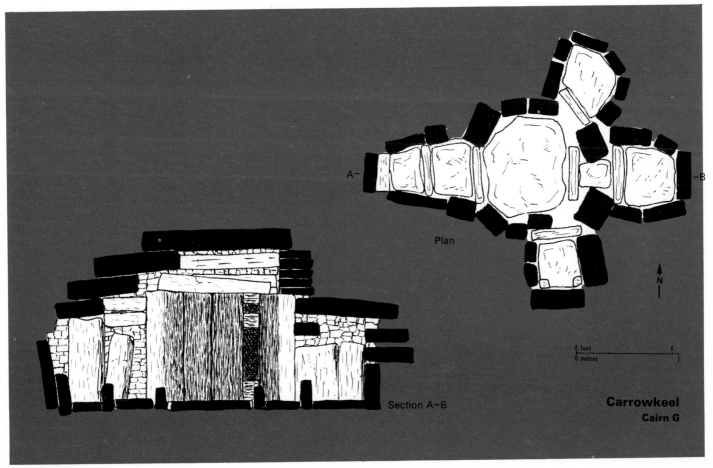

Plan

A– –B

Section A–B

0 feet   6
0 metres   2

N

Carrowkeel
Cairn G

Bryn Yr Hen Bobl ANGLESEY

Settlement, platform and passage grave
c. 2500–2000 BC

BIBLIOGRAPHY
Hemp, W. J., 'The chambered cairn known as Bryn yr Hen Bobl, near Plas Newydd, Anglesey', *Archaeologia* LXXXV, 1936, pp. 253–92
Lynch, Frances, 'The Megalithic Tombs of North Wales and The Contents of Excavated Tombs in North Wales', in T. G. E. Powell, editor, *Megalithic Enquiries in the West of Britain*, Liverpool, 1969, pp. 117–19, 161–6
Lynch, Frances, *Prehistoric Anglesey*, Llangefni, 1970, pp. 47–50
Piggott, Stuart, *The Neolithic Cultures of the British Isles*, Cambridge, 1954, p. 180

This site is picturesquely situated on a terrace that overlooks the Menai Straits. From it an extensive view of the Caernarvonshire mountains can also be obtained. Three main phases of activity are represented on the site but apparently there was cultural continuity.

The earliest remains are of a settlement. Part of this was exposed outside the cairn on the southern side but its extent has not been determined, neither have house sites been revealed. During the time of the settlement there were considerable oakwoods in the neighbourhood and hazel and hawthorn were also common. The inhabitants had sheep, ox and pig. They used, and probably made, pottery as well as artifacts in flint (scrapers and arrowheads) and stone (polished axes). But of particular interest is the fact that this was an industrial site. Rough-outs for stone axes, which were quarried in the Graig Lwyd, Caernarvonshire factory, were brought here for finishing.

The next stage in the history of the site was the construction of a raised platform of stones, 330 feet long, 40 feet wide and 2 feet high (100 m × 12 m × 60 cm). This is a unique monument and the fact that it bonds into the cairn of the megalithic tomb shows that it predates that structure.

Finally the passage was constructed. The covering cairn is kidney-shaped and it is 130 feet (40 m) in maximum diameter. It is surrounded at the base by a drystone wall and a short distance in from this, and concentric with it, there is another stone wall. There is a funnel-shaped forecourt before the entrance to the chamber. This is also bounded by drystone walling but the portion adjoining the chamber is flanked on one side by two upright stones and on the other by one stone.

The rectangular chamber measures 8 feet long by 6 feet in average width internally (2·3 × 1·8 m). It is covered by a single capstone. Unburned human remains were found in the chamber but it is not certain that all of these were deposited during the Neolithic period. This is an unusual chamber but another site in Anglesey, Pant y Saer, provides a good parallel.

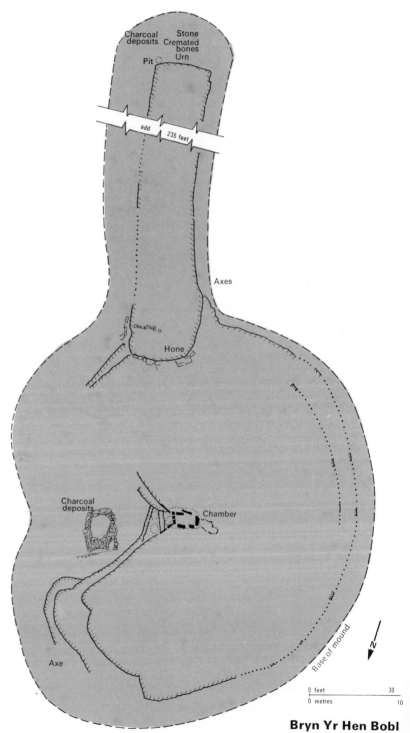

A-B Section

Plan

Charcoal deposits

Pit

Stone Cremated bones Urn

add   235 feet

Axes

Hone

Charcoal deposits

Chamber

Axe

Base of mound

N

0 feet   30
0 metres   10

Bryn Yr Hen Bobl

Barclodiad Y Gawres ANGLESEY

Passage grave
c. 2500–2000 BC

BIBLIOGRAPHY
Lynch, Frances, *Prehistoric Anglesey*, Llangefni, 1970, pp. 34–40
Piggott, Stuart, *The Neolithic Cultures of the British Isles*, Cambridge, 1954, pp. 193–222
Powell, T. G. E. and Daniel, G. E., *Barclodiad Y Gawres: The Excavations of a Megalithic Chamber Tomb in Anglesey*, Liverpool, 1956

Barclodiad y Gawres stands on a headland that overlooks a sheltered beach on the south-western side of the Island of Anglesey. Indeed, on a clear day the Wicklow hills of Ireland are visible and it is likely that the builders of this tomb came from Ireland at some stage in the centuries before 2000 BC.

The entrance to the passage is from the north. This consists of a cuspidal area that is formed by curving inwards the sides of the cairn. The passage, about 23 feet (7 m) long, has a maximum width of four feet (1·2 m) and a minimum width of two feet (60 cm). It once had seven orthostats on each side,

but the western side has been damaged and only two of its orthostats remain. At one point on the eastern side of the passage, close to the chamber, one of the orthostats is set obliquely so as to form a small niche for a pillar stone, two feet three inches in height (70 cm). No roofing stones survived.

The chamber is cruciform in plan and it is formed from orthostats. Internally it measures 18 feet across and 15 feet in depth (5·5 × 4·6 m). The central area is polygonal in plan. The roof (now destroyed) may have been corbelled above the tops of the orthostats and a large stone, possibly the capstone, survives. The end recess, about four feet (1·2 m) square was bounded by three orthostats but one of these is now missing. There is a small sillstone across the front. The eastern recess is also bounded by three orthostats. The western is the largest recess of the three. It is rectangular and there is a sill and other stones across the front. On the southern side a gap between two orthostats leads into a small rectangular annexe.

Only the base of the mound remains. This appears to have been circular. There was a band of compact stones marking the circumference but a definite kerb did not exist. A pile of loose stones was heaped up around the tomb on the outside and between this and the band of stones at the circumference there was a layer of redeposited peat. It is possible that the whole upper part of the mound was built up from peat.

The backstones of the eastern and western recesses and three stones near the junction with the passage and chamber bear pocked designs. Only spirals occur in the recess, but they are scarce on the other stones where the principal motifs are lozenges, chevrons and zig-zags.

The burial rite was cremation, the burned bones being placed in the recesses; in the western recess there were also fragments of a bone or antler pin. The remains represent at least two individuals, probably young men.

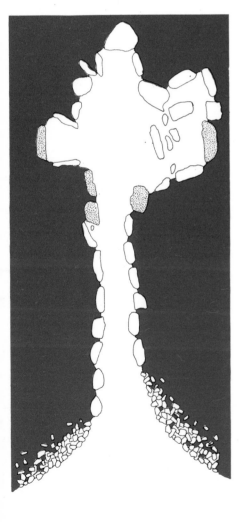

Decorated stones

0 feet 10
0 metres 3

Reconstruction of Chamber

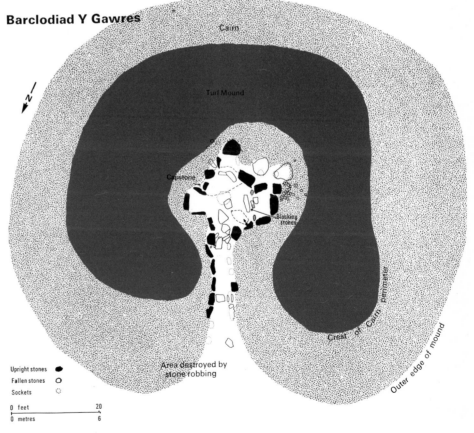

Barclodiad Y Gawres

Cairn

Turf Mound

Capstone

Blocking stones

Crest of Cairn perimeter

Area destroyed by stone robbing

Outer edge of mound

Upright stones ●
Fallen stones ○
Sockets ◌

0 feet 20
0 metres 6

Bryn Celli Dhu ANGLESEY

Henge and passage grave
c. 1800 BC

BIBLIOGRAPHY
Hemp, W. J., 'The Chambered Cairn of Bryn Celli Dhu',
 Archaeologia 30, (2nd series), 1930, pp. 179–214
Lynch, Frances, 'The Megalithic Tombs of North Wales',
 in T. G. E. Powell, editor, *Megalithic Enquiries in the
 West of Britain*, Liverpool, 1969, pp. 111–12
Lynch, Frances, *Prehistoric Anglesey*, Llangefni 1970, pp.
 58–65
O'Kelly, Clair, Bryn Celli Dhu, Anglesey: A Reinterpreta-
 tion, *Archaeologia Cambrensis*, 1969, pp. 17–48

About 3000 BC people set out from Brittany and landed in considerable numbers in the Boyne area of eastern Ireland. Some groups, who may have been blown off course, reached North Wales, or there may have been a secondary movement by passage-grave builders from Ireland (compare with BARCLODIAD Y GAWRES). The tomb plan suggests that Bryn Celli Dhu, Anglesey, has more affinities with Brittany than with Ireland. But this tomb plan must be due to the conservatism of passage-grave society. Bryn Celli Dhu was one of the last passage graves that was built as it is later than a Late Neolithic–Early Bronze Age henge monument.

The henge monument is a circular area about 69 feet (20·6 m) in diameter. This was enclosed by a ditch that averaged 17 feet across at the top and about six feet in depth (5·2 × 1·8 m). As the ditch has been only partially excavated the position of the entrance, or entrances, has not been located. Neither did any evidence for a bank come to light but it is most likely that one existed, presumably on the outside of the ditch. It is even possible that it was removed by the builders of the tomb who could have used the material for the mound. There was a pit in the centre of the henge. This was at least four feet six inches (1·4 m) in diameter at the mouth and the same in depth. The pit was filled with clay and stones, the bottom was scorched with fire and there were fragments of human bone present. There were two stones over the mouth of the pit, one of which was decorated, but these seem to have been deposited by the passage-grave builders. On the inside of the ditch there appears to have been a row of irregularly spaced pits. Some of these held upright stones and occasionally at the base human bone had been deposited.

After a long enough period of time had elapsed for sod to form over the area and the ditch partially to silt up, a passage grave was erected. The passage is 26 feet (8 m) long but the outer eight feet (2·4 m) may not have had a roof. It is formed from seven orthostats on each side but at the outer end the orthostats are doubled. It is possible that this was a structural necessity to give support to a large capstone or lintel that, it may be assumed, spanned the entrance at that point. The orthostats in the passage vary in size. Some are five feet (1·5 m); others are only about three feet (approx. 1 m) in height. The low orthostats may have been topped with drystone work in order to level up the height of the sides of the passage. Three capstones survive but originally there may have been a fourth.

The chamber is polygonal in shape, with six orthostats and two capstones. Internally the chamber measures about eight feet long and six feet six inches in height (2·4 × 2 m). There is an upright pillar in the northern side of the chamber. The circular mound, of stones and earth, is much denuded but originally it covered an area 85 feet (26 m) in diameter. It has a kerb of up to 80 stone blocks.

On the south side of the chamber one of the orthostats has a spiral and one of the stones that overlay the central pit in the henge (the 'pattern stone') is decorated on both faces, and across the top, by meanders.

Cremated bone was found on the floor of the chamber and at the inner end of the passage. Elsewhere a flint scraper, *petit tranchet* derivative arrowheads and a stone bead were found. Outside the entrance features, such as post-holes and setting of small stones, came to light. This area also produced loose quartz stones.

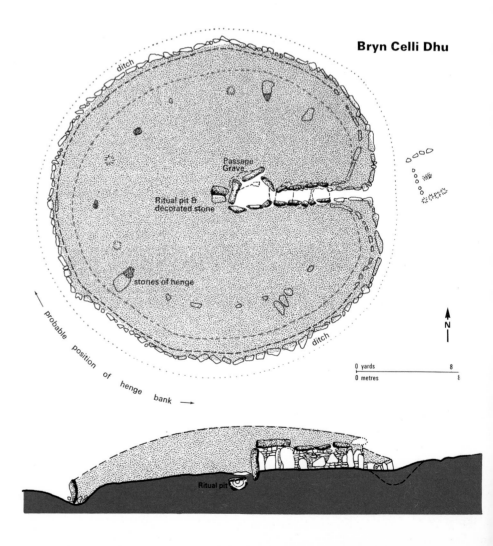

Bryn Celli Dhu

ditch

Passage Grave

Ritual pit & decorated stone

stones of henge

probable position of henge bank →

ditch

N

0 yards   8
0 metres   8

Ritual pit

Maes Howe ORKNEY ISLANDS

Passage grave
c. 2200–1800 BC

BIBLIOGRAPHY
Childe, V. Gordon, 'Excavations at Maes Howe', *PSAS* LXXXII, 1947–8
Petrie, George, 'Notice of the Opening of a Tumulus, called Maes-how, at Stenness in Orkney', *Archaeological Journal* XVIII, 1861, pp. 353–8
Henshall, Audrey Shore, *The Chambered Tombs of Scotland*, vol. 1, Edinburgh, 1963, pp. 219–22 with pp. 121–34
Royal Commission on the Ancient Monuments of Scotland, *Twelfth Report with an Inventory of the Ancient Monuments of Orkney and Shetland*, Edinburgh 1946, pp. 306–13

The magnificent megalithic passage grave of Maes Howe stands in the southern part of Mainland which is the largest of the Orkney islands. It is built from the local flagstones of Old Red Sandstone. This rock, which readily splits into rectangular forms, partly accounts for the exceptional regularity and perfect finish of its architecture.

The cruciform plan and corbelling of the chamber and the enormous circular covering mound link Maes Howe with Newgrange and other Irish passage graves. It is generally assumed that it was built by settlers who had followed the sea route up the west coast of Scotland, possibly using the Stromness region as their port of entry. The affinities with NEWGRANGE suggest that this tomb also was built in the mid-3rd millennium BC. In the 12th century AD on more than one occasion Vikings took shelter in the chamber, having entered through the roof. They left graffiti that included a dragon and a runic inscription recording that they had carried off treasure.

The tomb is entered from the south west by a long passage, the inner 36 feet (11 m) of which are floored, walled and roofed with huge flagstones. A large block that stands in a recess just inside this portion was probably used to close the entrance. The 15-foot (4·6 m) square chamber is walled with upright slabs above which rises a corbelled roof, the inner edges of the stones sloped to make a smooth-faced vault.

The apex is missing, but was probably about 15 feet (4·6 m) high and finished with a single capstone. This fine corbelled vault is supported by four buttresses so placed in the corners of the chamber as to form three apparent recesses, one on each side and one at the inner end. From each of these a narrow opening gives on to a small rectangular cell with the floor raised well above the main chamber. It is recorded that in the 19th century these cells contained a fragment of human skull and animal bones. They could be closed by slabs now lying on the chamber floor.

The chamber is covered in loose rubble contained by a neat drystone wall. The main mass of the mound is of clay and stones, but two low revetment walls show that it was built in an orderly fashion.

This remarkable monument is further distinguished by standing in a level oval area demarcated by a 45-foot (14 m) wide ditch. The material from the ditch may have been used for the cairn.

There are several smaller passage graves in the Orkney islands (and other forms of megalithic tombs). There is a peculiar type known as the stalled cairn, which is found in some numbers on Rousay; the gallery is divided into segments by projecting pairs of tall slabs. Their builders probably came by eastern seaways via Caithness, in contrast with the western approach of the passage-grave people. The finest example is Mid Howe.

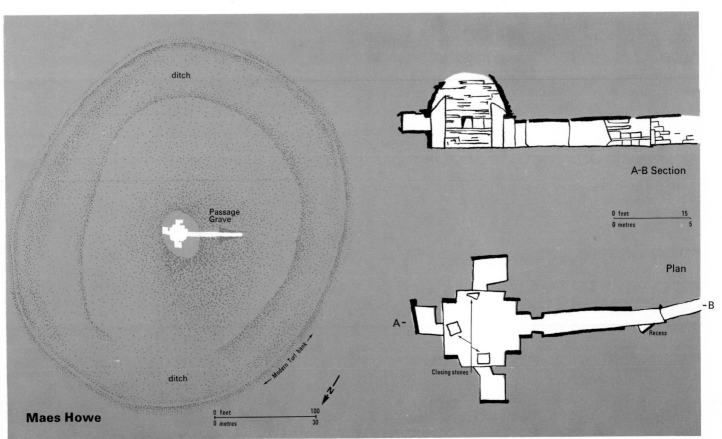

Maes Howe

A-B Section

Plan

0 feet 15
0 metres 5

0 feet 100
0 metres 30

Skara Brae ORKNEY ISLANDS

Settlement
c. 1800 BC

BIBLIOGRAPHY
Childe, V. Gordon, *Skara Brae*, London, 1931
Childe, V. Gordon, *Ancient Dwellings at Skara Brae, Orkney*, Edinburgh, 1950
Piggott, Stuart, *The Neolithic Cultures of the British Isles*, Cambridge, 1954
Royal Commission on the Ancient Monuments of Scotland, *Twelfth Report with an Inventory of the Ancient Monuments of Orkney and Shetland*, Edinburgh, 1946

This very well-preserved village was excavated in 1927–30 by V. Gordon Childe. It is situated on the Bay of Skail on the main island (Mainland) of Orkney. Skara Brae was inhabited by a self-sufficient stone-using community around the early part of the 2nd millennium BC. Furniture was made from stone slabs. This, and the fact that the houses themselves survived reasonably intact, provides us with a very complete picture of the way of life of the village.

The excavator distinguished three main phases of occupation but there was cultural continuity throughout. The first phase was a small encampment represented by a fireplace and occupation refuse. During the second phase stone huts were constructed. These were poorly built and eventually they were demolished. It was during the third phase that the settlement was elaborated into a group of eight substantial, drystone-built houses. A main passage, slab-roofed, runs through the 'village' with

possessions of the owners. There was a hearth in the centre of each house and in at least one instance there was a seat beside this. For fuel peat was burned.

The economy of the village was based on fishing and raising sheep and cattle. The inhabitants used flat-bottomed bowls and other vessels handsomely decorated by groove and incision. The motifs included lozenges, triangles, and in at least one instance a spiral. Stone vessels were also used. Tools included bone adzes and chisels as well as points and awls. Pins of bone, antler and possibly ivory may have fastened cloaks, and for personal adornment the villagers wore beads of stone and bone.

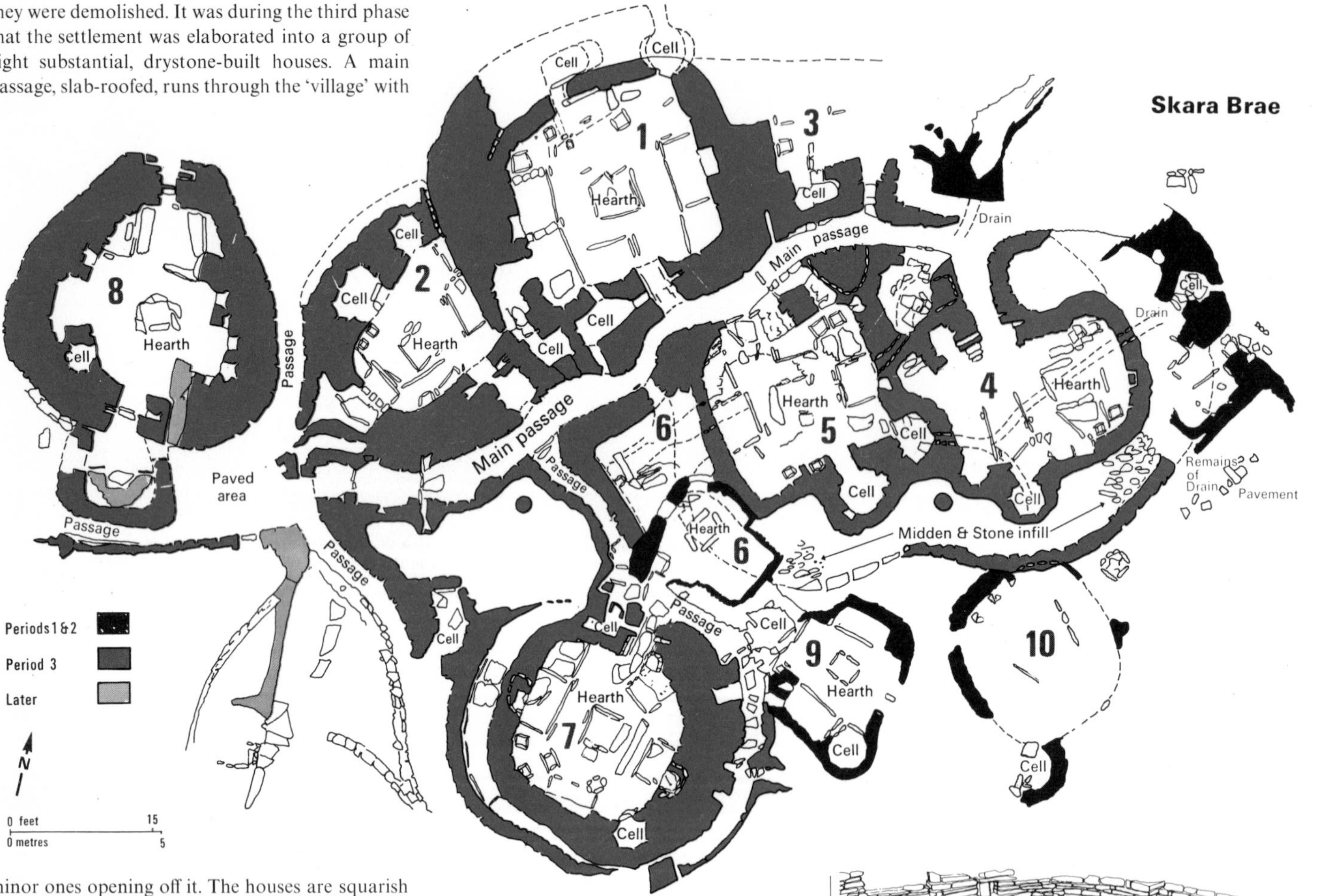

Skara Brae

minor ones opening off it. The houses are squarish in plan, measuring 15 to 20 feet (4·6–6 m) across. The exact nature of the roofs is not known but the rooms may have been spanned horizontally by ribs of whale, covered with thatch or skins.

The absence of wood meant that stone was used for furniture and as a result a fairly complete picture of the furnishing has emerged. This was built-in and normally each hut had two beds, a dresser with two shelves, and wall cupboards. One of the beds was larger than the other and this was probably used by the man. Above the beds were recesses in the walls which must have been used for keeping the personal

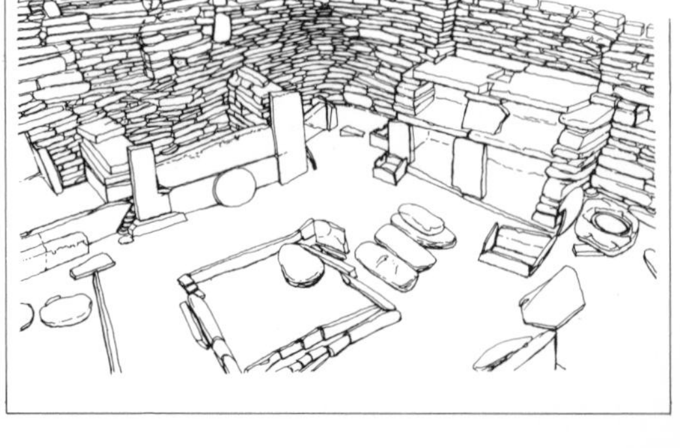

Skara Brae, Hut 1, interior
showing hearth and furniture

44

Cairnpapple SCOTLAND

Henge monument, and Bronze Age cairns
c. 2000–1500 BC

BIBLIOGRAPHY
Atkinson, R. J. C., Piggott, C. M. and Sandars, N., *Excavations at Dorchester, Oxon*, part I, Oxford, 1951, esp. pp. 81–107
Piggott, Stuart, 'The Excavations at Cairnpapple Hill, West Lothian, 1947–8', *PSAS* LXXXII, 1947–8
Wainwright, G. J., 'A review of the Henge Monuments in the light of recent research', *PPS* XXXV, 1969, pp. 112–33

A characteristic of the Late Neolithic and Early Bronze Age people of Britain was the emphasis that they placed on ritual. A site that clearly demonstrates this is Cairnpapple, in West Lothian, Scotland, where people of successive Early Bronze Age cultures practised various forms of ritual. The nature of the rites that were carried out by the Beaker Folk in the henge monument is not known, but the subsequent Food-Vessel and Urn people constructed, and enlarged, a cairn for burial purposes. Cairnpapple also throws considerable light on the cultural sequence in Scotland during the first half of the 2nd millennium BC.

The first use of the summit of Cairnpapple Hill, which commands an extensive view of the Firth–Clyde isthmus, took place during the Neolithic period (before 2000 BC). At that time seven holes were dug in the form of an irregular arc, possibly to hold upright stones. Thirteen deposits of cremated bone were found in and near them. The arc opened to the west and three holes in front of it may also have held upright stones.

A henge monument was built at the beginning of the metal age. This enclosed the features already mentioned and it consisted of an oval area that measured 145 by 125 feet (44 × 38 m). This was delimited by a ditch that had a bank on the outside. Between the bank and ditch there was a flat area, or berm. There were entrances on the north and on the south.

Excavation revealed various features within the oval area. Concentric with the edge of the ditch there was a setting of 24 holes. These may have held standing stones originally. In the centre there was an unexplained complex of irregularly shaped pits. A short distance to the west of this feature there was a standing stone eight feet (2·4 m) in height. At its base there was a grave. This was subrectangular in shape and it measured seven by four feet (2·1 × 1·2 m). The grave contained a burial but only the teeth survived. It was accompanied by two pottery vessels of beaker type and a fragment of a similar vessel. There was a setting of stones around the edge of the grave and the whole may have been covered by a small cairn. On the east side of the enclosure, just on the outside of the line of the holes, there was another grave, perhaps a child's. It, too, contained a beaker.

Later Food-Vessel people built a kerbed round cairn 50 feet (15 m) in diameter overlying the main grave and part of the central pit complex of the Beaker period. This cairn covered two cists, a central one with an inhumation burial and a vase-type food vessel, and one off-centre containing the cremated remains of a youngish adult, probably a woman.

The Food-Vessel cairn was subsequently buried beneath a round cairn that was double its size. This enlarged cairn was also kerbed and it was constructed to cover two burials. Both were cremations and they were under inverted pottery vessels of the collared urn type.

Finally, four extended inhumation burials may give evidence for the use of the site during the Iron Age.

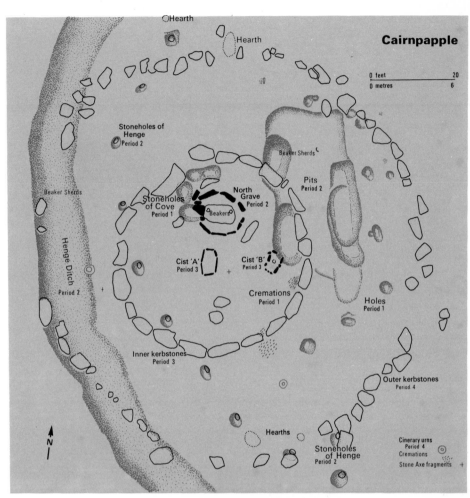

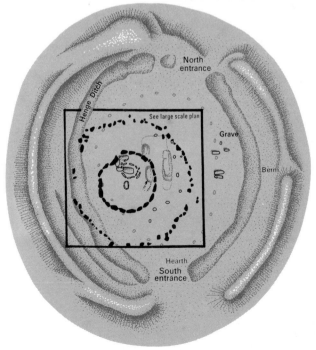

45

Mousa SHETLAND

Broch
c. 300 BC–AD 400

BIBLIOGRAPHY
Cruden Stewart, *The Brochs of Mousa and Clickhimin, Shetland*, Edinburgh, 1951, pp. 7–9
MacKie, Euan W., 'The Origin and Development of the Broch, and Wheelhouse Building Cultures of the Scottish Iron Age', *PPS* XXXI, 1965, pp. 93–146
Paterson, J. Wilson, 'The Broch of Mousa: A Survey by H.M. Office of Works', *PSAS* LVI, 1921–2, pp. 172–83
Scott, Lindsay, 'The Problem of the Brochs', *PPS* XIII, 1947, pp. 1–36

In the course of the Iron Age farmers in Scotland, especially in the remote north west, built for themselves well-protected homesteads in the form of circular, drystone-walled citadels. Sometimes they were high towers displaying a scale of architecture hitherto unknown among Iron Age communities in Britain. The citadel is often surrounded by outer defence works such as ditch and bank. These brochs are a Scottish phenomenon and in that country about 500 are known. They overlook low-lying fertile tracts of land usually close to the sea. The inhabitants were self-sufficient. They practised mixed farming and they manufactured many of their everyday requirements such as textiles and pottery.

The most impressive broch of all stands at Mousa, Shetland. The tower of this broch is 43 feet 6 inches (13·3 m) high. At the base it is 50 feet (15 m) in external diameter but at the top it narrows to 40 feet (12 m). In profile the sides are curved externally while internally the walls taper outwards from the base. The rectangular entrance is at ground level. This has a paved floor. At a lower level there are three chambers, or cells, within the thickness of the walls. In addition to the ground floor, there may have been two additional floors so that when in use the structure was three storeyed.

The upper part of the wall is hollowed. The space between both shells is spanned by flagstones and as a result galleries are formed.

The stairway is in the hollow of the wall. This would have been for security purposes, and entrance to the presumed floor that the lower scarcement supported would have been by ladder. For security purposes the entrance to it is 7 feet (2·1 m) above ground level. The stairway, 3 feet (approx. 1 m) wide, leads up to the top of the tower.

Interior corbelling was used to bring about a slight inturning of the wall at the top. It is not known how the broch was roofed.

Outside the tower there are the remains of a wall and originally there may also have been huts.

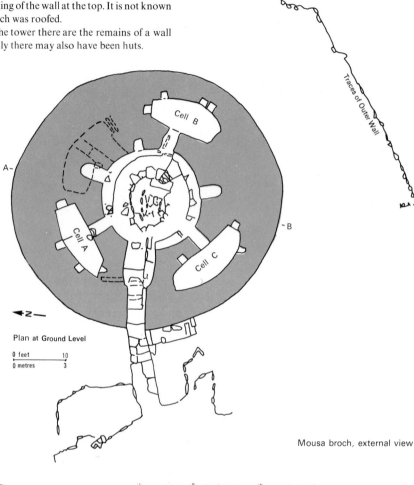

Plan at Ground Level

0 feet 10
0 metres 3

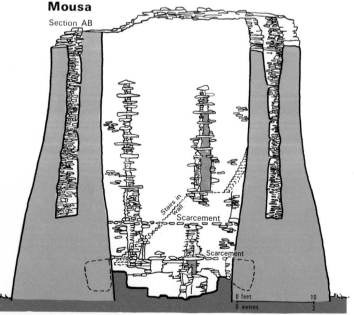

Mousa

Section AB

Stairs in wall
Scarcement
Scarcement

0 feet 10
0 metres 3

Mousa broch, external view

FRANCE

France has one foot in the Mediterranean and the other in the English Channel. At some periods Brittany was more an Atlantic coast province than a French peninsula, while the north was open through the Low Countries to the North European Plain and to movements along the Danube and Rhine. On the other hand Mediterranean influences, sometimes from Italy, sometimes from Iberia, flowed up the natural highway of the Rhône valley, or, less strongly, westward down the Garonne.

The famous cave dwellings of the Palaeolithic hunters were concentrated in three regions: the Dordogne, the central Pyrenees and along the Côte d'Azur. Le Vallonet cave, near Menton, is the oldest inhabited site in Europe, perhaps a million years old, and the other sea caves on this coast, the Grimaldi caves and the Observatory, near Monaco, and Lazaret, in the suburbs of Nice, contain early occupations representative of Neanderthal man and his predecessors. Lazaret cave is notable, as containing the only Lower Palaeolithic house or shelter in a cave. There Acheulean man lay on bear skin couches, supported on a stuffing of seaweed. Most of the Dordogne and Pyrenees caves on the other hand, were only formed by springs active in the last, Riss-Wurm, or *Eemian* interglacial, about 90,000 years ago, much later than those on the southern coast of France. It is from the finds in these caves, principally from those in the Dordogne, that popular ideas of Cave Men were formed.

During the Upper Pleistocene, after 70,000 BC, most of central and western Europe was periglacial steppe and almost uninhabitable, except in the summer (especially between 30,000–10,000 BC), but the proximity of the Atlantic and the southern latitude gave to south-western France damper but also less severe climatic conditions, and made it a favourite habitat for the reindeer, the bison and their hunters. In the principal caves there are thick deposits belonging to this later period, and these contain the flint tools of the hunters, and the broken bones of the animals they sought in far greater profusion than less favoured sites, and illustrate the dense and relatively stable population supported by this region for many thousands of years. It is in these conditions of abundance that there flourished the palaeolithic animal art of the Magdalenian – the cave painting and also cave engraving and rock sculpture for which the cave of LASCAUX, and the cave and shelters of the LES EYZIES DISTRICT and the French Pyrenees, are celebrated.

The discovery of many rich palaeolithic deposits stratified one upon another in the caves has concentrated attention on problems which can be solved by their investigation in the vertical plane; on problems, that is to say, related to the thickness and contents of different layers in the cave – the relative ages of a series of archaeological units known as cultures. The main French Palaeolithic cultures after the Acheulean are the Mousterian, attributed to Neanderthal man (60,000–39,000 BC) and a series of later cultures made by modern man (*Homo sapiens sapiens*), Chatelperron (starting 33,000 BC), Aurignacian (starting 30,000 BC), Gravettian (starting 24,000 BC), Solutrean (starting 17,000 BC), Magdalenian (starting 15,000 BC).

Open air huts or tents, houses or settlements of this period have only recently been recognized and excavated in France. These apparently exist in some numbers, in the Dordogne and east of Paris, and tell us much more about the social life and economic organization of the hunters. In open air sites (especially Pincevent near Montereau), which were perhaps only occupied for one or two seasons, houses and rooms, kitchen, butcher's shop and bedroom are spread out for the archaeologist to study. In the accumulated rubbish heaps of a permanently occupied cave, which represent many generations of occupants, the debris is less easily related to the human situation.

The profusion of caves and visible monuments, such as megaliths, has also distracted archaeological attention from the buried open-air settlements of later periods, though these are beginning to be excavated as the result of the increasing industrialization of the south of France. The earliest agricultural communities of France are recognized in the caves of the foothills along the Mediterranean coast, where users of a type of 47 pottery known as Impressed Ware appear to represent immigrants coming by sea, at about 5000 BC. In the earlier stages the pottery is decorated in a number of different ways which are impressed before the pottery is fired. A particular variety is Cardial decorated pottery, decorated with the serrated edge of the common cockle or Cardium shell. This style is common at the beginning of the tradition, but dies out entirely after a time, and the ratio of plain to decorated pottery becomes greater and greater. Finally the pottery style is abandoned or more probably transformed into that of a second style of predominantly plain pottery identified as the Chassey culture, one of the most long-lasting French Neolithic cultural traditions. The earliest radio-carbon dates for Chassey type pottery are about 3500 BC, so that the cultural tradition represented by these forms had already existed for about 1500 years in southern France. But the change in pottery, if not in the people making it, heralded a great expansion of Neolithic farmers, and an increase in population. By 2900 BC this agricultural people had spread throughout southern France from Marseilles to Toulouse, and 500 years later they occupied as well all eastern France, the Paris basin and the Channel coast. While the main located Impressed Ware sites are usually small caves, the Chassey settlement at Toulouse – one of the earliest – is a camp, with more than 100 houses enclosed by a ditch of the causewayed type, known from contemporary camps in Britain.

Between 4000–3000 BC other parts of France have a different cultural history. The Paris basin and the flat plains of northern France and Belgium form part of the territory of groups of efficient farmers, coming immediately from Germany but building large farmhouses and using Linear pottery in the tradition of the farmers in central Europe or the Danube. Two further traditions are identified on the Atlantic coast before 3000 BC. In Brittany the first farmers, travelling apparently by sea from Spain, introduce a form of megalithic or dry-walled chambered tomb, used for communal, periodic burials and known as a passage grave; and in the La Rochelle–Charente district, another farming group construct ditched camps on the chalk downs like those found in England (including the AVEBURY DISTRICT), and also bury their dead in megalithic communal tombs.

Such tombs dominate prehistory in Brittany and on the Atlantic coast, in the Paris basin and the coastal hills to the west of the Rhône valley for the next 2000 years, changing their shape and use and contents, representing first one agricultural people then another, containing Beaker pottery after 2000 BC and later funerary offerings, including copper and bronze tools and ornaments. The other burial tradition, after about 1600 BC, is that represented by the small round mound or tumulus constructed of earth or stones, under which single bodies of chieftains are buried, usually after cremation. Apart from a small group of immigrants from England, found mainly in Finistère, where they create what is known as the Breton Dagger Grave culture, barrows and burial mounds with cremations are found in grave fields or barrow cemeteries in eastern France, mainly in the territory bordering the Rhine and represent the outer edge of a much larger central European Bronze Age culture.

Excavated settlements are lacking both for the megalith users and for the tumulus peoples of eastern France and their successors, the Marnian Celts of Burgundy and the upper Paris basin (whose chariot burials beneath similar mounds or tumuli represent the latest inhabitants of pre-Roman France) so we can at present say very little about their ways of life. The answers may lie among the many camps and fortified sites recorded by French archaeologists, both in the Rhône valley and in other districts. Some of these undoubtedly represent settlements of Bronze Age and Neolithic date, as well as those more complex sites which belong to the confused period immediately before the Roman conquest, and perhaps also to the Middle Ages.

Inset map right. Generalized distribution of Megalithic chambered tombs (Stuart Piggott, *Ancient Europe*, London, 1965).

English Channel

Channel Is.
La Hougue Bie ✳

✳Barnenez
Finistère
○
Brittany
✳Castle Coz
✳
Carnac✳ Locmariaquer
✳ **Gavr' inis**

Loire

La
Rochelle

Atlantic Ocean

✳ ✳

Les Eyzies. .**Lascaux Cave**

✳ **Dordogne**

Toulouse.
St Michael du Touch ✳

✳ ✳

Muri Gallici ○
Main Megalithic site ✳

Pyrenees

Seine

Paris
✳✳
✳
✳✳

Vix✳

Burgundy

Saône

Rhône

Alps

Languedoc
✳
✳ ✳

Arles✳ ✳**Grotte des Fées**

Menton
Monaco
Nice

Marseilles

Rhine

0 miles   62
0 kilometres   100

Mediterranean Sea

49

Les Eyzies District FRANCE

Caves and shelters with painting, engraving, sculpture
c. 15,000–10,000 BC

BIBLIOGRAPHY
Daniel, G. E., *Les Eyzies and Carnac,* 1955
Sieveking, A. and G. de G., *The Caves of France and
    Northern Spain,* 1962
Graziosi, P., *Palaeolithic Art,* London 1960

Les Eyzies is a village in the Dordogne, south east of Perigueux. The French call it the capital of prehistory, because of the numerous important prehistoric caves and shelters found in the district.

The village lies between the river Vezère and a line of steep overhanging limestone crags, into which a number of houses are built. These towering rocks are a feature of the neighbourhood and contain the prehistoric sites. Many living places, containing accumulations of prehistoric occupation debris, are rocky overhangs providing cover from wind and rain, rather than real caves. These are known as shelters (*abri*). A number are in the crags behind the village, including the Cro Magnon shelter, which in 1868 yielded burials of the variety of *Homo sapiens* known as Cro Magnon man, creator of cave art. It is now the garage of an hotel. Abri Pataud is another shelter of the same sort, where a team from Harvard University excavated for 15 years. The Les Eyzies Museum, which has some of the most important finds from the district, is in a house built under another rocky overhang. The major prehistoric occupation sites are some distance from the village. They include two big shelters at Laugerie-Basse and Laugerie-Haute, and further away Laussel, Le Moustier and La Madeleine.

Laugerie-Basse and La Madeleine, which lie on the river bank opposite Tursac, are the main living places of the hunters who were responsible for much of the cave art. These people are known as Magdalenians, after the La Madeleine shelter. Both shelters have been excavated and found to contain numerous works of miniature art carved on bone, antler or stone, some of which are in the Les Eyzies Museum and in another museum on the site at Laugerie-Basse. Laugerie-Haute is a Solutrean living site, with a long sequence of earlier Gravettian and a mysterious Proto Magdalenian industry, not found elsewhere, stratified *beneath* the Solutrean deposits. The Le Moustier cave and shelter, at a village of this name some miles away, provides the principal Middle Palaeolithic sequence in the district. Here, in fact, is the type-site for the Mousterian culture of Neanderthal man.

There are also four major caves just outside Les Eyzies containing Palaeolithic art: La Mouthe, Les Combarelles and Font de Gaume, and also the Cap Blanc shelter with its famous sculptured horses, which are finer than any other French Palaeolithic sculpture. Font de Gaume is the most important local cave for Palaeolithic art. It is also well lit and looked after. The cave is decorated, on either side of the main corridor, with a frieze of painted (and engraved) bison, now rather faded, with, upon their bodies, a further frieze of engraved mammoth, once assumed to be much later in date. This is an example of the phenomenon referred to as Superposition (see LASCAUX). One bison was hidden until recently under stalagmite, and now that this has been removed, can be seen in its original bright colours. There is also one of the very rare 'scenes' in the art of the caves – a painting of two reindeer. The female is kneeling, or attempting to rise and the male is muzzling or licking her head. Les Combarelles, close to Font de Gaume, is a narrow cave with a large number of very fine animal engravings, and some curious engraved human 'caricatures'. La Mouthe has a small number of clear engravings including a fine ibex, and a famous painted tectiform symbol, thought to illustrate a Magdalenian tent. The cave's historic importance lies in the fact that it was sealed by a prehistoric occupation deposit when it was first excavated, and so provided a guarantee of authenticity to the cave art within. Cap Blanc is a shelter and not a cave and contains some fine sculptured animals, principally six almost lifesized horses. In the Gorge d'Enfer, a small side valley near the Laugerie shelters, which is now a national park, there is a further cave with, on its ceiling, a single, very impressive large bas-relief sculpture of a salmon, one of the main sorts of fish caught by the Magdalenians for food. Above the salmon is a tectiform symbol resembling a trap. There are two deep cuts in either side of the fish, dating from an attempt to remove the sculpture clandestinely in modern times.

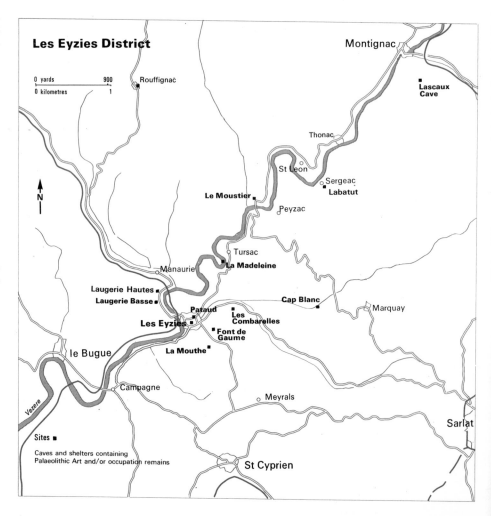

Lascaux FRANCE

Painted cave
c. 15000–13,000 BC

BIBLIOGRAPHY
Laming, A., *Lascaux*, London, 1959
Sieveking, A. and G. de G., *The Caves of France and Northern Spain*, 1962

Lascaux cave near Montignac, found by accident in 1940, is deservedly the most famous prehistoric painted cave in France.

The cave had been sealed in antiquity shortly after it had been painted. Many if not all the paintings were as fresh as the day they were finished. The cave walls are a sparkling creamy white which shows up the animals admirably. Beyond the cave entrance is a broad hall nearly 50 feet (15 m) long which can be taken in at a glance. Its walls are decorated with a number of friezes of animals evidently disposed with care to make the best of available space. The chamber beyond it has further friezes on the upper walls and ceiling (the floor has been deepened in modern times to improve access). Another corridor and a further room to the right have fine paintings of groups of animals, often carefully related to one another, such as a group of stags' heads painted as if seen swimming across a river.

At the end of the main hall there is a line of six very large bulls painted in black outline, some of them 16–18 feet (4·8–5·5 m) in length. The head of one of these animals, wonderfully observed, must be the most famous of all palaeolithic paintings. Under the bulls' legs and upon their bodies are other animals, small, rather fat, horses and cows painted in a different style. In a space between two of the bulls which face one another is a small group of red deer painted more stiffly and in a slightly different technique.

Looking at all these elements from a distance, it is plain that each group of animals, even when it over-

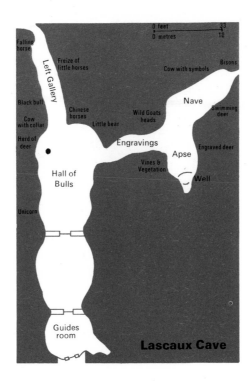

Cave paintings in the Hall of Bulls, Lascaux

laps the others, adds to the total composition in a balanced and deliberate manner. The styles are different, but not more so than those of six different impressionist painters, to whom one Danish prehistorian compared them. It seems self-evident that the cave was painted, perhaps by different artists, but the greater part of it as a unified conception, within a short time. There seems to be no question of the superpositions representing paintings thousands of years apart, as was thought to be the case with the first painted caves to be recognized. Indeed, it has been generally accepted since the discovery at Lascaux that most, if not all, developed animal paintings in French caves must belong to the hunters of the Magdalenian culture. The purpose of the animal paintings is, perhaps, more obscure today than when the first cave paintings were recognized.

The most generally accepted explanation is that the paintings formed part of a rite of sympathetic magic and that their creation ensured the continuance of a plentiful food supply in the form of the favourite game animals of the Palaeolithic hunters.

The reindeer, which forms the principal animal diet of the hunter, is absent at Lascaux and seldom depicted in the cave art; so that the sympathetic magical interpretation of the paintings appears to lose much of its force.

Due to the large number of people that visited Lascaux between 1945–63 it was in some danger of being seriously damaged by the growth of algae over the paintings. This peril has now been averted, but the cave is still closed to the public.

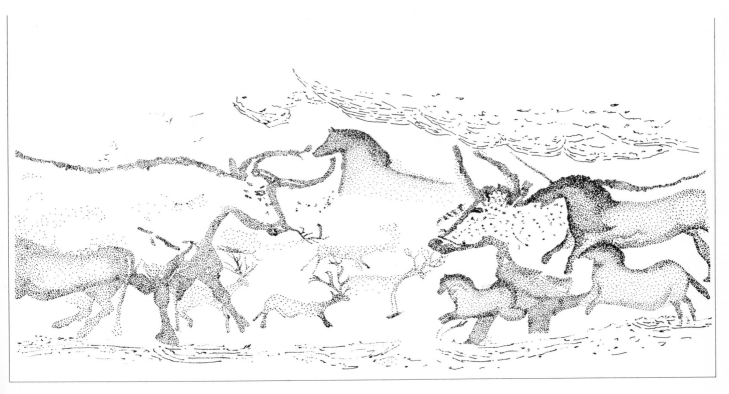

La Hougue Bie JERSEY

Passage grave
c. 2500 BC

BIBLIOGRAPHY
Hawkes, Jacquetta, *The Archaeology of the Channel Islands*
vol. II: The Bailiwick of Jersey, 1938

La Hougue Bie is one of the finest passage graves in western Europe, comparable in scale and in many details of design to the great tombs of NEWGRANGE in Ireland and MAES HOWE in Orkney. Like these tombs it is a large circular mound or *hougue* (like how[e] in north of England and Orkney place names, the word is from the Norse *haugr* meaning a hill, an eminence), containing a cruciform burial chamber and a long entrance passage of megalithic construction. The huge mound made of loose stones, earth and also apparently of masses of limpet shells, is 180 feet (55 m) in diameter and 40 feet (12 m) high and must have been higher still before it was levelled for the construction of the two medieval chapels, the Jerusalem Chapel and Notre Dame de la Clarté, that now stand on the top.

The tomb and passage, inside the mound, are also of considerable size. Their total length is 67 feet (20 m), and the 30-foot (9 m) main burial chamber lies immediately beneath the summit of the mound. The passage and tomb appear to be deliberately oriented east–west. These details are of importance. They show that La Hougue Bie belongs to a relatively early stage in tomb design, when the size of passage and tomb combined is still related to the total size of the mound, and the direction from which the tombs were approached was considered of some importance.

The burial chamber itself is broken up by large uprights supporting the massive blocks in the roof, and there are further burial chambers opening off it, one on either side, and a third terminal chamber at the far end. The side cells are separated from the main chamber by two uprights and by a recumbent sillstone, on top of which there was a blocking stone, which has since fallen down. The terminal cell also has a recumbent sillstone and when this was excavated it was found to be resting on a quernstone, used for grinding corn. One of the side walls and the capstone of the northern side cell have been decorated with a large number of basin-shaped hollows technically known as cup marks.

When La Hougue Bie was opened it was found that two of the capstones or roofing stones near the entrance had collapsed, blocking the passage. But the tomb inside was almost empty and had plainly been robbed. Only a few human bones and other fragments remained. These included pieces of a number of the so-called vase supports, saucer-topped pottery stands of a kind well known in Brittany. Some of these have their saucers charred and appear to have been lamps; others were used to contain ritual offerings. Two stands were found carefully placed one on either side of the innermost part of the main chamber. Very large numbers of such vase supports are found at the Er-Lannic stone circles and other ritual sites in southern Brittany, where they appear to have been deliberately broken.

La Hougue Bie is not the only or the earliest passage grave in Jersey. There are others at Gorey and at Mont Ubé nearby, and also overlooking St Ouan's Bay, but the earliest grave of this type is a corbelled structure of drystone walling at La Sergenté (St Brelade) which is usually referred to as the Beehive Hut. This closely resembles corbelled structures at Barnenez near Morlaix in Brittany, dated between 3800 and 3500 BC. La Hougue Bie seems likely to have been built several hundred years after this and still to have been in use a thousand years later when the Breton type of vase supports were in use, and when similar monuments were being constructed in Brittany and Ireland.

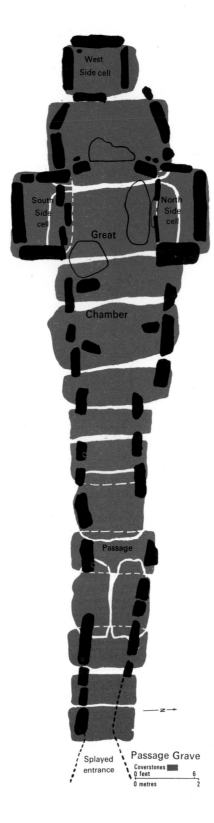

West Side cell

South Side cell

North Side cell

Great

Chamber

Passage

Passage

Splayed entrance

Passage Grave
Coverstones
0 feet   6
0 metres   2

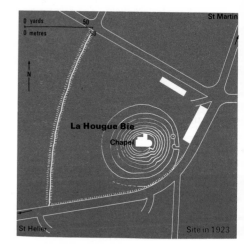

0 yards   50
0 metres   50

St Martin

N

La Hougue Bie
Chapel

St Helier

Site in 1923

Gavr'inis FRANCE

Passage grave
c. 3000–2500 BC

BIBLIOGRAPHY
Péquart, M. and Le Rouzic, S. J., *Corpus des Signes Gravés des Monuments Mégalithiques du Morbihan*, 1927
Giot, P. R., *Brittany*, London, 1960

Gavr'inis, a fine megalithic passage grave (see CARNAC and LA HOUGUE BIE) on one of the smaller entirely barren islets in the enclosed Gulf of Morbihan, Quiberon Bay, is the most important monument in Brittany for megalithic art. Many of the islands in the gulf contain important or picturesque megaliths, and it seems that the coastline was flooded after some of these were already built, because the important stone circles of Er-Lannic, on the adjoining island to Gavr'inis, are half under water at high tide. Gavr'inis itself may have been built on a coastal hill rather than on an island.

The tomb is covered by a large round mound of stones 30 feet (9 m) high. It has a long, east–west passage, ending in a square burial chamber and is paved, walled and roofed with megalithic slabs, with a small amount of drystone masonry filling the interstices between the orthostats and between these wallstones and the roof. Of the 29 orthostats, 23 are decorated. In addition, a small slab set in the masonry above upright 6 is engraved with a hafted axe design, and the sillstone on the threshold is engraved on its three exposed faces. Whereas many Breton megalithic monuments are decorated with isolated or fragmentary engraved designs, so that we wonder if they were originally painted as well, every stone at Gavr'inis is completely covered with decor-

ation. There are a number of different motifs or types of design on the stones but these are carefully related to one another, and to the shape of the stone block. The designs are heavily cut or pecked into the stone with a hammer. Most of the motifs are abstract, the principal elements being such things as maze patterns, spirals, groups of concentric semicircles and other forms of overall, flowing linear decoration, but this is used in a manner often suggestive of anthropomorphic intentions.

It is hard to look at the swirling figures on stones 9, 10, 15 and 20 without seeing them as inhabited in some way by individuals or groups of people, in the same way that the carvings of Australian aborigines may represent individuals, often in a ritual dance. In the Gavr'inis designs there are also wholly naturalistic elements, principally axe designs (stone 21) resembling pointed polished Neolithic axes. Fragments of such axes have been found with the northern stone circle at Er-Lannic, the neighbouring ceremonial monument, where they were buried with quantities of broken pottery vessels, the relics of some ritual feasting like that which is supposed to have taken place in the British circles and henges (see STONEHENGE DISTRICT and AVEBURY DISTRICT). It seems clear that Gavr'inis was one of the tombs related to the Er-Lannic community, in use between 3000 and 2500 BC.

Right Decorated stone from Gavr'inis

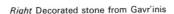

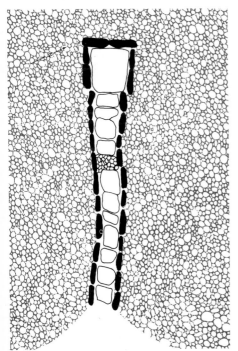

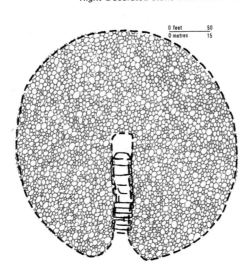

53

Grotte Des Fées FRANCE

Rock-cut gallery grave
c. 3500 BC

BIBLIOGRAPHY
Daniel, G. E., *The Prehistoric Chambered Tombs of France*,
1960

Between 3000 and 1000 BC, during the Neolithic and Bronze Age, a very great many megalithic tombs were built in southern France, in the central massif west of the Rhône, and on the Atlantic coastal plain. Here, they take the place of the common round barrow or tumulus, the earthen mound or cairn of stones covering a single grave, which represents the Bronze Age rise in population in eastern France, as in Britain, Holland and Germany. Commonly, these southern French megaliths consist of a few large upright stones, roofed with one or two equally heavy capstones, covered by a low round mound. But there are also more unusual structures, outstanding among which is the Grotte des Fées, a colossal tomb, over 120 feet (37 m) long internally, beneath a large oval mound.

The Fairies' Cave, as it is called, is one of a group of tombs known as the Arles caves or grottos, because they are cut into the rocky hillside, instead of being erected upon it. They are nevertheless of megalithic construction, being roofed or partly roofed with heavy slabs of stone, and set into mounds or barrows of earth, in the same way as the above-ground structures. These tombs are found in two small hills in the low-lying marshlands of the Rhône delta, north east of Arles: the Grotte des Fées on one hill, the Montagne de Cordes, and the other much smaller tombs in a low rise known as the Plateau du Castelet. When the tombs were constructed these hills must have been islands in the mouth of the Rhône, and their coastal and insular position both suggest that the tomb builders arrived by sea.

The design of the Grotte des Fées is on the grandest scale. At the west end, the tomb is approached down a steep flight of steps cut into the rock. A rock-cut archway leads into the 40-foot (12 m) long antechamber, a parallel-sided passage, which was once roofed, but is now open to the sky. Another doorway at the far end opens into the darkness of the immense burial chamber. This is a slightly tapering rectangular room, nearly 80 feet

(24 m) long and nine feet (2·7 m) wide. It is a carefully fashioned artificial cave entirely cut out of the rock with 11-foot (3·4 m) high walls, sloped inwards from floor to ceiling to give additional height. This tripartite plan is common to the other rock-cut tombs at Arles. In addition the Grotte des Fées has two bottle-shaped side chambers opening off the antechamber, and also today open to the sky. One of the side chambers has a groove at the top of the wall to receive a capstone, and a broken block of stone nearby may have been used for roofing; the antechamber could have been roofed with wood, or else with stone blocks since removed for more modern buildings.

Grotte des Fées
(Arles District)

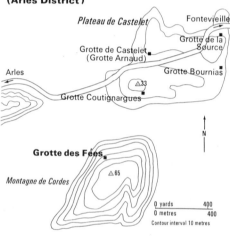

Contour interval 10 metres

The remaining Arles grottos are only a few hundred yards away on the Plateau de Castellet, which is traversed by the Arles–Fontvieille road. There are three tombs of nearly identical design: the Bounias Cave, the Grotte de la Source, and the Grotte de Castelet (Grotte Arnaud). All of these are rock-cut trenches, approached by sloping ramps, with tapering rectangular burial chambers, roofed with immense megalithic slabs. These tombs are each between 40 and 60 feet (12–18 m) long. Nearby there is also a smaller, wedge-shaped, burial chamber, lacking a ramp, built above ground, with walls of small slabs of drystone, inclined inwards at the top: a design clearly related to that of the rock-cut tombs. Surrounding each of the tombs, and also the Grotte des Fées itself, are slight mounds of earth and stone, the remains of circular tumuli which once covered the tombs, except for the entrance ramps, which would have remained open for periodic burials.

The Grotte des Fées was early robbed of its contents and no archaeological finds remain to identify those who used it; but the other tombs have been excavated. Only a few fragmentary burials and funerary gifts were found and these usually identified only the latest users of the tombs, generally belonging to the Beaker culture, or to contemporary groups (1900–1700 BC). A few arrowheads and pottery found at Bournias are apparently earlier and connect the tombs with the Chassey culture or, more probably, with the ancestral Impressed Ware culture. It seems likely that the Arles tombs were constructed between 4000 and 3500 BC, by some of the first farmers to arrive in the Arles district, travelling by sea along the coast or perhaps from Sardinia or Majorca. The related design of these tombs suggests that they belonged to a few closely related families probably in the neighbouring settlement sites or villages, which have been identified on the Plateau de Castelet.

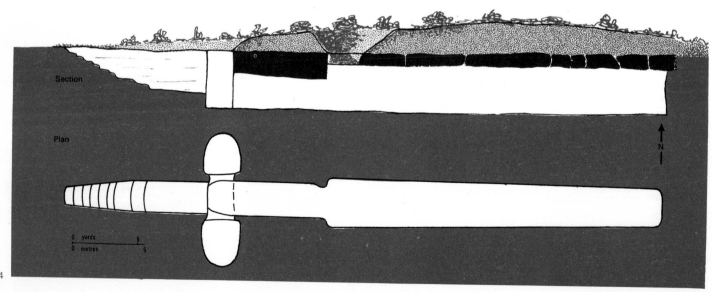

Section

Plan

Carnac and Locmariaquer Districts

Stone alignments,
passage graves and other megalithic tombs
c. 3800–2000 BC

BIBLIOGRAPHY
Daniel, G. E., *The Prehistoric Chambered Tombs of France*, 1960
Giot, P. R., *Brittany*, London, 1960

The districts of Carnac and Locmariaquer in southern Brittany are known for their prehistoric tombs and for a unique type of structure, the stone alignments. These are avenues generally about a mile (1·6 km) in length and 100 yards (91 m) wide, built of multiple rows of tall upright stones or menhirs. The best alignments, those just outside Carnac, run in a generally easterly direction for about four miles (6 km), and are associated with a number of prehistoric tombs – actually overrunning the tomb at Manio which is earlier in date than the alignments. There are really three separate structures running in line. The Menec alignment, north of Carnac, has 11 parallel rows of stones and is about 1,200 yards (1,097 m) long; the Kermario alignment, 400 yards (366 m) further east, has 10 rows and is approximately the same length (the Manio tomb is at the east end of this alignment); and the third alignment, at Kerlescant, has 13 rows of stones and is about 1,000 yards (914 m) long.

Kerlescant Tomb

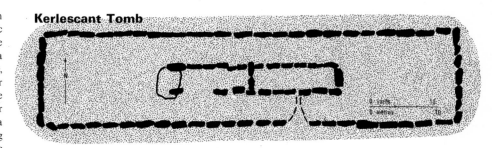

Carnac & Locmariaquer District

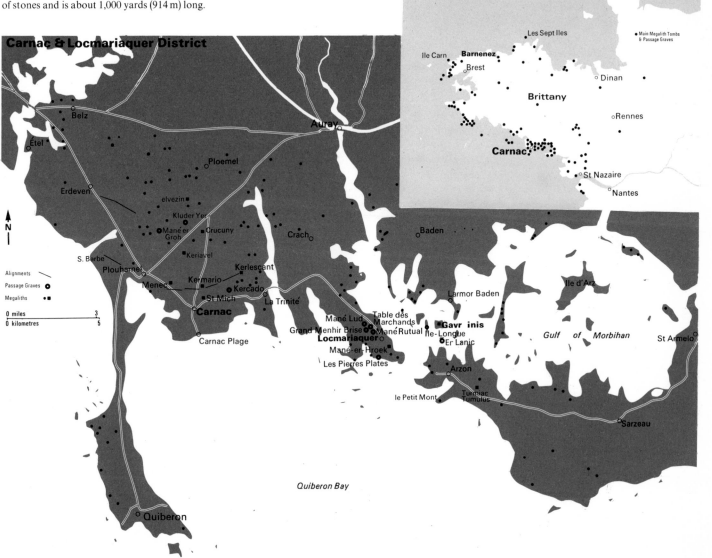

These are impressive monuments. Many of the stones stand considerably higher than a man and some 14–20 feet (4–6 m) high. The Menec alignment has 1,100 standing stones, and Kermario almost as many. The three alignments do pursue a roughly similar general north-east direction, but their purpose does not seem to have been processional, as each alignment has a different number of avenues and these narrow at the *eastern* ends, while the stones are larger at the *western* ends. It seems likely that each alignment had a circle or a square of standing stones at the western end, and these may be the ceremonial monuments towards which the avenues are aimed. Another, large, less well-preserved alignment near Erdeven runs in a generally south-east direction, and has particularly large granite pillars at its western end.

Though many of the Carnac tombs nowadays consist of upright blocks of stone roofed by megalithic slabs and resembling card houses, nearly all were once covered by long or round mounds (barrows) of earth and rubble. The finest surviving barrow of the sort in the district is the gigantic Tumulus de Saint Michel, on the outskirts of Carnac, which is 380 feet (116 m) long and 35 feet (11 m) high. Like LA HOUGUE BIE in Jersey it has been christianized by a chapel, placed on top of the barrow.

St Michel tumulus contains a few closed megalithic chambers, which can now be visited by a tunnel dug for the excavators. There were a large number of beautifully polished axes of jadeite and other rare hard rocks in the main burial chamber. Similar funerary gifts are found with other large barrows with closed burial chambers, such as the magnificent Mané-er-Hroek tomb at Locmariaquer.

The age of these princely burials with ritual axes has been much debated. There are a series of radiocarbon dates for St Michel which would suggest that the tomb was built very early in the Neolithic period, perhaps between 3500 and 3000 BC. But the earliest megalithic tombs at Carnac and Locmariaquer are the passage graves, usually found under round barrows, but distinguished by their structural division into an entrance passage and a burial chamber. There are nearly 100 passage graves in the Carnac–Locmariaquer and adjoining districts, and these are of many different designs.

Small, almost individual, passage graves, with carefully defined entrances, narrow passages 20–30 feet (6–9 m) long, and single small burial chambers, either square, circular or polygonal (8–10 feet, 2·4–3 m in diameter) are among the earliest. They may be built and roofed either of megalithic stones, or provided with walls and a corbelled vault of small drystone masonry. A ruined chamber at Ile-Longue, the adjoining island to GAVR'INIS, is the only certain corbelled or beehive tomb in south Brittany, but there is another equally early structure at Kercado, 200 yards (183 m) or so south east of the Kermario alignments. This is a fine circular barrow about 10 feet (3 m) high and nearly 100 feet (30 m) in diameter, containing a megalithic passage grave with a square chamber, and several engraved stones. A hafted stone axe is lightly engraved on the underside of the large capstone roofing the burial chamber. Kercado is radiocarbon dated to 3800 BC, as early as the earliest of the dated passage graves at Barnenez and elsewhere on the north Brittany coast, so we have clear evidence that these simple, clearly defined chambered tombs are among the first to be built by the passage-grave settlers.

But the finest megaliths are three found at Locmariaquer. Two large passage graves beneath barrows, Mané Lud and the Table des Marchands, and an enormous standing stone now broken in four pieces, the Grand Menhir Brise, are north of the town. Mané Rutual in the town itself, and Les Pierres Plates to the south are long passage graves, which have been deprived of their barrows, and Mané-er-Hroek, also south of Locmariaquer, is another magnificent barrow, with a closed central chamber, like the St Michel monument described at Carnac. These are all monuments of some size. The Mané Lud passage grave is in a long barrow 260 feet (79 m) long. The Table des Marchands whose barrow is restored, is roofed by a single capstone of enormous proportions, 20 feet by 13 feet (6 × 4 m). The Mané-er-Hroek mound is oval in shape and 340 feet by 180 feet (104 × 55 m). These sites are also particularly distinguished by their megalithic art. Mané Lud has eight stones engraved with designs, including a number interpreted as ships on the two stones in the passage at the entrance to the chamber. The Table des Marchands has some fine engravings on the underneath of the capstone, and a magnificent orthostat (supporting stone) with a brilliant design depicting the sun surrounded by ranks of corn sheaves. Mané-er-Hroek has an engraved slab set up in the central chamber. But the finest designs are highly stylized female representations and shield shapes on different stones at Les Pierres Plates, thought to be engravings of a female deity.

Vix FRANCE

Hill Fort
c. 600–50 BC

BIBLIOGRAPHY
Joffroy, R., *Le Tombeau de Vix*, 1958
Wheeler, R. E. M. and Richardson, K. M., *Hill Forts of Northern France*, Society of Antiquaries Research Report No. XIX, 1957

The oppidum of Vix is on the top of Mont Lassois, a commanding height beside the river Seine, north west of Dijon, two miles (3·2 km) north west of Châtillon-sur-Seine. The slopes of Mont Lassois are steep and it is an excellent defensive position, strategically well placed beside the river. It was occupied in two separate periods in the Early Iron Age. In the 6th century BC the hillfort was occupied by a Hallstatt D people, and in the 1st century BC a Gaulish tribe of La Tène III culture refortified the hill.

The earlier occupation is the more extensive. The natural defences were strengthened by a ditch and rampart at the base, surrounding the hill and running to the river with internal embankments or levées which climb up the shallow slopes facing the river and protect it against waterborne attack. Here and at the foot of the slope to east and south of the hill thick occupation deposits occurred. As with other Hallstatt fortresses in eastern France, the main archaeological interest of this site lies in the extraordinary quantity of Greek pottery, like amphorae and domestic vessels, found in all

the different Hallstatt levels. The pottery was almost certainly supplied by the Phocean Greek colony of Massilia, the modern town of Marseilles, and the richness and importance of the Hallstatt tribes in the district must have been a direct result of the strategic position on the trade routes of the colony. It has been suggested that Greek traders used Mont Lassois as an entrepôt in the overland trade in British tin, travelling up the Seine and then down the Rhône to Marseilles. The importance of the Greek connection is illustrated by the finds in the

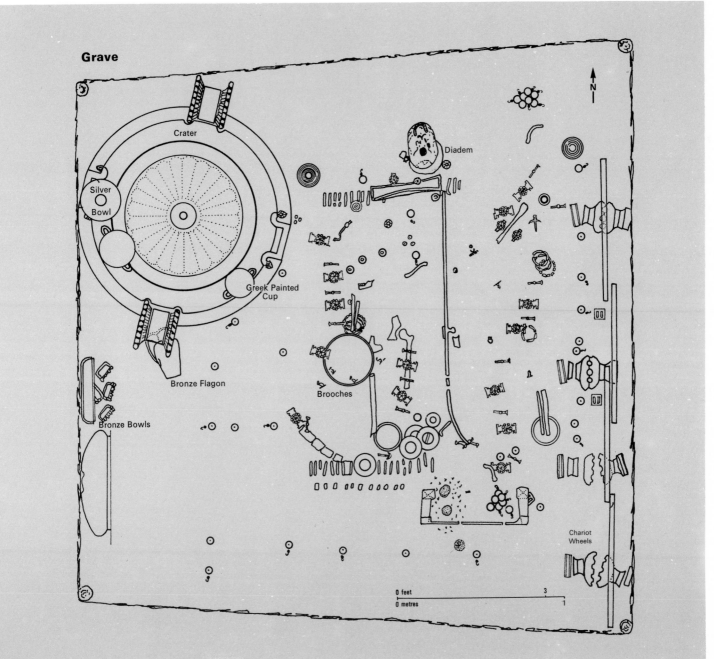

Grave
Crater
Silver Bowl
Greek Painted Cup
Bronze Flagon
Bronze Bowls
Brooches
Diadem
Chariot Wheels

0 feet 3
0 metres 1

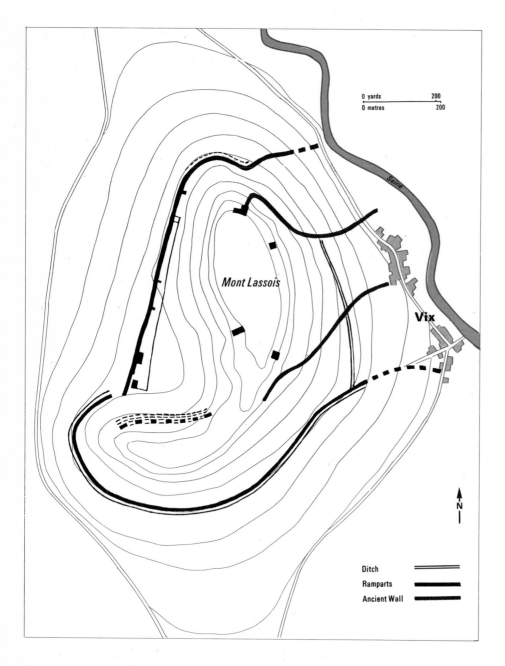

0 yards 200
0 metres 200

Mont Lassois

Seine

Vix

N

Ditch
Ramparts
Ancient Wall

famous Vix princess's burial, excavated in January 1953 from a tumulus at the foot of Mont Lassois beside the Seine, described as one of the most spectacular finds of postwar European archaeology. Besides the princess herself, crowned with a golden diadem, the grave contained her jewelry, the dismembered parts of her funerary cart or chariot (most notably the four wheels stacked up in a line against the side of the grave), and also a series of funerary gifts or offerings. Among these was the magnificently decorated archaic Greek bronze crater, more than 6 feet (1·8 m) high, the largest extant Greek bronze vessel of this period. With this great wine vessel was a fine painted pottery drinking cup, imported from Massilia in about 520–510 BC. So the burial should have taken place within a few years of this date.

A profound change in the native culture took place shortly after 500 BC when the Hallstatt people were replaced by those of the La Tène culture. At the same time Massilia declined in importance, and Greek imports in the district were replaced by Etruscan. Perhaps as a result of the loss of the Greek trade the Vix stronghold was deserted, and not reoccupied for some centuries.

Julius Caesar's Gallic Wars were the occasion for the refortification of Mont Lassois. In *De Bello Gallico* Caesar describes the method of fortification used in the Gaulish fortresses, known as the *murus gallicus*. This is a wall or rampart of large stones specially strengthened with heavy balks of timber placed longitudinally and at right angles to the wall and nailed together. From Caesar's description it seems that this construction was a remarkably good defence against the battering ram, the Romans' principal siege weapon. A map of *murus gallicus* forts (identified by the iron nails used to fasten the reinforcing timbers) shows that these are all outside southern Gaul, most of them being in eastern France. The *murus gallicus* at Vix is on the periphery of the plateau on the western side of Mont Lassois. It is associated with a La Tène III Celtic occupation deposit of the 1st century BC. From Caesar's commentaries and other documents it can be shown that the fortress was the oppidum or headquarters of the tribe called the Lingones. (See also HEUNEBURG.)

GERMANY AND THE NETHERLANDS

The earliest certain evidence for the presence of men (hominids) in the region is the fossilized lower jaw found in the Mauer Sands near Heidelberg (Germany). It represents a pithecanthropine (*Homo erectus*) of advanced type. Unfortunately no implements were found with the mandible, but it can be dated by the associated fauna to the first (Günz–Mindel) interglacial and hence to the opening of the Middle Pleistocene period. (The old system of four glacial periods, Günz, Mindel, Riss and Würm, based on the Alps, is oversimplified but still provides the best framework for Palaeolithic chronology in western and central Europe. See table at end of Glossary.)

At Steinheim, near Stuttgart (Germany), a complete skull was found in association with an early Acheulean hand axe possibly belonging to the first phase of the hand axe cultures (sometimes called Chellean or Abbevillian). Steinheim man, identifiable as a proto-Neanderthaloid, lived during the second, Mindel–Riss, interglacial. These two finds, both belonging in cultural terms to the Lower Palaeolithic, support the impression that our area was on the extreme northern limit penetrated by man during Middle Pleistocene times. The succeeding Middle Palaeolithic sequence of cultures (Later Acheulean, Micoquian and Mousterian) are represented by a large enough quantity of finds to be regarded as a phase of true colonization. In the final interglacial (Riss–Würm) the first occupation of the upland regions and the high Alps was achieved. At this time innovations made in the Mousterian and Szeletian of eastern Europe (p. 75) were influencing southern Germany, particularly the Altmühl cultural groups (WEINBERGHÖHLEN).

During the final glaciation the indigenous Neanderthalers with their Mousterian tradition were displaced by the arrival of men of *Homo sapiens* stock and Upper Palaeolithic blade- and bone-tool cultures. Representational art, immediately characteristic of the Aurignacian culture, appears for the first time in our area.

The succession of the Aurignacian, Gravettian, Solutrean and Magdalenian cultures in the south, and the Hamburg, Federmesser and Ahrensburg on the north-west European Plain led to economic diversification and to a highly successful adaptation to harsh glacial conditions. There was a growth in population, a proliferation of art styles, and a degree of economic stability hitherto unknown. The sharp climatic changes that came with the ending of the final glaciation upset that stability. Warmer conditions led to the afforestation of the region, while the melting of vast masses of ice caused the sea to rise and flood much of the hitherto habitable North Sea and Baltic areas. About 5900 BC Britain became separated from the continent. The rise in sea level also caused a rise in ground-water level and so the formation of raised bogs in the north. These were strongly to effect the later settlement of the north-west European Plain.

In the course of the Boreal period Mesolithic cultures, derived from the Upper Palaeolithic traditions, developed regional groupings. Specialized reindeer hunting was replaced by a more varied food quest – for large and small forest animals, edible plants and freshwater and marine fish and shellfish. Settlements increased in size and density.

New peoples introduced mixed farming to central Europe in about 4400 BC. The Bandkeramik, or Linear pottery culture (p. 76) of these Neolithic settlers was characterized by villages of from six to thirteen wooden longhouses (averaging 325 feet by 80 feet, approx. 100×25 m). Of these, Köln–Lindenthal near Cologne is a well-known example. The villagers, often called Danubians since they had spread westward on the line of the great river, grew wheat by a slash-and-burn method that involved intermittent shifting of village sites as well as of fields. They kept cattle, sheep and pigs. In their arts, crafts, settlements and whole way of life these pioneer farmers established a quite remarkable degree of cultural uniformity and stability over their vast range from eastern Europe to east France and Belgium.

By the middle of the 4th millennium (Middle Neolithic) this early uniformity had largely broken down into regional groupings. Contacts with the western Neolithic spreading up the Rhône valley and into the basin of the Lower Rhine contributed to this diversification, producing such cultures as the Michelsberg, Altheim, Aichbühl, Cortaillod and Horgen cultures, while the Stichbandkeramik and Rössen cultures represent a continuation of the Danubian tradition into these later Neolithic times. Meanwhile on the northern plain the first farming culture of the Funnel-Necked Beaker culture was probably due to the acculturation of the local Mesolithic peoples by the Danubians.

See p. 49 for generalized distribution of megalithic chambered tombs.

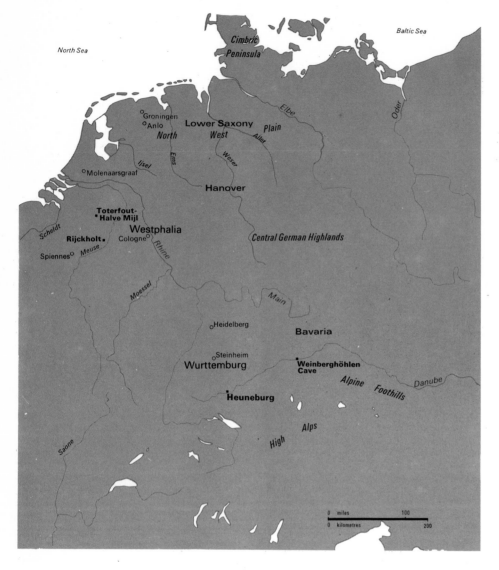

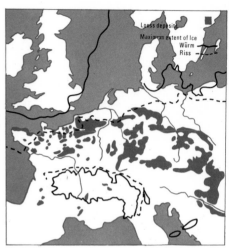

Demographic pressures may have led to a decrease in the size of individual settlements and to the fortification of settlements (Altheim and Michelsberg) and the siting of villages on defensible peninsulas and marshes – such as the Swiss lakeside settlements. They may also have caused a striking revival in the importance of hunting as a source of meat.

An economic advance in some ways contrasting with this general pattern was the beginning of industrial specialization represented by flint mining. This activity, which sprang up right across Europe from Britain to Poland and Hungary, is well represented in our region by RIJCKHOLT, and also by the Spiennes mines of Belgium.

Another change was in burial rites, as megalithic tombs were adopted in a broad area including southern Belgium, and northern Holland, Westphalia, Lower Saxony, Hanover and the Cimbric peninsula.

As over so much of Europe (p. 77), these later Neolithic cultures were to be dominated from about 2500 BC by invasions of Corded Ware/Battle Axe peoples; internment in megalithic tombs was superseded by their rite of single burial under low round barrows. The cultivation of cereals appears to have been increased with the help of the plough; but discoveries such as the cattle coral at Anlo in the Dutch province of Drente prove that stockbreeding was also important. The Corded Ware peoples appear to have been the first to introduce wheeled vehicles and made-up roads.

The uncertain origins of the Bell–Beaker culture (pp. 77, 85) means equivocation as to how the Beaker people reached our area. They may have spread up the Atlantic coast and mingled with the Corded Ware people in the Rhine basin; on the other hand a westward spread from central Europe may have been more significant. One thing is sure – that it was the Bell–Beaker people who introduced the use of metal implements in the north-west European Plain. Their settlements are little known, but at Molenaars-graaf in southern Holland, the occupants of a long, oval house made their living by mixed farming together with hunting.

With the Early Bronze Age a range of bronze tools became a necessary part of the economy: in our region such tool kits are first in evidence in the valleys of southern Germany. The rise and spread of mining and metallurgy and the increase in trade that went with it, can be seen as an integrating factor in the prehistory of Europe. It helped to create brilliant cultures in central Europe and to introduce new ideas and materials from the Aegean and the Near East. Large barrow cemeteries (TOTERFOUT-HALVE MIJL) show that population was again increasing.

The Middle Bronze Age was another period of regional variations, among them the Hilversum culture of Holland is of interest as it was introduced between 1400 and 1200 BC from England, thus reversing the usual westward cross-channel movements. These people placed the cremated remains of their dead in large urns below round barrows. The dominant power was, however, that of the Tumulus culture with its heart-land in Bavaria, Württemberg and the old Únětice area (The HEUNEBURG). Bronze tools and weapons were far more specialized and numerous, including a variety of axes, spears, swords and personal ornaments.

After about 1200 BC the Tumulus culture, in which the dead were commonly laid at full length under barrows, was superseded by the urnfield cultures with cremation burial in low mounds or flat cemeteries. This Late Bronze Age saw further advance in the skill of bronzesmiths who could now turn out beaten bronze vessels, shields and armour.

Actual urbanization, or the development of centres of permanent economic and political administration, did not take place in our area until the Iron Age. The growth of fortified settlements such as The Heuneburg was largely due to unrest in the east. Cimmerian migrations, spurred on by Scythian pressures, seem to have caused a rapid expansion of chariot warfare. Its importance for the élite is shown by their splendid horse trappings and by burial in wagons and chariots in wooden mortuary houses (as in the Hohmichele barrow near The Heuneburg).

In the La Tène period the transformation of hill forts into oppida and true towns is one sign of the transference of power northward to the middle Rhine. On the north-west European Plain the same growth of population led to the first settlement of the salt mudflats – in spite of their occasional flooding by the North Sea. As a protection, villages of wooden, rectangular houses were built on artificial platforms or terpen. A striking example has been excavated at Ezinge, near Groningen.

Caesar's invasion of Switzerland in 58 BC marked the end of the prehistory, senso stricto, of our area. The Roman armies found a Europe hardly inferior to that of the Middle Ages in technical and social development. The rural way of life was deeply rooted in the prehistoric past. Millennia of adaptation to growth, cultural change and immigration had produced a stable economy of permanent village farming.

The Weinberghöhlen by Mauern GERMANY

Palaeolithic cave dwelling
c. 40,000–15,000 BC

BIBLIOGRAPHY
Bohmers, A., 'Die Höhlen von Mauern', *Palaeohistoria* I
Groningen, 1951

The Weinberghöhlen, a complex of four limestone caves, are on the southern slopes of the Frankish Jura. They lie opposite the village of Mauern, between Ingolstadt and Donauwörth, at a height of some 65 feet (20 m) above a dry valley that carried the Danube until the time of the Riss–Würm interglacial. The excavation of the caves yielded a significant stratification of Middle to Upper Palaeolithic occupations, and threw some light on settlement in the corridor between the two great land-ice masses of Scandinavia and the Alps.

The caves have been labelled A–D by the excavator. Cave A, the most westerly of the complex, provided a vertical stratigraphy of Mousterian, Altmühl, and early Magdalenian material. The middle cave, B, which is connected to cave A by a small passage deep in the limestone matrix, displayed an Altmühl and Magdalenian occupation sequence, but cave C had no prehistoric remains. Cave D is situated under the entrance to cave B and was first discovered in the course of excavation. Largely filled with later sediment, this small cave was inhabited by Mousterian and Altmühl peoples. For the total complex, the following composite section represents the stratigraphic sequence:

Layer A humus with Medieval, Iron Age, Bronze Age, Neolithic, and Mesolithic material mixed together

Layer B loam – sterile

Layer C loess with frost-shattered fragments of limestone – sterile

Layer D grey loam lens in the loess (layers C + E) with many rounded pebbles and the early Magdalenian occupation

Layer E loess – sterile

Layer F organic cave loam, grey in colour and containing many rounded limestone pebbles. The final Middle Palaeolithic Altmühl was located in this layer

Layer G organic cave loam, brown in colour, and containing the cultural remains of the Mousterian occupation

The Mousterian habitation was represented by a few large hearths and a concentration of 544 pieces of flint and many food bones, scattered primarily near the entrance to cave D. The levels with the

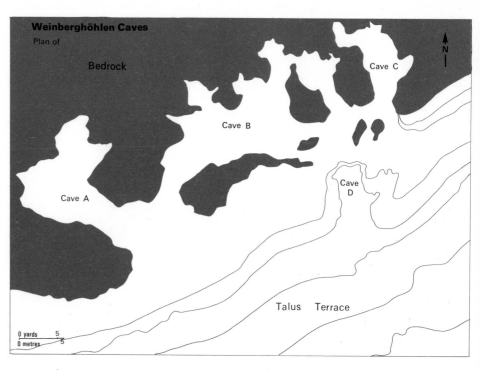

hearths were highly compacted, presumably as a result of the occupation. Inside the cave, there were very few finds. The people of the Altmühl group, however, appear to have lived deeper in the cave and to have abandoned and reoccupied the site over a longer period of time. The Magdalenian settlement was represented by an exceptionally thick culture layer containing 193 flint tools, 12 bone tools, 25 bored animal teeth – possibly a necklace, 1,662 pieces of flint waste, and a great number of animal bones largely confined to the entrance of cave B. Near the entrance, in a natural depression in the rock, a number of vertebrae and a nearly complete skull of a mammoth were found. The fractured tusks lay three feet one inch (95 cm) nearer the entrance. In direct association with this skeleton, a rectangular rock was surrounded by a concentration of flint tools. Red ochre, brought from a source just over three and a half miles (6 km) away, and a surface hearth completed the settlement remains. They suggest that the Magdalenians were more numerous than the Middle Palaeolithic inhabitants, but that they lived in the caves for a shorter time.

Rijckholt-Sint Geertruid

THE NETHERLANDS

Neolithic flint mines
c. 4500–2500 BC

BIBLIOGRAPHY
Layard, N., 'Recent Excavations on the Neolithic Site of Sainte-Gertrude, Holland', *Proceedings of the Prehistoric Society of East Anglia*, vol. V, 1925, pp. 34–55
Felder, W., Jaarverslag Werkgroep Prehistorische Vuursteenmijnbouw, Vijlen, Limburg, 1965–70
Engelen, F. H. G. et al., 'Eerste Internationale Symposium over Vuursteen 26–29 April 1969, Maastricht', *Grondboor en Hamer* no. 3, Maastricht, 1971
Clason, A. T., 'The Flint-Mine Workers of Spiennes and Rijckholt-St Geertruid and their Animals', *Helinium* XI, no. 1, 1971, pp. 3–33

In 1881, the Belgian archaeologist M. Du Puydt discovered the first traces of prehistoric flint mining on the eastern bank of the middle terrace of the Meuse (Maas) river, four miles (7 km) south south east of Maastricht. Excavations have been conducted on the terrace slope, in a dry valley to the north, on the plateau above the terrace, and currently from the slope into the chalk, in order to map the extent of the shaft and gallery complex.

It now appears that there were three phases of mining. At first flint was taken from surface formations exposed by erosion. The numerous round-to-oval depressions scattered throughout the terrain are the remains of this phase. Among them the oval Grand Atelier de Puydt measures 177 feet by 43 feet (54 × 13 m) and is three to five feet (1–1·5 m) deep in flint waste. Actual underground mining began with the driving of horizontal floor galleries from the middle terrace into the chalk slope of the upper terrace. The so-called Abri, 650 feet (approx. 200 m) north of the Grand Atelier de Puydt, cutting into three bands of fresh flint, is most probably another floor gallery of the same type.

Quite clearly, this method of mining was abandoned in favour of the shaft and gallery system. It was more efficient than that of the open pits and perhaps safer. Prof. Waterbolk's excavations on the high terrace exposed ten new shafts. More recently the shafts and galleries of five of these have been cleared and an additional 65 discovered. The shafts, seldom more than three feet (approx. 1 m) across, were sunk through the terrace gravel and underlying chalk to a depth of 33 to 53 feet (10–16 m). The miners reached the workings, and also removed waste and mined flint, by means of ropes, the wear marks of which are clearly visible on the chalk. Radiating from the shafts, tunnels around two feet (60 cm) high were driven to a maximum distance of 49 feet (15 m). Deeper in the chalk, where the quality is better, the prehistoric miners excavated larger and more extensive galleries. The waste from each gallery was deposited in the one previously abandoned. Frequently, such galleries were driven so far as to break into those of an earlier mine.

In addition to the waste and rubble of subsequent shafts and galleries, the mine systems have yielded about 14,500 picks, cores, both polished and unfinished flint axes, antler axes, and animal bones. Two human skulls have also been found. Radiocarbon dates for the mines range from 3140 BC to 3050 BC.

The finds and the structural elements of the shaft and gallery complex illustrate the importance of fresh flint for the manufacture of large tools. The earliest exploitation was by terminal Mesolithic populations who apparently passed this trait on to the Bandkeramik peoples. All of the actual underground mining activities, and certainly the intensive and specialized industry at Rijckholt, Banholt, Mheer, and such Belgian sites as Rullen, Saint Pietersvoeren, Saint Maartensvoeren, Remersdaal, Obourg, Mesvin, Spiennes, and other localities are dated to the Middle Neolithic. In the Late Neolithic, either the demand diminished or it was met from other sources.

While plans are being made to turn the site into a state park, visitors are advised to contact Mr W. Felder, Vijlen, Limburg for an appointment.

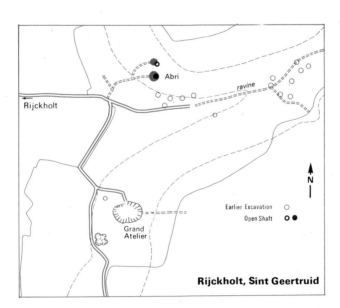

Rijckholt, Sint Geertruid

Toterfout-Halve Mijl THE NETHERLANDS

Bronze Age barrow cemetery
c. 1600–1100 BC

BIBLIOGRAPHY
Glasbergen, W., 'Barrow Excavations in the Eight Beatitudes. The Bronze Age Cemetery between Toterfout and
Halve Mijl, North Brabant. The Excavations'. *Palaeohistoria* II, Groningen, 1954, pp. 1–134
Glasbergen, W., 'Barrow Excavations in the Eight Beatitudes. The Bronze Age Cemetery between Toterfout and
Halve Mijl, North Brabant. II. The Implications'. *Palaeohistoria* III, Groningen, 1954, pp. 1–204
Butler, J. J., *Nederland in de Bronstijd*, Dishoeck, Bussum,
1969

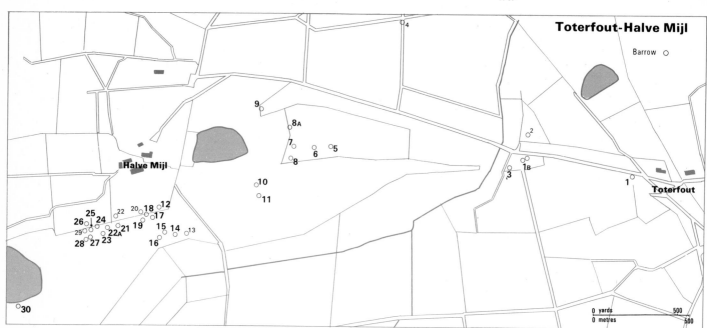

Between 1840 and 1846 the schoolmaster and amateur archaeologist P. N. Panken discovered and explored an extensive group of Bronze Age barrows situated between the hamlets of Toterfout and Halve Mijl, Veldhoven, North Brabant. The area is known locally as the Acht Zaligheden or Eight Beatitudes. In a survey, conducted a century after that of Panken, 34 of the barrows could be located. Between 1948 and 1951 they were completely and meticulously excavated under the auspices of the State University of Groningen.

Three of these tumuli proved to be bell barrows and therefore among the earliest in the cemetery. Tumulus 1 had an oval ring ditch and the barrow consisted of sods carefully laid over a cremation grave without an urn. Tumulus 18 was a ring-ditch bell barrow with a tangential extension, and was built over a primary deposition of a cremation in a Hilversum cinerary urn. Tumulus 9 was the only barrow of this type in the centre of the cemetery. In addition to the bell barrows of English type, the Toterfout–Halve Mijl complex is characterized by five types of post-circle barrows, defined according to the number of post rings and the spacing of the posts. Single widely spaced post circles were found in tumuli 3, 6, 7, 14, and 15. A single closely spaced post circle characterizes tumulus 12, and double closely spaced post circles were found at tumuli 22A, 23, 24, 25, 27, 28. Triple closely spaced post circles were found at tumuli 18 and 30 and a circle of close-set stakes characterizes tumulus 10. All these are simple, one-period barrows; 5, 8, 8A, 9, 16, 17, 19, and 26 are two-period barrows, displaying various combinations of the above elements. Finally, tumulus 22 had three or four periods of construction and use.

Of interest as throwing light on burial practices

Structural Ground Plans of different Barrow types

1. Intermediate single closely spaced postcircle in foundation trench

2. Single closely spaced postcircle in foundation trench

3. Single widely spaced postcircle

4. Circle of wide spaced paired postcircle

5. Single closely spaced postcircle

6. Double closely spaced postcircle

7. Triple closely spaced postcircle.

8. Quadruple and multiple closely spaced postcircle

9. Circle of close-set stakes

are the four small post or stake holes sometimes found defining the area of the central, primary grave. Found in tumuli 1B, 5, 8, 10, 11, 14, 15, 19 and 21, they have been interpreted as traces of rectangular mortuary houses, which were removed before the barrow itself was built. Additional elements are the 'ritual pits', temporary stake circles, offerings, and occasional grave gifts such as tubular bone ornaments, bone pins, and arrowshaft polishers.

A careful study of the stratigraphy of the monuments, the associated finds, and the radiocarbon datings has indicated that the Toterfout barrow cemetery displays all three phases of the burial custom of the Hilversum culture. Phase I, dated *c.* 1600–1350 BC is situated in the eastern part of the cemetery and is characterized by the ring-ditch barrows. Phase II, dated *c.* 1350–1250 BC is found toward the centre of the complex and is defined by barrows with single widely spaced post circles. Finally, predominantly multiple post-circle monuments of Phase III date between *c.* 1250 and 1100 BC.

From this time range it is clear that the barrows all belong to the Hilversum culture of the south Dutch Early and Middle Bronze Age. It was long ago recognized that some English cremation urns and barrows resembled those of the Hilversum culture, and it was assumed that they were proof of an immigration from Holland in Late Bronze Age times. It was the evidence from the Toterfout–Halve Mijl cemetery that led to the reversal and drastic redating of this supposed migration. The Hilversum culture is now accepted as an offshoot from the English Wessex culture. Recently, the discovery of round houses, resembling those of the south English 'Deveral–Rimsbury' type, in a number of Hilversum settlements, has added a new element to the picture.

The Heuneburg GERMANY

Iron Age hill fort settlement
c. 600–400 BC

BIBLIOGRAPHY
Bittel, K. and Rieth, A., *Die Heuneburg an der oberen Donau im frühkeltischer Fürstensitz*, Kohlhammer-Koln, 1951
Dehn, W., 'Die Heuneburg an der oberen Donau und ihre Wehranlagen', *Neue Ausgrabungen in Deutschland*, Mann Berlin, pp. 127–45
Kimmig, W., *Die Heuneburg an der oberen Donau, Führer zuvorund frühgeschichtlichen Denkmälern in Wurttemberg und Hohenzollern*, Stuttgart, 1968

Situated on a terrace promontory of the western bank of the upper Danube, the Heuneburg lies half-way between the present towns of Hundersingen and Binzwangen, in the state park Talhof, Baden-Württemberg. The hillfort has a commanding view over the valley some 200 feet (approx. 60 m) below. Outer fortifications, consisting of a double bank and ditch system, date from the earliest Halstatt occupation of the Burg. This is bridged by an earthen causeway curving directly in front of the western wall and leading to the gate. The gate was perhaps defended by a flanking bastion. The western wall was first constructed in the 'timber-frame' technique and then, following its destruction by fire, in the 'timber-box' (Holzkasten) technique. Two or, more frequently, three rows of carefully squared studs were deeply anchored in the ground. The horizontal joists, joined with wooden pegs, were placed on a stone footing, and the intervening space filled with dirt and stone rubble. Up to five layers of beams and filling were constructed on this foundation and the outer and inner walls faced with roughly shaped stones. Although no definite traces have been found, a wooden rampart may have crowned the wall. Later greatly admired as the *murus gallicus* des-

cribed by Caesar, this technique of defensive wall building originated and was developed in central Europe. (See also VIX.)

Mediterranean ideas (or perhaps artisans) were, however, responsible for the wall of sun-dried mud bricks built on the north-west, south, and south-east sides of the Burg. Some 13 feet (4 m) high, this wall was constructed on top of a massive limestone base 1,640 feet (500 m) long. The requisite 35,000 cubic feet (approx. 1,000 cu m) of limestone were transported four miles (6·5 km) from its source to the Heuneburg. The north-west mud-brick wall is further characterized by eight quadrangular bastions placed at regular intervals of 33 feet (10 m). A similar bastion is to be found on the south-east wall. The mud-brick wall and bastion system enclosed the larger part of the Burg but was absent on the west side above the double bank and ditch system and its extreme north-east and south-east ends were joined by a length of wood and stone wall. When finally burned, it was not renewed but flattened and replaced by a 'timber-box' wall of wood and stone.

The settlement remains are situated in an enclosed roughly triangular area measuring 980 feet by 490 feet (approx. 300 × 150 m). Excavations in the south-

east corner yielded 24 habitation levels, beginning with a disturbed Late Bronze Age village. Following a hiatus of seven centuries, the Heuneburg was occupied around the beginning of the 6th century BC as the centre of a local nobility. In the course of the succeeding 200 years, the fort with its equally carefully planned settlement was constructed. The houses were placed almost directly against the wall usually having their long sides parallel with it. Small alleys, sometimes no more than three feet (approx. 1 m) wide, gave access to the houses and made space for drainage trenches. All the houses were of wood but varied in plan and details of construction. The earliest were erected upon a grid of sleeper beams and the following two building periods were characterized by quadrangular post-hole structures. Finally, the La Tène phase had three-aisled houses.

The great days of the Heuneburg faded around the close of the 5th century BC. The latest walls were burned down and never rebuilt. It seems that the fall of the Heuneburg is contemporary with that of other fortified settlements in the southern German and Swiss highlands. This collapse is perhaps to be connected with the beginning of the Celtic migrations.

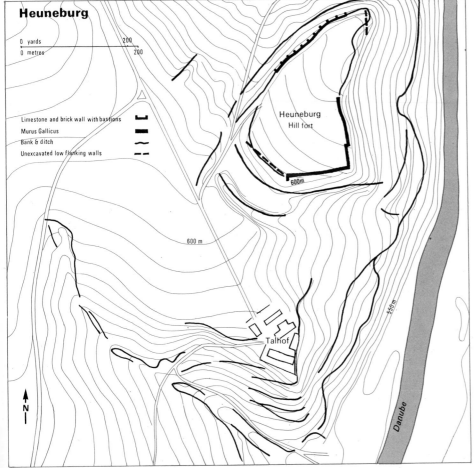

Heuneburg

0 yards 200
0 metres 200

Limestone and brick wall with bastions
Murus Gallicus
Bank & ditch
Unexcavated low flanking walls

Heuneburg
Hill fort

600 m

600 m

Talhof

Danube

N

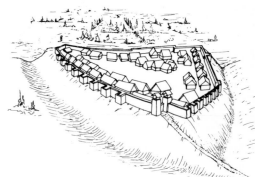

Reconstruction of the hillfort at the Heuneburg

SCANDINAVIA

Scandinavia is larger than commonly realized. North Cape lies as far from the southern-most Danish islands in one direction as Sicily does in the other. Denmark and the southern tip of the Scandinavian peninsula lie in the area originally occupied by deciduous forests, while the rest of the peninsula is covered by the coniferous forests that still extend eastward to Siberia, and in the north thin out to arctic steppe. All of the peninsula and most of Denmark were covered by ice during the last phase of the great Ice Age. The earliest inhabitants entered in the period 12,000–8000 BC following after the retreating ice. They were primitive hunting communities; those in the south flourished best and left behind them the fine flint and bone work of the Maglemose and Ertebølle cultures and the shell heaps of the latter.

Shortly after 4000 BC (even earlier according to some estimates) there occurred a great change in south Scandinavia. Hitherto the area had been culturally isolated, but now it was drawn into the stream of European development. Influences travelled along the valleys of the rivers connecting the Baltic and North Sea with the various head-waters of the Danube drainage basin, where European culture had its main fermenta-tion and growth outside the Mediterranean area. Other contact routes were the Atlantic seaways – but these had little importance except in the Neolithic and Viking periods – and the coniferous forests, through which the primeval hunter-fisher people of central and northern Scandinavia had their contacts eastwards.

As a result of migrations and influences from the south the people came from now on to base their existence on crops, especially barley and wheat, and on herds of cattle, sheep, and pigs. Large axes were made of polished flint. Longhouses have been excavated on Langeland, but the people left as their most enduring legacy burial chambers of large stones, the so-called MEGALITHIC TOMBS, of which some thousands still stand in south Scandinavia. These are the tangible vestiges of a religious idea which at that time affected the various peoples of Atlantic Europe from Spain to Sweden, regardless of their different origins.

For some centuries after the middle of the 3rd millennium BC we find over large parts of Europe the strange situation that different peoples with quite different habits and equipment occupied the same regions together. In south Scandinavia the different peoples were: 1. the declining remains of the megalithic civilization; 2. the Single Grave culture of Jutland; 3. the Boat Axe culture of south Sweden; 4. the Pitted Ware culture. The Single Grave and Boat Axe peoples were mutually related and were in the habit of burying their dead singly, accompanied by a pot or a battle axe of polished stone. In Jutland they built the many barrows, which, with additions from the Bronze Age, give the region the character of a land full of grave mounds. The Pitted Ware culture had something to do with the cultures east of the Baltic, and its most striking item of equipment was its ferocious, rod-like flint arrowheads.

Meanwhile the northern and central parts of the peninsula were still inhabited by hunter-fisher groups similar to those which had been there during the Mesolithic period. They have left behind them, as well as their camp sites, many pictures of wild animals, hammered or polished on to the rocks of their native fells. Circumscribed by a harsh nature, they continued in their original pattern of life untouched by the changes that were slowly creating civilization in other parts of the world. For them the first important change was the domestication of the reindeer some time during the early centuries AD.

To return to south Scandinavia, after about 2000 BC the various populations fused together to create a retarded Neolithic culture into which the use of metal slowly penetrated. The people were skilled in the working of flint, out of which they made beautiful daggers. Their burials were in stone cists, or in the barrows and stone chambers of their predecessors.

After about 1500 BC the bronze founders of the west Baltic area began to develop a marked regional style. This grew into the school of metalwork known as the Northern

See p. 49 for generalized distribution of Megalithic chambered tombs

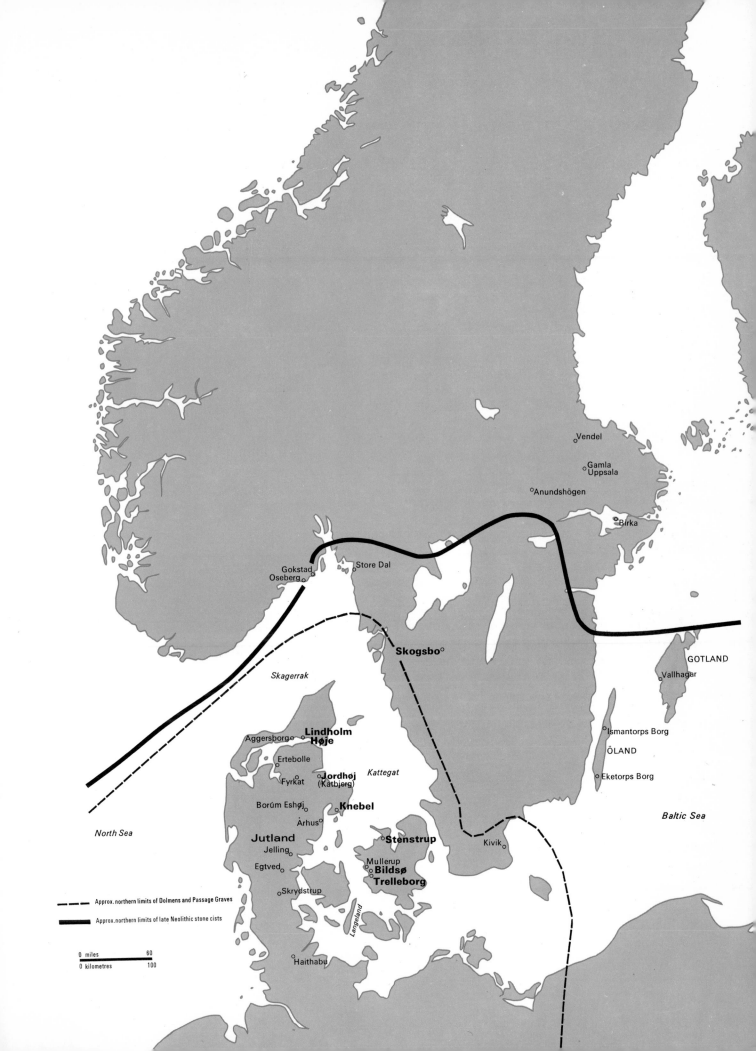

Vendel

Gamla
Uppsala

Anundshögen

Birka

GOTLAND

Vallhagar

Gokstad
Oseberg

Store Dal

Skogsbo

Ismantorps Borg

ÖLAND

Skagerrak

Eketorps Borg

Baltic Sea

Lindholm
Høje

Aggersborg

Ertebolle

Kattegat

Fyrkat

Jordhøj
(Katbjerg)

Knebel

Borúm Eshøj

North Sea

Århus

Stenstrup

Kivik

Jutland

Jelling

Mullerup

Egtved

Bildsø
Trelleborg

Skrydstrup

Langeland

Haithabu

- - - Approx. northern limits of Dolmens and Passage Graves

⸻ Approx. northern limits of late Neolithic stone cists

0 miles   60

0 kilometres   100

Bronze Age, which enjoyed an uninterrupted craft tradition for close to a thousand years. Its development was divided into six main stages by the great Swedish archaeologist, Oscar Montelius, whose approach to the problem has been a model for later scholars. Burial was in barrows, and the most remarkable finds are the great log coffins from Egtved, Borum Eshøj, and Skrydstrup, in which the clothing and hair of the dead were preserved intact. Another interesting feature is the scribings of mythological scenes, found on natural rock faces in parts of Scandinavia.

The Northern Bronze Age had spent itself by about 500 BC, and iron came gradually into use. The Iron Age falls naturally into two major epochs dividing at about the 3rd century AD. The earlier appears to have been a period of prosperity, when south Scandinavian culture was more integrated with the European than ever before, and was much influenced by the great Celtic and Roman civilizations. The period has left few monuments other than cairn cemeteries, as at Store Dal and Vallhagar.

The later Iron Age is the earliest into whose spirit we are able to enter. Nordic mythology, and the tense, detailed ornament of its metalwork give a feeling of its heroic, but rather ruthless and destructive spirit. Scandinavia became severed from the rest of Europe, where the Christian religion was spreading, and the centre of gravity within Scandinavia moved northward to previously marginal regions. This northward expansion was made possible by the new iron technology, with better tools, better carpentry, ships, weapons and so on, than ever before. The final phase of the Iron Age, after 800 AD, is known as the Viking period, when the warrior spirit reached its climax and the Scandinavians burst out of their isolation to spread terror in Christian Europe.

The later Iron Age has left a great variety of monuments. Mention may be made of the very large barrows at royal cemeteries such as Vendel, Gamla Uppsala, and Jelling, and of the many ship-shaped settings of standing stones, sometimes over 160 feet (50 m) in length, of which some surround cremation graves. On occasion real ships were buried under barrows – the most famous are those from Gokstad and Oseberg. In Sweden there are many stone forts, especially on the islands of Gotland and Öland, and Denmark possesses four great 10th-century military camps with circular earthen ramparts. In the Viking period trade developed to such a level that we find the first towns around the Baltic. Some have been found by excavating under modern towns such as Århus. Haithabu, near the town of Schleswig, and Birka, near Stockholm, were abandoned at the end of the Viking period, so their protective embankments and cemetery mounds are still visible. A particularly fascinating type of monument are the stones with runic inscriptions, many of which in Sweden are decorated with mythological and historical scenes.

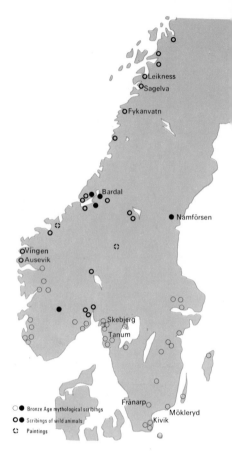

○● Bronze Age mythological scribings
○● Scribings of wild animals
⟡ Paintings

This rather remote site at Vingen is one of the purest examples of the schematized animal style

Rock Scribings

c. 5500–400 BC

BIBLIOGRAPHY
Hallström, G., *Monumental Art in Northern Europe from the Stone Age: 1. The Norwegian Localities*, Stockholm, 1938
Hallström, G., *Monumental Art of Northern Sweden from the Stone Age: Nämforsen and other Localities*, Stockholm, 1960
Hasselrot, P. and Ohlmarks, A., *Hällristningar*, Stockholm, 1966
Davidson, H. R. E., *Pagan Scandinavia*, London, 1967

Among the most remarkable prehistoric remains of Scandinavia are the many rock scribings, or petroglyphs, hewn into, or more rarely painted upon rock faces. These are found all over the peninsula, and fall into two main groups – a northern one with representations of wild animals, and a southern, in which mysterious scenes from myth and legend appear to be depicted.

The finest of the wild-animal scribings are outline drawings in naturalistic style. The artists were masters of the creation of life and movement by the simplest of means, and preferred to work in full natural size. Another style is represented by badly proportioned, rather amusing animals, whose bodies tend to be rectangular or oval and often are filled with geometric patterns. These latter sometimes appear to indicate internal organs like an X-ray picture. Important sites with stylized animals are found at Vingen and Ausevik in Norway and Nämforsen in Sweden. The scribings of wild animals are very ancient and are the work of the early hunter-fisher inhabitants of Scandinavia. Comparable works of art are found in Finland, in the Soviet Union near Lake Onega, by the White Sea, and even in Siberia.

The second main group of scribings is associated with the south Scandinavian Bronze Age cultures, as is shown among other things by the fact that identical motives are found on rock faces and on datable bronzes. These scribings are found mainly in the more southerly part of Scandinavia, and in Denmark, where suitable rock faces were confined to Bornholm, they can be found on loose blocks used in grave mounds or found alone. The richest area of Bronze Age scribings straddles the Swedish–Norwegian border in Bohuslän and Østfold, with a remarkable concentration of sites in Tanum parish. An unusually sophisticated set of pictures can be seen on the stones of a burial cist at Kivik in Skåne (Scania), which was discovered in the 18th century. It was largely destroyed but has been reconstructed as well as circumstances permit.

These scribings were made by agricultural peoples, and their subjects are quite different from those of the hunters. They show highly stylized

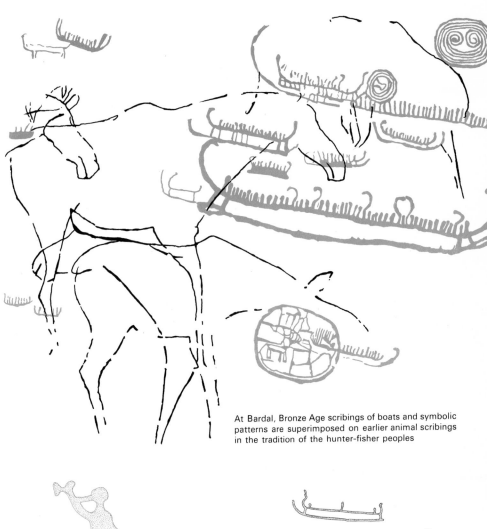

At Bardal, Bronze Age scribings of boats and symbolic patterns are superimposed on earlier animal scribings in the tradition of the hunter-fisher peoples

Hauge, Rolvs Island, S.E. Norway. A phallic giant sailing majestically in a boat and blowing a horn gives a good impression of the Bronze Age scribings as scenes from a forgotten mythology

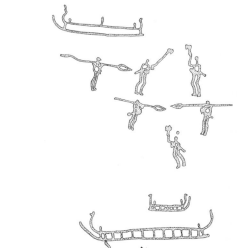

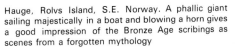

Smørsten (the Butter Stone) in Tanum parish. A small but clear group with six men in combat with axes and spears and six typical ships

representations of ships, men with shields, battle axes, or other weapons, sometimes carts or ploughing scenes, as well as many other less frequent motives; these are accompanied by symbolic figures such as the cross-in-circle, footprints, spirals, and in particular cup marks.

At some sites the two main styles are found on the same rock face. Sometimes, as at Bardal, the styles were clearly successive, but at other sites the composition of the pictures and the sharing of motives makes it appear that the two schools came into contact with one another.

Leikness: one of the richest and stylistically purest groups of scribings in the naturalistic style. The lines are not sunken but almost level with the surface of the granite, upon which they have been laboriously polished as smooth tracks. The animals are only visible because the lichen, which covers the rock, does not grow on the polished areas. Elk, reindeer, bears, a whale, and a long-necked bird are superimposed in lively profusion

Megalithic Tombs

Passage graves, dolmens and other forms
c. 3500–1500 BC

BIBLIOGRAPHY

Nordman, C. A., 'Jaettestuer i Danmark. Nya fund.' *Nordiske Fortidsminder*, 2, no. 2, Copenhagen, 1918, pp. 55–118

Becker, C. J., 'Die mittel-neolitischen Kulturen in Südskandinavien', *Acta Archaeologica* 25, 1954, Copenhagen, 1955, pp. 49–150

Kjaerum, P., 'The Passage Grave Jordhøj', *Kuml* 1969, Copenhagen, 1970, pp. 9–66

Glob, P. V., *Danish Prehistoric Monuments*, London, 1971

Tombs built of giant stones, or megaliths, are a phenomenon associated mainly with the Atlantic coasts of Europe. The Scandinavian tombs, together with the related Dutch–north German group, are the north-western extremity of a great swathe extending all the way from the Iberian peninsula to Sweden. It is perhaps because of their position at the end of this swathe that the Scandinavian tombs were constructed over a rather shorter period and are less various in their architectural details than those of many parts of western Europe.

The simplest type of chamber is illustrated by an example at Bildsø in western Sjaelland (Zealand), where three simple rectangular chambers can be seen in a long mound retained by a kerb of very large stones. These chambers are of a type which is rectangular and usually of the size necessary to accommodate a single burial with its grave goods. But though the chambers are small, they were built of very large stones, four or five in number fitted neatly together, plus a still larger capstone. These closed chambers have yielded finds from an earlier period than any other megaliths in Scandinavia – the middle of the 4th millenium BC according to the newest estimates. To judge from their construction they were not intended, like later megaliths, for the dead of the whole community.

With increasing expertise in the handling of boulders and a growing desire to conform to the Atlantic custom of communal burial, the inhabitants learned to build larger chambers. These were often polygonal, with an indication of a short entrance passage or portico. One of the finest examples of this type of chamber can be found at Knebel in eastern Jutland.

More evolved megaliths had a long roofed passage and a chamber large enough to require several roofing stones. These are known as passage graves, and a good example is Jordhøj, near Katbjerg in eastern Jutland. The chamber was completely sealed

Bildsø

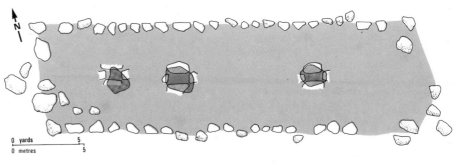

0 yards 5
0 metres 5

Skogsbo

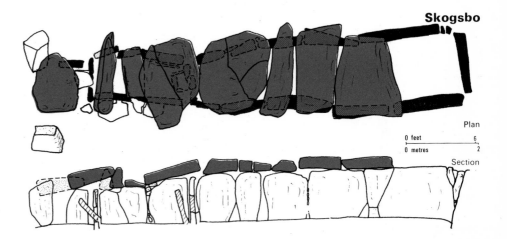

Plan

0 feet 6
0 metres 2

Section

Jordhøj

Section

Plan

Knebel

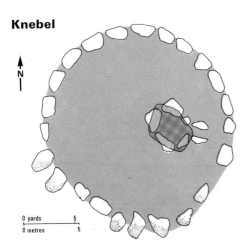

0 yards 5
0 metres 5

when opened in 1890. The excavator's eye was met by various mouldered planks – the remains of wooden coffins – among which lay a number of pottery vessels and flint implements. All bones had decayed away. These finds were, however, from a period hundreds of years after the chamber had been built. Those from the first period of the tomb lay outside the entrance, where large quantities of pottery were found during renewed excavation in 1964–5. The sherds came from pots which had been placed in a complete condition before the entrance, no doubt as a sort of sacrifice to the dead.

The passage grave motive had a number of variations. One of these is two chambers sharing an end stone in common but each having its own passage. One such double passage grave can be seen at Stenstrup in north-west Sealand. The mound is

(24 m) in diameter and 15 feet (4·6 m) high. Each chamber has four roofing stones, and the construction is relatively sophisticated in that a row of extra blocks have been inserted between the uprights and the roofing stones to make the chamber higher.

Another variant has an extra chamber situated behind the main chamber and entered through it. It should be noted that some passage graves have rectangular chambers instead of the oval ones illustrated here. The largest of the Scandinavian passage graves are found in the Swedish province of Västergötland.

There seems to be little difference in age between the enlarged dolmens, the passage graves, and the more elaborate variations of the passage graves. They all stopped being built in the early 3rd millenium BC, and when a new type of stone tomb appeared at about 2000 BC there was no direct continuity of building tradition.

This new type, the stone cist, is best represented by some of the larger Swedish examples, such as that at Skogsbo, Norra Säm parish. Västergötland. This is a long gallery divided into segments by crosswalls, in which there are round openings – so-called portholes. Although this cist resembles in many ways certain west European gallery graves, the latter are earlier and a direct connection is therefore unlikely. When all factors are taken into account, it seems that the most probable source of this new wave of megaliths lay in Poland and the Ukraine. The earliest were connected with the Single Grave culture, and they continued to be built far into the retarded Late Neolithic of the south Baltic region.

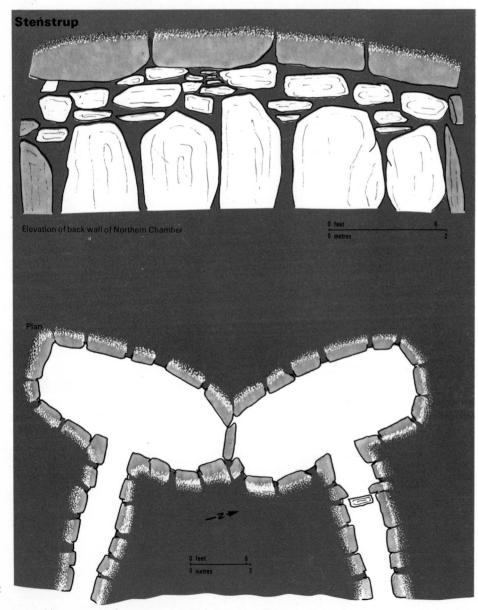

Stenstrup

Elevation of back wall of Northern Chamber

0 feet 6
0 metres 2

Plan

0 feet 6
0 metres 2

Lindholm Høje NORTH JUTLAND

Later Iron Age cemetery
c. AD 500–900

BIBLIOGRAPHY
Ramskou, T., Series of excavation reports in *Acta Archaeologica* 24, 1953, pp. 186–96; 26, 1955, pp. 177–85; 28, 1957, pp. 193–201, Copenhagen

On a hill across the fjord from Ålborg lies a remarkable cemetery with graves from the 6th to 10th centuries AD, and an adjacent settlement with house remains. The complex was excavated in 1952–9, during which time about 700 graves were discovered, over 90 per cent from the period AD 700–1000.

The earliest burials were inhumation graves under very small mounds. They were situated near the top of the hill and date from the 6th century. After about the year 600 the inhabitants of the village went over to disposing of their dead by cremation. The remains were surrounded by settings of stones – often quite large stones – and the method was to burn the corpse inside the enclosure and then to cover the area with a thin layer of soil, which sealed and protected the remains. The objects found amid the cremated bones were such things as melted glass beads, small knives, brooches, bone combs, gaming pieces. There were none of the sumptuous grave goods characteristic of princely burials. The finds are exhibited in Ålborg Historical Museum.

The stone settings of the 7th century were triangular, round or rectangular, and are found close to the still earlier inhumations. In the 8th century oval settings came into fashion, and in the 9th century – the beginning of the Viking period proper – these gave way to pointed-oval 'ship settings' (to be compared with the real ships found in princely graves). Ship settings are found especially in a swathe around the southernmost part of the cemetery, and they normally pointed north and south.

After 900 inhumation burial again began to come into vogue, and a number of log-coffin burials were found from the latest period of use of the cemetery.

During the whole of this time there was continual deposition of sand blown in from the north coast, which meant that later settings were constructed at a higher level than their predecessors and often overlapped them. The stones of earlier burials were often dug up and used again, so that the complex as it now stands is by no means complete. Places where it was ascertained that a stone had been removed were marked with squared paving slabs.

A big cemetery implies the existence of a settlement of importance, and several buildings lay within the excavated area. The positions of the most important wall trenches and post holes have been preserved by marking them with cement. The buildings include long houses with convex sides as at TRELLEBORG, and four straight-sided buildings placed around a central yard. There were also small sunken huts for weaving in. The site continued to be inhabited for about a hundred years after the cemetery had gone out of use.

View of Lindholm Høje from the south

Trelleborg WESTERN ZEALAND

Viking fortification
10th century AD

BIBLIOGRAPHY
Christiansen, T. E., 'Traeningslejr eller Tvaengsborg', *Kuml* 1970, Copenhagen, 1971, pp. 43–63
Nørlund, P., *Trelleborg*, Copenhagen, 1948
Olsen, O., 'Trelleborg Problemer', *Scandia*, vol. 28, 1962, pp. 92–112
Glob, P. V., *Danish Prehistoric Monuments*, London, 1971

This remarkable monument was the object of very large-scale excavations in 1935–42 and is now a national monument open to the public.

The most imposing part of Trelleborg is the circular bank, 564 feet (172 m) in diameter and 16 feet (4·9 m) high. It had four entrances pointing in the direction of the points of the compass. Outside it a ditch on the eastern and south-eastern sides gives additional protection. There was no ditch on the other sides, as the fortress originally stood on a slight cape extending into an area of shallow water. This estuary has now silted up and been drained, and the site is surrounded by fields. On the landward side there was an outer bailey, enclosed by a smaller bank and ditch concentric with the inner one, except where it widens out to enclose the site's cemetery.

The excavation showed that the bank had originally been bounded without and within by great timber palisades. The four gateways had been roofed passages, and in one of them was found the iron key to the gate itself. The ditch was then a water-filled moat crossed by a bridge midway between the south and the east gates, from which the passage continued along the berm between wall and moat. Within the inner bailey the opposite gates were connected by roadways of sleepers, which crossed at the centre, dividing the camp into four quadrants. In each of these four buildings had been laid out with great precision in a square. Four smaller buildings stood at the centres of the north-east and south-west squares and just within the north and west gates. The outer bailey contained 15 longhouses arranged radially, and a cemetery where the majority of the dead were men, confirming the military character of the whole construction.

The longhouses of Trelleborg were of a standard plan. The sides were bowed and were built of vertical planks which had stood in a trench. Outside the wall was found an extra row of post holes whose significance has been interpreted in various ways. The excavators' interpretation is illustrated by a full-size reconstruction on the site. The posts were thought to have belonged to a sort of colonnade or gallery around each house. A newer interpretation is that the rafters instead of stopping at the eaves were carried down and their ends buried in the ground. This is supported by the fact that further excavation at Trelleborg and other similar sites in Denmark has shown that the outer posts leaned inward at an angle of about 30° and were buried deeper than the wall footing itself. This would have given the construction great stability and made it possible to reduce the number of internal posts, as indeed seems to have happened, for there are hardly any traces of posts inside the houses to support the roof. There is also evidence for a long pre-existing tradition for this type of construction.

Trelleborg was built in the later part of the 10th century, and gives an idea of the level of organization and discipline in the armies that ravaged England in the time of Ethelred the Unready.

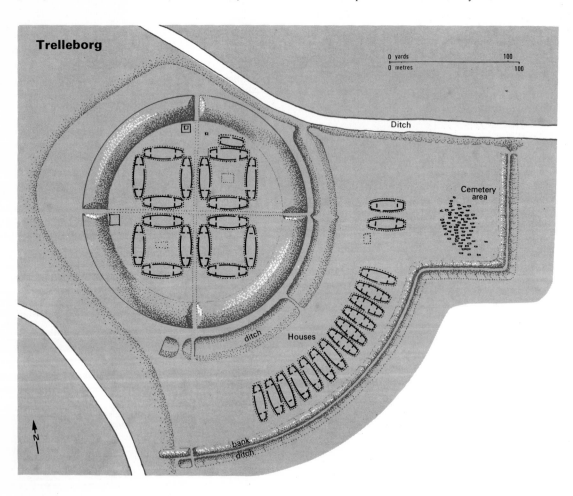

Trelleborg

0 yards 100
0 metres 100

Ditch

Cemetery area

Houses

ditch

bank
ditch

N

EASTERN EUROPE

East Europe must be considered a traditional geographical unit rather than a cultural one. Even so a division into eastern and western Europe is more a convention than the expression of any geographical reality. This survey will be mainly concerned with territories lying within the borders of modern Bulgaria, Rumania, Hungary, Czechoslovakia, Poland and the European part of the USSR.

The structure of east Europe as it emerged with the ending of the Pleistocene Age allowed easy contacts between human groups living throughout its vast area. Wide plains or hilly country traversed only by a few ranges of low mountains stretched to the Urals in the east. To the west there was no natural barrier. The only high mountains, the Carpathians, did not isolate south-eastern Europe from surrounding lands. The great Danube valley and numerous other waterways and passes facilitated movement and trade. Permanent settlements developed mainly in the loess and steppe-forest areas. Natural conditions favoured cultural advancement. Rivers and lakes provided plentiful sources of fresh water, and there was an abundance of wood for house building and utensils. These factors did much to shape human life in great areas of Europe.

Other natural resources that were to be of importance through prehistoric times were good supplies of flint (especially from Krzemionki in Poland) and of copper, gold and tin from the Carpathians and Transylvania.

There is little to be said of the earliest human settlement during early Pleistocene times, though the site known as Vértesszóllós, not far from Budapest, dating from the second (Mindel) glaciation of the European system, yielded human remains apparently of advanced *Homo erectus* type. By the last interglacial period men of Neanderthaloid stock had introduced their Mousterian industries and continued to develop them through the first half of the final glaciation. There are a number of cave dwellings, including the well known one of Krapina (Croatia) which yielded the remains of no fewer than thirteen Neanderthaloid skeletons. Men of modern type entered the region as bearers of Upper Palaeolithic hunting cultures identified with the Aurignacian and Gravettian of western Europe. Caves at Szeleta and Istállóskó, both near Miskolc, Hungary, have industries showing a mingling of Aurignacian with the old Mousterian tradition of the Neanderthalers. However, these men seem to have died out here as in the west by about 30,000 years ago.

The Gravettian is highly developed in the region and may indeed have originated there. Both Aurignacian and Gravettian remains are found in cave dwellings, but the most interesting sites in east Europe are the huts built by Gravettian mammoth hunters, most commonly in southern Russia and Moravia. These, the earliest known houses, were usually sited beside rivers, and were sometimes constructed with hides and mammoth bones MEZHIRICH and Kostenki, near Voronezh, both USSR).

The Gravettian culture was further distinguished by excellent carved or modelled figurines, most of them representing women or animals (Dolní Věstonice, Czechoslovakia; Kostenki and Gagarino, USSR). There was, on the other hand, no cave art to compare with that of western Europe.

In the Mesolithic period of post-Pleistocene times there were both temporary and permanent settlements throughout the area. The industries were characterized by microlithic tools evolving out of the Palaeolithic tradition. Some are identified with the Azilian and Tardenoisian of the west, but the Swiderian was a distinctive culture originating in the Polish area. In various ways, but particularly in the beginning of permanent settlements, this Mesolithic epoch can be seen as a preparation for the great advance to the farming economy of the Neolithic age.

Between the 6th and 3rd millennia BC Neolithic cultures emerged, partly derived from the old hunting and fishing cultures, but stimulated by strong influences radiating from the early centre of farming in western Asia. Features characteristic of the pastoral tribes of the Asian–European borders also contributed to the complex origin of the east European Neolithic. Of the several distinct farming traditions that developed, their

Ural
Mountains

Volga

Baltic Sea

Moscow

Gagarino

Voronezh

Biskupin ○   ○ Włocławek
Gaj ○   ○ Warsaw   Kostenki

Závist ○   Stara Słupia
                          ○ Krzemionki   Dnieper   Don

                    ○ Ojców   Kolomyscina
Staré Hradisk ○
Býčí Skála ○   ○ Předmosti   Carpathian Mountains   Mezhirich ○
            ○ Kulna   Vladymirovka ○   Volga
         ○ Liseri   ○ Aggtelek
                    ○ Miskolc
                    ○ Bodrogkesztur   Caspian Sea
Vértesszőllós ○   ○ Cucuteni
   Lengyel ○   Ariusd ○   ○ Poiana
○ Krapina
         Sarmizegethusa   ○ M nteoru
         (Gradistea
          Muncelului)
                    ○ Glina   Black Sea   0 miles   300
                 ○ Cernavodă   0 kilometres   5
Rabisza ○   Danube
                                                                    Adriatic Sea
      ○ Baco-Kiro

Karanovo ○   ○ Azmaska

nature affected by differences in climate and the raw materials available, the Linear Ware Körös culture of Hungary, the Cucuteni–Tripolje of Rumania and the Ukraine and the Rumanian Vinca culture are the most important.

One of the distinguishing features of these different groups of farming communities can be seen in the form of their houses. In general the peoples of eastern Europe preferred rectangular plans (or later trapezoidal) in contrast with the round house usual in the prehistoric west. The materials varied locally, the sharpest division being between the south (Bulgaria and much of Rumania) where the earliest settlements were built largely of mud, producing 'tells' comparable to their Asian counterparts, and the more northerly regions where wooden houses were the rule. Clay and wood building was, however, practised in the Ukraine. In KARANOVO we shall examine one of the largest and longest-lived of the many tell villages.

Among these farmers agriculture and stockbreeding flourished, they were skilled workers in flint and polished stone, and accomplished potters. As well as in their pottery, these peoples showed their aesthetic gifts in small figurines – among which those from Cernavodă, Rumania, are outstanding. By the 3rd millennium BC contacts with western Asia became increasingly important in connection with the diffusion of copper.

During the centuries on either side of 2000 BC the migrations of the Indo-European peoples caused upheavals in many parts of Eurasia. Those entering our region soon split up, settling down in regions later to be found occupied by Slavs, Germans and Balts. Among the movements probably to be attributed to Indo-Europeans was that of the warrior Corded Ware people, who characteristically buried their dead singly under circular mounds or kurgans. They may have come from south Russia and Poland but spread across Europe, merging their traditions with those of the old farming communities. They also met and sometimes mingled with the Bell–Beaker people who were spreading through much of Europe – from homelands that may have been either Iberian or central European. These Bell–Beaker people did much to propagate the use of copper. (See also pp. 24, 30, 48, 63, 85.)

Rather later in date was the Únětice culture which flourished during the first half of the 2nd millennium. It was involved with a great development of metallurgy (first copper then bronze) in Transylvania, the Hungarian Plain and Western Poland.

Although local differences remained, the mid-2nd millennium saw the first signs of a unification of culture throughout Europe – at a time when the Aegean was replacing western Asia as the main centre of cultural inspiration. A significant change of this time was the appearance of cremation burial, probably as the result of internal cultural evolution.

Another event of fundamental importance was the emergence of the Lusatian culture in Poland and north Czechoslovakia. Its genesis was a complex one, including Danubian and eastern (Trzciniec) elements. It was fully developed by 1200 BC and had spread into central Europe. Its people were farmers and skilled bronze workers. That tribal life was highly organized is suggested by their fortifications (BISKUPIN). Lusatian territory largely coincided with that of the earliest West Slavic lands of later times. Under the pressure of Germans, Celts and Scythians, however, the culture suffered a crisis, when its fortified settlements were destroyed and left temporarily uninhabited.

By the 8th century BC, when the Lusatian culture was still at its height, eastern Europe entered upon its Hallstatt Iron Age. A few centuries later the expansion of the Celtic peoples introduced their La Tène culture (p. 57) as far east as southern Poland and Czechoslovakia. With the growth of the Roman Empire, the territories of present-day Rumania, Bulgaria, part of Hungary and the southern coasts of the USSR were brought within its frontiers. Lands outside the empire felt Roman influence and developed economically. This is shown, for instance, by the creation of great centres of metal working in the Polish regions of STARA AND NOWA SŁUPIA. In these independent lands, large states, most of them Slavonic, were to be established in the early Middle Ages.

Mezhirich USSR

Upper Palaeolithic settlement
c. 14,000 BC

BIBLIOGRAPHY
Pidoplicko, I., Lubin, I., Timčenko, N., 'Kvoprosu chozjaistvie, bytie i kulture pozdniepaleolitičeskov naselienia v sviazi s raskopkami v s. Mezhirich' (To th problem of economics, life and culture of Late Palaeo lithic inhabitants in light of the excavations at Mezhirich in: *Materiały i Issledovania po Archeologii SSSR* (Studie in the archaeology of USSR), no. 185, *Paleolit i neoli* vol. 7, Leningrad, 1972, pp. 189–92

This important settlement of mammoth hunters of Gravettian culture lies about 90 miles (145 km) south east of Kiev. Having been first detected by the exposure of mammoth bones, excavation began in 1966. By stripping down layer by layer over a wide area it has been possible to prove that the bones were no mere food waste, but had been used in the construction of the huts.

The one hut that has been fully excavated is circular in plan with a single entrance. It had been raised on the basal bones of mammoth skulls, the lower jaws projecting as a facing. Both pine poles and large bones were used for the framework and to support the conical roof. For the sake of warmth the interior was lined with hides. A central hearth was still covered by an eight-inch (20 cm) layer of ash. It appears that the hunters did some of their flint knapping by the fireside, as both finished and unfinished implements were found near the hearth.

A second, smaller, hut has been found a few yards from the first, and there are signs that others stood nearby.

Finds from both huts include ornaments of amber and other materials, and carved bone figurines. The flint industry is of the characteristic Gravettian type, including backed blades and scrapers. Bone awls and needles are numerous.

Reconstruction of mammoth bone hut at Mezhirich

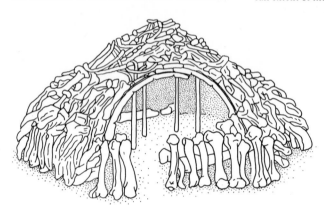

Mezhirich seems to have been occupied all the year round, and the large number of mammoth slaughtered, including many young ones, (it is calculated that the large hut had bones from at least 100 animals) suggests that human hunters played a large part in making the breed extinct.

The structural remains of the larger hut have been taken to the museum of the Zoological Institute of the Ukrainian Academy of Science in Kiev. The reconstruction is accessible to the public. Meanwhile excavation is continuing and it is hoped to find the full extent of the settlement.

Karanovo BULGARIA

Settlement mound or tell
c. 4500–2000 BC

BIBLIOGRAPHY
Georgiev, G., 'Main periods of cultural development in Neolithic and Bronze Ages in Bulgaria in light of the most recent archaeological discoveries', *Swiatowid*, Warsaw, 23, 1960, p. 309
Mikov, V., 'The Prehistoric Mound of Karanovo', *Archaeology* 12, 1959, pp. 87–8
Mikov, V., 'Razkopkite na selišcata mogila pri Karanovo'. (Excavations at settlement mound at Karanovo), in: *Poslednije archeologičeski razkopki w Bułgaria* (Recent archaeological excavations in Bulgaria), ed. D. Dimitrov, Sofia, 1955, p. 9

Karanovo, near Nova Zagora in southern Bulgaria, is one of the biggest of the very numerous tells in this country: 43 feet (13 m) in height with a diameter of 590 to 820 feet (180–250 m). Excavation, in progress since 1957 but still far from complete, has proved this to be a most important site for our understanding of the Bulgarian Neolithic period. The stratification shows seven distinct phases.

The earliest, Karanovo I, represents the first farmers of early Neolithic times. The houses were small, square, and single-roomed, the clay wells reinforced inside with wattlework. The floors were of wooden planks with a hearth near one wall; each house contained a quernstone. Outside was a small storehouse for food. These dwellings were arranged regularly in parallel lines and the space between them had a covering of planks with a layer of sand above. The inhabitants decorated their pottery with both painted and incised designs, and modelled crude female figurines.

In Karanovo II painted wares were no longer made and new forms of pottery and figurines appeared. Graves of this period were found near the settlement. In Karanovo III (Late Neolithic) the houses were similar to those of the previous phases but had two or even three rooms. Households evidently had their own religious observances for portable altars were found in some rooms. The pottery

Karanovo

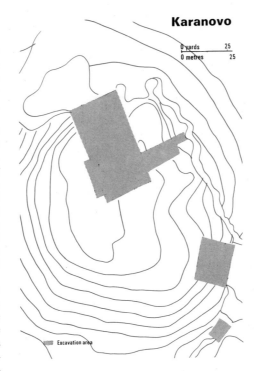

0 yards 25
0 metres 25

Excavation area

was now more varied and figurines resembling Cycladic types indicate connections with the Mediterranean. Little is known of Karanovo IV except that it belongs to the period when pottery was ornamented with spiral and meander designs encrusted in white.

Karanovo V and VI can be said to belong to a Chalcolithic Age since copper was coming into use, and indeed in VI was used on quite a large scale, for shaft-hole axes, pins and daggers. Silver and gold were also employed. The houses, still built of clay and wattle, were now of rectangular shape, with one or two rooms. Pottery was produced in great quantity; a single house was found to contain a hundred vessels. Figurines were carved from both bone and marble. These phases probably fall within the second half of the 3rd millennium BC.

There may have been a break in the continuity of settlement before the occupation of Karanovo VII. This is an Early Bronze Age culture, though most tools were still made of stone, flint and bone. Some authorities believe it represents the arrival of a new group of people. The rectangular houses were now larger than before with one apsidal wall and sometimes a porch – very much in the megaron style. It is of interest that hearths, quernstones, pottery and other utensils were all concentrated in one room, the other being quite empty.

Kujavian Megalithic Tombs

POLAND

c. 2500 BC

BIBLIOGRAPHY
Chmielewski, W., *Zagadnienie grobowców kujawskich w świetle ostatnich badań*, Łódź, 1952 (summary: Le Problème des sépultures de Cuyavie dans la lumière de récentes études, pp. 104–9)

The Kujavian graves lie in two regions of northern Poland, one the Kujawy district (including the Chełmice area) between Inowrocław and Włocławek, and the other western Pomerania. Some 76 now survive, particularly where they are protected by woodland. Large numbers have been destroyed; until not very long ago nine miles (14 km) of road in the Kujawy district were paved with stones taken from these monuments. They were always built on the highest spot in their area, and often near a river or lake. Essentially the Kujavian graves were elongated mounds enclosed by standing stones large enough to qualify as megaliths, but not very large. Some are triangular in outline, others trapezoidal. The dimensions vary widely: some are no more than 20 feet (6 m) long while others are over 330 feet (100 m). That at Wietrzychowice measures 381 feet (116 m), and that at Gaj, in the Koło district, about 427 feet (130 m). In spite of the length, the mounds were probably never more than 10 feet (3 m) in height. The grave illustrated is at Świerczynek, Nieszawa district.

Almost invariably the mounds were built on an east–west axis with the burials at the larger, eastern end. The bodies were usually interred singly in sunken graves, but there might be as many as 10 such graves under one mound. This does not seem to mean true collective burial such as is found in many megalithic tombs elsewhere. The Gaj tomb was found to have a burned wooden structure, probably a mortuary house, at the larger end. In some mounds there were lines of stones thought to mark the place where mourners ate the burial feast.

Excavations have established the order in which these monuments were constructed. First the pit was dug, the body laid in it and covered with earth or stones. Next a low mound of earth was raised, similar in outline to that which the completed form was to assume, and the stone blocks were placed in position along the sides. Finally more earth was piled to bring the mound to its full height.

It is surprising that although an immense amount of labour was put into building the Kujavian tombs, the grave goods were, so far as is known, very modest. A few amber beads were found in one grave, pottery in another. The builders belonged to the Funnel Beaker (Trichterbecher) culture, dating from the middle of the Polish Neolithic period.

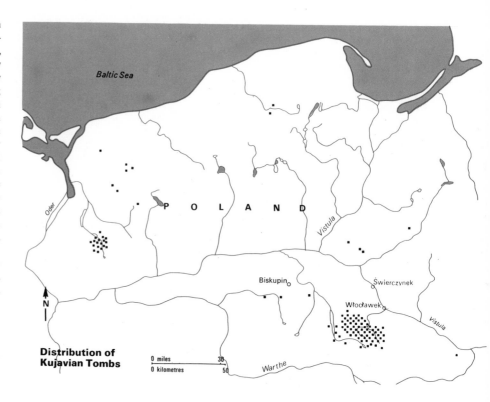

Distribution of Kujavian Tombs

0 miles 30
0 kilometres 50

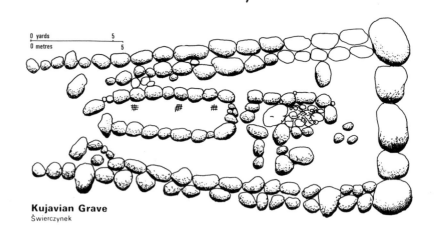

Kujavian Grave
Świerczynek

Biskupin POLAND

Fortified settlement
c. 550–400 BC

BIBLIOGRAPHY
Kostrzewski, J., Lubicz-Niezabitowski, E., Jarón, B., *Osada babienna w Biskupinie w pow. żnińskim*, (Marshy Settlement at Biskupin near Żnin), Poznań, 1936
Rajewski, Z., *Biskupin*, Warsaw, 1970 (summaries: English, French, German)

This site is in flat country near Gniezno (Znin), 140 miles (225 km) west of Warsaw. It was occupied from Neolithic times to the Middle Ages, but by far the most important stage in its history was that of a late Lusatian settlement of the 5th–6th centuries BC (Early Iron Age).

What is now a peninsula in a lake was at that time an island; the village occupied the greater part of it – an area of about five acres (2 hectares). It was enclosed by an earthen rampart reinforced with a wooden framework and palisade. This rampart was itself protected on its outer side by a breakwater of several rows of piles driven obliquely into the bottom of the lake. The entrance through the ramparts was on the south-west side, and was a complex structure with a wooden guard room above. An oak causeway 394 feet (120 m) long linked the island with the mainland.

Inside these stout defences a road encircled the settlement from which diagonal roads, surfaced with wood, led between the houses. A small square was used for a market and meeting place. There were altogether over 100 houses arranged in 13 rows; each row was covered by a single, unbroken, thatched roof.

The individual houses, constructed of oak and pine, consisted of a main room with a stone hearth, and a separate sleeping room. A porch, where cattle were kept in winter, spanned the front of the house. The entrance was always on the southern side.

It has been calculated that the building of this fortified village took 247,000 cubic feet (approx. 7,000 cu m) of wood and about 353,000 cubic feet (approx. 10,000 cu m) of earth, reed and clay.

The first Lusatian settlement was soon destroyed, probably by flooding, but soon after this a second, similar though a little smaller, was built inside the ruined ramparts. In the second half of the 5th century it was destroyed for a second time, either once again by flooding or by Scythian invaders. This was evidently a severe blow to the community for when it was again rebuilt the village was both smaller and poorer.

The inhabitants of Biskupin grew four varieties of wheat, barley, peas, broad beans and lentils; they also cultivated flax and poppies. Cattle, pigs and horses were bred, but hunting and fishing (in spite of the proximity of the lake) were of relatively little importance. Among the principal crafts were iron working, potting and weaving. Excavation is not complete, but has revealed the greater part of the settlement. Large quantities of metal objects and pottery have been found, and, because of the dampness of the ground, not only horn and bone artifacts have survived but also wooden tools, utensils, house timbers and plant and animal remains. Many of these things are exhibited in a popular museum close to the site.

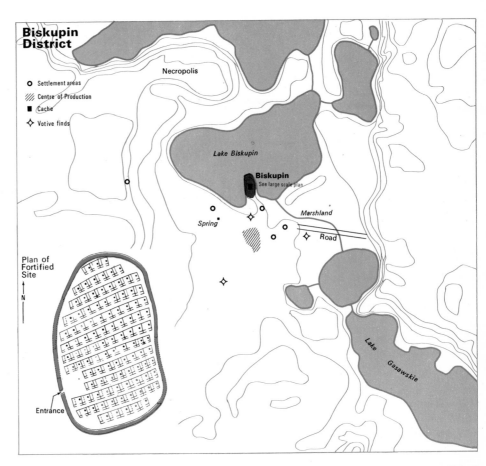

Biskupin District

- ○ Settlement areas
- ⧅ Centre of Production
- ■ Cache
- ✦ Votive finds

Necropolis

Lake Biskupin

Biskupin
See large scale plan

Spring

Marshland

Road

Lake Gasawskie

Plan of Fortified Site
N

Entrance

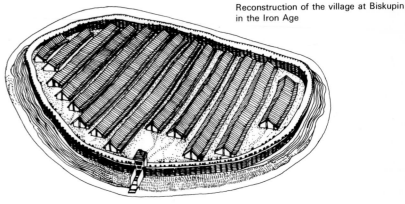

Reconstruction of the village at Biskupin in the Iron Age

Závist CZECHOSLOVAKIA

Celtic oppidum
c. 450–200 BC

BIBLIOGRAPHY
Filip, J., *Keltove ve středni Evvropě*, Prague, 1956, p. 326
Jansovà, L., 'Hradiště nad Závisti. Výzkum brány na jihovýchodnim úpati Hradiště v r. 1966' (summary: Die Erforschung des Tors am Hradiště oberhalb Závist), *Arheologické rozhledy*, 19, 1967, pp. 597–605

Závist, near Zbraslav, 11 miles (18 km) from Prague, is the greatest Celtic oppidum in Czechoslovakia and one of the largest in the entire region. It stands on two hills some 1,000 to 1,300 feet (approx. 300–400 m) high divided by a ravine and overlooking the river Moldau. The whole oppidum covers as much as 420 acres (170 hectares) and is enclosed by five and half mile (9 km) long walls that are led across the gorge.

The main fort (Hradiště) is enclosed within its own walls and comprises an acropolis with an outer stronghold some 165 feet (50 m) lower, overlooking the steep slope down to the Moldau. The walls, built of stone laced with wood, stand to a height of 20 feet (6 m) and are as much as 33 feet (10 m) thick on the acropolis. The gates are of an elaborate plan. This hillfort contained buildings in earth and stone and also water cisterns. The stray find of a carved stone head, similar to Celtic sculptures found in France, suggests that there may have been a sanctuary of some kind among the buildings. A residential quarter was found below Hradiště on the southern side of the hill.

The fort on the other hill is named Sance – meaning 'ramparts'. It, too, has its own walls, but they appear to have been thrown up in haste, presumably in some time of danger.

Excavations, begun in 1963, have been largely concentrated on the Hradiště area. They prove that the site was already occupied in the Neolithic and Bronze Ages. The acropolis was fortified at the turn of the Hallstatt–La Tène periods in the 5th century BC and the buildings inside probably date from the same time. It was only later that the whole double oppidum was surrounded by the outer wall. In the early Middle Ages Slavonic tribesmen built some modest huts on the site.

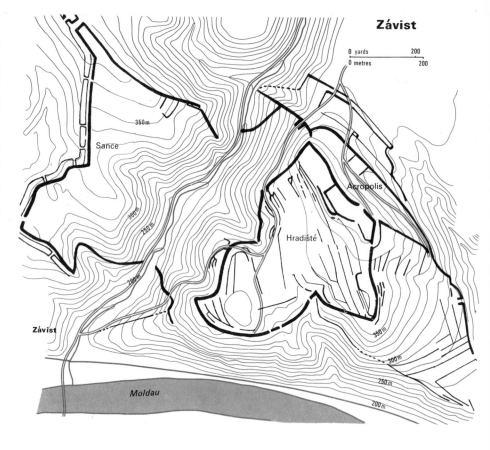

Závist

0 yards 200
0 metres 200

Stara and Nowa Słupia POLAND

Iron-working centre
c. 200 BC–AD 300

BIBLIOGRAPHY
Bielenin, K., *Starożytne hutnictwo świętokrzyskie*, (Ancient Metalurgy in Góry Świętokrzyskie), Warsaw, 1960
Bielenin, K., 'Das Hüttenwesen im Altertum im Gebiet der Góry Świętokrzyskie', *Praehistorische Zeitschrift*, 42, 1964, pp. 77–96
Bielenin, K., 'Krótkie podsumowanie dziesięcioletnich badań nad starożytnym hutnictwem żelaza w połnocno-wschodnim rejonie Gór Świętokrzyskich' (Short summary of 10 years research on the iron metallurgy in Góry Świętokrzyskie), in: *Liber Josepho Kostrzewski octogenario a venatoribus dicatus*, Wrocław, 1968, pp. 263–75

The greatest iron-smelting centre in prehistoric Europe was located at Stara and Nowa Słupia near Kielce. It covers an area of about 190 square miles (approx. 500 sq km) at the foot and on the slopes of the Świetokrzyskie range of mountains. More than 440 smelting sites have been recorded, all of them marked by heaps of dross, often reaching almost to the ground surface. These appear as large flattened masses, covering anything from 540 to 1,600 square feet (approx. 50–150 sq m) apiece. They are composed of blocks of dross, each one the left-over of a single smelting process.

Excavation has proved that the furnaces were usually arranged in regular rows with up to four in each row. Each of these smelting sites was more or less closely associated with a settlement.

There are revealing data on the amount of raw material processed in the furnaces. In the area of one modern village (Jeleniów in the Opatów district) some 100 smelting sites with approximately 9,500 furnaces were found. In these 112 tons (approx. 114,000 kg) of iron were extracted from 1,870 tons (approx. 1,900,000 kg) of ore. This amount of smelting consumed roughly 1,970 tons (approx. 2,000,000 kg) of charcoal. The immense output of the centre as a whole was due to an abundance of ore in the neighbourhood.

This site has been known since the 19th century, and in the 1930's the dross, which was proving a nuisance to farmers, was sold to ironworks as it still contained pure iron. Systematic excavations were begun in 1955.

A study of finds on the site itself, together with an analysis of the iron from La Tène artifacts from many parts of Poland, have proved that the industry began in the late La Tène period of the 2nd to 1st centuries BC. The time of its greatest prosperity was, however, in the 1st to 3rd centuries AD. Its later history is obscure, but the industry certainly flourished again between the 6th and 12th centuries.

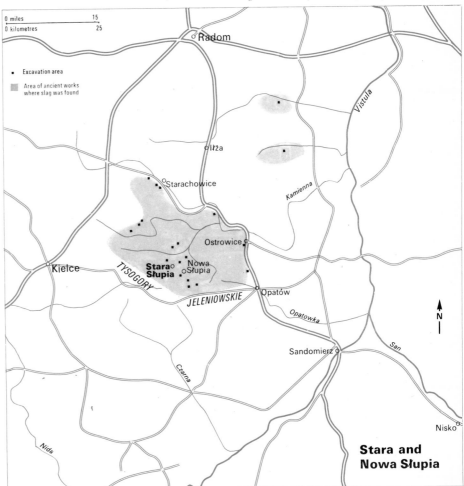

Stara and
Nowa Słupia

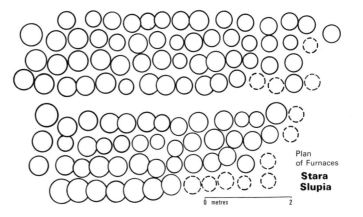

Plan
of Furnaces
**Stara
Słupia**

83

Sarmizegethusa RUMANIA

Dacian capital
c. 100 BC–AD 106

BIBLIOGRAPHY
Daicoviciu, C., Daicoviciu, H., *Sarmizegethusa. Die daki-schen Burgen und Siedlungsstätten in Orăştie-Gebirge*, Bukarest, 1963
Daicoviciu, H., 'Il tempio-calendario dacico di Sarmize-getusa', *Dacia*, 4, 1960, pp. 231–54
Studii şi cercetări de istorie veche, 1, 1950, pp. 137–42; 2, 1951, pp. 95–126; 3, 1952, pp. 281–310; 4, 1953, pp. 153–217; 5, 1954, pp. 123–59; 6, 1955, pp. 195–238 (excavation reports, French summary from vol. 3)
Materiale şi cercetări arheologice, 3, 1957, pp. 255–77; 5, 1959, pp. 379–401 (French summary)

Sarmizegethusa (King's Seat), or Grădiştea Mun-celului, in southern Rumania, was the royal capital of the Dacian state. It is situated at a height of 3,940 feet (1,200 m) on terraced slopes deep among the southern Carpathian mountains.

The Indo-European Dacians had occupied the territory of Rumania during the 1st millennium BC, but this capital was established only in about 100 BC, flourishing until its destruction by the Romans in AD 106.

The walls of the citadel are of irregular, geometric plan, following the lines of several terraces built at different levels. They are of typical Dacian construc-tion, some 10 feet (3 m) thick, with dressed-stone facings filled with rubble and bound together by timbers. There are two gates.

Outside the walls a wide, partially stone-paved road leads to terraces that supported the houses of the élite of the king's subjects and also a sacred enclosure occupying two terraces and containing a number of sanctuaries. Three of these are rectan-gular, but two are of a much rarer circular type. The largest of the rectangular sanctuaries is 164 feet (50 m) long and enclosed by a wall. Inside are the stone bases for no less than 60 wooden columns. This structure was demolished in Dacian times, some of the materials being re-used for the second rectangular sanctuary, probably built during the second half of the 1st century BC. It is thought that these buildings with their many columns were not roofed but possibly represented sacred groves.

A third, much smaller, rectangular sanctuary is situated on the same terrace with the two circular shrines. The larger of these is 98 feet (30 m) in diameter, and consists of an outer ring of andesite blocks with a ring of small andesite pillars immed-iately inside. This inner ring is composed of runs of six taller and more slender pillars separated by one that is shorter and thicker. There are 30 of these runs of six, and it seems that the total of 180 stand for one half of the Dacian year. The small circular shrine is only 39 feet (12 m) in diameter and is enclosed by a ring of stone blocks that may have some astro-nomical significance.

Close to the 'calendar' sanctuary lies a most remarkable composite stone disk that appears to represent the sun. It is made up of ten wedge-shaped slabs radiating from a circular slab at the centre; a drainage hole and basin suggest it was used for blood sacrifices.

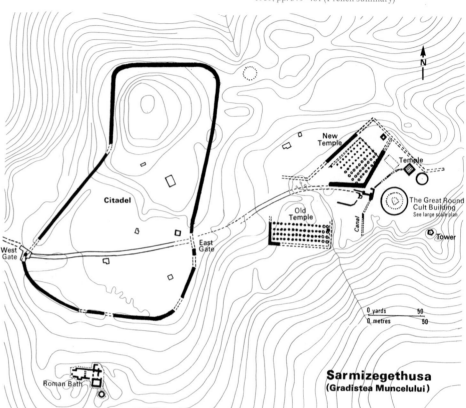

Sarmizegethusa
(Gradistea Muncelului)

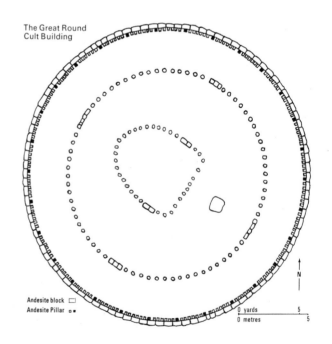

The Great Round Cult Building

Andesite block
Andesite Pillar

IBERIA

As a well-defined geographical unit, the Iberian peninsula invites comparison with Anatolia. It is isolated from the rest of Europe by a great mountain range, and comprises high inland plateaus, some of which are arid and all of which suffer extremes of heat in summer and cold in winter, while the coastal areas, mostly well watered and with milder climates, are separated from the interior and from each other by further mountain ranges.

Both these great peninsulas are well placed to serve as land bridges connecting Europe with a neighbouring continent – Africa or Asia. The Iberian peninsula, however, has not in fact filled this role to anything like the same degree as Anatolia. Whereas the latter was the connecting link between the early agricultural cultures of the Near East and south-eastern Europe and their urban successors, the former merely faced across the Straits of Gibraltar, in later prehistoric times, a north-western Africa which was poor and isolated and had a limited capacity to transmit to or receive from the outside world. Only in early and middle Palaeolithic times did Africa play a vital part in sending primitive human cultures of its own creation across the Straits, through Spain into western Europe. The earliest men of 'modern' type seem to have reached the Iberian peninsula overland through central Europe, bringing with them cave art, or along the coasts of the Mediterranean, in late Palaeolithic times, and thereafter their cultures were transmitted in some degree to north-western Africa. This pattern was maintained throughout later prehistory: from the 6th millennium BC onwards the eastern and southern coastal regions of the peninsula, with their fertile soil and mineral wealth, attracted successive waves of settlers bearing by Mediterranean sea routes first the agricultural arts and then the metallurgical skills of the Near East.

The early development of relatively advanced Neolithic and Copper Age communities in the Iberian peninsula, about 5000–2000 BC, was a most uneven process. The attractions of the fertile and temperate region near the mouth of the Tagus brought the new cultures to it almost as soon as to coastal Andalusia, but the inland plateaus for long remained largely in the hands of the Mesolithic hunters and their descendants who became pastoralists, and even in the mountainous areas near the east coast the rock paintings, naturalistic at first, later schematized, not only bear witness to a survival of Upper Palaeolithic art and magic in Mesolithic times but its practice long after the installation of farming communities near the coast. In spite of the geographical difficulties of the peninsula and the resulting isolation of its provinces, the interplay of its indigenous cultural groups and the new cultures on the coast, from the 4th millennium onwards, shaped two highly original groups. These eventually permeated the greater part of the peninsula and in due course exercised a most powerful influence over a large part of Europe beyond the Pyrenees, and to a much more limited degree in north-western Africa. The first of these groups developed the megalithic communal tomb in a number of forms, as an adaptation of the practice of successive communal burial which had perhaps been introduced from lands in and around the east Mediterranean, along with the use of caves, rock-cut tombs and circular vaults built of drystone walling, for this purpose, and the worship of a mother-goddess. The primary centres of this culture were in Andalusia and southern Portugal, but the megalithic cult was spread, by migration or by missionary enterprise, during the 4th and 3rd millennia BC, to the Iberian north west, Biscayan France, Catalonia and Languedoc, and from there to various parts of northern Europe.

The second dynamic group has often been referred to by archaeologists as the Beaker Folk. Its origins probably lay in the Mesolithic hunting and early Neolithic pastoralist communities of the interior of eastern Spain (but see p. 61); these were nomads armed with bows and after about 2500 BC they began to move into the fertile coastal areas of Andalusia and central Portugal which were at that time occupied by a settled agricultural population whose rulers controlled metallurgy based on the copper and other ores of Andalusia and southern Portugal. These rulers could command the construction of forts like those of LOS MILLARES (Almeria), Vila Nova de São Pedro (Santarém) and Zambujal (Torres Vedras) (see under THE EARLY METAL AGE ON THE LOWER TAGUS). The Beaker Folk, however, seem eventually to have overpowered such forts and squatted among their ruins, learning from the local population something about the techniques of metallurgy and developing their own form of copper dagger. The distinctive tradition of decorated pottery from which the Beaker Folk derive their name was subsequently spread to all parts of the Iberian peninsula except the south west and the basin of the Guadiana and beyond the Pyrenees to most parts of western and central

Upper Palaeolithic caves

East Coast (Mesolithic) Rock paintings
c 8000-4000 BC

Megalithic Tombs
c 4000-1500 BC

Fortified settlements
c 3000-1000 BC

Europe, together with their metallurgical knowledge and their distinctive forms of weapons, archer's equipment and clothing.

After about 1800 BC the Iberian peninsula ceased to exercise a powerful influence beyond the Pyrenees and began to stagnate, perhaps as a final result of desiccation during a phase of dry climate which at an earlier stage had driven many of the Beaker Folk to migrate. Parts of the peninsula now received new forms of metalwork and pottery from beyond the Pyrenees, and in the temperate regions of the north west these influences, coming from western France and the British Isles, mainly as a result of trade contacts, shaped a local Atlantic Bronze Age which lasted far into the 1st millennium BC. In the south east a new semi-urban culture, very different from that of Los Millares, takes its name from the fortified settlement and cemetery of EL ARGAR (Almeria). This seems to owe something to renewed contacts with the eastern Mediterranean, but its Early Bronze Age ceramic and metal forms persisted without much change until after the end of the 2nd millennium. Other conservative groups existed in western Andalusia, southern Portugal and on the eastern seaboard of Spain; some of these may have participated in the activities of seafaring communities on Sardinia, Corsica and the Balearics which sometimes impinged on New Kingdom Egypt (The Peoples of the Sea). Among all these peoples tin bronze, which became general north of the Pyrenees in the Early Bronze Age, was slow to replace the arsenical copper which had been introduced into southern Spain during the 4th millennium BC.

From about 800 BC the north-eastern parts of the peninsula were being settled by groups of invaders, from southern France or the Rhineland, some of whom were Celtic-speaking, while all participated in the Urnfield culture, of central European origin. The historic Iberian culture of the Mediterranean seaboard of Spain seems to have arisen after these newcomers had been absorbed by the natives. In western Andalusia a semi-urban culture with roots in the local Early Bronze Age became, by the beginning of the 1st millennium BC, the centre of Iberian civilization and its wealth in gold, silver, copper and tin, some of it obtained by trade with north-western Spain and even with the British Isles, attracted Phoenician merchants through whom the fame of the Kingdom of Tartessus reached the Near East. The resulting oriental stimulus raised the metalwork, jewelry and pottery of TARTESSUS to a standard not seen in the peninsula before and the fierce tribes of the interior, partly Celtic in character, developed, under its influence, a characteristic Early Iron Age culture of their own which diverged increasingly from the Hallstatt and La Tène tradition of the regions beyond the Pyrenees. Early Greek efforts at trade and colonization on the Spanish coasts were overshadowed by those of the Phoenicians and, after about 500 BC, the Carthaginians, but in the north east they played an important part in shaping the local Iberian culture, as seen at ULLASTRET. In the north west the warlike semi-Celtic tribes long preserved their independence even from the Romans, and maintained a Castro culture in which local Early Bronze Age and truly Celtic elements were combined (see THE CITÂNIA OF BRITEIROS).

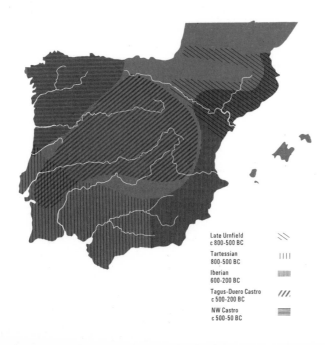

Late Urnfield
c 800-500 BC

Tartessian
800-500 BC

Iberian
600-200 BC

Tagus-Duero Castro
c 500-200 BC

NW Castro
c 500-50 BC

Altamira and the Cantabrian Caves SPAIN

Cave dwellings and painted caves
c. 75,000–8,000 BC

BIBLIOGRAPHY
Breuil, H. and Obermaier, H., *The Cave of Altamira at Santillana del Mar, Spain,* tr. M. E. Boyle, Madrid, 1935
Leroi-Gourhan, A., *The Art of Prehistoric Man,* London, 1968
Maringer, J. and Bandi, H.-G., *Art in the Ice Age,* London, 1953
Sieveking, A. and G. de G., *The Caves of France and Northern Spain: a Guide,* London, 1962

With the onset of the final glaciation the caves of the Pyrenees and their extension westwards in the Cantabrian mountains came to be frequented by human groups very similar in culture to those of southwestern France. The two most famous are Castillo and Altamira, both about 19 miles (30 km) west or south west of Santander. The former is notable because it contained stratified remains of human occupation going back to the beginning of the last glaciation, when hand axes of Acheulean tradition were still in use alongside of Mousterian flake tools, as well as a large number of Upper Palaeo-

Engraved stag on the painted ceiling at Altamira

lithic paintings and engravings of various Solutrean (*c.* 19,000–16,000 BC) or Magdalenian (*c.* 16,000–10,000 BC) styles. Altamira is notable not only for its splendid ceiling with bisons painted in the late polychrome style, which are among the highest achievements of Palaeolithic art, but for the fact that the discovery of the painted ceiling in 1879 by Don M. de Sautuola was the first occasion in Europe on which the possibility of Palaeolithic cave paintings was recognized. As it happened, though De Sautuola was supported by some specialists in his country from the first, European and particularly French prehistorians of the day refused to accept that the Altamira paintings could be so ancient. It was not until a series of discoveries in French caves, in 1895 and 1901, had demonstrated the contemporaneity of cave paintings with engravings on bone or reindeer horn found in Upper Palaeolithic occupation layers in these caves that E. Cartailhac published his retraction and went with H. Breuil to study the Altamira paintings and prepare a monograph on them.

The cave of Altamira contains a large number of paintings and engravings of various dates distributed throughout its length. The area immediately within the entrance, which is easily approached, was inhabited from late Solutrean to late Magdalenian times (about 17,000–10,000 BC) and a radiocarbon date of about 13,500 BC obtained from samples collected in this area appears to relate to a middle Magdalenian phase of this occupation. The painted ceiling with its polychrome bisons covers a side

chamber branching off to the left near the entrance and in no way constitutes a deep sanctuary, difficult of access like those found in some French caves such as LASCAUX and Trois Frères – Tuc d'Audoubert (pp. 47, 51). The walls of a wide serpentine gallery in the middle part of the cave and a narrow passage towards its end carry paintings in a simpler, earlier style, probably late Solutrean, with black outlines, and engravings, some of which are primitive in style though probably not earlier than the Solutrean. Others, mostly representing deer, are in a shaded style which is distinctive of the Cantabrian caves, appearing also at Castillo and Cándamo San Román. Breuil supposed that the polychrome paintings belonged to the end of the Magdalenian, but Leroi-Gourhan now assigns them to the middle phase of this culture.

The Upper Palaeolithic cultures of the northern Spanish coast seem to have been derived from southwestern France, but with some delay, so that their earlier phases are not well represented in the Cantabrian caves; the carved bone figurines which characterize the earlier phases of Palaeolithic art beyond the Pyrenees are hardly found in Spain. However, the isolation which caused this retardation also caused local cultural forms to develop, like special types of beautifully flaked projectile points and shaded engravings on cave walls or on bone fragments, which are probably late Solutrean in date. Though the art shows that much the same range of Upper Pleistocene cold-loving animals was hunted by the cave dwellers as in southern France, reindeer were usually scarce and some of the elephants were not woolly mammoths but smooth-coated animals which apparently still lived in the warmer areas south of the northern mountain ranges (Castillo, Pindal). The end of the Ice Age drove many of the bearers of the Magdalenian culture northwards, the remainder evolved the much inferior Azilian culture, and the artistic tradition passed to other hunting communities in Mediterranean Spain.

Bay of Biscay

Painted ceiling

Entrance

Shaded engravings

Terminal Passage

0 feet 80
0 metres 25

Altamira Cave

Los Millares and El Argar SPAIN

Los Millares: Settlement and cemetery
c. 2500–1800 BC
El Argar: Settlement and cemetery
c. 1700–1000 BC

BIBLIOGRAPHY
Almagro, M. and Arribas, A., *El Poblado y la Necrópolis Megalíticos de los Millares*, Madrid, 1963
Blancé, B., 'The Argaric Bronze Age in Iberia', in *Revista de Guimarães*, 1964, pp. 129–42
Leisner, G. and V., *Die Megalithgräber der Iberischen Halbinsel*, I: Der Süden, Berlin, 1943
Savory, H. N., *Spain and Portugal*, London, 1968, chs. VI–VIII

Thanks to a Belgian mining engineer, L. Siret, who devoted his spare time for many years during the late 19th century to the exploration of the ancient settlements and burial places around Almería, the late prehistory of a limited area in what is now one of the most arid regions of the Iberian peninsula is better known to us than that of any other part of southern Spain. The study of Siret's finds in the light of modern work elsewhere shows that Neolithic farming had begun near Almeria by the 5th millennium BC; the chief early site is El Garcel, where the pottery suggests maritime connections with lands around the south-east Mediterranean, which would explain the appearance, even at this early stage, not only of wheat but of cultivated vines and olives. At a later stage the same connections brought the practice of communal burial in caves or in circular stone cists, which later developed into passage graves, suitable for successive burials, with beehive chambers formed of drystone walling or with sides formed of upright slabs, and corbelled roofs; further inland, in the province of Granada, rectangular cists developed in the same way into megalithic passage graves. By this time, from about the middle of the 4th millennium BC, copper slag is found in the settlements (Tres Cabezos, Campos, Parazuelos, La Gerundia, Tabernas and Almizaraque).

In the mid-3rd millennium one settlement, at Los Millares, became outstandingly important. It is known chiefly from the cemetery outside it, containing about 80 communal tombs, mainly of the 'tholos' type, with circular covering mound and an entrance passage, built of orthostats and divided into two or three segments by septal slabs which have 'port holes'. These are sophisticated structures which were sometimes adorned with coloured wall plaster internally and had well-built revetment walls and ritual enclosures in which stood cult pillars. The grave goods included a distinctive range of ritual objects of ivory, bone and stone, as well as pottery vessels, sometimes painted, on which Eye Goddess symbols, derived from oriental mother-goddess cults, appear. The settlement at Los Millares – like all the other Almerian sites, incompletely explored – covered about 12 acres (5 hectares) and was built on a spur, the tip of which was defended by a wall of rough masonry, bonded with clay, with semi-circular bastions; the inspiration here, too, probably came from lands adjoining the south-east Mediterranean. In-

side was an uncertain number of circular huts, generally about 15 feet (4·6 m) in diameter and others that were rectangular. Beyond the extramural cemetery was a line of forts, like those of the Tagus estuary (see THE EARLY METAL AGE ON THE LOWER TAGUS). There is evidence suggesting that the Beaker Folk overran the Almerian sites as they did those of the Tagus estuary, towards the end of the 3rd millennium BC, and put an end to the Millaran culture. Certainly when semi-urban culture develops again in the area, in the Early Bronze Age (about 1700 BC) it is entirely different in character.

The small fortified settlement and cemetery of El Argar is the best known of the Early Bronze Age sites explored by Siret, but others at El Oficio, Ifre

and Bastida de Totana share its character. The choice of high, isolated hills contrasts with Millaran practice, and the houses within are rectangular and densely built, sometimes in tiers bedded into the hillside. The dead were no longer buried in communal tombs but singly in cists or big jars, very often within the settlement and sometimes under the floors of the houses, and all traces of the mother-goddess cult disappeared. With some modification under influences derived from the interior of Spain, this retarded Early Bronze Age culture survived into the 1st millennium BC. Further inland, near Orce and Galera, a culture in some respects more akin to the Millaran survived in the same way, with large, sometimes walled settlements of circular houses, throughout the 2nd millennium BC.

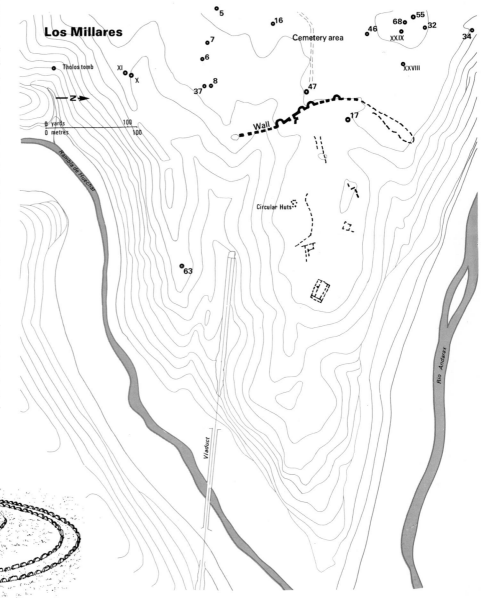

Reconstruction of a tholos tomb at Los Millares

The Early Metal Age on the Lower Tagus PORTUGAL

Settlement and tombs
c. 4000–1000 BC

BIBLIOGRAPHY
Blance, B., *Die Anfange der Metallurgie auf der Iberischen Halbinsel*, Berlin, 1971
Leisner, V., *Die Megalithgräber der Iberischen Halbinsel: Der Westen*, parts 1–3, Berlin, 1956–65
Do Paço, A. and Sangmeister, E., 'Vila Nova de São Pedro, eine befestigte Siedlung der Kupferzeit in Portugal', in *Germania*, XXXIV, Frankfurt-am-Main, 1956, pp. 211–230

The earliest Neolithic farmers of the Iberian peninsula had probably discovered the attractions of the fertile limestone country around the mouth of the Tagus by about 5000 BC. Their characteristic flint implements and pottery have been found with multiple burials in several caves in this area, like those of Escoural, Furninha and Casa da Moura. It was not until more than a millennium later that their successors began constructing communal tombs – first of all megalithic passage graves, but later on rock-cut tombs, as at Palmela, Alapraia and São Pedro de Estoril. Later still 'tholos' passage graves like those of Andalusia were built wholly or partly of drystone masonry, as at São Martinho, Barro and Monge, and at Praia das Maçãs the two traditions were combined in a two-period monument. During the early part of the 3rd millennium BC a highly original Copper Age culture, distinguished by local types of ritual objects, usually made of limestone, quite different from the engraved slate plaques and croziers of the contemporary Alemtejan megaliths, flourished around the Tagus estuary. Some of the finer pottery associated with this culture suggests contacts with the Early Cycladic civilization of the east Mediterranean.

Metal is extremely rare in the earlier tombs and settlements of the Lower Tagus and the main mineral exploitation at this time seems to have been located

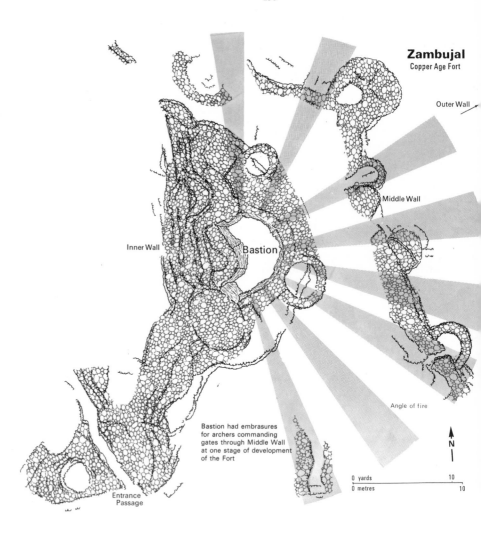

Zambujal
Copper Age Fort

Outer Wall

Middle Wall

Inner Wall

Bastion

Angle of fire

Bastion had embrasures for archers commanding gates through Middle Wall at one stage of development of the Fort

Entrance Passage

N

0 yards 10
0 metres 10

in southern Alemtejo and Andalusia. But about the middle of the 3rd millennium strong influences from these regions were reaching the Tagus estuary and an impetus seems to have been given to the fortification of settlements, possibly as centres of power for alien overlords who controlled supplies of copper ore. Defences, as at LOS MILLARES, consisted of massive walls, sometimes bonded with a mixture of clay and powdered limestone and reinforced by bastions from which archers would enfilade attackers; the inspiration for them probably came ultimately from Palestine and neighbouring lands. The best known of these fortified sites, Vila Nova de São Pedro, had three roughly concentric lines of defence; within it was a well-built potter's kiln, and many copper weapons and tools were found on this site. Most of the exploration here, however, was not conducted with modern excavation technique and the plan is far from complete. The recent scientific excavation of a similar site, Zambujal (Torres Vedras), carried out by Professor Sangmeister and Dr Schubart for the German Archaeological Institute in Madrid, has revealed a similar concentric system of

defence which was many times restored and elaborated, with the refinement of a large hollow bastion on the inner wall which had embrasures through which the gaps in the middle wall could be commanded by archers. The dwellings in these and other sites are not well known, but seem generally to have been round or oval huts. The enemy who probably overthrew these forts, and squatted among their ruins, was the Beaker Folk. These were pastoralists, armed with the bow, who later spread far and wide in Europe, spreading metallurgical knowledge and cultural forms which they had acquired from the more advanced communities in due course, and pottery of Beaker tradition occurs with secondary burials in many of the communal tombs of the lower Tagus area. Much of this, however, is of a late Beaker style, mass-produced locally and on the Lower Guadalquivir, and seems to have influenced the development of later Tartessian wares. With it are found simple gold ornaments which stand at the beginning of a long local development, culminating in the elaborate jewelry of TARTESSUS, early in the 1st millennium BC.

---

0 miles 25
0 kilometres 40

N

Furninha

Casa da Moura

Outeiro de São Mamede

Pragança

Vila Nova São Pedro

C. da Fornea
Gruta da Ermegeira

Castro de Ota

Zambujal

Barro

Castro de Pedro de Oiro Alenquer

Cabeço da Arruda

C. de Penedo

Serra das Mutelas

Tagus

Praia das Maçãs
São Martinho

Casainhos

Folha das Barradas

Bela Vista
Colares
Estria
Monte Abraão

Monge

Carenque

Atlantic Ocean

Quinta do Anjo
C. de Chibannes
C. de Rotura

- Cave
- Fortified settlements
○ Rock cut tomb
▽ Megalithic tomb
● Tholos tomb

90

Tartessus SPAIN

Kingdom
c. 1000–500 BC

BIBLIOGRAPHY
Arribas, A., *The Iberians*, London, 1962
Blazquez, J. Ma., *Tartessos y los Origines de la Colonización Fenicia en Occidente*, Salamanca, 1968
Maluquer de Motes, J., (ed.), *Tartessos, V, Symposium Internacional de Prehistoria Peninsular*, Barcelona, 1969
Savory, H. N., *Spain and Portugal*, London, 1968, ch. IX

Carambolo

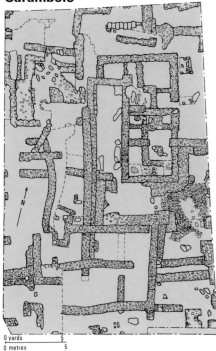

In late classical times the lower basin of the Guadalquivir and some lands adjoining it were considered to be the richest part of the Iberian peninsula on account of their agricultural as well as their mineral wealth, and some of the richest Roman colonies were located there. But even in the 7th and 6th centuries BC the coastal region of the peninsula, beyond the Pillars of Hercules, had acquired a reputation among the Greeks as a rich source of precious metals, copper and tin controlled by native rulers who were hospitable to strangers. It was from this shadowy kingdom of Tartessus, to which early Greek writers refer, that the 'ships of Tarshish' mentioned in the Old Testament, appear to have got their name. These ships were Phoenician merchantmen: in fact, archaeological evidence from chance finds and from partial excavations of a number of settlements and cemeteries in Andalusia makes it clear that it was mainly the Phoenicians who were responsible for opening up a market on the southern coasts of Spain for objects of Semitic or Greek manufacture, and that in the early stages, at least, Ionian Greeks only played a minor role.

Phoenician influence in Andalusia naturally declined after the middle of the 7th century BC, when the Assyrians had completed their conquest of Tyre and Sidon; but by this time a rich Tartessian culture, served by local manufacturing centres which produced jewelry, metal vessels, pottery and engraved ivory ornaments of largely oriental inspiration had developed – a phenomenon, in fact, rather like that which accompanied the growth of Etruscan civilization about the same time. Though this was certainly an urban culture, its identified towns have no historical fame and modern excavation has so far done no more than explore limited areas in a few of them. On the north side of one of these sites, on the hill of Carambolo near Seville, was a densely built settlement of rectangular houses, with several phases of construction, occupied, apparently, in the 8th and 7th centuries BC, and on the top of the hill was found a famous hoard of Tartessian gold jewelry, buried in the ruins of an oval hut with Tartessian pottery. A copper-mining settlement of this period has been found at Rio Tinto and well-equipped cremation burials have been found at Acebuchal near Carmona. The Tartessians were trading partners of the Phoenicians and had their own ships, possibly copies of Phoenician merchantmen; the Greek tradition that they traded up the Atlantic coasts as far as Brittany and in this way procured tin, much of which may have come from Cornwall, has archaeological confirmation, notably the great bronze hoard found in the harbour at Huelva. Tartessian trade may well have been the intermediary through which east Mediterranean types of shield and cauldron came to be imitated by the Irish bronze industry.

The rich culture of the Tartessians owed much to oriental influence, but rested on strong local foundations – a semi-urban native culture the roots of which go back to the Copper Age and at least to the 3rd millennium BC, when western Andalusia was occupied by a distinct culture, founded originally on the rich agricultural possibilities of the region but soon exploiting its mineral wealth. This culture is known, fragmentarily, from local types of megalithic or 'tholos' tombs with very long entrance passages – as at Matarrubilla and the Cueva de Romeral. The apogee of Tartessian culture, however, in the 7th and 6th centuries BC, was brought to an end by the expansion of Carthaginian power in Andalusia, which at the same time curtailed the influence of the Ionian Greeks in the same area. Thereafter its place is taken by a generalized Ibero–Punic civilization stretching throughout southern Spain.

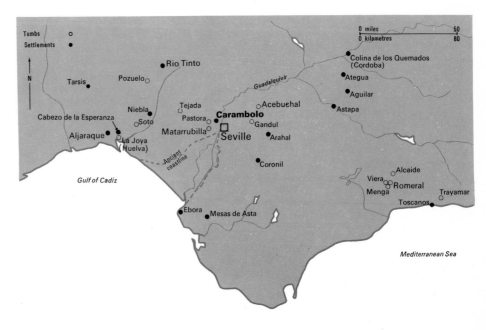

Ullastret SPAIN

Iberian town
c. 600–200 BC

BIBLIOGRAPHY
Arribas, A., *The Iberians*, London, 1962
Dixon, P., *The Iberians of Spain*, Oxford, 1940
MacKendrick, P., *The Iberian Stones Speak*, New York
    1969
Oliva Prat, M., *Ullastret, Guia de las Excavaciones y se
    Museu*, Gerona, 1970
Pericot, L. and Ripoll Pesello, E., (ed.), *Prehistoric Art o,
    the Western Mediterranean and the Sahara*, Chicago
    1964, section II

The Mediterranean coastal regions of Spain, with their different climate, had already begun to develop a different cultural personality from those near the Biscayan coast, well before the end of the Upper Palaeolithic. This is reflected in the rock-shelter paintings found in the ravines of remote mountainous areas behind the east coast of Spain, with their dramatic and impressionistic art, which probably began in the local Epigravettian groups of the final Upper Palaeolithic but belongs mainly to the Mesolithic (about 10,000–5000 BC). The hunters and warriors with their bows, portrayed in these paintings gave way gradually to settled agricultural communities which were established during the 5th millennium BC and in due course were using communal burial places, in caves or megalithic tombs. In Catalonia and Valencia Bronze Age cultures were backward, but in the early part of the 1st millennium BC invaders from central Europe, some of whom were Celts, introduced the pottery and burial customs of the Urnfield Culture. After these foreigners had been absorbed by the natives a distinctive Mediterranean culture emerged, in which the houses and settlement forms were of local Bronze Age origin and a non-Indo-European language was used – Iberian.

About 600 BC Ionian Greek colonies were being founded on the Mediterranean coast, at Massilia, Emporion (Ampurias) and Rhode (Rosas), after a long period during which Phoenician and Greek traders had been visiting the area. These contacts led to the growth of larger Iberian towns, and the practice there of sophisticated arts such as sculpture and the manufacture of wheel-turned and painted pottery. Greek influence was particularly strong in Catalonia and Valencia during the 4th century BC, large quantities of Greek red-figured and Campanian pottery were imported and local Iberian civilization reached its highest development, with Iberian mercenaries much in demand in the Greek world. Thereafter the growth of Carthaginian power and the ensuing clash with Rome brought with it the collapse first of Greek and then of Iberian civilization in Spain.

The fortified hill settlements of the Iberians have been identified in a zone stretching from Languedoc (Ensérune) through Catalonia (Creueta, Palamós, Burriach, Puig Castellar, Sobra, Olius, Pedrera de Balaguer), Aragón (Azaila, Mazaleón, Calaceite), Valencia (Liria, Montgó, Mogente), to Andalusia; many originated as settlements of the Late Bronze Age Urnfield Culture. One of the largest and best explored is Ullastret, which occupies a hill nine

miles (14 km) south of Emporion, and covers 10 acres (4 hectares). It was defended originally by a line of massive trunconic towers, built at the beginning of the 6th century BC, which were later connected by a curtain wall, which has so far been exposed only on the western and southern sides of the settlement. The walling is 'Cyclopean', made of large, shaped blocks carefully fitted together without mortar. The main entrance, at the south end, is flanked by sharply inturned walls and a trapezoid bastion which replaced an earlier circular tower. The rectangular drystone houses are built densely on either side of streets or butted against the town wall, as in other Iberian settlements, and a temple of Hellenistic type was built in the 'acropolis'. There was a small

marketplace, and a number of cisterns for water collected from the roofs. The houses usually contained silos in which grain and other cereals were stored, and in which amphorae of Greek or Punic type are found. The pottery found on the lowest levels includes Urnfield ware and imported Ionian grey ware and painted pottery. At a later date Greek pottery and coins are so plentiful on the site that it has been suggested that it should be identified with a Greek city, Cypsela, mentioned in early classical texts, but it was probably a town of the Indigetes, as the Iberian weapons and numerous Iberian inscriptions (on stone, pottery and lead sheets) suggest. It seems to have been destroyed by fire early in the 2nd century BC.

Ullastret

0 yards   50
0 metres   50

N

Gate

Gate

Gate

Early Towers
(6c. BC)

Museum

Acropolis

Main
gate

Market
Place

The Citânia of Briteiros PORTUGAL

Hill fort
c. 500 BC–AD 300

BIBLIOGRAPHY
Cardozo, M., *Citânia de Briteiros e Castro de Sabros*
 Guimarães 1971
Hawkes, C. F. C., 'North-western Castros: Excavatio
 Archaeology and History', in *Actas do II Congress*
 Nacional de Arqueologia, Coimbra, 1971, pp. 283–6
Maluquer de Motes, J., in *Historia de España*, ed. R. M
 Pidal, tome I, vol. iii, Madrid, 1947–54
Savory, H. N. *Spain and Portugal*, London, 1968, ch. X

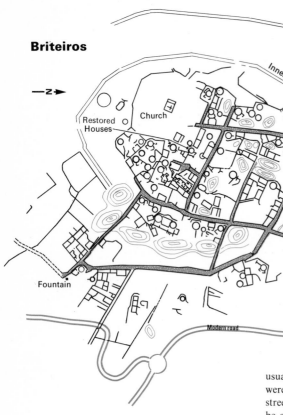

Briteiros

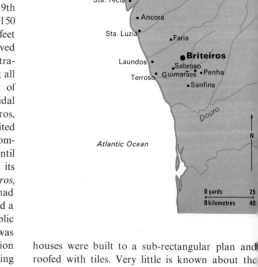

The north-western areas of the Iberian peninsula were generally the most backward in prehistoric times. The Atlantic climate of this region and its vegetation, with much in common with that of north-western Europe, fostered a degree of cultural community with lands across the Bay of Biscay which culminated at the beginning of the Early Iron Age with an actual immigration of Celtic-speaking people. These new arrivals reached the interior of northern Spain by land or by sea and ultimately spread into the mountainous north west, mixing with the local pre-Celtic communities to produce the Castro culture in which points of resemblance to Hallstatt and early La Tène forms can be seen alongside features derived from the more developed urban civilizations of southern Spain, for example in the jewelry made from local gold.

The warlike semi-Celtic tribes of the inland plateaus of Spain supplied many mercenary soldiers, often mounted men, to Greek and Carthaginian armies. They built hillforts defended by single drystone walls, without ditches but sometimes with rows of stone pillars (*chevaux de frise*) erected outside them as an obstacle to attackers. The carefully built 'Cyclopean' walling, bastions and other elaborations of the entrance defences on some of these sites probably reflect Greek and Punic influence. In Galicia and northern Portugal large numbers of *castros* can be seen and some of the small ones, like Cameixa and Cespón, may have been built in the 5th century BC. In these early forts dwellings were

usually built of perishable materials and as they were scattered and not arranged densely along streets, as in Iberian settlements, they continued to be circular in plan, as in Britain. Later, probably from the end of the 3rd century BC, bigger *castros* like Terroso, Sanfins, Sabroso and Briteiros were built and the walls of circular houses were being constructed of carefully shaped and fitted granite blocks.

The Citânia of Briteiros is an example of a large *castro*, the plan of which is better known than most because it was extensively excavated in the late 19th century by Martins Sarmento. He cleared about 150 houses and restored two of them: the largest is 36 feet (11 m) in diameter and some have elaborately carved door frames, while a few have vestibules of trapezoid plan and one has stone benches running all round the interior. The low walls were built of granite blocks arranged in oblique or helicoidal lines; the roofs were probably of thatch. Briteiros, unlike many other *castros*, continued to be inhabited after the Roman conquest, (which was not completed until the end of the 1st century BC) and until the end of the 3rd century AD; consequently its layout is more sophisticated than most *castros*, with a system of streets and squares, such as had existed in the Iberian towns of eastern Spain, and a stone gutter carried water from a spring to a public fountain. Like some other *castros*, Briteiros was enlarged at some time in its history by the addition of outer, roughly concentric lines of wall enclosing a large space which was probably intended originally to receive livestock, like the similar enclosures at many hillforts in south-western Britain, but housing tended at Briteiros to spread into the middle enclosure. In the Roman period at Briteiros some houses were built to a sub-rectangular plan and roofed with tiles. Very little is known about the burial custom at Briteiros or the other *castros* of northern Portugal and Galicia. The objects from Sarmento's excavations, and more recent ones by Dr Mario Cardozo, are preserved in the Martins Sarmento Museum at Guimarães.

CENTRAL MEDITERRANEAN

Italy with its islands sits firmly astride the sea routes of southern Europe, and its role through the past has been an important one accordingly, long before it developed its own civilizations in the 1st millennium BC. Geographically the region divides into three. Alt'Italia – the mountainous Alpine fringes and the flat alluvium of the Po valley – is part of continental Europe, as is clearly shown by much of its prehistory and history. The peninsula, still part of the continent, is more Mediterranean, open as it is to the length of the Adriatic, Ionian and Tyrrhenian Seas; geologically it consists largely of Tertiary limestones and marls but there are important exceptions, the metal ores of Tuscany, the areas of recent or actual volcanic activity of Latium and Campania (Vesuvius), and the ancient crystalline mass of Calabria. The islands, both the larger ones of Corsica (geographically if not politically part of the region), Sardinia and Sicily, and the many smaller ones like Elba, the Pontine, Lipari and Egadi groups, Pantelleria, Malta and Gozo, and Tremiti, show similar if stronger geographical and geological influences.

The first two regions, together comprising the mainland, have yielded archaeological material of great interest and in considerable quantity, as the many fine Italian museum collections amply demonstrate, but the sites are on the whole unspectacular – 'sites' rather than 'sights'. It has not been easy to assemble a worthwhile representative selection.

The contrast when one comes to the islands is very marked. The *domus de gianas* (rock-cut tombs) of Sicily, *nuraghi* (towers) and *tombe di giganti* (megalithic tombs) of Sardinia, the *torri* (smaller, simpler towers than *nuraghi*) and statue menhirs of Corsica, and above all the temples of Malta, are all very distinctive of their particular areas, though there are clearly points of basic similarity. Here the difficulty lies in reducing the list of worthy sites to manageable proportions. What we are seeing are the combined, or rather opposed, effects of the sea. It allows people and ideas to spread widely and freely, but at the same time it shields local developments from outside disturbance. On the mainland there are statue menhirs near La Spezia, gallery graves in Apulia, rock-cut tombs in Campania and Latium, but none of these developed so exuberantly as in the islands.

But it was the mainland which nurtured civilization.

Italian prehistory begins well back in the Lower Palaeolithic, at a time when the human race was represented by *Homo erectus*. Hand axes regarded as typical of his handiwork have come from many parts of the peninsula, notably from the living floor at Torrimpietra, 16 miles (26 km) west of Rome. Early in the last Ice Age a closer relative of ours, *Homo sapiens neanderthalensis*, was certainly in the country, as shown not only by Mousterian flintwork but also by Neanderthal skulls from Monte Circeo and from Saccopastore, at the very gates of Rome. Later, men physically indistinguishable from ourselves replaced them, leaving Upper Palaeolithic tools in caves from the Riviera to the Egadi islands, then probably still part of Sicily. For these early days, the changes of coastline due to higher or lower sea levels have to be borne carefully in mind. Equally, the changes of climate would affect markedly the food resources available to these hunters and food gatherers.

At a date perhaps around 6000 BC, farmers came by sea from the east and spread round all the coasts. Their material equipment, now including that very useful cultural indicator pottery, comes first from caves, but later open villages were built, spreading gradually further inland. The Foggia plain and the Matera district were particularly popular for crop raising and stockbreeding, the bases of the new economy. The size of some of these villages, Passo di Corvo near Foggia for example, amply demonstrates the rise in population. By the later 4th millennium, the food surplus was already such as could support the architectural achievements of the Maltese temples.

Archaeological thinking on the spread of metallurgy is in a state of some confusion at the moment. Several independent centres of development in Europe are now

Alps

Alps

Val Camonica

Milan

Turin

Emilia

Genoa

Bologna

Riviera

La Spezia

Arno

Florence

Ancona

Tuscany

Gola del Sentino

ELBA

Perugia

Belverde

Corsica

Adriatic Sea

Ajaccio

Tiber

Tarquinia

TREMITI

Caere

Veii

Rome

Passo di Corvo

Latium

Foggia

Monte Circeo

Sassari

PONTINE

Naples

Apulia

Anghelu Ruju

Palmavera

Sant'Antine

Campania

Matera

Taranto

Sardinia

Losa

Orrubiu

Barumini

Cagliari

Calabria

Tyrrhenian Sea

Ionian Sea

Sa Domu S'Orcu

Castello di Lipari

LIPARI

Grotta Addaura

Palermo

Milazzo

EGADI

Mediterranean Sea

Sicily

PANTELLERIA

Pantalica

Syracuse

Castelluccio

Mediterranean Sea

96

GOZO

Hal Saflieni

MALTA

Tarxien

Po

Adige

0 miles   25
0 kilometres   200

Etruscan Territory

Etruscan influence

suggested and whether north Italy was the home of one of these, or whether its copper working was introduced from outside, either central Europe or the Aegean, is as yet far from clear. The appearance of the rock-cut tomb in its many forms falls within this period too.

Certainly by the full Bronze Age, the south had been drawn into the trading network of Mycenae. Our loss of information from the destruction in 1899 of the major port in this trade, the Scoglio del Tonno at Taranto, is immense. New influences were apparent at this period in the north also, connecting the terramara settlements of Emilia with antecedents in Hungary. Elsewhere, however, local developments were barely interrupted, whether in the direction of elaborate pottery, in the Apennine culture, or of monumental architecture, in nuraghic Sardinia.

Uncertainties too cloud the end of the Bronze Age, in particular the significance of the spread of cremation as a burial rite. Three moments of time are involved, roughly the 13th, 11th and 10th centuries, and three possible points of origin in each, Italy itself, central Europe and the Aegean area. That already gives twenty-seven alternative interpretations of the record! Iron working too could have reached Italy at this period from either north east or south east.

However it came about, the position in the early 8th century is fairly clear, with the progressive Villanovan culture holding a strip of rich territory between the mouths of the Po and the Tiber. In Sardinia the *nuraghe*-builders were developing rapidly, though in greater isolation, broken only by occasional though far-reaching trade contacts with Spain, Sicily and Cyprus. Elsewhere – in Sicily, the lower peninsula and the remoter parts of the north – progress was less noticeable.

Then three interrelated phenomena completely transform the scene. First, the Greeks, driven by economic and social pressures in their homeland, start colonizing the southern coastlands in the later 8th century, establishing in the region for the first time the attributes of true civilization – city dwelling, complex societies and economics, and the art of writing. In the islands the Phoenicians were following a parallel course. Secondly, drawing heavily on these traditions either through the colonies or direct from the east, the Etruscans a century later build their own intriguing civilization on sound Villanovan foundations. Thirdly Rome, as the leader of a staunch native-Latin group, taps both Etruscan and Greek sources to its own advantage, eventually by military power conquering and absorbing both. From this moment, the central Mediterranean was no longer a recipient and transmitter of prehistoric cultural influences, but an initiator of, and leader in, world history.

Grotta Addaura SICILY

BIBLIOGRAPHY
Bernabò Brea, L., *Sicily*, London, 1957, pp. 32–3

Cave with engravings
Probably *c.* 10,000 BC

It is paradoxical that of the innumerable Italian caves, it is those furthest from the centres of Upper Palaeolithic art in France and Spain which should offer the best examples of that art south of the Alps. The island of Levanzo, with its Grotta dei Genovesi, is now separated even from Sicily, lying off its western tip. No great rise in sea level would make the Monte Pellegrino near Palermo an island too, with the three caves of Addaura at the foot of its northern cliffs and the Grotta Niscemi on its eastern slope.

The Addaura caves overlook the modern road and shore one mile (1·6 km) east of Mondello, five and a quarter miles (8·5 km) north of the centre of Palermo. Permission to visit them must be obtained beforehand from the archaeological authorities in Palermo – enquire at the Museo Nazionale.

The centre cave of the three is a shallow one. On the smooth slab of rock forming its eastern side a large number of animal and human figures are clearly incised. They were revealed when an accidental explosion of ammunition, stored here in the later stages of the Second World War, detached a crust of stalagmite. Three styles have been recognized, and their order determined by superpositions. But having said that, one must admit that no firm date can be given to any of the styles. This cave yielded no archaeological material, though its eastern neighbour had an Upper Palaeolithic deposit.

The earliest engravings are lightly incised, mainly animals and well drawn. The latest are again of animals, less competently executed. Interest centres on the intermediate group, including a deer and a fascinating group of human figures. These are boldly and convincingly incised, standing full face or in profile, crouching, or lying, apparently painfully tied up. Two have their arms upraised. Hands, feet and faces are little more than suggested. Some at least appear to have bird or dog heads, perhaps masks. One is particularly spaniel-like. Several interpretations of the scene have been offered, all of them more or less hazardous. We cannot even be sure that the individual figures were drawn as part of a single scene. And the relationships, cultural and chronological, with the cave art of continental Europe are no more easy to determine.

Grotta Addaura: the mysterious scene engraved on the cave wall

Matera ITALY

Caves and ditched villages
Late 5th – early 1st millennium BC

BIBLIOGRAPHY
Trump, D., *Central and Southern Italy before Rome*, London, 1966, pp. 39, 48, 147

The city of Matera in southern Italy, as well as boasting a fine archaeological collection in its museum, has a wide range of prehistoric sites in its immediate neighbourhood.

Two miles (3·2 km) to the south east, the Grotta dei Pipistrelli opens high in the wall of the great gorge below the city. It yielded rich material of the Middle Neolithic, 5th to 4th millennia BC. A smaller cave just below the main one apparently served as its cemetery or, better perhaps, burial vault. Many skeletons were recovered. Such natural caves are the obvious ancestors of the rock-cut tombs which continued the same collective burial rite.

Of the same period, villages or homesteads in the open, surrounded by single ditches, have been recognized on three eminences on the top of the escarpment overlooking the Taranto road. La Murgecchia is just across the gorge from Matera, Murgia Timone beyond the side gorge and Tirlecchia, with two enclosures, some two miles (3·2 km) east of that. Their pottery is mainly of two classes, painted with broad red swags on buff, or scratched with geometric designs on a dark polished surface. Further north again, but still within four miles (6·4 km), Sette Ponti in the valley by the Altamura road and Serra d'Alto on its isolated hilltop were Neolithic settlements of larger size and of a slightly later phase, characterized by pottery with delicately painted designs and curiously contorted handles.

The Copper Age seems not to be represented here, but an interesting Early Bronze Age cist grave was found at Parco dei Monaci, four and a half miles (7·2 km) to the south east of the city. It contained a flanged axe and two daggers, one a simple flat blade, the other with a cast hilt. Two rock-cut tombs of the Bronze Age were cut into the site which had long

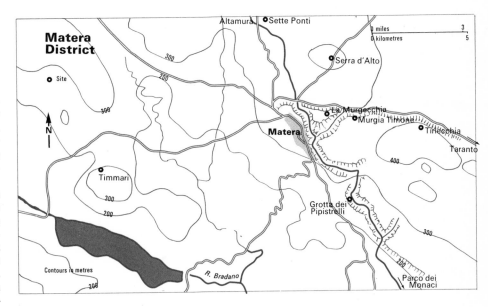

before held the Neolithic homestead on Murgia Timone. A few late finds suggest that burials were still being added well into the Iron Age.

Seven miles (11·3 km) west of Matera, the small plateau at Timmari supported both a village of the Final Bronze Age and its associated Urnfield cemetery. The great number of cinerary urns implies a long use, and this is confirmed by occasional imports of Sicilian Iron Age painted pottery. Finds of painted pottery of the full Iron Age, Apulian Geometric Ware, carry the story of the Matera area down to the end of prehistory.

Val Camonica ITALY

Rock-engravings
Late 3rd–2nd millennium BC

BIBLIOGRAPHY
Anati, E., *The Camonica Valley*, London, 1964

In the Val Camonica, the valley of the upper Oglio, many of the rock surfaces smoothed by the glacier which passed this way in the Ice Age were employed as 'canvases' by prehistoric artists. The greatest interest centres about the village of Capo di Ponte, 34 miles (55 km) north of Brescia. The zone of Naquane, east of the village, has been designated a National Park so that the engravings are both adequately protected and readily accessible to visitors.

The art consists of designs of very varied form engraved or pecked on the smooth stone. No less than 876 have been counted on one face, admittedly a large one. They include human and animal figures, huts, wagons and ploughs, weapons, tools, nets and a range of geometrical or abstract forms, including solar disks and labyrinths. Most interesting are the scenes frequently portrayed, the huts and fields of a village, some of the huts with their occupants clearly drawn within; a farmer following a two-ox plough; a horse and rider being led by a servant; a hearse drawn by two horses; fighting warriors in elaborately plumed helmets; worshippers raising their arms to the sun disk, and many others.

Study by Anati suggests that four periods are represented, distinguished by technique, content and superposition. In the earliest, figures and symbols tend to be isolated and lightly engraved. These may go back to the Neolithic. In phase two, dated to the Copper Age by, for example, the appearance of tri-angular dagger blades and halberds, compositions begin, especially sun-worshipping scenes, and the lines are more deeply incised. The Bronze Age phase three takes these developments much further. There are fewer human figures in this group. By contrast, phase four sees a proliferation of portrayals of human beings and they achieve much greater vitality and activity. Some could be called crowd scenes, and few figures now stand alone. The forms of armour and weapons place this group in the Iron Age, with some clear Etruscan influence. Thereafter decline and disappearance were rapid.

As well as rock faces over several miles of the valley's course, isolated blocks were also similarly decorated. The Masso di Cemmo, one of the finest with its axes, daggers, stags and wagons, is still in situ, two thirds of a mile (1 km) west of Capo di Ponte. The earlier and more formal Masso di Borno is now in Milan. Art such as this goes a long way towards bringing life to the prehistoric past.

Naquane: a detail of the engravings on the Great Rock

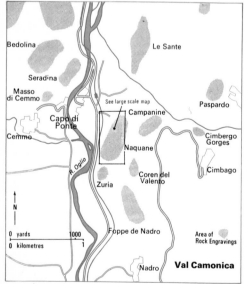

Val Camonica

Castello Di Lipari LIPARI ISLAND

ensive settlement
000 BC–today

BIBLIOGRAPHY
Bernabò Brea, L., *Sicily*, London, 1957
Cavalier, M., *Il Castello di Lipari*, Palermo, 1958

ari had three very considerable advantages for
prehistoric inhabitants. Its position just off the
its of Messina gave it a commanding position
r trade routes. Its volcanic deposits included
h-grade obsidian, a very desirable material be-
e the introduction of metallurgy. Its rocky prom-
nce above the harbour offered a magnificent
ensive site for early settlement. Add to this the
quent increment to its deposits of volcanic ash
wed from neighbouring Vulcano and Stromboli,
nteracting the effect of natural erosion, and its
portance to the archaeologist will be evident.
earch has continued at intervals from 1950 to the
sent day.

he oldest of the upstanding remains, part of the
uit of walls, dates back no earlier than the 13th
tury AD. Below ground, the story can be extended
k into much more remote periods. This is best
strated in a sector of the excavations in front of
cathedral (A), kept open for the purpose. Beneath
level of the modern street can be seen the
ction of two roads of Hellenistic date, one with
ntral drain.

ower again are oval huts of four prehistoric
ses running back to the Early Bronze Age, 18th
15th centuries BC. Perhaps the most important
iod of the citadel's history was the one im-
diately following this, through the second half of
2nd millennium. Then the island offered a port
call for the Mycenaean traders bringing back
per from Tuscany and Sardinia. Their activities
documented by their well-dated pottery from a
prisingly early 1500 BC down to about 1250 BC.
Where soundings could be made without destroy-
these remains, they penetrated another 16 feet
m) through successive Copper Age and Neo-
ic deposits to the rock, a truly remarkable and
mplete sequence. The wealth of finds from these
other trenches is admirably displayed in the
seum on the site.

elow the citadel to the west, a Middle to Late
nze Age cemetery of inhumations in large jars
cremations in urns was located in the Piazza
nfalcone. It is reconstituted in the museum. Late
olithic material in quantity came from the Diana
rict, just outside the town on the same side.
er sites in the islands, and on the promontory
Milazzo, have also contributed generously to the
seum collections.

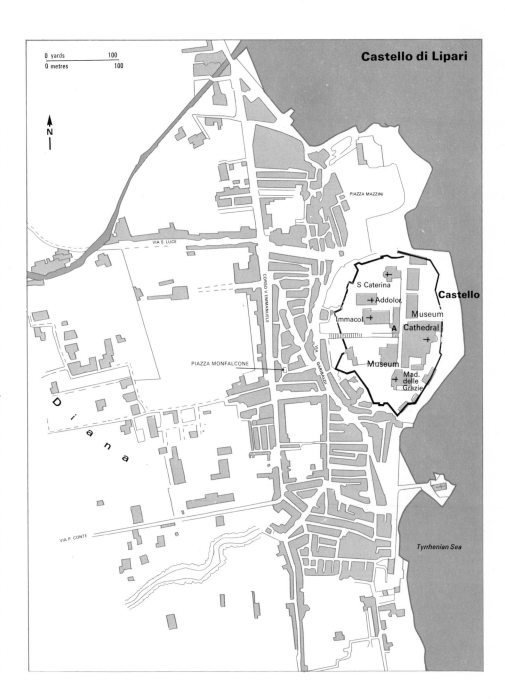

Castello di Lipari

Castelluccio SICILY

Village and cemetery of rock-cut tombs
c. 1800–1400 BC

BIBLIOGRAPHY
Bernabò Brea, L., *Sicily*, London, 1957, pp. 109–10
Guido, M., *Sicily, an Archaeological Guide*, London, 196

the Cava della Signora, a nearby side valley. They are of simple form, much simpler than those of ANGHELU RUJU for example. By being cut in steep or vertical slopes, they needed no shaft or entrance passage. A small doorway, with provision for a blocking slab or slabs, opens into a modest antechamber or even directly into the main oval burial chamber. Where the contents were found intact, they showed that the burial rite was collective inhumation, the tomb being opened for successive depositions. Earlier remains were simply swept to the back. Each interment was accompanied by pot-

tery offerings and, rarely, copper ornaments. O
sword fragment was found.

The best-known tomb is just as simple inside, b
its entrance is enlarged into a porch, 15 feet 6 inch
(4·7 m) wide, four pillars of solid rock being left
support the roof. Two of the tombs were closed wi
blocking slabs bearing designs carved in relief. The
spirals have suggested comparison with TARXIEN
Malta, of much earlier date, and the grave stelae
MYCENAE. Some curious bone slips from the tomb
carved with a row of oval bosses, certainly ha
parallels in Bronze Age Greece.

Castelluccio: the entrances to two of the rock-cut tombs

The modern village lies eight miles (13 km) north west of Noto and 22 miles (35 km) west south west of Syracuse, 1,150 feet (350 m) above sea level on a ridge of limestone between deeply incised valleys. The inhabitants of its Early Bronze Age predecessor were attracted by the natural defences of the site. Though nothing is left above ground, in 1890 some rich rubbish deposits of about 1800–1400 BC were found.

The cemetery, however, survives, consisting of several hundred tombs cut in the limestone walls of

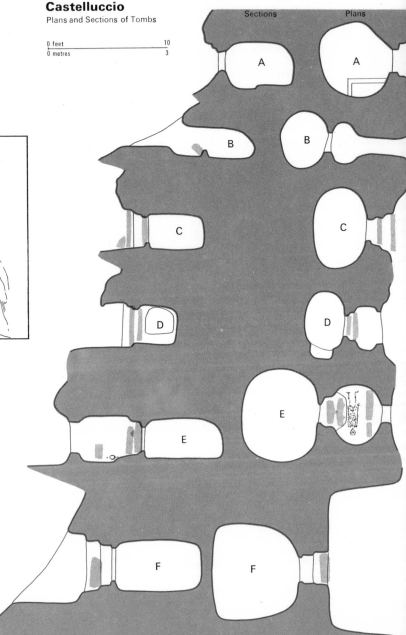

Castelluccio

Plans and Sections of Tombs

0 feet — 10
0 metres — 3

Sections   Plans

antalica SICILY

wn and cemeteries of rock-cut tombs
h–8th century BC

BIBLIOGRAPHY
Bernabò Brea, L., *Sicily*, London, 1957, pp. 162–4
Guido, M., *Sicily, an Archaeological Guide*, London, 1967,
  pp. 192–5

teen miles (26 km) inland from Syracuse, a trib-
ry joins the River Anapo. The two streams occupy
p valleys, gorges almost, cut into the limestone.
e plateau between, further protected by a wall
d ditch across the neck of land connecting it to
el ground, was occupied by a populous village
wnship from the 13th to the 8th centuries BC,
nning the local Late Bronze to Iron Age.

Within the village, Orsi identified and excavated
hieftain's palace, in a vaguely Mycenaean style,
5 feet (35 m) long and 36 feet (11 m) wide. Its
aight walls and right angle corners contrast
rkedly with the more usual oval buildings of the
nze Age in this part of the world. But it is the
eteries which make the site so impressive. The
k slopes to the south in particular are honey-
mbed with the tombs of a vast necropolis. The
lier tombs, still with oven-shaped chambers, are
uped mainly to the north and north west. There
lowed a period to which few tombs can be at-
buted, perhaps the result of a reduced popula-
n. The great cemeteries then spread to the east
avetta), south and west (Filiporto), bringing the
al number of tombs to over 5,000. These later
mbs tend to have rectangular chambers and flat
lings. All are in cliffs, so required no shaft or
trance passage.

A wealth of material, now in the National Museum
Syracuse, was removed from these tombs. They
ply not only a large population – many were
used over and over again – but a comparatively
h one. Much of south-east Sicily may have been
led from the palace on the hill in the period when
e coastal plains were felt to be vulnerable to
stile assault. Weapons of bronze, indeed, figure
ominently among the finds, though bronze was
w common enough to be used for a wide range
ornamental and domestic articles as well – such
safety pins, mirrors, knives and razors. The
ttery, usually wheel-made, has a distinctive red
lished slip in the earlier phase. Later, influence
m Greek Geometric becomes apparent, the result
trade with the colonies now appearing on the
ast.

During the 8th century, power and wealth passed
the Greek city of Syracuse and Pantalica faded
t of existence. The site was reoccupied by small
lages in the Byzantine period, but the site has
nce then lain empty.

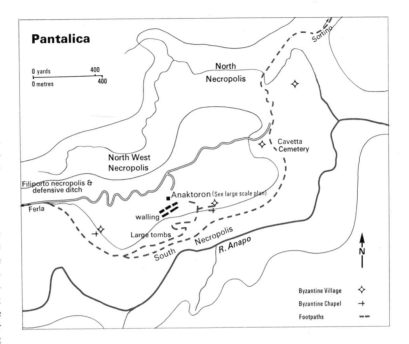

Pantalica

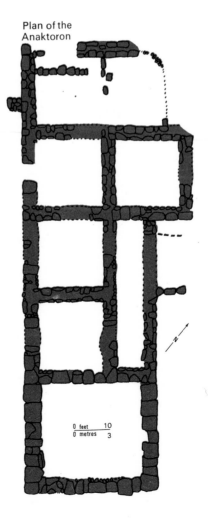

Plan of the
Anaktoron

Gola Del Sentino ITALY

Caves, village, cemetery
2nd millennium BC

BIBLIOGRAPHY
Trump, D., *Central and Southern Italy before Rome*, L[ondon], 1966, p. 144

The Sentino is a tributary of the Esino in the Marche. Shortly before joining that river, it cuts an impressive gorge 2 miles (3·2 km) long and 1,970 feet (600 m) deep through a range of limestone hills. Modern Fabriano lies five and a half miles (9 km) to the south west, Ancona 31 miles (50 km) to the east north east. Probably, however, it was not the scenery but the series of commodious caves in its cliffs, and perhaps the mineral spring near the outlet of the gorge, which attracted early man.

A village of the Middle Bronze Age once stood at Spineto, just under a mile (1·5 km) south of the gorge's entrance, but nothing can be seen today. The attractive Apennine Culture pottery, with its dotted band meanders and spirals, is preserved in the National Museum at Ancona, like most of the other finds from the area. Again there is nothing above ground to mark the Final Bronze Age cemetery of Pianello di Genga, though the site is easily identifiable in the mouth of the gorge. Its several hundred cremation burials of around 1000 BC made it the obvious type site for the early Italian 'proto-Villanovan' Urnfields. The cemetery had been dug through the deposits of an earlier village, which in turn overlay material apparently of Neolithic date.

Half way down the gorge, and opening high in its left wall, is the great cave of Frasassi. It is still something of a pilgrimage centre and contains a full-sized church, with room to spare. Its continuing popularity may explain why its deposits yielded no recognizable stratigraphy. They were mainly of the Apennine Culture, if rather later in date than Spineto, but included material spanning a wide range of time.

Where the northern cliff bends away from the river, the Grotta del Mezzogiorno was less disturbed, a Roman level overlying one of the Final Bronze Age, with a little earlier material on the cave floor. Several other caves, Baffoni, le Monache, Leonardo, have been investigated in the gorge, with less important archaeological results. The little 11th-century church of San Vittore delle Chiuse, just below the gorge, perhaps deserves a passing mention too.

The open villages above the gorge could well represent mixed-farming communities and economies, but the cave sites give strong support to the view that the Apennine Culture, during the latter part of the 2nd millennium BC, was primarily based on pastoralism.

Gola del Sentino

Belverde ITALY

Caves and rock carvings
3rd–early 1st millennium BC

BIBLIOGRAPHY
Trump, D., *Central and Southern Italy before Rome*, London, 1966, pp. 118–9
Calzoni, U., 'Topografia e scavi nelle stazioni preistoriche della Montagna di Cetona (Belverde)', *Quaderni dell'Istituto di Studi Etruschi*, I, 1954; II, 1962

Belverde di Cetona cannot be regarded as a typical site of its period, the Bronze Age, but its uniqueness has its own interest. It lies five miles (8 km) south west of Chiusi, itself an Etruscan site with tombs which repay a visit. The approach is by a sign-posted turning south of the Cetona–Sarteano road.

Monte di Cetona, 3,766 feet (1,148 m) high, is an outlier of the Monte Amiata group, one of the richest areas in Tuscany for metals. From its slope, a ridge of travertine projects towards the quaint medieval village of Cetona. A fortified site probably of the Late Bronze to Iron Age (it has not been investigated) uses the escarpment as one side of its defences, the others now being represented by a crumbled bank of stone.

Below the cliff, geologically recent erosion has left a tumble of great blocks, toppled from above. The alternation of dark crevices and exposed pin-nacles apparently attracted the attention, indeed awe, of early inhabitants. The spaces between and beneath the rocks – one cannot rightly call them caves – yielded to Calzoni in the 1930's a vast quantity of material, now displayed in the Perugia Museum. It included pottery from the Late Neolithic through to the Early Iron Age, the Apennine wares of the later 2nd millennium preponderating. A remarkably high proportion of the vessels were recovered complete, or at least restorable, some containing carbonized cereal grain, beans, acorns and the like. These, and the rich finds of bronze-work, strongly imply votive deposits.

Then the tops of the fallen blocks were sculpted into rectangular basins, steps, and other geometrical forms. The modern names of 'the Observatory', 'the Amphitheatre', etc. are fanciful, but the labour involved, often in almost inaccessible positions, again hints at a strong religious motivation.

The atmosphere of sanctity was revived in the Middle Ages when a hermitage (still standing) was erected at the eastern end of the site. The rock crevices came back into use as convenient cells for tranquil meditation.

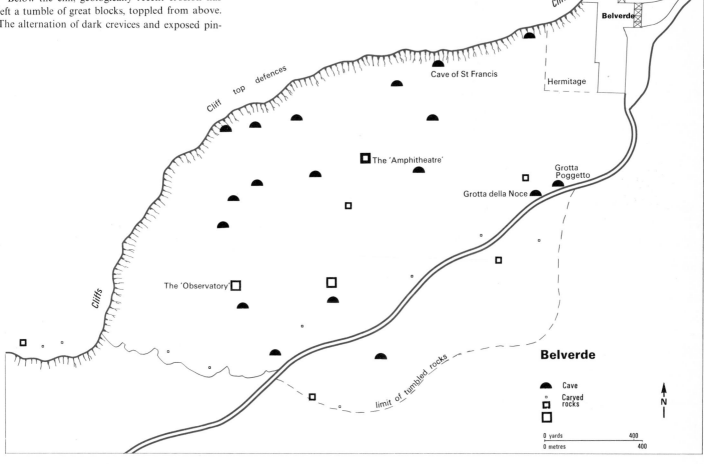

The 'Amphitheatre'

Cave of St Francis

Belverde

Hermitage

Grotta Poggetto

Grotta della Noce

The 'Observatory'

limit of tumbled rocks

Cliff top defences

Cliffs

Belverde

Cave
Carved rocks

0 yards 400
0 metres 400

N

105

Tarquinia ITALY

City and cemeteries
10th century–308 BC

BIBLIOGRAPHY
Hencken, H., *Tarquinia and Etruscan Origins*, London, 1968

This site, formerly the leading city of the Etruscans, lies on hills overlooking the coastal plain 43 miles (70 km) north west of Rome. Any visit falls into three parts.

Logically the first should be the ancient city, two miles (3·2 km) north east of the modern town and now completely deserted. It is not on the first promontory beside the river Marta as one might expect, but in a position of greater security on the second. By the 3rd century BC it had five miles (8 km) of walls around it, but it is unlikely that anything near the whole of the area enclosed was ever built on. The heart of the city was always on the better-defended western tip. Parts of the walls and gateways survive, together with a monumental temple base, the Ara della Regina. But the main impression here is of desolation.

Paradoxically the cemeteries offer a remarkable contrast. They began modestly on low hills east of the city, whence material from graves of the 10th to 7th centuries BC is of prime importance in the study of the Villanovan period in Italy. Later, the ridge of Monterozzi south of the city, now with the modern town on its tip, was developed as the main necropolis, an Etruscan city of the dead opposite that of the living. Air photographs show that the whole of this area was once pimpled with burial mounds, many of which have been levelled by agriculture. But a substantial number had chambers cut deeply enough beneath the surface to escape the plough, and it is these which draw the visitors in their thousands to the site. A guide from the museum is necessary as the tombs are kept locked.

The Tarquinian practice was to fresco the rock-cut chamber beneath the mound. Preservation of the paintings has therefore been on the whole excellent, the colours and scenes often as bright as when they were painted in the 6th to 2nd centuries BC. Most commonly one is shown the funeral ceremonies of the deceased, but even these seem happy affairs;

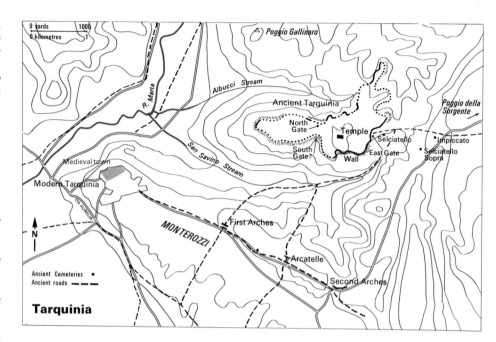

Tarquinia

dining, dancing and games appear, as well as the more formal offerings or leave-takings. Then there are a few delightful scenes from life, notably one showing fishing and wildfowling. More sombre, and usually of later date, are those with demons of the underworld. When so little of Etruscan civilization stands above ground, it is particularly fortunate that this wealth of documentation concerning a fascinating people has survived in their earthfast tombs.

Thirdly, the medieval village of Corneto, renamed Tarquinia in 1922, is of interest in its own right. The fine 15th-century Palazzo Vitelleschi houses the museum. Here the great terracotta horses from the façade of a long vanished temple on the Acropolis must on no account be missed.

Caere-Cerveteri ITALY

City and cemeteries
9th century–351 BC

BIBLIOGRAPHY
Cerveteri, Guidebook to the Museums and Monuments,
Ministero della Pubblica istruzione, Rome

Very little is left of the Etruscan city here, 22 miles
(35 km) north west of Rome, its last remains obliterated by the medieval and modern village on the
same site. A small museum has recently been opened
in the Orsini castle. As at TARQUINIA it is the
cemeteries which hold the major interest.

The main group is on the Banditaccia, the next
ridge to the north west, a veritable city of the dead.
Indeed, many of the tombs are grouped into streets,
like so many terraced houses, and some of their
interiors were carved or built in close imitation of
domestic architecture. They thus throw valuable
light on Etruscan dwellings, otherwise poorly preserved and little investigated. Most remarkable of
all is the unique Tomb of the Stuccoes, cut deep in
the rock as a rectangular chamber with sleeping
niches set in its walls. Each niche has its double
pillow, several have stools to climb in by, one even
a pair of slippers, likewise in relief plaster, still wait-
ing to be reclaimed by their owner. All the walls and
the two central pillars are decorated with more
stuccoes of everyday tools, weapons and domestic
animals, an invaluable picture of life in the 4th
century BC.

Other tombs are more impressive externally, with
mounds up to 130 feet (40 m) in diameter, and many
have internal fittings of interest, if less startling than
the Tomb of the Stuccoes. The area within the
enclosure may contain the most monumental group
of tombs, but the cemetery extends far beyond its
fence in both directions. Beyond it is a bare rock
face honeycombed with graves going back to the
Villanovan period. Further on, the main funeral
road cut into the rock can still be followed back
towards the city. To the east of the enclosure stands
the great Tomb of the Chairs and Shields, a particularly good example of a tombhouse. South west
are a number of such tombs lining another funeral
way. Some have traces of paintings on their walls,
many are carved in relief and one has engraved the
name of Tarchnas (Tarquin), a famous one in
Etruscan history.

There was once a second cemetery area south east
of the city on Monte Abetone. This is less easy of
approach, but the climb to the Campana Tomb is
worth the effort, and there are one or two more
further out in this direction. Immediately below the
tip of the modern settlement lies the oldest Etruscan
tomb so far discovered, known as the Regolini-
Galassi after the priest and general who found it.
This tomb dates from the late 7th century BC. It
yielded a famous treasure of highly artistic gold
jewelry, now preserved in the Vatican.

Caere had two ports, Alsinum and Pyrgi. The site
of the latter, seven miles (11·3 km) to the west at
Santa Severa, repays a visit. Here are the foundations of a temple which yielded three inscribed gold
sheets, two written in Etruscan and one, giving an
extremely useful parallel text, in Phoenician. Also to
be seen are the wall foundations of the Roman
military colony, a magnificent 14th-century castle
and, on calm days, traces of the old harbourworks
beneath the sea.

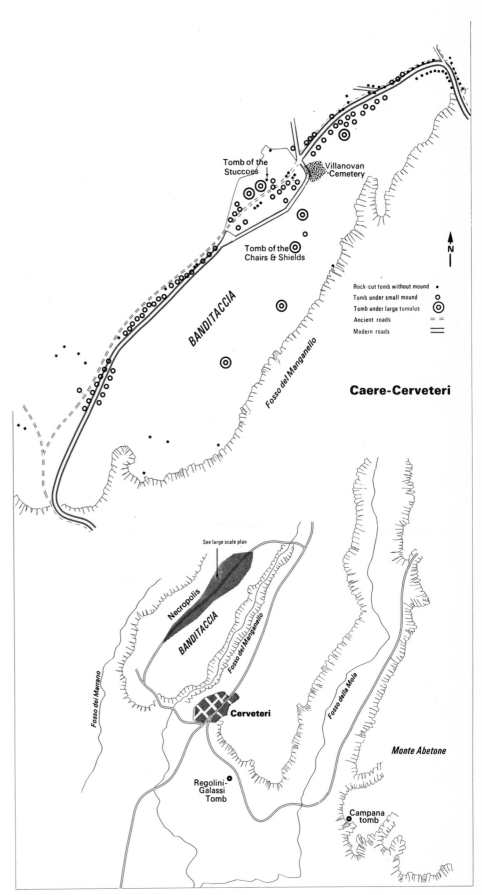

Caere-Cerveteri

Rock-cut tomb without mound
Tomb under small mound
Tomb under large tumulus
Ancient roads
Modern roads

Tomb of the Stuccoes
Villanovan Cemetery
Tomb of the Chairs & Shields
BANDITACCIA
Fosso del Manganello

See large scale plan
Necropolis
BANDITACCIA
Fosso del Marrano
Fosso del Manganello
Fosso della Mola
Cerveteri
Monte Abetone
Regolini-Galassi Tomb
Campana tomb

Veii ITALY

City and cemeteries
10th century–396 BC

BIBLIOGRAPHY
Ward Perkins, J. B., Veii: 'The historical topography of an ancient city', *Papers of the British School at Rome* 39, 1961, pp. 1–123

Only nine miles (14·5 km) north of Rome, Veii was its first and most formidable enemy among the Etruscan cities. Though the story of the '10-year siege' by Camillus has obviously been influenced by that of Troy, itself literature rather than history, the conflict was obviously fierce, and on its outcome depended Rome's growth to power.

The site now stands empty, but all the more impressive in its desolation, with many hints of former greatness. The usual approach is from Isola Farnese on its south side. A narrow road drops to the valley floor, whence a path crosses the stream above a spectacular waterfall. Here are the remains of the Temple of Apollo of about 500 BC, the source of a series of magnificent terracottas.

A track climbs to the plateau, one and a half miles (2·5 km) long and up to two thirds of a mile (1 km) wide, formed by the cutting of the gorges of the Cremera to the north and Valca to the south. Over the whole of this area the cultivated fields yield sherds of Etruscan and Roman pottery. At the tip, the Piazza d'Armi formed the citadel, separated by a ditch from the rest of the city. Its steep sides fall 200 feet (60 m) or more to the valleys below. In the stream banks below it to the north can be seen the remains of a Roman bath.

Higher up the Cremera, the Ponte Sodo gives a fine example of the use of 'lateral thinking' in the Etruscan period. Where the Romans would have bridged the river, the Etruscans diverted it through a rock-cut tunnel, running their road across its now dry bed. At the western end of the site, they pierced the ridge to divert the Cremera into the Valca at need, to protect the more sorely threatened flank of the city. The entrance to this tunnel and some of the shafts, up to 165 feet (50 m) deep, can still be seen. At this western end of the city, two stretches of the walls which fell to Camillus in 396 BC have been exposed by excavation, either side of the main west gate.

Outside the walls, the Etruscan road system can be traced as long abandoned hollow ways, sometimes for many miles. Beside the roads were the cemeteries, but only the Campana Tomb, to the east of the Ponte Sodo, attracts visitors. It is one of the earliest painted tombs, going back to the 7th century. No trace of the very important Villanovan cemeteries to north and east of the city shows on the surface. For their contents, as for the other material recovered from the site, one must visit the Villa Giulia Museum in Rome. The famous Apollo of Veii, with his frightening inscrutability, can perhaps be left to make the last comment on this ancient city.

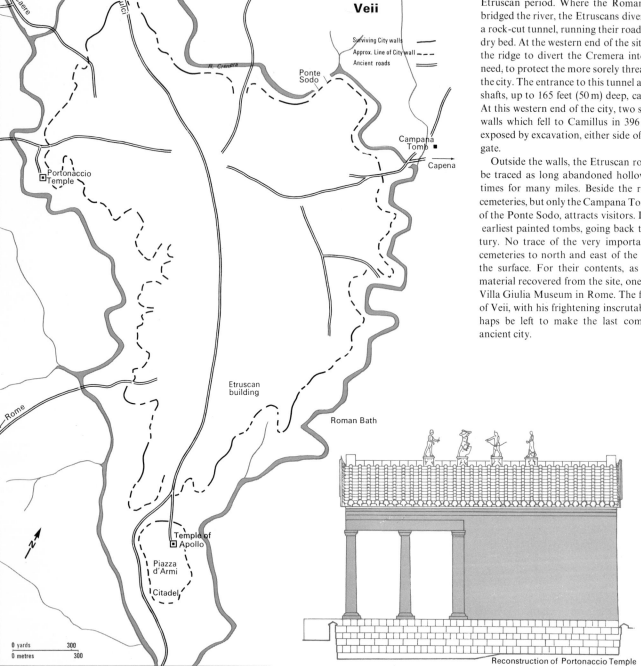

Veii

Surviving City walls
Approx. Line of City wall
Ancient roads

Caere
Vulci
R. Cremera
Ponte Sodo
Campana Tomb
Capena
Portonaccio Temple
Rome
Etruscan building
Roman Bath
Temple of Apollo
Piazza d'Armi
Citadel

0 yards 300
0 metres 300

Reconstruction of Portonaccio Temple

Anghelu Ruju SARDINIA

Cemetery of rock-cut tombs
c. 2500–2000 BC

BIBLIOGRAPHY
Guido, M., *Sardinia*, London, 1963, pp. 49–51
Taramelli, A., Alghero, 'Nuovi scavi nella necropole pre-istorica, Anghelu Ruju', *Monumenti Antichi dei Lincei* XIX, 1909, co. 397 ff

The Copper Age in Sardinia is represented best by a large number of rock-cut collective tombs known locally as *domus de gianas*, roughly 'fairies' houses'. They occur singly or in groups, the most famous being the cemetery of some 35 tombs at Anghelu Ruju, five and a half miles (9 km) north of Alghero. The site is on the edge of a flat sandstone plateau overlooking a steep-sided valley, just over three miles (5 km) from the sea. The parent settlement is unknown. A new road is under construction right past the site and access, at least from the main Sassari road to the north, is already easy.

The tombs vary considerably in plan but a common pattern is readily recognizable. A shaft or sloping passage, sometimes stepped, leads down from the rock surface to the doorway of a roofed antechamber. This is often quite small. A second similar doorway gives onto the main burial chamber on the same axis. In all but the simplest tombs, other smaller cells open out of the end, or sides, or both, of the main chamber, and it is in the number and distribution of these cells that the greatest variation lies.

Not surprisingly, the main chamber is often the more elaborately decorated. The doorways to the side chambers are occasionally carved in relief to imitate wooden post and lintel construction. Even more are rebated to receive a blocking slab. A few walls have bulls' horns, also in relief, (better shown on tombs from other sites). One of the finest tombs here had two pillars of rock left to support the roof of a substantially larger main chamber. Both have broken off but one still lies on the floor and on this, too, can be made out two pairs of horns.

Burial was by collective inhumation. The finds were mainly of the Sardinian Ozieri Culture, but there was also an intrusive element from southern France, including Beakers and Fontbouisse ware. Ozieri, too, was attributed to external, specifically east Mediterranean, influences, but recent research suggests that these may have been exaggerated. Flint and obsidian were much used for arrowheads, and copper, though scarce, was known, and especially used for daggers. There were also marble figurines of schematic form. Further controversy surrounds the tomb plans, concerning the extent to which similarities to tombs elsewhere, HAL SAFLIENI and CASTELLUCCIO for example, are indicative of cultural contact, rather than parallel local development. The date should lie in the second half of the 3rd millennium BC.

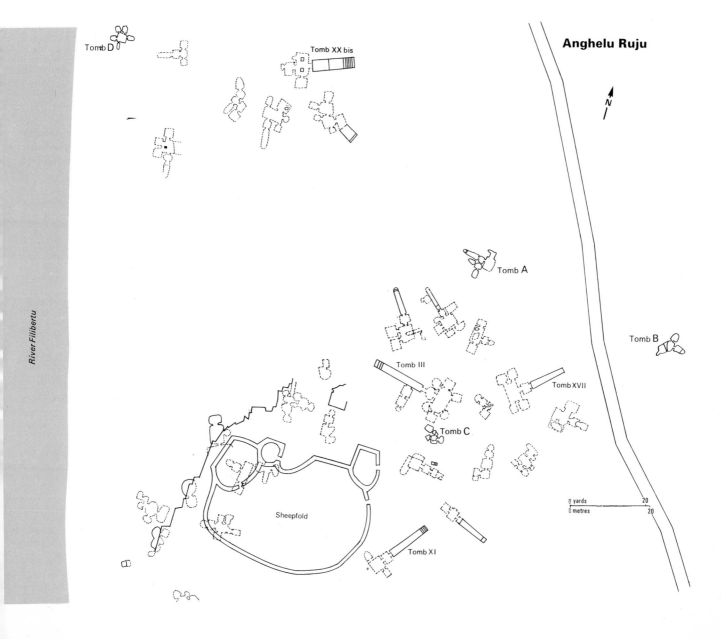

Anghelu Ruju

Barumini SARDINIA

Nuraghe and village
c. 17th–6th century BC

BIBLIOGRAPHY
Guido, M., *Sardinia*, London, 1963, pp. 121–4
Lilliu, G., 'Il nuraghe di Barumini e la stratigrafia nuragica',
   Studi Sardi, XII–XIII, 1952–4, p. 90 ff

Six thousand five hundred nuraghi (towers) are already known in Sardinia and the total may go appreciably higher. It is no easy matter to choose one to represent the rest. A short list would certainly include Palmavera (Alghero), Sant'Antine (Torralba), Losa (Abbasanta), Orrubiu (Orroli), and Sa Domu S'Orcu (Domusnovas). But Su Nuraxi (Barumini), 34 miles (55 km) north of Cagliari, has not only an interesting elaborate plan but also a history archaeologically substantiated by excavations made in the 1950's.

The nucleus of the site is a single tower, originally 56 feet (17 m) high, built from massive blocks of the local basalt. The external walls sloped inwards and were crowned by a projecting platform, the fallen supports of which can be seen lying on the ground. The entrance was at ground level, but the staircase to the upper storeys in the thickness of the wall began 11 feet 6 inches (3·5 m) off the floor, presumably approached by a ladder which could be drawn in by the defenders. Inside were three superimposed corbel-vaulted chambers, the lowest 25 feet (7·6 m) high and 15 feet (4·6 m) in diameter, the highest now represented only by its floor. A radiocarbon date was obtained for this tower, placing it surprisingly early, about 1800 BC.

Some time later – the early 8th century BC is suggested – four more towers were added, with connecting walls enclosing both the original tower and a small open courtyard with a well. At least three towers were built even further out and by this time a surrounding village had begun to grow. Then more towers were built and the outer ones linked by a continuous curtain wall. In the same period, the walls of the inner keep were considerably thickened. The village too expanded, though many of the visible huts belong to a reoccupation of the site after its destruction by the Carthaginians in the 6th century.

It is difficult to avoid the terms of medieval castle architecture in describing the nuraghi. They offer an extraordinarily clear example of a similar, here socio-political, need calling forth a remarkably similar, here architectural, material response.

Nuraghi are unique to Sardinia, though related monuments can be recognized in the torri of Corsica and the talayots of the Balearics, both smaller and simpler than the nuraghi. We have from the island three other associated classes of antiquity. The *tombe di giganti* in which the inhabitants of the nuraghi buried their dead are gallery graves with great concave façades. The sacred wells are subterranean corbelled vaults of magnificent cut masonry. And through the remarkable bronze votive figurines we are given a fascinating glimpse of the men and women of prehistoric Sardinia.

Barumini

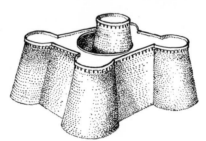

Reconstruction of Nuraghe Complex

Central Tower

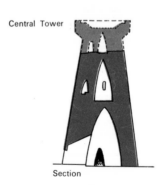

Section

Plan

0 yards 5
0 metres 5

Hal Saflieni MALTA

Rock-cut temple and cemetery
c. 4000–2500 BC

BIBLIOGRAPHY
Evans, J. D., *The Prehistoric Antiquities of the Maltese Islands*, London, 1972, pp. 44–60
Trump, D., *Malta, an Archaeological Guide*, London, 1972, pp. 58–65

The Hypogeum, a short distance from the head of Grand Harbour in Malta, consists of a complex series of artificial caves cut into the limestone.

The earliest, and most roughly cut, chambers surround the entrance, before which there once stood some megalithic structure, perhaps a temple like TARXIEN. The finds here go back to the Zebbug phase around 4000 BC. It was constructed as a burial place, an irregular and earlier form of the rock-cut tombs we see at CASTELLUCCIO for example. As these chambers became filled with interments, more were cut deeper into the rock beyond them, characterized by more recent grave goods and a finer finish to the walls.

Then the site was given what we might regard as a funeral chapel, two rock-cut replicas of the megalithic temple chambers we see above ground. Two more were smoothly hewn and painted in red ochre with running spirals. Ochre was used on the relief carved walls too, and there is a panel of black and white chequers in addition. Simpler side chambers held more interments, which appear to have encroached on the main chambers towards the end of the site's active life.

By that time a lower storey of chambers had been cut, penetrating over 33 feet (10 m) below the modern surface. These were found empty by the excavators and had probably served for storage only. Nearby and presumably associated, a great rock-cut water cistern served the needs of the religious ceremonies. This remained open and in use long after the time, about 2500 BC, when the rest of the site was sealed off and forgotten.

The finds included vast numbers of human bones, though of the 6,000 estimated by the excavator, very few now survive. There was also a great quantity of pottery and personal possessions such as beads and amulets, particularly in the form of small polished axes. The most famous object, and the most problematical, is an elegant terracotta figurine of a lady apparently asleep on a bed.

Though in general this site must be related both to the rock-cut tomb tradition, and to that of the Maltese-built temples, it is unique, and correspondingly baffling.

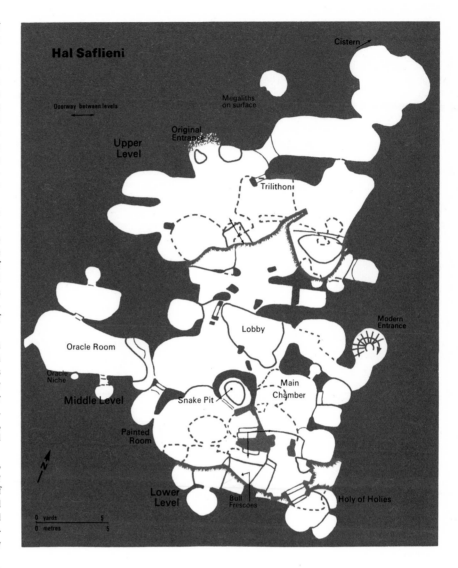

Hal Saflieni

Cistern

Doorway between levels

Megaliths on surface

Original Entrance

Upper Level

Trilithon

Oracle Room

Lobby

Modern Entrance

Oracle Niche

Middle Level

Snake Pit

Main Chamber

Painted Room

Lower Level

Bull Frescoes

Holy of Holies

0 yards 5
0 metres 5

N

Tarxien MALTA

Megalithic temple and cemetery
c. 3300–2500 BC

BIBLIOGRAPHY
Evans, J. D., *The Prehistoric Antiquities of the Maltese Islands*, London, 1972, pp. 116–38
Trump, D., *Malta, an Archaeological Guide*, London, 1972, pp. 65–75
Zammit, T., *Prehistoric Malta, the Tarxien Temples*, Oxford, 1930

A few hundred yards east of the Hypogeum, the largest of Malta's prehistoric temple complexes was discovered in 1915. The first and southernmost of the four temples has a concave façade opening onto a court with a cistern, probably original, at its centre (1). Shrines at either end contain slab floors perforated presumably for libations.

The restored entrance leads into a transverse, elliptical chamber (2) into which are set a number of slabs as screens, altars, etc., decorated with designs in relief. The running spiral is the commonest motif, and two blocks with friezes of animals are worthy of note. To the east once stood a three-dimensional statue of an extremely corpulent woman originally some eight feet (2·5 m) high, surely the goddess of the temple. Destruction of her upper half by farmers (before the excavation) has at least taken some of the weight off her feet. To her right is a spiralled altar block in which a cubby hole held a flint knife blade and the horn core of a goat. Animal bones found in the niche above seemed to lend support to this suggestion of animal sacrifice. A doorway opposite the first leads into a second oval chamber, with a fine decorated central altar.

The eastern apse was modified as an entrance to the central and largest temple, 79 feet (24 m) long internally. This consists of three oval rooms, the first (3), though undecorated, being the most impressive. Its walls of orthostats, with horizontal courses above, are monumental, and reddened by the fire which destroyed the site. A carved stone bowl in the western apse copies closely a pottery form. A chamber in the thickness of the wall to the east has relief carvings of two bulls and what is usually taken

to be a sow with piglets. The passage to the inner chambers is barred by a septal slab with a relief oculus motif. The next chamber has two magnificent stone screens and the terminal one a neat little cupboard.

The next temple (4) to the east is less well preserved but does illustrate the skill of stone carving and also has an 'oracle hole' penetrating the wall. East again, beyond a square court (5), are the scanty remains of a smaller and earlier temple (c. 3300 BC) (6). Otherwise the complex falls within the period 3000–2500 BC, the central temple being the latest.

Very considerable quantities of material, including an intrusive Bronze Age cremation cemetery, were recovered from the site, and are now preserved in the National Museum at Valletta. But the temple's greatest importance is probably as a type site for this extraordinary class of monument, unique to Malta. Examples at Hagar Qim and Mnajdra near the south coast and the Ggantija on Gozo are hardly less fine.

The evidence, such as it is, would point to the worship of a Mother Goddess concerned with both fertility and death. Libation and animal sacrifice are attested and there are strong hints of some sort of priesthood. Beyond this we cannot go.

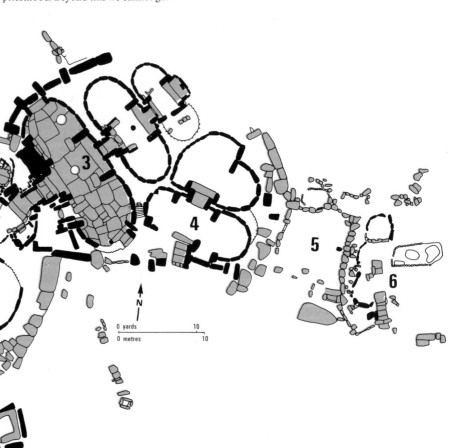

Tarxien

GREECE AND THE AEGEAN

From the central massifs of Greece a series of limestone mountain ridges run south-eastwards into the Aegean. As they near the sea the valleys between them open into cultivable coastal plains forming natural areas of settlement, often more accessible by sea than from each other, and open therefore in early times to influences from the Near East rather than from the rest of Europe. The mountains continue beneath the Aegean, their peaks forming groups of island stepping stones to Asia Minor. Crete lies separate from the rest of the islands, and is much larger and therefore capable of supporting an independent culture.

In the north the great plain of Thessaly was the home of a Neolithic population from a very early date, but it forms an area apart, and consequently shares only marginally in the chief trends which distinguish the phases of the Greek Bronze Age. Nevertheless it is at the Late Neolithic settlement of DIMINI, near modern Volo, that we can perhaps first observe a recurrent phenomenon in the early history of Greece, the settlement of invaders of more advanced or more dynamic cultures, arriving by sea and occupying the fertile coastal plains.

In Crete a separate and lively Neolithic civilization, centred on KNOSSOS, was transformed soon after 3000 BC (whether as a result of immigration we cannot tell) by the incipient knowledge of metal working, learned no doubt from more advanced civilizations further east. The distinctive Cretan civilization that now emerged (called Minoan after the legendary king Minos) at first flourished in the eastern parts of the island at such places as Vasiliki, Palaikastro, Mochlos, and Myrtos. But with the exploitation of local sources of copper the rich Mesara plain did not long lag behind. The coast near PHAISTOS in that area, and ZAKRO in the east, may already have been points of departure for trade with Egypt. Middle Minoan saw the rise, as centres of social and economic organization, of the great palaces at Knossos, Phaistos, MALLIA, and Zakro, and the development of Minoan civilization to its first peak.

As in Crete, knowledge of metal working in mainland Greece came from further east, no doubt via the Aegean islands, which in the Early Bronze Age developed their own little Early Cycladic civilization, based on maritime activities supplementing their local agricultural and mineral resources. On the mainland, however, progress was less rapid. There the corresponding civilization, known as the Helladic, began a little later. The transition from its Early to its Middle phase was marked by disturbances, probably caused by the influx of the first Greek population (see LERNA).

The M.M. III phase (see end table) is marked off from what precedes it by the destruction of many places in Crete; yet it is the beginning of a new era of prosperity, the Second Palace period, which extends to the close of L.M. I and sees an expansion of Minoan civilization to a number of the Aegean islands, best attested so far at Phylakopi in Melos, in Kea, in Kythera, and most strikingly in the volcanic island of Thera (Santorini). Mainland Greece is unaffected by Minoan influence until the very end of the Middle Helladic, the transition being illustrated in the Shaft Graves at MYCENAE. Whether the occasion of this rather sudden transformation was the conquest of Mycenae and other places in southern Greece by invaders is a matter of debate. The result of it is the rise of the Late Helladic (Mycenaean) civilization, which though obviously borrowing freely from Crete and soon equalling the Minoan in splendour, owes some features to its M.H. antecedents. The distribution of the distinctive and monumental Mycenaean beehive tombs not only in the Argolid (Mycenae, TIRYNS, Dendra, etc.) but in many other parts (for example, near Volo, at Vapheio in Laconia, at Kakovatos in Triphylia, at ORCHOMENOS and in Messenia) implies the rise of a number of flourishing principalities; and this is at least compatible with the theory of small invasions from outside Greece providing a new impetus. The principal Mycenaean centres figure in the epics of Homer and in Greek literature generally as the homes of the great heroes, and there is no doubt that such traditions embody memories of the real glories of the Mycenaean age.

The Minoan palaces all suffered violent destruction at the end of L.M. IB, as did some overseas Minoan sites, and it is now widely believed that this was caused by the cataclysmic eruption (of a magnitude perhaps unparalleled in world history) of the island of Thera. Knossos, unlike the other palaces, was reoccupied for perhaps another 50 years, but under Mycenaean rulers. (This is the period of the Linear B tablets at Knossos, written in the mainland language, Greek.) The centre of Aegean civilization shifted from Crete to the mainland, which continued for two centuries to develop and to expand its influence and prosperity. The Argolid, commanded to north and south by Mycenae and Tiryns, was the chief focus; but there were others too (in Laconia and Messenia) in the Peloponnese, and for a time Orchomenos and Thebes in central Greece may have rivalled Mycenae. Iolkos (by Volo) is still unexplored, but was doubtless another important centre. Whether the king of Mycenae ruled all Greece we cannot be sure. Probably he could call on the other princes for support at least in wartime, like Agamemnon in Homer. Some at least of the Aegean islands (for example, Melos and Rhodes) became thoroughly Mycenaean in culture, and less concentrated influence spread far beyond the Aegean. Some Mycenaeans reached and even settled in Sicily and south Italy; but they were far more active in the eastern Mediterranean, trading with Cyprus (the prime source of their essential metal, copper), with Syria and Palestine, and with Egypt. This eastward intercourse was facilitated by a balance of power between the Hittite and Egyptian empires; but by L.H. IIIB we find a recession, along with evidence within Greece itself of destruction and desertion of settlements, besides the strengthening of fortifications, which suggests some threat of danger from without. The last century of the Greek Bronze Age (L.H. IIIC) is one of disruption and decline, the causes of which may lie partly in exhaustion of economic resources at home. The immigration of the Dorian Greeks and the introduction of iron are now seen as only contributory or even consequential rather than causal factors in the collapse of Mycenaean civilization.

SUMMARY OF AEGEAN BRONZE AGE CHRONOLOGY

Note: It is a convenient custom to use initials for the Early, Middle, and Late phases of the Minoan, Cycladic, and Helladic civilizations. Late Helladic is alternatively called Mycenaean.

B.C.	3000	2900	2800	2700	2600	2500	2400	2300	2200	2100	2000	1900	1800	1700	1600	1500	1400	1300	1200	1100
CRETE				Early Minoan I			E M II		E M III			MM I	MM II	MM III	LM I A	LM I B	LM II	LM III		
AEGEAN ISLANDS	Neolithic			Early Cycladic								Middle Cycladic								
MAINLAND GREECE				Early Helladic								Middle Helladic			LH I	LH II	LH III A	LH III B	LH III C	

0 miles 60
0 kilometres 100

Ionian Sea

Peneios

Larissa

Thessaly

Iolkos
Dimini Volo

Spercheios

Acheloos

Euboea

Orchomenos
Gla **Euboea**
Boeotia
Thebes *Channel*

Patras *Corinthian*
Gulf

Corinth Athens

Alpheios **Mycenae** **Argolid**
Dendra **Tiryns**
Lerna Nafplion
Kakovatos **Triphylia** *Gulf of*
Argos

Eurotas
Messenia Sparta
Pylos Vapheio
Laconia

Aegean Sea

KYTHERA

LEMNOS Troy

LESBOS

SKYROS

CHIOS

ANDROS SAMOS

TENOS NIKARIA

KEA MYKONOS

CYCLADES

PAROS NAXOS

Phylakopi KOS

MELOS

THERA
(SANTORINI)

KARPATHOS

CRETE

Chania Heraklion Amnissos
Tylissos **Knossos** **Mallia**
Hagia Vathypetro Mochlos
Triada **Phaistos** **Gournia** Palaikastro
Kamilari Vasiliki **Kato Zakro**
Myrtos

115

Dimini GREECE

Fortified Neolithic settlement
c. 3300–3000 BC

BIBLIOGRAPHY
Wace, A. J. B. and Thompson, M. S., *Prehistoric Thessaly*, Cambridge, 1912, pp. 75–85 and 243–8
Piggott, Stuart, (ed.), *The Dawn of Civilisation*, London, 1961, p. 197

The Late Neolithic settlement of Dimini lies on a slight eminence nearly three miles (5 km) west of modern Volo, on the Gulf of Pagasae. The site, covering about one and a half acres (5,000 sq m) was protected by at least six roughly concentric walls of undressed limestone, which must have given a maze-like impression to a stranger penetrating their narrow gates and passages. Where the walls lie close together the interspace may perhaps have been filled with earth. Within the little citadel are several large houses of a kind known as the *megaron*. The main room with a central hearth was entered through an open porch, and sometimes an antechamber. Here is an early form of the banqueting hall of the Mycenaean palaces (see PYLOS, MYCENAE, TIRYNS). Already the plan of Dimini implies an aristocratic society contrasting with the open village communities of the earlier Neolithic Age in Thessaly. Megaron A can hardly be other than a chieftain's house, while humbler people probably lived outside the walls.

Although Sesklo, a few miles further west, may have been fortified already in the Middle Neolithic, Dimini is still exceptional. The walls may imply no more than less peaceful times; but this could well be the stronghold of some small but vigorous immigrant group arriving by sea and establishing themselves in reach of good harbourage and with control over a cultivable area inland. The inhabitants used a highly distinctive pottery (Dimini Ware), the distribution of which, radiating from Dimini itself to some other Thessalian sites, is not incompatible with the immigrant theory, though foreign derivations of the style formerly proposed are no longer tenable. Carbon 14 dating suggests that Dimini flourished in the later 4th millennium BC. There are some Bronze Age building remains and a number of M.H. (see table in Introduction) cist graves. A Mycenaean beehive tomb is built into the northwest slope of the hill.

Reconstruction of the fortified settlement at Dimini, looking eastward

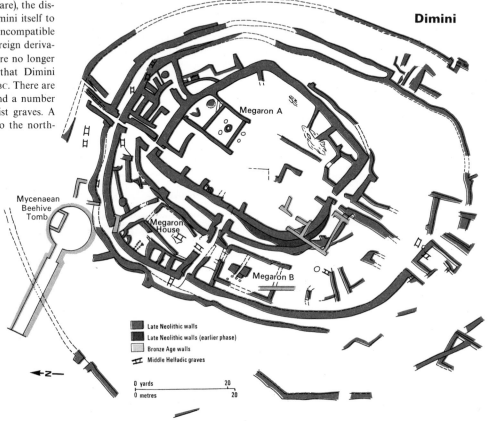

Dimini

Megaron A

Mycenaean Beehive Tomb

Megaron House

Megaron B

■ Late Neolithic walls
■ Late Neolithic walls (earlier phase)
☐ Bronze Age walls
Ⅱ Middle Helladic graves

0 yards   20
0 metres   20

Lerna GREECE

Neolithic to Middle Bronze Age settlement
3300–1500 BC

BIBLIOGRAPHY
Excavation reports in the journal *Hesperia* vols. XXIII,
1954 to XXIX, 1960

The site of Lerna lies by the village of Myloi at the west corner of the Gulf of Argos, opposite the modern town of Nafplion. It is an artificial mound composed of settlement debris, rising hardly 25 feet (7–8 m) above sea level. Just to the north runs the stream Amymone, carrying the waters of the adjacent Lerna spring to the sea. Though only 520–590 feet (160–180 m) in diameter, it is one of the larger prehistoric mounds of southern Greece, and doubtless owed its importance to its position on the route from the Argolid to the southern Peloponnese which (like the modern railway) here inevitably followed the narrow strip between sea and mountains.

After a long period of Neolithic occupation (Lerna I and II) the site seems to have been deserted for a time before it was levelled off and reoccupied in E.H. II (see table in Introduction). This new settlement (Lerna III) has a double ring of walls with gates and towers, within which a succession of substantial buildings can be traced. Latest and most important of them is the House of Tiles (so named from being roofed with flat clay plaques) measuring 82 feet by 39 feet (25 × 12 m), with walls nearly three feet (1 m) thick. (The only known E.H. II building of comparable scale is at TIRYNS.) This building

was perhaps still under construction, and the whole citadel undergoing reorganization, when it was destroyed by fire, and its site covered by a low tumulus surrounded by a single ring of stones, as though to mark it off as a forbidden area. The subsequent Lerna IV was not a fortress, but an open settlement of smaller buildings, some of them of apsidal *megaron* plan. Cylindrical rubbish pits (*bothroi*) were peculiarly numerous in this settlement. Lerna IV saw the introduction, alongside wares characteristic of E.H. III, of a grey pottery, which was sometimes wheel-made, like the Minyan Ware typical of Middle Helladic. The clearly M.H. settlement of Lerna V (with matt-painted pottery and intramural burials) follows without a break.

At the transition from Middle to Late Helladic two rectangular shaft graves (found empty – perhaps deliberately despoiled in the Bronze Age) were cut into the tumulus over the House of Tiles; but the settlement did not continue into the Mycenaean period. The legend of the killing of the Hydra of Lerna by Herakles could conceivably embody a memory of the destruction of the place by the growing power of Mycenae and Tiryns.

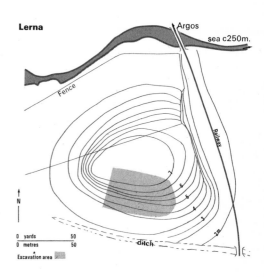

Lerna

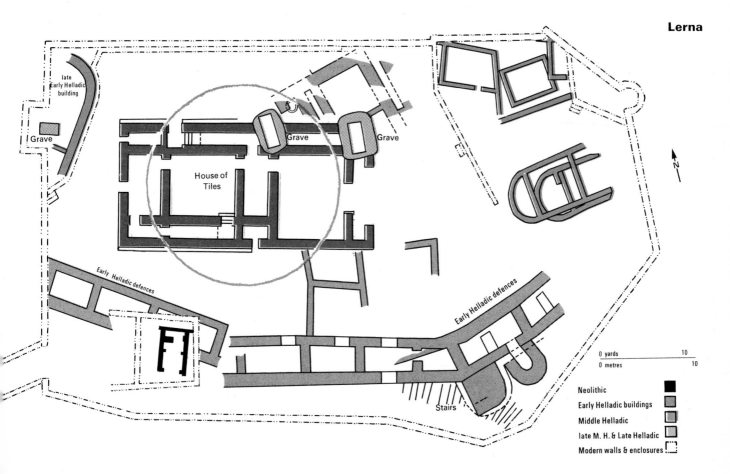

Lerna

House of Tiles

Grave

Grave

Grave

late Early Helladic building

Early Helladic defences

Early Helladic defences

Stairs

0 yards 10
0 metres 10

Neolithic
Early Helladic buildings
Middle Helladic
late M. H. & Late Helladic
Modern walls & enclosures

Mycenae GREECE

Mycenaean palace-citadel and royal tombs
c. 1600–1100 BC

BIBLIOGRAPHY
Schliemann, H., *Mycenae*, London, 1878; new edition, Ne
York, 1967
Wace, A. J. B., *Mycenae, an archaeological history and guid*
Princeton, 1949
Mylonas, G. E., *Mycenae and the Mycenaean Age*, Princ
ton, 1966

In Homer, Agamemnon, commander-in-chief of the Greek heroes, has Mycenae for his city; and it is well placed to be the chief stronghold of Mycenaean Greece. It lies in a recess of the hills at the northeast edge of the Argive plain; to the south the Gulf of Argos affords a sea approach from Crete and the Aegean; to the north Mycenae controls the road to Corinth and so to central Greece. In the Bronze Age it may be that trade between the Aegean and the Adriatic also was routed through the Argolid to the Gulf of Corinth, to avoid the southern capes of the Peloponnese, a notorious hazard for ancient and medieval shipping. Mycenae itself is on an easily defensible eminence, with commanding views, and a copious water supply near by.

Although the hill was occupied through most of

the Bronze Age, almost all that survives – the great walls, the palace and many houses both inside and outside the citadel – is of Mycenaean age. The transition from the modest stronghold of earlier times to this Mycenae 'rich in gold' is revealed in the burials made in the two Grave Circles that are a famous feature of the site. While Circle B, outside the citadel, had both humble graves of ordinary M.H. (see table in Introduction) type followed by far richer early Mycenaean burials, the deep-cut Shaft Graves of Circle A, just inside the Lion Gate, represented an altogether new degree of wealth. The six shafts, with carved grave slabs above them, contained the bodies of 19 men, women and children of the royal house. Some of the princes had been buried with face masks and breast plates of gold,

and all with a spectacular profusion of grave good gold and silver vessels, sumptuous swords and da gers, huge golden diadems, ornaments and oth elegant possessions. Many of these treasures (now the National Museum at Athens) show stro Minoan influence. They date from the 16th centu BC (L.H. I), marking the brilliant opening Mycenaean civilization.

There was probably a Mycenaean palace on t citadel from this time onward, but the existi remains are chiefly of L.H. IIIA and B. The *megar* is clearly recognizable; a small court west of it w approached by a staircase of which one flight is we preserved. The layout of other rooms is now los much must have been destroyed when the site wa levelled for a post-Mycenaean temple of Athena,

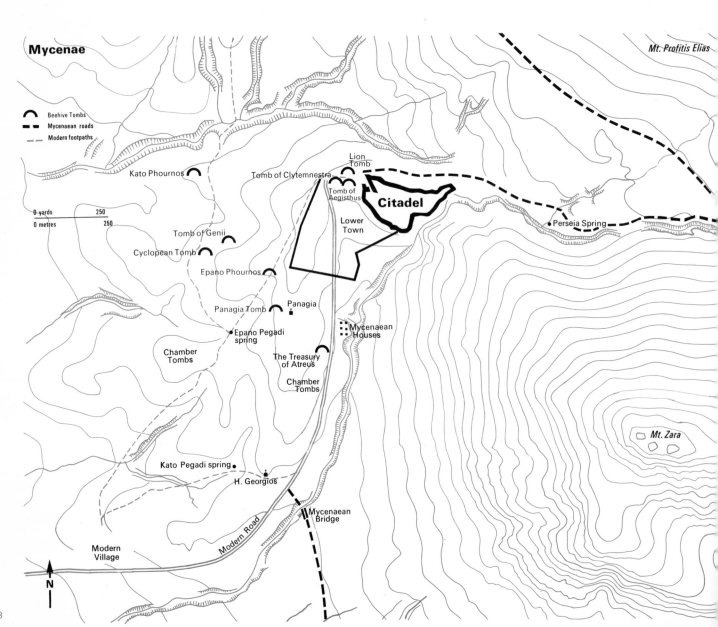

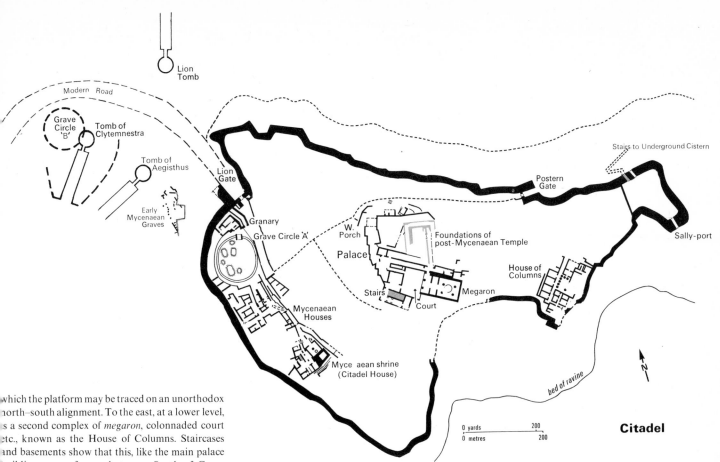

Lion Tomb

Modern Road

Grave Circle 'B'

Tomb of Clytemnestra

Tomb of Aegisthus

Early Mycenaean Graves

Lion Gate

Granary

Grave Circle 'A'

W. Porch

Palace

Stairs

Court

Mycenaean Houses

Mycenaean shrine (Citadel House)

Foundations of post-Mycenaean Temple

Megaron

Postern Gate

Stairs to Underground Cistern

Sally-port

House of Columns

bed of ravine

N

0 yards 200
0 metres 200

Citadel

which the platform may be traced on an unorthodox north–south alignment. To the east, at a lower level, is a second complex of *megaron*, colonnaded court etc., known as the House of Columns. Staircases and basements show that this, like the main palace buildings, was of several storeys. South of Grave Circle A are remains of houses, and of a unique building (formerly called the Citadel House) containing a small temple or shrine with frescoed walls and numerous clay idols.

In L.H. IIIA the 'Cyclopean' fortifications probably followed the outcrop of hard limestone which forms a natural boundary of the citadel on the west. In L.H. IIIB the circuit was enlarged on the south west to include the royal Grave Circle A, the surface of which was terraced up to form a precinct surrounded by a new wall of limestone orthostats as in the drawing. Towards the end of L.H. IIIB was added an eastern extension of the citadel, with a small opening through the wall at the south-east corner, and an underground cistern approached by a stepped passage through the walls, to ensure water in case of siege. The monumental Lion Gate, with its surmounting relief, the main entry, is of L.H. IIIB.

After the period of the Shaft Graves the kings of Mycenae were buried in beehive tombs, of which nine are known in this vicinity. The numbers assigned to them on the map indicate their probable chronological order. The Treasury of Atreus, the finest and best preserved, is probably of the late 14th century BC. Non-royal burials were in unlined rock-cut chamber tombs, of which two groups are known. Substantial houses have been excavated beside the modern road south west of the citadel, and there must have been a considerable settlement on the slopes above them. These extra-mural houses seem all to have been destroyed in L.H. IIIB, and never rebuilt, though the citadel was still occupied in L.H. IIIC.

There are various traces of Mycenaean-built roads in the vicinity, including the abutment of a bridge in 'Cyclopean' masonry about half a mile (800 m) south of the citadel. There was a Mycenaean lookout post on the peak of Prophitis Elias (2,648 feet, 807 m) immediately to the north east.

Grave circle A, Mycenae, as it probably appeared about 1200 BC

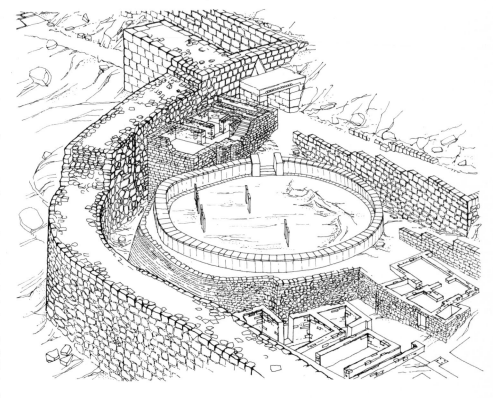

Orchomenos and Gla GREECE

Bronze Age settlement and Mycenaean fortress
Orchomenos, c. 3000–1250 BC
Gla, 13th century BC

BIBLIOGRAPHY
Schuchhardt, C., *Schliemann's Excavations*, London, 1891
   pp. 299–303
Frazer, Sir J. G., *Commentary on Pausanias*, London, 1898
   vol. V, pp. 120–130 (Gla) and 180–91 (Orchomenos)
Kenny, E. J. A., 'The ancient drainage of the Copais',
   Liverpool Annals of Archaeology and Anthropology, vol.
   XXII, 1935, pp. 189–206
Hope Simpson, R., *A Gazeteer and Atlas of Mycenaean sites*
   (Univ. of London Inst. of Classical Studies, Bulletin Sup-
   plement no. 16, 1965), pp. 113 and 116.

Nowadays the waters of the Kephissos and other streams which enter the Copais basin from the north west are drained by artificial channels to a tunnel debouching in Lake Hylike to the east, thus leaving a fine arable plain. In classical times, when drainage was only by the natural swallow holes at the base of the surrounding rocky hills to the north east and east, Copais was a lake or fen, famous for wildfowl and eels. In Mycenaean times, according to ancient literary tradition (supported by archaeological evidence), the area was drained and cultivated by the people of Orchomenos. All round the eastern half of the basin have been found remains of dikes, reinforced with 'Cyclopean' walls, planned to channel the waters against the rocky edges of the plain to the swallow holes. From near Topolia (also called Kastron) two dikes formed a stone-lined canal 200 feet (60 m) wide, running east north east, which appears to have been the main emissary. Vertical shafts for an uncompleted tunnel through the hills towards the sea at Larimna may represent a further project for getting the waters directly to the sea.

That the dikes must be Mycenaean is inferred not only from the 'Cyclopean' masonry, but because at no other period was there such intensive occupation around Copais. Orchomenos, on a rocky spur to the west, doubtless dominated this fertile area; in Homer it is mentioned as a city of unusual wealth. Extensive Early and Middle Helladic (E.H. and M.H. see table in Introduction) settlement remains, and a number of M.H. cist graves, have been excavated on the lower slopes of the hill. The Mycenaean levels have unfortunately been badly eroded, but fresco fragments imply buildings of palace scale, and the total inhabited area covered a space of over 1,650 feet by 650 feet (500 × 200 m). In the south-east slope is the beehive tomb known since antiquity as the Treasury of Minyas, comparable in size and excellence of finish (perhaps also in date) with the Treasury of Atreus at MYCENAE. Its side chamber has a stone ceiling beautifully carved with a repeating design of spirals and palmettes.

There were substantial smaller settlements at Pirgos, Stroviki, and Topolia. The spur opposite the last, at Ayia Marina, was strongly fortified, and two more forts, Chantsa and Ayios Ioannis – the latter larger than TIRYNS – guarded the north-east end of the great dikes and the pass from Larimna and the sea. These strongpoints were all doubtless controlled from headquarters in the colossal fortress of Gla (ancient name probably Arne). This rises from the plain like an island, its natural rocky cliffs defended by 'Cyclopean' walls nearly 20 feet (6 m) thick, and still in parts standing 10 feet (3 m) high. The buildings in the central enclosure were probably barracks, while the highest part of the citadel, on the north, is occupied by the so-called palace. This though including a *megaron* at the end, is not comparable in plan with Tiryns or PYLOS: it could well have contained the quarters of the commander or officers of the fortress. Gla and its subsidiary forts clearly defended the eastern approaches to the Copais basin, and also protected the drainage works vital to its Mycenaean prosperity. Tradition relates that Thebes (with the aid of Herakles) in fact overthrew the power of Orchomenos by breaking the dikes and flooding the cultivated land.

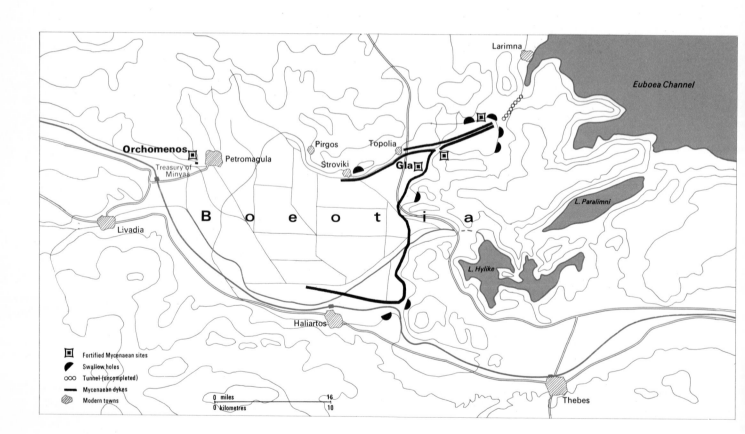

Legend:
Fortified Mycenaean sites
Swallow holes
Tunnel (uncompleted)
Mycenaean dykes
Modern towns

0 miles 16
0 kilometres 10

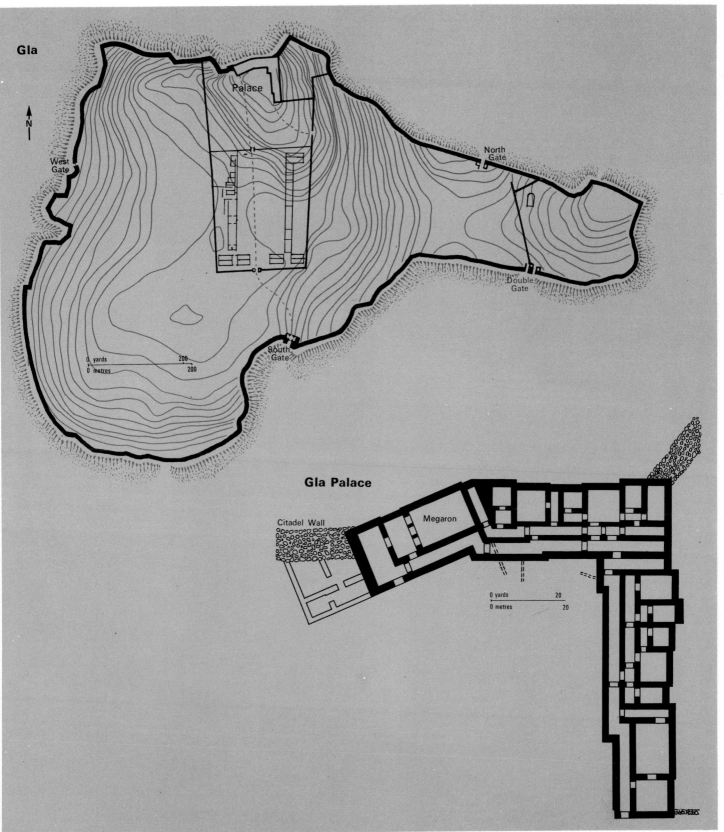

Gla

N

West
Gate

Palace

North
Gate

Double
Gate

South
Gate

0 yards 200
0 metres 200

Gla Palace

Citadel Wall

Megaron

0 yards 20
0 metres 20

Tiryns GREECE

Mycenaean fortress-palace
c. 1600–1100 BC

BIBLIOGRAPHY
Schliemann, H., *Tiryns*, London, 1886
Mylonas, G. E., *Mycenae and the Mycenaean Age*, Princeton, 1966

The fortified citadel of Tiryns crowns a limestone outcrop some eight miles (13 km) south east of Mycenae and a mile (1·6 km) from the sea. It commanded the route from the sea near Nafplion to Argos, Mycenae and the whole fertile Argive plain. Like MYCENAE, Tiryns was occupied throughout the Bronze Age, but although excavations showed that a large circular building stood on the higher, southern end of the outcrop in Early Helladic times (E.H. see table in Introduction), the surviving walls of Tiryns, already a byword in Homer, as well as the royal residence they protect, are all Mycenaean.

The first Mycenaean fortifications enclosed only the southern summit. In its final form the citadel had its main entrance by a ramp (A) on the east side, leading to an open gap through the outer wall. Once inside this, the visitor turned south between massive piles of masonry to a gate (B) similar in size and construction to the Lion Gate at Mycenae. Beyond it, a more decorative entrance (C) with columned porches without and within, gave upon a courtyard (D); and from this a similar gatehouse (E) led to the inner court, flanked on either side by columned porticoes and closed on the north by the *megaron* (F). Here the porch had an ornamental stone bench, and in the main hall the plaster floor was painted with octopuses and dolphins, the walls with a boar hunt and other scenes.

The tremendous walls on the east and south contained store chambers (K, K) opening off passages roofed with corbelled stone. To the west a bastion enclosed a narrow stair (L) winding down to a postern gate – the shortest way to water supplies outside the citadel. Against siege, however, two tunnel-like passages (M) through the west wall of the lower citadel led to hidden spring chambers.

The relation of Tiryns to Mycenae is interesting. In Homer it is not within the personal domain of Agamemnon, the commander-in-chief of the Greeks, who ruled from Mycenae. There are legends in which the two cities are at enmity. But it is difficult to believe that the two fortresses were not planned by a single authority, the more so because Tiryns commands the sea approach to the whole area.

Like Mycenae, Tiryns suffered severe damage in L.H. IIIB, but was not fully overthrown before the end of the Bronze Age. Even then the great walls remained a landmark, and like the Lion Gate at Mycenae have never been wholly lost to view. Greek tradition said that they were built by the Cyclopes, who were brought from Asia Minor for the work. Some influence from Hittite fortifications is not indeed improbable (see BOGHAZKÖY).

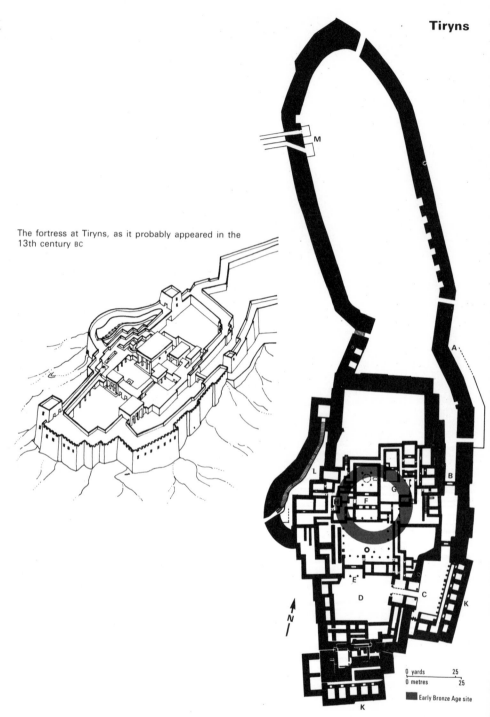

The fortress at Tiryns, as it probably appeared in the 13th century BC

Tiryns

0 yards 25
0 metres 25

■ Early Bronze Age site

Pylos GREECE

Mycenaean palace
13th century BC

BIBLIOGRAPHY
Blegen, C. W. et al., *The Palace of Nestor*, 2 vols., Princeton, 1966 and 1969
Mylonas, G. E., *Mycenae and the Mycenaean Age*, Princeton, 1966

The Mycenaean palace site identified as Pylos, the seat of the Homeric hero Nestor, and capital of the south-western Peloponnese, lies in the hill country at Ano Englianos, about three miles (5 km) from the coast and seven and a half miles (12 km) north of the classical and modern Pylos on the Bay of Navarino, of which it commands a fine view. The place was occupied from at least the Middle Helladic (M.H. see table in Introduction) period, but the palace itself, which is all that has been fully explored, belongs wholly to L.H. IIIB. Earlier in Mycenaean times the hilltop had been fortified, though not in the massive manner of MYCENAE and TIRYNS, and a gateway (R) is still identifiable at the east end; but these fortifications seem to have been dismantled by the 13th century BC.

As at Tiryns, the *megaron* (A) with a courtyard (B) before it, forms the focus of the buildings, with corridors and service rooms compactly arranged around. This is the best preserved of all Mycenaean palaces. The hall, with its huge flame-decorated hearth, and with marks where the throne stood against frescoed walls, makes it easy to imagine the place in its banqueting days. The picture is enhanced by the stores for oil (G) and wine (H), and by the vast number of wine cups in the pantries. Just within the entrance gate (C), to the left, is an office or archive room (D) in which were found hundreds of clay tablets inscribed in Linear B – the first major find of such writing in mainland Greece. East of the court is a group of rooms, including a bathroom (E) with built-in clay tub, perhaps intended as a guest

suite. South of them is a group identified as the queen's apartments (F). To the east of the main court and guest suite is an enclosed yard (K) in which a spout delivered water brought by some form of aqueduct (L) from a source perhaps a mile (1·6 km) away across a valley. The buildings (M) beyond this courtyard are probably workshops. West of the *megaron* complex, and perhaps rather earlier in date, is a large hall (N) with internal columns, approached from another court through a large entrance porch with pantries etc., beyond it on the north west.

Several beehive tombs have been excavated in the neighbourhood, the nearest of them lying only 300 feet (91 m) north east of the palace.

Pylos

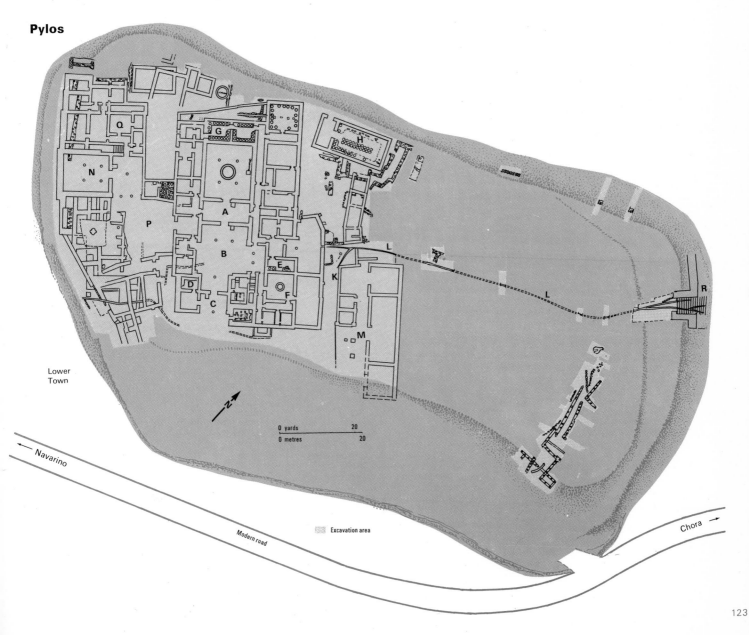

Lower
Town

0 yards   20
0 metres   20

Navarino

Modern road   Excavation area   Chora

Knossos CRETE

Prehistoric settlement and Minoan palace complex
c. 6000–1380 BC

BIBLIOGRAPHY
Evans, A. J., *The Palace of Minos at Knossos*, vols. I–IV,
  London, reprinted 1964
Pendlebury, J. D. S., *A Handbook to the Palace of Minos*,
  London, 1954
Hood, Sinclair, *The Minoans*, London, 1971

The Palace of Knossos stands on a low eminence about five miles (8 km) south and slightly east of Heraklion (Candia). It is in a saucer of gentle hills and is cut off from any sight of the sea. The Kairatos stream flows northward past the east side of the Palace in a little ravine. At its mouth there was a harbour town in Minoan times, and only two miles (3·2 km) to the east was the town of Amnisos, mentioned in the Odyssey as a landing place. It had many fine houses and was probably the main harbour for Knossos. To the south the peak of Mount Juktos shows above the Hill of Gypsades. This was the traditional burial place of the Cretan Zeus and there was a shrine on the summit.

The knoll was selected for a settlement as early as 6000 BC when some of the first Neolithic farmers to cross to Crete constructed huts and store pits there. Later a village of mudbrick houses was built and in time formed a tell above the natural rise. Remains of this earliest settlement can be seen in pits in the central court of the Palace.

Knossos has little to show from the Early Minoan Bronze Age (E.M. I–III, see table in Introduction) of the 3rd millennium BC, although the site was certainly inhabited during this time. In about 2000 BC, great social changes brought royal houses to power, and the first palaces were built here and at Phaistos and Mallia. This phase (later M.M. I–M.M. II some-

times called the Old Palace Age) has not left many conspicuous remains, chiefly because the old palace was engulfed by the later one – which seems to have been built on much the same plan. There are, however, foundations of houses to be seen in the West Court near the modern entrance and some masonry in the main palace.

It is generally accepted that the destruction of the three old palaces in about 1700 BC (M.M. IIB) was due to one of the violent earthquakes to which Crete is prone. Minoan civilization was by now coming to full flower and its creators were vigorous and prosperous enough to rebuild their towns and palaces and enter into their greatest age (M.M. III–L.M. II).

Knossos Palace

Almost all that is now to be seen of the Palace of Knossos dates from this last age of the New Palaces – and the reconstructions made by Sir Arthur Evans after his excavations at the beginning of the 20th century. During this period the royal house at Knossos established a hegemony over most of Crete.

The history of the final phase of the palace and its destruction are much disputed. One view is that most Minoan centres were destroyed by the great volcanic eruption on Thera in about 1450 BC, but that Knossos alone (surprisingly?) revived and continued to flourish, under Mycenaean Greek rule, until about 1380 when it was destroyed, perhaps again by earthquake. A minority view is that the Greeks took possession in about 1400 and that under them Knossos continued as a prosperous, essentially Mycenaean, palace state until about 1180 when it was destroyed by the Dorians. Whatever the true story may be, the Linear B writing tablets found in such number in the Palace leave virtually no doubt that the capital of Minoan Crete had been seized by Greek speakers from the mainland.

The labyrinthine nature of the ruins of Knossos struck later Greek visitors as it does present-day tourists. The essence of the plan, repeated in the other palace, is that it is inturned upon the great Central Court that runs north and south. This divides the Palace into two wings, a western and an eastern, that can themselves conveniently be divided into two parts. The west side of the court was given over to cult rooms – the famous Throne Room with its griffin frescoes and lustral tank, the Triple Shrine and the Pillar Rooms. Two staircases led up to a suite of state rooms on the first floor. Separated from this cultic centre by a north–south corridor are the western magazines still preserved with their huge storage jars (*pithoi*) and stone-lined storage 'boxes' let into the floors.

While the west wing is bisected by a north–south passage, in the east wing an east–west passage divides the royal apartments from the workshops and studios of the palace craftsmen that lay to the north. Foundations for the quarters of the king and queen were cut into the slope of the ancient tell, so that the back was two storeys below the Central Court, and had at least three, and probably four storeys. The architecture here, with its Grand Staircase, light wells and elaborate water supply and drainage is brilliantly original.

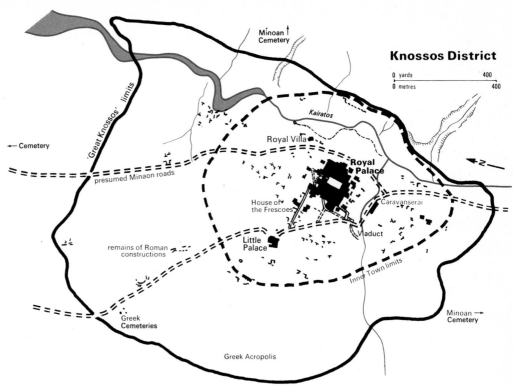

Knossos District

The palace had an entrance in each of its four sides. Most traffic probably came from the harbour road through the northern entrance and by the road from the south coast that approached the Palace along a monumental viaduct and a stepped portico. The western entrance, used by modern visitors, was certainly of ceremonial significance for it was linked with the 'theatre' at the end of the Sacred Way, and led past bull-leaping frescoes to the Corridor of the Procession where the walls displayed over 500 life-size figures of girls and young men bearing offerings.

Today the attention of the visitor is focused on the main Palace, but it should be imagined as the centre of a complex of buildings the remains of which can still be visited. The paved Sacred Way leads westward down to the so-called Little Palace, an elegant building that served ritual and ceremonial purposes; to the north east is the Royal Villa, in fact probably one of many houses of wealthy courtiers, while to the south is the Rest House or Caravanserai for both men and animals. Further to the south are the remains of the elaborate Temple Tomb, probably a royal mausoleum dating from late Middle Minoan times. Finally one has to picture the hill slopes (and notably those of Gypsades) covered with the clustering houses of the town, neat two or three-storey dwellings, some stonebuilt, some timber framed.

The originals of the Knossos frescoes, together with most other finds, are in the wonderful Archaeological Museum of Heraklion. The treasures from all the main Cretan sites are here – and this is where the unique spirit of Minoan civilization can best be understood.

Reconstruction of the Royal Palace at Knossos seen from the south east

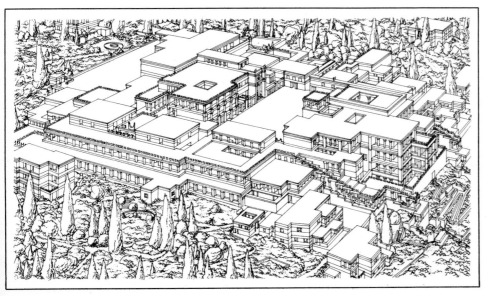

Tombs of Kamilari CRETE

Tholos tombs
c. 2700–1700 BC

BIBLIOGRAPHY
Branigan, Keith, *The Tombs of the Mesara*, London 1970
Levi, Doro, *La Tomba a Tholos di Kamilari*, Annuario della
Regia Scuola, pp. 39–40, Athens, 1962

The Kamilari tombs lie about 6 miles (9·6 km) south of Hagia Triada (PHAISTOS) and the same distance from the west coast of the projecting plain of the Mesara. They have been selected as the best-looking example of a class of *tholos* tombs the great majority of which are here in the Mesara, but which includes some outliers to the north and east.

These tombs can usefully be divided into two groups, an earlier one of E.M. I–II date (see table in Introduction), and a later one of E.M. III–M.M. I, built when the Mesara was losing the cultural lead it had enjoyed in the earlier period.

There is no Neolithic prototype for the *tholos* in Crete and foreign origins have therefore been sought – in Libya, the Cyclades and Anatolia, and even in Syria. It is equally uncertain whether the Cretan tombs can themselves provide an origin for the later Mycenaean *tholoi* of the mainland (MYCENAE). A good case can be made for it, despite the time gap between them.

In the Mesara the *tholoi* are almost invariably on high ground near a contemporary Minoan village. They served as burial places for the whole community, but as two or more might be in use together, it is possible that they belonged to clans.

The inside diameter of the chambers ranges from eight feet to 43 feet (2·4–13 m), the later group tending to be smaller than the earlier. Most are entered through an antechamber and a low doorway with large slabs for jambs and lintel. Sometimes, however, the jambs are of built masonry. Other rooms may adjoin the antechamber. Typically the walls have facings of unshaped stones filled with small stones and clay, but in rare instances the facing stones are shaped and laid in courses. The most disputed point is whether these tombs were true *tholoi* in the sense of having corbelled vaults. The most likely answer appears to be that the walls were indeed brought in by corbelling, but that the apex

was finished in wood. Possibly some of the small, late chambers had a complete stone vault.

The dead were buried with their heads to the east, accompanied by such personal possessions as jewelry, bronze tools and daggers and by male and female figurines. The very numerous cups and jugs may have been used by relatives for funerary 'toastings'. Old burials were treated with little respect, the bones being bundled into the antechamber or other ossuaries and the gravegoods looted. It seems that after the decay of the body the dead were regarded as spirits; their cult was associated with various aspects of the Cretan female deity, the symbols of the bull, double-axe, birds and horns of consecration appearing among the grave goods.

There are three tombs at Kamilari, interest focusing on the large Kamilari I with an inside diameter of 25 feet 1 inch (7·65 m); II has a diameter of 16 feet 5 inches (5 m); III is destroyed, but may have been partly built into the hillside. All belong to the later group, Kamilari I and III dating from M.M. I, and II possibly from as late as M.M. II. The large *tholos* has uniquely fine masonry, the facing stones carefully shaped and bonded, the courses regular; the door is exactly built and closed with a big slab. The walls still stand to a height of six feet six inches (2 m) and are conspicuously corbelled in. Next to the antechamber there is a rectangular building with several rooms and part of what may have been an enclosure wall.

The finds made in Kamilari I are as remarkable as its structure. It seems that up to 500 bodies had been buried and there were over a thousand pottery cups. Personal possessions included scraps of gold jewelry and many sealstones. Most exceptional were rough clay models of ritual enactments, including four figures ring-dancing on a base bearing horns of consecration. Kamilari II yielded a bronze double-axe, apparently ritually broken.

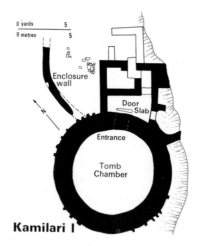

Kamilari I

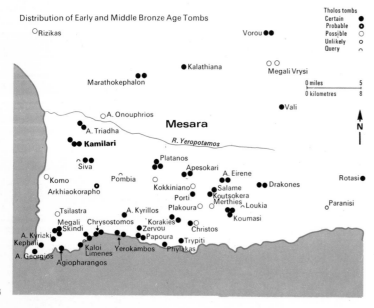

Distribution of Early and Middle Bronze Age Tombs

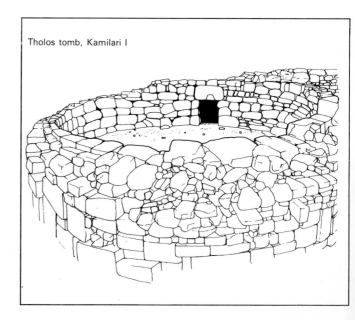

Tholos tomb, Kamilari I

Mallia CRETE

Minoan palace
c. 2000–1450 BC

BIBLIOGRAPHY
Charpouthier, F., Demargne, P., reports by these and others in *Études Crétoises*, Paris from 1928 onwards
Tiré, C. and van Effenterre, H., *Guide des Fouilles Francaises en Crète*, Paris, 1966
Marmatos, S., *Crete and Mycenae*, London, 1960

The third in size of the four principal Minoan palaces lies close to the sea 20 miles (32 km) due east of KNOSSOS. It is on a strip of fertile coastal plain, near the foot of hills that run up to the heights of Dicte. As, unlike Knossos and Phaistos, its name was not recorded by Homer or other Greek tradition, this Palace has been called after a small modern town a mile to the west. To the south is the Hill of the Prophet Elias which seems to have had a Minoan sanctuary on its summit.

The French excavators and some of their followers have claimed that Mallia still represents the character of the old, Middle Minoan (M.M., see table in Introduction), building, most of the rooms having been merely adapted and re-used after 1700 BC. There is little evidence for this, but it is true that the architecture tends to be simple, largely lacking such advanced features as light wells.

Although the Palace has the regular north–south Central Court, the arrangement of quarters round it shows the freedom of the royal architects to vary their plans. The east side was occupied by store rooms with an elegant portico masking their fronts. The north had a simpler portico and behind it a columned hall and open courts. The west wing was the most important, with the royal apartments to the north, the main cult rooms in the centre and tiers of shallow steps (corresponding to the 'theatres' at Knossos and PHAISTOS) on the south. Nearby is a large circular limestone table with a ring of small depressions on the outer rim and a larger one in the centre. It is usually regarded as an offering table for the rites of the goddess, but may have been used for a game of religious purport. Another unique feature is the sunken altar in the middle of the Court. Eight stone-built, cylindrical containers in the south-west

corner of the Palace are often called cisterns but are more likely to have been granaries – following an Egyptian model.

There are entrances from the south and south east, but the most striking approach is by Sea Street, a paved way adorned with huge *pithoi*, leading into the north wing of the Palace.

To the north west of the Palace, under a plastic roof, is a series of semi-basement rooms, the chambers at each end surrounded by benches. This may possibly have been an assembly place for the councillors of Mallia.

A variety of houses, some dating back to M.M. times, have been excavated in the Minoan town. On its north-east edge is a large rectangular tomb which probably belonged to the royal family. In one of the small internal compartments was found the famous golden bee pendant dating from late M.M. times.

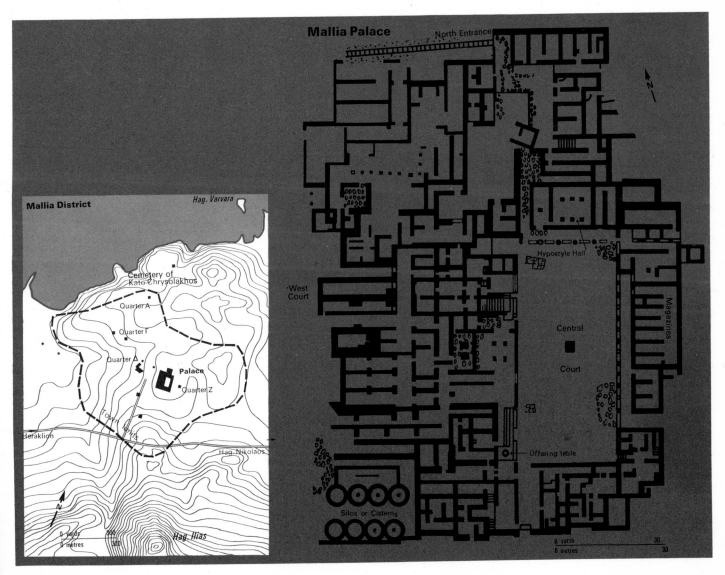

Mallia Palace
North Entrance
West Court
Hypostyle Hall
Central Court
Magazines
Offering table
Silos or Cisterns

Mallia District
Hag. Varvara
Cemetery of Kato Chrysolakhos
Quarter A
Quarter Γ
Quarter Δ
Palace
Quarter Z
Heraklion
Hag. Nikolaos
Hag. Ilias

Phaistos and Hagia Triada CRETE

Minoan palace
c. 2000–1450 BC

BIBLIOGRAPHY
Levi, Doro, *The Recent Excavations at Phaistos*, Lund, 1964

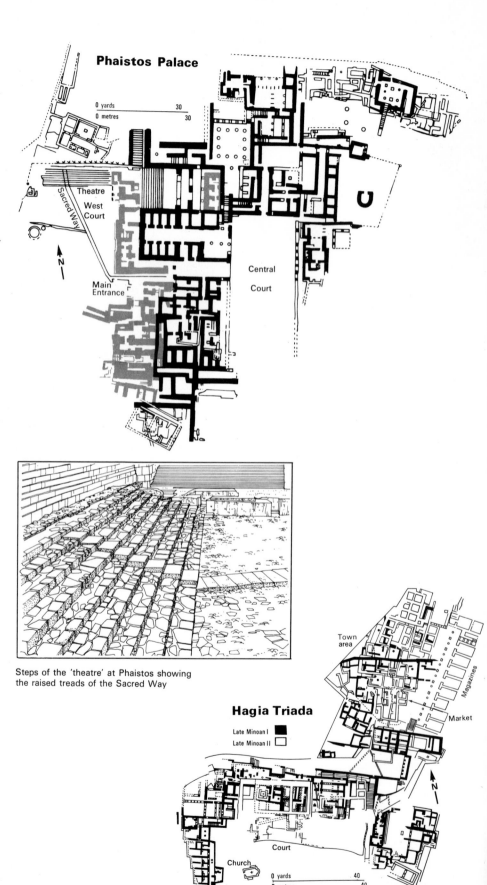

Phaistos Palace

Steps of the 'theatre' at Phaistos showing the raised treads of the Sacred Way

Hagia Triada

Late Minoan I
Late Minoan II

This Palace has a much finer situation than that of KNOSSOS. It stands on the edge of a hill with a splendid view of the fertile plain of Mesara to the east and of Ida and its range to the north. The Geropotamos, the largest stream in Crete, flows past its northern side to reach the sea some four miles (6·4 km) to the west.

Phaestos was second in size to Knossos and had in many ways a similar history. Here, too, there was a Neolithic settlement mound that was levelled for the building of a first palace in about 2000 BC. The destruction in about 1700 BC appears to have been even more complete for the ruins were flattened and covered with broken tiles before the new palace was built over them. In the ensuing period this capital of the south came under the control of Knossos. The final destruction seems to have coincided with that of MALLIA and KATO ZAKRO in about 1450 BC.

In spite of the total destruction, excavation has revealed a considerable part of the Old Palace, particularly the paved West Court, the foundations of the western façade with its south-west angle and what appears to be a small shrine in the north-east corner of this court.

Today the most striking remains at Phaistos are the Sacred Way diagonally crossing the West Court and running on raised treads up the steps of the 'theatre'; the adjacent broad flight of steps leading to the upper floor of the main royal apartments and a porticoed court that may have been the royal garden. The residential quarter of the palace may have been set here to the north west of the Central Court in contrast with the south-east position at Knossos to allow cool winds from Ida to relieve the intense summer heat.

The rooms of the Palace were not frescoed, very few treasures and no tablets were found there (other than the famous Phaistos Disk with its spiral of unknown script); the magazines were small and poor. Some authorities therefore believe that it was never finished. An explanation may be found in the 'Villa' of Hagia Triada (Holy Trinity) two miles (3·2 km) to the west. This place was so sumptuous that it can be assumed to have been a royal dwelling. It may have been built after the destruction of the Old Palace at Phaistos and in fact to have been the residence at the time of the final destruction. Certainly it was charmingly frescoed, contained many treasures including a great hoard of copper ingots, and had a record office.

The area seems to have recovered its prosperity some time after the destruction of Palace and Villa, perhaps under Mycenaean occupation. From this period dates a large hall, the ruins of which overlie the site of the residence at Hagia Triada, and also a big store and market to the north of it. Of this same post-Palace age is the famous Hagia Triada sarcophagus with funerary scenes that best reveal Minoan ritual – with priests, priestesses, musicians, bull sacrifice and the symbols of the doubleaxe and horns of consecration. This and other finds are in the Archaeological Museum of Heraklion.

128

Kato Zakro CRETE

Minoan palace
c. 1700–1450 BC

BIBLIOGRAPHY
Platon, Nicolas, *Crete*, London, 1971
Hood, Sinclair, *The Minoans*, London, 1971, pp. 65–7

The Palace of Zakro is the most easterly of all major Minoan sites. It lies on the lower slopes at the end of the mountain spine, with a deep ravine running behind it to the west. It overlooks the neat little bay of Zakro after which it has been named. The sight of this natural anchorage opening its arms to the seaways and the Levant evokes thoughts of maritime trade – and indeed Zakro certainly became an important port. Copper ingots found in the Palace most probably came from Cyprus, elephant tusks from Syria.

Zakro was the last of the four palaces to be excavated (during the 1960's) and was also the last to have been established. Although there was much early settlement in the region, the Palace seems to date from the period after 1700 BC. Its final destruction in about 1450 BC appears to have been by burning; for some reason it had not been so thoroughly evacuated or looted as most other establishments and many marvellous finds, particularly of cult vessels, have been made there.

One characteristic of Zakro not brought out by the plan is the fact that while the Central Court and the western wing are on relatively level ground the buildings to the north mount a steep slope. It is the smallest of the four palaces – as indicated by the fact that the Central Court is 98 feet (30 m) long in comparison with the 171 feet (52 m) of KNOSSOS and PHAISTOS and the 164 feet (50 m) of MALLIA. The layout comes closest to that of Knossos, for the royal apartments are to the east of the Court and the state and cult rooms, including a shrine (A) and large Lustral Basin (B), to the west. Many of the ritual vessels were found in rectangular bins of hard mudbrick, now restored. On one side of this treasury is the shrine, and on the other a little room (C) where Linear A inscribed tablets had been kept in wooden boxes. To the north of the court was a kitchen with a dining hall over it and adjacent stores for food, oil and wine. A two-storey block to the south served as a pottery store and also probably as workshops for craftsmen in stone, ivory and faience.

One cult vessel, a *rhyton* of carved chlorite, must be mentioned for its unique architectural interest. It shows one of the peak sanctuaries that were probably the chief holy places of the Cretans during their Palace era. Nobly horned mountain goats flank the peak, lying on the high centre part of a triple shrine – similar to the one facing the Central Court at Knossos. Masonry, horns of consecration, sacred pillars and an altar table are clearly shown.

Kato Zakro

steeply rising ground

Kitchen

Central
Court

C A B

West
Wing

Treasury

0 yards 20

0 metres 20

Gournia CRETE

Minoan Town
17th–12th centuries BC

BIBLIOGRAPHY
Hawes, H. D., *Gournia, Vasiliki and other Prehistoric Sites on the Isthmus of Hierapetra*, Philadelphia, 1903
Marinatos, S., *Crete and Mycenae*, London, 1960. References in this and most other general works on Cretan archaeology

The compact little town of Gournia covers the crown and slopes of a low hill on the isthmus formed by the Bay of Mirabello. Backed by craggy mountains to the south it commands a view of the great Bay and its cliffs.

The ruins make a totally different impression from those of the palatial sites, for, apart from the large house on the summit, these are the streets and dwellings of artisans and other humble people. The place has a rough and rustic air, chiefly because there is little ashlar masonry to be seen, the walls and paving being of unshaped stone. It should be remembered, however, that the houses were neatly plastered, and this, the most completely preserved of Minoan towns, would have been as seemly as many Mediterranean hill towns of today.

Gournia seems to have been founded only after the disaster of 1700 BC and to have been destroyed in that of c. 1450. It was, however, at least partially reoccupied after the period of the Mycenaean Greek rule in KNOSSOS and new houses then built on the edge of the town are thought to show mainland influence.

The street plan was based on an upper road round the top of the hill connected with a lower road circling the extensive east quarter of the town. Very narrow cross streets, sometimes stepped, ran between them.

Along these narrow but carefully paved streets the houses were close packed. They had up to five or six small rooms on the ground floor and might have upper floors reached by outside steps. It is thought that in some houses the ground floor served only as a basement store. In one dwelling a carpenter's kit was found; others were identified with potters, bronzesmiths and oil pressers.

The large building that dominated the town from the hilltop is sometimes described as a palace, sometimes as a governor's house. It is badly preserved, partly because ashlar masonry was taken from it for building the houses of the final occupation. It had a big entrance hall and magazines along the west side against the road. The main entrance was from a spacious square, identified as a public market and meeting place. At the top of the hill, a little to the north of the palace, but approached from a public street stood a one-roomed shrine that was found complete with its ritual furniture, including a snake-entwined clay idol of the Goddess, and ritual stands with snakes and horns of consecration. The shrine itself dates from before 1450 but the furnishings may be later.

Near Gournia are two historically important sites dating back to Early Minoan times before 2000 BC: the port of Mochlos on the east side of the Bay of Mirabello and the settlement and proto-palace of Vasiliki, four miles (6·4 km) to the south east.

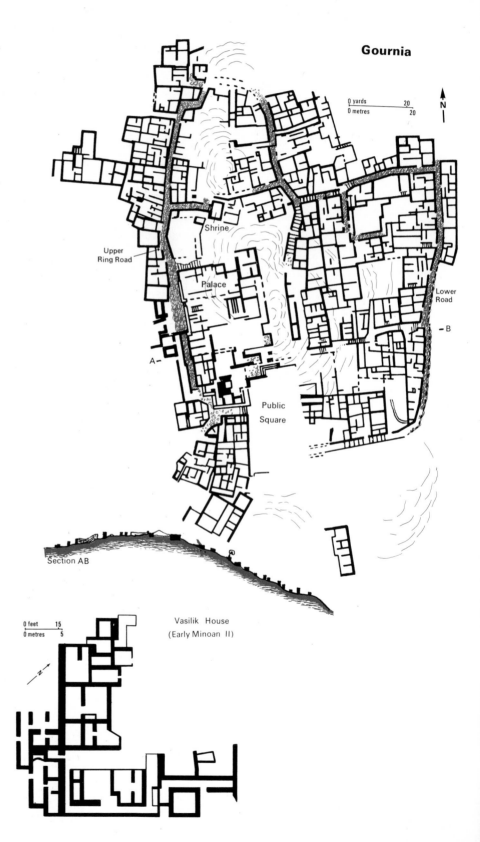

Gournia

Shrine

Upper
Ring Road

Palace

Lower
Road

A—

—B

Public
Square

Section AB

Vasilik House
(Early Minoan II)

ANATOLIA AND
SOVIET ARMENIA

Anatolia is the name now generally applied to the entire Asiatic territory of the Turkish Republic. An approximate rectangle, almost a thousand miles (approx. 1600 km) long, it consists of a central plateau, separated by mountains from coastal plains and valleys, with highland country in the east of which Soviet Armenia is an extension. Thus, geography and climatic differences have created natural divisions in the country, which, until recent times, obstructed its political unification and are reflected in its regional history.

The art of writing was unknown in Anatolia until the 19th century BC, when the cuneiform script was introduced from Mesopotamia. In the absence of written records, however, the movements and character of its more ancient peoples have been partially reconstructed from archaeological evidence. Their anonymity has been remedied by the use of convenient labels and a prehistoric chronology formulated in accordance with archaeological convention. The earliest phase in the transition from hunting to food producing is now referred to as Proto-Neolithic and appears to have begun in about 9000 BC. In Anatolia it is represented only by rock shelters in a restricted area near Antalya. More plentiful are traces of early farming communities, characteristic of a true Neolithic culture, which reached maturity about two millennia later. Located by deep soundings at Mersin, Tarsus, Sakjegözi and elsewhere, these at first seemed to be confined to the fringes of the so-called Fertile Crescent east of Taurus. But the more recent discovery of two sites, Hacilar and ÇATAL HÜYÜK on the plateau itself, have revealed the full and remarkable development of this culture in Anatolia during the 7th and 6th millennia BC. A pastoral and agricultural economy, supplemented by hunting, was already represented at the second site by a socially well-organized township, precociously advanced craftsmanship and the paraphernalia of religious ritual.

In Anatolia the Chalcolithic Age, which occupied the remainder of the 6th millennium BC, the whole of the 5th and much of the 4th, was notable for the growth and wide distribution of agricultural societies, now related by trade or migration with other countries of the Near East. Its principal innovations included the ornamentation of pottery with painted designs, and the smelting of copper to make small implements, now used alongside their flint or obsidian prototypes. Throughout the southern provinces, from Cilicia to the upper Tigris, pottery sequences resemble those of Mesopotamia and North Syria, but at plateau sites like Hacilar, painted ornament seems to acquire a vitality of its own and clay figurines show a remarkable talent for modelling. At Mersin (Level XVI), a settlement is systematically planned as a military fortress, with slit-windows in its defensive walls and standard accommodation for the garrison. The Early Bronze Age, which accounts for the 3rd millennium BC, shows an even more formidable advance in technology, as well as social and political organization. Regional divisions have now become apparent and a pattern of separate provinces can be distinguished, each controlled by a native dynasty. Advanced metallurgy and improved trading facilities have contributed to the accumulation of material wealth in their metropolitan centres. Archaeologically this is illustrated by the more spectacular finds at representative sites; 'treasures' of luxury articles, contrived from precious metals and rare materials, supplementing the evidence of civic planning and monumental architecture. Thus at TROY, huge *megaron* buildings and Priam's Treasure (which may or may not be associated with the controversial Dorak Treasure from Lake Apollyont), emphasize the importance of a north-western province: the wealth of a central Anatolian province is proved by the contents of the famous Royal Tombs at ALACA HÜYÜK and Mahmutlar: a south-west province centres around BEYCE-SULTAN, with its religious installations. Other provinces, less well defined, include Cilicia, which has plateau connections through the Taurus passes, and in the extreme east, a highland province, first identified at Karaz near the sources of the Euphrates, is now linked with early settlements found by Russian archaeologists in the Ararat

Plain and in the Kura–Araxes valleys, at which an Early Trans-Caucasian culture has been recognized during the 3rd millennium BC.

The Middle Bronze Age (*c.* 1900–1600 BC) is notable for the appearance of Assyrian merchant colonies on the outskirts of several Anatolian cities, including Kanesh (KÜLTEPE), and their introduction of written records. At Kültepe many thousands of cuneiform tablets have been found in the Assyrian karum (merchants' meeting place), and others with an historical content in the palaces of the indigenous (Khattian) rulers on the main mound. The merchants' houses too have produced fine examples of contemporary craftsmanship, including engraved cylinder seals, which were now used in Anatolia for the first time. All the evidence suggests that in Anatolia the Assyrians found themselves in contact with a culturally sophisticated people; a pattern of city states with common political conventions and religious beliefs.

The form of certain names in the Kültepe tablets first indicates the arrival in Anatolia of an Indo-European people subsequently known to history as the Hittites. Their infiltration from the north east seems to have taken place during the century preceding 1750 BC, by which time they can be seen to have become a dominant military caste, controlling important cities in Cappadocia and the 'bend' of the Halys river. (All of the peninsula to the south and west of these provinces was already occupied by an

immigrant people called Luvians, speaking a different Indo-European dialect, with which the so-called Hittite hieroglyphs are associated.) During the century which followed, a dynasty of Hittite rulers was founded, with its capital at Hattusas (Boǧhazköy). The history of the Hittites, customarily divided into an Old Kingdom and an Empire period, is intermittently recorded in their own Neshite language on the tablets constituting their national archive, discovered at Boǧhazköy earlier in the present century. Hittite kings boasted of their campaigns against the rival powers of Mesopotamia and Egypt, but they also referred to neighbour states in Anatolia: Kizzuvadna which is Cilicia, Lukka Lands including Lycia, Arzawa and Assuwa in the hinterland of the Aegean coast, as well as a people called Ahhiyawans who have been equated with Homer's Achaeans.

The Empire of the Hittites ceased to exist in about 1200 BC. They were swept from their homeland on the plateau by Phrygian invaders from south-east Europe, the remains of those settlements and fortresses have been found by excavators, overlying the ruins of older Hittite cities. One of these is Gordion on the Sangarius (Sakarya) river which they made their capital. From the 11th century BC, fugitive Hittites reappear as part-occupants of small city states in Taurus and North Syria, previously outposts of their own empire. Carchemish on the Euphrates was the most important of these; but excavations at Sam'al (Zincirli), Sakjegozi, Malatya and more recently at Karatepe in the Cilician foothills, have produced architecture and sculpture testifying to the ephemeral prosperity of these Neo-Hittite states. For a time, their most reliable ally against the military threat from Assyria was the east Anatolian state called Urartu; a kingdom at first centred on Lake Van, but later extended by conquest to include large parts of what are now Soviet Armenia and Azarbaijan. Here again, excavations in our own time have produced evidence of a powerful and technologically advanced people, whose history could be reconstructed from cuneiform inscriptions in their own language on rock faces and fine masonry façades. Their art owed something to that of Assyria, but their buildings, skilfully adapted to the more dramatic background of alpine scenery, created an architectural precedent. In classical times, their country became the homeland of the Armenians.

Troy TURKEY

Walled city
c. 3000–300 BC

BIBLIOGRAPHY
Blegen, C. W., *Troy*, 4 vols., Princetown, 1950–8
Blegen, C. W., *Troy and the Trojans*, London, 1963
Akurgal, E., *Ancient Civilizations and Ruins of Turkey*, Istanbul, 1969 and 1970, p. 47 ff
Lloyd, Seton, *Early Highland Peoples of Anatolia*, London, 1967

The mound called Hissarlik, commonly identified with the site of Homeric Troy (Truva in Turkish) is 20 miles (32 km) south west of Çanakkale, from where it can be reached by motor road. It covers a low shoulder of rock overlooking the marshy valley of a river known to history as the Scamander (Küçük Menderez), which reaches the sea three miles (4·8 km) away. From the top of the mound the view is impressive. With Mount Ida behind and the 'Plain of Troy' in the foreground, one sees beyond almost the entire setting of the Dardanelles campaign in 1915, from Imbros to 'the Narrows'. As for the site itself, 19 years of excavation have left a tangle of fragmentary walls which the most well-informed guide must find difficulty in identifying.

Schliemann's deep trenching, which involved the destruction of so much archaeological evidence, lasted from 1870 to 1890, and was resumed more methodically by Dorpfeld in 1893–5. Dorpfeld recognized nine principal periods of occupation, and these, divided into no less than 30 subphases, formed the basis of Carl Blegen's stratigraphical conclusions, after his scientific re-excavation of the site from 1932 to 1938. Today, little is to be gained by recollecting Schliemann's predictably naive interpretations of what he found, since the history of the fortress, from its first foundation in about 3000 BC, is now reasonably well known. The main occupations are numbered from the bottom upwards. The Troy I settlement was less than 295 feet (90 m) in diameter, but it boasted a substantial enclosure wall, with a single gateway flanked by stone towers, one of which remains standing to a height of four feet eleven inches (1·5 m). Buildings inside already provide at least one example of the *megaron* plan, long afterwards adapted by the Greeks for their temples. The city walls were slightly extended during the Troy II period, which represents the second phase of the Early Bronze Age (2500–2200 BC), and the strongly protected south gateway is at times supplemented by others, again reflecting the *megaron* plan. A very large *megaron*, whose timber roof must have spanned almost 30 feet (9·1 m), served as a council chamber, and, buried beneath the floor of a palace to the south west of this, Schliemann found the nine caches or hoards of gold jewelry and other objects, which he fancifully called Priam's Treasure.

Most of it disappeared in Berlin during the second World War. The most obvious signs of prosperity and aggrandisement were found in the Late Bronze Age fortress, Troy VI (1800–1300 BC), the finely built stone substructure of whose walls are in part still standing. It is thought to have been destroyed during an earthquake, though its walls were rebuilt in Troy VIIA, which Blegen considered to be contemporary with the events of the Homeric legend. Many of the Troy VIIA buildings were demolished when the summit of the mound was relevelled for rebuilding in classical times. Those which survive enigmatically suggest a much impoverished settlement.

This is not the only enigma connected with Hissarlik. The area enclosed by the VIIA fortress still hardly exceeded five acres (2 hectares) and can hardly be thought to have accommodated the 50,000 soldiers of Priam and his allied armies. Schliemann indeed found traces of a substantial wall enclosing a greatly extended outer town, which he called Ilium (an alternative name for Troy in the *Iliad*): but this could be dated no earlier than Hellenistic times. Here we see one of the main problems which the excavations have posed. Another is the dates, varying between 1250 and 1180 BC, which different scholars attribute to the Trojan War, unmentioned in Hittite records.

Troy

Troy I
Troy II
Troy VI
Troy IX

Great Hall
Private Houses
Temple of Athena
Palace (Royal Residence)
Old Gate (blocked up)
Servants Quarters
Pithoi (jars)
Fortified Gateway
Tower
Pillar Hall
Theatre B
Sanctuary
Bouleuterion
Theatre C

N

0 yards 50
0 metres 50

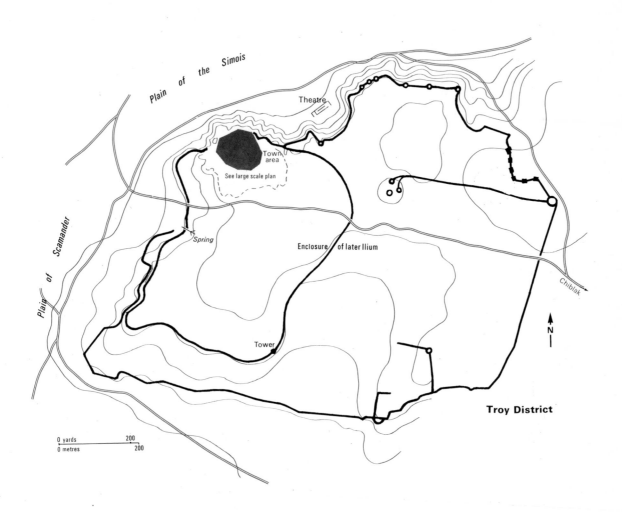

Plain of the Simois

Theatre

Plain of Scamander

Spring

Town
area
See large scale plan

Enclosure of later Ilium

Chiblak

Tower

N

Troy District

0 yards   200
0 metres   200

Kültepe TURKEY

City mound and adjacent suburb
c. 2300–700 BC

BIBLIOGRAPHY
Ozguc, Tahsin, *Kültepe-Kanis*, Turkish Historical Society
  Ankara, 1959
Lloyd, Seton, *Early Highland Peoples of Anatolia*, London
  1967

Kültepe (ancient Kanesh), which has proved one of the most productive and historically important sites on the Anatolian plateau, is reached by car from Kayseri. Twelve miles (19 km) out on the main road to Sivas, a track turning left across the railway on its way to the modern village passes close to the foot of an enormous mound created by the ruins of the Hattian city. This was at first thought to be the source of the famous Cappadocian tablets by which scholars were so greatly intrigued in the early years of the present century. It was not until 1925 that Hrozny traced them to an outlying suburb of the city, now covered by cultivated fields, where a colony of Assyrian merchants had established themselves during the early centuries of the 2nd millennium BC. The tablets were their business archives.

Hrozny's excavations at Kültepe have been resumed during the past two decades by the Turkish archaeologist Tahsin Özguc, both in the commercial colony (*karum*) and in the city mound itself. Many hundreds of tablets have been added to the Assyrian archives, and historical documents of even greater importance have been recovered from the palaces and other public buildings of the city's native Anatolian rulers. The Kanesh *karum* was one of several similar stations, established by the expanding kingdom of Ashur, to facilitate the exchange of its own products against metal ores and other raw materials obtainable in Anatolia. Its status resembled that of a chamber of commerce, through the authority of which prices could be fixed, debts settled and transport arranged by caravans of donkeys. The contents of the tablets create a lively picture of the various activities involved. The quarters allotted to the merchants by their foreign neighbours, with whom they were on friendly terms, were annexed to the town by an enclosure wall which increased its total area to almost 125 acres (50 hectares). The character of their timber-framed buildings – warehouses, offices and dwellings – can be gathered from the excavated ruins themselves or from many published reconstructions. Their contents included fine examples of

contemporary craftsmanship: brightly ornamented polychrome pottery, later giving way to the graceful shapes of 'red burnished ware'; objects in bronze or more precious metals from graves; terracotta rhytons in grotesque animal forms; figurines or stone plaques carved in relief with religious scenes, and above all, an abundance of cylinder seals with regionally peculiar designs, in which the mythical imagery of the Plateau alternates with that of other countries linked to it by trade.

Historical events in Assyria mentioned in the *karum* tablets have helped to establish its chronology. Early occupations of the suburb (Levels IV and III) predate the arrival of the Assyrians, of whose presence there begins to be ample evidence in about 1950 BC (Level II). A hundred years later the *karum* was destroyed by fire, but continued to exist on a diminished scale for a further century (Level IB), after which (1750 BC) some more serious disaster put an end to its activities. Coinciding with its final disappearance was the destruction of public buildings on the main mound, including the palace of a native king called Anitta, who had made Kanesh his capital, and whose name was associated by the Hittites with the beginnings of their own history.

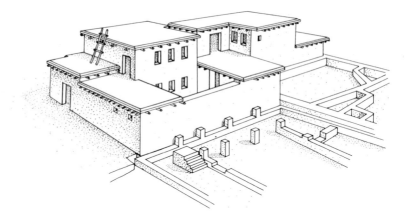

Reconstruction of Assyrian Merchants' house
in the *Karum* at Kültepe

Karatepe TURKEY

Citadel
8th century BC

BIBLIOGRAPHY
Bossert, H. T., Cambal, H. and Alkim, U. B., Excavation
    reports in the Turkish Historical Society *Belleten*, 1946
    and 1967
Lloyd, Seton, *Early Anatolia*, Harmondsworth, 1956

In an attractive setting among the wooded foothills
which rise behind the coastal plain of Adana, within
sight of the Ceyhan river, a local ruler in the 8th
century BC built himself a modest fortress and
decorated its two gateways with sculptures. In 1945,
the location of its ruins was pointed out by a Turkish
schoolmaster to two archaeologists, Bossert and
Alkim, and in 1947, after clearing away much scrub-
oak and undergrowth, they were able to make a
sensational discovery. They had exposed a gateway,
flanked on either side by guardian figures in the
form of paired lions. Their surface, and that of the
adjoining stone slabs, were covered by long inscriptions, identically worded, one in the familiar script
of the Phoenicians and the other in the so-called
Hittite hieroglyphs, which had hitherto proved un-
decipherable. Like the Rosetta Stone, this could
provide access to a whole new literature, represented by some hundreds of inscriptions found
elsewhere.

Excavations which took place during the following years revealed well-preserved lines of sculptured
wall slabs in the gate-chambers. Depicted on these
was a bewildering variety of subjects and, although
quite ambitious scenes such as a banquet or a sea
battle were attempted, their design and workmanship were uneven in quality to say the least of it,
and there appeared to be little coherence in the
arrangement of the slabs. Traces of three main
stylistic influences have since been detected in them.
One is the Anatolian culture of the Hittite Empire,
now hardly more than a waning memory; the second
is Egyptian influence acquired through the medium
of Phoenician art; and the third that of Assyrian
traditions, with which these Iron Age principalities
were increasingly in contact.

Compatible with the hybrid character of these
sculptures is a passage in the bilingual inscription
itself, in which the builder of the fortress, a prince
called Azitawandas, gives particulars of his own
political status and genealogy. He appears to be a
vassal of the King of Adana, or (in the Phoenician
text) of the Danunians, a people who have been
equated by historians with the Homeric Greeks. He
claims, furthermore, to be a descendant of the individual called Mopsus, whom Greek tradition
credits with the foundation of several Greek colonies
in south-west Asia Minor before or after the Trojan
War. Since Mopsus is also mentioned in Hittite
records of the reign of Arnuwandas III (1220 BC
onwards), he has fairly been described as 'the first
figure of Greek mythology to emerge into historic
reality'.

Within its defensive wall, the citadel at Karatepe
measures about 980 feet (300 m) in diameter. Excavations within its gates have produced some further
sculpture and inscriptions, together with domestic
objects typical of the 8th century BC. The Turkish
excavators also extended their investigations to a
neighbouring site called Domuztepe, which, unlike
Karatepe, proves to have been already occupied in
the 12th century BC and could therefore well have
been a small city founded by the Greek ancestors of

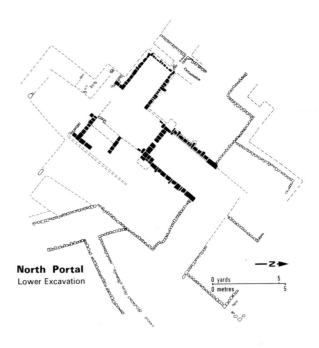

North Portal
Lower Excavation

0 yards 5
0 metres 5

→N→

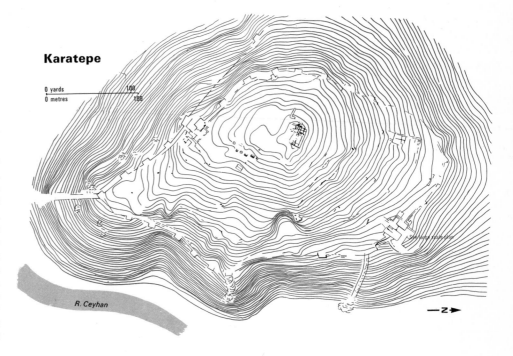

Karatepe

0 yards 100
0 metres 100

R. Ceyhan

→N→

Azitawandas. But none of these finds rivalled in importance his portal sculptures with their inscriptions. Where necessary the reliefs have now been
restored to their original positions and are exhibited
beneath protective roofing. Modern visitors, travelling 52 miles (84 km) from Adana by road, may
therefore study the eccentricity of their designs in
an authentic setting.

Gordion TURKEY

City mound and burial tumuli
c. 1700–8th century BC

BIBLIOGRAPHY
Young, Rodney S., excavation reports published annually
   in *American Journal of Archaeology*
Akurgal, E., *Ancient Civilizations and Ruins of Turkey*, p.
   47 ff
Lloyd, Seton, *Early Highland Peoples of Anatolia*, London,
   1967

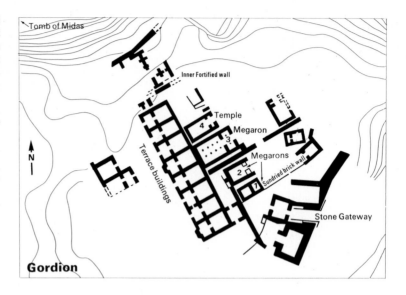

Gordion

Gordion, capital city of the Phrygians, is situated 12 miles (19 km) north west of Polatli, on the left bank of the Sakarya (ancient Sangarius) river. The city mound itself measures 1,640 feet by 1,150 feet (500 × 350 m), and from its flat summit one obtains a view of the surrounding valley, with its many burial tumuli dating from Phrygian and later times. The most prominent of these is that known traditionally as the Tomb of Midas, a vast mound of earth still standing to a height of over 165 feet (50 m). R. S. Young's excavations for the University Museum of Pennsylvania, begun in 1950, have been mainly concentrated on the Phrygian levels in the main mound, with an interval in 1955, during which the Great Tumulus was investigated and its tomb chamber exposed.

The city excavations have involved much labour, since later occupations in Hellenistic and Achaemenian times had first to be studied and a sounding made elsewhere in the Hittite levels beneath. Eventually, however, an extensive area of the Phrygian city, dating from the 8th century BC, has been completely cleared. It is approached by a formidable stone gateway, deeply recessed between towers in the city wall. Facing successive courtyards inside are public buildings with timber-framed walls on a stone socle, mostly conforming to the *megaron* plan, consisting merely of a 'hall' and 'portico'. In the first court, Megaron 2 was paved with a geometrically patterned mosaic of coloured pebbles; the earliest known example of this technique. Its gabled façade was crowned by an *acroterion* ornament and two limestone heads of lions, which have survived. The largest building of all, measuring 98 feet by 59 feet (30 × 18 m), is Megaron 3 in the second court, whose side galleries and roof were supported on tall wooden posts. Megaron 4, which Young identified as a temple, stood upon its own, slightly raised terrace. The excavated group is completed by a range of eight large and identical megara, facing south west.

In 1955, after experimenting with smaller tumuli, Young turned his attention to the Tomb of Midas. He located the actual burial chamber by drilling vertically from above; then approached it by a tunnel at plain level. Measuring 20 feet by 17 feet (6·2 × 5·2 m), its walls and roof principals were constructed from huge balks of juniper wood, up to two feet (61 cm) thick, and an outer stone wall supported a covering mound of stone rubble. Inside the tomb, the skeleton of a man, about 60 years old and only five feet three inches (1·6 m) tall, lay among the decayed coverlets of a collapsed bed. Around him was tomb furniture, including nine wooden tables and two screens with skilfully inlaid ornament; a bronze *situla* (ritual bucket) of an Assyrian type, in the form of a lion's head; three huge bronze cauldrons on tripods, of Urartian design; 166 smaller bronze vessels; strange wall ornaments, or perhaps horse trappings, of embossed leather, and 145 bronze *fibulae* (ornamental safety pins). One strange aspect of the tomb, in view of the Midas legend, was that it contained no single object

of gold or, for that matter, silver. The only personal ornaments were the *fibulae*, more than 70 of which had been contained in a linen bag. The excavator himself is loth to believe that the burial could have been made *after* the Cimmerian conquest of Phrygia, during which Midas is said to have committed suicide. He prefers to think of the tumulus as the resting place of an earlier king, Gordios, who died between 725 and 720 BC.

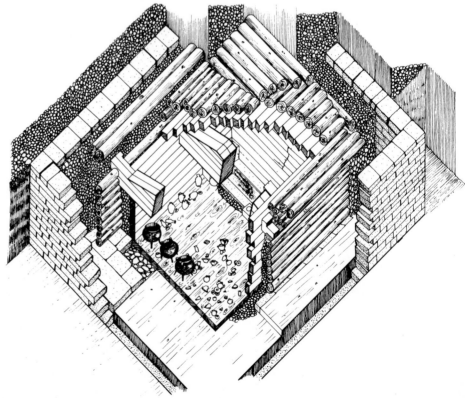

Burial chamber in the Tomb of Midas at Gordion, sectioned to show interior

Çatal Hüyük TURKEY

Neolithic township
c. 6500–5700 BC

BIBLIOGRAPHY
Mellaart, J., *Çatal Hüyük: A Neolithic Town in Anatolia*,
London, 1967

To the south east of Konya on the Anatolian plateau, a wide expanse of fertile farmland is irrigated in part by the Çarsamba Çay, a stream which flows out into the plain near the town of Çumra, carrying the surplus waters of the Beysehir Lake. As might be expected, the water courses of this Konya Plain are punctuated by the remains of ancient settlements, one of which, 13 miles (21 km) north east of Çumra, is the double mound called Çatal Hüyük. Its eastern part represents an occupation by Neolithic people from the mid-7th millennium until about 5700 BC, and its excavation by J. Mellaart in the years 1961–3 may be said to have transformed our whole conception of human life and behaviour in that period.

In the first place, the settlement is no mere village, but a township covering an area of over 15 acres (6 hectares), (three times the size of Homeric Troy). The houses, of sun-dried brick, were arranged contiguously like the cells of a honeycomb and entered by ladders from their flat roofs, which provided communal living space for the inhabitants. There were other strange features of the buildings, some of which seemed to be religious shrines, decorated inside with heads or horns of animals, either real or imitated in plaster. The wall faces also were covered with mural paintings, repeatedly renewed after replastering. Frequently depicted were hunting scenes, probably with some ritual significance, in which the physical appearance and dress of the men and women proved no less interesting than the stylized presentation of animals. Other ritual appointments included raised platforms with human burials beneath. The obvious comparison between these mural designs and the cave paintings of Palaeolithic times would here suggest a people newly adapting themselves to life in artificial dwellings and an economy now partly dependent on the products of agriculture. To prove this, it could be shown that no less than 14 different food plants were cultivated. As shown by the murals, art and crafts-

manship had also reached a high standard of attainment. Stylized human or animal figures were skilfully carved in stone or modelled in clay, sometimes distinguished by religious imagery. The bone handles of tools and implements were similarly ornamented. Weapons included polished maces, arrows and lances with tanged obsidian heads. Pottery shapes in the upper levels could be seen to have prototypes in wooden vessels and basketry, which, like the products of spinning and weaving, had been miraculously preserved. Shells from the Mediterranean, metal ores and other materials not locally available suggested extensive trade. Further evidence of agriculture was provided by deposits of food grains in the houses; while the position of the site on an ancient watercourse, subject to regular flooding, could have been exploited for the purpose of artificial irrigation.

As the excavator has pointed out, there was nothing to suggest that this precociously advanced civilization had its origin elsewhere than in southwest Anatolia. But he also agrees that it may well have been a short-lived phenomenon, since the picture we have so far gained of the succeeding Early Chalcolithic culture showed symptoms of temporary retrogression. The unique attainments of Neolithic man in this setting accordingly deserve further investigation. The excavations have till now covered only a small section of the mound, and, when the unique technical problems relating to conservation, (particularly of the fragile mural paintings), have been solved, Mellaart's work at Çatal Hüyük will no doubt be continued.

Reconstruction of part of the Neolithic township at Çatal Hüyük

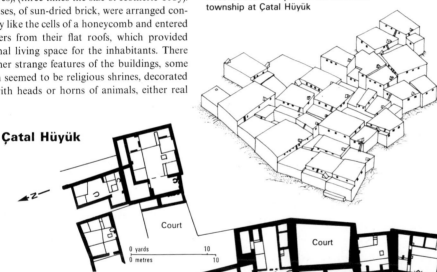

Çatal Hüyük

Court

0 yards 10
0 metres 10

Court

Court

Court

Court

Court

Court

Excavation area

15 m
10 m
5 m

N

0 yards 50
0 metres 50

Beycesultan TURKEY

City mound
c. 4750–1100 BC

BIBLIOGRAPHY
Lloyd, Seton, *Beycesultan*, British Institute of Archaeology
in Ankara, vols. I–III, 1962–73
Lloyd, Seton, *Early Highland Peoples of Anatolia*, London,
1967

Below its source at Dinar (Apameia) the Meander river winds its way over a broad expanse of upland country, once the territory of the Bronze Age state called Arzawa, which so often resisted the westward expansion of the Hittite kingdom. Near Çivril the stream crosses the line of an ancient highway, coming up from the deep valley which leads to Miletus and the sea, and here a great mound marks the site chosen by the Arzawans for an important city – perhaps their provincial capital known today as Beycesultan. British excavations (1954–9) have revealed its history, starting in the early 5th millennium BC as a cluster of mudbrick houses at the river crossing. By Arzawan times in the 19th century, continuous rebuilding and expansion of the settlement had created a hill almost 66 feet (20 m) high. The road still passed between its twin summits, but city walls now spread far out on either side at plain level. Public buildings on the west summit were protected by an inner enclosure wall, and the elevation to the east was entirely occupied by a residential palace, of which some 80 chambers have now been excavated.

The construction of this Middle Bronze Age palace finds parallels elsewhere in Anatolia at all periods; a timber framework with fillings of mudbrick above and undressed stone below. Peculiarities here are tree trunks laid transversely to create foundations, and the use of an upper storey for the main reception rooms, which recalls the Minoan palaces of Crete. The building had been evacuated or looted before its total destruction by fire, for which the Hittite army was perhaps responsible during a campaign in the mid-18th century BC. The excavation of its ruins – piles of charred wood, calcinated limestone and semi-vitrified brickwork – presented an unenviable archaeological problem, though in the end providing evidence for a reliable reconstruction. The site had been partially levelled by squatters who occupied the site for the remainder of the Middle Bronze Age.

By means of an immensely deep sounding in the western part of the mound, 40 successive occupation levels could be studied, from the beginning of the Late Chalcolithic period onwards (c. 4750–1100 BC), and these afterwards served to establish stratigraphic criteria for the whole south-western province of Anatolia. One conspicuous find, at a level dating from the final phase of the Early Bronze Age, were rectangular shrine chambers arranged in pairs, complete with the appointments of religious ritual and much votive pottery. The model for dwelling houses from this time onwards appears to have been the *megaron*; a form of building already to be seen in the first and second settlements at TROY, and similar shrines adapted to this form in the Middle Bronze Age were found in another part of the site.

During the Late Bronze Age (c. 1400–1200 BC), the eastern summit was once more occupied by a small walled settlement with an orderly arrangement of buildings along parallel streets. The larger houses were again of the *megaron* type, by that time familiar in Greece, and accommodation for horses was in evidence. This settlement too was eventually

destroyed by fire and only a solitary farmhouse survived into the 12th century. The whole mound then remained uninhabited until the 10th century AD, when the west summit was briefly adopted as their home by a Byzantine community. The site of the Arzawan palace became a Christian burial ground.

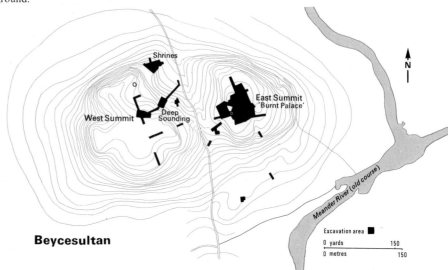

Beycesultan

Excavation area ■

0 yards 150
0 metres 150

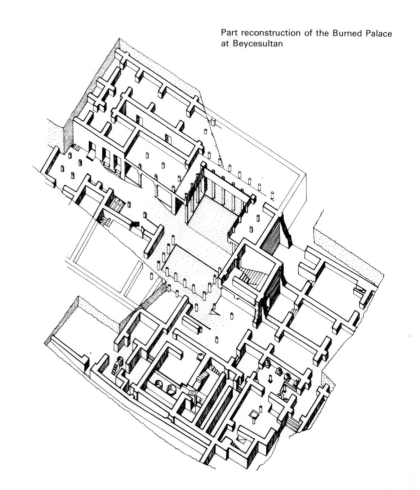

Part reconstruction of the Burned Palace
at Beycesultan

Alaca Hüyük TURKEY

Walled city and royal tombs
4th millennium–1st millennium BC

BIBLIOGRAPHY
Kosay, Hamit, *Les Fouilles de Alaca Hüyük, 1937–9*,
Turkish Historical Society, Ankara, 1966
Lloyd, Seton, *Early Highland Peoples of Anatolia*, London
1967

The ruins of an important Hittite city, perhaps ancient Kussara, lie beneath the mound called Alaca Hüyük (or Höyük, called by early travellers 'Eyuk'), 20 miles (32 km) north east of the capital at Boğhazköy, from which it can easily be reached by road. Today partly covered by a modern village, its ancient walls enclosed an area of about 10 acres (4 hectares), with two monumental gateways, now destroyed. One of these, dating from the early years of the Empire, was flanked by portal sculptures in the form of rather crudely designed sphinxes, which still retain their dignified position at the old entrance to the city. A collection of contemporary relief sculptures from buildings nearby have been taken to the Ankara Museum. Unlike the facing slabs or orthostats of later times, some of these are carved on the actual blocks of masonry. They differ from the sculptures of BOĞHAZKÖY in that they are carved in lower relief and represent secular subjects such as animals, hunted or in conflict, as well as conventional religious scenes. Beyond this gate, inside the city, Turkish excavators have been able to plan the foundations of an imposing building, since identified as a temple. Its colonnaded loggia faced an open piazza, approached through its own inner gateway. In an area immediately to the west of this gateway, where only scanty remains of the Hittite period were to be found, the Turks made a deep sounding, eventually reaching the remains of an earliest Chalcolithic settlement. As it proved, the spot was well chosen, for in 1937, at a level dating from the second phase of the Early Bronze Age (c. 2450 BC), they came upon 13 Royal tombs, whose contents, now in the Ankara Museum, remain one of the most spectacular finds yet made in Anatolia.

The graves of this early Anatolian aristocracy, measuring up to 20 feet long by 10 feet wide (6 × 3 m), were lined with stone walling and roofed with timber, showing traces of ritual sacrifice in the filling above. Funerary ritual was also suggested by some of the objects which they contained; s'range, openwork grilles of bronze, sometimes called 'standards', and finial ornaments in the form of animals, including stags. Dead rulers of both sexes were often buried together – not always simultaneously – and were accompanied by their personal possessions; men by their weapons, women by their ornaments or toilet articles and both by domestic vessels, and other objects made of gold, silver and even iron, which is known to have been much more valuable at that time. When aligned with contemporary treasures found at TROY and elsewhere, they create a repertory of Early Bronze Age luxury goods which suggest an advanced knowledge of metallurgy and a wide variety of rare materials obtainable by trade. This cemetery at Alaca is no longer an isolated phenomenon, since others with less pretentious grave goods have more recently been found at Horoztepe and Mahmutlar in the Pontic area to the north east.

Alaca Hüyük

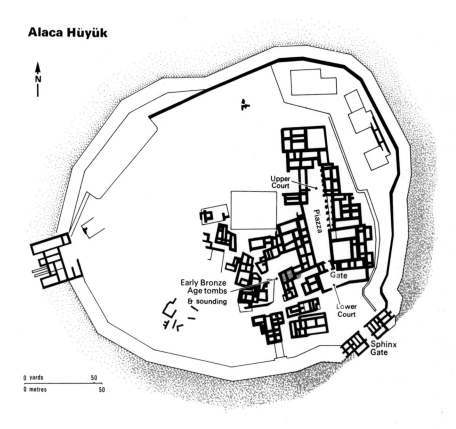

Alaca Hüyük
Excavation area

The small local museum near the site at Alaca Hüyük is worth visiting, since it contains pottery and objects characteristic of each level encountered by Dr Hamit Koşay in his sounding, from the initial, 4th-millennium settlement to the Phrygian aftermath of the Hittite occupation.

Yazilikaya TURKEY

Rock-cut sanctuary
13th century BC

BIBLIOGRAPHY
Gurnet, O. R., *The Hittites*, Harmondsworth, 1952
Lloyd, Seton, *Early Anatolia*, Harmondsworth, 1956
Bittel, K., *Guide to Boghazköy*, Ankara, 1972

Yazilikaya is the name given by the Turks to the famous rock sanctuary which seems to have been a primary focal point for the religious beliefs and seasonal ritual of the imperial Hittites. One and a quarter miles (2 hm) north east of BOĞHAZKÖY, a high outcrop of rock faces a shallow valley, where a spring of water may once have risen. In the rock itself, deep clefts create roofless chambers, whose almost vertical walls are decorated with the hieratic imagery of an ancient cult. In Hittite times they could only be approached through a complex of religious buildings, the foundations of which still protrude from the pavement of the natural terrace outside. The German excavators found that their plan followed the architectural formula of temples in the nearby city, with monumental gateways leading through a colonnaded courtyard to the principal rock galleries, and they attributed their construction to King Hattusilis III (1275–1250 BC), with modifications by his son, Tudkhalias IV (1250–1220 BC).

The larger of the galleries (A) themselves is entirely surrounded by sculptured reliefs, arranged in a single register at eye level, with simple stone benches and pedestals for offerings beneath. A pageant of over 60 deities here provides the subject of the sculptures, each figure carefully depicted with its conventional attributes, standing on its appropriate cult animal or identified by a group of hieroglyphs. The processions – gods on the left and goddesses on the right, – converge on a major scene in the furthest recess of the gallery (40–46), where a confrontation takes place between the principal members of the pantheon, overlooked on the rock face opposite by the figure of King Tudkhalias IV. On the extreme right, two apotropaic figures of demons guard the passage leading to a smaller gallery (B), invested by its narrow confines with an atmosphere of religious mystery. Here, three subjects are depicted. On the west face, 12 minor deities, hurrying to take part in some ritual, are subordinated to the two striking designs opposite: first, the beautiful figure of a young king in the protective embrace of his god; secondly the enigmatic device of a huge dagger thrust into the rock, its pommel ornamented with animal figures and a symbol of divinity. Beyond this are niches for funeral urns and the name of Tudkhalias IV, conspicuously carved in hieroglyphs near an empty pedestal, suggests that a free-standing statue is now missing.

The details and implications of these sculptures have been exhaustively studied by archaeologists over the past half-century. Latterly, some have been puzzled by the fact that the arrangement of the figures and the orthography of their titles conform more closely to Hurrian religious conventions than to those of the Hittites. This has been attributed to the initiative of Queen Puduhepa, the Hurrian wife of Hattusilis III, who is said to have 'reorganized the Hittite state cult according to Hurrian rites'. Nevertheless, as one Turkish scholar comments,

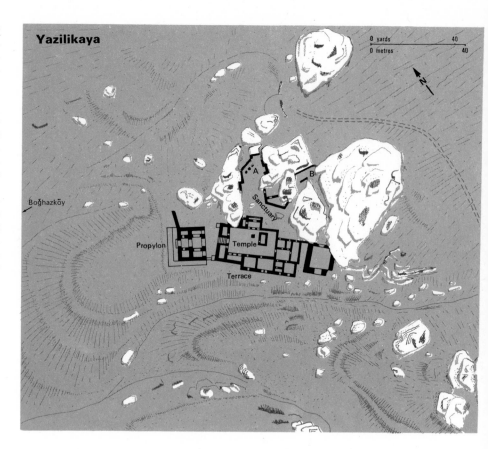

'the deities themselves are depicted entirely according to Hittite iconographic principles.... The artistic style of the reliefs is wholly Hittite in character.'

Although the Yazilikaya sanctuary is now accessible by car and much visited, these natural shrines, open to the sky and often carpeted with grass and flowers, still retain something of the tranquility associated with places where ancient peoples have worshipped.

Sculptured reliefs nos. 41–46 in the larger gallery (A) at Yazilikaya

Boğhazköy TURKEY

Walled city and citadel
c. 1900–700 BC

BIBLIOGRAPHY
Bittel, Kurt, Illustrated Guide to the city of Hattusas, Ankara Museum, 1969
Lloyd, Seton, *Early Highland Peoples of Anatolia*, London, 1967

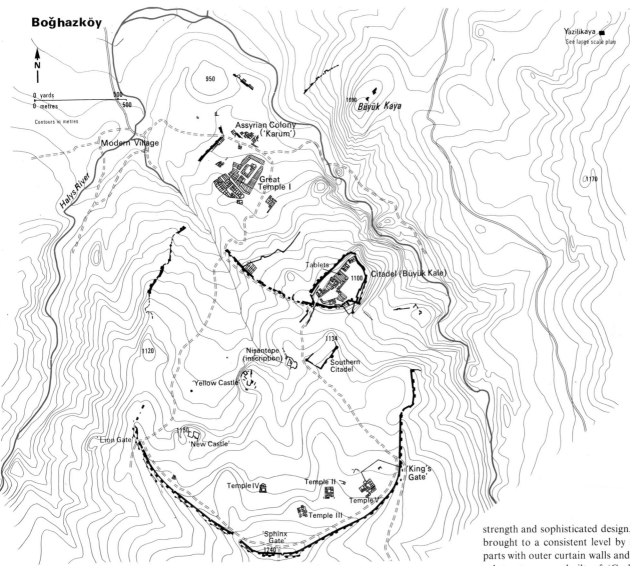

Boğhazköy

Centrally placed in the 'bend' of the Halys (Kizil Irmak) river, 125 miles (200 km) from modern Ankara, the ruins of Hattusas (Khattushash), fortified capital of the Hittites, are now known to the Turks as Boğhazkale. The city, founded on the site of an earlier settlement in about 1900 BC, soon gained importance owing to he presence of a *karum* or colony of Assyrian merchants. Later destroyed in a war between rulers of the indigenous 'Hatti', it was rebuilt in the 17th century and adopted as his capital by the second king, Hattusilis (Khattushilish) of a newly created Hittite dynasty. He extended his territory to 'make the sea his frontier' and in 1595 BC his son, Mursilis, even reached Babylon. In these days of the Hittite Old Kingdom, the foundations were laid of the Hittite Empire, which, from 1400 BC shared the hegemony of the Near East with Egypt and Assyria. In about 1200 BC Hattusas and the

Hittite state itself were destroyed by Phrygians who occupied the Anatolian plateau. Only the citadel at Boğhazkale survived as a minor Phrygian stronghold.

The site of Hattusas is strategically placed in rocky terrain at the head of a broad and fertile valley. The older part of the city occupies a spur of the hills above the modern village of Boğhazköy, rising sharply towards the high citadel rock, Büyükkale at its south-east end, to which its ancient walls are connected. In the 14th century, as required by the increasing size and importance of the imperial capital, the fortifications were extended over the high ground to the south, to include a total area of over 300 acres (approx. 120 hectares). A century later, the hill called Büyükkaya to the east was also enclosed and connected to the old city by a bridge. The new walls to the south were of remarkable

strength and sophisticated design. On foundations brought to a consistent level by stone-faced ramparts with outer curtain walls and sally-ports, their substructure was built of 'Cyclopean' masonry with rubble-filled casemates and projecting towers. Tower-flanked gateways with eliptical arches were ornamented with sculptures, including the famous warrior relief now in the Ankara Museum. In the town, remains of five temples have been recognised of which Temple I in the old city is far the most impressive. A huge complex of store-rooms and priests' quarters surround the main building which, with its colonnaded courtyard, twin shrines and external windows has no parallel in contemporary architecture elsewhere. Surviving walls and pavements are of finely dressed stonework. But it is to the buildings within the citadel that the German excavators have paid most attention during the past 20 years; for here, in a range of store-rooms known as Building A, Hugo Winkler in the years 1931–3 discovered over 3,000 cuneiform tablets representing the archives of the Hittite kings. Among other remains of the Empire period is the basement of a columned audience hall measuring 105 feet (32 m) square.

Sardis TURKEY

Walled city and acropolis
c. 1200 BC–AD 615

BIBLIOGRAPHY
Mitten, D. G., 'A New Look at Ancient Sardis', in *The Biblical Archaeologist*, vol. XXIX, 2, 1966
Butler, H. C., *Sardis I: The Excavations* and *Sardis II: The Artemis Temple*, Princeton University, 1910–14
Hanfmann, G. M. A., *Excavations at Sardis*, Harvard University, 1962

As capital of Lydia, a small state occupying the fertile valley of the Hermos (Gediz Çay) east of Smyrna, Sardis was traditionally founded by Greeks of the Homeric age, but gained importance under the Mermnadae, a native dynasty founded by Gyges (680–652 BC). It prospered under his successors, Ardys, Sadyattes, Alyattes and finally under Croesus, whose wealth became a byword, partly owing to Lydian sources of gold and the invention of minted coinage. Captured by Cyrus the Great, it became the western stronghold of the Achaemenian Empire, connected with Susa by the Royal Road. Following Alexander's conquests, the Seleucids made it a Greek city and, in 133 BC it came as a welcome gift to the Romans from the last Pergamene king. Generously rebuilt by Tiberius after an earthquake in 17 BC, its prosperity again increased in the following centuries, and, as an early centre of Christianity it ranked among St John's Seven Churches of Asia, later acquiring the status of a Byzantine bishopric. Sardis was destroyed by Sasanian Persians in AD 615, but survived as a minor

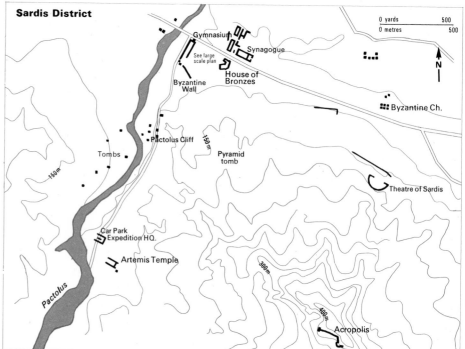

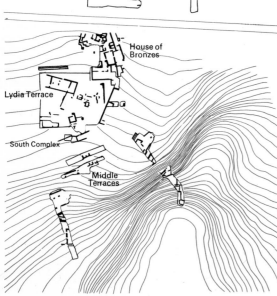

fortress, to be occupied alternately by Turks and Crusaders in the Middle Ages.

Sardis is situated 65 miles (105 km) from Smyrna astride the Ankara main road, at a point where a stream called Pactolus (Sart Çay) flows out into the open plain from between broken hills of soft conglomerate. That to the east of the river forms the acropolis, from which the city fans out northwards in terraces. At its summit are remains of Byzantine and even Lydian fortifications. Near its foot to the west are the ruins of the Artemis Temple, built in Hellenistic times on the site of a Lydian shrine dedicated to Cybele. This was excavated by Americans early in the present century, who also examined 1,000 chamber tombs of the Lydian nobility in the western escarpment. From 1958 onwards, other Americans resumed their work in the Roman town. A deep sounding near the old river crossing revealed a Lydian occupation, and beneath it Late Bronze Age levels with sub-Mycenaean and Protogeometric pottery. North of the highway, much work has been concentrated on the 3rd century Gymnasium-Synagogue complex, part of which has been ingeniously and expensively reconstructed.

Four miles (6·4 km) to the north of Sardis, between the Hermus and the Gygaean Lake (Mermere Gölü), is the Lydian royal cemetery, known locally as Bin Tepe. Of the ninety-odd tumuli the largest, the Tomb of Alyattes covers an area 1,165 feet (355 m) in diameter, but has been heavily plundered in antiquity. Another, identified by the excavators as the tomb of Gyges, has been examined by the Americans, who found retaining-walls of fine ashlar masonry.

Karmir-Blur USSR

Walled city and citadel
8th century BC

BIBLIOGRAPHY
Piotrovski, B. B., *Karmir-Blur: Results of the Excavations,*
4 vols. in Russian, Erevan, 1950–5
Barnett, R. D., Summaries of 2 vols. of the Russian report
in *Iraq,* vols. XIV and XXI
Piotrovski, B. B., *The Ancient Civilization of Urartu,* London, 1969

The site now called Karmir-Blur, representing the remains of Teishebaini, a fortified Urartian city, occupies a prominent position on the outskirts of Erevan, the present capital of Soviet Armenia. A similar site, Arin-berd (ancient Eribuni) is to be found on the opposite side of the town to the south east. Both, at different times, were capitals of Aza, the Trans-Caucasian province of Urartu beyond the Araxes river; the seat of a Viceroy, responsible to the Urartian kings. Teishebaini was built by Rusa II, son of Argishti II, to replace the earlier 8th-century BC capital after its destruction. One of its functions seems to have been the collection of tribute, which was processed in its workshops before being transferred to the central seat of government at Tushpa (Van). Starting in 1939, Karmir-Blur was excavated for 26 years by Russian archaeologists under the direction of Boris Piotrovski, whose astonishingly rich finds have created a detailed and impressive picture of Urartian civilization at the peak of its development.

The hill upon which Teishebaini stood, overlooking a tributary of the Araxes, was crowned by a strongly fortified citadel, about half of which (1½ acres, 6,000 sq m) was occupied by the palace, a building with more than 120 rooms; workshops, storerooms, wine cellars and well-stocked granaries.

Some of these, accommodated in the heavy stone substructure, were only accessible from the main (upper) storey, whose high windows admitted light and air. The huge outer walls – 12 feet (3·7 m) thick and up to 30 feet (9·1 m) high – with crenellated parapets and towers at their intersections, must have made a striking picture. Inside, some of the rooms were decorated with mural paintings, others contained ranges of colossal storage jars for grain or wine, inscribed either in Urartian hieroglyphs or cuneiform with the nature and quantity of their contents. Outside the citadel was a residential quarter, where dwellings of standard designs were disposed along parallel streets, some superimposed in a single building, like flats.

Piotrovski's account of his finds in the palace makes compulsive reading: jewelry and vessels of gold, silver or bronze; (in one wine store, a pile of 86 bronze drinking cups, inscribed with the names of Urartian kings, in addition to 1,036 jugs of polished red pottery); statues and cult figures in bronze and ivory; horse trappings and metal parts of chariots; armour and weapons, including iron swords with ornamental bronze hilts – and so on. One group of bronze objects – possibly the finest in the whole collection, consisting of huge circular shields, helmets and quivers, decorated in repoussé

with human and animal figures – had a special significance. They bore the names of 18th-century kings and had evidently been rescued from the ruins of Erebuni after its destruction. In a different category, smaller finds had great scientific interest. A catalogue could be made of cereals, food plants and botanical species whose remains were identifiable. Apart from the skeletons of horses and other large animals, the bones of small rodents – and even wéevils – were found in storage jars.

Teishebaini was sacked and burned in about 590 BC. A litter of clay lamps showed that it was a night attack and the identity of the attackers was proved by scores of Scythian arrowheads embedded in the walls. The season of the year was fixed by the contents of the stomachs of donkeys, temporarily accommodated on the roof of the citadel. Some of the more spectacular discoveries are intelligently displayed in a new museum on the site of Erebuni. Others are in the Hermitage, Leningrad, or elsewhere.

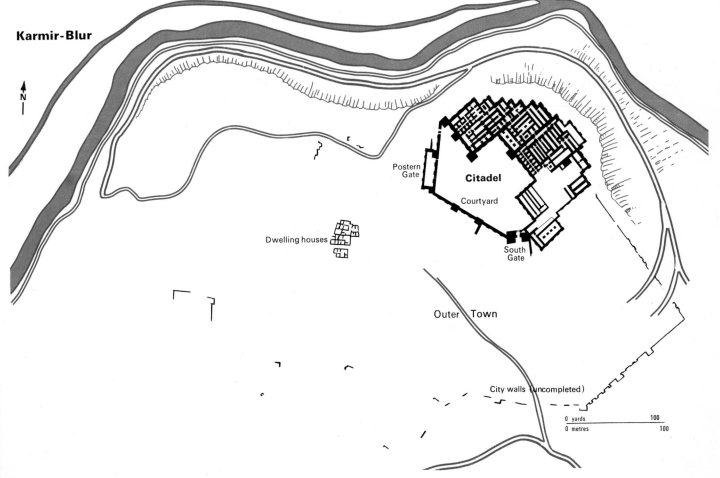

EGYPT

In ancient times the land of Egypt was just the alluvial margins of the 600-mile (966 km) stretch of the River Nile between Aswan and Cairo, and the triangular area of swamps and fields, the Delta, across which the Nile finds its outlets to the Mediterranean Sea. It is a land sharply delineated by the contrast between the rich green farmlands watered by the river and the arid sand and rock deserts which lie immediately beyond. To the east these rise to a line of broken mountains, anciently exploited for gold, which effectively isolate the valley from the Red Sea; to the west they merge into the vast plateau of the Sahara Desert. In ancient times the fertility of the valley was greatly enhanced by the annual rise and flood of the river waters, which both saturated the fields for a short period and left a deposit of rich silt on them. Today a series of barrages, the largest of them at Aswan, evens out the annual variation in flow so that agriculture is now dependent on mechanical irrigation.

Egyptian civilization in its characteristic form emerged from prehistory about 3100 BC, and, although the nature of Egyptian society underwent a process of slow change over the centuries, many of its outward features survived into a period, 3000 years later, when the country was ruled by the Greek-speaking Ptolemies, and after them by the Roman emperors. Much of our knowledge of ancient Egypt concerns the history and culture of the Egyptian court, which centred around a hereditary divine kingship at the head of a powerful administrative machine. Its families of kings, or Pharaohs, are now, for convenience, grouped into thirty-one dynasties which carry us down to the conquest of Egypt by Alexander the Great in 332 BC. Ordered rule under the divine pharaohs was, however, twice interrupted. The Old Kingdom (Dynasties 3–6) collapsed through social revolution in about 2280 BC. After a little more than two centuries order was restored under Dynasties 11 to 12, the Middle Kingdom. The second collapse, beginning late in the 18th century BC, was largely due to the infiltration of the Asiatic Hyksos, who for a time ruled much of Egypt. The New Kingdom was established by about 1575 BC and flourished for some 500 years (Dynasties 18 to 20).

About the secular and everyday side of society we are much less well informed, despite the apparent wealth of illustration on tomb walls. From ancient times through to the present, though political boundaries have altered, the population of Egypt has continued to live on the same limited areas bordering the river. It has thus proved difficult to learn through archaeology much about the cities, towns, and villages of Pharaonic Egypt which were built very largely of perishable sun-dried mudbricks. Their fate, when not built over, has frequently been systematic destruction by peasants who have found them to contain chemically rich earth (*sebbakh*) which could be used as a fertilizer on their fields. EDFU supplies a good example of an ancient town mound largely quarried away by this process. Only in rare cases on the desert edge, such as at EL-AMARNA, can we see an ancient Egyptian urban layout preserved on any scale.

The principal feature in towns, and often the only one to have survived, was the temple, not a place for collective popular worship but conceived as the house of the gods. Only the temple staff was normally allowed to enter, but the temple must nevertheless have acted as a cohesive focal point for the community living around it. It was a manifestation of court culture, its scenes of ritual depicting only the king making offerings to the gods, as well as, in the most prominent place, smiting all his enemies. There were two main phases of non-funerary temple building in stone: the New Kingdom and the period covering Dynasty 30 to the Roman emperors of the 1st century AD. To the former belong most of the temples at Thebes, including KARNAK and LUXOR, also ABU SIMBEL and the surviving temples at ABYDOS; DENDERA and Edfu are well-preserved examples from the latter period. Temple land and other sources of revenue made them important centres for economic activity. This is reflected in the large warehouse blocks often found within temple precincts, as in the case of the temple of Sety I at Abydos. In temple religion ceremonies of a processional nature were prominent, and

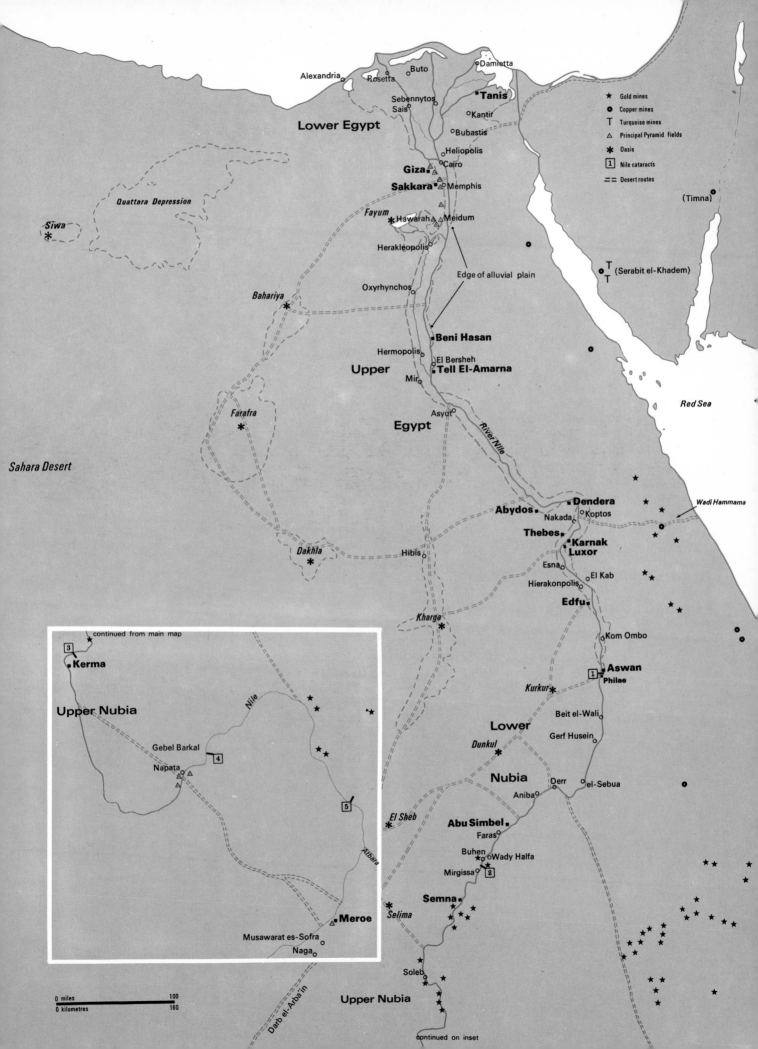

Alexandria
Rosetta
Buto
Damietta
Tanis
Sebennytos
Sais
Kantir
Lower Egypt
Bubastis
Heliopolis
Cairo
Giza
Sakkara
Memphis
Quattara Depression
Fayum
Hawarah
Meidum
Siwa
Herakleopolis
Edge of alluvial plain
Oxyrhynchos
Baharia
Beni Hasan
Hermopolis
El Bersheh
Upper
Tell El-Amarna
Mir
Farafra
Asyut
Egypt
River Nile
Red Sea
Sahara Desert
Abydos
Dendera
Nakada
Koptos
Wadi Hammama
Dakhla
Hibis
Thebes
Karnak
Luxor
Esna
El Kab
Hierakonpolis
Edfu
Kharga
Kom Ombo
continued from main map
3
Kerma
1 **Aswan**
Philae
Kurkur
Beit el-Wali
Upper Nubia
Nile
Gerf Husein
Gebel Barkal
4
Dunkul
Napata
Lower
Derr
el-Sebua
5
Nubia
Aniba
Atbara
El Sheb
Abu Simbel
Faras
Buhen
Wady Halfa
Mirgissa
2
Meroe
Semna
Musawarat es-Sofra
Selima
Naga
Soleb
0 miles 100
0 kilometres 160
Darb el-Arba'in
Upper Nubia
continued on inset

(Timna)

T
T (Serabit el-Khadem)

★ Gold mines
○ Copper mines
T Turquoise mines
△ Principal Pyramid fields
✳ Oasis
1 Nile cataracts
== Desert routes

this influenced both the plan of the temple itself, and of the layout of subsidiary shrines within the temple enclosure. Outside the temple they could follow paved avenues often connecting the temple to stone landing places on the river or a canal.

The ancient Egyptians placed considerable importance on making adequate preparations for the existence they believed they would enjoy after death. A secure space had to be provided for the body and for the burial equipment which could be used by the dead owner and which could be supplemented by pictures of agricultural and domestic activities to supply the sort of environment familiar in life. Of almost equal importance was an offering place where, on a simplified and reduced scale, the dead owner could benefit from the same kind of offering ceremony as performed for the gods in their temples. It is because tombs and offering chapels were for preference built on the dry desert margins, and for eternity, that the religion of the dead represents such a disproportionate amount of our knowledge of ancient Egypt. Important groups of rock-hewn tombs are at BENI HASAN and THEBES, and at GIZA and SAKKARA are fine court cemeteries of decorated *mastaba*-tombs, rectangular buildings on level ground which were particularly favoured in the earlier periods. The power and divinity of kings was made manifest in tombs of a special type and on a larger scale. Down to the beginning of Dynasty 18 the burial chamber was protected by a stone or brick solar symbol in the form of a pyramid, which could, as at Giza, attain gigantic proportions. Attached to pyramids were full-size decorated temples with a processional causeway leading down from their desert sites to the edge of the cultivated land. In the New Kingdom pyramids were abandoned. Instead, royal burial chambers were cut into the sides of the Valley of Kings at Thebes, and the mortuary temples constructed separately in a row along the edge of the desert. After the New Kingdom royal tombs tended to be placed actually within the precincts of the main local temple, as at TANIS.

Despite its situation in Africa, Egypt belonged more to the interrelated cultures of the eastern Mediterranean. The Egyptians' attempts to build an empire here, particularly in the New Kingdom, were limited to the coercion of princes who ruled states with an urban culture as ancient and often as sophisticated as that of the Egyptians themselves. By contrast the Nile valley to the south of Egypt, called Nubia, was primarily a land of pastoralists with cultures not dissimilar to that of Egypt in prehistoric times. It was repeatedly conquered by the Egyptians and either held by garrisons in fortresses, such as at Buhen, Mirgissa, and SEMNA, or, in the New Kingdom, made the object of an elaborate policy of cultural integration. The Egyptians were partly interested in the mineral resources of Nubia, and also concerned with the native kingdoms which from time to time came to represent a political force of some magnitude. The Kingdom of Kush centred at KERMA was one of these. The legacy of Egyptian culture left behind in Nubia eventually produced, after a period of independence, a kingdom whose capital came to be the great city of MEROE. Its court modelled itself on that of the Pharaohs, building temples and pyramids in a style which borrowed much from Egypt. Endowed with a vigour of its own it managed to outlive the gradual fading of Egyptian culture into the Hellenistic world.

Sakkara EGYPT

Cemetery
c. 3100 BC–Roman period

BIBLIOGRAPHY
Lauer, J.-P., *La Pyramide à Degrès*, vols. 1–3, Cairo, 1936–1939
Emery, W. B., *Archaic Egypt*, Harmondsworth, 1961
Preliminary reports on the excavations of the Egypt Exploration Society are published annually in the *Journal of Egyptian Archaeology*, beginning with vol. 51, 1965
Aldred, C., *Egypt to the End of the Old Kingdom*, London, 1965. (The library of early civilizations)

Shortly before reaching Sakkara visitors usually pass through an extensive area of low earth mounds and palm groves. These, with some stone foundations, are all that survives of the city of Memphis which served as an effective capital during most of Egypt's ancient history. A small museum houses some of the sculpture found locally, including a colossus of Rameses II. Sakkara, on the edge of a low desert plateau behind, was the principal cemetery for Memphis, and thus contains tombs from all ancient periods. But except for some enormous shaft tombs of Dynasty 26, and the animal cemeteries, the visible portions of the cemetery are of Dynasties 1 to 6. Considerable areas are still covered with heaps of gravelly debris and await serious exploration.

The earliest part is to the north and dates to the very beginnings of Egyptian history. Here lies a densely packed cemetery of mudbrick *mastaba* tombs of Dynasties 1 to 3, including a row of elaborately panelled examples overlooking the cultivation which probably belonged either to members of the royal family or to high officials of Dynasty 1. The central part of Sakkara is dominated by the Step Pyramid of King Djeser (*c.* 2700 BC) of Dynasty 3. This is the earliest known monumental stone building in Egypt. It stands within an enclosure containing also a complicated arrangement of real and dummy stone buildings, apparently designed to enable the ceremonies of kingship to be re-enacted for eternity. A similar but unfinished complex belonging to a successor lies to the south west, and there are possible traces of others. As the Old Kingdom progressed the surrounding area was gradually filled with *mastaba* tombs, accompanied by three royal pyramid complexes of Kings Userkaf and Unas of Dynasty 5, and Teti of Dynasty 6. A small section of the long causeway leading up to the pyramid of Unas has been restored, and contains some interesting carved reliefs. Alongside is a pair of boat pits similar to those at GIZA. Of the *mastaba* tombs, many possess beautifully decorated chapels with richly varied scenes of agriculture, hunting, and manufacturing. The most visited are those of Ti and Mereruka.

In the period between about the 7th to 1st centuries BC the northern part of Sakkara became one of the principal centres for the mass burial of sacred animals, a phenomenon peculiar to this period, although individual tombs of the sacred Apis bull of Memphis extend back into the New Kingdom. Underground catacombs have been found for dogs, ibises, falcons, baboons and cows, as well as for the Apis bulls of this late period, interred in a catacomb called the Serapeum, now open to the public. Slightly north of the Serapeum are the current British excavations at Sakkara, to which we owe a considerable increase in our knowledge of this practice, and which have raised hopes of discovering the Asklepion, a divine healing centre of this period.

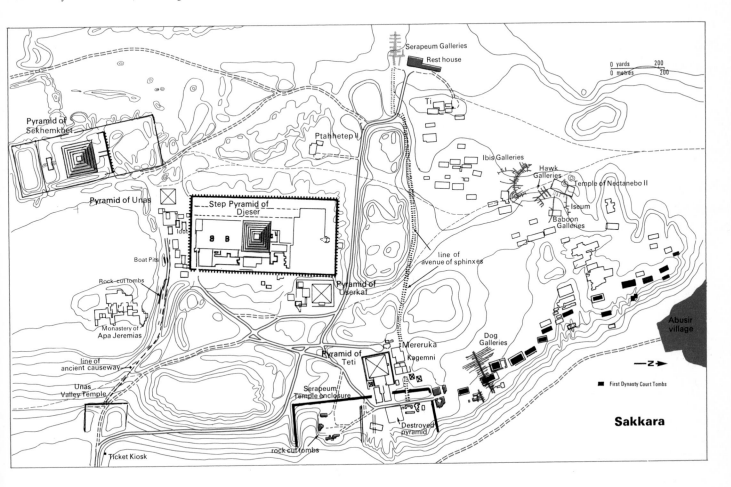

Giza EGYPT

Pyramids
c. 2600–2520 BC

BIBLIOGRAPHY
Edwards, I. E. S., *The Pyramids of Egypt*, 2nd. ed., London, 1961, Harmondsworth, 1961
Hassan, S., *The Great Sphinx and Its Secrets*, Cairo, 1953
Junker, H., *Giza I–Giza XII*, Vienna, 1929. Published as parts of the Österreichische Akademie der Wissenschaften, Phil. hist. Klasse, Denkschriften
Reisner, G. A., and Smith, W. S., *A History of the Giza Necropolis, II, The Tomb of Hetep-heres*, Cambridge, Mass., 1955

Most of the Old and Middle Kingdom royal pyramids were situated along the edge of the low desert plateau running both north and south of Sakkara, between Abu Rawash and Dashur. Giza is one of the sites, containing the pyramids of three kings of Dynasty 4: Khufu (Cheops), Khafra (Chephren), and Menkaura (Mycerinus), and dating to between about 2600 and 2520 BC. That belonging to Khufu, the Great Pyramid, is the largest known. When originally cased in smooth white limestone it was 481 feet 5 inches (146·7 m) high, and measured about 755 feet (230 m) along each side of the base. Khafra's is the second largest, and still retains some of the original smooth casing towards the top. Each pyramid contained at least one burial chamber, and stood surrounded by various ancillary structures.

These were principally subsidiary pyramids and a mortuary temple linked by a causeway to a smaller temple on the edge of the valley. The valley temple of Khafra, built of huge monoliths of limestone and granite, is almost completely preserved. Beside it and a little to the rear is the Great Sphinx, carved from a knoll of limestone rock, which represents a recumbent lion with the head of a king, probably Khafra himself. It has its own temples in front, and by the New Kingdom had come to be regarded as a statue of the sun god Horemakhet (Harmachis).

A large concrete building against the south side of the Great Pyramid marks the position of a long narrow pit which was found, in 1954, to contain a well-preserved and full-size funerary boat for Khufu's use in the next world. When restored it will

be housed inside the concrete building. An adjacent pit remains to be opened, and several more open boat pits can be observed on the east sides of both Khufu's and Khafra's pyramids.

The royal pyramids are surrounded on all sides by the stone *mastaba* tombs of courtiers and officials of the period. The principal sectors were laid out on a strict grid pattern. Some contained small decorated chapels, and all had at least one offering place in the form of a false door, of which many examples from sites of this period have found their way into museums. Some fine portrait sculpture has also been found in some of them.

Later burials at Giza were rare, and the cemetery, unlike SAKKARA, has been left largely undisturbed since the end of Dynasty 6.

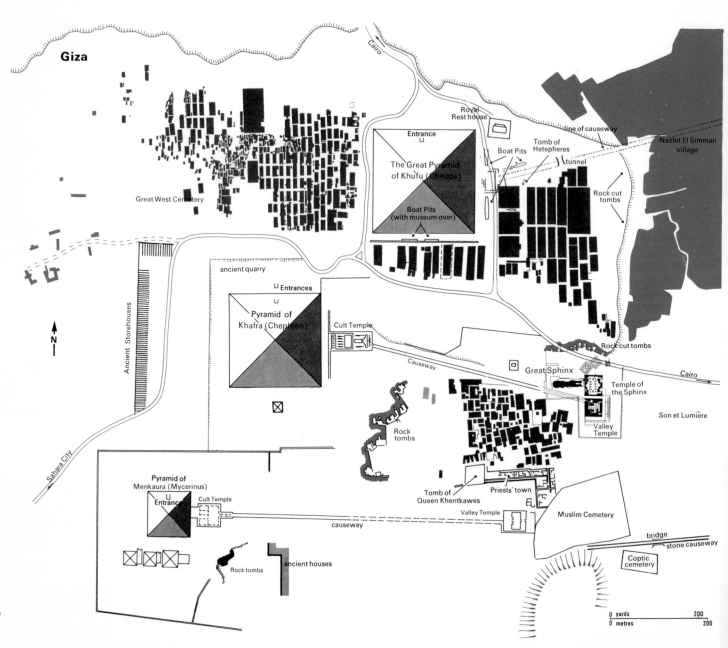

Beni Hasan EGYPT

Rock tombs
c. 2000–1890 BC

BIBLIOGRAPHY
Newberry, P. E., Griffith, F. Ll. et al., *Beni Hasan*, I–IV, London 1893–1900, Archaeological Survey of Egypt memoirs 1, 2, 5 and 7
Garstang, J., *The Burial Customs of Ancient Egypt*, London, 1907
Davies, N. M., *Ancient Egyptian paintings*, vol. I, Chicago, 1936, plates VII–XI

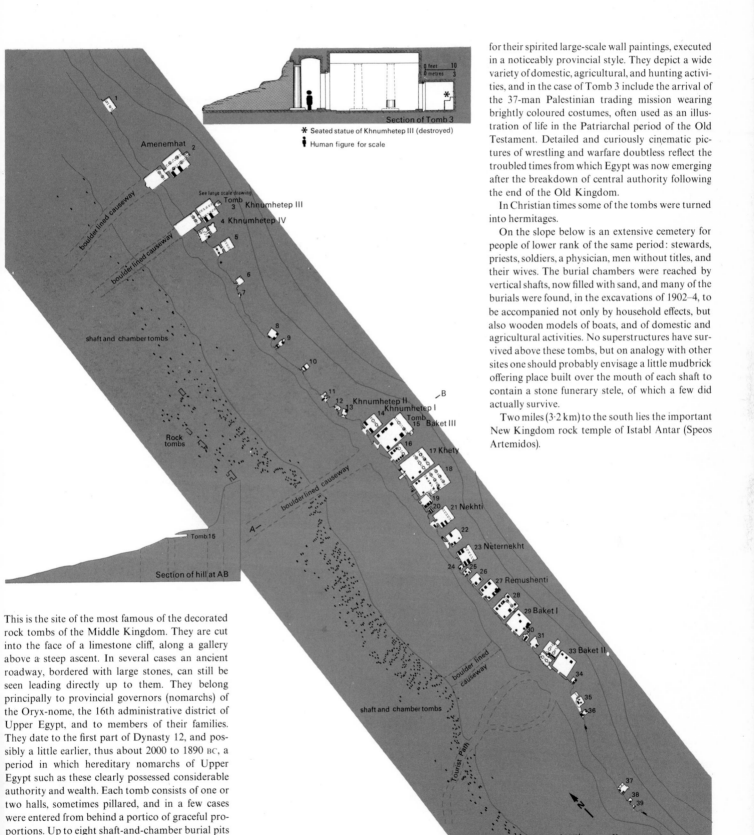

Section of Tomb 3

✻ Seated statue of Khnumhetep III (destroyed)

👤 Human figure for scale

for their spirited large-scale wall paintings, executed in a noticeably provincial style. They depict a wide variety of domestic, agricultural, and hunting activities, and in the case of Tomb 3 include the arrival of the 37-man Palestinian trading mission wearing brightly coloured costumes, often used as an illustration of life in the Patriarchal period of the Old Testament. Detailed and curiously cinematic pictures of wrestling and warfare doubtless reflect the troubled times from which Egypt was now emerging after the breakdown of central authority following the end of the Old Kingdom.

In Christian times some of the tombs were turned into hermitages.

On the slope below is an extensive cemetery for people of lower rank of the same period: stewards, priests, soldiers, a physician, men without titles, and their wives. The burial chambers were reached by vertical shafts, now filled with sand, and many of the burials were found, in the excavations of 1902–4, to be accompanied not only by household effects, but also wooden models of boats, and of domestic and agricultural activities. No superstructures have survived above these tombs, but on analogy with other sites one should probably envisage a little mudbrick offering place built over the mouth of each shaft to contain a stone funerary stele, of which a few did actually survive.

Two miles (3·2 km) to the south lies the important New Kingdom rock temple of Istabl Antar (Speos Artemidos).

This is the site of the most famous of the decorated rock tombs of the Middle Kingdom. They are cut into the face of a limestone cliff, along a gallery above a steep ascent. In several cases an ancient roadway, bordered with large stones, can still be seen leading directly up to them. They belong principally to provincial governors (nomarchs) of the Oryx-nome, the 16th administrative district of Upper Egypt, and to members of their families. They date to the first part of Dynasty 12, and possibly a little earlier, thus about 2000 to 1890 BC, a period in which hereditary nomarchs of Upper Egypt such as these clearly possessed considerable authority and wealth. Each tomb consists of one or two halls, sometimes pillared, and in a few cases were entered from behind a portico of graceful proportions. Up to eight shaft-and-chamber burial pits were cut in the floor. Many tombs are undecorated or unfinished, but the halls of some, intended as places of commemoration and offerings, are famous

Karnak and Luxor EGYPT

Temples
Principally *c.* 1550–924 BC

BIBLIOGRAPHY
Nims, C. F., *Thebes of the Pharaohs*, London, 1965
Kamil, J., *Luxor, A Guide to Ancient Thebes*, London, 1973
Barguet, P., *Le Temple d'Amon-Re à Karnak*, Cairo, 1962
  (Recherches d'archéologie, etc., 21)
Preliminary reports on excavation and reconstruction work
  at Karnak are published annually in *Kêmi*, beginning
  with vol. 19, 1969

The ancient city of Thebes lay on the east bank of
the river, apparently in the vicinity of Karnak,
although little of it has been located and excavated.
That it did not remain a provincial town of no particular importance seems entirely due to the political
success of its governors who on two occasions, in
Dynasty 11 and at the beginning of Dynasty 18,
became kings of united Egypt following a civil war.
From early Dynasty 18 Thebes was Egypt's first
city, although kings increasingly resided at or near
Memphis. What gave to Thebes its lasting importance was the wealth and effort bestowed on its
temples. The principal one was for the originally
local god Amen. This expanded to become the
centre of the largest complex of temples to have
survived in Egypt.

Despite the bewildering impression created by
the existing ruins the plan has a unifying theme in
the form of processional avenues, some of them
sphinx-lined. These provide a basic unity within the
main enclosure, and also serve to unite a number
of originally independent holy places outside, Luxor
among them. The temples are primarily a creation

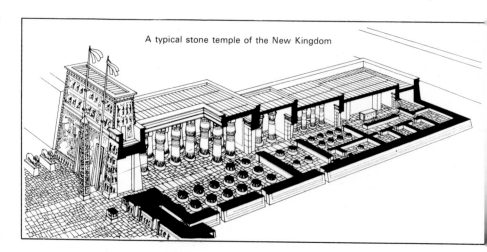

A typical stone temple of the New Kingdom

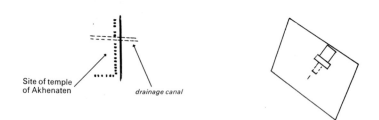

Site of temple
of Akhenaten

drainage canal

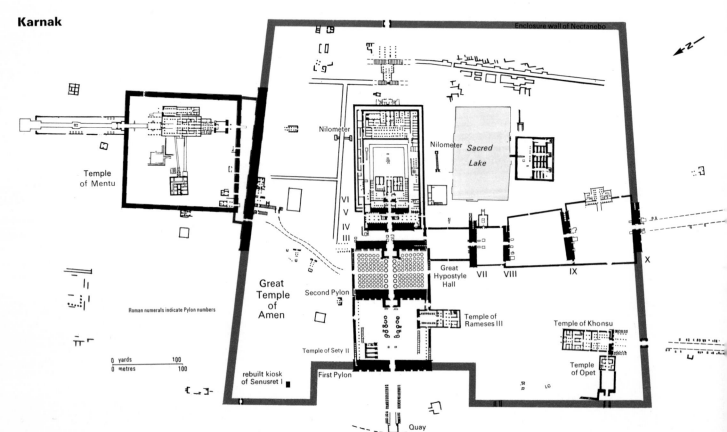

Karnak

Enclosure wall of Nectanebo

Temple
of Mentu

Nilometer

Nilometer   *Sacred
              Lake*

VI
V
IV
III

Great
Hypostyle
Hall   VII VIII   IX   X

Great
Temple
of
Amen

Roman numerals indicate Pylon numbers

Second Pylon

Temple of
Rameses III

Temple of Khonsu

0 yards   100
0 metres   100

Temple of Sety II

Temple
of Opet

rebuilt kiosk
of Senusret I   First Pylon

Quay

site of ancient basin

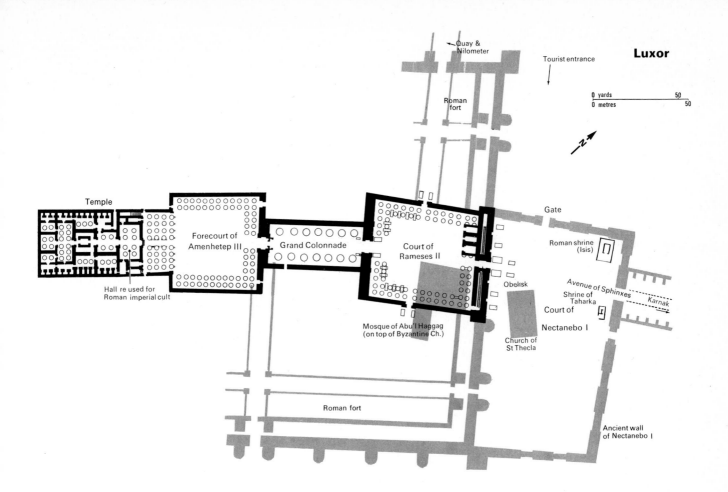

Temple

Forecourt of
Amenhetep III

Grand Colonnade

Court of
Rameses II

Hall re used for
Roman imperial cult

Mosque of Abu'l Haggag
(on top of Byzantine Ch.)

Roman fort

Quay &
Nilometer

Roman
fort

Tourist entrance

Luxor

0 yards 50
0 metres 50

Gate

Roman shrine
(Isis)

Obelisk

Church of
St Thecla

Avenue of Sphinxes

Shrine of
Taharka

Court of
Nectanebo I

Karnak

Ancient wall
of Nectanebo I

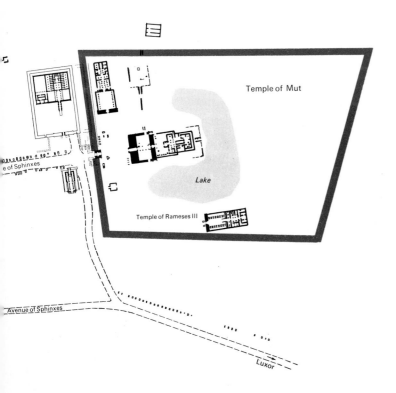

Temple of Mut

Lake

Temple of Rameses III

e of Sphinxes

Avenue of Sphinxes

Luxor

of the New Kingdom. The great temple of Amen grew slowly in a westward direction, from a building erected by Tuthmosis III and Hatshepsut (about 1490 to 1436 BC) in front of the Middle Kingdom temple (now destroyed), via the Great Hypostyle Hall of Sety I and Rameses II, to the unfinished entrance pylon of Sheshonk I of Dynasty 22 (about 945 to 924 BC).

An additional source of complexity is the way in which blocks from old buildings were regularly used again in fresh ones. The task of dismantling and rebuilding Karnak is still progressing, and has yielded many thousands of re-used blocks from a temple to the Aten erected by Akhenaten to the east of the main temple, as well as blocks from various small structures, some of which have been rebuilt in the north-west corner of the main enclosure. One is a beautiful kiosk of early Dynasty 12.

Luxor temple is a distant part of the Theban complex, and again intended primarily for the cult of Amen. The rear part is the work of Amenhetep III, the front of Rameses II. As Thebes decayed this became the main centre of occupation, first as part of a Roman fort, and the temple was gradually buried. The medieval mosque of Abu'l-Haggag still perched almost at roof level is a survival of this.

Western Thebes EGYPT

Temples and cemeteries
c. 2000–1087 BC

BIBLIOGRAPHY

Riefstahl, E., *Thebes in the Time of Amunhotep III*, Norman, Oklahoma, 1964

Winlock, H. E., *The Rise and Fall of the Middle Kingdom in Thebes*, New York, 1947

Thomas, E., *The Royal Necropolis of Thebes*, Princeton, 1966

Hölscher, U., *The Excavation of Medinet Habu*, 5 vols., Chicago, 1934–54. (University of Chicago, Oriental Institute, publications 21, 41, 54, 55, 66)

Werbrouck, M., *Le Temple d'Hatshepsout à Deir el Bahari*, Brussels, 1949

Piankoff, A., *The Tomb of Ramesses VI*, 2 vols., New York, 1954. (Bollingen series 40)

Desroches-Noblecourt, C., *Tutankhamen*, London, 1963

Černý, J., 'Egypt from the death of Ramesses III to the end of the Twenty-first Dynasty', *Cambridge Ancient History*, revised ed., vol. II, ch. XXXV, Cambridge, 1965

The striking cliffs and their foothills on the west bank became the main cemetery for the city of Thebes lying opposite. The earliest tombs so far located are a few of the Old Kingdom, and they form the beginning of a long and numerous sequence extending to the very end of ancient Egypt. A great many had their chapels cut into the convenient slopes and cliff faces, and have tended to survive better than others erected on more level ground. The most famous of the private rock tombs are those made for court officers of the New Kingdom. Because much of the rock was too poor for carving a lively and sophisticated school of wall painters arose whose colourful portrayals of court events and personal episodes have become justly famous.

The kings of Dynasties 11 and 18 to 20 (the New Kingdom) also chose burial at Thebes. Of Dynasty 11 the finest tomb was that of King Nebhepetra Menthuhetep II at Deir el-Bahari with an attached terraced temple. The royal tombs of the New Kingdom were confined, for security, to a single network of valleys, known collectively as the Valley of Kings. It was carefully policed by men who have left innumerable graffiti in the Theban hills. These tombs developed a style of funerary decoration quite different from the more secular spirit of private tombs. Their offering cults were carried out in a row of temples along the edge of the cultivation where the dead king became fused with a form of the god Amen. The terraced temple of Queen Hatshepsut at Deir el-Bahari is an unusually fine example of architecture fitted to a natural setting. Other well-preserved mortuary temples are those of Sety I and Rameses II of Dynasty 19, the latter's usually called the Ramesseum, and that of Rameses III of Dynasty 20 at Medinet Habu. Amenhetep III's must have been one of the finest, but all that survives is a pair of quartzite colossi from the entrance avenue, often known as the Colossi of Memnon.

A welcome change from the funerary monuments are the remains of the little village of Deir el-Medina where lived the workmen and artists responsible for cutting and decorating the royal tombs of the New Kingdom. A large amount of inscribed objects have combined to give a remarkably detailed picture of the life and economy of this community.

Beyond Medinet Habu lie the mounds marking the edges of a huge harbour excavated by Amenhetep III, the Birket Habu. This was part of a complex (called Malkara) containing palaces and a temple which probably amounted to an entirely new urban and commercial development for Thebes. It seems to have been abandoned by the end of Dynasty 18.

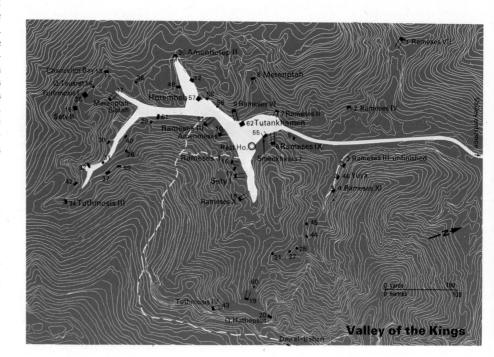

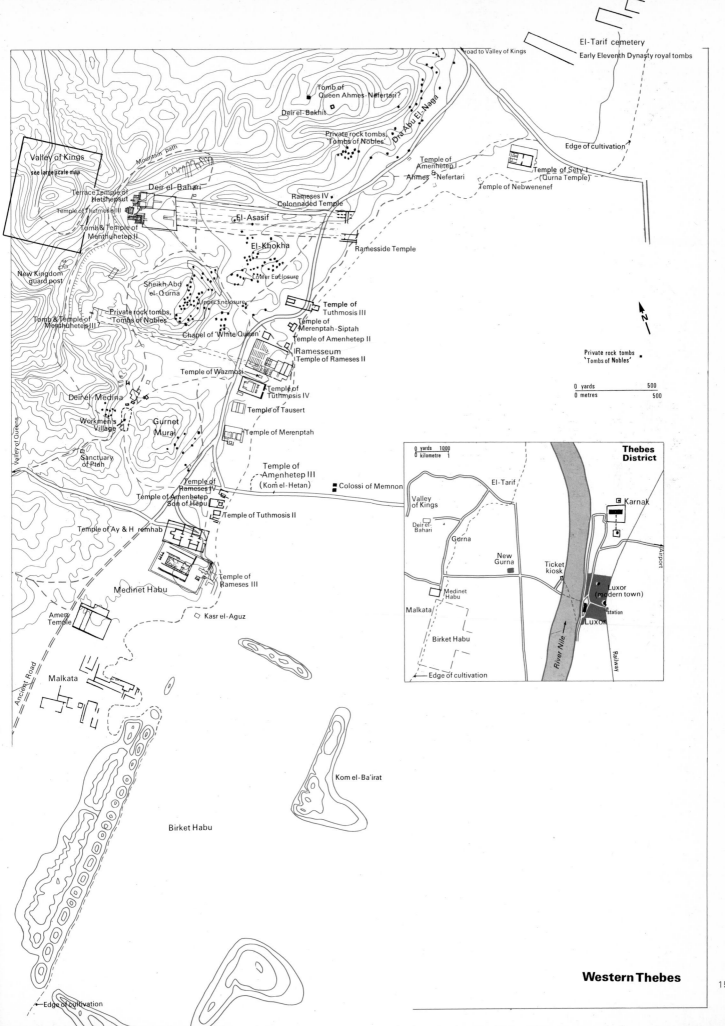

El-Tarif cemetery
Early Eleventh Dynasty royal tombs

road to Valley of Kings

Tomb of
Queen Ahmes-Nefertari?

Deir el-Bakhit

Private rock tombs,
'Tombs of Nobles'

Dra Abu El-Naga

Temple of
Amenhetep I
& Ahmes-Nefertari

Temple of Sety I
(Qurna Temple)

Edge of cultivation

Temple of Nebwenenef

Valley of Kings
see large scale map

Mountain path

Deir el-Bahari

Terrace Temple of
Hatshepsut

Temple of Thutmosis III

Rameses IV
Colonnaded Temple

El-Asasif

Tomb & Temple of
Menthuhetep II

El-Khokha

Ramesside Temple

New Kingdom
guard post

Lower Enclosure

Sheikh Abd
el-Qurna

Upper Enclosure

Temple of
Tuthmosis III

Tomb & Temple of
Menthuhetep III

Private rock tombs,
'Tombs of Nobles'

Temple of
Merenptah-Siptah

Temple of Amenhetep II

Chapel of 'White Queen'

Private rock tombs
'Tombs of Nobles'

Ramesseum
(Temple of Rameses II)

Temple of Wazmosi

N

Deir el-Medina

Temple of
Tuthmosis IV

Workmen's
Village

Temple of Tausert

0 yards   500
0 metres   500

Gurnet
Murai

Temple of Merenptah

Sanctuary
of Ptah

Valley of Queens

Temple of
Amenhetep III
(Kom el-Hetan)

Colossi of Memnon

Temple of
Rameses IV

Temple of Amenhetep
Son of Hapu

Temple of Tuthmosis II

Temple of Ay & H'remhab

Thebes
District

0 yards   1000
0 kilometre   1

Valley of
Kings

El-Tarif

Karnak

Deir el-
Bahari

Gurna

New
Gurna

Ticket
kiosk

Medinet Habu

Malkata

Birket Habu

Edge of cultivation

Luxor
(modern town)

station

Luxor

River Nile

Airport

Railway

Medinet Habu

Temple of
Rameses III

Amen
Temple

Kasr el-Aguz

Ancient Road

Malkata

Kom el-Ba'irat

Birket Habu

Edge of cultivation

Western Thebes

155

Abydos EGYPT

Town temples and cemeteries
c. 4000 BC–Roman period

BIBLIOGRAPHY

Kemp, B. J., 'Abydos', in *Lexikon der Ägyptologie*, ed. W. Helck and E. Otto, Band I, 1, Wiesbaden, 1972, columns 28–41

Calverley, A. M., *The temple of King Sethos I at Abydos*, vols. 1, London and Chicago, 1933

David, R., *Religious Ritual at Abydos* (*c. 1300 BC*), Warminster, 1973

Frankfort, H., *The Cenotaph of Seti I at Abydos*, 2 vols., London, 1933, (Egypt Exploration Society, memoir 39)

The importance of this provincial town on the edge of the desert lay in the process, still not properly understood, whereby, by the beginning of the Middle Kingdom, it had become the principal centre for the cult of Osiris. Osiris was a god slain and then resurrected to become ruler of the netherworld. Although at first primarily associated with the royal funerary cult, by the Middle Kingdom he had come to represent the hope of eternal life to ordinary people, and his cult remained popular into late antiquity. Abydos became a centre of pilgrimage, in death as well as in life, and each year a dramatized re-enactment of the life-cycle of Osiris was performed in and around the temple.

The site of the ancient town is adjacent to the modern village of Beni Mansur. Most of it has been removed by *sebbakh* (fertilizer) digging except for a section in one corner, the Kom es-Sultan. The temples of Osiris, too, have been destroyed to their foundations leaving little to see other than the great brick enclosure wall of a late period. Across the desert behind stretch extensive cemeteries, either excavated or plundered, from all periods of Egyptian history. In the distance, on Umm el-Qa'ab, lie the modest tombs of the kings of Dynasty 1, though the part they may have played in the religious history of Abydos is very unclear.

The kings of the Middle and New Kingdoms also chose to share in the religious aura of Abydos, by having a funerary cult established there. At first this took the form of imitation tombs at Abydos South, but was superseded by temples nearer to the ancient town. The finest was built for Sety I of Dynasty 19 (1309–1291 BC) with painted reliefs of the greatest delicacy. It has at the back a separate suite of rooms for the cult of Osiris. Immediately behind is a subterranean structure, the Osireion, probably a combination of dummy tomb and representation of the primeval mound of creation. Also within the brick enclosure wall, in the south-east corner, is a well-preserved set of warehouses. A short distance along the desert edge is a much more ruined temple of Rameses II lying within an enclosure still thickly buried in sand.

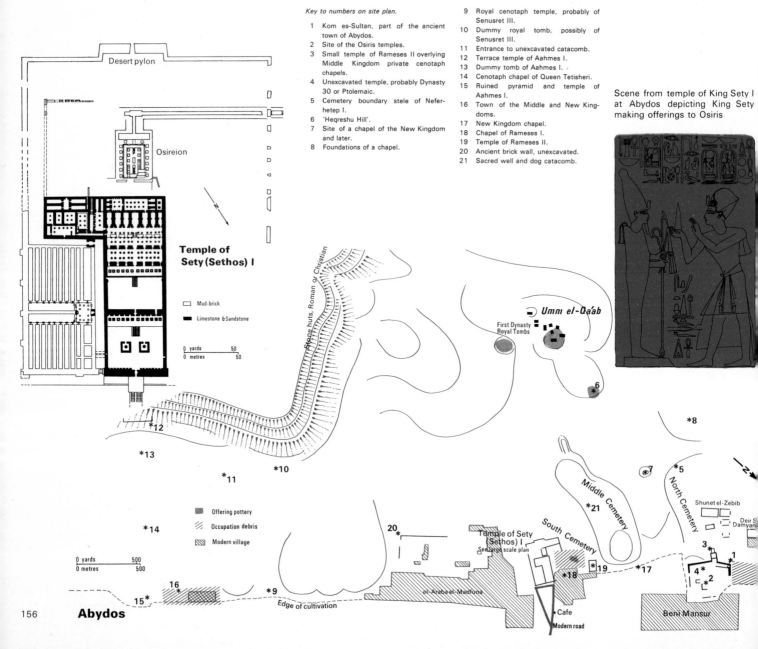

Key to numbers on site plan.

1 Kom es-Sultan, part of the ancient town of Abydos.
2 Site of the Osiris temples.
3 Small temple of Rameses II overlying Middle Kingdom private cenotaph chapels.
4 Unexcavated temple, probably Dynasty 30 or Ptolemaic.
5 Cemetery boundary stele of Neferhetep I.
6 'Heqreshu Hill'.
7 Site of a chapel of the New Kingdom and later.
8 Foundations of a chapel.
9 Royal cenotaph temple, probably of Senusret III.
10 Dummy royal tomb, possibly of Senusret III.
11 Entrance to unexcavated catacomb.
12 Terrace temple of Aahmes I.
13 Dummy tomb of Aahmes I.
14 Cenotaph chapel of Queen Tetisheri.
15 Ruined pyramid and temple of Aahmes I.
16 Town of the Middle and New Kingdoms.
17 New Kingdom chapel.
18 Chapel of Rameses I.
19 Temple of Rameses II.
20 Ancient brick wall, unexcavated.
21 Sacred well and dog catacomb.

Scene from temple of King Sety I at Abydos depicting King Sety making offerings to Osiris

Desert pylon

Osireion

Temple of Sety (Sethos) I

☐ Mud-brick
■ Limestone & Sandstone

0 yards 50
0 metres 50

Stone huts, Roman or Christian

Umm el-Qa'ab

First Dynasty Royal Tombs

*6

*12

*13

*10

*11

*8

*7 *5

Middle Cemetery

North Cemetery

Shunet el-Zebib

Deir S. Damyan

*21

■ Offering pottery
▨ Occupation debris
▥ Modern village

0 yards 500
0 metres 500

*14

20*

Temple of Sety (Sethos) I
See large scale plan

South Cemetery

3*
*4 1
*2

16* *9

15*

*18 *19 *17

el-Araba el-Madfuna

Cafe

Modern road

Edge of cultivation

Beni Mansur

El-Amarna

City and tombs
c. 1365–1350 BC

BIBLIOGRAPHY
Aldred, C., *Akhenaten*, London, 1968. (New aspects of antiquity.)
Samson, J., *Amarna. City of Akhenaten and Nefertiti*, key pieces from the Petrie Collection, London, 1972
Peet, T. E., Woolley, C. L., Frankfort, H., Pendlebury, J. D. S. et al., *The City of Akhenaten*, 3 parts in 4 vols., London, 1923–51. (Egypt Exploration Society, memoirs 38, 40, 44)
Davies, N. M. de G., *The Rock Tombs of El-Amarna*, 6 vols., London 1903–8. (Egypt Exploration Fund, Archaeological Survey of Egypt, memoirs 13–18)

In about 1370 BC, at the height of the New Kingdom, Amenhetep IV, later called Akhenaten, came to the throne, a son of Amenhetep III. His reign of 17 years is marked by an extraordinary personal attempt by the king to introduce a major change in Egyptian theology. Its purpose appears to have been to substitute for the complexities and subtleties of conventional theology the simpler notion that all life and divine power emanated from a single direct source, the sun's disk, called since much earlier times the Aten. It was also probably accompanied by a reappraisal of kingship, to emphasize its divine and non-human properties. This is reflected, particularly in statuary, in the strange distortions of the king's appearance.

He planned an entirely new capital city, called Akhetaten, 'The Sun Disk's Horizon', now known as el-Amarna. A series of boundary stelae cut high up in the cliffs set its limits as a great desert-filled bay in the cliffs on the east bank of the Nile, and a broad tract of agricultural land on the west. The city, as built, straggled along the edge of the river and has thus been partly lost under modern fields. It was built almost entirely of mud brick, and remains only partially excavated. In the centre were temples of brick and limestone built as series of open courts packed with altars, appropriate for direct worship of the visible sun. Alongside were administrative quarters, and a small royal residence connected by a bridge over the central avenue to an enormous brick and stone building, either a very formal palace or another temple. Since all stonework was robbed anciently this bridge is now one of the few easily recognizable features on the site. To north and south stretched residential suburbs through which ran broad avenues parallel to the river. The suburbs were a chaotic mixture of rich men's estates and dwellings of the lowly. They were interrupted by other palaces, including one at the north end, with a massive double wall, which was perhaps the main royal residence.

In the cliffs behind, in two main groups, are the unfinished tombs of some court officials, decorated by carvings in the new style which subordinated everything to depictions of the royal family and their temples. In a side valley some distance to the east is a further group of tombs, all unfinished except one, the tomb of the king himself.

Early in the reign of his successor, Tutankhamen, the city was abandoned, and eventually the stone buildings were demolished to supply building stone, particularly for the temples of nearby Hermopolis where many of the blocks have been recovered. Akhenaten's theological innovations were ignored.

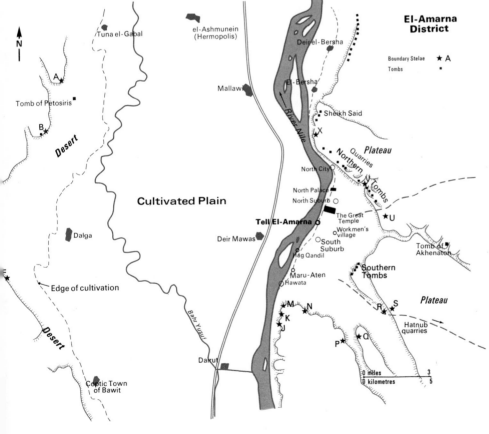

Tanis EGYPT

Temples and royal cemetery
c. 1050–730 BC

BIBLIOGRAPHY
Montet, P., *Tanis. Douze années de Fouilles*, Paris, 1942
Montet, P., *La Nécropole Royale de Tanis*, 3 vols., Paris, 1947–60
Van Seters, J., *The Hyksos*, New Haven and London, 1966, ch. 9

This is almost the only Delta site to have been made the object of a prolonged major excavation, principally by a French expedition. It lies near the village of San el-Hagar in the far north-eastern corner of the Delta, beyond the limits of the fertile alluvium, in a desolate area of salt marshes. It was an important city for the kings of Dynasties 21 and 22, many of whom were buried there, and may, indeed, have been largely created by them. Lying near the coast it may have had commercial importance, although there is no direct evidence for an ancient port.

Excavations have so far been concentrated in the great temple enclosure. It had been anciently robbed for stone so that little more than the foundations of a complex of temples has been recovered, spanning the period from Psusennes I, in the 11th century BC, to Ptolemy IV (221–203 BC). A striking feature are the fragments littering the ground from an avenue of granite obelisks. The most famous discovery, in 1939, was that of the royal tombs of some of the kings of Dynasties 21 and 22, in subterranean burial chambers in one corner of the temple enclosure. Some were relatively intact, though affected by damp, and yielded a splendid collection of gold and silver coffins and masks, jewelry and vessels. They inevitably suffer from comparison with the not dissimilar Tutankhamen treasure, but they display, nevertheless, some fine craftsmanship. The collection is in the Cairo Museum.

Tanis has also provided a major archaeological puzzle. Although no buildings or strata can for certain be ascribed to a period earlier than Psusennes I the site has produced a very considerable amount of

Tanis

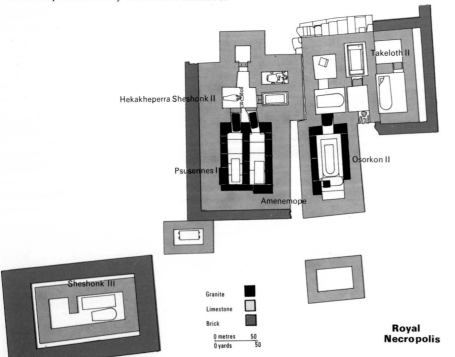

Royal Necropolis

Granite
Limestone
Brick

stone monuments of earlier periods, including at least 18 obelisks of Rameses II and a fragment from a colossus of his probably reaching 92 feet (28 m) in height, and many sphinxes and statues of the Middle Kingdom. On the evidence available it would seem that the kings of Dynasties 21 and 22, unwilling or unable to commission sufficient new stone monuments to embellish their temples, collected a large number from elsewhere and transported them to Tanis, which must have come to resemble a veritable museum of Egyptian sculpture. On this interpretation there are no grounds for indentifying Tanis with either the Hyksos capital of Avaris, or the late New Kingdom city of Per-Rameses, the Biblical 'Raamses'.

Considerable mounds await excavation outside the temple enclosure, on some of which stone columns and blocks have been observed.

Abu Simbel EGYPT

Rock temples
1290–1224 BC

BIBLIOGRAPHY
Macquitty, W., *Abu Simbel*, London, 1965
Desroches-Noblecourt, C., and Kuentz, C., *Le Petit Temple d'Abou-Simbel*, 2 vols., Cairo, 1968

The New Kingdom empire in Nubia seems to have been much more ambitious in conception than anything before: nothing less than complete integration into Egypt. The central feature of this was the building of stone temples, often in places where the population can have scarcely been more than a small village. The last of the great temple builders in Nubia was Rameses II (1290–1224 BC). Much of his work was confined to Lower Nubia, and to sites where the proximity of sandstone cliffs to the river enabled part or all of the temple to be rock hewn. This was fully within the spirit of Egyptian architecture, but had never been so consistently developed. The main temple at Abu Simbel is by far the largest and most ambitiously conceived, cut into a high cliff which inscriptions call a 'Holy Mountain'. The

others were at Beit el-Wali, Gerf Husein, el-Sebua, and Derr. The el-Sebua temple also preserved remains of mudbrick buildings, including priests' houses, within an enclosure wall in front of the temple, and it is not unlikely that others, including Abu Simbel, were similarly provided. A contemporary cemetery lies a short distance from Abu Simbel.

The larger temple has an impressive façade, with two pairs of colossal seated statues of the king, each over 65 feet (19·8 m) high. At the rear of the temple, which faces due east towards the rising sun, is a group of four rock-hewn statues to whom the temple was dedicated: Rameses II himself, Ptah, Amen, and the sun god Horakhty. Of the interior wall scenes the most important is a complex com-

position depicting the Battle of Kadesh, fought against the Hittites. A short distance downstream is a smaller rock temple dedicated to Queen Nefertari, Rameses II's principal queen. Colossal standing statutes of the queen and her husband flank the entrance. Adjacent to both temples are numerous commemorative rock stelae and graffiti of New Kingdom officials, and even earlier visitors of the Middle Kingdom long before the temples were built.

To safeguard them from the waters of the great reservoir behind the new Aswan dam the temples were separated from the mountain, cut into large blocks, and, by late 1968, had been re-erected on the top of the cliff. They are accessible from Aswan by plane or hydrofoil.

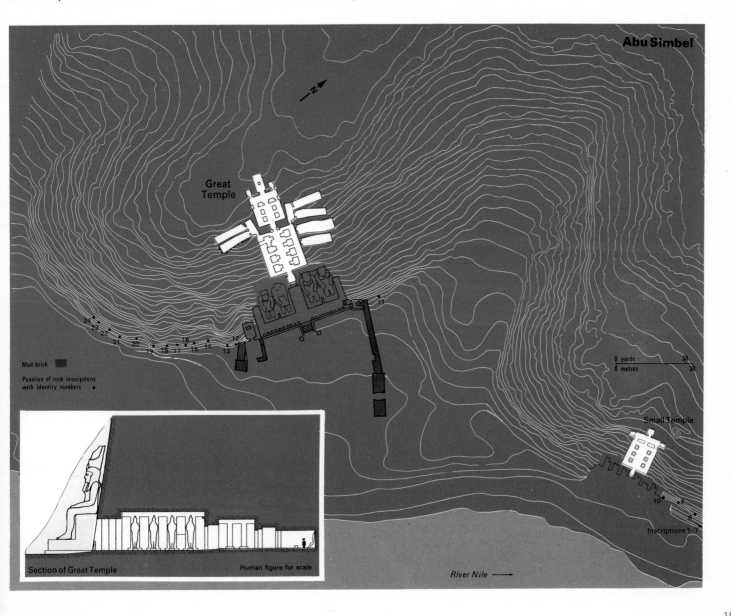

Abu Simbel

Great Temple

Small Temple

Mud-brick

Position of rock inscriptions with identity numbers

Inscriptions 1–7

0 yards 30
0 metres 30

Section of Great Temple

Human figure for scale

River Nile →

Edfu EGYPT

Temple
237–57 BC

BIBLIOGRAPHY
Fairman, H. W., 'Worship and festivals in an Egyptian
    temple', in *Bulletin of the John Rylands Library*, vol. 37
    no. 1, (Sept. 1954), pp. 165–203
Reymond, E. A. E., *The Mythical Origin of the Egyptian
    Temple*, Manchester, 1969
Bruyère, B., Michalowski, K, et al., *Tell Edfou*, 1937, 1938,
    1939, 3 vols., Cairo, 1937, 1938, 1950. (Fouilles franco-
    polonaises)

Most of the provincial towns of Upper Egypt seem to have had a relatively uninterrupted and uneventful history. Edfu is one of them. Over the centuries the slow and piecemeal rebuilding of houses on the remains of their predecessors created a mound, or tell. Part of this is still occupied by the modern town, other parts have been quarried away for *sebbakh* (fertilizer), but a little has remained available for archaeologists, and can be glimpsed away to the right as the visitor prepares to enter the temple enclosure. Only the upper levels, of the Ptolemaic, Roman and Byzantine periods have been excavated. These provide a good example of the densely packed and tangled town layouts of the 'organic' type which is the opposite to geometrical town planning in the classical tradition. Beneath it must lie similar layers

of the earlier periods. The *sebbakh* digging has revealed that the town mound had at some time encroached upon an Old Kingdom cemetery which now lies partially exposed.

The rising ground level of the town mound did not apply to the temple enclosure. Thus by the Ptolemaic period this had become like a great well in the middle of the town. In the reign of Ptolemy III, in 237 BC, a grandiose project was begun to replace the old temple. This was to last for over 180 years, into the reign of Ptolemy XI, and to produce what has survived as the most complete temple from ancient Egypt. It was dedicated to the local god, the hawk-headed Horus of Edfu. It must have stood inside an enclosure containing other religious structures, including a sacred lake, with a ceremonial avenue

leading away to the south, but this is all well buried beneath the present town. The temple architecture is typical of the Ptolemaic period, with a screen wall rather than a pylon separating the forecourt from the first columned hall. Also typical of the period is the rich variety in the designs of the capitals of columns, many of them having elaborately interlaced floral designs. Inside and outside the walls are covered with religious scenes and inscriptions, the latter written in a deliberately complicated script to render them unintelligible to all but a priestly few. When translated they are found to include summaries of rituals and of myths, among them a complicated mythological history of the temple building at Edfu imagined to be standing on the very site of the primeval hill where creation first took place.

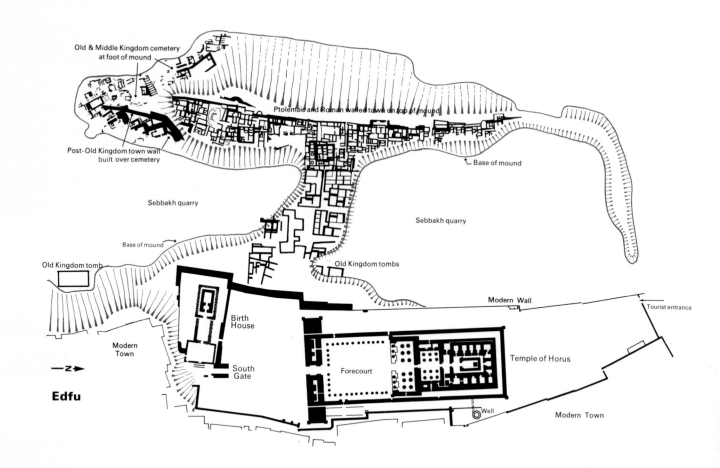

Edfu

Dendera EGYPT

Temple
116 BC–AD 117

BIBLIOGRAPHY
Daumas, F., *Dendara et la Temple d'Hathor*, Cairo, 1969.
(Recherches d'archéologie 29)
Fischer, H. G., *Dendera in the Third Millennium BC*, Locust
Valley, NY, 1968
Petrie, Sir W. M. F., *Dendereh*, London, 1900. (Egypt
Exploration Fund, memoir 17)

Like EDFU, Dendera was a provincial town, also a nome (province) capital, with a long and relatively uneventful history which has not, however, continued into modern times since, unlike Edfu, the site is no longer inhabited. Its main deity was the goddess Hathor. The principal attraction is the fine Ptolemaic temple standing almost intact inside its enclosure which, too, preserves an unusually clear idea of what else lay inside a temple enclosure. Visitors enter the great mudbrick enclosure wall through a tall sandstone gateway erected as late as the Roman emperors Domitian, Nerva, and Trajan (AD 81–117). On the right is a row of smaller buildings. Two of them are birth houses (*mammisi*), a standard component of Ptolemaic temple layouts wherein was celebrated the divine birth of the king. Between them is an unusually well built early Christian church which typifies the situation in so many Egyptian temples, whose sanctity was taken over by the Christians. Beyond these are the foundations of a brick sanatorium in which divine healing was practised. Then comes the sacred lake on which rites were enacted. Finally, behind the main temple is a smaller temple, with its own gateway in the east wall, to celebrate the birth of the goddess Isis. The main temple is unusual in lacking the stone pylon and forecourt possessed, for example, by Edfu. But otherwise it exemplifies the Egyptian temple tradition of a succession of ever smaller and darker halls leading by one central axis to the shrine.

From the high roof of the front part of the temple a fine view of the surroundings can be obtained. The town mound has been reduced more or less to ground level by *sebbakh* (fertilizer) digging and has not been excavated. To the east can be seen the stone gateway, of Roman date, which is all that survives of another temple, probably either for the local god Ihy or for Horus of Edfu, both of whom are known to have had their own temples here. On the desert immediately behind stretches the considerable cemetery for Dendera, a large part of it containing mudbrick *mastaba* tombs of the Old Kingdom, and of the ensuing First Intermediate Period. Towards the west is a catacomb for animal burials, similar in date to the animal catacombs at SAKKARA.

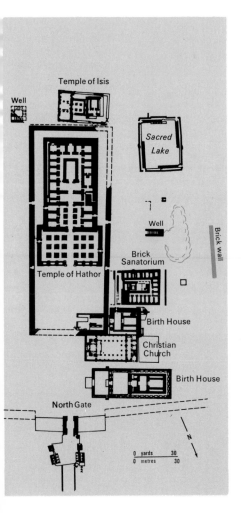

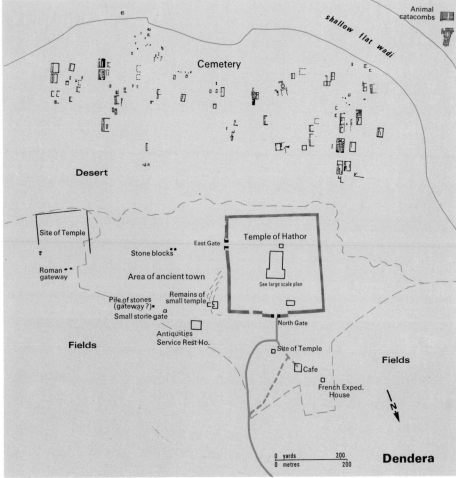

Aswan and Philae EGYPT

Town, cemetery, quarries and temples
c. 2600 BC–Roman period

BIBLIOGRAPHY
De Morgan, J. et al., *Catalogue des Monuments et Inscriptions de l'Egypte Antique*, vol. I, part 1, Vienna, 1894
Engelbach, R., *The Aswan Obelisk*, Cairo, 1922
Preliminary reports on the excavations of the German Archaeological Institute on Elephantine are published in *Mitteilungen des Deutschen Archäologischen Instituts Abteilung Kairo*, vol. 26, 1970, pp. 87–139; vol. 27, 1971, pp. 181–201
Lyons, H. G., *A Report on the Temples of Philae*. Cairo, 1908

In ancient times Egypt's southern frontier lay at the First Cataract, a barrier of rocks and islands which interrupts the flow of the Nile. The frontier town and administrative capital of the southern-most nome (province) was on the southern tip of the island called Elephantine by the Greeks. A portion of the town mound remains, with foundations of a Ptolemaic temple on top. This was dedicated to the ram-headed god Khnum, the leading deity of the area, who figures prominently in local inscriptions and graffiti. It lies behind a small museum containing antiquities from here, and from the archaeological surveys of Nubia. The principal ancient necropolis was on the west bank, in a stretch of cliffs called Qubbet el-Hawa. Thick sand drifts cover the lower unexcavated parts, but in galleries towards the top are some large decorated rock tombs of local governors of Dynasties 6 and 12, some with steep causeways running straight down to the water's edge.

Numerous graffiti, by their content and nature, attest ancient activity in the area. They show how expeditions bound for Nubia landed on the east bank at some point opposite Elephantine, then followed a valley southwards parallel to the cataract, to rejoin the river, and presumably a fresh set of boats, at Konosso whence navigation upstream was unimpeded. The road was protected from attack from the east by a massive mudbrick wall, probably of the Middle Kingdom, and by a fortress on Bigeh island. If camping en route, a narrow defile and a short crossing took them to a naturally protected camp site on the island of Sehel, where an impressive collection of graffiti and rock stelae can be seen. Some commemorate the clearing of obstructions from the natural channels to aid the passage of boats. Expeditions bound for Nubia by the overland desert route to the west followed a still discernible road, past a little rock shrine, visible from far away, called Tingur.

Many graffiti in the Aswan area commemorate quarrying, for which Aswan was famous. The main quarries for red granite lay on the east bank, in two principal zones. That on the north still contains an unfinished New Kingdom obelisk. Those to the south, whose exit was north along the valley taken by the railway, contain unfinished statues and sarcophagi. Sandstone and quartzite quarries, again with an unfinished obelisk, are in Gebel Saman on the west bank.

In Ptolemaic and Roman times a cult of the goddess Isis was built up on the island of Philae, and came to be represented by a picturesque group of temples. These now lie in the turbulent waters between the old and new Aswan dams, and are to be moved to the nearby island of Agilkia.

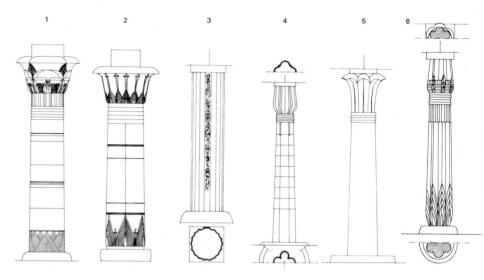

1 Composite column, with innumerable variations of detail on the capital

2 Bell-shaped, or single papyrus column with open capital

3 Fluted column

4 Date palm column

5 Lotus column

6 Papyrus column with closed-bud capital. Note the triangular section of the stalks

Philae

- Brick
- Stone

N

Main Gate

ramp

Temple of Harendotes

Temple of Isis

Enclosure wall

Birth House

Temple of Hathor

Temple of Imhotep

Kiosk of Trajan

Temple of Arsenuphis

Gate of Nectanebo

0 yards 50
0 metres 50

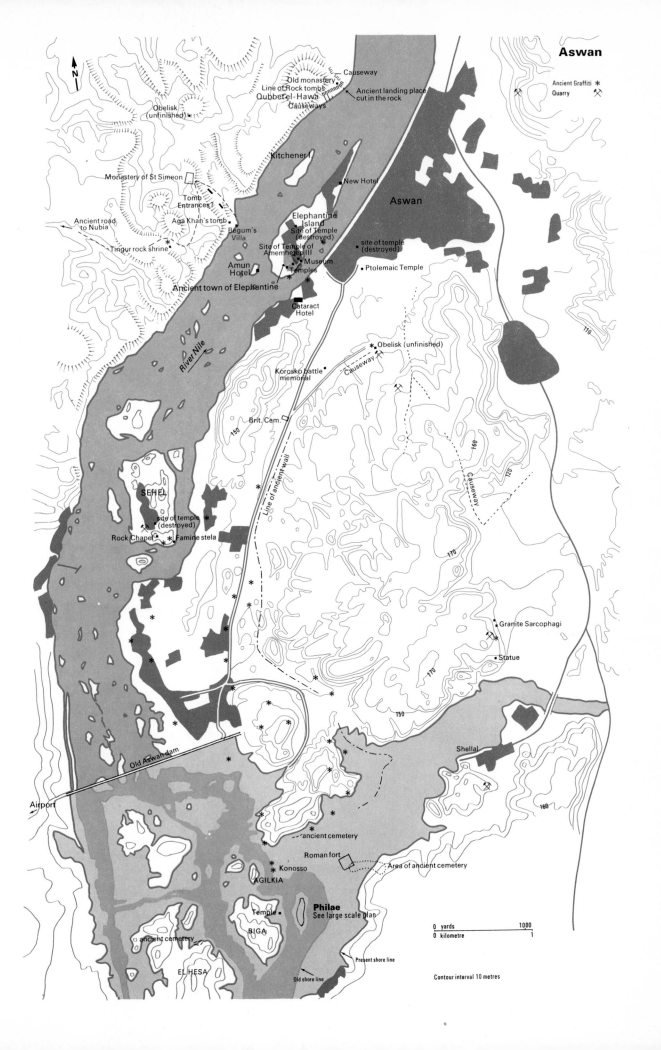

Aswan

Ancient Graffiti ✳
Quarry ⚒

Old monastery
Line of Rock tombs
Qubbet el-Hawa
Causeways
Causeway
Ancient landing place
cut in the rock

Kitchener I.

New Hotel

Aswan

Monastery of St Simeon

Tomb
Entrances?

Obelisk
(unfinished)

Elephantine
Island
Site of Temple
(destroyed)

site of temple
(destroyed)

Ancient road
to Nubia

Aga Khan's tomb

Begum's
Villa

Site of Temple of
Amemheten III

Museum
Temples

Ptolemaic Temple

Tingur rock shrine

Amun
Hotel

Ancient town of Elephantine

Cataract
Hotel

River Nile

Obelisk (unfinished)

Korosko battle
memorial

Causeway

Brit. Cem.

150

160

170

Causeway

SEHEL

site of temple
(destroyed)

170

Rock Chapel
Famine stela

Granite Sarcophagi

Statue

170

150

Shellal

Old Aswan dam

160

Airport

ancient cemetery

Roman fort

Area of ancient cemetery

Konosso

AGILKIA

Temple

Philae
See large scale plan

BIGA

0   yards   1000

0 kilometre   1

ancient cemetery

EL HESA

Present shore line

Old shore line

Contour interval 10 metres

163

Semna SUDAN

Fortresses
c. 1870–1780 BC

BIBLIOGRAPHY
Dunham, D. and Janssen, J. M. A., *Semna Kumma*, Boston 1960. (Second Cataract Forst, vol. 1)
Vercoutter, J., 'Semna South fort and the records of Nile levels at Kumma' in Kush, 14, 1966, pp. 125–64
Lawrence, A. W., 'Ancient Egyptian fortifications' in *Journal of Egyptian Archaeology*, 51, 1965, pp. 69–94
Smither, P. C., 'The Semneh Despatches' in *Journal of Egyptian Archaeology*, 31, 1945, pp. 3–10

Early in the Middle Kingdom the Egyptians invaded Lower Nubia and continued to hold it until some date after about 1780 BC. Access to the gold and other minerals of the Nubian hills and deserts was thereby secured, and some check could be kept on the growing power of the native kingdoms of the northern Sudan, particularly the Kingdom of Kush. The Egyptian presence was maintained by elaborately planned and massively constructed mudbrick fortresses built on the river banks. The Egyptian garrisons who lived inside remained culturally quite separate from the indigenous population. Aniba, Buhen, and Mirgissa were the largest. In the reign of Senusret III (1878–1843 BC) the area thus occupied was extended for a further 30 miles (48 km) upstream to the Semna Gorge, at the head of the Second Cataract area. Here, where the river narrows to flow between two rocky headlands, a pair of mudbrick fortresses was erected. Each was planned so as to make maximum use of the uneven terrain, and provided with stone-lined passages down to the water's edge to safeguard the water supply in time of siege. Inscriptions left here by Senusret III proclaim this the Egyptian frontier, north of which no Nubian could proceed by boat or on foot unless he were an envoy or heading for an officially designated trading port at Mirgissa.

The role of the forts was made more effective by a surveillance system which operated patrols into the surrounding deserts. Detailed intelligence reports on papyrus, a group of which (the Semna Despatches) have survived, were sent back to Thebes. An observation post north of Semna and a checkpoint on the road leading past Kumma were marked by ancient graffiti. Other graffiti measured the high-water level of the Nile in the late 12th and early 13th Dynasties. These show a greatly varying flood level, in some years reaching a height of 20 to 25 feet (6·7–7·6 m) above the modern one.

The greatly extended New Kingdom empire reduced the strategic value of Semna. Nevertheless both sites continued to be occupied, and were graced with little sandstone temples, one dedicated partly to Sunusret III. Taharka, a king of Dynasty 25, built a further brick temple in Semna fort. The whole area has now disappeared beneath the waters of the great reservoir, Lake Nasser. The two sandstone temples were dismantled in 1964, to be rebuilt in the grounds of the new museum at Khartoum.

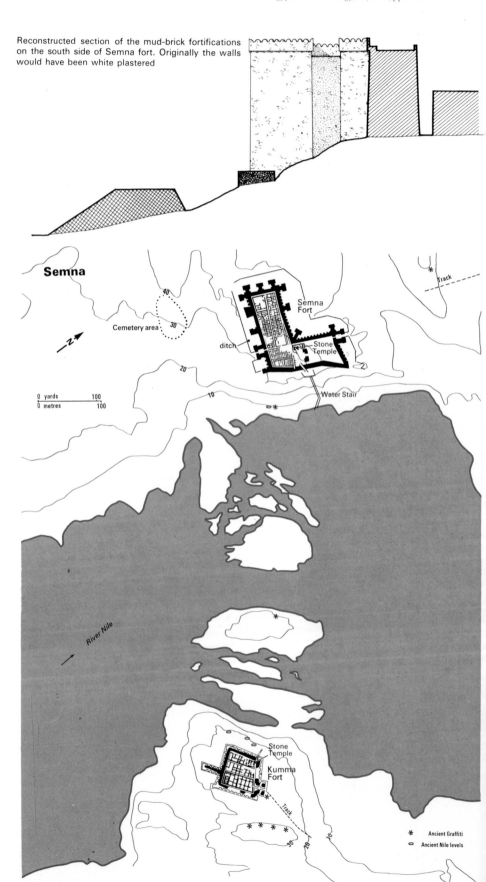

Reconstructed section of the mud-brick fortifications on the south side of Semna fort. Originally the walls would have been white plastered

Kerma SUDAN

Castle and cemetery
c. 1650–1530 BC

BIBLIOGRAPHY
Reisner, G. A., *Excavations at Kerma*, I–V, 2 vols., Cambridge, Mass., 1923. (Harvard African Studies, vols. 5 and 6)
Hintze, F., 'Das Kerma-Problem' in *Zeitschrift für Ägyptische Sprache*, vol. 91, 1964, pp. 79–86
O'Connor, D. B., 'Ancient Egypt and black Africa – early contacts,' *Expedition*, University Museum of Pennsylvania, 14, no. 1, Fall 1971, pp. 2–9

In the century or so between the end of the Middle Kingdom and the beginning of the New Kingdom, thus the late 17th and early 16th centuries BC, the Kingdom of Kush which had figured so prominently in the military records of the Middle Kingdom became the dominant political force of Nubia, extending its sway probably over most of Lower Nubia as well. At the same time much of Egypt was ruled by a dynasty of Palestinian origin, the Hyksos. The centre of the Kushite kingdom was at Kerma. Situated at the northern end of one of the most fertile areas of the northern Sudan, and 150 miles (241 km) south of Semna, it was also within easy reach of the great overland trade and communications route which bypasses southern Egypt, the Darb el-Arba'in. The kings of Kush maintained diplomatic relations with the Hyksos, employed Egyptians in their service,

occupied some of the old Middle Kingdom forts, and even repaired the little garrison temple at Buhen. Their culture was a distinctive one, with a taste for Egyptian-type glazed objects and finely made red and black polished pottery. They also acquired much old Egyptian statuary, some of it royal, which for many years misled scholars into thinking that Kerma had been an Egyptian trading post.

Practically all of the ancient town has been reduced by denudation to a layer of potsherds and rough stone utensils. But at the south end stands the remains of a massive brick castle, still over 60 feet (18 m) high. Its great solid mass was clearly to support at some considerable height above the ground a series of apartments, reached by a single broad staircase. A confused sequence of foundations

was excavated on the west side. The latest phase seems to have represented a courtyard in front of the great staircase, and opposite, a building representing one of the earliest uses in the Nile valley of baked brick, its piers possibly to support a balcony.

The cemetery, only partially excavated and published, contains many hundreds of tumulus graves. The northern part, the least known, probably represents earlier cultural periods. The southern part contains the royal cemetery of the Kings of Kush, including two funerary temples, one encased in sandstone. The elaborately constructed tumuli, with brick frameworks, had contained, in addition to the main burial, subsidiary burials and sacrificial human burials, in one case (K X) amounting to at least 322. The kingdom and its culture were terminated by the Egyptian invasions of early Dynasty 18.

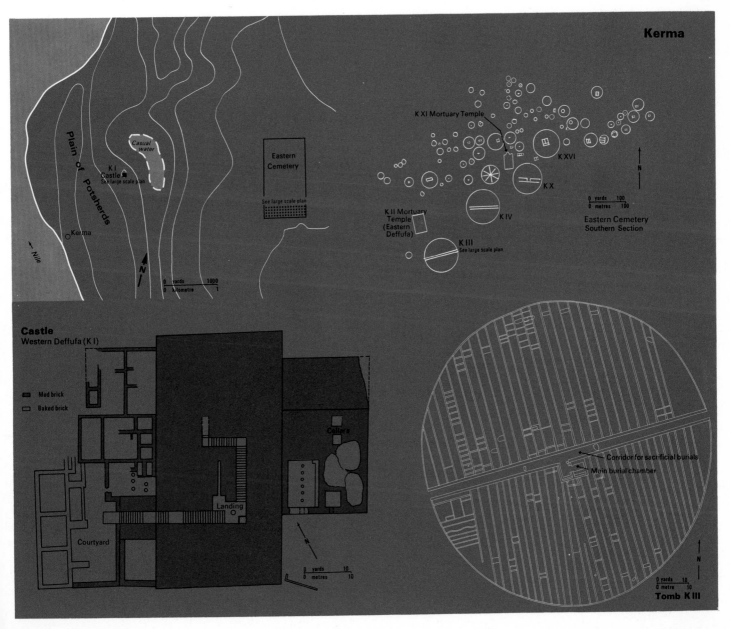

Meroe SUDAN

City and cemeteries
c. 750 BC–AD 320

BIBLIOGRAPHY
Garstang, J., *Meroe. The city of the Ethiopians*, Oxford, 1911
Shinnie, P. L., *Meroe. A civilization of the Sudan*, London, 1967. (Ancient Peoples and Places, vol. 55)
Dunham, D., *Royal Tombs at Meroe and Barkal*, Boston, Mass., 1957. (Royal Cemeteries of Kush, 4)
Dunham, D., *The West and South Cemeteries at Meroë*, Boston, Mass., 1963. (Royal Cemeteries of Kush, 5)

For a brief period in the late 8th and early 7th centuries BC, long after the end of the New Kingdom empire in Nubia, a line of Sudanese kings, following a successful invasion, included Egypt in their rule until defeated and expelled by the Assyrians. They form Dynasty 25. Thereafter, until the 4th century AD, they dominated the northern Sudan, ruling from the great city of Meroe. Although the culture of their people was basically an indigenous one, with its own religion and distinctive pottery, and eventually its own alphabetic script, the kings borrowed and adapted from ancient Egypt a number of characteristic features. These were particularly the style of temple architecture, and pyramidal tombs, and they gave to the Meroitic court the dignity and cultural authority of the Egyptian Pharaohs.

Meroe itself lies a short distance from the east bank of the Nile, some 125 miles (201 km) downstream from Khartoum, on a flat plain broken by low hills, and nearly opposite one of the trans Bayuda Desert crossings. Its centre was the royal enclosure, surrounded by a massive stone wall, and containing a number of palaces and other separate buildings of mudbrick, baked brick, and stone. Excavation uncovered a series of superimposed levels representing a long and continuous occupation. Most of the buildings were relatively small, but probably of several storeys. A number of widely scattered temples in brick and stone lie outside the enclosure. Although their architecture is Egyptian-inspired their layouts must reflect local cult practices. Picturesque names given to some of them, such as Sun Temple, Lion Temple, and Temple of Isis only obscure the fact that very little is known of their precise function. The two most important seem to have been the Temple of Amen, the most obviously Egyptian-like, and the misnamed Sun Temple, a particularly fine specimen of a type of temple closely associated, as here, with a great earthen water reservoir called a *hafir*. The rest of the city remains largely unexcavated, extending around the royal enclosure on the east, south, and north. Its stratified levels reach a depth of 30 to 40 feet (9–12 m). Around its edges lie extensive slag heaps from a contemporary iron industry using local ferricrete sandstone.

Over a wide expanse of desert east of the city are scattered the tumulus tombs of the ordinary people, burials in a traditional mode uninfluenced by Egyptian practices. But on three distant low hills, called collectively Begrawiya, are the court cemeteries. These contain numerous pyramids for the later kings of Meroe (Begrawiya North) and for other royalty, also *mastaba* tombs and more tumuli.

Other important Meroitic sites are at Musawarat es-Sofra, Naga, and Napata near which are further pyramid cemeteries.

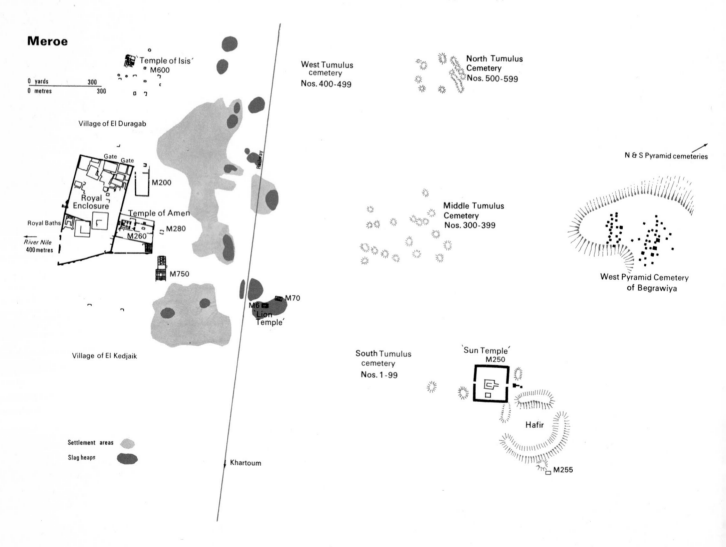

Meroe

0 yards 300
0 metres 300

Temple of Isis
M600

Village of El Duragab

Gate Gate
M200

Royal Enclosure

Royal Baths
River Nile
400 metres

Temple of Amen
M280
M260

M750

M70
M6
'Lion Temple'

Village of El Kedjaik

Settlement areas
Slag heaps

Railway

Khartoum

West Tumulus cemetery
Nos. 400-499

North Tumulus Cemetery
Nos. 500-599

Middle Tumulus Cemetery
Nos. 300-399

South Tumulus cemetery
Nos. 1-99

N & S Pyramid cemeteries

West Pyramid Cemetery of Begrawiya

'Sun Temple'
M250

Hafir

M255

MESOPOTAMIA, IRAN AND THE ARABIAN GULF

The Mesopotamian plain is bounded on the north east by the Zagros ranges along the Iranian border and slopes gradually up to the Arabian massif on the south west. On the west it is cut off from the Mediterranean by the highlands of Palestine and Lebanon and the Amanus range, separated only by the 'Syrian saddle' through which the Orontes flows to the sea. North east of a line joining Hit on the Euphrates with Samarra on the Tigris is a rolling steppe through which the rivers have cut trough valleys. South east of this line the land consists of recent alluvium, but the deposition of silt by the rivers has been compensated by episodic subsidence of the underlying rock structure, and there is no reason to believe that the shoreline of the Gulf has changed substantially since human settlement began. Subsidence may at times have outstripped deposition and contributed to widespread flooding, of which there is archaeological evidence at UR and other ancient cities and, probably, a historic tradition in the Flood legends.

The climate is continental in type, with hot summers and relatively cold winters. Rainfall occurs in the winter and spring months and is almost entirely derived from depressions moving eastwards from the Mediterranean. Most of these are intercepted by the coastal highlands, and they find free passage only across the Syrian saddle. Consequently rainfed agriculture is possible only in a belt some 60 miles (approx. 100 km) wide across the northern rim of the plain and in the foothills east of the Tigris. Elsewhere cultivation is dependent on irrigation, using the waters of the Tigris and Euphrates and their tributaries, and north of the Hit–Samarra line is restricted to their relatively narrow flood plains. The central plain outside the river valleys, known in the west as the Syrian Desert, between the two rivers as the Jazira, is habitable only by nomadic herdsmen, the modern Bedouin. In the southern alluvium the rivers have built levées and most of the land between them can be irrigated, although the very gradual drop in land level makes drainage difficult and both ancient and modern irrigation systems have been severely affected by salination. The history of Mesopotamian climate is still little known, but the distribution of ancient sites suggests that during the last 10,000 years there have been only minor variations in rainfall affecting marginal areas. There is evidence, however, for the progressive desiccation of the Arabian peninsula after the end of the Neolithic Wet Phase about 4000 BC, and this may have led to increased movements of nomadic population northwards into the Syrian Desert and their gradual penetration into the settled lands. Certainly such infiltration has been a recurrent feature of Mesopotamian history since the earliest records some 5,000 years ago.

Commerce and communications were also stimulated and controlled by geographical factors. The scarcity or complete lack of many raw materials encouraged the development of long-distance trade. Obsidian from the area of Lake Van was imported for tool making as early as 7000 BC, and copper found on 6th-millennium sites must have come from Turkey or Iran; in the later prehistoric period there was a growing demand for luxuries such as gold, silver and semi-precious stones. This brought ever-widening trade by land and, by the middle of the 3rd millennium, considerable sea traffic down the Gulf to the shores of Arabia and eastwards to the Indus valley. But the pattern of land routes was largely dictated by natural conditions. Eastward the Zagros ranges could be crossed by a limited number of passes, of which the most important was the road to Kermanshah up the Diyala valley. In the plain only the rainfall zone afforded sufficient water and forage to permit a free choice of routes, which nevertheless converged on important foci such as the passage to the Mediterranean by the Orontes valley, controlled successively by Aleppo and Antioch, and the crossing of the Tigris at Mosul/Nineveh. In the south the waterways must have served as the main arteries of transport, and in central Mesopotamia, although neither the Euphrates nor the Tigris was conveniently navigable in both directions, the caravan routes followed their valleys; desert travel was commercially impracticable until the camel came into widespread use as a beast of burden late in the 1st millennium BC. The great highways from the east, north and west thus converged at the northern end of the alluvial plain, and obviously influenced the location there of a series of important capitals, from KISH in the 3rd millennium to Islamic Baghdad.

Our first evidence of permanent settlements dependent on agriculture and herding goes back to the 8th millennium BC in the foothills of the Zagros, where the plants and animals that were first domesticated were already to be found in the wild state. Only small sites such as the hilltop village of Jarmo have so far been found and excavated. It is probable that larger communities also existed, but in this and subsequent periods our knowledge of Mesopotamian history is often limited by the fact that a well-favoured site was usually occupied for thousands of years and its oldest levels lie buried beneath the remains of many later cities. The next stage seems to have been the extension of agriculture into the rainfed northern plain, which took place some time before 6000 BC. Again we rely principally on the evidence of small sites such as Hassuna, after which the culture of this phase is named; we know the existence of a settlement beneath the later city of Nineveh, but not its extent, although its position at the Tigris crossing suggests that it would have been an important centre. The first large villages or small towns that have been excavated lie further south, at Baghouz on the Euphrates, at Tell as Sawwan near Samarra in the Tigris valley, and at Choga Mami near Mandali on the eastern rim of the plain, where perennial streams emerge from the mountains. These 'Samarra' settlements date from the 6th millennium and mark a further advance in agriculture, the introduction of at least primitive irrigation systems, which can be inferred from their geographical position and from the discovery of irrigated varieties of barley and linseed.

In the southern alluvium at this time there were probably marsh-dwelling communities dependent on hunting and gathering, but the first agricultural settlement is attested about 5000 BC at the site of ERIDU, one of the holy cities of later Sumer. We are ignorant of contemporary developments in the northern alluvium, later Akkad or Babylonia, and cannot say whether the techniques of irrigation were transmitted from central Mesopotamia by people seeking new land, or by imitation from one community to another. But once established they led to a rapid increase in wealth and population that made the alluvium the economic and political centre of Mesopotamia. In the 5th and 4th millennia successive cultures, named after the sites of al 'Ubaid, near Ur, and URUK (Warka), mark stages in the Sumerian development of urban life and increasing influence in other regions of the Near East. Later 'Ubaid pottery has been found along the Arabian shores of the Gulf and throughout northern Mesopotamia as far as the Mediterranean, while direct contacts in the Uruk period extended even further, to Egypt and the Iranian plateau. At home monumental temples of unbaked brick – for building stone was scarce – accommodated the households of the gods, the centres of religious and, at first, secular administration, and about 3500 BC pictographic writing was invented to record their economic transactions. This was gradually formalized into a syllabic 'cuneiform' script in which the first literary and historical texts were written in the early 3rd millennium. Although the language of these documents was Sumerian, some of the personal names reveal the existence of a Semitic-speaking element in the population, perhaps representing the first of the many waves of people of Arabian origin who infiltrated into Mesopotamia.

At the same time secular administration of the numerous city states passed to dynastic rulers, originally perhaps war leaders who nonetheless held office as the earthly representatives of divine patrons, as did all later Mesopotamian kings. Later records reflect the temporary supremacy of one or other dynasty; but it is notable that by the end of this Early Dynastic period the hegemony was traditionally associated with the kingship, not of one of the great religious centres in the south, but of KISH in the northern alluvium, at the crossroads of Mesopotamia. This area was also more exposed to Semitic infiltration than Sumer, and about 2360 BC a Semitic-speaking official at the court of Kish usurped the throne and subsequently founded a new capital, Agade, nearby. Taking the name of Sargon (True King), he established, and his successors for a century maintained, the first Mesopotamian empire, exercising direct control over the northern plain as well as the alluvium, and campaigning from the Mediterranean to the Gulf. The Akkadian empire disintegrated under the pressure of invasion by tribes from the Zagros, but after a period of anarchy it was reunited under

For map of Iran and the Arabian Gulf see p. 186

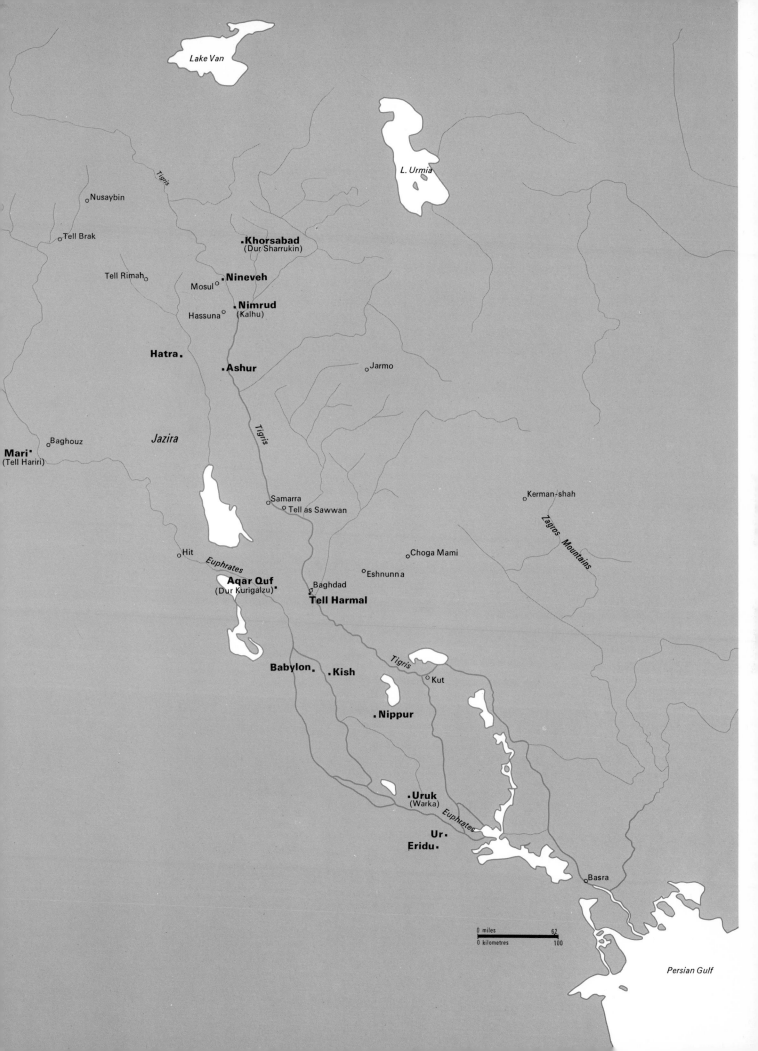

Lake Van

L. Urmia

○ Nusaybin

○ Tell Brak

.Khorsabad
(Dur Sharrukin)

Tell Rimah ○

Mosul ○ **.Nineveh**

Hassuna ○ **.Nimrud**
(Kalhu)

Hatra.

.Ashur

○ Jarmo

Tigris

Jazira

○ Baghouz

Mari .
(Tell Hariri)

Tigris

○ Samarra

○ Tell as Sawwan

○ Kerman-shah

Zagros Mountains

○ Choga Mami

○ Hit

Euphrates

○ Eshnunn a

Aqar Quf
(Dur Kurigalzu) .

Baghdad

Tell Harmal

Babylon. **.Kish**

Tigris

○ Kut

.Nippur

.Uruk
(Warka)

Euphrates

Ur .
Eridu .

○ Basra

0 miles 62

0 kilometres 100

Persian Gulf

the Third Dynasty of Ur, the only occasion when we know that all Mesopotamia was under the rule of a Sumerian city, and the last time that the Sumerians appear as a political force. It is interesting that part at least of the administration was centred on NIPPUR, home of Enlil, chief of the gods, and also the northernmost city of Sumer.

Ur fell just before 2000 BC, and by 1800 a new struggle for supremacy was developing in which the main protagonists were BABYLON, successor to Kish and Agade, MARI on the Euphrates, Eshnunna in the Diyala plain and ASHUR on the upper Tigris, with the kings of Elamite Susa in south-western Iran and of Aleppo in Syria as changeable allies. All these cities controlled important routes, and in Mesopotamia two of them, Ashur and Babylon, were ruled by dynasties of desert origin representing yet another infiltration of Semitic peoples. When this conflict was resolved by the victories of Hammurabi, the centre of political power was established in Babylonia and remained there for six centuries, first under his heirs at Babylon and, after about 1600 BC, under the Kassites, intruders probably of Iranian origin who founded a new capital, Dur Kurigalzu, modern AQAR QUF near Baghdad. In the mid-2nd millennium the northern plain, never under Kassite control, emerged for the first time as a separate political entity. Indo-Aryan rulers, the Mitanni, dominated a confederacy of northern peoples from their capital near Nusaybin, and were succeeded from the 14th century by the kings of Ashur, who now controlled the important centre of NINEVEH and its fertile hinterland. About 1200 BC the whole Near East was thrown into turmoil by the onslaught of the Peoples of the Sea on the Levant coast, and the insurgence of Aramaean tribes in the Syrian Desert and on the borders of the settled lands. Out of this confusion Assyria emerged as the dominant power, first in northern Mesopotamia and, during most of the three centuries from 900 to 600 BC, in Babylonia and Sumer, Syria and the Levant, and finally even in Egypt and western Iran. Although Ashur, the old tribal capital, remained the religious centre of Assyria, her rise to imperial power was marked by the transference of the administration to a series of new capitals further north, Nineveh, NIMRUD (Kalhu) and KHORSABAD (Dur Sharrukin), which were in the heart of the most productive and populous district; the first and last choice among them was Nineveh, which was also the great centre of communications.

The phenomenon of the Late Assyrian Empire cannot be explained by its native resources, but their inadequacy undoubtedly contributed to its sudden collapse; after the fall of Nineveh in 612 BC Assyria was never again a political entity. Babylon under Nebuchadrezzar briefly inherited its metropolitan status, but thereafter Mesopotamia was only the richest province of foreign empires. The advantages of its wealth and position were recognized for the Seleucid, Parthian and Sassanian dynasties, maintained winter capitals at Seleucia and Ctesiphon in Babylonia. Many ancient cities renewed their prosperity, and in the first six centuries AD when Mesopotamia was a frontier province between east and west, new foundations such as HATRA attest the military and political importance of the desert region and its inhabitants, now Arabic-speaking tribes. But it was not until the Abbasid Caliphs founded their capital at Baghdad that Mesopotamia was reborn as the centre of the civilized world.

Eridu IRAQ

Sumerian city
c. 5000 BC

BIBLIOGRAPHY
Safar, F., *Sumer*, Baghdad, Directorate General of Antiquities, 1947, 1950
Lloyd, S. and Safar, F., *Sumer*, Baghdad, Directorate General of Antiquities, 1948

Eridu, (modern Abu Shahrain), lies 196 miles (315 km) south east of Baghdad and 22 miles (35 km) south of the Euphrates. According to Sumerian legend it was the first of the five cities that existed before the Flood, and it was the centre of the worship of Enki, god of the sweet waters that were vital to the prosperity of Sumer. It was served by canals fed from the Euphrates which then passed by UR, 12 miles (20 km) to the north east; an ancient reference to Eridu 'on the shore of the sea' probably implies that it stood on a lagoon connected by waterways to the Gulf. Certainly fishing played an important part in its economy, for deposits of fishbones have been found among the offerings in successive shrines. Its historical importance lies in the series of superimposed temples that have been ex-

cavated there, spanning the whole period of south Mesopotamian prehistory from about 5000 to the early 3rd millennium BC. They demonstrate continuity of religious observance on the same spot and, associated with the uninterrupted development of the site from small village to large city, are a convincing argument for the indigenous origin of Sumerian civilization, although the population was probably an amalgam of groups with originally different ways of life, hunters and fishers as well as farmers. The importance of Eridu in the early 3rd millennium is attested by the discovery of a large palace, one of the earliest known examples of a royal residence separate from the religious precinct, but its history is virtually undocumented. The Sumerian revival under Ur-Nammu of Ur about 2100 BC saw

the construction, as at Ur, Warka and other religious centres, of a ziggurat overlying the high terrace on which the 4th-millennium shrines had stood, and which in turn enclosed the remains of their predecessors. But the ziggurat was never completed and there is little evidence of occupation after this date; Eridu, on the extreme south-western edge of the alluvial plain, was an inhospitable site and the excavations have shown that even during its occupation the encroachment of sand dunes was a recurrent menace. The mounds of the ancient city now extend over an area some 1,300 feet by 1,000 feet (approx. 400 × 300 m), and are dominated by the ruins of Ur-Nammu's ziggurat, but the excavated buildings have once more been covered by blown sand and nothing is visible of their plan.

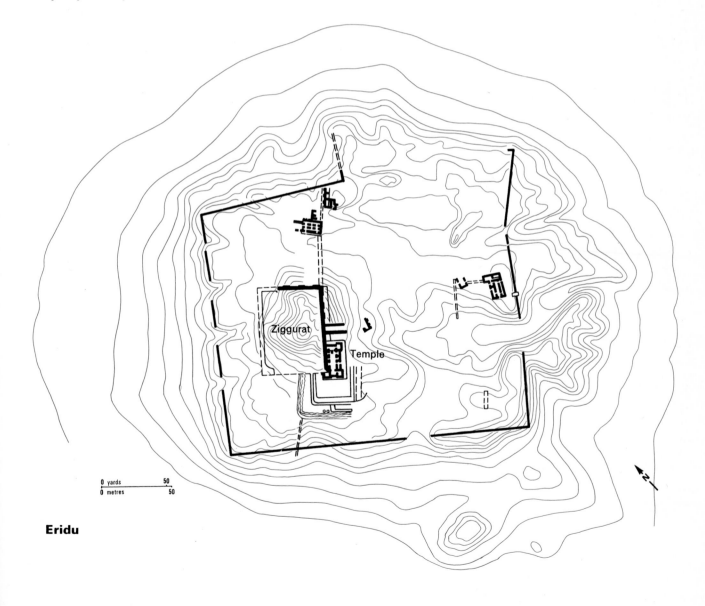

Eridu

Uruk IRAQ

Sumerian city
c. 4500 BC–AD 300

BIBLIOGRAPHY
Lenzen, H., *Vorlaüfiger Bericht über die Ausgrabungen in Uruk-Warka*, Berlin, 1956–68
Schmidt, J., *Vorlaüfiger Bericht*, Berlin, 1972
Lenzen, H., *Archaeology*, New York, 17, 1964

Uruk (modern Warka, Erech of Genesis), lies 155 miles (250km) south east of Baghdad and 12 miles (20 km) from the Euphrates, of which a branch skirted the ancient city. Pottery found there includes some of the earliest known in Sumer, *c.* 5000 BC, and in the 4th millennium there were apparently two settlements, Kullabs and Eanna, each centred around an important sanctuary. Eanna outstripped Kullaba, and by 3500 BC was endowed with a unique complex of vast temples elaborately decorated with pilasters and cone mosaics; this latest phase of Mesopotamian prehistory is known as the Uruk period, and marks the first appearance of major cities. The two sites coalesced to form one large unit, surrounded from the early 3rd millennium by a city wall 6 miles (9·5 km) long. The rulers of Uruk intermittently aspired to leadership in Sumer until the rise of the UR Empire, about 2100 to 2000 BC. After its fall political power passed northwards to Semitic Babylonia and Assyria, but all Mesopotamian over-lords maintained the Sumerian holy cities, and Uruk remained a great religious centre until the Seleucid period. Less is known of its secular buildings, but there was certainly an extensive and prosperous Parthian occupation at the beginning of the 1st millennium AD.

The heart of the city is a complex of three vast buildings. On the east stand the ziggurat and precinct of Eanna, dedicated to the goddess Inanna. Originally laid out by Ur-Nammu of Ur about 2100, it was reconstructed by many rulers down to Cyrus of Persia in the 6th century. The temples of 4th-millennium Eanna lay south west of the ziggurat, and 650 feet (approx. 200 m) to the west is another vast sanctuary of many courtyards, the Bit Resh or Principal Temple, dedicated to Anu, god of the firmament and his wife Antu. This is a Hellenistic building, the last of a series of which the earliest lie outside its boundary to the south west. Here the ruins of the 4th-millennium White Temple stand on a high terrace that incorporates a succession of earlier shrines; this was the centre of Kullaba. South of the Bit Resh is a second huge Seleucid temple, Irigal. On a mound near the city wall to the west are the ruins of the early 2nd-millennium palace of Sinkashid, and much of the southern sector is covered by Parthian ruins, dominated by the temple of Gareus.

Uruk

0 yards 500
0 metres 500

Ur IRAQ

Sumerian city
c. 4500–400 BC

BIBLIOGRAPHY
Woolley, C. L., *Excavations at Ur*, London, 1955
Woolley, C. L., *Ur Excavations II*, Oxford, 1934, V, 1939, X, 1951, IV, 1956, VIII, 1965; with M.E.L. Mallowan, IX, 1962
Mallowan, M. E. L., 'Ur in Retrospect', ed. D. J. Wiseman, *Iraq*, XXII, London, 1960

Ur (modern Muqayyar) lies 186 miles (300 km) south east of Baghdad beside an ancient bed of the Euphrates, which now passes 9 miles (15 km) to the north. Like URUK and ERIDU, it was one of the great religious centres of ancient Sumer, and the site was occupied as early as the 4th millennium BC. The prehistoric settlement, explored in a limited area, was interrupted by the famous Flood Deposit, but this was not necessarily the result of a complete inundation. The city's wealth in the early Sumerian period is attested by the discoveries in the Royal Tombs, *c.* 2500 BC, and in the 21st century it was the centre of the last revival of Sumerian power under Ur-Nammu and his dynasty, who ruled much of Mesopotamia. At this time its merchants traded down the Gulf to the Indian Ocean. Its sack by the Elamites about 2000 and the shift of political power to Babylonia ended its temporal importance, but its religious buildings received the pious attention of many later rulers and it remained prosperous until the Achaemenid period, though it seems to have been abandoned before the time of Alexander.

The site is now dominated by the ziggurat, the best preserved in Mesopotamia, which was first constructed by Ur-Nammu and finally rebuilt by Nabonidus of Babylon in the 6th century; its bottom stage has recently been restored. The temple of the moon god Nannar stood on the summit, and round the base was a large courtyard, with a second smaller one to the north east, both surrounded by service chambers for the business of the shrine. In the angle of the outer walls there was originally a storehouse, and immediately to the south east a complex, the Giparu, containing two temples of Nannar and his consort Ningal, small chapels and the living quarters and tombs of the high priestesses. A short distance to the east a smaller building, Ehursag, was apparently a palace for royal use on religious occasions, and beyond it lay the underground mausolea of Ur-Nammu's successors. The site of the earlier Royal Tombs is just south west of the mausolea. Outside the temenos buildings of many periods have been excavated. The outer city wall was built about 2100 BC. Just inside it on the north was a harbour, and a palace built by Nabonidus for his daughter, the High Priestess Bel-shaltinannar. About 2,000 feet (approx. 600 m) south east of the ziggurat is a quarter of streets and private houses of the early 2nd millennium, which gives a rare impression of an ancient Mesopotamian city.

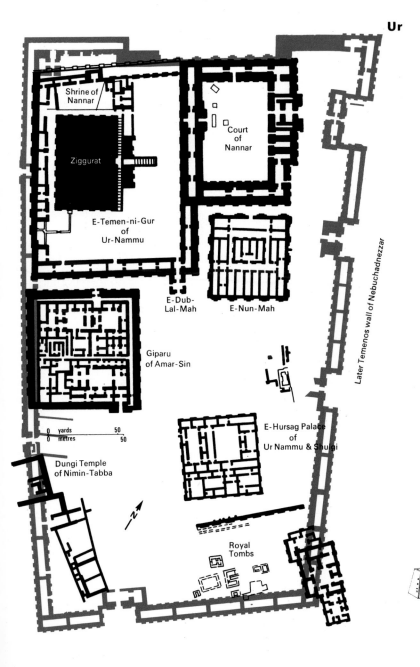

Ur

Shrine of Nannar

Court of Nannar

Ziggurat

E-Temen-ni-Gur of Ur-Nammu

E-Dub-Lal-Mah

E-Nun-Mah

Later Temenos wall of Nebuchadnezzar

Giparu of Amar-Sin

0 yards 50
0 metres 50

Dungi Temple of Nimin-Tabba

E-Hursag Palace of Ur Nammu & Shulgi

Royal Tombs

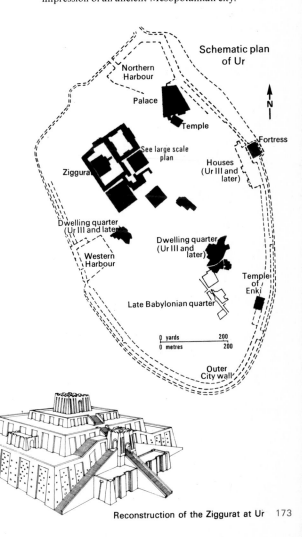

Schematic plan of Ur

Northern Harbour

Palace

Temple

N

Fortress

See large scale plan

Ziggurat

Houses (Ur III and later)

Dwelling quarter (Ur III and later)

Dwelling quarter (Ur III and later)

Western Harbour

Temple of Enki

Late Babylonian quarter

0 yards 200
0 metres 200

Outer City wall

Reconstruction of the Ziggurat at Ur

Nippur IRAQ

Sumerian city
c. 4500 BC–AD 600

BIBLIOGRAPHY
Hilprecht, H. V., *Explorations in Bible Lands during the 19th century*, Edinburgh, 1903
McCown, D. E. and Haines, R. C., *Nippur, I*, Chicago, 1967
Haines, R. C., *Sumer*, Baghdad, Directorate General of Antiquities, 1956, 1958
Kudstad, J. E., *Sumer*, Baghdad, Directorate General of Antiquities, 1966, 1968

Nippur (modern Nuffar) lies 93 miles (150 km) south east of Baghdad and close to the modern town of Afak, on the ancient course of the Euphrates known at the Shatt al Nil. It is the northernmost of the principal religious cities of Sumer, and was occupied from at least 4000 BC. At the beginning of history in the early 3rd millennium it was already the centre of the worship of Enlil, chief deity of the Sumerian pantheon, and its religious pre-eminence remained the principal factor in its later history. Though situated in a prosperous region it never achieved political supremacy, but the temple of Enlil was richly maintained by all the rulers who claimed to control the country as his earthly representatives. The earliest temple so far discovered was built, with the nearby ziggurat, by Ur-Nammu of UR about

2100 BC, and sacked by the Elamites when his dynasty fell a century later. It was almost immediately rebuilt, and restored on at least three later occasions before the conquest of Mesopotamia by the Persians in 539 BC. The prosperity of the city is illustrated by many thousands of clay tablets of all periods, largely economic texts, including the records of a banking house that flourished under the Achaemenid Empire. Later remains are largely eroded, but in the Parthian period the ziggurat was used as the foundation for a massive fortress, and surface finds attest Sassanian and medieval Islamic occupation.

The site is an irregular conglomeration of massive mounds, divided by the ancient Shatt al Nil. Recent excavations have been confined to the mounds

north east of the watercourse, which contained an extensive religious quarter and a scribal district. The remains of the ziggurat stand out in the middle of this sector, crowned by a modern ruin, and the Enlil Temple lies immediately to the north within the same precinct; to the south west stood the temple of Inanna, queen of heaven. Most of the archives were found in the scribal district, south of the precinct and separated from it by a gully, and a number of private houses have been excavated here.

The city wall has been exposed at several points, but its outline on the plan is largely reconstructed from an ancient map of about 1900 BC found on the site; this is one of the rare examples of ancient cartography that can be related to a known area.

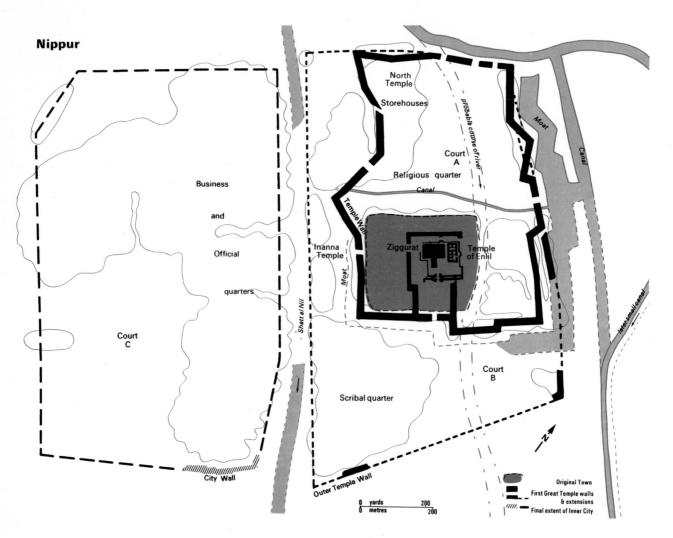

Kish IRAQ

Sumerian city
c. 3500–500 BC

BIBLIOGRAPHY
Mackay, E., Chicago Field Museum of Natural History, Anthropology Memoirs, 1925, 1929
Gibson, A. McG., *The City and Area of Kish*, Miami, 1972
Moorey, P. R. S., *Iraq*, London, 1964

Kish is situated 53 miles (85 km) south of Baghdad and 9 miles (15 km) east of BABYLON, on an ancient branch of the Euphrates and in the northern alluvial plain of Mesopotamia where the river valleys and other major highways converge. It was the first of a series of capitals that lay in this area. Almost nothing is known of prehistoric settlement, but its importance in the early 3rd millennium is reflected in the later legend that names it as the first seat of kingship after the Flood, and the title 'King of Kish', assumed by many rulers of other cities, was an especial claim to hegemony in Sumer. The population was a mixture of Sumerians and Semites, and the Semitic Sargon, who founded the city and empire of Agade, was a court official in Kish. The foundation of Agade led to a decline in its importance, though it was periodically independent until the early 2nd millennium, when it came under the control of Babylon. Hammurabi and his successors restored some of its buildings, but little is known of the city after their time, and when Babylon became a great metropolis in the 6th century BC Kish was little more than a suburb. It continued as a prosperous small town at least until the Sassanian period.

Kish was a twin city, now represented by a series of mounds extending over two and a half miles (4 km) from Uhaimir in the west to Ingharra in the east, along the ancient watercourse. Each of these was originally the focus of a separate settlement with its own temple and ziggurat. The most important standing buildings are the temples at Ingharra, ancient Hursagkalama, which were founded by Nebuchadrezzar in the 6th century. They are of typically Babylonian layout, with central courtyards surrounded by rooms, and ornate internal and external façades. The main gateways face north east, and lead straight through the courtyards to the entrances of the shrines; the large temple, probably of Inanna, has two ante-cellas and a number of vestries and treasuries. The other rooms would have housed the temple personnel and its stores. In the angle between the two buildings to the south was probably a high terrace or ziggurat, with a larger mound marking the site of a second ziggurat behind it. On a small outlying mound south of Ingharra can be seen the ruins of an early 3rd-millennium palace, dating from the greatest period of Kish's power.

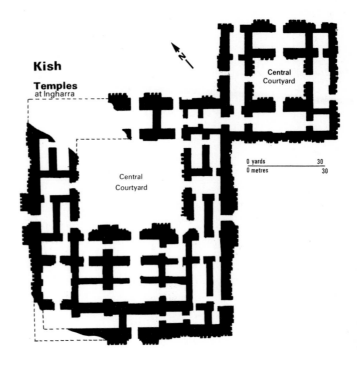

Kish
Temples at Ingharra

Central Courtyard

Central Courtyard

0 yards 30
0 metres 30

Mari SYRIA

City
c. 2800–1750 BC

BIBLIOGRAPHY
Parrot, A., *Mission Archéologique de Mari: Le Palais*, Paris, 1958, 1959; and *Mission Archéologique de Mari: Le Temple d'Ishtar*, Paris, 1956
Parrot, A., *Studia Mariana*, Leiden, 1950
Saggs, H. W. F., *Everyday Life in Babylonia and Assyria*, London, 1965

Mari (modern Tell Hariri) overlooks the west bank of the Euphrates 7 miles (11 km) above Abu Kemal. The site derived its ancient importance from its position on the valley trade route that linked southern Mesopotamia with Syria. It was occupied before 3000 BC, and a number of typically Sumerian statues attest its cultural links in the mid-3rd millennium, though the names inscribed on them show that its rulers and population were Semitic. By the early 2nd millennium it was an independent state of considerable wealth and standing. It was controlled briefly by Shamshi-Adad I of Assyria about 1800 BC but after his death the native ruler Zimri-Lim recovered his throne, only to be defeated by Hammaurabi of Babylon about 1760. The site then declined greatly in importance, although there was a

Late Assyrian settlement there in the 1st millennium.

Excavations have revealed a number of temples and the largest and most complete Mesopotamian palace known before the Late Assyrian period. A series of shrines dedicated to Ishtar, dating from before 2500 to 1800 BC, stood near the west wall of the city, and in the centre was another group around a small ziggurat. On the east lay the palace, which in its final 18th-century form contained more than 260 rooms and courts and measured 650 feet by 400 feet (approx. 200 × 120 m). It was entered by a gate on the north east, which led through guard chambers and an entrance court to the main courtyard with the earliest throne room on the south side, which was originally decorated with paintings of about 2000 BC.

To the west lay a second courtyard where the famous mural painting, the Investiture of Zimri-lim (c. 1780 BC) originally adorned the façade of a second royal reception suite of two large halls. The private royal apartments opened off this court to the north west, and the rest of the building was occupied by living quarters for government officials and servants, offices and storehouses. The palace housed not only the king but his whole administration, and the most important discovery in it was the archive of many thousands of cuneiform tablets that give a detailed and vivid picture of its day to day operation in government, diplomacy and economic life. Beneath this building an earlier palace of the mid-3rd millennium, also well preserved, is still in course of excavation.

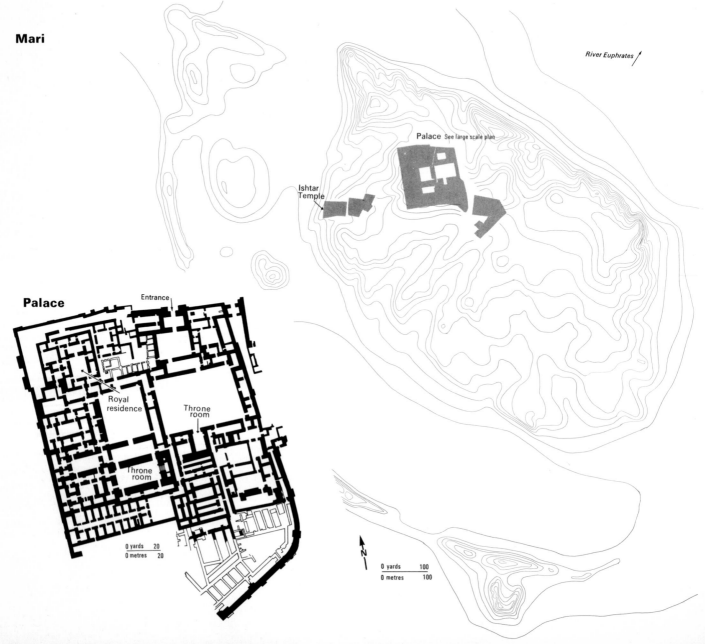

Mari

Palace See large scale plan

Ishtar Temple

River Euphrates

Palace

Entrance

Royal residence

Throne room

Throne room

0 yards 20
0 metres 20

0 yards 100
0 metres 100

N

Babylon IRAQ

Capital of Babylonia
c. 2000–539 BC. Occupied c. 2000–200 BC

BIBLIOGRAPHY
Koldewey, R., *The Excavations at Babylon*, London, 1914
Parrot, A., *Archéologie Mesopotamienne*, vol. I, Paris, 1946
Baqir, T., *Babylon and Borsippa*, Baghdad, 1959
Saggs, H. W. F., *The Greatness that was Babylon*, London, 1962

Babylon stands on the Euphrates 56 miles (90 km) south of Baghdad. It is first mentioned in the late 3rd millennium, but was relatively unimportant until it became the capital of a Semitic dynasty after the fall of the Ur Empire about 2000 BC. Under Hammurabi (1792–50 BC) it controlled all Mesopotamia, but its power later declined and it was first sacked by the Hittites about 1600 and then taken over by the Kassites, who later founded a new administrative capital at Aqar Quf. Babylon suffered from an Elamite invasion that overthrew the Kassites about 1170, and many monuments including the famous stela with Hammurabi's 'Law Code' were removed to Susa. Thereafter it maintained its independence until it came under Assyrian rule in the 7th century, and reasserted it, in alliance with the Medes, to achieve the downfall of Assyria in 612. The 6th century saw the creation, under Nabopolassar and then Nebuchadrezzar, of the great metropolis whose ruins we now visit. It was captured by Cyrus the Persian in 539, but remained the centre of the Achaemenid empire's richest province. Alexander, who may have intended it as his capital, died there in 323, and it remained an important city in later periods until it was finally superseded by the neighbouring town of Hilla in medieval times.

The road from Baghdad passes through the north wall of Nebuchadrezzar's city, skirting a mound known as the Summer Palace, and a fork leads past the Hellenistic theatre to the museum, containing models of the principal buildings. Behind the museum is a stretch of the elevated Procession Street that led from the Ishtar Gate on the north to the ziggurat and temple of Marduk. Of these nothing is now visible, but on the north-west side of the

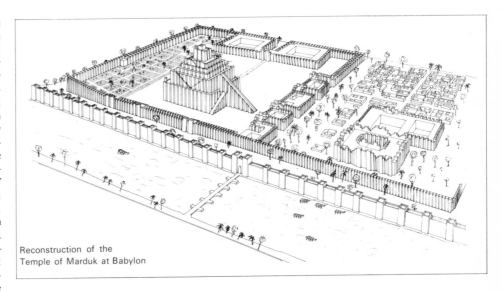

Reconstruction of the
Temple of Marduk at Babylon

Procession Street lie the ruins of Nebuchadrezzar's palace. The main entrance on the east led through three courtyards surrounded by official residences, offices and store rooms, to the royal quarters, with the throne room on the south side of the third court. Some vaulted structures north of the first court are said to be the remains of the legendary Hanging Gardens. East of the Procession Street stands the excellently restored temple of Ninmakh, and to the north the foundations of the Ishtar Gate, decorated with lions, bulls and dragons in relief. This was originally surmounted above road level by similar façades in glazed brick, now in the Berlin Museum.

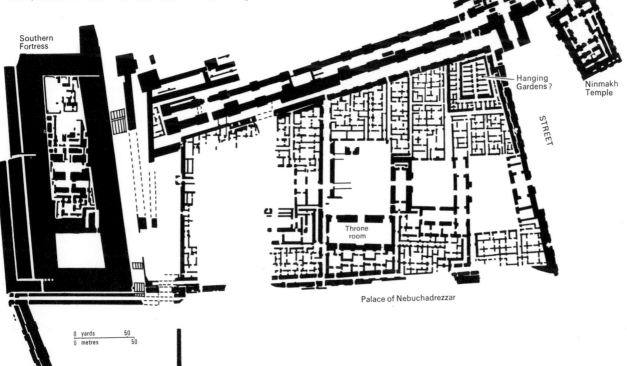

Southern
Fortress

Ishtar
Gate

Hanging
Gardens?

Ninmakh
Temple

STREET

Throne
room

Palace of Nebuchadrezzar

0 yards 50
0 metres 50

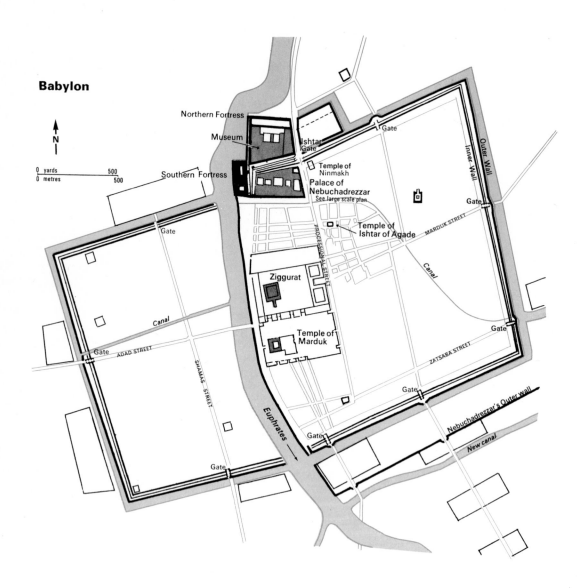

Babylon

N

| 0 | yards | 500 |
| 0 | metres | 500 |

Northern Fortress

Museum

Ishtar Gate

Southern Fortress

Temple of Ninmakh

Palace of Nebuchadrezzar
See large scale plan

Temple of Ishtar of Agade

MARDUK STREET

Outer Wall

Inner Wall

Gate

Gate

Gate

Gate

PROCESSIONAL STREET

Canal

Ziggurat

Temple of Marduk

ZATSABA STREET

Canal

Gate

ADAD STREET

SHAMAS STREET

Gate

Euphrates

Gate

Gate

Gate

Nebuchadrezzar's Outer wall

New canal

Tell Harmal IRAQ

Old Babylonian town
c. 1800 BC

BIBLIOGRAPHY
Baqir, T., *Sumer*, Baghdad, Directorate General of Antiquities, 1946, 1948
Baqir, T., *Tell Harmal*, Baghdad, 1959

Tell Harmal is situated in a southern suburb of Baghdad known as Baghdad Jadida, just south of the modern road leading to Baquba. It was a small walled town of no especial political importance, and its main period of occupation falls in the early 2nd millennium, when it formed part of the kingdom of Eshnunna in the Diyala plain east of Baghdad. Its ancient name signifies the 'place of writing' and it appears to have been specifically a centre for priests and scribes. Excavations there yielded a large collection of tablets now in the Iraq Museum. They include literary, legal and economic documents as well as one of the most famous of Babylonian mathematical texts which anticipates the theorem of Pythagoras.

The town was surrounded by a massive brick wall with buttressing towers, the outline of which has been restored. The ancient gateway, preserved as the modern entrance, leads to a street with a temple of typical Old Babylonian plan on its north side; the lower parts of its walls have also been preserved in cement. The temple doorway is flanked by projecting towers, and gives access through a gate chamber into a courtyard. Facing the entrance at the west end is the façade of the principal shrine, with the door protected by two seated lions, copies of terracotta originals now in the Iraq Museum. Steps lead into a broad ante-cella, from which a second doorway opens into the cella; a niche in the rear wall marks the position of a dais for the cult statue, facing worshippers as they entered the courtyard. Another similar but smaller sanctuary opens off the north-west corner of the court, and other rooms on this side were probably priests' lodgings and domestic quarters. Elsewhere on the site can be seen the remains of dwelling houses, of which a characteristic example, with an internal courtyard, has been preserved on the south side of the street opposite the temple. In the south-east corner a pair of shrines of a different type has been completely reconstructed. The façade, again decorated with pilasters, is pierced by two doorways each leading into a long nave with the entrance to a broad cella at the far end; the divine statue again stood on a dais inset in the rear wall, facing the length of the shrine. Each unit includes a small vestry or store, and from the nave of the southern temple a stair leads to the roof, with its characteristic parapet and the ventilation shafts still found in old houses in Baghdad.

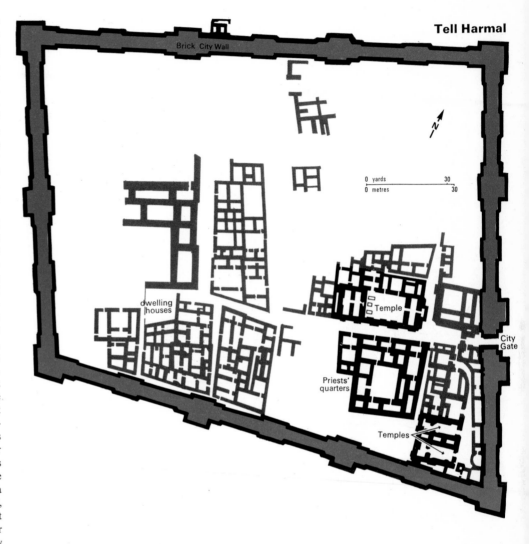

Tell Harmal

Brick City Wall

dwelling houses

Temple

City Gate

Priests' quarters

Temples

0 yards 30
0 metres 30

Aqar Quf IRAQ

Kassite capital
c. 1500–1150 BC

BIBLIOGRAPHY
Baqir, T., *Iraq*, Supplements 1944, 1945 and vol. VIII, 1947
Baqir, T., *Aqar Quf*, Baghdad, 1959

Aqar Quf (ancient Dur Kurigalzu) lies 9 miles (15 km) west of Baghdad and just north of the modern highway to Jordan. The site may have been a border fortress of Babylonia in the 3rd millennium BC but the visible remains are of the late 2nd millennium. It was refounded by the Kassite king Kurigalzu in the 15th century BC and remained the administrative capital of southern Mesopotamia until the fall of the dynasty about 1170. Political control then reverted to Babylon, but occupation on the site continued through much of the 1st millennium. It is one of a long series of capital cities, from 3rd-millennium KISH to Abbasid Baghdad, that all lay in northern Babylonia, the narrow waist of Mesopotamia where its great highways meet.

The most conspicuous feature of the site, visible for miles around, is the core of the ancient ziggurat. Built of sun-dried brick interspersed with layers of reed matting, it still stands to a height of 187 feet (57 m) above the plain. The baked brick face of the lower stage and its upper pavement have been restored, together with the axial stairway; two other stairs rose to meet it from the corners of the façade,

as at UR. In front of the ziggurat was a lower platform, surrounded by a series of courtyards forming part of the religious precinct. One room has been restored and serves as a small museum. The Kassite palace lay beneath a second large mound, 3,000 feet (approx. 900 m) south west of the ziggurat, which has been only partly excavated. On the north is a corner of the outermost courtyard that served the administrative and reception area. Opening off it were two long chambers originally decorated with painted friezes of courtiers entering through their doorways. To the south a depression marks the site of a second courtyard, one of many in the whole building, that was surrounded by triple rows of rooms in some of which, at the south corner, can still be seen low vaulted chambers opening off a central passage. This was the royal storehouse and treasury, in which were found many examples of Kassite art now in the Iraq Museum, including a decorated ceremonial macehead, a gold bracelet with paste inlay, fragments of inlaid glass vessels and a graceful and lifelike terracotta figurine of a lioness.

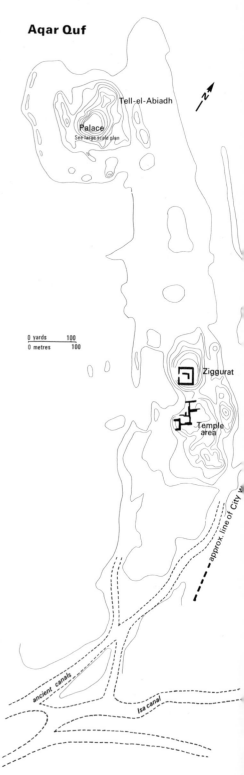

Aqar Quf

Tell-el-Abiadh

Palace
See large scale plan

0 yards 100
0 metres 100

Ziggurat

Temple area

approx. line of City wall

ancient canals

Isa canal

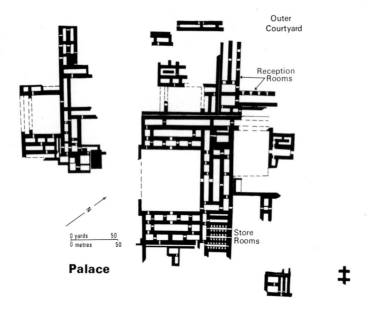

Outer Courtyard

Reception Rooms

Store Rooms

Palace

0 yards 50
0 metres 50

Ashur IRAQ

Ancient capital of Assyria
c. 2000–884 BC. Occupied *c.* 2500–612 BC

BIBLIOGRAPHY
Andrae, W., *Das Wiedererstandene Assur*, Leipzig, 1938
Parrot, A., *Archéologie Mesopotamienne*, vol. I, Paris, 1946
Smith, S., *Early History of Assyria*, London, 1928
Oates, D., *Studies in the Ancient History of Northern Iraq*,
   London, 1968

Ashur (modern Qala'at Sharqat) occupies a spur overlooking the Tigris 186 miles (300 km) north of Baghdad, at the point where the ancient highway following the river northwards entered the rainfall zone and could diverge into a choice of routes with adequate water and forage. It is also exposed westward to the steppe, and has thus a twofold historical role as a focal roadstation and a point of nomadic intrusion into the settled lands. There is no evidence of prehistoric settlement, but by the mid-3rd millennium there was a temple of Ishtar, in which the presence of Sumerian statues suggests that the site was a military or commercial outpost of the south. It was later under the control of Agade and UR, but a Semitic-speaking tribe had settled there, and made it their independent capital about 2000 BC. Ishtar remained important but a new deity, Ashur, the personification of the city, gained pre-eminence as the patron of the new kingdom. It was now a great trading centre, with merchant colonies as far as KÜLTEPE (p. 136) near Kayseri in Turkey, and a usurper, Shamshi-Adad I, briefly included it in a north Mesopotamian empire about 1800. After a period of obscurity the Assyrian kingdom, now including the rich lands around NINEVEH, re-emerged as a power in the 14th century. From the 10th to the 7th centuries it conquered the whole Fertile Crescent, but during this time the administration was removed successively to NIMRUD, KHORSABAD and Nineveh, close to the centre of wealth and population, although Ashur remained the religious capital where many of the kings were buried. When the Medes overthrew Assyria it was one of the first cities to fall, in 614 BC, and was only reoccupied when the Parthian Empire restored central control in Mesopotamia.

A track, leaving the modern road on the lip of the river basin, passes over the west gate with the latest palace adjoining it on the north west. Beyond are two mounds representing the twin ziggurats attached to the temple of Anu and Adad, and on the south side, the site of the Ishtar Temple. Between the Anu-Adad Temple and the prominent mass of the principal ziggurat, dedicated first to Enlil and then to Ashur, lay the Old Palace, founded in the 3rd millennium. On the headland the ruined Turkish police post masks the site of the precinct of Enlil which became the temple of Ashur.

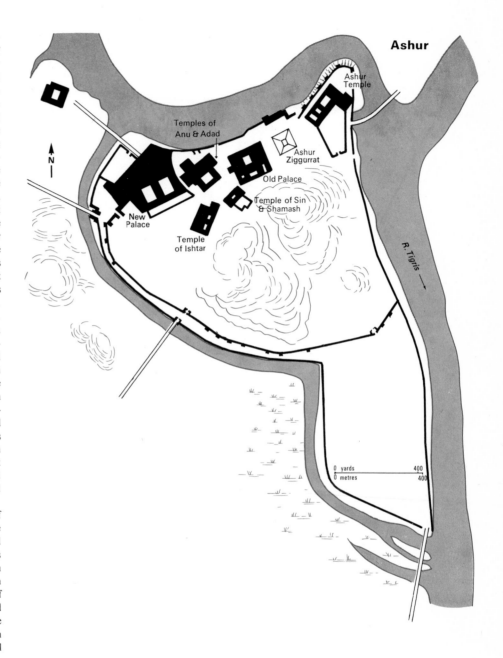

Ashur

Ashur Temple

Temples of Anu & Adad

Ashur Ziggurrat

Old Palace

Temple of Sin & Shamash

New Palace

Temple of Ishtar

R. Tigris →

N

0 yards 400
0 metres 400

Nineveh IRAQ

Capital of Assyria
c. 700–612 BC. Occupied *c.* 6000 BC–AD 600

BIBLIOGRAPHY
Layard, A. H., *Nineveh and its Remains*, London, 1849, 1850
Layard, A. H., *Nineveh and Babylon*, London, 1882
Campbell Thompson, R., *Annals of Archaeology and Anthropology*, Liverpool, 1931, 1932, 1938
Oates, D., *Studies in the Ancient History of Northern Iraq*, London, 1968

Nineveh lies 250 miles (400 km) north of Baghdad just across the Tigris from Mosul. This is the main crossing of the Tigris in the northern plain, and at the centre of a rich agricultural region, ancient Assyria. Excavation on the principal mound, Kuyunjik, has shown that it was occupied from the 6th millennium onwards. By the mid-3rd millennium it possessed a temple of Ishtar which became one of the great shrines of Mesopotamia, maintained by successive kings who controlled this strategic point: the Agade dynasty about 2300 BC, Shamshi-Adad of ASHUR about 1800, and in the mid-2nd millennium the rulers of Mitanni, a king-dom centred around Nusaybin, who sent the goddess on a diplomatic visit to Egypt. With the revival of Assyrian power in the late 2nd and 1st millennium Nineveh was often a royal residence and was finally established as the capital about 700 by Sennacherib, whose successors lived there until its destruction by the Medes in 612. There was intermittent occupation for another thousand years, but the main settlement now lay in the plain beneath Kuyunjik. In the Parthian period Nineveh had a Greek city constitution and a temple of Hermes near the river crossing, and the Ishtar temple survived until at least AD 200, but before the Islamic conquest the site had become a suburb of Mosul.

The city wall has a circumference of over seven and a half miles (12 km), and five gates have been excavated. The flanking towers of the Nergal Gate in the north wall are a modern reconstruction, but the original bull colossi still flank the entrance. The first, ashlar-faced stage of the east wall on either side of the Shamash Gate, by the Erbil road, has been rebuilt to parapet height; above and behind this there was a second stage of unbaked brick. On the mound of Kuyunjik the throne-room suite of Sennacherib's palace has been re-excavated and roofed, with some of its relief slabs depicting the king's conquests still in position; many sculptures of Sennacherib and his grandson Ashurbanipal were removed to the British Museum and the Louvre in the 19th century. No other buildings are now exposed on the citadel. The mound of Nebi Yunus, the site of the imperial arsenal a mile (1·6 km) south of Kuyunjik, has long been covered with houses grouped around a mosque, containing the reputed tomb of Jonah.

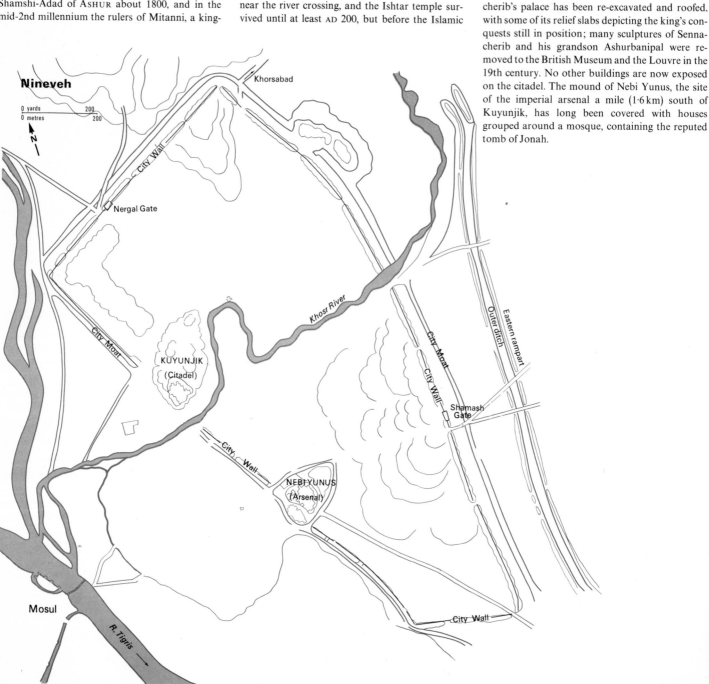

Nineveh

0 yards 200
0 metres 200

N

Khorsabad

City Wall

Nergal Gate

City Moat

Khosr River

KUYUNJIK
(Citadel)

City Wall

NEBI YUNUS
(Arsenal)

City Moat

City Wall

Outer ditch

Eastern rampart

Shamash Gate

City Wall

Mosul

R. Tigris

Nimrud IRAQ

Capital of Assyria
884–c. 710 BC. Occupied c. 2500–612 BC

BIBLIOGRAPHY
Layard, A. H., *Nineveh and its Remains*, London, 1849, 1850
Layard, A. H., *Nineveh and Babylon*, London, 1882
Mallowan, M. E. L., *Nimrud and its Remains*, London, 1966
Oates, D., *Studies in the Ancient History of Northern Iraq*, London, 1968

Nimrud, Assyrian Kalhu and Calah of Genesis, overlooks the east bank of the Tigris 19 miles (31 km) south of Mosul. Surface finds indicate that the site was occupied from at least the early 3rd millennium BC, but it first appears in history as a town founded by Shalmaneser I of Assyria about 1250 BC. It was refounded and greatly enlarged by Assurnasirpal II (884–59 BC), whose successors resided there until the late 8th century, when the capital was transferred first to KHORSABAD and then to NINEVEH. It was a provincial capital in the 7th century, and was sacked twice during the Median invasions that overthrew Assyria in 614–12. A few survivors lingered on, but it was deserted when Xenophon marched by in 401 BC. There was a Hellenistic village on the ruined citadel, but that too was abandoned about 150 BC.

The road from Mosul passes through a low ridge marking the outer city wall, which encloses an area about one and a quarter miles (2 km) square, and terminates at the north-west corner of the citadel beneath the eroded ziggurat. The temple of Ninurta, patron god of Kalhu, adjoined the ziggurat on the south, and beyond it lay the outer, public courtyard of the North-west Palace, built by Assurnasirpal II. The restored south façade is decorated with reliefs depicting tribute bearers, and two doorways flanked by winged lions and bulls lead into the throne room. Many of the reliefs from this and other chambers were removed to the British Museum in the 19th century, but the throne dais that stood at the east end is now in Mosul Museum, with a stela found outside the east door which commemorates the completion of the palace in 879 BC. It records a feast given to the people of Kalhu, 63,000 in number including 47,000 workers transported from conquered territories. South of the throne-room other reception rooms lined with sculptures have been restored by the Iraqi Antiquities Department. Most of the citadel was occupied by palaces and temples, of which the largest, dedicated to Nabu, god of writing, is still partly exposed near the south-east corner. Here two stone-paved chambers with raised platforms were the shrines of Nabu and his consort, and surrounding rooms housed the domestic and business activities of the temple. North of the Nabu Temple an original gate leads through the outer city to the imperial arsenal, founded by Shalmaneser III (859–824 BC), which housed barracks, workshops and stores as well as a royal palace. On the south can be seen a stone gate, built about 675 BC, and within the arsenal were found the sculptured throne dais of Shalmaneser, and many carved ivory plaques, originally furniture or harness ornaments, which are now in the Iraq Museum.

Plan of City Walls

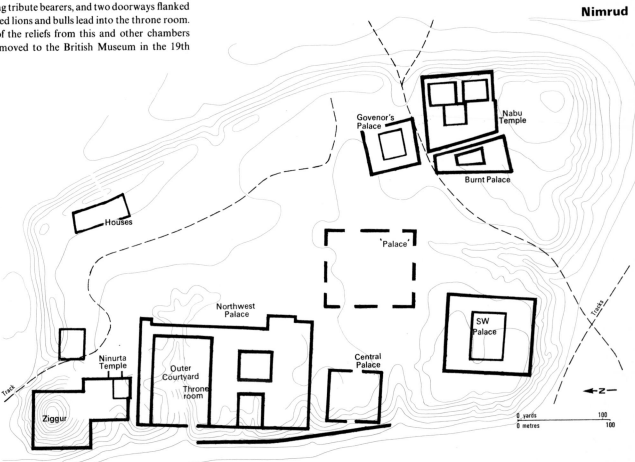

Nimrud

Khorsabad IRAQ

Capital of Assyria
c. 710–705 BC. Occupied *c.* 710–612 BC

BIBLIOGRAPHY
Place, V., *Ninive et l'Assyrie*, Paris, 1867, 1870
Loud, G., Frankfort, H. and Jacobsen, T., *Khorsabad, I*, Chicago, 1936
Loud, G. and Altmann, C. B., *Khorsabad, II*, Chicago, 1938
Safar, F., *Sumer*, Baghdad, Directorate General of Antiquities, 1957

Khorsabad (ancient Dur Sharrukin), 12 miles (20 km) north east of Mosul in northern Iraq, was founded by Sargon II, king of Assyria 721–705 BC, as a new capital to replace NIMRUD (Kalhu) where his predecessors had resided since the early 9th century. No trace of earlier occupation has been found on the site and there was, at most, a village there. After Sargon's death his son Sennacherib removed the administration to NINEVEH, and we know nothing of the history of Khorsabad in the 7th century. It presumably shared the fate of the other Assyrian royal cities and was sacked during the Median invasions of 614 and 612 BC; there was only a brief and impoverished reoccupation and, as at Nimrud, a village stood on the ruined citadel in the Hellenistic period. Unlike Nineveh, Khorsabad was never an important centre of communications and its sudden rise and decline apparently reflect only the whim of a single monarch.

The city wall encloses an approximate square of 1·1 miles (1·75 km) each side, and was pierced by seven gates, now visible as mounds rising from the low ridge that marks the line of the fortifications. A vast complex including the royal palace, a number of temples and a ziggurat stood on a terrace straddling the north-west wall, and immediately overlooking the modern highway from Mosul to Ain Sifni. Little of the palace plan can now be traced, but the ruins of the modern excavation house overlie its small internal courtyard with the throne-room immediately to the north east. Many of its stone reliefs were removed in the 19th century, but portal figures and friezes depicting processions of courtiers can be seen in the Iraq Museum. South of the terrace and linked to it by a stone bridge, of which the abutments are still visible, was the temple of Nabu, and along its cityward sides were four large residences occupied by the vizier and other ministers; this whole official area comprised a citadel separated by massive walls from the outer city. Just outside the citadel on the south west, and close to the modern road, a temple dedicated to the Sibitti, the Pleiades, was recently excavated and restored. A second large mound on the south-west city wall marks the headquarters of the arsenal, the outer bailey of which occupied all this corner of the city. Like the arsenal of Kalhu it contained a secondary royal palace, only a small part of which has been excavated.

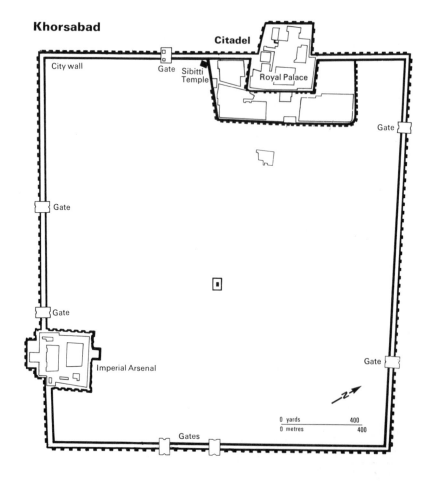

184

Hatra IRAQ

Parthian frontier city
c. 250 BC–AD 250

BIBLIOGRAPHY
Safar, F., *Sumer*, Baghdad, Directorate General of Antiquities, 1952
Al Asil. N., *Illustrated London News*, November 17, 1951

Hatra lies 62 miles (100 km) south west of Mosul on the west bank of the Wadi Tharthar. It is the westernmost point in the Mesopotamian steppe at which the water supply can support a community of any size, and is the focus of many desert tracks. It was one of the earliest settlements of the Arabic-speaking tribes who infiltrated into Mesopotamia about 200 BC, and under the Parthian empire it became the capital of a client kingdom under Arab rulers, with the dual importance of a religious centre for the nomad tribes and a fortress threatening the communications of invading Roman armies. It was unsuccessfully besieged by Trajan and Septimius Severus, but briefly accepted a Roman garrison about AD 240 after the Parthian dynasty had been overthrown by the Sassanians. It was finally abandoned after being sacked by the Sassanian Shapur I about 258, though Arabic inscriptions attest a brief reoccupation in the 12th century.

From the modern road skirting the city on the east a track leads through the wall, past a number of tower tombs, to the main gate of the central enclosure. Facing the entrance, at the far end of a vast courtyard, is a partly restored temple, set on a podium and surrounded by a double colonnade. This is the best surviving example of the Hellenistic style of architecture current at Hatra until the late 1st century BC. Immediately behind it is the wall of the inner precinct, pierced by two gates with a colonnaded temple between them. The precinct is subdivided by a wall abutting on the façade of a massive complex of temples in the later Iranian style of the 1st century

AD. There are two main units, each with a great open-ended hall or *iwan*, flanked by smaller iwans and other vaulted chambers one of which, off the south great iwan, is a museum of sculpture. Nearby is the entrance to a square temple with a vaulted ambulatory, dedicated to Shamash, the sun god. The major shrines housed the worship of a trinity of celestial deities, father, mother and son, and a pair of halls at the north end of the complex was apparently devoted to Mithras. Outside the central enclosure are a number of smaller shrines dedicated to various deities, some of which appear to have been tribal sanctuaries. In them were found many of the finest statues of kings, members of the royal family and military and religious officials that are now in the Mosul and Baghdad museums.

Temple Precinct

0 yards 100
0 metres 100

Siege works?

City Walls

Dwelling Houses and small Temples

Temple Precinct
See large scale plan

Tower Tombs

0 yards 500
0 metres 500

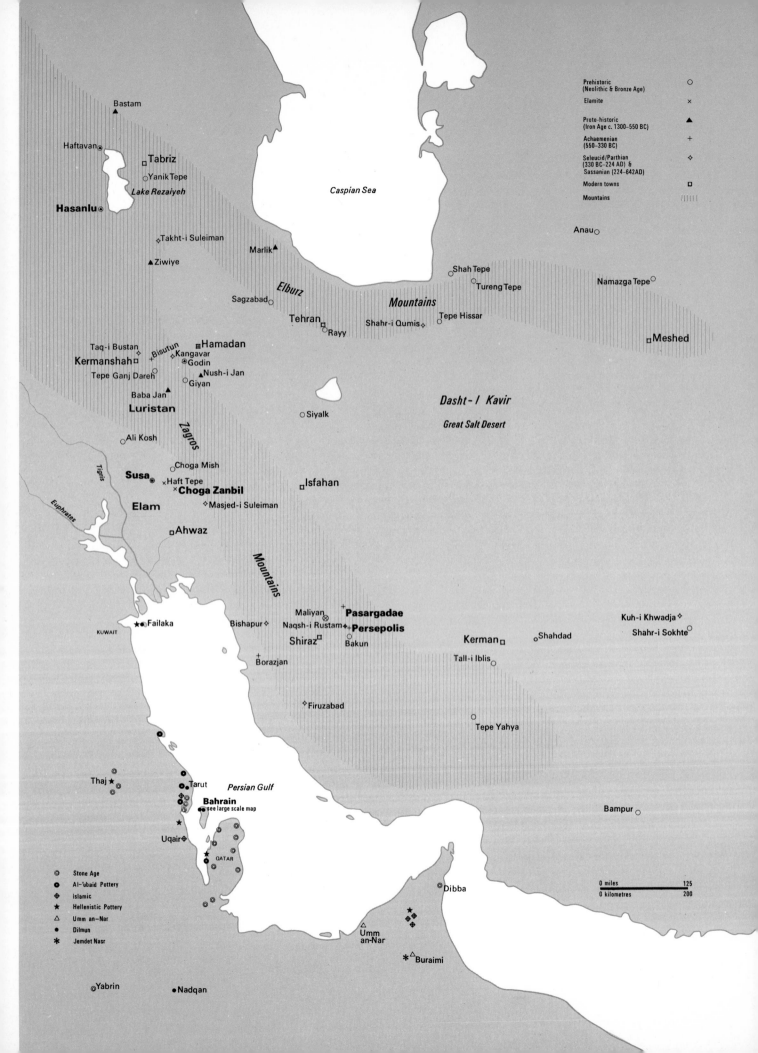

Bastam ▲

Haftavan ⊙
□ **Tabriz**
⊙ Yanik Tepe
Lake Rezaiyeh

Hasanlu ⊙

◇ Takht-i Suleiman
Marlik ▲
▲ Ziwiye

Elburz

Sagzabad ⊙

Mountains

Shah Tepe ⊙
Tureng Tepe ⊙

Anau ⊙

Namazga Tepe ⊙

Caspian Sea

Tehran ◻ ♦
Rayy

Shahr-i Qumis ♦
Tepe Hissar ♦

□ **Meshed**

Taq-i Bustan ⊙
╳ Bisutun
Kangavar ♦
Godin ⊙
Kermanshah □
Tepe Ganj Dareh ⊙
▲ Nush-i Jan
Giyan ⊙
⊞ **Hamadan**

Baba Jan ▲

Luristan

Zagros

Siyalk ⊙

Dasht - I Kavir

Great Salt Desert

Ali Kosh ⊙

Choga Mish ⊙
Susa ⊛
╳ Haft Tepe
╳ **Choga Zanbil**

Isfahan ⊙

Elam
◇ Masjed-i Suleiman

Tigris

Ahwaz

Euphrates

Mountains

Maliyan
⊗
Naqsh-i Rustam
✛ **Pasargadae**
Bishapur ⊙
✛ **Persepolis**
Shiraz ◻
Bakun ⊙

Kuh-i Khwadja ◇
Shahr-i Sokhte ◇

★⊙ Failaka
KUWAIT

Kerman ◻
Shahdad ⊙

Borazjan ✛

Tall-i Iblis ⊙

◇ Firuzabad

Tepe Yahya ⊙

⊙⊙
Thaj ★
⊙⊙

⊙⊙
Tarut
⊕⊙
⊕⊙⊙
Bahrain
see large scale map
★
Uqair ⊕
⊙⊙
⊙⊙
★
QATAR
●

Persian Gulf

Bampur ⊙

⊙ Dibba

★
◇◇
◇

⊙⊙
Umm
an-Nar △
✳ △ Buraimi

⊙ Yabrin
● Nadqan

⊙ Stone Age
⊙ Al-'ubaid Pottery
⊕ Islamic
★ Hellenistic Pottery
△ Umm an-Nar
● Dilmun
✳ Jemdet Nasr

0 miles   125
0 kilometres   200

Bahrain and the Arabian Gulf

c. 2800–0 BC

BIBLIOGRAPHY
Bibby, T. G., *Looking for Dilmun*, New York and London, 1970
Annual Reports in *Kuml* (Journal of Jutland Archeological Society), Aarhus, Denmark, 1954 onwards

In recent years the eastern half of the Arabian peninsula, particularly the coastal strip bordering the Arabian Gulf and the islands off its shore, have revealed extensive traces of cultures analogous to those of south Mesopotamia (p. 167). Most noteworthy among these is an urban civilization, settlements of which are found from Kuwait in the north (Failaka island) to the edge of the Rub' al-Khali (Nadqan) to the south.

The civilization flourished in the centuries around 2000 BC and has been plausibly identified with the Dilmun of the Mesopotamian records, an independent kingdom trading a variety of eastern goods, especially copper, to Sumer and Babylonia, and playing a surprisingly prominent role in their mythology. The Dilmun civilization seems to have had its centre on the island of Bahrain, where numerous sites, including the 3rd- and 2nd-millennium temple site of Barbar and about 100,000 burial tumuli of the same period, testify to the island's prominent role. The largest site on Bahrain, and in the whole area, is that of Qala'at al-Bahrain, a large low tell covering some 45 acres (18 hectares) on the northern coast of the island, and crowned by a prominent Portuguese castle.

The tell of Qala'at al-Bahrain shows seven major building phases: City I is unwalled, with stone-built houses flanking streets running due north-south and east-west. The pottery of its earliest phase shows virtual identity with that of the Umm an-Nar culture of the Oman, and close parallels with Bampur IV–VI and Yahya VA and IVB, and can be dated to about 2800 BC, but an indigenous type of pottery, red ovoid vessels with applied chain-pattern horizontal ridges, soon develops. The city shows traces of destruction by fire.

City II is walled, but the streets follow essentially the same pattern, and the pottery is a development of the foregoing, with raised plain ridges. Round steatite stamp seals of a distinctive pattern are numerous (and even more so in a small contemporary settlement on Failaka) as well as quantities of copper, some ivory, and chert weights of Indus Valley type and weight. Probably about 2300–1800 BC. City III possesses a rebuilt wall following the same line, large stone buildings with exceptionally thick walls, and a pottery identical with that of the Kassite period of Mesopotamia. Probably about 1700–1200 BC. City IV has large stone buildings with walls preserved to a height of 12 feet (3·7 m), bath-tub coffins and agate seals of 'neo-Babylonian type, and offerings below the floors of snake-skeletons in lidded bowls accompanied by a single bead. About 1000–600 BC. City V extends beyond the original city wall, and yielded glazed and red-washed bowls, sherds of imported black-on-red Attic ware, a hoard of silver coins imitating tetradrachms of Alexander and terracotta animal and human figurines, some Hellenistic, some Indian, and some resembling those of Thaj, a walled city on the Arabian mainland. About 300–0 BC. City VI is of 10th-century Islamic date, and Phase VII comprises the Portuguese castle of 16th-century date.

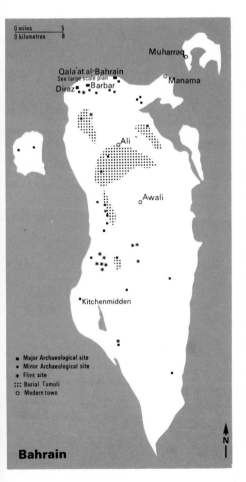

Bahrain

- ■ Major Archaeological site
- ▪ Minor Archaeological site
- ✴ Flint site
- ⫶⫶⫶ Burial Tumuli
- ○ Modern town

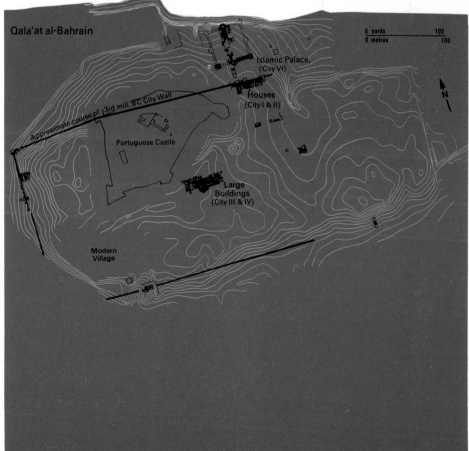

Qala'at al-Bahrain

Prehistoric Cultures of Iran

c. 7000–550 BC

BIBLIOGRAPHY

Dyson, R. H., 'Problems in the Relative Chronology of Prehistoric Iran', *Chronologies of Old World Archaeology*, ed. R. W. Ehrich, Chicago, 1965

Dyson, R. H., 'A decade in Iran', *Expedition*, 11, Philadelphia, 1969

Porada, E., *Ancient Iran*, London, 1965

Dyson, R. H. et al., in *Expedition*, 13, Philadelphia, 1971

The earliest Neolithic settlement in Iran has been found at the site of Tepe Ganj Dareh in western Iran dating from before 7000 BC. The villagers built their houses out of sun-dried mudbrick, herded goats and made lightly fired pottery vessels. In the 5th and 4th millennia BC much of Iran was influenced by the Ubaid and Uruk cultures of Mesopotamia and small villages became sizeable towns. At SUSA particularly fine elegant pottery was produced (Susa A) and similar painted pottery has been found at Tall-i Bakun and other sites in western Iran. Round the edge of the great salt desert in the centre of the Iranian plateau, another culture flourished at sites such as Siyalk (Level III), Tepe Hissar (Level I) and at Sagzabad. The pottery from these sites is often finely decorated with designs of animals and birds.

In the 3rd millennium BC there was a great diversity of early Bronze Age cultures. The Early Transcaucasian is characterized by black polished pottery; in the north east the arrival of the first Iranian tribes is heralded by the grey Gurgan pottery found at Tepe Hissar. Shah Tepe and Tureng Tepe. In central western Iran the Giyan (or Godin III) culture lasted for almost a thousand years. In the south west the kingdom of Elam with its capital at Susa flourished until it was finally destroyed by the Assyrians in 640 BC. In southern Iran various cultures existed but their relationship with each other is not yet fully understood. Towards the end of the 3rd millennium BC there was an important civilization in south-east Iran. This thrived at sites such as Shahr-i Sokhte and Tepe Yahya and provides a link between the civilizations of the Indus valley and of Mesopotamia.

By about 1200 BC Iranian tribes from the north east had conquered most of Iran. These people rode horses and used iron tools and weapons and were the ancestors of the Medes and Persians. During the 1st millennium BC the west of Iran was divided among the Urartians, Mannaeans, Medes, Elamites and Persians. But at the same time deep in the Zagros mountains horse-riding tribes manufactured the animal-style Luristan bronzes.

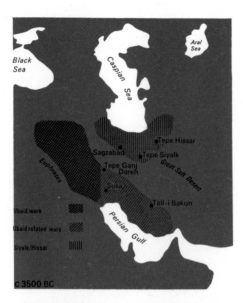

Choga Zanbil IRAN

Religious city
c. 1350–640 BC

BIBLIOGRAPHY
Ghirshman, R., Tchoga Zanbil, 4 vols., Paris, 1966–70

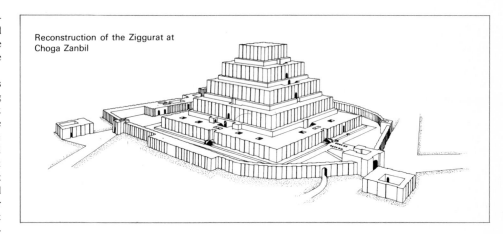

Reconstruction of the Ziggurat at Choga Zanbil

In the middle of the 13th century BC King Untash-Gal of Elam, (the south west corner of Iran) founded a holy city about 25 miles (40 km) east of SUSA the capital of Elam. He called this city Dur-Untash, the town of Untash.

The city had three concentric fortification walls and at its centre was a ziggurat, a square building made of sun-dried mudbricks which had about six stages. The lowest stage is 330 feet (100 m) square and in the thickness of the walls there were temple shrines dedicated to the god Inshushinak, the head of the Elamite pantheon. The ziggurat is now 92 feet (28 m) high but originally must have been almost twice that. Covered staircases on all four sides led up to the sanctuary on the top, which no longer survives. At the foot of the ziggurat were altars. Built into the innermost encircling wall were temples dedicated to the other important Elamite gods, and more temples were built in the space between the inner two fortification walls.

The outer wall is about 1,300 yards (1,200 m) long and 875 yards (800 m) wide and much of the area enclosed was probably never built on. In the north-east corner the remains of a large gatehouse, a temple, and three or four palaces have been excavated. In the south-western palace are five underground chambers reached by steep flights of stairs and roofed with true barrel vaults made of baked bricks and bitumen mortar. In each chamber there was a platform on which rested the ashes of cremated bodies. It is possible that these were the burials of some of the Elamite kings.

Shortly after the death of King Untash-Gal the importance of Choga Zanbil declined; but it was still occupied when the Assyrians devastated Elam in 640 BC.

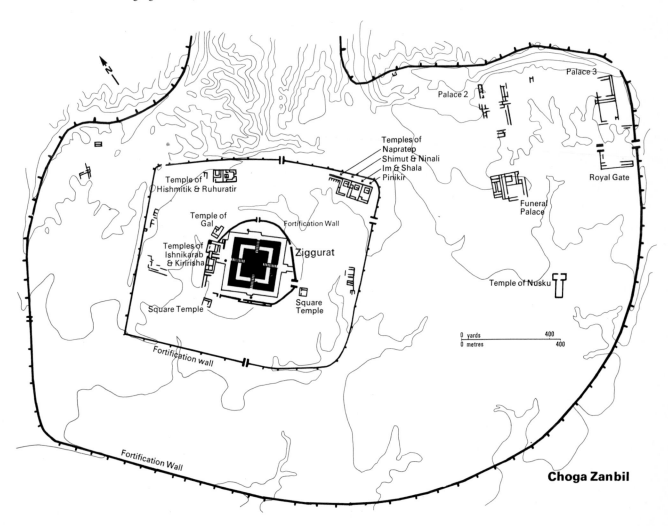

Choga Zanbil

Hasanlu IRAN

City site
c. 1000–800 BC

BIBLIOGRAPHY
Dyson, R. H., 'Problems of protohistoric Iran as seen from Hasanlu', *Journal of Near Eastern Studies*, 24, Chicago, 1965, pp. 193–217
Young, T. C., 'Thoughts on the architecture of Hasanlu IV', *Iranica Antiqua*, 6, Leiden, 1966, pp. 48–71
Porada, E., *Ancient Iran*, London, 1965

The mound of Hasanlu lies in the north west of Iran, just to the south of Lake Rezaiyeh, at the end of one of the few passes from Mesopotamia to Iran. The region was occupied from at least the 6th millennium BC but the most important discoveries made at Hasanlu come from Level IV, which was a strong fortified town built in about 1000 BC. It was destroyed in an enemy attack in about 800 BC, perhaps by the Urartians, who extended their power south of Lake Rezaiyeh at about this time.

The mound is a typical Near Eastern tell. The buildings were made of sun-dried mudbricks and were built on top of the ruins of earlier houses and so the mound rose in height. The five buildings so far excavated in Level IV all have basically the same plan, consisting of an antechamber, a columned hall, and storage rooms and work rooms at the sides. Most also have an entrance portico with a central column. The basic plan is known in the preceding level, level V, dating to the end of the 2nd millennium BC. No written documents have been found which tell us the name, history or function of the site. The buildings may have been the palaces of the rulers of the city, each palace built by successive rulers.

Because the citadel was destroyed in battle and by fire the remains and finds are extremely rich. Among the fallen debris of the violent conflagration, the bodies of defenders and looters alike have been discovered. One extraordinary find was a gold bowl, still clasped to the body of a man who was killed by a falling beam. The bowl was decorated in repoussé with scenes of gods and heroes, perhaps related to those of the Hurrians who lived in northern Mesopotamia. Other finds include numerous bronze bowls, carved ivory, and iron tools and weapons.

Gate
City wall
Bead House
South House
Burnt Building I
Burnt Building 2
Courtyard
Burnt Building 4

0 yards 20
0 metres 20

Hasanlu

Pasargadae IRAN

BIBLIOGRAPHY
Nylander, C., *Ionians in Pasargadae*, Uppsala, 1970
Stronach, D., *Excavations at Pasargadae*, forthcoming

Royal palaces of Cyrus the Great
c. 550–500 BC

Pasargadae was founded by Cyrus the Great (559–530 BC), who founded the Persian empire and conquered the other great powers of the Near East: Media in 550 BC, Lydia in 547 BC, and Babylon in 539 BC. The palace city of Pasargadae was built shortly after the conquest of Lydia and the masons probably came from there. The architectural style is a mixture of various traditions; the Persians themselves had no previous experience of monumental architecture and had to borrow from other countries – the design of the columned halls came from Media, the masonry techniques from Lydia and the sculpture perhaps from Mesopotamia. Yet despite these borrowings the site has a definite character of its own.

The buildings at Pasargadae are scattered over an area of some one and a quarter miles (2 km), but still seem to be the result of one unified plan. At the north is a stone terrace platform which forms part of a fortified area. To the west of this is a religious area with a large fire altar and a stepped platform on which the king stood when worshipping the sacred fire. South of the terrace platform is a square stone tower, called the Zendan-i Suleiman (the prison of Solomon) which may have been a shrine or sanctuary. There is a similar tower at Naqsh-i Rustam, the burial place of the later Persian kings near PERSEPOLIS. Palace P and Palace S have central columned halls, columned porticos and corner towers. The columns were made of stone but the walls were of sun-dried mudbrick. The doorways were made of stone and carved with relief sculpture. Palace P is set in a garden with flowing streams in carved limestone water channels and basins and there are two small pavilions which may have been the entrances of this garden.

Further east across a bridge is a gatehouse, Gate R. The east and west doors were supported by enormous stone bulls like those found in Assyrian palaces; on the north door a four-winged figure wearing an Egyptian type of crown has survived. On the palaces and the gatehouse are inscriptions in three languages. Elamite, Babylonian, and the specially invented Old Persian script, saying 'I, Cyrus, the Achaemenian'.

About two thirds of a mile (1 km) south west of the palaces is the tomb of Cyrus; according to ancient authors this was surrounded by gardens. It stands about 33 feet (10 m) high and is set on a plinth of six steps reminiscent of the ziggurats of CHOGA ZANBIL and of Mesopotamia. The tomb chamber is a gabled stone hut and above the door traces of a rosette are visible. The building has an impressive simplicity, which made it a suitable resting place for the founder of the Persian empire.

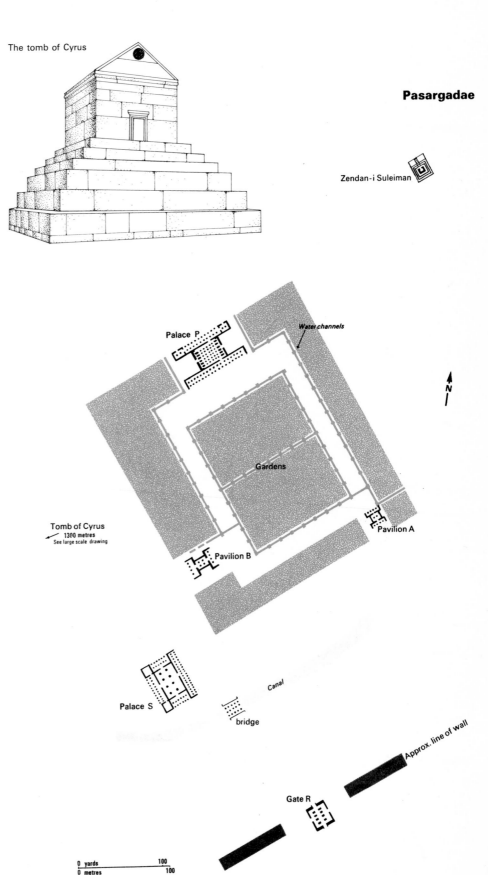

The tomb of Cyrus

Pasargadae

Zendan-i Suleiman

Palace P

Water channels

Gardens

N

Tomb of Cyrus
1300 metres
See large scale drawing

Pavilion A

Pavilion B

Palace S

Canal

bridge

Approx. line of wall

Gate R

0 yards 100
0 metres 100

Persepolis IRAN

Royal city and tombs
c. 510–330 BC

BIBLIOGRAPHY
Schmidt, E. F., *Persepolis*, 3 vols., Chicago, 1953–71

The ceremonial city of Persepolis was founded by the Persian king Darius I (522–486 BC). Darius seized the Persian throne in 522 BC and gained control of the Persian empire which stretched from the Nile to the Oxus and from the Indus to the Bosphorus.

Persepolis is situated at the northern edge of a large fertile plain in southern Iran, about 30 miles (50 km) south of Pasargadae, the earlier Persian capital. On a stone terrace platform about 40 feet (12 m) high and about 550 yards by 330 yards (500 × 300 m) in area a dozen buildings were constructed over some 60 years. The entrance staircase was at the north-west corner of the terrace and led up to a gatehouse. Like the gatehouse at PASARGADAE the doors were supported by huge stone bulls derived from earlier Assyrian prototypes, and in general the architecture is similar to that of Pasargadae. The palaces had central columned halls and often had one or more columned porticos. The walls were made of sun-dried mud-bricks on stone foundations. Some of the columns were made of finely carved stone and the capitals were shaped like the foreparts of two animals joined in the middle.

The palaces were reached by staircases and on the sides of the staircases numerous relief sculptures were carved. (All the sculptured reliefs at Persepolis are connected with the king.) The reliefs on the largest building, the Apadana, show representatives from throughout the Persian empire bringing precious gifts and rare animals to the king. This ceremony may have taken place at Persepolis during the Persian New Year festival each spring. Other carvings on the doorways and staircases show the king walking under an umbrella, the king fighting a lion or bull, the royal guard of Persian and Median soldiers, and the nobles at the Persian court.

Darius I was buried at Naqsh-i Rustam 4 miles (6 km) north of Persepolis, where, high in the cliff face, are carved four tombs, which belonged to Darius I and three of his successors. They are shaped like a Greek cross: the bottom arm is blank, the middle shows a palace façade with columns and a door leading to the burial chamber and the upper part shows a dais which is supported by 30 figures each from a different part of the empire. On the dais the king stands worshipping the sacred fire beneath the winged symbol of the god Ahuramazda. In front of the tombs is a stone tower like the Zendan-i Suleiman at Pasargadae.

The architecture and sculpture of Persepolis and Naqsh-i Rustam are essentially Persian, but include many borrowings from other lands such as Egypt, East Greece, Assyria and Babylonia, all of which were included in the Persian empire.

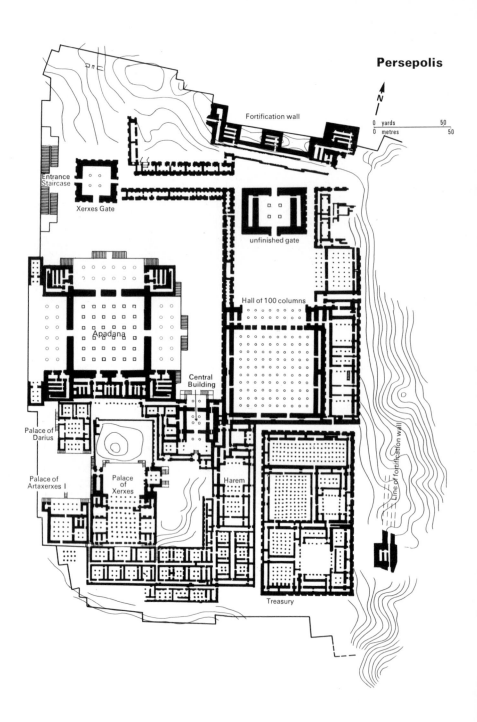

Persepolis

N

0 yards 50
0 metres 50

Fortification wall

Entrance Staircase

Xerxes Gate

unfinished gate

Hall of 100 columns

Apadana

Central Building

Palace of Darius

Palace of Artaxerxes I

Palace of Xerxes

Harem

Line of fortification wall

Treasury

Right
The tomb of Darius I, carved in the cliff of Naqsh-i Rustam near Persepolis

Susa

Elamite city
c. 3500 BC–AD 1000

BIBLIOGRAPHY
Amiet, P., *Elam*, Auvers-sur-Oise, 1966
Mémoires de la Délégation en Perse, vols. I–XLVI, Paris
    1900–72
Porada, E., *Ancient Iran*, London, 1965

Susa is situated in Khuzistan, or Elam as it was
called in antiquity, the geographical extension of the
Mesopotamian plain to the south-east. It lies on the
Royal Road, an important route along the foothills
of the Zagros mountains leading to the Mediterranean Sea. From the end of the 4th millennium BC
Susa was the capital of Elam. Under Persian rule
(550–331 BC) it became the administrative centre of
the whole empire.

The ruins at Susa cover an area of more than three
quarters of a square mile (2 sq km) and consist of
four mounds, Acropolis, Apadana, Royal City and
the Artisans' Town. Each mound is built up of the
superimposed ruins of mud-brick buildings. The
earliest settlement was on the Acropolis mound
where the foundations of a large temple platform
of the 4th millennium BC have been discovered. This
is the Susa A period which is distinguished by a
particularly fine painted pottery, elegantly shaped
with beautiful stylized animal and floral painted
designs. At times Susa was controlled by the Mesopotamian kings and at times Elamite armies ravaged
the Sumerian and Babylonian cities. As a result of
one of the Middle Elamite campaigns (*c.* 1160 BC)
the Stele of Naram-Sin (2254–2218 BC) and the Law-
code of Hammurabi (1792–1750 BC) were brought
from Babylonia to Susa, where they were discovered
by the French excavators of the site. They are now
in the Louvre Museum. The remains of the 2nd
millenium BC have been completely removed from
the Acropolis but still remain on the Royal City
mound, which was a suburb of the Acropolis at this
time. More impressive buildings of this period are
preserved at the nearby city of CHOGA ZANBIL.

Elam retained its independence until it was
ravaged and destroyed by the Assyrians in about
640 BC. Thereafter Elam was incorporated into the
Persian Empire under Cyrus. Darius I (522–486 BC)
built an extensive palace on the Apadana mound
and indeed in the Bible Susa is always called
Shushan the palace. The palace, like all Achaemenian art and architecture, is a blend of foreign
styles, in this case mainly Mesopotamian and
Iranian; it consists of rooms grouped about open
courtyards in the Babylonian and Assyrian manner
but has the added feature of a columned hall or
Apadana, similar to those found at PERSEPOLIS and
at PASARGADAE. The walls of the palace were
decorated with glazed brick reliefs showing brightly
coloured soldiers and animals. Later another small
palace was built on the plain just the other side of
the Shaur River. The Artisans' Town is a suburb
dating from Achaemenian and later times. After
Alexander the Great captured Susa in 331 BC it
remained important and the site was still occupied
well into the Islamic period.

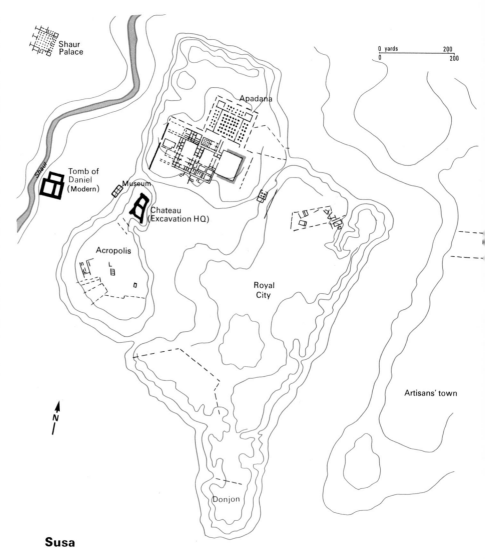

Susa

SYRIA, LEBANON AND PALESTINE

The mountains of the Levant, which modify the climate of the various regions, have played as large a part in shaping the history of settlement and migration in the country as did the rivers of Mesopotamia and Egypt. In most parts of its hinterland the mountains form a double chain running parallel to the coast, rising in some places precipitously to 10,000 feet (approx. 3,000 m), but elsewhere they are relatively low. Against these mountains come moisture-bearing winds from the sea, creating a strip of forested or arable land. At a few points the mountain barrier is broken and the rain storms sweep further inland – at the plains of Esdraelon and Akkar for example, but principally in the far north, where the Syrian saddle permits the winds and rain to penetrate far round the nothern part of the Fertile Crescent. The reverse east sides of the mountains lie in the rain shadow and are mostly barren and uninhabited slopes, but some of the winds, passing high over the first chain of mountains, break on the second line. Thus all the highlands receive adequate rainfall for agricultural purposes, but in antiquity most of them were heavily forested, the Lebanon especially being famous for its cedar wood. Generally the highlands are cold and wet or snow-covered in winter, but contrastingly hot and dry in summer.

On some parts of the coast the mountains fall directly to the sea, but rarely there is a broad coastal plain. The coastline itself, fringed either with sand-dunes or rock, has very few natural harbours, and the climate is hot and humid. Between the two mountain chains is the great Rift Valley which runs right through Palestine to the Gulf of Aqaba and beyond. At the level of the Dead Sea it is some 1,300 feet (approx. 400 m) below the Mediterranean sea level. This Valley is continued in a topographical sense in the Lebanon by the valley of the Beqa'a and these long troughs between the mountains contain the sources of the three main rivers of the Levant, the Orontes, the Litani and the Jordan. The Valley creates a distinctive zone, where the climate is generally warm in winter and very hot in summer, and the inhabitants lead a rather different way of life to that of the dwellers on the mountains and coast. Further east, beyond both mountain chains, the land generally maintains a high plateau level only gradually descending towards Arabia and Mesopotamia, but rapidly passing into an arid region where grazing of flocks is carried on by nomads in spring but which is uninhabitable for lack of water at most other times of year. Along the eastern edge of the Mediterranean the limits of settlement under conditions suitable even for dry farming hardly extend inland for more than 75 miles (120 km) at any point; beyond this the desert makes a natural frontier.

The main routes through the region run usually north–south along the coast, the ridges, the Rift Valley and the inland plateaus; and are crossed by shorter, but important, east–west passes. Many of the great cities lie at the junctions.

The rivers themselves are not practicable routes, whether for river transport or for traffic along their banks. Apart from the three main rivers, the limited number of perennial streams mostly drain in a westerly direction from the mountains, either to the sea or to the Valley, and appear not to have lent themselves to irrigation or canalization in the past after the fashion of the Nile, the Tigris and the Euphrates.

Due mainly to the topographical variety of the mountains, plains and valleys the regions of the Levant have rarely been politically united and in the past this has led to the development of numerous small states. The original siting of major cities was governed to a large extent by the occurrence of springs and has often resulted in continuous occupation of the same spot over many centuries and therefore in the rise of debris mounds or tells. The archaeological reconstruction of the past depends to a large extent on the excavation of the ruins contained in these tells and long sequences of occupation have been revealed.

Archaeology in the Levant begins with the remains of the Palaeolithic period, illustrated by excavations at MOUNT CARMEL, and the region has added greatly to our knowledge of hominid development. The evolution to a food-collecting Mesolithic stage is brilliantly illuminated in all its phases by the Natufian culture, with the earliest traces of village settlement, agriculture, a diversified economy and the first widespread evidence for a single type of burial ritual. The first Neolithic settlements probably date to the 9th millennium BC, and at an early stage quite numerous large villages appear, the most remarkable so far known being that of JERICHO with its unique defences. Clearly defined patterns of buildings, burial and social customs, and accompanying advances in agriculture and herding to cater for a large concentration of population also justify its description as a town. The Neolithic period in the Levant, with its increasingly well-defined archaeological phases continues well into the 5th millennium after which there was an increasing tendency to diverse regional cultures among peoples who were making metal implements for the first time. The beginnings of urbanism at the end of the 4th millennium may well have been stimulated by newcomers from the north and east, perhaps influenced by new ideas spreading from the great cities which had appeared in Mesopotamia a few hundred years earlier. During the 3rd millennium many large and well-planned defended towns were built, each presumably controlling, and dependent for food on, the agricultural villages of its adjacent territory. From this period, these 'city states' make a recurrent theme in Levantine organization.

An interlude beginning in the 24th–23rd centuries is indicated by a marked decline in urban standards and a reversion to semi-nomadism in Palestine, and changes in the urban tradition in Syria, but in the early years of the 2nd millennium the pendulum swung back again toward city life. There is evidence for new practices – in warfare, in the production of new styles of artifacts and probably in agriculture to suit bigger populations in larger towns. All this becomes familiar in the great cities such as HAZOR and RAS SHAMRA, which illustrate the apogee of Canaanite civilization. Literacy and wealth acted as a background for the increasing role of the neighbouring great powers, and thanks to texts discovered in the ruins of contemporary cities as well as the remains themselves, a great deal is known of the politics, the history, religion and culture of the Middle and Late Bronze Ages. At the end of the 2nd millennium there is a depressed period when many of the major cities were engulfed in the various troubles besetting the Mediterranean world, which include the invasions of the Sea Peoples and the Philistines. The subsequent establishment of the Phoenician and Israelite kingdoms is described in the Biblical accounts; the histories of JERUSALEM and LACHISH reflect the ups and downs of these and other states and the effects of Egyptian, Assyrian and Babylonian ambitions. The epoch ended with the Babylonian invasion in 588–587 BC and the exile and dispossession of many of the inhabitants. The later history of the Hellenistic and Roman periods reflects the rising influence of the countries of the western Mediterranean.

The Levant does not have the easy agricultural wealth of Egypt, for there is much hard hill country and it has always been relatively impoverished. The main products in antiquity were olive oil, grain, grapes, sheep and cattle; the timber resources were already considerably depleted by the end of the 3rd millennium but continued to be exploited right down to the present century. The area is not particularly rich in minerals, though copper and iron were mined in the Arabah, copper and turquoise in Sinai and bitumen was obtained from the Dead Sea. Utilization of a commanding position in the east Mediterranean meant commerce became the most profitable activity of the rulers and merchants of the rich cities of the coast, particularly BYBLOS and Ras Shamra and later Tyre and Sidon; and also of those cities such as QATNA which organized the traffic on the great inland routes to Mesopotamia. The Levant is the link between Asia and Africa, and as such has always had an exciting political and cultural role.

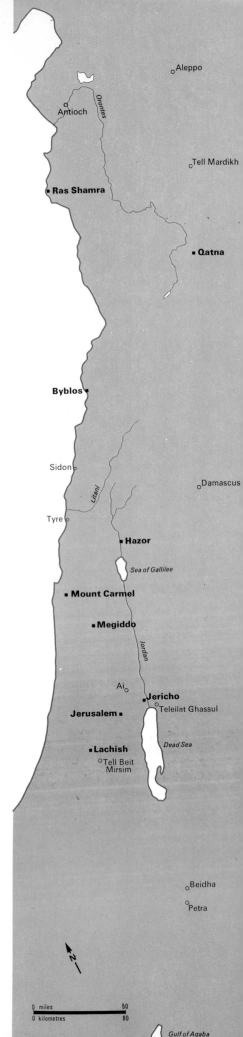

Mount Carmel ISRAEL

Cave sites
Perhaps 150,000/100,000–9000 BC

BIBLIOGRAPHY
Garrod, D. A. E. and Bate, D. M. A., *The Stone Age of Mount Carmel*, vol. I, Oxford, 1937

The excavation between 1929 and 1934 of a series of caves at Mount Carmel was one of the first in the Levant to deal with the material remains of earliest prehistory. The report, which included descriptions of the human skeletal remains recovered, is still one of the very few definitive works published on the subject and it thus remains fundamental to the study of man's evolution and development in Western Asia from Lower Palaeolithic to Mesolithic times.

The caves are located a little way up the face of low limestone bluffs in the Wadi el-Mughara at the point where the stream leaves the foothills of the Carmel Range to flow across the narrow coastal plain to the sea. There must have been abundant water and game in the area and a defensive virtue in the position of the caves which made them choice sites for occupation for such prolonged periods. In the Mesolithic period the surrounding territory clearly provided wild cereals for harvesting, fish and shell food from the sea as well as game to encourage a more diversified economy.

Two caves, Tabun and Skhūl, provided evidence of a sequence of cultures from Lower to Middle Palaeolithic in deposits up to 82 feet (25 m) deep. They also yielded a number of Neanderthaloid skeletons of unusually varied physical type. Perhaps even better known are the deposits in the cave of Mugharet el-Wad. The early deposits here were of Middle and Late Palaeolithic date, but the upper deposits revealed a great deal of information on the Mesolithic culture of Palestine, the Natufian. The cave itself, with chambers and corridor stretching 233 feet (71 m) into the hillside, was at least partly in use at this period, but much of the evidence comes from the sloping terrace before it. Here traces of hearths were found in an area partly artificially levelled, set with kerb and boundary stones and a small area of paving, with a number of large cup-marks or basins hollowed in the rock. With these, worked implements of flint and bone, stone pestles, mortars and querns and the debris of foodstuffs were found, the bonework in particular showing a high technical and aesthetic competence. As well as these domestic traces, remains of at least 59 bodies were found in the cave and on the terrace. In the chamber itself groups of bodies were found in an extended position, but the normal form of burial seems to be illustrated on the terrace where the dead were placed in pits in a contracted position, and occasionally had ornamental headdresses of shells. Other sites, such as that of Eynan in the Huleh region confirm that this is the normal Natufian burial practice and thus some of the earliest evidence for a widespread funerary ritual. The evidence from the Carmel caves is fundamental to the understanding of the transition to a sedentary Neolithic village-farming way of life. Objects, mainly of flint and bone, are in the Palestine Archaeological Museum in Jerusalem and the Ashmolean Museum in Oxford.

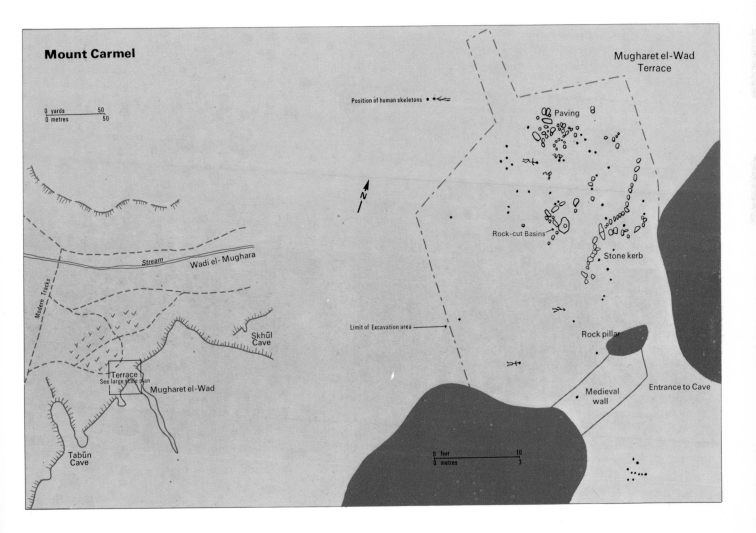

Jericho ISRAEL

Settlement site
c. 9th millennium to late 2nd millennium BC

BIBLIOGRAPHY
Kenyon, K. M., *Digging up Jericho*, London, 1957
Kenyon, K. M., *Excavations at Jericho*, vols. I and II, London, 1960–5

In a geographical sense, Jericho is one of the most remarkable of ancient sites. It lies in a hot and barren zone in the rain shadow of the Judaean hills, 650 feet (approx. 200 m) below sea level, and relies for its existence on the water issuing from a powerful spring which maintains an oasis-like environment. The earliest settlement is Mesolithic, with artifacts comparable to those of the Natufians at MOUNT CARMEL, but Jericho is most famous for the advanced Neolithic culture revealed by the excavations in the 1950's. Around 8000 BC a town 8 to 10 acres (3–4 hectares) with small round houses built of mudbrick and perhaps domed, was defended by a stone-built city wall with at least one very large tower built against its inner face. The tower is a remarkable monument for the period, with an internal flight of steps running from top to bottom. Later a wide rock-cut ditch protected the wall's outer face as well. The people of this and the succeeding period (when houses were rectangular) practised a mixed agricultural, herding and hunting economy and perhaps primitive irrigation. They made no pottery vessels, and placed considerable emphasis on the preservation of the skulls of their dead who were for the most part buried beneath the floors of the houses. The later pottery-using phases of the Neolithic are less well illustrated on the site, and it may have been deserted during the early Chalcolithic period.

The history of the settlement takes up again in the late 4th and 3rd millennia BC. Throughout the Early Bronze Age Jericho was defended by a series of mudbrick walls whose history has been traced in detail through 17 successive phases. An important series of building levels within the walls and burials without them in the cemetery have been found. The history of this period ends in decline and destruction. During the Middle Bronze Age a medium-sized town arose with fresh prosperity and had an elaborate defence sytem of mudbrick walls crowning steep plastered slopes with high stone revetments at the foot. This glacis and rampart type of defence common in the 2nd millennium is thought to have been introduced as a counter measure to the introduction of the the battering ram as a military weapon. The remains of the Late Bronze Age, much sought after in order to correlate the archaeological record with the Biblical account of the campaigns of Joshua are hardly preserved and provide no evidence on the subject, though there are tombs of the period in the cemetery. After this date the archaeological remains are of slight importance.

Objects from the site are displayed in the Palestine Archaeological Museum in Jerusalem, and in the Ashmolean Museum in Oxford.

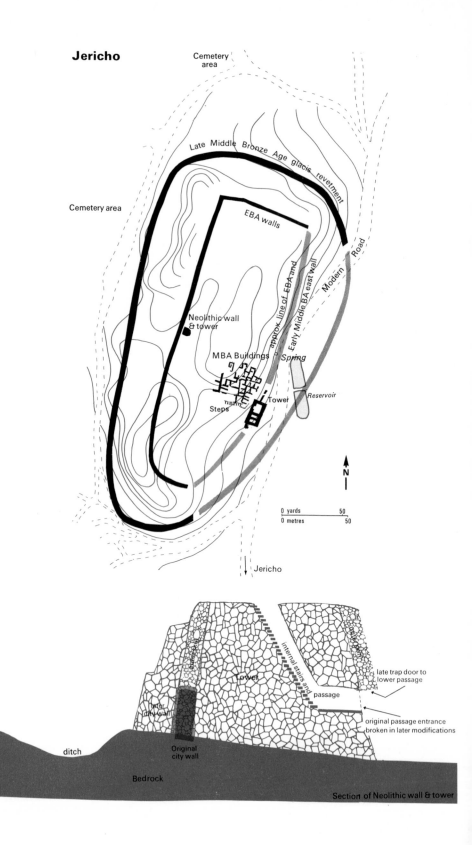

Section of Neolithic wall & tower

Byblos LEBANON

Town and trading entrepôt
c. 5th millennium BC to present day

BIBLIOGRAPHY
Dunand, M., *Fouilles de Byblos*, vols. I and II (text and plates), Paris, 1937–50

Byblos lies almost at the mid-point of the east Mediterranean shore line, on a low rocky promontory with valleys and bays on either side, fertile fields to the rear and the once-forested mountains of Lebanon in the hinterland. The combination of a spring, good rainfall, fields, easily exploitable timber and a sheltered harbour for small ships made Byblos not just an important Neolithic and Chalcolithic settlement, but the main centre for Egyptian exploitation of raw materials in the northern Levant as early as the 3rd millennium BC. The *objets d'art* found in the ruins prove almost continuous Egyptian interest in the politics, commerce and the cult of the tutelary goddess of the city throughout the Bronze Age. From approximately 3500 BC buildings of the inhabitants covered most of the promontory, and a thousand years later there was a prosperous city which appears to have been defended by stone-built ramparts. The houses were large, built of stone and wood, of regular pattern and layout and densely packed within the walls. The town certainly contained temples in which objects were dedicated by the Egyptian kings. Probably the central complex of temples originated at this period – two or perhaps three temples in a sacred area which continued to be used for this purpose almost to the end of the site's history. The temples are poorly preserved and difficult to date precisely, though the Middle to Late Bronze Age Obelisk Temple, dedicated to a male deity, the remains of which have been rebuilt slightly to the south of their original find spot, is more comprehensible. Like many of the major Levantine sites Byblos seems to have gone through a troubled period towards the end of the 3rd millennium, but subsequently revived in the Middle Bronze Age under a line of Egyptianized princes whose rock-cut shaft graves, stone sarcophagi and rich possessions have been found near the west cliffs of the promontory.

Byblos, later history is less important, for Tyre and Sidon to some extent usurped her role in the eastern Mediterranean in the 1st millennium, but the medieval walls round the harbour town on the north side of the ancient site, and the Crusader castle and church illustrate the history of Byblos as much as the remains of all periods, including the Neolithic hut floors, Chalcolithic jar burials and Bronze Age temples which are preserved on the promontory.

The finds from Bylos are displayed in the National Museum in Beirut.

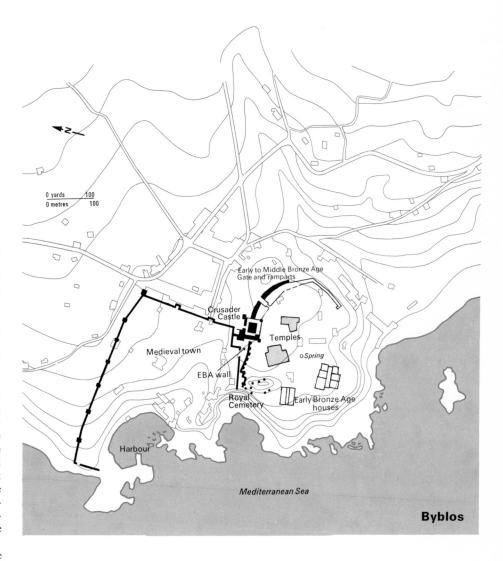

Ras Shamra SYRIA

Neolithic village and Canaanite city
c. 7th millennium to 12th century BC

BIBLIOGRAPHY
Schaeffer, C. F. A., *Ugaritica*, vols. I–VI, Paris, 1939–69

The original settlement of the 7th millennium BC on the site of Ras Shamra appears to have been on a low hill with streams at its foot, the inhabitants getting their living from the local fields and the fishing on the adjacent coast and at the small harbour of Minet el-Beida. During the early centuries of its history there is some evidence of contact with Cyprus, but principally the site was under Mesopotamian cultural influence, and lies at the end of a route to the east through the Ansariyeh Mountains. Successive settlements were of varying prosperity, though the earliest defensive ramparts seem to have been built in the 5th millennium. Late in the 3rd millennium the town seems to have been entirely destroyed, and for a short subsequent period the land was used for burials only.

The great epoch of the town begins in the 2nd millennium but it is principally the remains of the 14–12th centuries, when the town was at its most prosperous, that have been excavated. At this date ramparts enclosed an area of about 50 acres (20 hectares). Much of the area within the walls was occupied by rather spacious houses, usually containing the family burial vault below the ground floor or courtyard. Remarkable public buildings existed also. On the higher acropolis area in the north east are two temples dedicated respectively to the Canaanite deities Baal and Dagon, and nearby there was a priest's library containing mythological and ritual texts. In the lower, western part of the town a very large palace was found which contained a tremendous archive of texts whose contents indicated that the building was not solely a residence for the royal family but the centre for local admini-

stration and international affairs. These texts are also a basic source for the study of ancient Near Eastern scripts and language.

The history of the Canaanite town clearly dates back to the very beginning of the 2nd millennium when the temples were first built, and the site is firmly identified as Ugarit from the 18th century onwards. Ugarit's links by sea with Egypt, Cyprus, Crete and the Aegean were very close. It acknowledged Hittite overlords in the 14th–12th centuries and appears to have been destroyed in the early 12th century perhaps by an invasion of the 'Peoples of the Sea'. Thereafter the site was unoccupied except for sporadic settlement in the 5th–4th centuries BC. The impressive remains of the Late Bronze Age buildings have been preserved on the site, and the other finds are in the museum in Damascus.

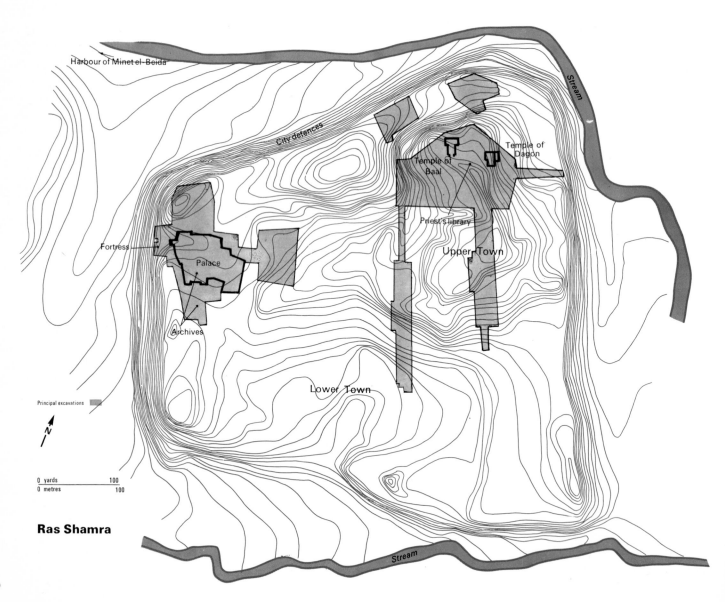

Ras Shamra

Hazor ISRAEL

Town
c. 2800–2nd century BC

BIBLIOGRAPHY
Yadin, Y., *Hazor*, vols. I–IV, Jerusalem, 1958–61
Yadin, Y., *Hazor*, The Schweich Lectures, 1970, London,
  1972

Hazor, probably the most important of Canaanite cities, held a strategic position in the Jordan Valley on the east side of the hills of north Galilee. The best routes to the north and to Damascus from Palestine run by its slopes, and others lead into the hill country behind. The main part of the site is an isolated spur on the north bank of a stream in the sides of which a number of springs provided the water supply. Buildings of Early Bronze Age 2 and 3 have been discovered here, pottery of the late 3rd millennium BC and slight occupation from the beginning of the Middle Bronze Age. But the important history of the site begins in the 18th century BC when a brick wall nearly 26 feet (8 m) thick was built around the spur; and a shoulder of land to the north and east, an area of a further 200 acres (80 hectares), was enclosed by massive earth ramparts over 98 feet (30 m) wide at the base. At least four different series of temples existed in the city, as well as palatial buildings on the spur, with houses and Middle Bronze Age graves over the whole area. It has been estimated that the population of the city at its zenith must have exceeded 25,000 people. The affairs of Canaanite Hazor are illuminated by texts from Mari and Egypt, the former showing Hazor as a major importer of tin in the 18th century. The city was totally destroyed in the late 13th century, and when settlers reoccupied it in the following century, they built an impoverished town restricted to the original spur. The great rampart or lower city area was never again included within the walls.

Only the upper west end of the spur was fortified by Solomon, who built a casemate wall (a double wall with internal chambers) and a six-chambered gateway. This citadel was partly destroyed in the 9th century and a larger one rebuilt with a wide single wall enclosing the whole spur, within which were contained a fort, a store building, and a huge rock-cut water system similar to that at MEGIDDO with steps descending round a rectangular shaft to a tunnel giving the only access to the water supply. The destruction by Tiglath Pileser III in 732 BC brought an end to an effective independent town, and afterwards Assyrian, Persian and Hellenistic forts and very slight traces of other habitations are found on the site. The finds from the site are displayed in the Israel Museum in Jerusalem, and many of the building remains are preserved at Hazor.

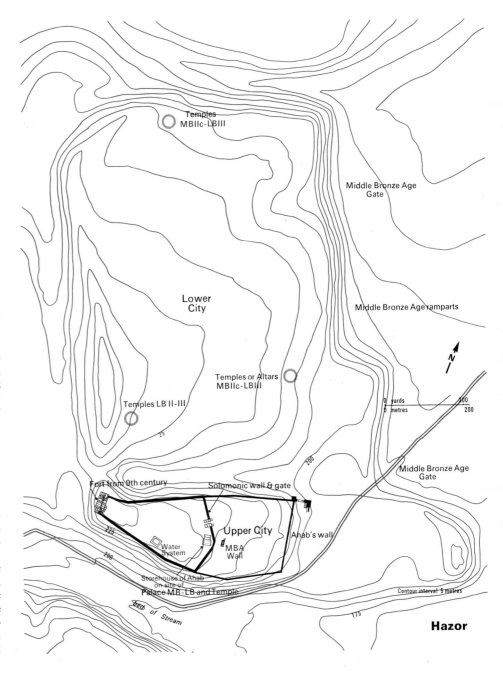

Hazor

Qatna SYRIA

Capital city
Principally late 3rd millennium to late 2nd millennium BC

BIBLIOGRAPHY
Du Mesnil du Buisson, R., *Le site archéologique de Mishrifé-Qatna*, Paris, 1935

The village of Mishrifeh lies 11 miles (18 km) north east of Homs in a shallow undulation of the inland Syrian plain. The village is hidden within great earthern ramparts forming a rectangular enclosure about half a mile (800 m) square, and which even today stand 40 to 65 feet (approx. 12–20 m) high and can be seen from far across the plain. On the outside to the north, east and south there are traces of ancient ditches, and nearby springs feed a small affluent of the Orontes which flows beneath the west side. There is a breach in the ramparts on all four sides in which elements of ancient gate systems have been disclosed. The ancient city probably extended over the whole area within the ramparts for the level there is now higher than that of the surrounding plain, and wherever the 1920's excavators dug, traces of ancient habitations and tombs were revealed.

The most important ruins lie on the north-west side of the central hill on a spur which was protected on the north by a rock scarp and a mudbrick wall. On the top, large buildings and courtyards were laid out. They have been interpreted as temples and a palace, but the visible evidence has proved less reliable than the evidence of the texts found there. These refer to a temple with a treasure of gold and lapis lazuli dedicated to the Mesopotamian goddess Nin-Egal; and a stone sphinx bearing the name of Princess Ita, a daughter of Ammenemes II, which was sent to the temple, suggests that it was built at least as early as his reign (1929–1895 BC).

This combined evidence – size of site, remains of important buildings, texts and its geographical position on a route from the Euphrates to the Mediterranean coast – tends to confirm Mishrifeh's identity with ancient Qatna. The land of Qatna and its rich pastures is often referred to in the 18th-century BC texts from Mari, and also in later inscriptions from Egypt and Anatolia. It was a part of the Egyptian Empire in the 15th century and Suppiluliumash, the Hittite king, claims to have destroyed it in *c.* 1360. It was taken by the 'Peoples of the Sea' in the time of Rameses III, and thereafter only relatively slight traces of the Iron Age, Seleucid, Roman and Byzantine periods are found at Mishrifeh. The date of its ramparts remains uncertain, but analogy with those at Tell Mardikh, just over 62 miles (100 km) to the north, suggests that they were built late in the 3rd millennium or early in the 2nd. There is occupation debris of the earlier date underlying the temple, as well as some tombs. Finds from Qatna are displayed in the museums in Aleppo and Damascus.

Qatna

Megiddo ISRAEL

Town
c. 5th millennium to *c.* 350 BC

BIBLIOGRAPHY
Lamon, R. S. and Shipton, G. M., *Megiddo*, vol. I, Chicago, 1939
Loud, G., *Megiddo*, vol. II, Chicago, 1948
Lamon, R. S., *The Megiddo Water System*, Chicago, 1935

Ancient Megiddo, overlooking the fertile Esdraelon Plain, held the entrance of the main pass to the south through the Carmel Range, and four other routes also converged at this point. It thus had local agricultural resources, and the economic and political rewards of a town on one of the great land routes of the ancient Near East.

The site appears to have been first occupied during the late Neolithic period, perhaps in the 5th millennium BC, and gradually thereafter a small town was established. Between *c.* 2700 and 2400 the slopes of the mound were terraced and a more stoutly built town was laid out, with rectangular houses, streets and covered drains, an outdoor altar and a series of temples. Whether this early town was defended is unknown, but analogy with neighbouring Taanach would suggest that it was. The inhabitants buried their dead on the slopes in rock-cut and natural caves. There is little evidence of occupation after this phase until about 1900 BC though some would argue that one or more of the temples were built in the interim; otherwise the continuity of Megiddo's history is assured only by the evidence from tombs.

Through most of the 2nd millennium Megiddo lay in Canaanite territory and was a flourishing town with strong defensive walls and city gates, temples, a palace and all the appurtenances of a wealthy Canaanite culture with contacts abroad. All this came to an end with a destruction in the 12th century. After a brief period of desertion and impoverished settlement, Megiddo again became important during the reign of Solomon, who constructed a casemate wall with a six-chambered gateway round the by then high summit of the mound to defend the town and its palaces or forts. It is now thought that the earliest stage of the defensive water system – a stone-built underground gallery approach to the spring at the foot of the mound – was built by Solomon, but the famous rock-cut shaft and tunnel belong in the reign of Ahab; these were obviously a major adjunct of the citadel's defence system. The Solomonic buildings were probably destroyed by the Egyptian, Shishak in about 926 BC, after which Ahab rebuilt the city wall in inset-offset style with a four-chambered city gateway and the famous 'stables' (perhaps storehouses) which cover nearly one-fifth of the total area. Megiddo's subsequent history includes a prosperous Assyrian phase when it was the capital of Galilee, and some scattered remains of the Babylonian and Persian periods. A visitor to the site can see in particular some remains of the cities of Solomon and Ahab, the water system and the deep cutting in which the early levels were exposed.

Finds from the site are displayed in the Palestine Archaeological Museum in Jerusalem and the Oriental Institute in Chicago.

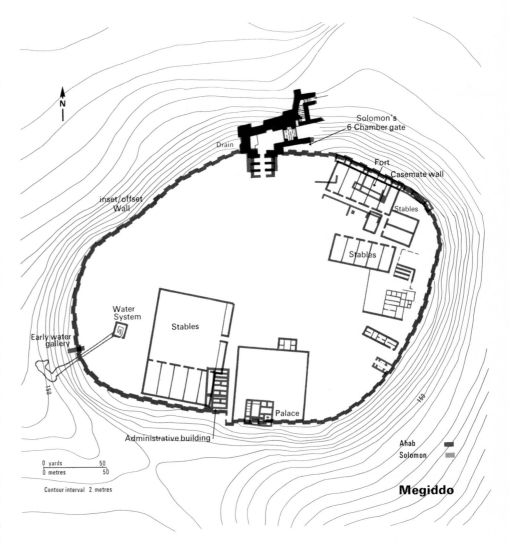

Lachish ISRAEL

Town
4th millennium–2nd century BC

BIBLIOGRAPHY
Tufnell, O., *Lachish*, vols. II–IV, London, 1940–58
Thomas, D. Winton, (ed.), *Archaeology and Old Testament Study*, Oxford, 1967

Controlling only minor routes through the foothills of the south Judaean hills, Tell ed-Duweir lies about 22 miles (36 km) inland on a low-lying spur. The adjacent seasonal watercourse and a deep well which dates back at least to the Iron Age seem to have provided the water supply of the early inhabitants. The agricultural land in the immediate vicinity is limited and the first settlements on the site are of an impoverished nature of Neolithic, late 4th and 3rd millennium BC dates, and mostly in nearby caves. The first attested establishment of a proper town dates to the Middle Bronze Age, perhaps *c.* 1750 BC, when a massive earthen rampart with a ditch at its foot surrounded the spur. The town of the Middle and Late Bronze Ages has hardly been revealed in excavation though an interesting 15th–13th century temple was found in the levelled ditch below the town.

After a violent destruction in the early 12th century the site seems to have been deserted until the 10th century when a town and sanctuary were established. As the identification of the site with Lachish is generally accepted, a correlation of the Old Testament and archaeological evidence suggests that it may have been Rehoboam who built the earliest Iron Age defences, a 20-foot (6 m) wide mudbrick wall on stone foundations. By the end of the 8th century the town was wealthy, with wide roads, public and private buildings and strong upper and lower defensive walls and gates. Sennacherib, King of Assyria, destroyed this city after a siege in 701 BC – an act of war celebrated on the reliefs in his palace at Nineveh, which as well as illustrating the capitulation of the inhabitants show the now vanished superstructure of the defences.

The city defences were rebuilt sometime after this catastrophe, but the houses within the walls were considerably poorer than before. Inscribed potsherds found within a guardhouse by the gate reveal the last stages of the defence of Lachish against the Babylonians, and in the Persian period, and a temple built by the inhabitants in the 2nd century BC belong to the final stages of the history of Lachish. The foundations of the walls and gates and of this late temple are the principal remains to be seen on the site, finds from which are to be found in the Palestine Archaeological Museum in Jerusalem and most large museums in Britain.

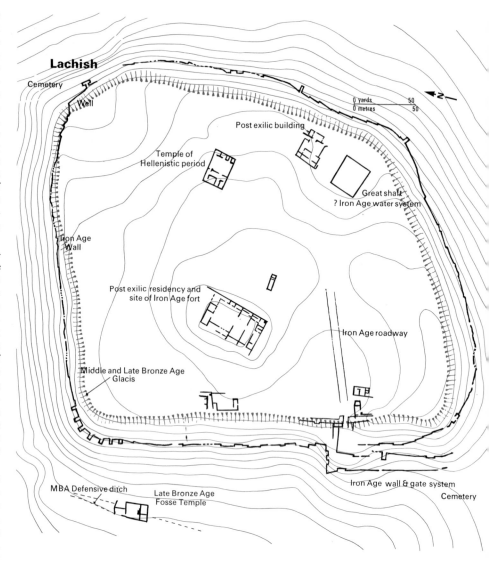

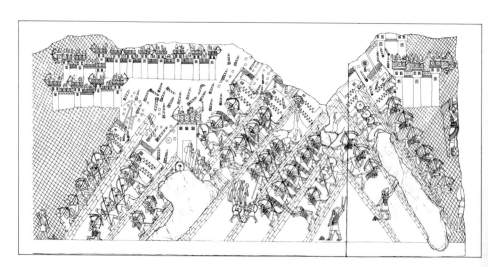

Reliefs on Sennacherib's palace at Nineveh showing the siege of Lachish

Jerusalem ISRAEL

Capital city
Principally c. 1800 BC to present day

BIBLIOGRAPHY
Kenyon, K. M., *Jerusalem*, London, 1967
Avigad, N., 'Excavations in the Jewish Quarter, Jerusalem',
Israel Exploration Journal, 20, Jerusalem, 1970

The history of Jerusalem has proved to be most difficult for archaeologists to reconstruct for their attempts have been hampered by Herodian, Roman and Byzantine quarrying and medieval and modern building, as well as the destructions and collapses of earlier dates, the effects of which are compounded on a site where stone rather than brick is the ordinary building material. As a result, few early buildings have survived.

The city is sited on the spine of the Judaean hills where vines and olives grow on the stony terraced slopes. The principal area of ancient settlement is the low spur of Ophel outside and to the south of the modern city, for this is adjacent to the water supply, the spring Gihon in the Kedron Valley. Apart from slight traces of Palaeolithic man and tombs dating c. 2000 BC on the Mount of Olives, and some pottery dated c. 3200 on Ophel, the earliest establishment of a proper settlement appears to be that of the Jebusites, c. 1800. Their massive stone defence wall has been found two-thirds of the way down the eastern slope of Ophel, and presumably their town covered most of the spur until it was captured by David c. 996. The Jebusites used the western slopes of the Mount of Olives opposite their city as a burial ground.

David seems to have utilized the Jebusite wall and not to have extended the town when he made it his capital, but by tradition, Solomon built his temple and palace on the higher ridge to the north. The date when the settlement was extended to the hill to the west has been uncertain, but the finding of fragments of a city wall suggests it was in the 8th century when possibly Hezekiah enclosed a part of a suburb which had already extended outside the walls and the rather cramped limits of the town of Ophel.

One of the few early monuments visible and still in use is the water tunnel constructed by Hezekiah against the threat of Assyrian invasion in 701. This is rock-cut, and curves underground from the Gihon spring to the Pool of Siloam whence it must have been accessible to the defenders of the town. It replaced an earlier system of Jebusite approach shafts adjacent to the spring. The city was destroyed by the Babylonians in 587 and the defences not reconstructed until Nehemiah's return exile 150 years later. The wall of the smaller post-exilic town was built along the top of the spur only and the extent to the west is not clear. Walls enclosing the north and west hills were in existence in the 2nd century BC. Most of the walls now visible were built by Suleiman the Magnificent, c. AD 1538–41 and are to a large extent based on Herodian and Roman footings, which can be seen particularly in the temple area and at the Damascus Gate.

Finds from the ancient city can be seen in the Israel Museum in Jerusalem and the Ashmolean Museum in Oxford; and the rock-cut inscription from Hezekiah's tunnel is in the Museum in Istanbul.

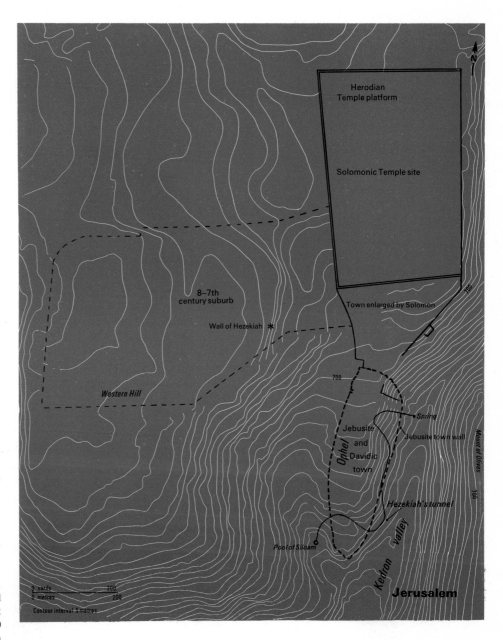

INDIA

Human occupation of the Indian subcontinent is first attested by the stone tools of hunting and gathering peoples in Middle Pleistocene times, the period of the second Himalayan interglacial around 250,000 years ago. Thenceforward, this basic form of human economy was to endure into postglacial times from around 10,000 BC, and virtually into the present, side by side with alternative and more complex societies with subsistence economics based on cultivated plants and domesticated animals, and with settlements ranging from the villages of stone-using farmers to the urban centres of civilizations with an elaborate technological background including metal working and literacy. Throughout its prehistory and history India has contained peoples at a diversity of cultural levels, often in close juxtaposition.

With the formation of modern climatic conditions from the 10th millennium BC, India, apart from the mountains of the Himalayas or in Baluchistan, would have been covered with woodland ranging in composition from tropical rain forest to that of dry deciduous type. Apart from forest reserves, the modern Indian landscape is man-made, the result of millennia of woodland clearance by man, cattle and goats for pasture, ploughing, building, domestic fuel and, with an ancient tradition of cremation, funeral pyres. The result has been changing patterns of rainfall, soil erosion, and desert areas, and while the process was active by the 4th millennium BC, pollen analysis suggests forest clearance and cereal cultivation in Rajasthan as early as the 8th millennium BC.

Today India has two contrasted areas of cereal cultivation – wheat in the Punjab and eastwards to the Middle Ganga, and rice lower down the river, in Bengal and on the coastal littoral. This duality is ancient: the Indus civilization of north-west India and the village communities that preceded it were based on wheat growing from the 5th millennium BC, but rice appears at the Indus civilization coastal towns of Rangpur and Lothal on the Gulf of Cambay at the end of the 3rd millennium, and a few centuries later it is the sole crop at HASTINAPURA on the Ganga, while Ashoka's empire of the 3rd century BC was based on the Lower Ganga and a rice crop.

North-west India belongs geographically, and largely in flora and fauna, to the westerly world of Afghanistan and Iran and beyond, and the first villages, of stone-using at first but soon, around 3000 BC, of copper-working agriculturalists, share cultural traditions with their counterparts to the west. But around this date village or town settlements such as Navdatoli on the Narbada were also flourishing, with mud-walled houses and copper working, and it would take a determined diffusionist to derive these from Baluchistan. We must be prepared, in the huge and diverse sub-continent, to find the independent emergence of animal management and plant domestication, and of technologies including metal working, in more than one place and at more than one time. Elsewhere in southern India stone-using hunter-gatherers or pastoralists (as in the central Deccan around 2700 BC), continued to exist side by side with more developed civilizations up to the early centuries AD, in what must have been heavily wooded areas.

The emergence of the Indus civilization in the north west before about 2500 BC can best be seen as a supreme example of indigenous achievement, and though links with the other contemporary civilizations to the west existed, we need not seek its origins there, any more than we should for the comparable phenomenon of Shang Dynasty China a millennium later. In the mature form in which we know it, it is individual and characteristically Indian, and MOHENJO-DARO or HARAPPA have as many dis-similarities from their western contemporaries as resemblances, and such features as cotton-growing certainly rank as distinctively Indian contributions.

The north west throughout history was an area of entrance and invasion, but though the first speakers of Sanskrit who called themselves Aryans must have reached this part of India from the west some time in the second half of the 2nd millennium BC, their archaeology is still unknown to us, and there are now grave chronological difficulties in seeing them as the destroyers of the Indus civilization. In the Upper Ganga region,

Charsadda ▪

▪ **Taxila**

Indus

Chenab

Ravi

Punjab

Sutlej

Himalayas

||||||| Indus Civilisation

✳ Indus sites

● Painted Grey Ware sites

0 miles   300

0 kilometres   500

Harappa ✳

✳

Kalibangan

Baluchistan

Indus

● **Hastinapura**

● Ahichchhatra

Delhi ○

✳

Mohenjo-Daro

✳ Chanhu-Daro

Ganges

Kausambi ●

Bengal

Ganges

✳ Lothal

Rangpur ✳

Gulf of Cambay

Arabian Sea

Bay of Bengal

▪ **Brahmagiri**

and often at sites associated with events in later Sanskrit legend, settlements with a characteristic black-on-grey painted pottery have been excavated, as at Hastinapura, dating from about 1000 BC onwards, with evidence of rice growing and iron working. This latter technology was apparently unknown to the early Aryans, and once again an independent mastery of the technique in ancient India seems likely: China again provides an instructive parallel situation. In southern India the cist burials, as at BRAHMAGIRI, are of iron-working peoples in about 200 BC, and with an ancestry of some centuries behind the technique there.

By the 4th century BC India was brought within the ambit of occidental history with the campaigns of Alexander to the Indus and TAXILA, for of the Achaemenid satrapy of the north west little is known, though Indian life became affected by Persian ideas in many spheres. The writing system of the Indus civilization was by now long forgotten (like Linear B in Dark Age Greece), and when literacy emerges, in the 3rd century BC, it is in the form of writing in a script derived from Aramaic, one of the official languages of the Persian court, and of its traders. Gautama Buddha had died around 500 BC, and in 321 BC the Mauryan Dynasty was founded, to be deeply influenced in its architectural styles and sculpture by Persian models. The third of the line, Ashoka, became a devoted Buddhist and when he wished to propagate his doctrine around 260–250 BC he adopted not only the Achaemenid rock-inscription form, but a derivative Aramaic script, Kharoshthi, for his Indian edicts, using Greek and Aramaic in his western province of Afghanistan. This, with its allied Brahmi script, restored literacy to India and so brought it however imperfectly into history, much as the propagation of Christianity centuries later brought literacy to the barbarian west.

Harappa PAKISTAN

Ancient city
Late 3rd millennium BC

BIBLIOGRAPHY
Allchin, B. and R., *The Birth of Indian civilization*, Harmondsworth, 1968, pp. 232–53
Burrow, T., 'Dravidian and the deciperment of the Indus script', *Antiquity*, XLIII, Cambridge, 1969, pp. 274–8
Clauson, G. and Chadwick, J., 'The Indus script deciphered?' *Antiquity*, XLIII, Cambridge, 1969, pp. 200–207
Fairservis, W. A., *The roots of ancient India*, London, 1971
Raikes, R., 'Kalibangan: death from natural causes', *Antiquity*, XLII, Cambridge, 1968, pp. 286–91
Wheeler, M., *The Indus civilization* (Supplementary vol. The Cambridge History of India, 3rd. ed.), 1968

Of the two great cities of the Indus civilization, Harappa lies 350 miles (563 km) north of its counterpart, MOHENJO-DARO, against an ancient silted-up bed of the river Ravi. Broadly contemporary with the southern city, within the last third of the 3rd millennium BC, it has traces of earlier occupation and of later use for a cemetery, but the extensive activities of brick robbers have reduced all but the citadel mound to fragments from which no street plan has been recovered: the citadel itself, however, measuring within its defences 1,200 feet by 600 feet (approx. 365 × 185 m), suggests that the accompanying town was no smaller than at Mohenjo-daro, which has a citadel of the same size. As elsewhere on Indus civilization sites, the buildings and defences were of fired bricks, or faced with these.

The citadel, up to 50 feet (15 m) high above the modern level, is a massive mud-brick podium, and its defences where excavated consisted of a primary rampart crowned with a great wall, 45 feet (14 m) wide at its base, of mud brick with battered sides, the outer faced with a fired brick casing. The defences included elaborate entrances and bastions, but no plan of internal structures could be traced. To the north and at a lower level lay an industrial area devoted to large-scale corn production and storage, with rows of circular brick working-platforms each holding at the centre the remains of a wooden mortar for pounding grain with a long wooden pestle. Beyond were granaries 50 feet by 20 feet (15 × 6 m) arranged in two rows of six, with provision for air ducts to keep the contents dry, as in Roman granaries of similar plan. Immediately under the shadow of the citadel a block of uniform little houses of regimented plan showed where the coolie labour for the municipal depot had its quarters.

South of the citadel a cemetery of the inhabitants of the city was partly excavated, with extended inhumations accompanied by pots and personal ornaments, one in a wooden coffin of rosewood and deodar. Not far away was another inhumation cemetery, in which the abundant pottery offerings were in a style wholly distinct in decoration and design from that of the Indus civilization, and the burials are not only later than the period of the city's occupation, but of an unknown and culturally distinct people.

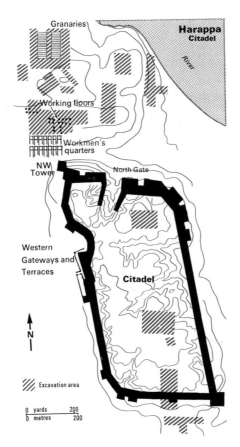

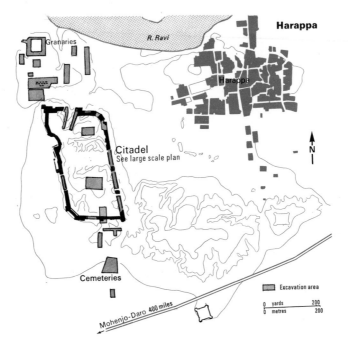

Mohenjo-Daro PAKISTAN

Ancient city
Late 3rd millennium BC

BIBLIOGRAPHY
See under Harappa

Corrected radiocarbon dates imply an overall time-span for the Indus civilization of about 2500–2100 BC in calendar years, and Mohenjo-daro, with HARAPPA, 350 miles (563 km) north, is one of the twin 'capital cities' of this anonymous people, with a still undeciphered script. It is known in its fully developed phases, contemporary with the Dynasty of Akkad and the 3rd Dynasty of Ur in Mesopotamia. Mohenjo-daro seems to have had an original nearly square plan, divided into 12 roughly rectangular blocks by main streets running north-south and east-west, with the central block on the west side occupied by a raised, defended, citadel, as at Harappa and at Kalibangan in Rajasthan. The buildings throughout are of fired bricks, and there are elaborate drainage and rubbish-disposal arrangements; the citadel, on a 20-foot (6 m) high brick podium, incorporated a municipal granary, a presumably ritual bath, and other buildings of unknown corporate function, but none a palace.

The site is approached by road from the railway station at Dokri, eight miles (13 km) away, and one enters the mounds with their excavated ruins from the east along an original street leading to the citadel, now crowned by a ruined Buddhist stupa of the early centuries AD. In the main excavated areas of the town, the street level today is one of the earlier in the stratified sequence, but as the street line of houses was strictly kept throughout the city's history, the house walls as they stand today represent centuries of successive rebuilding on old foundations, so that doors and drains open high above one's head onto vanished, later, street levels. Similarly, the brick-lined wells were continuously added to as the ground level rose with successive rebuildings on the debris of earlier buildings, and as excavated stand like factory chimneys high above the ground. Bathrooms and drains can be seen in the houses, as well as the main drains in the streets, with stone manhole covers for municipal inspection and clearance.

The citadel buildings include the Granary on the western edge, the Bath, 39 feet by 23 feet and 8 feet deep ($12 \times 7 \times 2 \cdot 4$ m), with surrounding ranges of rooms like monastic cells, other buildings interpreted as 'collegiate' in some form, and, to the south, a pillared assembly hall. However interpreted in detail, the implications combine to suggest a centre of religious and secular power.

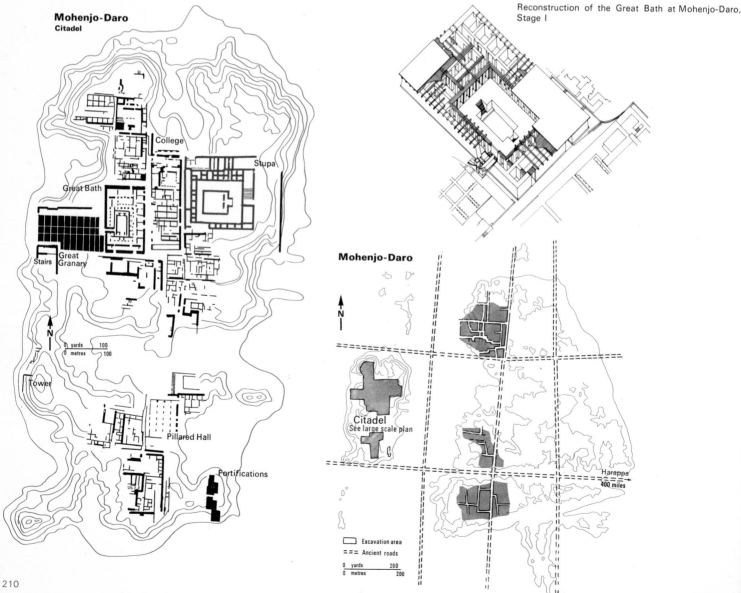

Reconstruction of the Great Bath at Mohenjo-Daro, Stage I

Mohenjo-Daro
Citadel

College

Stupa

Great Bath

Stairs Great Granary

Tower

Pillared Hall

Fortifications

Mohenjo-Daro

Citadel
See large scale plan

Harappa
400 miles

☐ Excavation area
=== Ancient roads

Hastinapura INDIA

Ancient city
5th century BC–15th century AD

BIBLIOGRAPHY
Lal, B. B., 'Excavation at Hastinapura and other explorations in the Upper Ganga and Sutlej basins 1950–2', *Ancient India*, X–XI, New Delhi, 1954–5, pp. 5–151

An objective of long standing in Indian archaeology has been to fill the gap between the end of the Indus civilization at the beginning of the 2nd millennium BC, and the historically documented Mauryan Dynasty from about 300 BC. Somewhere within this intermediate 1,700 years should lie the entry of the first Sanskrit-speaking Aryans from the west, the composition of the earliest Hindu religious works in verse and prose, and of the ancient traditional epic poems of the *Mahabharata* and the *Ramayana*. The gap has been partly filled by the identification of an archaeological culture with distinctive black-on-grey painted pottery, a knowledge of iron working and rice cultivation, and datable by corrected radiocarbon estimates between about 1150 and 450 BC in historical years. Although an interval of nearly a millennium separates this from the end of the Indus civilization, its distribution on over 30 sites south east of the Sutlej in the upper valleys of the Ganga and the Yamuna, many of them associated by name in legend with the *Mahabharata* epic, suggests that the pottery and the poem may be broadly contemporary, and both represent aspects of a long established and mature phase of Indo-European culture in northern India.

At Hastinapura in Meerut District, 60 miles (97 km) north east of Delhi by road, a group of dusty mounds up to 60 feet (18 m) high represent the accumulated debris of successive settlements from about 500 BC to the 15th century AD, eroded on the east by the now shrunk 'Old Ganga' river. Hastinapura was the starting place of the *Mahabharata* epic, and above an early occupation marked by a scatter of eroded potsherds, excavations revealed the Period II settlement to be that of people using the characteristic black-on-grey painted pottery, with rather miserable mud-walled houses and having domestic horses in addition to cattle and pigs, growing rice (the earliest evidence for its cultivation in India) and working in iron, copper, and glass. Around 300 BC this township was destroyed by a flood (as was the legendary Hastinapura in the epic) and replaced by the Period III settlement, of people using a distinctive polished black pottery typical of the period from about 500 BC to the end of the Mauryan dynasty around 185 BC and the formation of that of the Sungas. To them, with the Kushans, the fourth period on the site can be attributed, the fifth being the 11th to the 15th century AD.

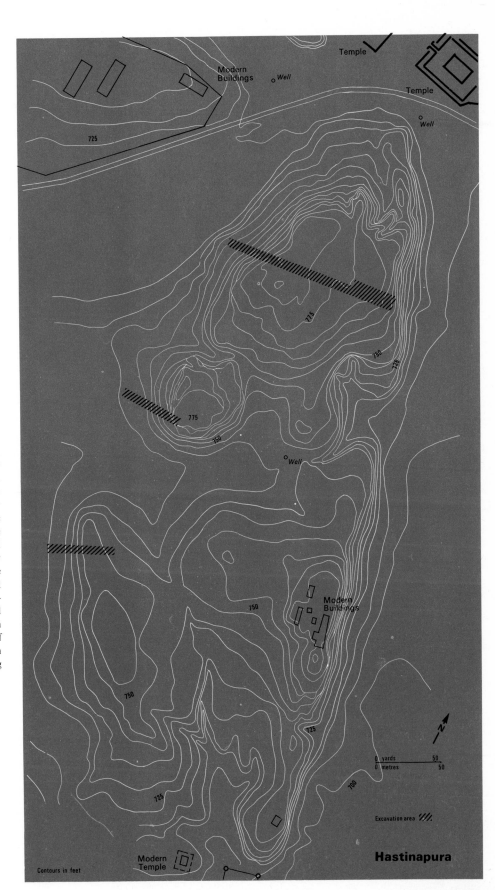

Hastinapura

Taxila PAKISTAN

Ancient cities
5th century BC–3rd century AD

BIBLIOGRAPHY
Marshall, J., *Taxila*, Cambridge, 1951
Marshall, J., *A guide to Taxila*, (4th ed.), Cambridge, 1960
Piggott, S., *Some ancient cities of India*, Bombay, 1945, pp. 20–31
Wheeler, M., *Flames over Persepolis*, London, 1968, pp. 91–122

When Alexander, carrying his conquests eastwards from Bactria to India, crossed the Indus and descended to the plain and the great city of Taxila, in 326 BC, he came at the invitation of the ruler of a township already some centuries old, perhaps founded in the 6th century BC. Ambhi, who called himself Taxiles, saw an advantageous alliance with the Greek forces against a rival, Poros, perhaps a chief of the Pauravas. After Alexander's withdrawal, Taxila came under the Mauryas, Ashoka being viceroy during his minority. After his death about 232 BC and the collapse of the Mauryan empire, a Graeco-Bactrian fortified town was built about 170 BC. This in turn was replaced by a walled city under Scytho-Parthian rule around the 1st century BC, itself succeeded in the 2nd-3rd century AD by a fourth Taxila founded by Kushan rulers.

The ruins of the first town are contained in the Bhir Mound, nearest the railway station and south of the Museum, and in the excavated areas can be seen some of the street plan and shoddily built houses of the 4th century BC, including a large house with courts and a three-pillared hall. Further south, in the centre of the town, is a public building with apsed end and a cross-hall with bases for wooden pillars.

The first phase of the new fortification seems to be represented by the mud-brick walls of the Kachcha Kot (Earth Fort) against the Tamra Nala stream to the north west, partly covered by the third town of Sirkap, a walled Hellenistic city with regular street plan partly excavated, containing a Buddhist temple and two large buildings, one, the Mahal, southwards in the Upper Town, with claims to being a palace. Classical architectural fragments including Corinthian pilasters, were found, and outside the Kachcha Kot to the north are the remains of a temple, probably a Zorastrian fire temple, with a portico having columns with Ionic capitals.

Of the fourth, Kushan, fortified town, at Sirsukh to the north west, there is little to be seen except the stone-built defences with half-round bastions and arrow slits.

The Museum contains finds from the excavations including sculpture, coins and gems.

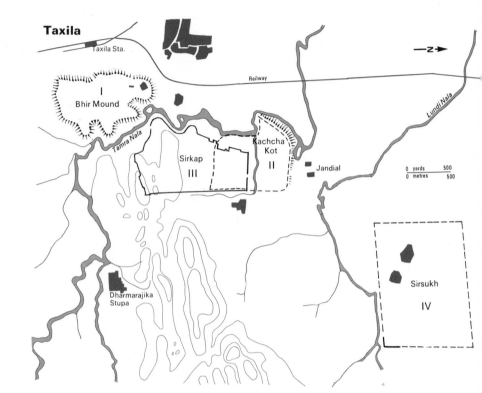

Brahmagiri INDIA

Ancient burials
2nd century BC

BIBLIOGRAPHY
Allchin, B. and R., *The birth of Indian civilization*, Harmondsworth, 1968, pp. 223–32
Wheeler, M., 'Brahmagiri and Chandravalli, 1947 . . .'
Ancient India, IV, New Delhi, 1947–8, pp. 181–310

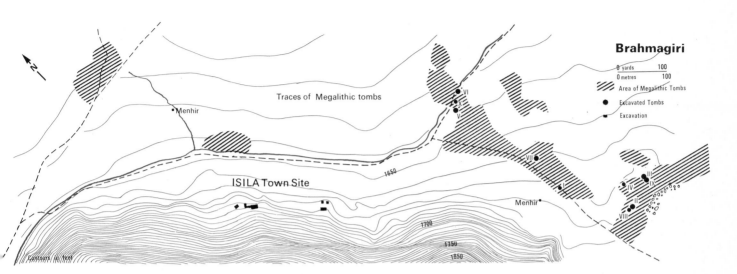

In southern India, beyond the Narmada and Godavari rivers, are considerable numbers of roughly made prehistoric burial monuments that, because of the use in some of them of often large stone slabs have been called 'megalithic tombs'. Unfortunately this phrase has emotive overtones when not used literally, associating these burials with other monuments in prehistoric western Europe, chronologically and culturally unrelated, and sharing only the use of large stones. At Brahmagiri a group of such burials was excavated and their chronology tied in not only to the native south Indian sequence, but to true historical dates obtained by Roman coins and imported pottery on such coastal trading sites as Arikamedu. The range of date was about 200 BC to about AD 50, and even if such structures may be somewhat earlier in other parts of south India, they are highly unlikely to approach the antiquity of the European monuments, of the 4th and 3rd millennia BC.

At Brahmagiri prehistoric occupation began with a local stone-using culture, having a little copper

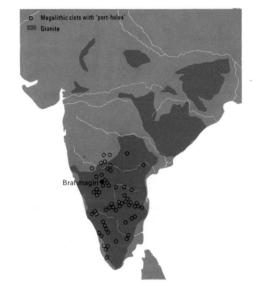

and going back to the earlier 2nd millennium BC in south India. At the site in question, in the Chitaldrug district, on the edge of the Ashokan town site of Isila, there follow burials in pits or cists within small circular stone enclosures, representative of an iron-using people from about 200 BC. The use of iron in south India may go back into the early 1st millennium BC, and in the Brahmagiri graves iron tools and weapons (swords, spears, sickles, knives) were found in some quantity. The graves are mostly constructed so as to have a symbolic 'entrance' on one side – a stone doorslab in the pit graves, or a perforated slab in the cists. In both we may be dealing with the idea of a hut or house for the dead, a simple concept expressed in wood or stone in many primitive cultures widely distributed in time and space, but there is no reason to think that apparent parallels, unsupported by other evidence of contact and chronologically disparate, have any significance. This locally prehistoric iron-using culture at Brahmagiri was succeeded by one representing the historical Andhra (Satavahna) Dynasty, established in the Deccan in the 1st century BC.

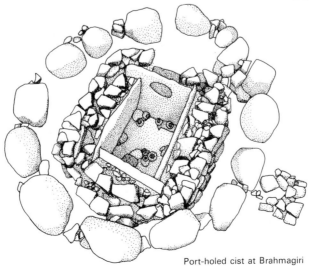

Port-holed cist at Brahmagiri

SOUTH EAST ASIA

The riverine and limestone landscape of central and southern China present the advantages to primitive life which are found in other parts of the world where the most ancient traces of man occur. In recent years the evidence for the antiquity and continuous presence of man in China has been greatly increased. A pithecine ancestor of the hominids was found in Yünnan associated with the bones of mastodon, and is assigned to the Pliocene period, about 15 million years ago.

The earliest hominid known in China is represented by a jaw and skull-cap found near together in reddish clay at Lan-t'ien, 28 miles (45 km) from Sian in Shensi. The morphology suggests an evolutionary stage preceding that of *Sinanthropus pekinensis*, and Lan-t'ien man is provisionally assigned to a time about 600,000 years ago. His tools included small and poorly flaked scrapers made from quartz. The Chou-k'o-tien caves which yielded the abundant remains of *Sinanthropus pekinensis* (Peking Man, now usually classified as *Homo erectus*) are thought to have been first inhabited about half a million years ago. Recently this site has produced further human remains, notably a skull cap and an upper arm. Peking man had a flattened skull and massive, projecting brow ridge, but his average brain size of about 1,000 cc was larger than that of the other well-known Asian representative of *Homo erectus*, Java man. Peking man's coarsely flaked stone tools, of which many bear marks of use, include very few with secondary working of the edge. The occupation of the Chou-k'ou-tien caves by *Sinanthropus* dates from Middle Pleistocene times.

The tools grouped as the Ting-ts'un culture resemble some categories of the Middle Palaeolithic of Europe, and are regarded as the work of human races of the late Middle Pleistocene or the early Late Pleistocene period. These men represent an advance on the Neanderthal man of western Asia and Europe but they retain primitive features which still ally them to *Sinanthropus*. It is notable that their remains occur from Mongolia to Kuangtung.

With the first appearance of races of *Homo sapiens* the features characteristic of the modern Mongol race, and even of its modern sub-divisions, are discernible. These men are traced in Kuangsi and Szechwan. The better known *sapiens* from Chou-k'ou-tien, known as Upper Cave Man, belongs with them. This Late Pleistocene race appears to have made the stone tools worked on elongated flakes (seldom qualifying clearly for the term 'blade'), scrapers and other unifacial tools, which for China represent the main Upper Palaeolithic industry. The sites extend from the Mongolian plateau to the hills of south-west China: whether the absence of these remains in the flood plains of the great rivers is a sign of avoidance of these regions, or results from destruction by the rivers, cannot yet be determined. Both the Middle Palaeolithic and the Upper Palaeolithic cultures belong to the period in which the loess, or yellow earth, of China was being deposited on the upper course of the Yellow River by winds coming from the north west. In caves tools of the Upper Palaeolithic have been found in the middle of loessic filling, dating some tens of thousands of years BC.

It is difficult to define the transition from this Upper Palaeolithic to the Neolithic cultures on the middle and upper course of the Yellow River, where food production was first achieved in China and whence it spread to the rest of the country. The earliest food-producing Neolithic is restricted closely to the area of the primary loess (the Yangshao culture), while the later phase (Lungshan culture) occupies the lower riverine plain of secondary, or redeposited loess and stretches some distance south and north along the east coast beyond the loessic zone.

Along the northern part of this Neolithic zone are found sites characterized by microlithic stone tools, which combine with polished stone axes, and mark the fusion or co-existence of the Upper Palaeolithic tradition with the new economy. When rudimentary pottery first appears in the north it is associated with stone assemblages of this kind. Food production was not necessarily the rule in pre-metal cultures which archaeologists of Siberia and East Asia sometimes term Neolithic. The first demonstrable Neolithic culture in the Yellow River valley certainly comprises farming, but in the Yangtze valley and the south and south east corded pottery marks numerous riverine sites where no sign of food production occurs, and it is speculated that a corresponding phase, not yet established archaeologically, must have been traversed also in the north. Millet was the staple of both the Yangshao and the Lungshan cultures along the Yellow River, and although rice was raised by Neolithic farmers in the south, it was not adopted in any northern region until the Bronze Age, and to the present day is of minor importance in the north. Most representative of the Yangshao culture are finely painted vases and bowls. There are two styles, separated sharply along the line of the eastern watershed of the T'ao valley in Kansu. It is the later phase of this pottery, typified by the magnificent painted urns of the Panshan cemetery, that has a generic resemblance to the Bronze Age painted potteries of Turkestan, particularly of Anau and Namazga, although there is no evidence of migration or specific cultural transfers. The central Yangshao, largely typified by the finds at Pan-P'o-Ts'un, begins earlier and develops independently. Its successor, the black-pottery Lungshan Neolithic, is interpreted by modern Chinese archaeologists to be a later stage of the Yangshao, and not an intrusive northern culture, as was formerly thought. Although aspects of continuity in the Yellow River valley may be defined, certain affinities of Lungshan culture connect with the north east and eastern Siberia, in a way which influence exercised from China hardly accounts for.

Throughout the history of the northern Neolithic, the Neolithic of the south and the south east continued unchanged, its corded bag-shaped pots persisting until historical times. It is arguable that a 'corded-pottery horizon' should be recognized over all China as a prelude to the initial stage of Neolithic settlement and food production. But in the most progressive area, on the Yellow River, it has not yet been possible to establish the existence of such a stage stratigraphically, and corded pottery remains a characteristic feature of the south and south east. The watershed between the valleys of the Yangtze and the Yellow River appears to mark a cultural boundary of increasing importance from the Upper Palaeolithic onwards. The distribution of polished stone axes conforms to it: subcylindrical axes of the common shape, and trapezoid flat axes being the concomitant in the north of Yangshao, and Lungshan respectively, while to the south the earlier stone equipment of roughly sharpened pebbles of Hoabinhian aspect gives way to beautifully working shouldered and tanged axes of polished stone which perhaps were not manufactured before the beginning of the Bronze Age in the north. The duration of the Chinese food-producing Neolithic is only very broadly estimated to be between the 5th or 6th millennium and the 3rd millennium. In view of the early date assignable to pottery in Japan, we may supposed that the ceramic art in China, being no later, goes back some millennia earlier still. Recent radiocarbon dating shows the Yangshao culture to have flourished in the 4th and 3rd millennia BC, while the Lungshan culture descends as late as the 2nd millennium.

In Japan the succession of prehistoric phases is markedly different from that observed in China. Stone industries of Middle and Upper Palaeolithic type are now well known, but their stadial position remains uncertain and is currently debated. Some of these stone cultures clearly antedate the appearance of pottery, and the 'pre-pottery phase' is now a well-established division of Japanese prehistory. The Jōmon Neolithic of Japan is the classical instance of a highly developed, pottery-using, and in part settled, culture which remained ignorant of food production during many millennia. The Jōmon culture extending from the 8th millennium until the late 3rd century BC, is related to the south-east Chinese tradition and to traditions recorded in the Soviet Maritime Province and in Kamchataka, and betrays no hint of communication with Yangshao or Lungshan. The elaboration of Jōmon pottery appears to exceed all possible bounds of hand potting.

The advent of bronze in China is peculiar for the advanced technology which was operated from the very beginning, as seen in the vessels and weapons from Cheng-chou and ANYANG. The tradition of a ceramic kiln in which a temperature for smelting and melting bronze was easily obtained undoubtedly goes far to explain the precocity and rapid progress of metallurgy. From 1027 BC, when a league of north-western tribes under leaders of the house of Chou overthrew Shang and occupied central China, until the mid-3rd century BC when Chinese armies occupied the southern seaboard, cultural history broadly shows the gradual move southwards of techniques and institutions founded by Shang and Chou in the northern provinces. Throughout this period a narrow but powerful artistic tradition based on linear design evolves along remarkably consecutive lines. Bronze was slow to displace stone as a material for tools in the remoter parts of the Chou territories, nor did iron later oust bronze for the manufacture of practical objects so rapidly as this occurred in the west. Iron was cast from the late 5th century BC, and a century or so afterwards long forged iron swords began to determine the fortunes of battle. The new iron weaponry gave essential assistance to the state of Ch'in when it finally united China by conquest. But the crossbow, a Chinese invention and a weapon of prime importance in the warfare of Ch'in and Han, was still cast of bronze, though necessarily with a precision which placed it beyond the attainments of the nomad bronze casters living north of the defensive walls.

It may be said of Chinese Bronze Age culture that it was less exportable than any of its equivalents in western Asia, the Mediterranean or Europe. Both in south China itself and in Japan bronze fails to make its appearance before about 200 BC. In Japan it marked the advent of the Yayoi culture in which bronze weapons closely copy those of Korea. The Korean forms were in turn inspired from China. The Yayoi people also introduced rice farming and wheel-made pottery into Japan. The subsequent period in Japan, termed *Kofun jidai*, Age of the Ancient Tombs, is analogous in some respects to the Hallstatt phase of central Europe, for it maintains high standards of bronzework inherited from the past, along with advanced iron metallurgy, and its monuments and grave goods reflect a social order in which power was shared by scores if not hundreds of local chieftains (ISHIBUTAI KOFUN). From the 3rd to the 7th century AD, while the central power was forming and the whole of Honshu was being finally occupied by the Japanese, an increasing flow of imported goods arrived from China, and with the imports came the influence of Chinese institutions. The state founded in the 6th century in Yamato, on the plain north of the modern city of Osaka, was in some essential respects a cultural satellite of the neighbouring mainland empire. The archaeologist notes how distinctly the independent artistic and technological character of the island tradition declares itself from the very beginning of this cultural symbiosis with China, which was destined to last until modern times.

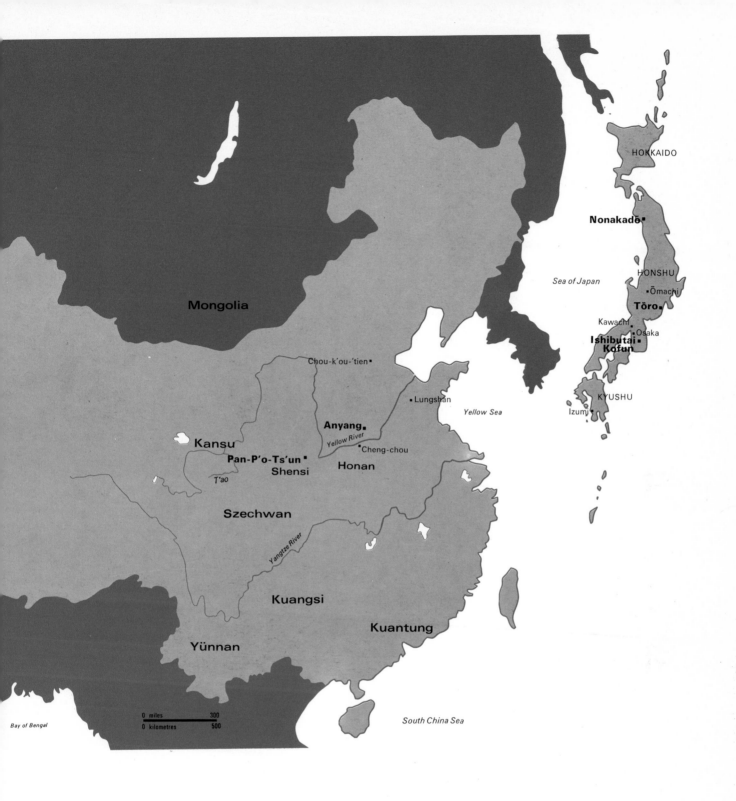

Mongolia

HOKKAIDO

Nonakadō▪

HONSHU

Sea of Japan

▪Ōmachi

Tōro▪

Kawachi▪

▪Osaka

Ishibutai▪
Kofun

Chou-k'ou-'tien▪

▪Lungshan

Yellow Sea

Anyang▪

Kansu

Yellow River

▪Cheng-chou

KYUSHU

Pan-P'o-Ts'un▪

Izumi▪

Shensi

Honan

T'ao

Szechwan

Yangtze River

Kuangsi

Kuantung

Yünnan

0 miles   300
0 kilometres   500

Bay of Bengal

South China Sea

217

Pan-P'o-Ts'un CHINA

Neolithic village
5th–4th millennium BC

BIBLIOGRAPHY
The Neolithic Village at Pan-p'o, Sian, Institute of Archaeo-
logy, Peking, 1963
Watson, W., *China before the Han Dynasty*, London, 1966

The Neolithic villages of the middle Yellow River
valley, particularly in Shensi, are of a size which
indicates an ancient population on a scale of that of
the great riverine civilizations of Mesopotamia and
Egypt. Pan-p'o is the first of such settlements to be
excavated extensively and so to give, for the first
time in East Asia, a tolerably complete picture of
the Late Neolithic culture and economy. It belongs
to the Yangshao culture of the central Chinese tradition, which began earlier than the related but distinct Yangshao of Kansu, and is to be dated probably
between the 5th and 4th millennium BC.

The most remarkable feature is the excellent preservation of house foundations and internal structures. Five building levels were distinguished by the
overlapping of floors, the houses in the two lowest
being nearly all square in plan, and sunk four steps
beneath the contemporary surface. The entrances are
separated from the interior by a threshold, and the
arrangement of fireplaces and internal postholes in
some cases indicates a ridged roof, in others a
conical one. A building almost 52 feet (16 m) wide,
in a late level, is interpreted as serving some communal purpose. The superstructures suggested by
the pattern of supporting pillars imply a rudimentary stage of the principles of the later Chinese
trabeate architecture with its interlocking of beams
over the pillar heads. The village was divided into
different areas for habitation, pottery making and
burials. Inside the houses ovens and storage spaces
were carved out of the virgin loess. Outside, storage
pits descended to as much as 20 feet (6 m) and were
lined with a layer of burned clay.

As in the Yangshao culture generally, the staple
was millet. A domestic bovid was known, but the
chief food animals were pig, sheep and/or goats. An
unusually large number of dogs were kept and may
have been eaten.

The site has been preserved as a museum in the
final stage of excavation. From the completeness of
the investigation Pan-p'o has become the type-site
for the central Yangshao, although it strictly represents a Shensi facies of this culture. In the decoration
of the black-on-red painted pottery a stylized representation of a fish is common, and not the intersecting circles used further east.

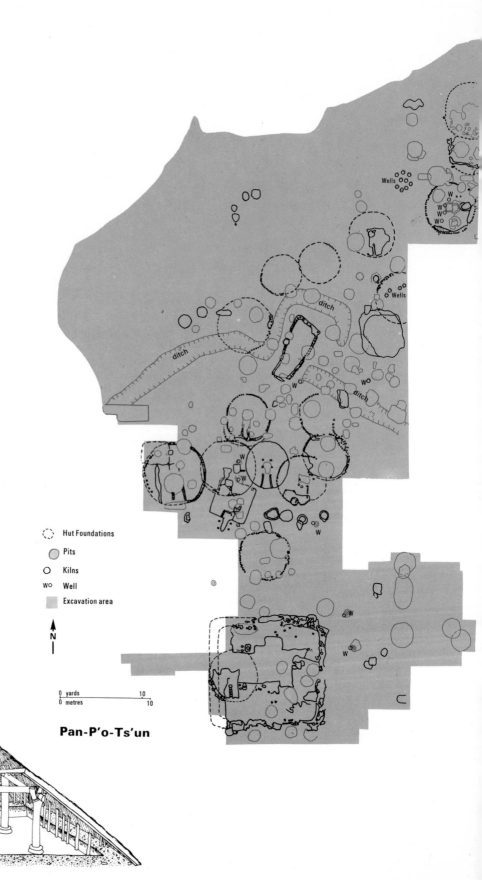

Wells

ditch

ditch

ditch

Wells

---- Hut Foundations

Pits

Kilns

W○ Well

Excavation area

N

0 yards 10
0 metres 10

Pan-P'o-Ts'un

Reconstruction of house
at Pan-p'o-t'sun

Anyang CHINA

Early Shang dynasty capital
c. 1500–1400 BC

BIBLIOGRAPHY
Cheng Tê-k'un, *Archaeology in China, vol. II: Shang China,*
    Cambridge, 1960
Watson, W., *China before the Han Dynasty,* London, 1966

To the north west of the town of Anyang in north Honan are habitation sites and tombs of the Shang kings, whose dynasty (c. 1500–1027 BC) appears second in the traditional list but is in fact the earliest attested by archaeological remains. The largest settlement was at the hamlet of Hsiao-t'un, two and a half miles (4 km) from Anyang, where excavations conducted from 1929 to 1937 and again in the early 1950s for the first time revealed the material context of the high Bronze Age of East Asia. Something of Shang history and institutions is recorded in the *Book of Documents* (c. 8th century BC), and the location of the capital, Great Shang, at the Waste of Yin (Yin being another title of the dynasty) was well known before the investigation of the place, just beyond the north limit of Hsiao-t'un, was taken in hand.

The site lies within a northward loop of the Huan river, which seems to have supplied its only defence, since no encircling wall has been traced. A bewildering conglomeration of house foundations, drainage systems and burials were well preserved in the loessic soil. Stratigraphy is limited to the distinction of remains antedating and postdating the great foundations of pisé, these representing, in the famous Sector C, structures interpreted as a palace built of timber pillars and beams erected during the flourishing late Shang dynasty of the 14th–13th centuries BC. Burials of animals and men represented the victims of foundation sacrifices. In the central space a whole company of soldiers and four charioteers with their companions, horses and vehicles, had been slaughtered and buried simultaneously. Many of these tombs contained fine bronzes, carvings in jade and bone and other materials, of a kind known long before from the depredations of antiquarians. Deposits of thousands of animal scapulae and tortoise carpaces used for divination by heat-cracking were found to be inscribed with the questions that had been put to divinities, which included ancestors' spirits: 'Will there be rain?' 'Is such and such a sacrifice acceptable?' 'Should a military campaign be conducted in such and such a direction?' The form of writing, in all essentials resembling the modern Chinese script, constitutes the earliest record of the Chinese language. The kings appear in the role of theocrats. The occurrence of their names in these oracular documents has confirmed the existence of all but two in the long list of Shang kings.

The evolved linear style of Shang art is seen to advantage on the bronze ritual vessels which were elaborately cast from piecemoulds. This material, together with that recovered from the great shaft graves and cruciform-shaft graves located a short distance to the north west at Hsi-pei-kang, Wu-kuan-ts'un and Ta-ssŭ-k'ung-ts'un, represents the first phase of the historical tradition, whose unreal stylizations were to dominate Chinese art until the Han dynasty (206 BC–AD 221). Pottery could fire at over 1,000°C and jade carvers were highly skilled. The Shang chariot has some affinity with the contemporary chariots of western Asia, while the bronze

socketed axe, bearing all the marks of a Shang invention, appears to have been transmitted directly to the Ural region of eastern Russia. Since the discovery of this capital, another and earlier Shang city has been excavated within a nine-mile (15 km) radius of the city of Cheng-chou in central Honan. It is estimated that the northward move of the capital took place about 1400 BC. The Shang dynasty is said to have been founded approximately in the 16th century BC, and the date of its overthrow by Chou was 1027 BC, according to a revised chronology. The traditional dates for these events are 1765 BC and 1122 BC. Recently a carbon-14 test has dated the late Shang tomb at Wu-kuan-ts'un to about 1085 BC.

1 Dog
2 Caprid
3 Pig
4 Bovid
5 Horse
6 Chariot
7 Child
8 Woman
9 Kneeling man
10 Stone pillar-footing
11 Find of ritual vessels
12 Grave of beheaded sacrificial victims
13 Find of a *lei*
14 Find of *ko* halberd etc.
15 Find of a *chüeh* etc.
16 Find of a *ting* etc.
17 Bird
18 Burial of a person upside-down (on head)
19 Kneeling victim holding shield and halberd (*ko*)
20 Kneeling victim holding halberd (*ko*)
21 Rammed earth foundation
22 Stone pillar-footing resting on a mound of rammed earth

Anyang

Sector C of excavations at Hsiao T'un

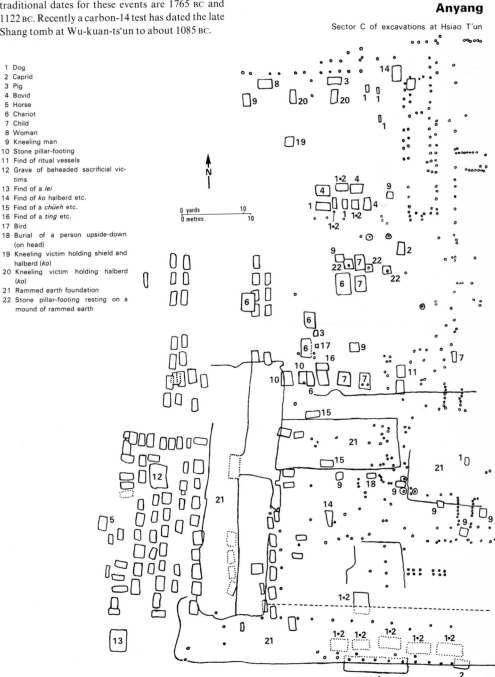

0 yards 10
0 metres 10

The Great Wall of China

BIBLIOGRAPHY
Lattimore, O., *Inner Asian Frontiers of China*, Boston, 195
Watson, W., *Cultural Frontiers in Ancient East Asia*, Edin
burgh, 1971
Herrmann, A., *An Historical Atlas of China*, Edinburgh
1972
Egami, N. and Mizuno, S., 'Inner Mongolia and the Regio
of The Great Wall', *Archaeologia Orientalis*, Series B
vol. 1, Tokyo, 1935

The 2,000-mile (3,220 km) Great Wall of China, as it is known today, shows largely the stone facing and the alignment given to it in the Ming reconstruction.

It differs from the first Great Wall, the continuous defence built by the emperor Shih Huang Ti of Ch'in after he had unified the country in 232 BC, in taking a generally more southerly route (marking the northern boundary of Hopei, Shansi and part of Shensi). The early wall passed north of the great loop of the Yellow River and so included the Ordos territory, a large part of which is excluded by the Ming wall.

The building of state walls are recorded for the southern state of Chou in the 7th–6th centuries BC. The walls built in the 5th–4th centuries by the northern states appear in the first place to be a development of the earth dikes erected against flood. In the era of the Warring States (453–232 BC) the state boundaries were often permanently guarded, and dikes and fortresses erected along them. Thus the first incentive to wall building was the internecine warfare of the Chinese, and not, as in later times, defence against barbarian intruders. The north-facing walls erected by the states of Chao, Yen and Ch'in were not planned in concert, but they provided much of the length of Shih Huang Ti's continuous bulwark. This was revetted with stone from the coast at least as far as the Lanchou district of Kansu (whereas earlier walls had used stone sparingly). Beyond and along the Kansu corridor leading to Tun-huang, the gate into central Asia, the wall was continued, though here unrevetted, in order to protect the military and trade route. Its crumbling mass of mud-dried brick may still be seen standing over considerable stretches.

On the Ming wall there are eight to 11 forts per mile (5–7 per km), at approximately equal intervals although the siting of these forts, like the siting of the wall itself, was adapted to the immediate advantages of the terrain. Whether Shih Huang Ti's wall forts were set so close together is not known, but in the strategically important north west they must have been very frequent. In the Ch'in and Han periods (232 BC–AD 221) the wall gave a decided advantage to the defenders, armed with crossbows, against mounted warriors who shot their bows from the saddle. The Chinese resembled the Romans in their efforts to found permanent veterans' colonies in the vicinity of the wall, to control the passage of nomads and to regulate their trade. The Wall was also an instrument of Chinese expansion and stabilization, preventing the exit of settled population no less than the irruption of mobile tribesmen.

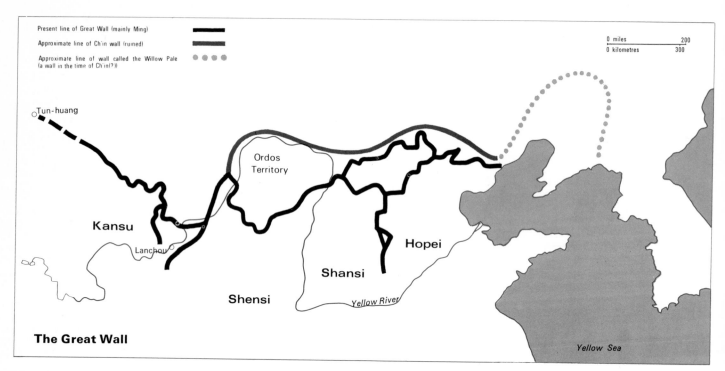

The Great Wall

Present line of Great Wall (mainly Ming)

Approximate line of Ch'in wall (ruined)

Approximate line of wall called the Willow Pale (a wall in the time of Ch'in(?))

0 miles 200
0 kilometres 300

Tun-huang

Ordos Territory

Kansu

Lanchou

Shensi

Shansi

Hopei

Yellow River

Yellow Sea

Nonakadō Stone Circle JAPAN

Ritual enclosure
1st millennium BC

BIBLIOGRAPHY
Kidder, J., *Japan before Buddhism*, London, 1966

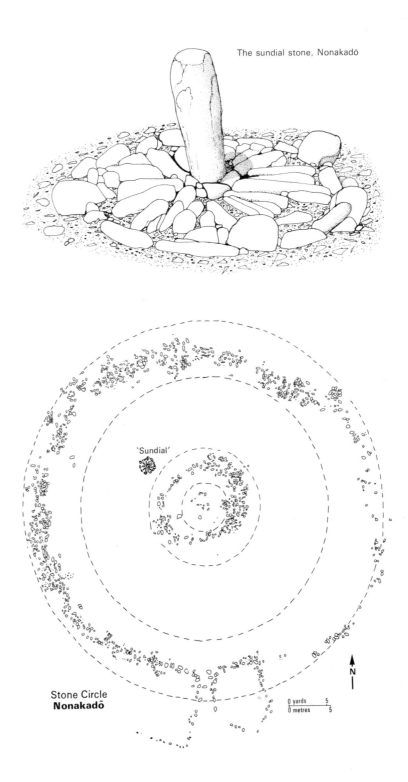

The sundial stone, Nonakadō

Situated at Ōyu in the Kazuno district of Akita prefecture, this monument is the best known of its kind in Japan. Together with another group of stones nearby called the Manza, it is laid out on a 560-foot (170 m) high river terrace. Like some similar structures known in Hokkaidō the perimeters at Ōyu are in fact oval, the two axes of the Nonakadō measuring 136 feet 2 inches (41·5 m) east–west and 126 feet 4 inches (38·5 m) north–south, while the Manza has a long axis of 149 feet 7 inches (45·6 m). The Nonakadō consists of two concentric settings of close-set stones forming belts up to 33 feet (10 m) wide, with two projecting parts in the south. Both of these perimeters contain a number of smaller stone settings of various design: oval, round and square, in some instances enclosing a standing stone and in others stones laid horizontally. The outer perimeter contains 33 such structures and the inner one 11, though in both cases the original number was higher. From the centre lying towards the north-west segment is the famous sundial, consisting of a standing menhir at the centre surrounded by long stones placed radially on their side, the whole enclosed by a circle of contiguous low-lying stones. The diameter of the sundial is about 36 feet (11 m) and the height of the standing menhir about 14 feet 9 inches (4·5 m). The Manza reproduces this scheme almost exactly, with a sundial forming also an independent circle in the north-west segment, but the perimeter is triple, the outer line enclosing 42 smaller structures and the inner five much damaged ones.

Excavations at these sites produced stone axes and sceptres, stone vessels and fragments of a local variety of late Jōmon pottery, dating from the 1st millennium BC. The purpose of the 'circles' has been disputed as between burial and some other ritual purpose, possibly connected with sun worship. Another oval setting of stones preserved in the Oshoro district of Hokkaidō is venerated by local Ainu, who make offerings of *sake* to it. It was formerly interpreted as having an astronomical function, but now is generally thought to be connected with the burials of the Ainu, and once to have contained stone-built burial chambers. Once again, associated pottery indicates the late Jōmon period. The presence of the Ōyu structures in the north of Honshu would thus record the wider extension of Ainu culture over Japan as it existed in early times. Stone structures of this kind are comparatively rare in Japan. One near Ōmachi in Nagano prefecture appears to be the southernmost, and underlines the late date of the phenomenon as a whole.

'Sundial'

Stone Circle
Nonakadō

0 yards 5
0 metres 5

N

Tōro JAPAN

Site of Yayoi culture
1st century AD

BIBLIOGRAPHY
Kidder, J., *Japan before Buddhism*, London, 1966

This site at Shikiji, Shizuoka City, of a village which flourished during the 1st century AD, fully excavated in 1947–50, has given the most comprehensive picture of rural life based on rice cultivation which can be cited for the prehistoric period in East Asia. In particular it throws new light on this middle period of the Yayoi culture of Japan.

The village appears to have consisted of some 10 to 20 houses only, of which 12 were identified and revealed as oval in plan. The largest measured 40 feet by 34 feet 9 inches (12·2 × 10·6 m), with the longer axis pointing north and south. Two granaries, of which one was eight feet six inches by seven feet ten inches (2·6 × 2·4 m), were raised above the ground on piles.

Wooden dishes, beakers, pestles, ladles, girdle ornaments and weaving instruments were recovered in considerable numbers, all retaining approximately their original shapes. For tools, stone and a little iron were used, bronze appearing only in the form of bracelets and rings. Fish-hooks were of horn. Some glass beads are a sure sign of the trade conducted from the place, and it is suggested that rice was cold. The pottery is typical of the Yayoi: tall red-surfaced vases with restricted neck and bowls on a high foot, all thrown on the wheel.

The outlines of wet-rice fields were recovered, each measuring from 800 to 2,800 square yards (670–2,340 sq m), lying to the south of the dwellings. The ridges separating the fields, about three feet (approx. 1 m) wide, were well supplemented by wooden stakes. The damp soil had preserved a remarkable number of vegetable traces, including, besides rice itself, beans, chestnut, wild grape, musk melon, cobicula and a kind of peach. Animal remains were identified as conger-eel (implying deep-sea fishing), clams, yellowfish, terrapin, wild boar, deer and a domestic bovid. The site has been kept as it was excavated, a museum installed, and one of the houses reconstructed. The abandonment of the site may have been sudden, possibly in consequence of flooding by the Abe and Warashina rivers. The signs of immediate contact with the East Asian continent which are frequent at Yayoi sites in western Japan are lacking at Tōro, but the evidence it provides of settled and comparatively complex farming is valid for the whole Yayoi culture. In two centuries this had ousted Jōmon culture and the food-gathering life from all southern and central Japan.

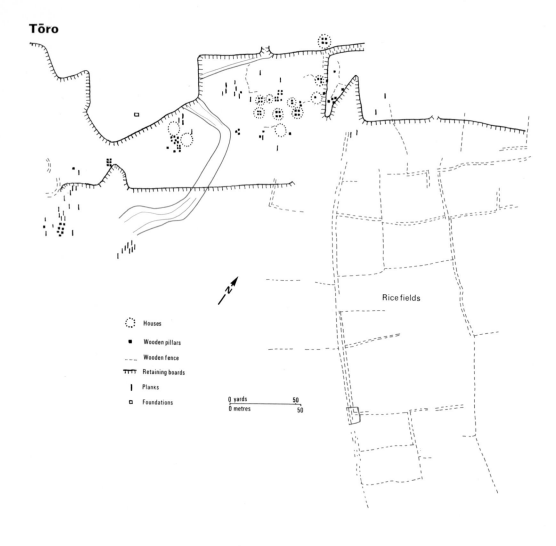

Tōro

Houses

Wooden pillars

Wooden fence

Retaining boards

Planks

Foundations

Rice fields

0 yards   50
0 metres   50

Ishibutai Kofun JAPAN

Tomb of the Late Predynastic period
7th century AD

BIBLIOGRAPHY
Kidder, J., *Japan before Buddhism*, London, 1966

Situated at Asukamurajima, Takaichi-gun, in Nara prefecture, this is one of the most celebrated of the *kofun* tombs characteristic of the proto-dynastic era of Japan, from the 3rd to the 7th century AD. The Ishibutai (meaning stone dancing platform) is an oblong chamber irregularly walled and roofed with huge undressed stones, the space enclosed measuring 25 feet 3 inches by 11 feet 6 inches by 15 feet 5 inches high (7·7 × 3·5 × 4·7 m). The covering of earth was removed long ago, but excavations by Hamada Kōsaku in 1933 showed that the original mound was rectangular, as made from the end of the early *kofun* era. The Ishibutai is dated to the 7th century AD belonging to the end of the second or to the third subdivision of the later *kofun* age. Tradition ascribes the tomb to the minister Soga-no-umako.

The tomb was surrounded by a bank with inner ditch, forming a circle of average 269 feet (82 m) diameter, the ditch varying from 18 feet to 27 feet (5·5–8·2 m) in width. The capstones of the chamber weigh 63 to 77 tons (64–78 tonnes). The excavators found fragments of both Sue and Haji pottery, as they combined at this time in west-central Japan. The tomb was restored in 1954 and presents an impressive spectacle.

Earlier *kofun* take advantage of features of the landscape to achieve height, beginning with the tombs of keyhole plan raised higher at the circular end. From the beginning some show a rectangular plan, but mounds with rounded ends and square mounds displace the keyhole design as the main types in the later period, except some tombs of emperors and powerful nobles, these being now increasingly differentiated from the numerous smaller rectangular tombs of the lesser gentry. The distribution of *kofun* extends from central Honshu to Kyushu, with special concentration in the metropolitan district (*kinai*) of Yamato, Yamashiro, Kawachi and Izumi. The tomb of the emperor Nintoku (AD 313–99) in Osaka urban prefecture, surrounded by a moat and wide bank, is the largest of all. The rectangular segment of its keyhole plan measures 1,000 feet (305 m) along its greater axis, and the diameter of the circular part reaches 804 feet (245 m) with a height of 115 feet (35 m). The stone-built burial chambers of the *kofun* are generally contained within the mound, at shallow depth below the surface. The earlier chambers take the form of long galleries walled with small unmortared stones, whereas the later chambers of large dressed slabs are higher, sometimes subdivided and covered by high corbelled roofs. The stone and pottery coffins and occasionally surviving wall painting of the later chambers are important documents of early Japanese art.

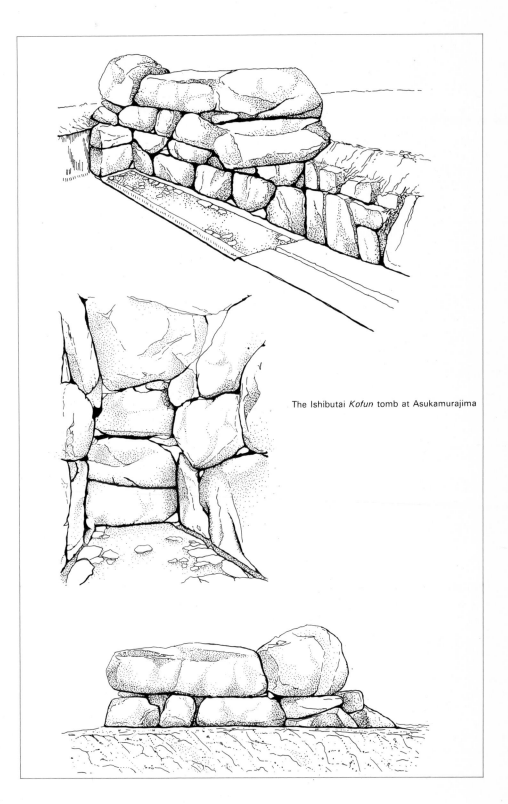

The Ishibutai *Kofun* tomb at Asukamurajima

NORTH AMERICA

The New World, and especially North America, has enormous diversity of terrain, climate, and resources, ranging from Arctic to subtropical. It is interestingly free of barriers to travel. Even the Pacific coast ranges and the Rocky Mountains are readily traversed because of the many low passes easily negotiated by foot travellers. The Appalachians pose even less of a problem. Except for the steppes or deserts of the south west and the Great Basin (between the Rockies and the Sierra Nevada), the land once teemed with game and provided rich subsistence resources for early man. A glance at the map shows the major physiographic zones. The archaeological culture areas correspond rather closely to these zones because the cultures were, of necessity, exploiting zonal resources. The Plains were rich in big game; east of the Mississippi large game and varied vegetable foods characterized the Woodlands. In the arid south west and Great Basin fewer large animals and scantier vegetable resources were available. The Pacific coast cultures looked to the sea or the rivers for staple foods, while the Arctic cultures have always been oriented to mammals of both land and sea.

The aboriginal American population has been recognized as Asiatic in origin. Human entry from Asia was accomplished before 12,000 years ago over Beringia, the landbridge between the new and old worlds. (There is evidence—see pp. 236, 256—that man was on the continent by 20,000 BC or even as early as 30,000 to 35,000 BC, but some students do not regard the evidence as adequate.) Beringia was exposed most of the time during the last major advance of the glacial ice, being more than 1,000 miles (approx. 1,600 km) wide at maximum exposure. From interior Alaska the emigrants followed the game southward along the eastern side of the Canadian Rockies and fanned out over the Western Hemisphere. Most of the American Indian physical variation probably developed through evolution of the small original population after the Bering bridge was recaptured by the sea as the glaciers melted.

For North America the prehistorians know of three major cultural stages that roughly correlate with the European Palaeolithic, Mesolithic and Neolithic stages. However, the European terms are not used in America. Instead the earliest American stage is spoken of as Palaeo-Indian, the next and longest is the Archaic, and the final one, called the Formative, is at a Neolithic level – characterized by agriculture, sedentary villages or towns, considerable religious and ceremonial development and the use of ceramics. The European invasion cut off the final or Formative stage before anything resembling the Mexican or Mayan civilizations had developed in North America.

Although ascribing dates that will hold for the entire country is impossible, it can be said that the Palaeo-Indian period, characterized by an association of artifacts with extinct fauna (mammoth, horse, dire wolf, long-horned bison), lasted perhaps until 7000 BC.

There are many dubious collections of crude, bifacially chipped flint tools usually occurring on old land surfaces and therefore not under stratigraphic control found in scattered locations over the American west. The accepted Palaeo-Indian remains, however, come largely from Great Plains locations where carefully chipped lanceolate points (believed to have been spear or lance points), scraper forms, and prismatic flake knives are found associated with the bones of extinct big game animals. The deposits are 'sealed' by Recent (Holocene) sediments. The chipped points are the Clovis fluted, Folsom fluted and after *c.* 7000 BC, a number of unfluted but distinctive forms called Hellgap, Agate, Scottsbluff, Eden, etc. became common. Two sites in the east – Debert in Nova Scotia and Bull Brook in Massachusetts – also yielded points very similar to Clovis fluted points; Naco, Arizona, is the best described Clovis location in the west.

With the extinction of the big game, the Archaic cultures developed and replaced those of the scattered Palaeo-Indian hunters. They were highly efficient with a wider hunting and gathering subsistence base. With selective and seasonal exploitation of both plant and faunal resources, there developed a great variety of tools and utensils.

Nets and twined and coiled basketry, millstones and mortar and pestle, for crushing or grinding of seeds and nuts, a variety of chipped stone points, knives and drills, and many specialized bone tools such as awls and fish hooks mark an altogether new technology geared to a new food-getting design. The Archaic way was adaptive and versatile and spread throughout the continent. It emerged earliest in the west where it dates from perhaps 8000 BC, at which time the residual big-game hunters were still in control of the plains east of the Rocky Mountains. Of course, the regional variants of the Archaic developed different tool kits in adjusting to varying environmental conditions, but as a uniform life style it was highly successful.

The Archaic persisted in the desert west until c. AD 1850, but was displaced over most of the eastern United States before the time of Christ by more complex cultures ultimately deriving from Mexico. By 300 BC Mexican influence was also felt in the American south west as the Pueblo and Hohokam cultures evolved from the last Archaic cultures.

The Mexican influences in both the south west and south east evidently included the idea of food production, by means of gardening. The staples were the domesticated plants endemic to the New World – maize, beans, cucurbits, and several plants now regarded as weed pests. Also pottery-making techniques were acquired. In the south east a heavy Mesoamerican influence can be detected in the temple mounds and ceremonial or religious practices. In the south west stone masonry from Mexico came into extensive use, but the religious concepts of the Mexicans were not accepted.

The food-producing Formative cultures – HOPEWELL (Burial Mounds) and Mississippian (Temple Mounds) in the east and Anasazi, Mogollon, and Hohokam in the south west – were the so-called high cultures north of Mexico. Both areas produced monumental remains. There were huge earthen mounds in the Woodlands of the east, and compact villages (pueblos) of stone all over the south west. The Adena–Hopewell cultures are sometimes lumped as Woodland. Early Woodland would represent the transition from Archaic, upon the introduction of pottery and possibly horticulture based on plants, now regarded as weeds, rather than on the maize, beans, and squash of the Christian era. Adena–Hopewell cultures are often called Middle Woodland. The historic tribes of the north east qualify as Late Woodland. The later Mississippian cultures began about AD 800, disappearing by 1700. These too are often classified as Early, Middle, and Late.

In the south west the Anasazi culture of the high plateau country of northern Arizona and New Mexico and adjacent regions of Utah and Colorado, is divided between a Basket-maker period lasting until about AD 700 and a subsequent Pueblo period with five sub-divisions extending up to modern times. North of PUEBLO BONITO, the zenith of Anasazi achievements came in Pueblo III, before 1300. East and south in the Rio Grande area Pueblo IV, up to about 1500, was equally brilliant, but the area of dominance was reduced over the Pueblo II and III distribution.

While the 'high cultures' developed, there was a lesser florescence in the Plains. The concept of horticulture and the three staples were transmitted largely by Mississippian expansion toward the edges of the Woodlands. The crops thrived in the light, fertile soils of the many river valleys of the Plains and several locally different semi-sedentary cultures arose. The historic tribes of the eastern Plains – Pawnee, Osage, Arikara for example – perpetuated the mixed horticultural and bison-hunting economy of the previous 800 to 1,000 years. There are scores of large villages – perhaps even towns – marking prehistoric settlements.

But some of the earliest, as well as very recent, sites of crucial importance are not monumental, being drab in the extreme. They were merely strata of midden or other accumulation in caves or in open situations, covered with recent sediment or soils. Excavating them destroys them; nothing can be seen or inspected on a visit. An exception occurs in the Plains where the huge villages (HUFF is an example), occupied by groups practising a mixed horticulture and hunting-gathering economy are to be found along the Missouri River and its tributaries. Here sod-covered, wooden lodges, often arranged in streets and surrounded by ditches and palisades, have been reduced by time to low, basin-shaped depressions. The depressions, when excavated, reveal house or lodge patterns, storage pits and other details.

Many of the earthen mound groups, scores of the stone villages of the south west and one or two Plains villages are preserved and can be inspected today.

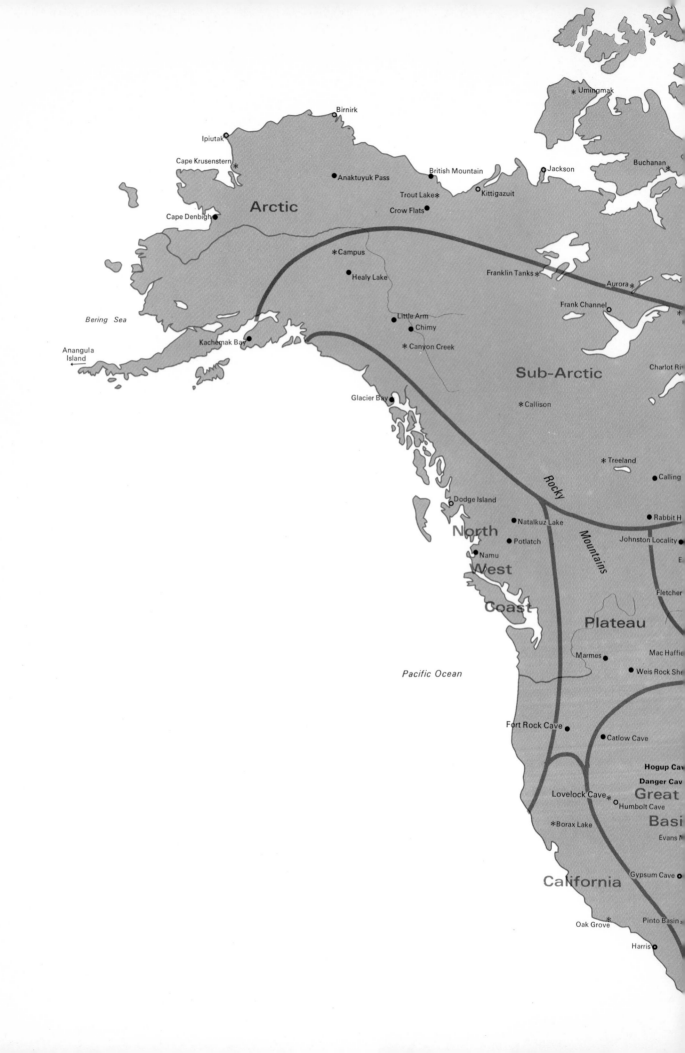

Umingmak *

Birnirk
Ipiutak
Cape Krusenstern *
Jackson
Buchanan

British Mountain
Anaktuyuk Pass
Kittigazuit
Arctic
Trout Lake *
Crow Flats
Cape Denbigh

* Campus
Healy Lake
Franklin Tanks *
Aurora *

Frank Channel
Bering Sea
Little Arm
Chimy
* Canyon Creek
Charlot Ri
Anangula
Island
Kachemak Bay
Sub-Arctic

* Callison

Glacier Bay
* Treeland
Calling

Rocky
Dodge Island
Natalkuz Lake
Rabbit H
North
Johnston Locality
Potlatch
Mountains
Namu
West
Fletcher

Coast
Plateau

Pacific Ocean
Marmes
Mac Haffie
Weis Rock She

Fort Rock Cave
Catlow Cave

Hogup Cav
Danger Cav
Lovelock Cave *
Great
Humbolt Cave
* Borax Lake
Basi
Evans
Gypsum Cave
California
* Pinto Basin
Oak Grove
Harris

Arctic

Naujan

arualik

Lemming

Schultz

Aberdeen

Silumiut

Saglak Bay

*Tyara

Henry Blake

Hudson Bay

Sub-Arctic

Debert

Dot Island

Sea Horse
Gully

Shethane Lake

Mistassini

Neck

Metabetchouan

God's Lake

Pelican Narrows

Bull Brook

Tailrace Bay

Abitibi Narrows

St Lawrence

Heron Bay

Eaka

Point Peninsula

Isle Royal

Great Lakes

Lamoka Lake

Harris Bison Runs

North East

Rosenkrans Ferry

Mortlach

Atlantic Ocean

Mississippi

Huff Village

Aztalan

Newark

Adena
Mound City

Williamson

Ludlow Cave

Effigy Mounds

Pictograph Cave

Starved Rock

Fort Ancient

Serpent Mound

Horner
Mummy Cave

Logan Creek

Ohio

Appalachian Mountains

Agate Basin

Hell Gap

Missouri

Graham Cave

Cahokia

Angel

Hardaway

Town Creek

Meserve

Modoc

Parrish

Finley

Signal Butte

Dalton

Hollywood

Lindenmeier

Plains

Eva

Etowah

Bilbo

Olsen-Chubback

South East

Mesa Verde

Folsom

Lipscomb

Spiro

Moundville

Mandeville

ali Ridge

Aligates Quarry

Jake Town

Turtle Mound

Tyuonyi
Bandelier
Pueblo Bonito

Poverty Point

on de Chelley

Emerald Mound

Weeden Island

Wupatki

Lubbock

Key Marco

Montezuma
Castle

Tularosa Cave

Midland

etown

South West

Marksville

Levi

Casa Grande

0   miles   400

Ventanta

Lehner
Naco

Bonfire

0   kilometres   600

● Older than 1000 BC

○ Younger than 1000 BC

✳ More than one period

Gulf of Mexico

Archaic Caves
of the Desert USA

Cave dwellings
From *c.* 8000 BC

BIBLIOGRAPHY
Willey, G. R., *An Introduction to American Archaeology*, vol. 1, Englewood Cliffs, NJ, 1966, ch. 2
Jennings, J. D., *Danger Cave*, Memoir 14 of the Society for American Archaeology, Salt Lake City, 1957
Jennings, J. D., *Prehistory of North America*, 2nd ed., New York, 1974

Ordinarily the dry steppes of the American west are not regarded as prime environments for human exploitation. Yet, 10,000 years ago, the Great Basin appears to have been occupied by a hardy, if sparse, population of hunters and gatherers. The most informative desert sites have been caves, so dry that perishable objects were preserved. As a result a very complete inventory of tools, foodstuffs, textiles, basketry, and cordage, made of bone and vegetable raw materials, allow a very detailed restoration of the subsistence base for these Archaic peoples.

The better-known caves are in Nevada (Lovelock), Oregon (Fort Rock, Roaring Springs) and Utah (Danger, Hogup). Caves are unspectacular, and malodorous; bats use them as roosts when man is absent. The strong odour of guano, the fine dust of centuries and the ashes of many fires make for disagreeable digging. Except for Danger, the caves cited above are situated on back country roads, and cannot be visited in ordinary vehicles. Danger lies only 300–400 feet (approx. 90–120 m) from U.S. Interstate 80, just east of Wendover. The cave is a Utah State Archaeological preserve, but has not been developed. Unless one merely wishes to stand in a large grotto, where man dwelt for 10,000 years, and beathe the musty, guano-scented air, there is no need to stop.

The outlines and dimensions of these caves, and simplified sketches of their stratified fills are provided. Some of the unusual artifacts, such as the duck decoys of rushes from Lovelock and the leathern moccasins from Hogup, are also portrayed in sketches. Commoner artifacts are also shown.

Unimpressive as they are, these caves and their contents typify Great Basin life from 8000 BC until about AD 1850. It should be noted that subsistence in western Nevada was based on the rich resources of the marshes and shallow lakes; fish, waterfowl, insect larvae, many bulbs, and seeds of marsh plants loomed large in the diet. The eastern Basin, in Utah, provided less variety and the diet appears to have been less varied.

An excellent display of Hogup Cave objects and an exquisite diorama is available at the Utah Museum of Natural History at Salt Lake City, Utah.

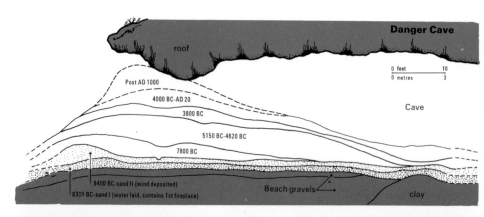

Danger Cave

roof

Post AD 1000
4000 BC–AD 20
3800 BC
5150 BC–4620 BC
7800 BC
8400 BC–sand II (wind deposited)
8300 BC–sand I (water laid, contains 1st fireplace)

Cave

Beach gravels

clay

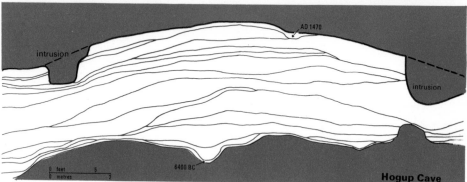

intrusion

AD 1470

intrusion

6400 BC

Hogup Cave

The plans below refer to Adena–Hopewell opposite.

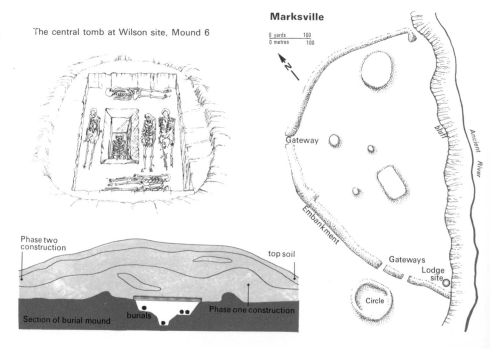

The central tomb at Wilson site, Mound 6

Marksville

Gateway

Embankment

Gateways

Lodge site

Circle

Bluff

Ancient River

Phase two construction

top soil

Section of burial mound

burials

Phase one construction

Adena-Hopewell USA

Burial mounds
c. 800 BC–AD 700

BIBLIOGRAPHY
Webb, W. S. and Snow, C. E., *The Adena People*, Reports in Anthropology and Archaeology, vol. 6, University of Kentucky, Lexington, 1945
Webb, W. S. and Baby, R. S., *The Adena People, No. 2*, Columbus, 1957
Morgan, R. G., 'Outline of Cultures in the Ohio Region', in *Archaeology of Eastern United States*, ed. J. B. Griffing, Chicago, 1952, pp. 83–98
Prufer, O. *et al.*, *The McGraw Site, A Study in Hopewellian Dynamics*, Scientific Publications of the Cleveland Museum of Natural History, vol. 4, no. 1, 1965

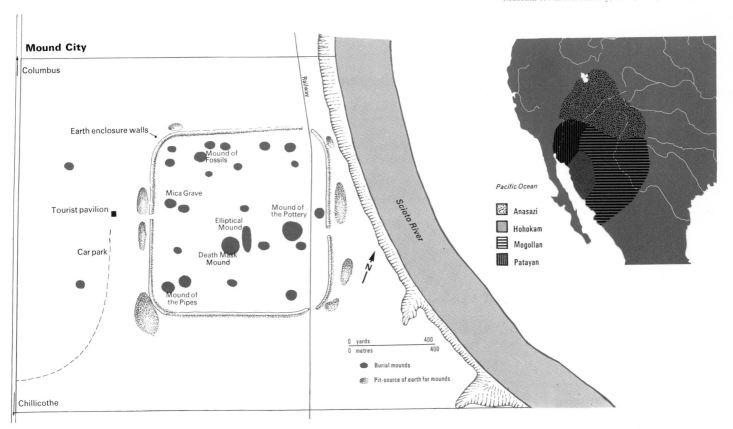

Through the North American midlands two related cultures, Adena and Hopewell, marked a tremendous transition from the eastern Archaic toward the Mississippian culture climax. Adena is the older, having developed by 800 BC; Hopewell, somehow related, can be recognized by 200 BC or slightly earlier.

Since their discovery the earthworks which characterized these cultures have been subject to vandalism, agricultural levelling, and inexpert archaeological study, and have been largely destroyed. But according to early 19th-century white traders and soldiers conical or domed mounds, and the enigmatic earthen embankments that formed vast geometric and naturalistic designs, were numerous – almost all of them along the continuous ridges that parallel the streams of Ohio and Kentucky. Nearly all have disappeared, except for one or two preserved as National Monuments.

So far as our knowledge goes the Adena–Hopewell cultures were created by an élite, possibly of priests, who ruled and imposed their religious ideas on the former Archaic populations. Both cultures had great interest in the dead. The large mounds were nothing but elaborate, costly tombs for important dead. Grave goods, showy, of great beauty and of many exotic materials were the work of skilled artisans, particularly among the Hopewell. The Adena were not so prone to bury grave furniture. The Hopewell imported or collected materials from all over the United States. Rich objects of obsidian from Yellowstone, copper from Lake Superior's Isle Royale, mica from either the Appalachian or Ozark mountains and sea shells from the Gulf of Mexico could be found in a single log-lined grave, beneath a mound of earth 30 feet high by 100 or more feet in diameter (9 × 30 m), that contained no other material.

Believed to have been agriculturally based, we find the Hopewellian sphere of influence increasing southward after AD 200 to 300, and large sites such as the Marksville group, near Marksville, Louisiana, were built. Later, in the Mississippian heartland, Marksville (or more properly Southern Hopewell) contributes to the final climax of eastern North American aboriginal culture.

Mounds National Monument, near Chillicothe, Ohio, is one of the few Hopewell sites being protected. Marksville is preserved as part of the Louisiana State Park system, is easily reached and well worth the effort.

Effigy Mounds
Pleasant Ridge Group
Marching Bears are 3 feet high
and 80-100 feet long

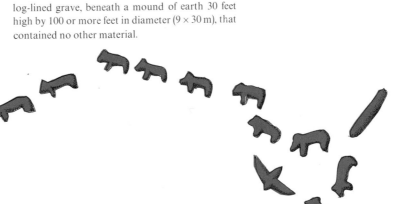

Snaketown USA

Town
c. 400 BC–AD 1200

BIBLIOGRAPHY
Gladwin, H. S. *et al.*, *Excavations at Snaketown – Material Culture*, Gila Pueblo Medallion Papers no. 25, Globe, Arizona, 1937
Gladwin, H. S., *Excavations at Snaketown IV: Reviews and Conclusions*, Gila Pueblo Medallion Papers no. 38, Globe, Arizona, 1948

South east of Phoenix, Arizona, on the Gila River, is the famous Snaketown site, the capital city of the Hohokam. The Hohokam reached the area by 400 BC, probably by direct migration from Mexico. They had taken the Gila, or at least had tapped it, for irrigation, diverting water to the dry first terrace of the river with a broad shallow canal by 300 BC. Knowledge of irrigation probably came with them from Mexico. Many think the Pima Indians of today are the lineal descendants of the Hohokam.

The huge settlement of 30 or more acres (12 hectares) has an estimated total of perhaps 5,000 houses, as they were built and rebuilt on the ruins of earlier ones. The continuous occupation of Snaketown from 400 BC to AD 1200 has made the site famous. It was here that the full history of Hohokam architecture, ceramics, art, and the evolution of many special artifacts were learned in the 1930's. Before that time no one suspected the glories of the transplanted Mexican culture. Special architectural features are the earthen pyramids, rude replicas of the elaborate ball courts of central America, and a low, round platform of clean clay – clean in that it contained no hidden trash or other debris.

The Mexican origins of the culture are also revealed in the frequent use of the snake on art objects, the presence of tiny bronze bells like hawk bells, slate mirrors faced with gleaming iron pyrites crystals, human figurines, and animal (deer?) effigies. The ceramics are singularly beautiful – the wares buff coloured, very thin but strong, and decorated with bands of red-painted conventionalized animal, human and geometrical figures. Many special effigy jars bespeak a Mexican origin. The network of irrigation ditches was enlarged through the centuries and the canal design changed from broad, shallow ditches, to deep, narrow ones, often cleaned, renewed and repaired.

Snaketown was revisited for a further study in the 1960's and it will one day be partially restored for public enjoyment. At present, the culture can be fully appreciated through the excellent display at the Arizona State Museum on the University of Arizona Campus at Tucson and one at Casa Grande National Monument, near Coolidge, Arizona.

Cliff Palace, Mesa Verde

Mesa Verde USA

Cliff village
c. AD 350–1300

BIBLIOGRAPHY
Kidder, A. V., *An Introduction to the Study of Southwestern Archaeology, with a Preliminary Account of the Excavations at Pecos*, Papers. Southwestern Expedition, Phillips Academy, no. 1, New Haven, 1924
Wormington, H. M., *Prehistoric Indians of the Southwest*, (5th edn), Denver, 1961

The famed Mesa Verde in south-western Colorado is the heartland of the Anasazi Pueblo. It has probably the greatest concentration of archaeological remains in North America, there being 800 known sites on Wetherill Mesa and over 1,000 on Chapin Mesa. These are only two mesas of the dozen long fingerlike units of the Mesa Verde itself. Moreover the sites attest to 800 or more years of occupancy, because they run the full range of Anasazi history from Basketmaker III to the final climax of Pueblo III, a period ending at about AD 1300.

But Mesa Verde's fame rests less on the time span of its ruins than on the multi-storied apartment-house villages rising storey upon storey under the ledges of its steep canyon walls. Along Chapin Mesa there are many, but the most famous is Cliff Palace. Notable for its many subterranean sacred rooms, called kivas, where religious and magical rites were performed by men (women being forbidden to enter) and its turretlike towers, the Palace is unique. The wonder of its creation, to say nothing of its preservation, is increased when the materials – stone slabs, mud mortar, and wood are considered. It is 325 feet (99 m) long, and nearly 100 feet (30 m) deep at the widest part of the vast cliff shelter that roofs it over. It was erected after about 1150; it was abandoned, for reasons not fully understood, in about 1300.

The Mesa Verde Anasazi were skilled artisans. All their minor crafts – pottery, turquoise jewelry, wooden and bone tools and utensils – display high technical skill. They gardened on the mesa tops, utilizing the scant water supplied with great ingenuity. The many kivas bespeak a strong ritual and religious bent, a tendency still seen in the modern Pueblo tribes of Arizona and New Mexico, the remnant of the Pueblo populations. Some of the modern tribes are descended from the Mesa Verde population.

Mesa Verde National Park preserves, for scientific research and public enjoyment, the hundreds of ruins in the mesa. Ruins can be visited (only in summer) on both Chapin and Wetherill Mesas.

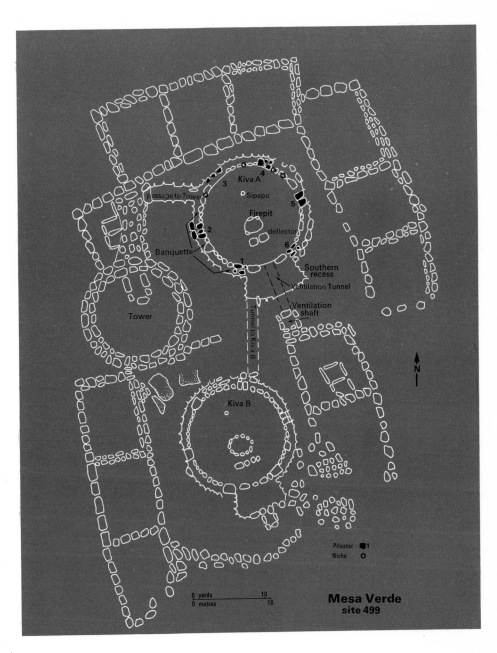

Mesa Verde
site 499

Pueblo Bonito USA

Small town
c. AD 350–1300

BIBLIOGRAPHY
Judd, N. M., *The Material Culture of Pueblo Bonito*, Smithsonian Miscellaneous Collections, vol. 124, Smithsonian Institution, Washington, DC, 1954

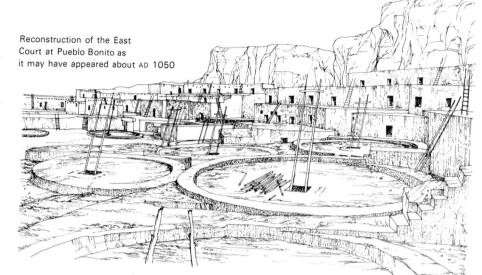

Reconstruction of the East Court at Pueblo Bonito as it may have appeared about AD 1050

Comparable in size and age and in aboriginal grandeur in MESA VERDE, Chaco Canyon in New Mexico is equally famous but is very different in many major ways. It lies in a long, broad wash; its many-storied towns are freestanding in the open; the architecture, although the same in material (mud, stones, and wood) is markedly superior in principle as well as in technical detail. The handicrafts – in variety, richness and execution – are also technically and artistically superior to comparable items from Mesa Verde.

Of all the many towns in Chaco Canyon, Pueblo Bonito is the best known and by far the largest. Being unprotected from the weather, Bonito was partially a crumbled ruin of mud and stone when first discovered by American soldiers in 1849. Some walls, however, were still standing. Originally Bonito was a huge multi-storied stepped apartment building, built in an arc. More correctly, the town is arranged around the circumference of a fully enclosed semicircle, with a plaza lying between the horns of the arc, while at the back of the circle there were four, even five storeys; nearer the plaza or central court, there is only one storey. Many kivas, completely subterranean, are scattered over the plaza or hidden within the circular terraced blocks of rooms toward the rear (east).

Pueblo Bonito represents the Pueblo II–III phase of the Anasazi culture. Construction began about AD 900 and was more or less continuously carried on (included are many remodelling projects) until after 1100, when population apparently began to decline. The exact cause of final abandonment is not known, but has been credited, among other reasons, to loss of arable fields, as a result of arroyo cutting with an attendant lowering of the water table making gardening impossible.

Vandalized and robbed by successive groups of soldiers, travellers, shepherds, and 'scientists' for 70 years, the noble ruins were finally excavated and studied with care, and extensive areas were rebuilt in the 1920's after the Canyon had been set aside in 1907 as a National Monument. There are some 600 rooms in the structure, built or rebuilt or abandoned during four separate building periods. Not all – perhaps less than half – were occupied at any one time, so the average population can be estimated at 800 to 1,200 people over the centuries.

Although Bonito is famous for the beauty and wealth of its ceramics and other minor arts, the excellent patterned masonry of the later buildings attracts greatest notice. The masonry of later periods consists of facing stones carefully applied to rubble cores – a Mexican technique – much at variance with the solid stone-and-mortar masonry of MESA VERDE (a technique used in the earliest block of rooms at Pueblo Bonito). The masonry and the artifacts show that Pueblo Bonito was Mesa Verdian in affiliation in the beginning, achieving its later flamboyance after Mexican stimuli were received. Scholars see the Mexican-style architecture and one or two 'great kivas' as evidence of direct contact with missionaries or traders from Mexico.

Other noteworthy items to be seen at Pueblo Bonito, and over much of the Chaco Canyon area, are old fields, a network of ancient 'roads', and many aboriginal water-control structures (dams, canals, etc.) discovered by various high-altitude sensor devices during the 1960's as a long-term study of the entire monument by the National Park Service got under way. Pueblo Bonito is perhaps most famous for having provided the wooden beams for Professor A. E. Douglass' completion of the prehistoric tree-ring calendar that provides the absolute chronology used in dating south-western sites.

Chaco Canyon is a National Monument open to the public; tens of thousands annually take advantage of this opportunity.

Pueblo Bonito

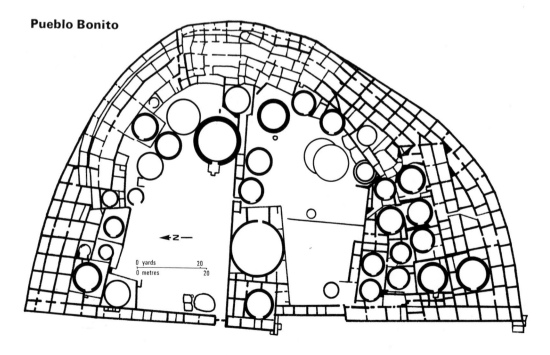

0 yards 20
0 metres 20

Bandelier National Monument USA

Cliff and cliff-side villages
c. AD 1300–1600

BIBLIOGRAPHY
Kidder, A. V., *An Introduction to the Study of Southwestern Archaeology, with a Preliminary Account of the Excavations at Pecos*, Papers, Southwestern Expedition, Phillips Academy, no. 1, New Haven; 1924

Near Santa Fe, New Mexico, in perhaps the most spectacular setting of any Pueblo ruin, lies Bandelier National Monument. The ruin was discovered by the great explorer and writer Adolph Bandelier: his charming novel, *The Delight Makers*, a reconstruction of the life of the inhabitants of the site, is well worth reading. It is in a deep gorge, cut by Rito de los Frijoles (Bean Creek) into soft volcanic tuff (consolidated ash). For nearly two miles (3·2 km) the tuff cliffs were used for housing. Rooms up to three storeys were carved into the cliff, and then other rooms of mud mortar and stone were built in front. The roof beams (or vigas) were supported on the cliffside by sockets carved into the cliff. This unusual and labour-saving trick of construction was also used at Montezuma Castle in Arizona, against a soft limestone cliff.

In addition to the cliffside ruins, and of about the same age, a huge vaguely D-shaped village of more than 100 rooms with three kivas was built in the valley floor. This ruin, called Tyuonyi, stands open ruins, not easily accessible to visitors, lie on adjacent plateaus and in other washes. They can be visited, however, by a network of footpaths, many of which are the aboriginal trails linking the towns together in prehistoric times.

Bandelier is very late in time, having been established after AD 1300 and abandoned about 1600. Thus its occupancy overlaps with Coronado's exploratory trek into the American south west, although there is no record that he visited the place.

Tyuonyi Pueblo
Bandelier

0 yards 20
0 metres 20

Kiva

Kiva

Kiva

Moundville, Cahokia and Etowah USA

Temple mounds
c. AD 700–1500

BIBLIOGRAPHY
Moorehead, W. K., *The Cahokia Mounds*, Bulletin of the University of Illinois, vol. 26, no. 4, Urbana, 1928
Moorehead, W. K., 'Exploration of the Etowah site in Georgia' in *Etowah Papers*, New Haven, 1932
Mound State Monument, Moundville, Alabama, Alabama Museum of Natural History, Paper no. 20, Moundville, 1932

Romantic as the Pueblos and cliff dwellings of the south west are, many people are more fascinated by the earthen tumuli that dot the southern states of the United States. The truncated pyramids with the steep ramp-stairways to their summits strongly suggest culture thrusts from Mexico more than a thousand years ago. Built and rebuilt and enlarged (as were the pyramids of Mesoamerica) over a cycle of years, these mounds rose 40, 50, 60 and even 100 feet (12–30 m) above the level valley floor or the river terrace setting along the wide fertile valleys of the Southland. Although the Mississippian culture began to evolve from Southern Hopewell by AD 500, its climax and the unique southern cult came in about 1500.

Usually thought of as cult centres of the late Mississippian culture, the pyramids are often grouped around a central square or plaza and normally each had a temple of wood, wattle and daub (or matting), and thatch construction upon its summit. Although the locations range from Moundville, Alabama, and Etowah near Marietta, Georgia, to Fort Ancient, Ohio and Aztalan in Wisconsin, the Mississippian cultures appear to have arisen or evolved in the 'Deep South' from an indigenous base with strong influences from some Mesoamerican source.

The most notable of all the temple sites is Cahokia, east of the Mississippi River at St Louis, Missouri. Here was a cluster or a series of groupings of pyramids (and burial) mounds, covering several square miles of the Mississippi river valley. The largest is 104 feet (32 m) high and covers 16 acres (6·5 hectares) and contains 22,000,000 cubic feet (approx. 623,000 cu m) of earth. It is called Monk's Mound because a monastery was built upon it early in the 19th century. The well, dug by hand to serve the monastery's needs, revealed the hill's artificial nature.

The richness of certain Mississippian artifacts rivals or exceeds even the fabled skills of the south-westerners. These extraordinary objects are associated with the southern cult and only with a few very late sites – Etowah, Spiro, Moundville and Macon being the most notable. The cult is characterized by bizarre articles of copper, shell, stone, wood, and clay that show a preoccupation with violence and death. The objects are done in re-

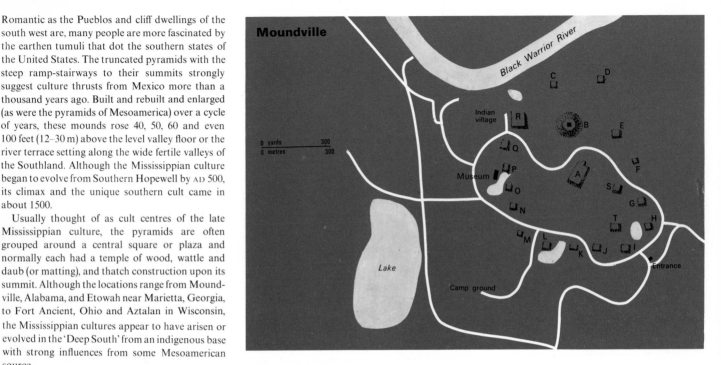

poussé, intaglio, incised, and sculptured techniques in a variety of symbolic, anthropomorphic and realistic motifs. Evidently the cult centres were supported by adjacent villages, where common folk tilled the rich, annually renewed soils (by floods, as was the Nile) of the valleys. From the villages there probably came food for the ruler priests, as well as corvée labour for the building of religious and public structures.

De Soto in the 16th century and a Frenchman, Du Pratz, in the early 18th century witnessed and described the mounds, temples, and the barbaric death ceremonies of the terminal Mississippian culture, as it crumbled beneath the cumulative weight of European diseases and warfare.

The Moundville, Etowah, Aztalan, Angel, Greenwood and Macon groups are all preserved as state or national parks or monuments and can readily be visited.

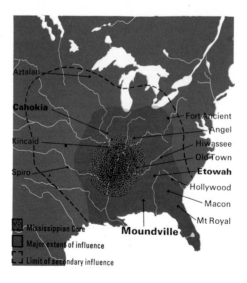

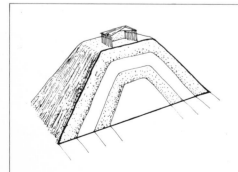

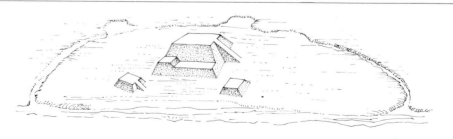

Left Cross-section of an idealized pyramid mound showing the constructional stages and temple on summit. *Right* Reconstruction of mounds at Etowah

Huff Village

c. AD 1400–1600

BIBLIOGRAPHY
Wood, Raymond W., 'An Interpretation of Mandan Culture History', *Bureau of American Ethnology*, Bulletin 198, Government Printing Office, Washington, 1967

One of America's most remarkable prehistoric villages, built by the ancestors of the historic Mandan tribe, is the Huff site, only some 20 miles (32 km) south from Bismarck, capital city of North Dakota. It was occupied at the time of Columbus' famous voyage; tree-ring dates and radiocarbon assays agree in setting the occupancy from about AD 1400 to 1600.

Preserved as a State Park, it is situated upon the right (west) bank of the Missouri River. This location may spell its doom. Unless the river changes its course it will continue to undercut the bluff of rich valley sediment the site is built on; each spring, until recently, huge slabs of earth splash into the flood waters carrying a part of an earth lodge ruin or other prehistoric material to destruction. Now a protective revetment is in place along the bluff. This expedient will at least reduce the effects of annual floods.

The village is large. House lodges even now number more than 100; the erosion of the Missouri has destroyed an unknown number. The dominant house type was a rectangular structure, built of vertical posts or poles with an entrance opening to the west. They were large, averaging 30 feet by 38 feet (9·1 × 11·6 m). The roof was supported by central posts or pillars arranged down the midline of the house. The covering for the houses is not definitely known, but they are believed to have been roofed with sod. The vertical walls were of wattle and daub. A most impressive component of the village was the encircling fortification, an earthen embankment, in which small posts set about one foot (30 cm) apart formed a palisade. Ten projecting bastions were equally spaced along its sides and at the two west corners.

The data show that in combining horticulture with food gathering and relying heavily on bison hunting, the Huff villagers followed a balanced subsistence pattern established a millennium earlier; it persisted among the eastern Plains villages until the bison were exterminated in the 1870's. Artifacts of bone, stone, wood, shell, and clay were varied and specialized, to meet the needs of the three bases of the villagers' economy. Huff Village, preserved as a North Dakota Historical Park, is easy to reach by a good road from the town of Mandan, North Dakota, and is well worth the visit.

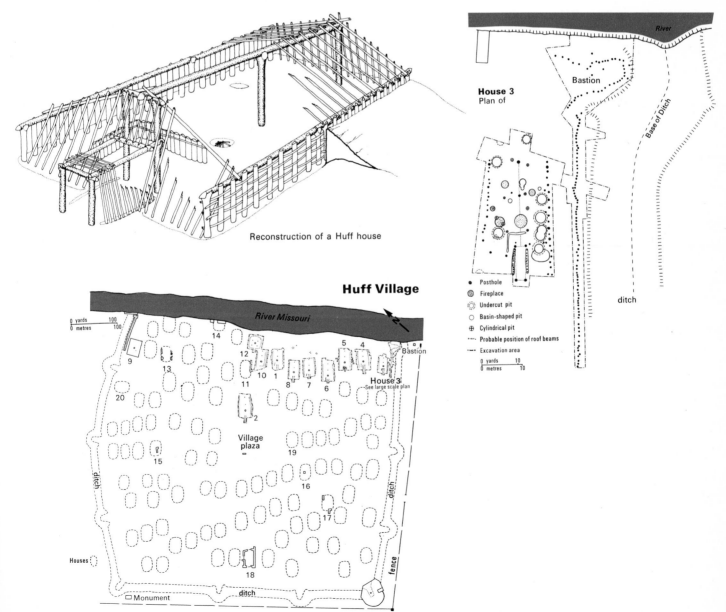

Reconstruction of a Huff house

House 3
Plan of

Bastion

Base of Ditch

ditch

- ● Posthole
- ⊕ Fireplace
- ○ Undercut pit
- ○ Basin-shaped pit
- ⊕ Cylindrical pit
- ···· Probable position of roof beams
- -- Excavation area

0 yards 10
0 metres 10

Huff Village

River Missouri

0 yards 100
0 metres 100

14

9
13
12
11
20
10 1
8 7 6
5 4
Bastion
House 3
—See large scale plan

2

Village plaza
19

16

17

15

Houses
18

ditch
fence
ditch

Monument   ditch

235

MESOAMERICA

Ancient Mesoamerica can be defined as the region of Mexico and central America which developed a distinctive form of civilization during the millennia before the European conquest. Its northern limit is the desert zone of Mexico, where settled life is impossible, and the southern frontier cuts across the present-day republics of Honduras and El Salvador, dividing the Maya-speaking peoples from the less advanced tribes of the Isthmus.

The oldest unambiguous evidence for man's presence in this area comes from Tlapacoya, in the Basin of Mexico, where there are lakeside camp sites dating from shortly before 20,000 BC. A few cave occupations and surface finds belong to the Late Pleistocene, and around the shores of the extinct lake which once filled the Basin of Mexico are several kill sites, dated 8000–7000 BC, where mammoths were driven into marshy ground to be speared and butchered.

Mesoamerica has no large animals suitable for domestication, but is rich in useful plants. The earliest attempts at cultivation are documented from dry caves in northeast Mexico, the valley of Oaxaca, and the Tehuacán valley in the state of Puebla. The stage of incipient agriculture, during which cultivated plants provided only a small proportion of the total diet, lasted from about 6500 to 2000 BC, and by the end of this period an efficient system of agriculture had developed on the basis of maize, beans, amaranth, squashes, chili peppers, and many fruits and vegetables.

The later stages of Mesoamerican prehistory are rather arbitrarily divided into three periods. The dates are only approximate, and vary slightly from one region to another.

The Formative, or Preclassic, period (2000 BC–AD 300) is the time during which the pattern of Mesoamerican civilization began to take form, with settled villages and the first pottery. During the 14th to 12th centuries, modest ceremonial buildings were constructed, and a little afterwards there is evidence for elaborate architecture, craft specialization, long-distance trade, and fine art. By this time, too, the lowland and highland ways of life had begun to diverge.

In the semi-arid uplands of Oaxaca, Puebla and the Valley of Mexico the first towns grew up, and were the forerunners of the later city states of highland Mexico. In the lowlands, shifting cultivation inhibited the growth of nucleated towns, and instead of

236

Northern limit of Meso-american Civilization AD 1500

Gulf of Mexico

La Quemada

El Tajín

Tula

Teotihuacán

Tenayuca
Tlatilco

Mexico City
(Tenochtitlán)

Tlapacoya

Pueblo

Cholula

Xochicalco

Chalcatzingo

Olmec
Heartland

Tres
Zapotes

La
Venta

San Lorenzo
Tenochtitlán

Tehuacán
Valley

Oaxaca Valley

Monte Albán

Mitla

Chichén
Itzá

Uxmal

Yucatan
Peninsula

BELIZE

Palenque

Tikal

Bonampak

HONDURAS

Copan

GUATEMALA

EL SALVADOR

Pacific Ocean

Limits of Maya Territory

0 miles 200
0 kilometres 300

cities we find 'ceremonial centres' occupied by small resident populations of administrators, priests and craftsmen serving a scattered peasantry living in the surrounding countryside.

Between 1200 and 400 BC one such area, the Gulf Coast plain, was the homeland of an advanced culture which has been given the name Olmec. Its major centres at La Venta, Tres Zapotes and San Lorenzo Tenochtitlán, were planned complexes of pyramids, platforms and courtyards with stelae, altars, colossal human heads carved in the round, votive pavements of imported serpentine blocks, and rich offerings of ceremonial jade objects. The full repertoire of Olmec culture is not found outside the Gulf Coast, but Olmec influence is strongly marked at certain sites in central Mexico, for example in some funerary offerings at Tlatilco (Mexico City) and in the carved reliefs at Chalcatzingo (Morelos).

During the Later Formative (300 BC–AD 300), hieroglyphic writing and complex calendrics made their appearance in several regions of Guatemala and Mexico. With these additions, all the significant traits of Classic Mesoamerican civilization are present in embryonic form.

The Classic period (AD 300–900) was a time of cultural and artistic climax. Many regional civilizations can be distinguished, but underlying this diversity was a common heritage marked by a series of shared customs, beliefs and artifacts. These include hieroglyphic writing and screenfold books, a ritual ball game played in an I-shaped court, blood offerings (self-mutilation as well as human sacrifice), temples on stepped pyramid platforms, arithmetical systems using a base of 20, similar gods and cosmological beliefs, and the use of a solar calendar of 365 days in combination with a 260-day ritual calendar. On the negative side, all Mesoamerican civilizations lacked the keystone arch, the plough, alphabetic writing, glass, explosives, and knowledge of the wheel for transport, potting, or mechanical devices. Iron remained unknown, and copper and gold were not introduced before AD 700.

During the Classic, the principal Maya centres attained their maximum size and complexity. Carved stelae were erected to commemorate the passage of time and the deeds of rulers: fresco painting (e.g. Bonampak), stucco modelling, jade carving and pottery decoration reached their fullest development.

Throughout the early Classic the dominant force in Mexico was the highland city of TEOTIHUACÁN, though there were important regional civilizations along the Gulf Coast (EL TAJÍN) and in the Valley of Oaxaca where the Zapotec peoples were established at MONTE ALBÁN and at hundreds of lesser sites. For a time, Teotihuacán influence was strongly felt in the Maya zone, but died away with the destruction of Teotihuacán in about AD 750. Classic Maya civilization outlasted Teotihuacán, but, for reasons not clearly understood, the sites of the central lowlands were abandoned between 800 and 900, and the area suffered severe depopulation.

The Postclassic (900 to the Spanish Conquest) is marked by the rise to prominence of new states. In the highlands, TULA became the capital of a Toltec empire which embraced much of northern Mexico during the 10th to 12th centuries. Toltec-related immigrants introduced new architectural ideas to the Maya of Yucatan, an area relatively unaffected by the collapse of Maya civilization further south, and Mexicanized dynasties ruled over the Maya population of highland Guatemala. In south-west Mexico, the rulers of the highland Mixtec cities increased their power and, by a mixture of diplomacy and force, succeeded in replacing the Zapotecs as overlords of many towns in the Valley of Oaxaca.

After the overthrow of Tula in the late 12th century, Chichimec tribes from the northern fringe of Mesoamerica broke into the Valley of Mexico where they established petty kingdoms at sites like Tenayuca. The most recent Chichimec immigrants were the Aztecs, who arrived some time in the 13th century. By 1428 they were powerful enough to initiate a programme of military expansion, and at the time of the Spanish conquest in 1519–21 they and their allies were in control of the greater part of Mesoamerica.

Note. Detailed information on all the following sites can be found in these books:

Marquina, Ignacio, *Arquitectura Prehispánica*, Instituto Nacional de Antropología e Historia, Mexico, 1951.
Handbook of Middle American Indians, (series ed. Robert Wauchope), University of Texas, 1964–

They are quoted as sources in individual site bibliographies only when they are the most complete source available.

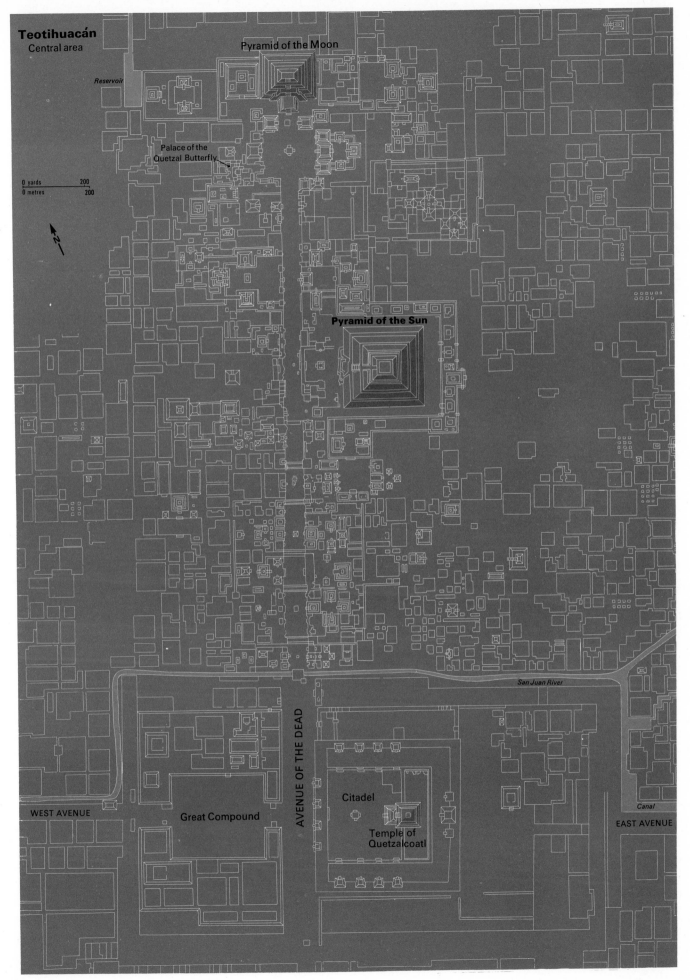

Teotihuacán
Central area

Reservoir

Pyramid of the Moon

Palace of the
Quetzal Butterfly

0 yards 200
0 metres 200

N

Pyramid of the Sun

San Juan River

AVENUE OF THE DEAD

Citadel

Temple of
Quetzalcoatl

WEST AVENUE

Great Compound

Canal

EAST AVENUE

239

This plan refers to Teotihuacán on p. 240

Teotihuacán MEXICO

City with civic-ceremonial district
2nd–8th centuries AD

BIBLIOGRAPHY

Teotihuacán Official Guide, Instituto Nacional de Antropología e Historia, Mexico

Millon, R., 'Teotihuacan: Completion of Map of Giant Ancient City in the Valley of Mexico', *Science*, vol. 170, 1970, pp. 1077–82

Bernal, Ignacio, *Teotihuacán: descubrimientos y reconstrucciones*, Instituto Nacional de Antropología e Historia, Mexico, 1963

Millon, R., Drewitt, B. and Bennyhoff, J. A., 'The Pyramid of the Sun: 1959 Investigations', *Transactions of the American Philosophical Society*, N.S., vol. 55, part 6

The city of Teotihuacán, in a side branch of the Valley of Mexico, was the largest urban site in Mesoamerica, with the possible exception of Aztec TENOCHTITLÁN. Between AD 300 and 750, when it was destroyed and abandoned, the influence of Teotihuacán art and architecture is apparent at nearly every important site in Mesoamerica although, in the absence of written records, it is impossible to define the frontiers of the area under its direct political control.

The locality was settled by 150 BC, but the city did not begin to take on its present form until the 2nd and 3rd centuries AD. By 600, it covered 7·7 square miles (20 sq km), had some 125,000 inhabitants, and was laid out to a precise grid plan with streets intersecting at intervals of 187 feet (57 m). At the centre was the ceremonial quarter, around which was a zone of elite residences, tailing off eventually into poorer suburbs. Within the city more than 500 craft workshops have been identified, and about 20,000 rectangular, single-storey residential compounds consisting of rooms, courtyards and small temples. Near the western edge of Teotihuacán was a zone occupied by foreigners from Oaxaca, and on the east was a residential or commercial quarter where the inhabitants had imported an abundance of Gulf Coast and Maya pottery.

The main ceremonial structures are aligned on the north-south Avenue of the Dead. Blocking the northern end of the Avenue is the Pyramid of the Moon, and further down, on the eastern side, is the still larger Pyramid of the Sun, containing more than 35 million cubic feet (about 1 million cu m) of fill. Its ruined façade and stucco covering have been removed, and the present shape is the result of inaccurate restoration in 1905–10. Where the Avenue of the Dead intersects with the main east–west street are two large compounds of rectangular plan. On the west, an unexcavated complex may have been a market or administrative centre: on the east is the Citadel, at whose inner end (still partially masked by a later building which once covered it entirely) stands a terraced temple platform ornamented with heads of Quetzalcoatl, the Plumed Serpent God, and of Tlaloc, the Rain God, who is recognizable by his spectacle-like eye mask.

In the outlying zone there are palace groups (Tepantitla, Tetitla, Atelolco etc.) with polychrome frescoes. One fresco at Tepantitla shows Tlaloc presiding over his paradise, where little figures are seen enjoying themselves with dancing, bathing and singing.

There is a museum near the centre of the archaeological zone.

Carved stone head of plumed serpent, Temple of Quetzalcoatl

See p. 239 for plan

Cholula MEXICO

City and temple
c. 200 BC–16th century AD

BIBLIOGRAPHY
Marquina, Ignacio, (ed.), *Proyecto Cholula*, Serie Investi-
  gaciones No. 19, Instituto Nacional de Antropología e
  Historia, Mexico, 1970
Marquina, Ignacio, *Arquitectura Prehispánica*, Instituto
  Nacional de Antropología e Historia, Mexico, 1951

Spanish conquistadors describe Cholula (near Puebla) as a city of more than 20,000 houses and 400 temples, one of which (now disappeared) was higher than any pyramid in the Aztec capital and was dedicated to Quetzalcoatl, the Plumed Serpent God. Very little remains of the 16th-century city, and archaeological activity has been concentrated in the area of the Great Pyramid on which stands the 18th-century church of Nuestra Señora de los Remedios.

Today the pyramid has the appearance of a natural hill, but its entire structure is artificial. More than three and a half miles (6 km) of tunnels have been driven into the mound to expose a sequence of buildings nesting inside one another. The earliest occupation of the site is represented by pottery and figurines of *c.* 200 BC found below the oldest pyramid. The first building, Structure A, was a five-tier platform with sides 390 feet (120 m) long. This was then covered by Structure B, a stepped pyramid in pure TEOTIHUACÁN style with a fresco on the façade depicting insects in red, black, yellow and blue. Structure C completely covers B, and is a unique nine-storey pyramid with steps on all four faces. Against this, and covering the lower tiers, are the courts and platforms of Phase D. These in turn are concealed by the final pyramid, a huge ruined adobe mound whose sides measure 1,150 feet (350 m) at the base, making this the largest building of prehispanic Mexico. Architectural and ceramic links with Teotihuacan prove that the whole pyramid sequence belongs to the Classic period when Cholula came under Teotihuacán domination.

South of the Great Pyramid, recent excavations have exposed a large square, the Patio de Altares, flanked by groups of buildings on the east and west. The square has many superimposed floors, and the buildings show many periods of reconstruction. Some of the façades have geometric relief ornament; others have polychrome frescoes with diagonal bands, interlace patterns and starlike motives executed in the style of Teotihuacán. In the square are three stone altars. Altars 1 and 3 have unusual upright slabs with borders of scrolls in a style resembling that of EL TAJÍN, and the recumbent altar, 2, is carved with plumed serpents. Like the Great Pyramid, the square and its buildings fell into disuse at the close of the Classic (*c.* AD 750), an event probably connected with the abandonment of Teotihuacán at about the same time.

The later history of Cholula is revealed in the deep trench west of the Great Pyramid, where stratified deposits cover all periods from Classic to early Spanish.

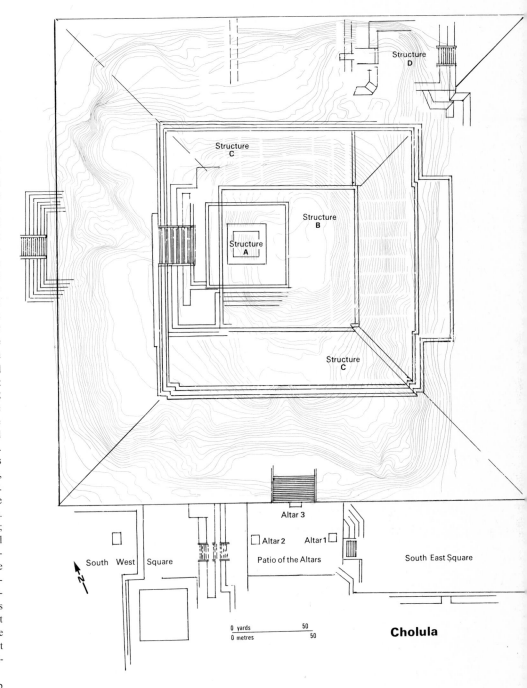

Cholula

Monte Albán MEXICO

Zapotec capital city, with ceremonial zone
c. 600 BC to 16th century AD

BIBLIOGRAPHY
Bernal, Ignacio, 'Mitla and Monte Albán: Official Guide',
(English and Spanish editions), Instituto Nacional de
Antropología e Historia, Mexico
Handbook of Middle American Indians, vol. 3, part 2, Uni-
versity of Texas Press, chs. 31–8
Paddock, J., (ed.), 'Ancient Oaxaca', Stanford, 1966
Caso, Alfonso, 'El Tesoro de Monte Albán', Memoria no. III
del Instituto Nacional de Antropología e Historia, Mexico,
1969

The hilltop city of Monte Alban, in the Valley of
Oaxaca, was the principal site in Zapotec territory
throughout the late Formative, Classic, and early
Postclassic periods. The first ceremonial buildings
(Monte Albán Period I) were constructed between
c. 600 and 100 BC. Most of them are now destroyed
or buried within later platforms, but to this period
belongs the Mound of the Danzantes, a pyramid
platform whose walls incorporate stone slabs carved
in bas relief with nude male figures in grotesque
postures. They have been variously interpreted as
dancers (danzantes) or even corpses. Several of the
slabs bear hieroglyphs, as do the nearby (and contemporary) Stelae 12 and 13. This is the oldest
writing known in Mesoamerica, and one can already recognize bar-and-dot numerals (later employed by the Maya), as well as day signs and some
evidence for the use of a 260-day ritual calendar.

The only significant building of Monte Albán II
(100 BC–AD 200) is Mound J, a platform in the shape
of an arrow. It may have been an observatory. In its
walls are slabs with long inscriptions thought to
commemorate the conquest of foreign chiefs who
are represented by inverted heads accompanied by
hieroglyphs for places and for names or dates.

Zapotec culture was at its finest during Period III

(200–900). The ball court, most of the existing platforms and the majority of the carved reliefs belong
to this phase, as do the finest of the painted tombs
(e.g. nos. 103, 104, 105, and 112). In the sculpture
and frescoes of Monte Albán III, features derived
from TEOTIHUACÁN are combined with purely
Zapotec hieroglyphs and iconography.

Monte Albán was abandoned as a functioning city
during the 10th century, though burials continued
to be made there. Zapotec culture continued to
evolve at MITLA and the smaller sites in the Valley
of Oaxaca, where one can speak of a Monte Albán
IV period, lasting to about 1200. Shortly after, during
the Monte Albán V phase, which continued up to
the Spanish conquest, much of the Valley came
under the control of Mixtec dynasties who introduced their own polychrome pottery together with
new styles of figure painting and metalwork. There
is no Mixtec settlement at Monte Albán, but the
newcomers re-used earlier tombs for their own
dead. It was they who left in Tomb 7 one of the
richest treasures ever discovered in Mexico, consisting of gold and silver objects, work in semi-
precious stones, and a series of bones carved with
hieroglyphs and calendrical inscriptions. The treasure is now in the museum of Oaxaca.

Carved slab, Mound of the Danzantes, Monte Albán

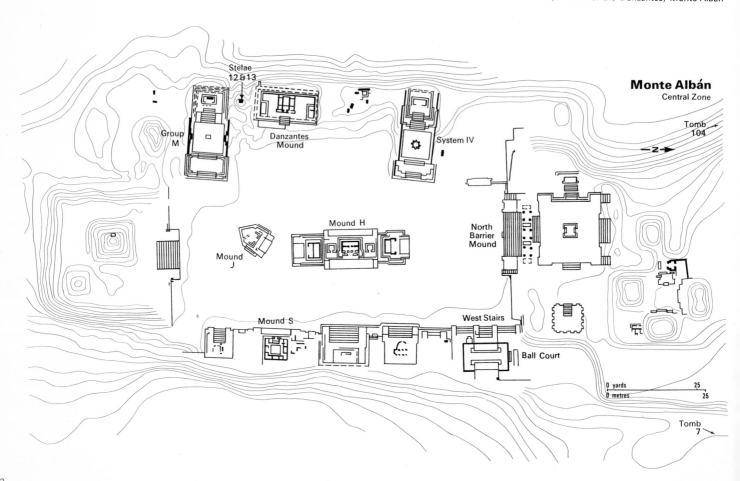

Monte Albán
Central Zone

Mitla MEXICO

Zapotec town
3rd–16th centuries AD

BIBLIOGRAPHY
Bernal, Ignacio, *Mitla and Monte Albán: Official Guide*, (English and Spanish editions), Instituto Nacional de Antropología e Historia, Mexico
Handbook of Middle American Indians, vol. 3, part 2, chs. 33–5
Paddock, J. (ed.), *Ancient Oaxaca*, Stanford, 1966

Archaeological Mitla is situated within the modern town of the same name in the Zapotec-speaking part of the Valley of Oaxaca in southern Mexico. Its history is intimately linked with that of its more powerful neighbour, MONTE ALBÁN. The earliest deposits at Mitla go back to 500 BC, and by the start of the Christian era the town stretched for more than two thirds of a mile (1 km) along both sides of the river. Between AD 200 and 900, when Monte Albán was the principal Zapotec centre in the Valley, the occupied area of Mitla was reduced, but it was at this time that the first of the surviving monumental buildings were constructed. To this period belongs the South Group, consisting of a shrine, a plaza flanked by pyramids on the north and south sides, and also a fine, underground cruciform tomb decorated with stone mosaics of the kind found in the palaces of the final period.

Shortly after 1000, at the time of the Mixtec invasions into the Valley, the hill to the west of Mitla was converted into a fortress by the addition of a great stone wall with an entrance passage.

With Monte Albán abandoned and the northern part of the Valley in Mixtec hands, Mitla became the centre of southern Zapotec culture and the residence of the Zapotec high priest. The town expanded in size, and was surrounded by a hinterland of farmsteads and terraced fields. Soon after 1200 the South Group fell into disuse, and new palace complexes were built north of the river. These survive in good condition and show several new architectural features which are not represented at Monte Albán and have no local antecedents. Low, range-style buildings form the sides of courtyards; roofs were carried on beams supported by stone columns; façades were ornamented with geometric patterns made of raised stone mosaic. Greek-key and stepped-fret designs are particularly characteristic of this work, and occur also at the nearby sites of Yagul and Zaachila. Beneath the Column Group are two cruciform tombs similar to the one in the South Group. Although Mitla seems to have remained under Zapotec control until the Spanish conquest, imported Mixtec polychrome vessels were found in the tomb below the South Group, and the building of the Church Group have some much-damaged frescoes executed in the detailed figurative style of Mixtec painted books.

The Museo Frissell (in the centre of the town) contains archaeological material from Mitla and the surrounding area.

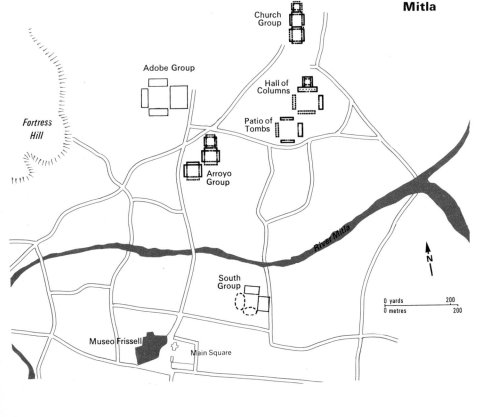

Mitla

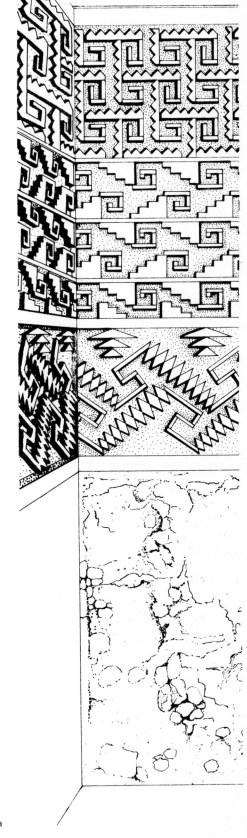

Stone mosaics decorating tomb at Mitla

Tikal GUATEMALA

Maya centre
c. 600 BC–AD 900

BIBLIOGRAPHY
Coe, W., *Tikal: A Handbook of the Ancient Maya Ruins*, University of Pennsylvania, Philadelphia, 1967
Tozzer, A. M., 'A preliminary study of the prehistoric ruins of Tikal, Guatemala', *Memoirs of the Peabody Museum of Archaeology and Ethnology, Harvard University*, vol. 5. no. 2, 1911
Haviland, W. A., 'Tikal, Guatemala, and Mesoamerican Urbanism', *World Archaeology*, vol. 2, no. 2, 1960, pp. 186–98

Tikal, in the Petén jungle of Guatemala, is not only the largest and most important lowland Maya site but also the most thoroughly investigated. Settlement began during the Formative period, in about 600 BC, and Tikal was continuously occupied until around AD 900 when, like the other Petén sites, it was all but abandoned.

Apart from one Late Formative pyramid, the visible remains belong to the Classic period. In the 5th century AD, Tikal came under the influence of TEOTIHUACÁN. Rich burials were accompanied by Teotihuacán pottery; Teotihuacán warriors appear alongside a Maya dignitary on Stela 31, and the Mexican Rain God is depicted on Stela 32. Three minor pyramids were built in the Teotihuacan manner.

Tikal took on its present appearance between AD 550 and 900. The nucleus of the site is the Great Plaza, flanked by Temples 1 and 2 which were built in about 700. Near the northern edge of the Plaza are two rows of stelae and altars, many of them finely carved. Their dates range from the 4th to the 8th centuries. Nearly half of them once stood elsewhere, and owe their present position to the revivalistic efforts of Postclassic survivors who continued to live at Tikal after the breakdown of Classic civilization.

Behind the stelae is the North Acropolis, a huge platform where an excavation 33 feet (10 m) deep exposed more than a dozen building levels which revealed the story of Tikal from 200 BC onwards.

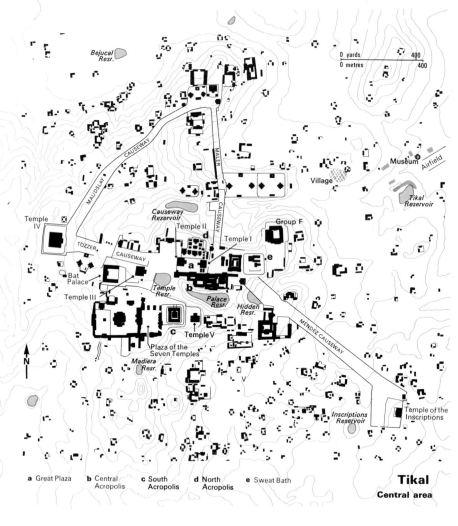

a Great Plaza b Central Acropolis c South Acropolis d North Acropolis e Sweat Bath

Tikal
Central area

General view of Temple I, Tikal

Some Early Classic structures, including façades with stucco masks of the Rain God, are partially exposed and offer the greatest concentration of Early Classic monuments at any Maya site.

The Central Acropolis is a residential or administrative complex consisting of small courtyards flanked by range-type structures, most of which were built between AD 500 and 900. East of the Great Plaza is another square containing a temple, a possible market area, a sweat bath, and a court for the ball game. The rather isolated Temple of the Inscriptions deserves a visit for the long text on its roof comb, and there are other important structures at the points of the triangle formed by the Maudslay, Tozzer and Maler causeways.

These buildings represent only the core of ancient Tikal. At the height of its power, greater Tikal had 40,000 inhabitants, and its nuclear area alone included more than 3,000 separate structures and some 200 stone monuments, not to mention reservoirs and rock-cut pits (*chultuns*).

Objects from the excavations are displayed in the site museum.

Palenque MEXICO

Classic Maya ceremonial centre
Mainly 7th–10th centuries AD

BIBLIOGRAPHY
Ruz, Alberto, *Palenque: Official Guide*, (English and Spanish editions), Instituto Nacional de Antropología e Historia, Mexico
Ruz, Alberto, 'Exploraciones en Palenque', in *Proceedings of the 30th International Congress of Americanists*, Cambridge, 1954, pp. 5–22
Marquina, Ignacio, *Arquitectura Prehispánica*, Instituto Nacional de Antropología e Historia, Mexico, 1951

The Maya ceremonial centre of Palenque is built on forested spurs of the Sierra de Chiapas, overlooking the plain of Tabasco and Campeche. Scattered finds of pottery indicate that the site was occupied during the later Preclassic and Early Classic periods, but most of the buildings were constructed between the 7th and 10th centuries AD.

The 'Palace' consists of a group of buildings set on an artificial platform with stairs on the north side. Courtyards of different sizes are surrounded by double galleries divided up into small rooms, and from the south-western patio rises a square, four-storey tower with an interior staircase. Pillars, walls and roof combs were covered with painted stucco reliefs portraying masks, hieroglyphs and religious scenes.

South west of the Palace is the Temple of the Inscriptions, erected in AD 692. The original eight-storey platform was converted at a later date into a three-tier pyramid, and part of this reconstruction can be seen at the foot of the staircase. The temple doorways are flanked by stucco reliefs of human figures, and inside the sanctuary are panels of hieroglyphs. Underneath the slab floor of the inner room is a stairway leading down to a funerary crypt some 80 feet (24 m) below. The walls of the crypt have stucco reliefs depicting nine richly arrayed priests, and most of the floor space is filled by a monolithic stone coffin with a carved lid. When opened, the coffin proved to contain a skeleton covered with jade ornaments. Since the coffin is too large to manoeuvre down the staircase, the burial crypt must have been built before the temple which now covers it.

On a terrace at the foot of the hills stand several important pyramids. The Temple of the Sun (dating to the 7th century) has a crested roof, and within the shrine is a carved panel showing priests making offerings to the sun, which is represented by a round shield and two crossed lances. The nearby Temple of the Cross has a similar panel, although in this case the object of worship is a cross rising from the mouth of an earth monster. In another version from the Temple of the Foliated Cross (c. 692) the offerings are made before a cross ornamented with maize leaves and a human head.

Within the archaeological zone are several more temples, a vaulted aqueduct, a ball court, and a museum containing a representative collection of sculpture and pottery.

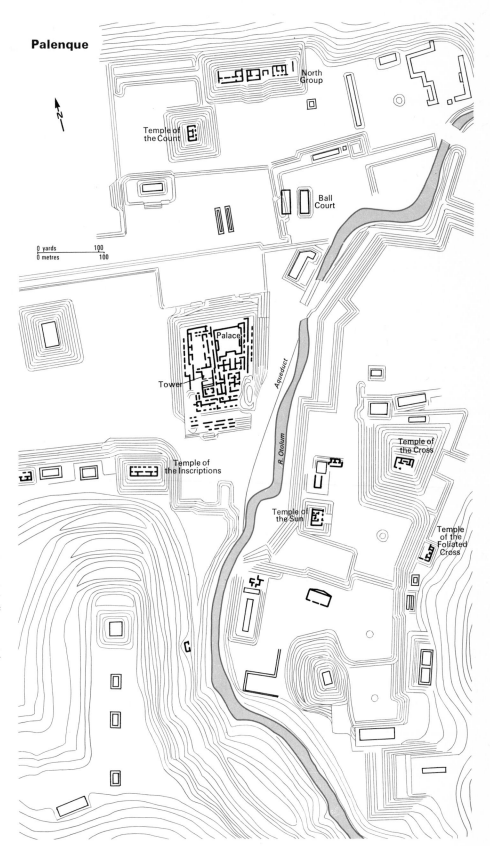

Palenque

0 yards 100
0 metres 100

North Group

Temple of the Count

Ball Court

Palace

Tower

Aqueduct

R. Otolum

Temple of the Inscriptions

Temple of the Cross

Temple of the Sun

Temple of the Foliated Cross

Copan HONDURAS

Maya ceremonial centre
4th–9th centuries AD

BIBLIOGRAPHY
Stromsvik, G., *Guide to the ruins of Copán*, Carnegie Institution of Washington Publication no. 577, 1947
Morley, S. G., *The Inscriptions of Copán*, Carnegie Institution of Washington Publication no. 219, 1920
Longyear, J. M., *Copán ceramics: a study of south-eastern Maya pottery*, Carnegie Institution of Washington Publication no. 598, 1952

Situated in a valley among the hills of western Honduras, Copan is one of the most beautiful of Maya sites, and is famous for its sculpture and hieroglyphic inscriptions. Its buildings, in green trachite instead of the usual limestone, are all of Classic date. The latest stela at Copan bears a date equivalent to AD 800 and the site was abandoned shortly afterwards, though finds of Postclassic pottery indicate occasional later visits to the ruins.

The nucleus of the site consists of an Acropolis, supporting a complex of courts, terraces and temples. At the eastern edge the Copan river has carried part of it away, cutting a vertical section some 100 feet (30 m) high through artificial fill with early floor levels visible within it. The principal structures on the Acropolis are Temple 11 (dedicated in 756, and remarkable for the panels of hieroglyphs on the entrance façade), Temple 22 (with elaborate 8th-century carving inside and out), and Temple 16, whose stairway is adorned with death's heads. At the base of this staircase is a table-shaped altar (Q). The inscription on its top includes the date 776, and around the vertical faces are 16 seated figures.

From Temple 26, on the north-east corner of the Acropolis, a unique 8th-century staircase descends to a court at ground level. The risers of the 63 carved steps are covered by an undeciphered inscription of about 2,500 individual glyphs, some of them wrongly placed during the reconstructions of the 1930's. The balustrades are decorated with celestial bird-and-serpent monsters, and there are seated figures at intervals of ten steps.

North of the Hieroglyphic Stairway is a ball court with carved parrot heads set into the upper edges of the benches. Below this was an earlier court in whose floor were three marker stones (one of them dated 514) carved with representations of ball players. Below this again was a third court, contemporary with early constructions on the Acropolis.

In the Main and Middle Courts stand sculptured altars and stelae, most of them with 7th- and 8th-century dates. The fine quality of the workmanship, the high relief, and the elaboration of detail are characteristic of Copan carving.

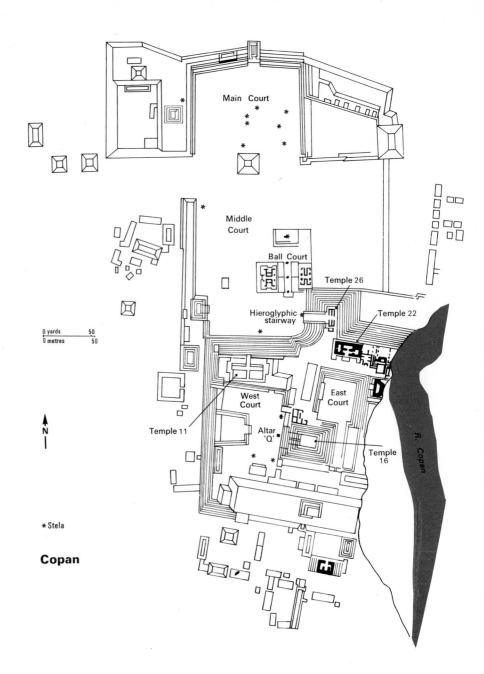

Main Court

Middle Court

Ball Court

Temple 26

Hieroglyphic stairway

Temple 22

0 yards 50
0 metres 50

West Court

East Court

Temple 11

Altar 'Q'

Temple 16

R. Copan

N

* Stela

Copan

Uxmal MEXICO

Maya centre
7th–10th centuries AD

BIBLIOGRAPHY
Ruz, Alberto, *Uxmal: Official Guide*, (English and Spanish editions), Instituto Nacional de Antropología e Historia, Mexico
Kubler, George, *The Art and Architecture of Ancient America*, Harmondsworth, 1962, chs. 7–9

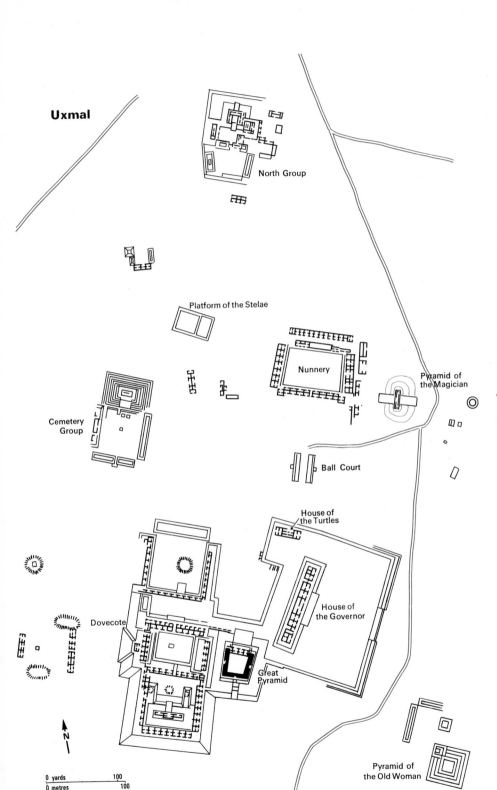

Uxmal

North Group

Platform of the Stelae

Nunnery

Pyramid of the Magician

Cemetery Group

Ball Court

House of the Turtles

House of the Governor

Dovecote

Great Pyramid

Pyramid of the Old Woman

N

0 yards 100
0 metres 100

In the 6th to 8th centuries AD the Maya of Yucatan created new styles of architecture. One of these styles, named Puuc after a nearby range of hills, is found at several sites in the north-west corner of the peninsula, and is characterized by buildings whose cement and rubble cores are faced with a veneer of thin, finely carved limestone slabs. Elaborate mouldings divide the exterior façades into two horizontal zones, the upper one decorated with rows of engaged half-columns and with relief designs made up of thousands of carved stone elements forming geometric fret and lattice patterns, sky serpents, human or divine figures, and stylized masks of the Long-nosed Rain God.

Uxmal, the largest of the Puuc sites, flourished from the 7th to the 11th centuries. Its best preserved temple, the Pyramid of the Magician, stands on a platform of elliptical ground plan, and was rebuilt five times. The earliest shrine is partially exposed at the base of the pyramid; three buildings can be recognized on the middle level, and the final version (Temple 5) stands alone on top of the monument. To the north west of this pyramid is the Nunnery Quadrangle, consisting of four long, elaborately decorated palace buildings enclosing a courtyard with an entrance to the south. Aligned on this entrance are two elongated mounds which are the collapsed side walls of a ball court. Beyond this is another group of buildings which includes the Great Pyramid (largely in ruins), the Governor's Palace (a long, low building standing on a terraced platform), and the Dovecote (a palace-type building with a crest formed by nine huge masonry triangles pierced by rows of openings). The names given to these structures were coined by the Spaniards, and are not indigenous.

In its later stages, the architecture of Uxmal shows signs of highland Mexican influence (phallic sculpture on one of the lesser temples and on one of the Nunnery buildings, skulls and crossbones on the altars in the Cemetery Group, and a Rain God face in Mexican style at the Pyramid of the Magician). The most recent inscription at Uxmal is painted on a capstone in the Nunnery Quadrangle and incorporates a date equivalent to AD 909. The site was virtually abandoned soon afterwards, though a few Postclassic sherds found above the patio of the Nunnery Quadrangle provide evidence of sporadic occupation in the 10th and 11th centuries.

Chichén Itzá MEXICO

Maya centre
7th–13th centuries AD

BIBLIOGRAPHY
Ruz, Alberto, *Chichén Itzá; Official Guide* (Eng. and Span.),
    Instituto Nacional de Antropologia e Historia, Mexico
Tozzer, A. M., 'Chichén Itzá and its Cenote of Sacrifice',
    *Memoirs of the Peabody Museum of Archaeology and
    Ethnology, Harvard University*, vols. 11 and 12, 1957
Morris, E. H. et al., *The Temple of the Warriors at Chichén
    Itzá, Yucatan*, Carnegie Institution of Washington
    Publication no. 406, 2 vols., 1931
Ruppert, K., *The Caracol at Chichén Itzá, Yucatan, Mexico*,
    Carnegie Institution of Washington Pub. no. 454, 1935

On the riverless limestone plateau of Yucatan, settlement is concentrated round the natural wells (*cenotes*) which tap the underground water table. Many *cenotes* also became votive sites, as at Chichén Itzá where the cult seems to have begun in the Early Classic and reached its apogee during the 12th to 16th centuries.

The oldest buildings (cf. UXMAL) are in the Puuc style of the 7th and 8th centuries AD, and have tall roof combs, stone mosaic decoration, and Rain God masks with long, curved noses. To this period belong the structures in the south-western corner of the site: the Red House, Nunnery, Church, Deer House, and the Akab-Dzib.

Native histories refer to one or more invasions by foreigners who ruled over all Yucatan from their capital at Chichén Itzá, and archaeological evidence demonstrates the arrival of newcomers in the 10th century, introducing new architectural ideas which can be matched at TULA, the Toltec capital in highland Mexico. Scenes showing Toltec victories over Maya warriors appear on wall paintings in the Temple of the Jaguars and on gold disks dredged from the *cenote*. Relief sculpture portrays Mexican soldiers and human sacrifice (e.g. on the frieze in the Ball Court), and there is a representation in stone of a typically Mexican skull rack, the *tzompantli* platform.

One probable transitional building is the Caracol (snail), a round structure on a large rectangular platform. A spiral staircase leads up to a small chamber with narrow slits in its wall, and there is little doubt that the building served as an observatory.

The principal Maya–Toltec monuments were constructed around the north-east periphery of the original site, with the main temple, the Castillo, placed squarely in the middle. Architecture and iconography combine features drawn from both cultures. Toltec plumed serpent columns support the lintels of the Warrior and Jaguar temples, and the same figure appears (with eagles and jaguars identical to those at Tula) on the Eagle and Venus altars beside the skull rack. But alongside these Mexican deities, notably in the Temple of the Warriors, are representations of the Maya Long-Nosed Rain God. In building construction, too, the Maya corbelled roof persists alongside the new column-and-beam technique.

Chichén Itzá was overthrown in the mid-13th century and lost its dominant position in Yucatan. No new buildings were erected, but a sparse population remained at the site, and offerings continued to be thrown into the *cenote* until after the Spanish conquest.

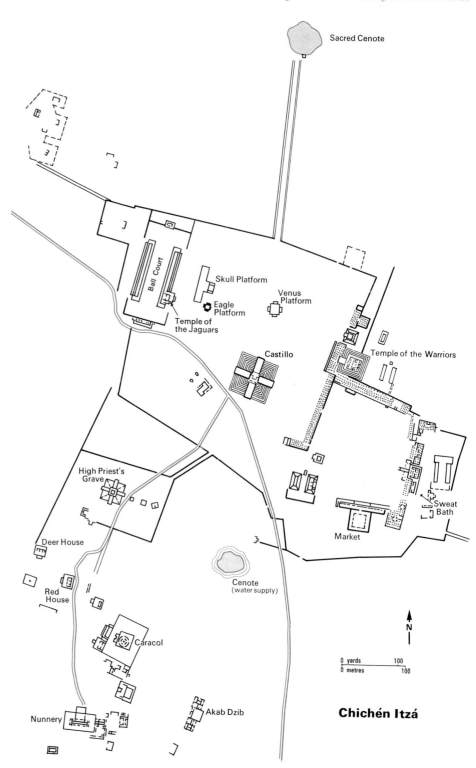

Chichén Itzá

El Tajín MEXICO

Ceremonial centre, Classic Veracruz civilization
Main buildings 7th-11th centuries AD

BIBLIOGRAPHY
Krotser, Paula H. and G. R., 'The Life Style of El Tajin',
American Antiquity, vol. 38, 1973, pp. 199–205
Payón, J. Garcia, *El Tajín: Official Guide*, (English and
Spanish editions), Instituto Nacional de Antropologia e
Historia, Mexico
Handbook of Middle American Indians, vol. 11, ch. 21

The site of El Tajin was the main centre of Gulf Coast civilization from about AD 100 until its destruction by fire somewhere around 1100. It is set among low hills in a hot and humid zone where shifting, slash-and-burn cultivation is the rule, and (like the great Maya sites in a rather similar environment) was a religious and governmental centre rather than a true city. Even so, it is a large site; the nuclear zone covers some 150 acres (61 hectares), and subsidiary mounds extend over at least two square miles (5 sq km). Much of El Tajin is still unexplored, but excavation has shown that most of the visible buildings were constructed between 600 and 900. During this period El Tajin was the dominant political power in eastern Mexico, and its distinctive art style influenced the other Classic styles of Mesoamerica.

Tajin art motifs, based on interlocking scroll patterns, occur on pottery and stone objects but are also well represented in the architecture of the parent site. The characteristic features of Tajin buildings are structural (incorporation of niches, flying cornices and false arches, and the use of columns to support roofs made of poured concrete slabs) and also decorative (scroll, step fret, Greek key and interlace designs, sometimes used in combination with sculptured panels showing realistic scenes).

The finest building at El Tajin is the Pyramid of the Niches, a quadrangular platform rising in six stages to an upper sanctuary approached by a staircase with decorated balustrades. Tunnelling revealed an earlier platform within the pyramid. Eleven ball courts are scattered throughout the site, and some of them have finely carved panels. Those of the South Court show ceremonies connected with the game itself, and include sacrificial scenes in which two men dressed in the padded costume of ball players are cutting out the heart of a third player under the watchful eye of a skeletal Death God.

On an elevated promontory to the north of the main group is Tajin Chico, a complex of 18 buildings which is still incompletely cleared. In this zone stands the Building of the Columns, a palace structure with six column drums carved with reliefs depicting priests, winged dancers, Eagle Knights, day signs, and bar-and-dot numerals. The Building of the Columns is one of the latest at El Tajin and was burned down after only a century of use.

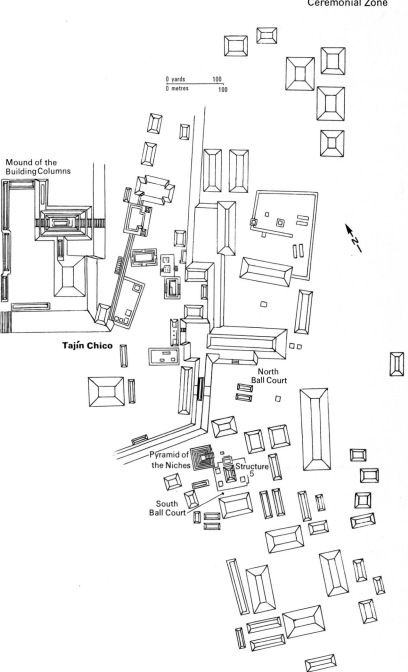

El Tajín
Ceremonial Zone

0 yards 100
0 metres 100

Mound of the
Building Columns

Tajín Chico

North
Ball Court

Pyramid of
the Niches

Structure
5

South
Ball Court

Xochicalco MEXICO

Hilltop city
6th–10th centuries AD

BIBLIOGRAPHY
Noguera, Eduardo, *Archaeological Sites in the State of Morelos: Official Guide*, (English and Spanish editions), Instituto Nacional de Antropología e Historia, Mexico
King, Jaime Litvak, 'Investigaciones en el Valle de Xochicalco: 1569–1970', *Anales de Antropología*, vol. VIII, 1971, pp. 101–24
Marquina, Ignacio, *Arquitectura Prehispánica*, Instituto Nacional de Antropología e Historia, Mexico, 1951

During the 6th and 7th centuries AD the major cultural regions of Mexico were in contact with each other, and the interchange of ideas and products stimulated the growth of new, eclectic art styles. One such style developed at Xochicalco, a fortified city which controlled much of the fertile terrain in the present-day state of Morelos.

The main site is on a hill which rises 426 feet (130 m) above the level of the plain and is linked by a paved causeway to a second hill which also has structures. The natural contours of Xochicalco hill have been modified into a series of stepped terraces with retaining walls, and the principal structures are grouped on a broad platform at the summit.

The most impressive building is the Pyramid of the Plumed Serpents, whose present outline conceals two earlier platforms. The reliefs on the façade were originally coloured red, black, white, yellow, blue and green. On the lower storey are plumed serpents, between whose undulating coils are several seated human figures wearing elaborate feather head-dresses. The cross-legged posture, the upraised hand, and the facial profile with the forehead sloping backwards from the bridge of the nose, are characteristic of Maya art. Some of the hieroglyphs in this panel incorporate numerals in Maya or Zapotec style (in which a bar is equivalent to five dots), while other glyphs are related to those used at a later date by the Aztecs and other Nahuatl-speaking groups. Above the serpent panel is a frieze of human figures surmounted by a row of stylized shells, symbols of Quetzalcoatl, the Plumed Serpent God. The second storey has a further series of glyphs and figures, but the restoration is somewhat conjectural.

Just south of the Serpent pyramid lies Structure A, which yielded three fine stelae carved with the faces of gods and with groups of hieroglyphs, some of them calendrical. The stelae, together with the rich offerings from the little chamber annexed to the south-west corner of Structure A, are now in the Anthropological Museum at Mexico City. Of the remaining structures, the most notable are the great I-shaped ball court, and the palace group (Structure B) with its little sweat bath. In various parts of the hill are underground passages and halls, one of which (Los Amates) has been cleared and restored for visitors.

Although the Xochicalco site was inhabited as early as 100 BC, the main occupation and the existing buildings are of the 6th to 10th centuries AD.

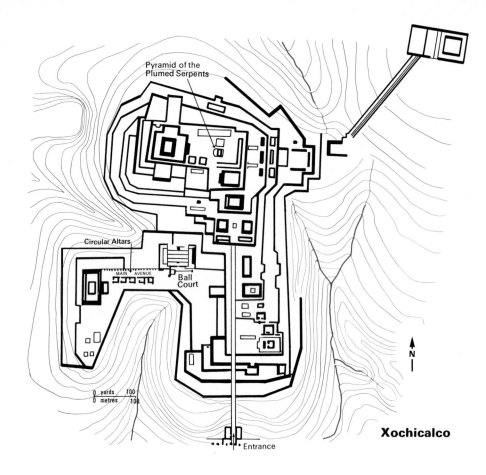

Pyramid of the Plumed Serpents

Circular Altars

MAIN AVENUE

Ball Court

0 yards 100
0 metres 100

N

Entrance

Xochicalco

Tula MEXICO

Toltec city
10th–12th centuries AD

BIBLIOGRAPHY
Del Rio, Pablo Martinez and Acosta, Jorge R., *Tula: Official Guide*, (English and Spanish editions), Instituto Nacional de Antropologia e Historia, Mexico
Dutton, Bertha P., 'Tula of the Toltecs', *El Palacio*, vol. 62, Santa Fe, 1955, pp. 195–251

The Toltec capital was founded in about AD 960, and was violently destroyed in the late 12th century. The site, lying just north of the Valley of Mexico, is still largely unexcavated, but the cleared and restored buildings around the central plaza illustrate all the principal features of Toltec art and architecture.

In the middle of the main square is a small altar or shrine; on the western side is a ball court, and on the east is Edificio C, a stepped pyramid in a rather destroyed condition. The important buildings are on the north side of the square. First comes the Vestibule, a great rectangular hall with a coloured frieze and three rows of columns which once supported roof beams (a typically Toltec building technique). Through the Vestibule is Edificio B, a stepped pyramid of five stages on which there once stood a temple supported by stone columns. Almost all the facing of the platform has disappeared, and the mound was cut into during the prehispanic period to provide material for a ramp down which the temple columns were hurled during the destruction. The re-erected columns are made of tenoned sections and take various forms: warrior figures, round pillars carved with plumed serpents, and square pillars with reliefs of warriors. Traces of paint were visible on the originals. Part of the façade remains in place at the rear of the platform, and consists of carved panels representing a procession of jaguars, front views of a plumed serpent, and birds of prey tearing at hearts.

Behind this pyramid is a length of wall surmounted by representations of conch-shell sections (symbol of the Plumed Serpent God, Quetzalcoatl, in his wind god aspect), and with a frieze of serpents devouring partially defleshed human beings. The Serpent Wall forms the south side of a square, flanked on the north by another ball court. West of Edificio B stands a complex ceremonial structure, the Burned Palace, with a frieze of warriors in procession. This building also yielded two Chac Mools, characteristic Toltec sculptures of reclining figures with offering trays on their stomachs.

Unexcavated mounds extend for a considerable distance, and indicate that Tula was a large city. The more important outlying buildings are Edificio 2 (a complex of rooms occupied in Toltec, Aztec, and Colonial times') and El Corral, which has a round, stepped platform, an altar decorated with skulls and crossbones, and some recently excavated Toltec houses.

Tula also has a small museum.

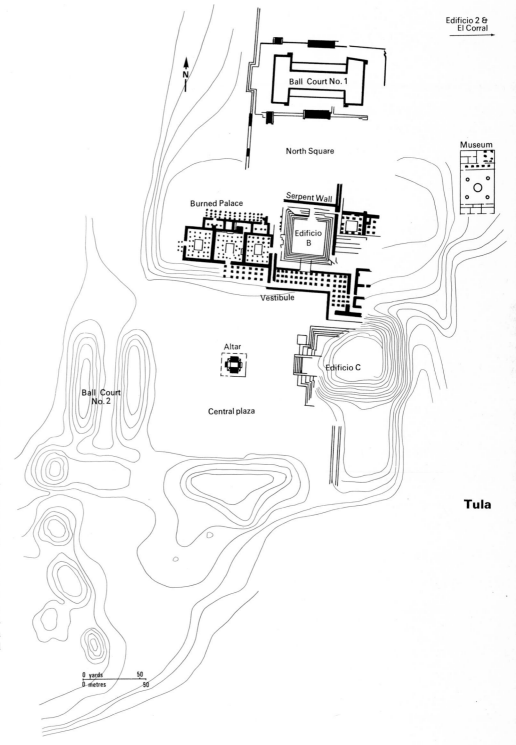

Tula

Tenochtitlán MEXICO CITY

Aztec capital city
AD 1345–1521

BIBLIOGRAPHY
Marquina, Ignacio, *El Templo Mayor de Mexico*, Instituto Nacional de Antropología e Historia, Mexico, 1960
Bray, Warwick, *Everyday Life of the Aztecs*, London, 1968
Soustelle, Jacques, *The Daily Life of the Aztecs*, Harmondsworth, 1964
Calnek, Edward P., 'Settlement Pattern and Chinampa Agriculture at Tenochtitlán', *American Antiquity*, vol. 37, 1972, pp. 104–15
(For the most recent discoveries, consult the volumes of the *Boletín* of the Instituto de Antropología e Historia, Mexico.)

The Aztec capital at Tenochtitlán was founded in AD 1345 on a muddy island in the lake which at that time filled the centre of the Basin of Mexico. In 1521 it was besieged and destroyed by the Spaniards, who then built colonial Mexico City on the same spot.

Documentary sources describe Tenochtitlán as a city of more than 150,000 people. It was laid out on a grid plan and covered more than 4·6 square miles (12 sq km), much of this being reclaimed swamp land converted into *chinampas* (rectangular garden plots surrounded by canals). The outer ring of *chinampa* suburbs enclosed the residential zone, at the heart of which was the main ceremonial precinct: a rectangular, walled enclosure containing the principal temple, subsidiary shrines, ball courts, and the wooden rack on which were skewered the skulls of sacrificed victims. Another centre existed at Tlatelolco, an independent Aztec foundation which had become physically and politically incorporated into Tenochtitlán. Canals reached to all parts of the island city, and five causeways linked it to the mainland.

Aztec Tenochtitlán is almost obliterated by later buildings. *Chinampa* cultivation is still practised at nearby Xochimilco, and part of the Tlatelolco centre has been exposed in the Plaza de las Tres Culturas where there are temple platforms and a building with carved day signs. In this area were found rows of skulls from a collapsed wooden rack.

The Great Precinct occupied the present cathedral square and the surrounding streets. Almost every excavation in this zone has revealed platforms, altars, frescoes, sculptures, and wooden stakes used to consolidate the marshy ground. Most of these excavations have been filled in, but the base of the main temple can still be visited. The four superpositions represent successive enlargements of the temple platform, and carved serpent heads are associated with the third stage.

Nothing is left of the twin shrines which once stood on the pyramid, but some idea of their appearance can be gained from a visit to the reconstructed Aztec temple at Santa Cecilia Acatitlán, near Tlalnepantla about eight miles (13 km) north of Mexico City.

Excavations for the new metro have unearthed numerous buildings, tombs and offerings. One group of buildings, a round shrine with five earlier structures beneath it, is preserved in the Pino Súarez metro station.

The Museo Nacional de Antropología is one of the world's great museums. In it are displayed the principal treasures of Mexican archaeology, among them the Calendar Stone and the colossal statue of the goddess Coatlicue from the ceremonial precinct of Tenochtitlán.

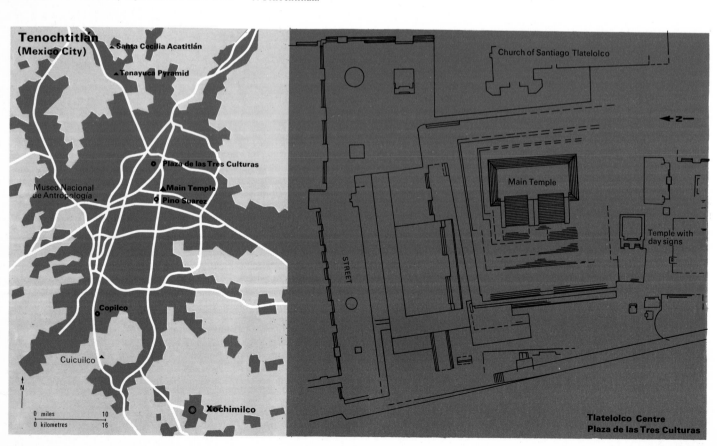

Tenochtitlán (Mexico City)
- Santa Cecilia Acatitlán
- Tenayuca Pyramid
- Plaza de las Tres Culturas
- Museo Nacional de Antropología
- Main Temple
- Pino Suarez
- Copilco
- Cuicuilco
- Xochimilco

0 miles 10
0 kilometres 16

Church of Santiago Tlatelolco
Main Temple
Temple with day signs
STREET
Tlatelolco Centre
Plaza de las Tres Culturas

La Quemada MEXICO

Fortress city
Main occupation *c.* AD 900–1100

BIBLIOGRAPHY
Noguera, Eduardo, *La Quemada – Chalchihuites: Guia Oficial*, Instituto Nacional de Antropología e Historia, Mexico
Handbook of Middle American Indians, vol. 11, ch. 32
Marquina, Ignacio, *Arquitectura Prehispánica*, Instituto Nacional de Antropología e Historia, Mexico, 1951

The fortress city of La Quemada lies on the ecological and cultural frontier which separated the nomadic and semi-nomadic Chichimec tribes of the northern desert from the settled, civilized communities of Mesoamerica proper. It occupies a favourable locality, taking advantage of an isolated hill which rises from the centre of one of the few fertile valleys in this arid zone, and at the same time it blocks the natural southward invasion route along the Rio Malpaso. La Quemada represents a late colonization, perhaps under Toltec influence, which attempted to impose the Mesoamerican pattern of civilization on a distinctly marginal region. The attempt had only limited success. Some rather ambiguous radiocarbon dates hint at several centuries of occupation, with the climax falling somewhere between AD 900 and 1100.

The highest part of the hill has been converted into a series of stepped terraces bounded, where the natural cliff defences are inadequate, by immense sloping walls made of rough stone slabs. Further north a curtain wall encloses a triangular area some 1,310 feet (400 m) across and, at the opposite end of the site, an important complex of buildings (the South Group) covers the lower, southern end of the mesa. Within the acropolis are rooms, walled courtyards and small pyramids which seem to be poor copies of those in use at the central Mexican cities. A larger pyramid with unusually steep sides is located on an esplanade a little apart from the other buildings. The architecture of La Quemada is distinguished by the use of irregular, horizontally laid slabs with the apparent absence of mortar. Early travellers noted that some structures were finished with stucco, but there are few traces of this today.

The South Group consists of a small pyramid and a broad, open terrace with a large hall at the eastern edge. This hall is the most imposing building on the site. Parts of the wall still stand to a height of 10 feet (3 m) and the roof was supported by 11 round, slab-built columns more than 16 feet (5 m) tall. The roofing technique appears in Mesoamerica during the Toltec period, and the hall at La Quemada may be a pale reflection of the pillared Toltec buildings of TULA and CHICHÉN ITZÁ.

From La Quemada a network of roads led to the smaller settlements in the valley, and traces of some of these are still recognizable. The fortress was already in ruins when the Spaniards passed through Zacatecas, and excavation has demonstrated that it was burned at the end of its period of occupation.

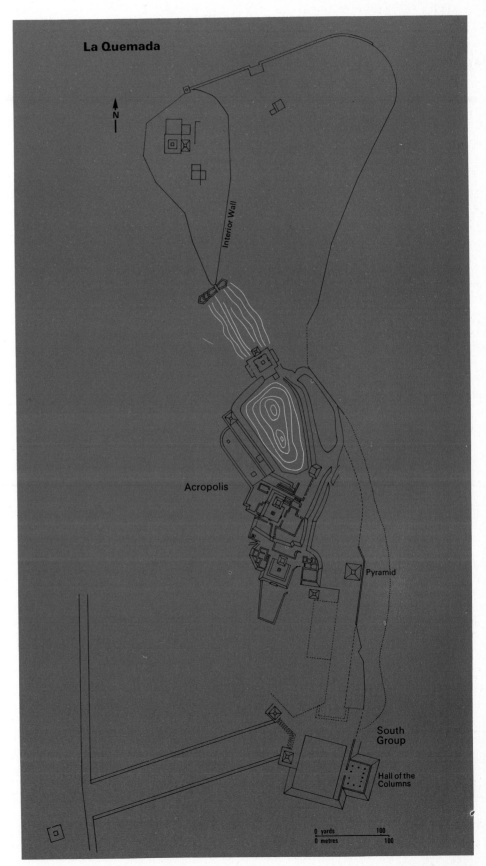

La Quemada

N

Interior Wall

Acropolis

Pyramid

South Group

Hall of the Columns

0 yards 100
0 metres 100

SOUTH AMERICA

It would be simple but inaccurate to say that South America consisted of the towering range of the Andes on the west with the vast lowland basin of the Amazon running eastwards from its foot to the Atlantic; but this highland–lowland dichotomy is nevertheless the most striking and influential feature of the continent's physiography.

The Andes run the length of South America, ranging in width up to 400 miles (approx. 645 km), sometimes dividing into two or even three parallel ranges with high intermontane plateaus and basins in between. On the western, Pacific shore are coastal lowlands, minimal in southern Chile and broadening to 100–200 miles (approx. 160–320 km) in Ecuador and Colombia.

East of the Andes is the great tropical forest basin of the Amazon, bordered on the north by the Guiana Highlands plateau and on the south by the Brazilian Highlands, which occupy most of southern Brazil. The Orinoco basin divides the Guiana Highlands from the northern end of the Andes, as the Paraguay–Paraná drainage does the Brazilian Highlands from the broad plateau of the central Andes. These two rivers flow into the La Plata estuary, which forms the northern boundary of the great flat plains of the Argentine Pampas. Thus the major river systems of South America – the Amazon, Orinoco and Paraguay-Paraná – divide its highlands into three blocks, of which only the highest, the Andean chain, has ever been the focus of indigenous civilization.

Culturally South America falls into nine major areas, corresponding in large part to the topographic divisions. From north to south these are (following Willey's scheme):

Caribbean, comprising the Lesser and Greater Antilles as far north as the Bahamas, north-west Venezuela and north Guyana.

Intermediate (so called from its position between the high cultures of Mesoamerica and Peru), comprising the Andean regions of Ecuador, Colombia and Venezuela, Panama, and the eastern parts of Costa Rica, Nicaragua and Honduras abutting the Mesoamerican culture area that reaches north and west into Mexico.

Amazonian, the huge drainage basin of the Amazon and its tributaries from the foothills of the Andes to the Atlantic coast of north-east Brazil and from central Venezuela and the coast of Surinam south to Bolivia.

Peruvian, comprising the Andean and Pacific coast regions of the modern Republic of Peru, together with small areas of southernmost Ecuador and north-western Bolivia around Lake Titicaca.

East Brazilian, consisting of the Brazilian Highlands plateau from the southern margin of the Amazon basin to Uruguay, and the Atlantic coastal lowlands on the eastern edge of the highlands.

South Andean, including south-west Bolivia, north-west Argentina and Chile south to the fjord country at about 40°S.

Chacoan, comprising the Paraguay–Paraná lowland basin and including Paraguay, south-east Bolivia and north-east Argentina adjoining.

Pampean, the great plains of Uruguay and Argentina south of the La Plata estuary, including Patagonia and northern Tierra del Fuego.

Fuegian, the fjord country of Chile from 40°S down to Cape Horn.

All of these areas contain vast numbers of archaeological sites, indicating a large and widespread population over the last 10,000 years, but relatively few have been excavated (although many have been, and are being, looted) and even fewer have been restored or have visible structures sufficient to attract a traveller who is not also a hardened archaeologist. A combination of topography, environment, demography and chance resulted in the emergence of complex societies whose buildings in stone or mudbrick still survive in only two of the areas, the Peruvian and the Intermediate; only the Peruvian area seems to have attained the level of true civilization, late in time, and

Caribbean Sea

Atlantic Ocean

Puerto Horminga

Orinoco

Orinoco

San Agustín

Quito
El Inga

Valdivia

Cerro Narrío

Amazon

Amazon

Amazon

Chan Chan

Huaca Prieta

Moche
River

Chavín de Huantar

Kotosh

Playa Culebras

Cajamarquilla

Lima

Huari Ayacucho

Machu Picchu
Cuzco

Lake
Titicaca

Tiahuanaco

Pacific Ocean

| 0 | miles | | 250 |
| 0 | kilometres | | 400 |

thus most of the sites that are worth visiting are in or near modern Peru, and date from around 1000 BC down to the Spanish conquest.

Man's occupation of South America begins, however, between 10,000 and 20,000 years ago, on the basis of radiocarbon dating. Recent work in Mexico suggests the presence of man there well over 20,000 years ago, and most current theories put the irruption of humans into the Americas across the Bering Strait area at some time after 26,000 years ago, a time when the lowered sea level of the Wisconsin (= late Würm in Europe) glaciation had exposed a landbridge joining Asia and America.

Several radiocarbon dates from central and southern Chile, from Laguna de Tagua and from Fell's Cave and Palli Aike on the Strait of Magellan, show that man had already penetrated to the far south of the continent by 9000 BC; earlier dates from Muaco in north-western Venezuela and the Ayacucho region of highland Peru indicate an occupation by 12,000–15,000 BC, and a date of nearly 20,000 BC has been claimed for the Ayacucho area.

By about 9500 BC hunting groups were well established over most of highland and plateau South America, exploiting the Pleistocene and post-Pleistocene large game animals, now extinct, which were hunted with spears tipped by fish-tailed, and later long lanceolate, stone points. By 7000 BC an economy based on plant collecting and small game as well as larger animals such as the camelids (the llama family) and deer had superseded the hunting tradition, with seasonal exploitation of different resources in upland and lowland environments. An important site for this period, having both the fish-tailed points of the hunting tradition and the stemmed points of the later hunting-collecting development, is that of El Inga, near Quito in highland Ecuador, where the artifacts are made of obsidian. In some areas of South America such a hunting and collecting economy continued for millennia with the development of coastal settlements exploiting marine resources for part of the year dating from at least 5000 BC.

By 4000 BC permanent villages based on marine resources and plant gathering were established on the coast of Peru. This region consists largely of desert, crossed by more than 40 short rivers descending from the western slopes of the Andes. The environmental contrasts are sharp, the habitable areas circumscribed; the desert has both marvellously preserved a rich variety of archaeological material, and in the past, by containing rising population densities within small areas of oasis, perhaps forced the development of stratified societies through territorial awareness and competition for land. In these coastal valleys domesticated plants were grown, including eventually maize, beans, squash, cotton, avocado, chili pepper and guava, all by 2500 BC, and the guinea pig was also kept for food.

These settlements still lacked pottery, which did not appear in Peru until after 2000 BC. The first ceramics in South America appear further north in the Intermediate area, though precisely where has not yet been established. The two regions with the earliest recorded pottery so far are coastal Colombia, where radiocarbon dates for the Puerto Hormiga site are 3000–2500 BC, and coastal Ecuador, where Valdivia has 20 radiocarbon dates covering 2700–1500 BC, one date of 3200 BC, and a recently dis-covered but undated early pottery horizon antedating the levels from which the carbon came. Pottery in highland Ecuador is at present undated, but typological studies on Cerro Narrio ceramics suggest that it may be as early as the coastal material. Suggestions that South American pottery originated in the Middle Jōmon culture of Japan around 3000 BC are not generally accepted.

A distinctively Peruvian cultural tradition was, however, emerging long before even the introduction of pottery. Between 2500 and 1800 BC sites such as Huaca Prieta existed on the coast, making complex decorated textiles and carved gourds, and at Playa Culebras artificial terraces faced with basalt blocks and supporting mudbrick houses characterized a large settlement which has produced some of the earliest maize known from South America, and at Chuquitanta a large building interpreted as a temple has been excavated.

Similar developments were taking place in the highlands: at Kotosh on the Upper Huallaga drainage, at 6,400 feet (1,950 m) a series of superimposed temples has been excavated by Japanese archaeologists. At the bottom of more than 43 feet (13 m) of deposit was the famous Temple of the Crossed Hands, built of stones set in mud mortar and placed upon a high platform; above it was the later Temple of the Little Niches, and no pottery was associated with either building. Both temples, and an even earlier phase below the Temple of the Crossed Hands, date to before 1800 BC; over them is built a later temple with radiocarbon dates ranging from 1800 to 1150 BC, and over that still later structures.

Not far north west of Kotosh, on the Upper Marañon drainage running parallel to the Huallaga, is the site of CHAVÍN DE HUANTAR, a similarly placed though larger and later temple complex with associated settlement. This is the type site for the Early Horizon (900–200 BC), marked by the emergence and spread of the Chavín art style and its derivatives. The style includes men, beasts and birds, often fantastic and with feline attributes and attached serpent heads. The glaring eyes and fanged mouths of Chavin art are not dissimilar to those of SAN AGUSTÍN, which may overlap the end of the Chavín Horizon in time. Chavín influence is found in restricted areas of the highlands and more widely along the north, central and south coasts of Peru, in the latter area in the well-known Paracas culture. Chavín pottery has been found as far north as the Cuenca basin of southern Ecuador.

The Early Horizon in Peru is followed by the Early Intermediate Period, apparently a time when regional political entities developed their individual art styles and ceramic traditions. These entities were based on and gave rise to the first Peruvian cities, such as MOCHE on the north coast, indicating a stratified and controlled society with sophisticated craft specialization developing under patronage.

The Middle Horizon (AD 600–1000) is marked by the emergence of one of these regional styles, that based on Tiahuanaco near Lake Titicaca, and its spread through much of southern Peru in association with the related Huari style. The archaeology of this period suggests that the emergence of the state in Peru began at this period, with control of food resources and population movement over a wide area.

In the succeeding Late Intermediate Period (AD 1000–1476) a number of such state organizations coexisted, the best known of which is the Chimu kingdom on the north coast of Peru with its capital at CHAN CHAN, but also including that based on Cajamarquilla in the Rimac valley near Lima.

Finally, from 1476 until its truncation by the Spanish conquest in 1534, one of these kingdoms, that of the Inca based on Cuzco in the south Peruvian Andes, spread inexorably along the Andes and the Pacific coast until it commanded an empire reaching from Quito to central Chile. Inca sites are numerous; the capital at CUZCO with its fortifications and ceremonial structures, and the late refuge settlement at MACHU PICCHU are both good examples of Inca architectural achievement.

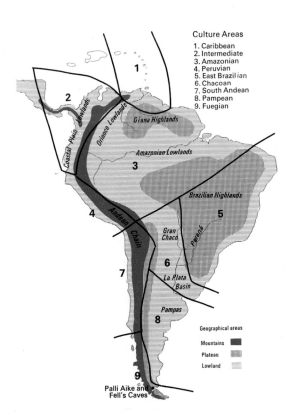

Culture Areas

1. Caribbean
2. Intermediate
3. Amazonian
4. Peruvian
5. East Brazilian
6. Chacoan
7. South Andean
8. Pampean
9. Fuegian

Geographical areas

Mountains
Plateau
Lowland

San Agustín COLOMBIA

Ceremonial centres and settlements

c. AD 0–500

BIBLIOGRAPHY
Reichel-Dolmatoff, G., *San Agustin*, London, 1972, with full
bibliography

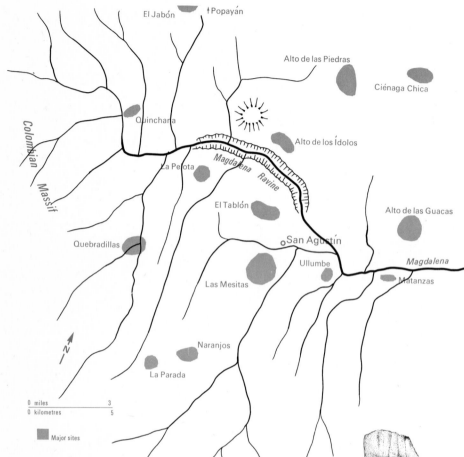

San Agustín

The San Agustín region is in the southern part of Colombia, on the headwaters of the Magdalena river but with easy access through passes to the Cauca, running parallel with the Magdalena, the Caquetá flowing into the Amazon and the Patis descending steeply to the Pacific coast. It lies near the point where the Andean chain trifurcates into the three cordilleras of central and north Colombia.

The archaeological label of San Agustín refers not to a single site but to several dozen scattered round the modern town of that name. They lie on either side of the Magdalena river at about 5,900 feet (1,800 m) on gentle slopes descending from the eastern flank of the Columbian massif. The climate is temperate with plentiful rainfall, and the heavily cultivated land can yield two maize crops in most years and a variety of tree and root crops. To these can be added the produce of the highland Andean and tropical lowland zones, both within a day or so's walk.

The remains consist of mounded tombs and monolithic stone sculptures but clearly these formed the ceremonial precincts of a large, dispersed population. Their date is still a matter of

One of the feline-
headed stone monoliths
at San Agustín

debate, but it would seem to centre on the period AD 0–500.

The main site to the south of the river is Las Mesitas, on a flat area between two affluents of the Naranjos river. The ground level has been artificially levelled, and on the plateau are several groups of earthen barrows covering stone constructions. The general technique of construction is remarkably like that used in the megalithic chambered tombs of Atlantic Europe.

Mesita A, one group, consists of barrows now some 80 feet (25 m) across and 13 feet (4 m) high, covering rectangular chambers with slab walls and roofs. Each central chamber contained one or more large sculptured stone statues, and near the barrows a number of freestanding statues are also found. Mesita B a short distance away consisted of three large barrows, heavily robbed; a number of trough-shaped stone sarcophagi of more than six feet six inches (2 m) were found here, and it seems likely that these barrows, like their European counterparts, were funerary monuments. A third group, Mesita C, is nearby, and beyond it the valley of the Lavapatas stream, where the bedrock has been carved into a series of pools, channels and reliefs.

North of the Magdalena the main site is called Alto de los Idolos, a large U-shaped hill open to the south; the central part is artificially built up. A number of barrows stand on the hill, with six large stone slab cists containing sarcophagi on the western arm. Part of the eastern arm is a deep midden packed with occupation material.

The most striking sculptures are the statues of humans with feline features, particularly fangs, which have been connected by scholars with jaguar shamanism.

258

Chavín de Huantar PERU

Ceremonial centre and settlement
c. 900–*c.* 300 BC

BIBLIOGRAPHY
Lumbreras, L. G., *Los Templos de Chavín*, Lima, 1970
Rowe, J. H., *Chavin Art, an inquiry into its form and meaning*, New York, 1962

Chavín lies in the uppermost reaches of the Amazon basin, not far east of the continental divide which runs along the Cordillera Blanca. The Río Mosna in whose valley the site stands is a tributary of the Puchka, which flows in turn into the Marañón, the great western branch of the upper Amazon.

The site occupies a triangular tongue of land bounded by the Mosna to the east, the smaller stream of the Wacheksa flowing into it on the north and north west and steeply rising hills to the south. Just across the Wacheksa to the north is the present town of Chavín.

Chavín lies at 10,430 feet (3,180 m) at a point where the valley of the Mosna narrows to less than two thirds of a mile (1 km). The area is intensively cultivated to a much higher level, although like much of the Andes there is a long dry season from April to December.

The extant structures comprise a complex of courts and 'temples', structures which are certainly not domestic and probably not defensive, but the foundations of a few rude dwellings are to be seen in the courtyard in front of the Templo del Lanzón, and extensive refuse deposits have been reported in the vicinity which suggest that Chavín was a substantial settlement during the period of florescence of the site in the 1st millennium BC. This period, 900–200 BC, is known as the Chavín Horizon, and is marked in northern and central Peru by the complex art style typified at Chavín de Huantar.

The ruins consist of a number of mounds and courts, partially excavated from the thick layer of mud and debris that covered them during a flood in 1945. The main structures are in the southern part of the site, the lower ones running out along the area between the streams. The principal structure and also the earliest is the complex comprising the Templo del Lanzón and the Piramide Mayor, the latter apparently enlarged southwards at a later date.

The Templo del Lanzón is a three-sided construction with an earth and rubble fill retained by vertical masonry walls. The masonry is well trimmed and squared but not finely dressed, and has alternate thick and thin courses, with the upper part of the wall in finer masonry. The three ranges are grouped around a small courtyard open towards the river, and in the centre of the main range a doorway and steps give access to a subterranean gallery. At the end of a narrow passage is a cruciform vault surrounding the tall stone carving of a feline deity known as El Lanzon. The rest of the structure and the area beneath the courtyard are also honeycombed with rectilinear networks of galleries.

The Piramide Mayor incorporates the southern range of the early structure, and consists of two further southward extensions also riddled with galleries and chambers, some containing stone carvings in the Chavín style. Other carvings including tenoned heads are set into the outer walls of the 'pyramid', which is the largest building at Chavin. On the eastern side is a monumental façade, consisting of a slab wall flanking a columned doorway.

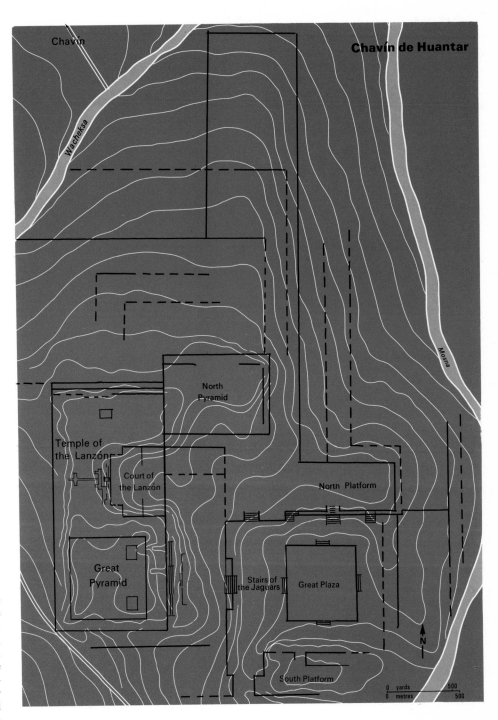

Both the columns and the lintel are carved in detailed incision and low relief. The doorway faces axially on to a sunken court on two levels, each reached by a number of shallow stairs, flanked to north and south by low platforms and facing east onto the river bank. There is a broad terrace between the pyramid and the courtyard.

Tiahuanaco BOLIVIA

Ceremonial centre and settlement
c. AD 600–1000

BIBLIOGRAPHY
Bennett, W. C. and Bird, J. B., *Andean Culture History*, 2nd edition, New York, 1964
Bennett, W. C. *Excavations at Tiahuanaco*, Anthropological Papers, American Museum of Natural History, vol. 34, part 3, New York, 1934

The site of Tiahuanaco lies at over 12,000 feet (3,660 m), in the broad and shallow valley of the Río Tiahuanaco just upstream from the modern town of the same name. The valley is one of a number that cut back into the high plateau of the Bolivian *altiplano* from the southern end of Lake Titicaca, and the site is located at the point where the valley narrows markedly like a funnel. The size of the present town, the largest settlement between La Paz and the Peruvian border, is an indication of the strategic importance of the site, controlling traffic from the lake basin up to the *altiplano* and then down into the basin of the Río Beni, a tributary of the Amazon, and with harsh upland climate ameliorated to some extent by the proximity of the lake.

Tiahuanaco has given its name to a widespread cultural 'Horizon' around the middle of the 1st millennium AD, marked by polychrome pottery beakers with humans, animals, and other designs and characteristic three-dimensional feline-head rimadornos. The visible remains are of a 'ceremonial centre', but the distribution of refuse beyond this area has suggested the existence of an urban zone of perhaps one square mile (2.6 sq km), with a population estimated at between 5,000 and 20,000 people.

The site lies north of the river in the valley bottom, and on first sight is not at all spectacular, consisting of a haphazard huddle of mounds and platforms within a shallow encircling ditch that encloses an area about 1,200 yards by 700 yards (approx. 1,000 × 600 m). The most obvious structure is the mound of the Akapana, roughly rectangular in plan with an oval central depression, just over 650 feet (approx. 200 m) a side and some 50 feet (15 m) high. A survey in 1904 showed that the mound had once been enclosed within a stone retaining wall of stepped plan, and it is thought to have had a stepped-pyramidal profile also. The central depression seems to have been for water, since a stone-built 'drain' runs from it through the mound to the south. The foundations of small structures on the top suggest that it could have been used as a redoubt.

Immediately to the north is the large rectangular platform of the Kalasasaya, about 443 feet by 427 feet (135 × 130 m), with a retaining wall of dressed stone slabs filled with smaller masonry. On the western side is an access stair leading to an interior sunken court, on the east another stair leading to the Sunken Temple, another sunken court, the walls of which are decorated with tenoned stone heads. In the north-western corner of the Kalasasaya stands the Gate of the Sun, a monolithic portal with numerous sculptures of a Staff God on the eastern face, balanced in the south-west corner by a statue known as El Fraile. To the west of the Kalasasaya is another enclosure known as El Palacio, some 197 feet by 180 feet (60 × 55 m) in plan and once surrounded by double walls.

A number of massive and superbly dressed stone blocks, including other monolithic portals, are scattered about the site; one of the latter has been re-erected on a small platform some distance west of the site centre. Only a few of the pillar-like stone statues remain at the site; others have been removed to the museum, to the town and to La Paz.

Evidence of settlement is found for some distance around the ditched enclosure but has never been systematically investigated.

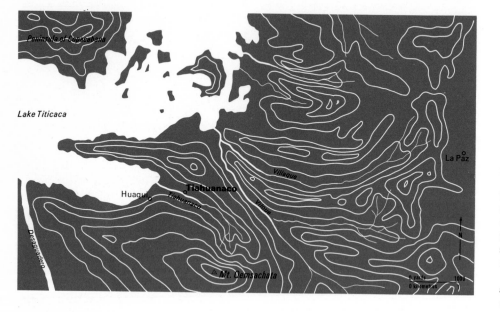

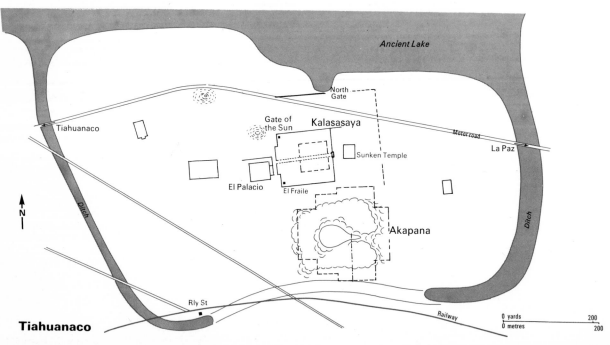

Tiahuanaco

Chan Chan PERU

Chimu capital
14th–15th centuries AD

BIBLIOGRAPHY
Platt, Simon, Mapping Chan Chan, *Illustrated London News*, 31 December, 1970
Holstein, O., 'Chan-Chan, Capital of the Great Chimu', *Geographical Review*, vol. 17, New York, 1927, pp. 36–61

The great urban site of Chan Chan, capital of the Chimú empire in the 14th and 15th centuries, lies on the desert north coast of Peru a short distance inland from the Pacific shore. The rainless coast is crossed by many river valleys that create fertile oases; the Moche valley is one of the largest of these and has long been an important focus of settlement, containing as it does the ruins of Moche, dating to the 1st millennium AD, Chan Chan, and the colonial and modern city of Trujillo.

The oasis area has long been extended beyond the actual river valley by means of irrigation canals, and although the irrigated area has shrunk since the Conquest, Chan Chan still lies on its northern edge. The ruins cover an area of 14 square miles (36 sq km), with a central core of two and a half square miles (6·5 sq km) which contains the 10 surviving walled compounds known as *ciudadelas* (fortresses), which formed the heart of the Chimu city. Two of the *ciudadelas*, called Rivero and Tschudi after early explorers, have been partly excavated and restored, together with an outlying pyramid compound called El Dragón.

The *ciudadelas* are basically similar in plan, and range in size from 1,300 feet by 650 feet (approx. 400 × 200 m) – Rivero – to 2,130 feet by 1,300 feet (approx. 650 × 400 m) – Gran Chimu. Each is surrounded by a wall of mudbrick adobes, laid in mud mortar and covered with mud plaster, 30 to 40 feet high (9–12 m) and 10 feet (3 m) thick at the base. Six of the 10 *ciudadelas* have a tripartite internal divi-sion and can be entered only through a single narrow gate in the north wall; at Rivero excavation showed this to be flanked by rows of niches, two with wooden 'guardian' statues some three feet (approx. 1 m) high.

The southernmost sector in each *ciudadela* is open and contains one or more *pukios* (walk-in wells) and small dwellings of perishable materials. The northern sector has an entry court, flanked by smaller courts and complexes of small rooms, which leads to a densely packed area of similar courts, some with rooms and others with a U-shaped struc-ture termed an *audiencia* at one end. The central sector has a smaller entry court and larger com-plexes of small rooms.

The courtyard walls and the outer walls have intricate friezes in mudbrick, depicting fish, animals, birds and other motifs familiar from Chimú pottery.

In eight of the *ciudadelas* a large platform stands by or beyond the central sector, surrounded by high-walled courts with up to three levels of internal chambers; in two cases these complexes were un-finished. They may have been burial platforms, and it has been suggested that each *ciudadela* was the seat of a new Chimú ruler, the old palace being left in perpetual maintenance as a cult centre, a practice attested slightly later among the Inca.

The core area is surrounded by small residences, cemeteries, irrigation canals and other structures, and at least one walled road running north-south has been mapped.

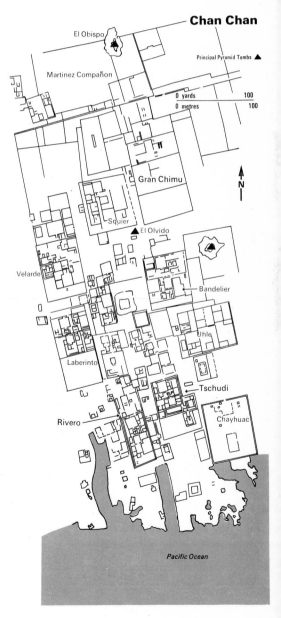

Chan Chan

El Obispo

Principal Pyramid Tombs ▲

Martinez Compañon

0 yards   100
0 metres   100

Gran Chimu

Squier

▲ El Olvido

Velarde

Bandelier

Uhle

Laberinto

Tschudi

Rivero

Chayhuac

Pacific Ocean

N

Moche Valley

1 Huaca del Sol
2 Huaca de la Luna
▲ Early Intermediate site
○ Early Horizon site

0 miles   3
0 kilometres   5

Huanchaco

Airport

Chan Chan

Laredo

Moche River

N

Trujillo

Buenos Aires

Pacific Ocean

Moche

Las Delicias

Salaverry

Huaca del Sol

Causeway

Ancient canal

Platform

Pyramid

Platform

N

0 yards   100
0 metres   100

Machu Picchu PERU

Inca town
15th–16th centuries AD

BIBLIOGRAPHY
Bingham, H., *Lost City of the Incas*, London, 1951

Reconstruction of Machu Picchu with the thatched roofs restored on buildings where these were known to have existed

This late Inca settlement was discovered by Hiram Bingham in 1912, and is, in his words, 'on an almost inaccessible ridge, 2,000 feet [610 m] above the Urubamba River. The ruins are of great beauty and magnificence and include palaces, baths, temples and about 150 houses. Carefully cut blocks of white granite, some of them 12 feet [3·7 m] long, were used in the construction of the walls.'

The site lies high in the Peruvian Andes, some 43 miles (70 km) north west of Cuzco, and its location on the top of a ridge renders it invisible from the Urubamba gorge below. The ridge is in fact a saddle between a block of highland and the towering pinnacle of Huaynac Picchu, around which the river describes a sharp bend. The surrounding area is covered in dense bush, some of it covering Pre-Colombian cultivation terraces, and these terraces reached almost to the centre of the site.

Machu Picchu is more of a village or small town than the 'lost city' it has become in the literature, but is thought to have been planned and built as a unit by mit'a labour working under the supervision of professional Inca architects. The buildings are of hard local granite, dressed with stone hammers and possible bronze chisels and axes, and fitted with such exactitude that the mortarless joints will rarely bear the insertion of a thin blade. This polygonal masonry is characteristic of the late Inca period, and varies in quality of surface dressing depending on its use in a building or retaining wall.

The saddle runs east–west, with a rise on both the north and south sides. That on the south is a steep rock which has been trimmed to provide a number of flat surfaces for buildings, particularly the Temple of the Three Windows, and the summit of the rock has been worked into the curious faceted block known as the Hitching-Post of the Sun. The flattish top of the ridge, which is fairly narrow, consists of

a number of small plazas, the largest and highest at the western end, the others stepping down a gentle slope to the north east, perhaps filling in a small stream valley that cuts back into the hillside. To the north of the plazas the broader northern rise is covered with a series of house blocks surrounded by terraces, and further terraces supporting houses descend the steep slope on the north side for a short distance. Bedrock outcrops in several places, and in most has been trimmed to a faceted form, although rarely brought down to floor level. Towards the eastern end of the site one such outcrop supports a round-walled building, and the rock itself has an enlarged and utilized fissure.

The houses which form the bulk of the buildings at Machu Picchu have stone walls with high steep gables. Stone pegs set into the outer gable wall were used to fasten the straw thatch, and the interior walls have a number of niches.

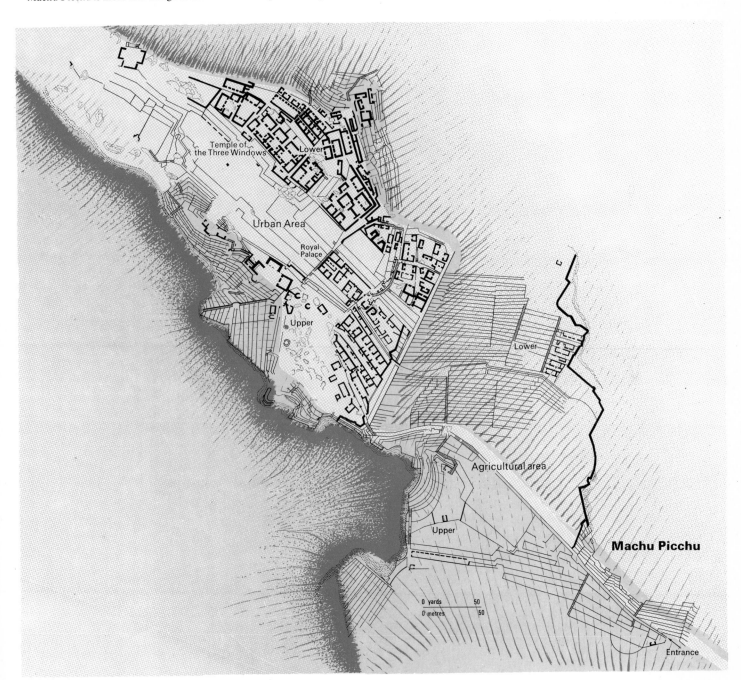

Cuzco PERU

Inca capital
AD 1430–1533

BIBLIOGRAPHY
Rowe, J. H., 'An Introduction to the Archaeology of Cuzco', *Papers of the Peabody Museum, Harvard University*, vol. 27, no. 2, Cambridge, Mass., 1944
Hemming, J., *The Conquest of the Incas*, London, 1970

The city of Cuzco was the capital of the Inca empire in the 15th and 16th centuries. It lies at the western end and head of a small but fertile valley on the eastern slope of the Peruvian Andes at just over 11,000 feet (3,080 m), on the Río Huatanay, a tributary of the Urubamba. The valley is surrounded by mountains of 13,000–16,000 feet (3,960–4,875 m), with a pass to the west into the plain of Anta, and the Inca and colonial cities were built on a glacial gravel fan of material washed down from the northern mountains. The local geology includes limestone, porphyry and basalt, all of which were used in the city.

The Inca capital, the form of which is partly preserved in the colonial layout, had a modified rectangular grid plan, each block being occupied by an inward-looking compound called a *cancha*. The walls surviving within the city range from superbly dressed and regularly coursed masonry through that with similarly high-quality dressing but irregular polygonal outline (the famous Stone of 12 Corners is of this type) to roughly trimmed but carefully fitted polygonal blocks: the entire range can be seen on the two sides of the street called Ahuacpinta, which runs along the eastern side of the Coricancha, the Golden Enclosure or Temple of the Sun (now the Monastery of Santo Domingo).

The Temple of the Sun was the oldest and most sacred of Inca shrines. It stands on a levelled piece of ground between two stream valleys, with a terrace built out over the slope and retained by the well-known curved wall that now supports the east end of the church of Santo Domingo. Around the monastery cloister a number of the halls of the temple enclosure survive in good condition to almost their original height, some 10 feet (3 m) above floor level. Some of the wall blocks retain the protuberances used for handling, and a number of channelled drains were cut through the eastern wall into Ahuacpinta street. The walls were faced with gold plates, which were removed by Pizarro's men in 1533.

The Plaza de Armas is the centre of colonial Cuzco, and stands on part of the main plaza of the Inca city. Many of the principal palaces and shrines stood in this area, and Inca *cancha* walls are preserved along many of the streets. The other important area of Inca ruins is on the hill to the north of the city, where they are not obscured by later building.

The principal structure on the hill is the fortress of Sacsayhuaman. This occupies a ridge overlooking the town, facing north on to a flat open area and separated from it by three lines of massive terraced walls with salients and re-entrant angles sheltering entrance doorways. On top of the ridge were three towers, the foundations of two of which remain, and the fortification walls continue around the steeply sloping southern side of the hill.

To the east of Sacsayhuaman is the amphitheatre of Kenko, the site also of the tomb of the great Inca Pachacuti, and to the north the baths of Tambo Machay.

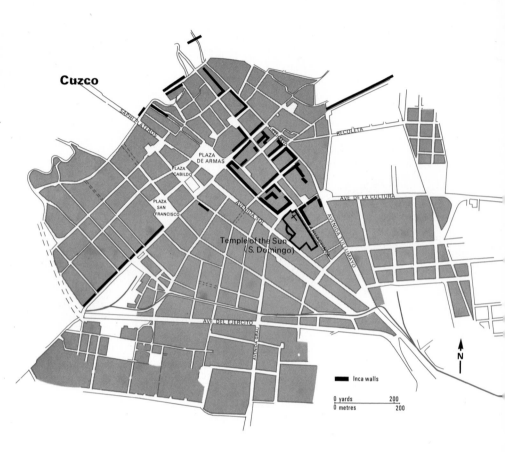

Cuzco

PLAZA DE ARMAS
PLAZA CABILDO
PLAZA SAN FRANCISCO
Temple of the Sun (S. Domingo)

Inca walls

0 yards 200
0 metres 200

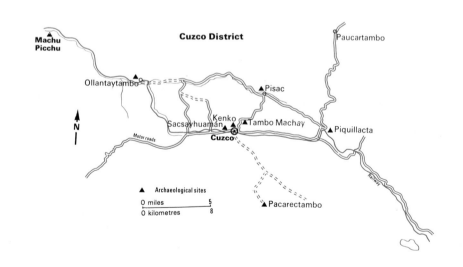

Cuzco District

Machu Picchu
Paucartambo
Ollantaytambo
Pisac
Sacsayhuaman
Kenko
Tambo Machay
Cuzco
Piquillacta
Motor roads
Pacarectambo
Railway

▲ Archaeological sites

0 miles 5
0 kilometres 8

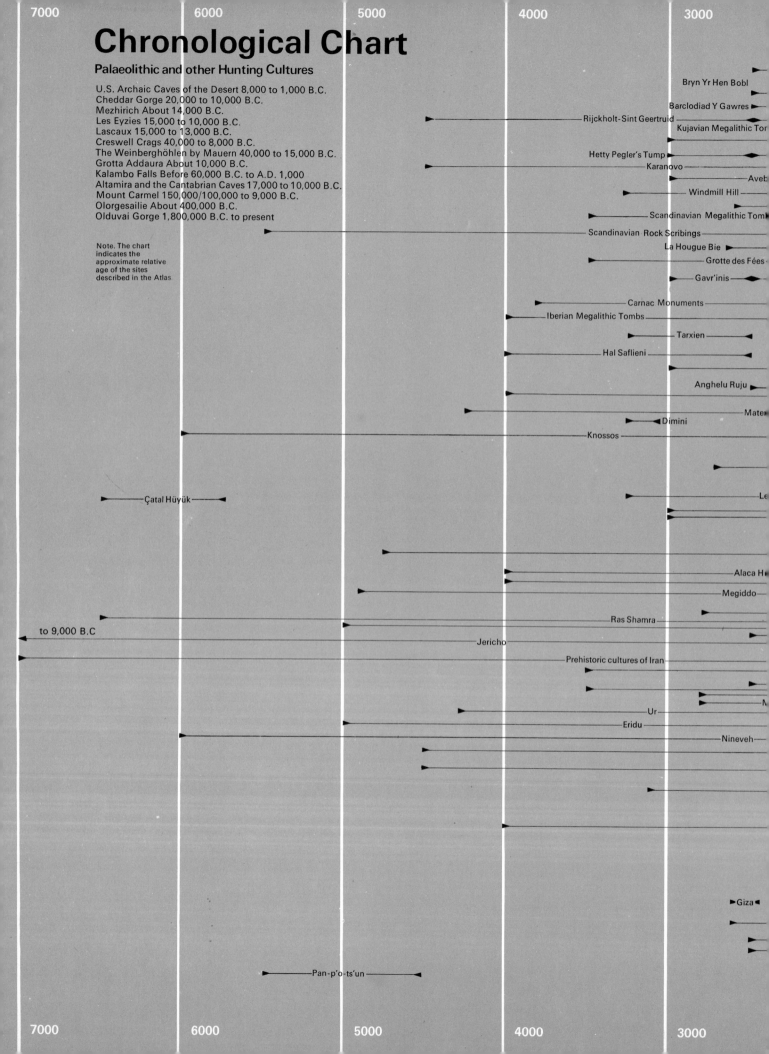

Chronological Chart

Palaeolithic and other Hunting Cultures

U.S. Archaic Caves of the Desert 8,000 to 1,000 B.C.
Cheddar Gorge 20,000 to 10,000 B.C.
Mezhirich About 14,000 B.C.
Les Eyzies 15,000 to 10,000 B.C.
Lascaux 15,000 to 13,000 B.C.
Creswell Crags 40,000 to 8,000 B.C.
The Weinberghöhlen by Mauern 40,000 to 15,000 B.C.
Grotta Addaura About 10,000 B.C.
Kalambo Falls Before 60,000 B.C. to A.D. 1,000
Altamira and the Cantabrian Caves 17,000 to 10,000 B.C.
Mount Carmel 150,000/100,000 to 9,000 B.C.
Olorgesailie About 400,000 B.C.
Olduvai Gorge 1,800,000 B.C. to present

Note. The chart
indicates the
approximate relative
age of the sites
described in the Atlas.

7000 6000 5000 4000 3000

Bryn Yr Hen Bobl
Barclodiad Y Gawres
Rijckholt-Sint Geertruid
Kujavian Megalithic Tor
Hetty Pegler's Tump
Karanovo
Aveb
Windmill Hill
Scandinavian Megalithic Tom
Scandinavian Rock Scribings
La Hougue Bie
Grotte des Fées
Gavr'inis
Carnac Monuments
Iberian Megalithic Tombs
Tarxien
Hal Saflieni
Anghelu Ruju
Mate
Dimini
Knossos
Le
Çatal Hüyük
Alaca H
Megiddo
Ras Shamra
to 9,000 B.C
Jericho
Prehistoric cultures of Iran
Ur
Eridu
Nineveh
Giza
Pan-p'o-ts'un

7000 6000 5000 4000 3000

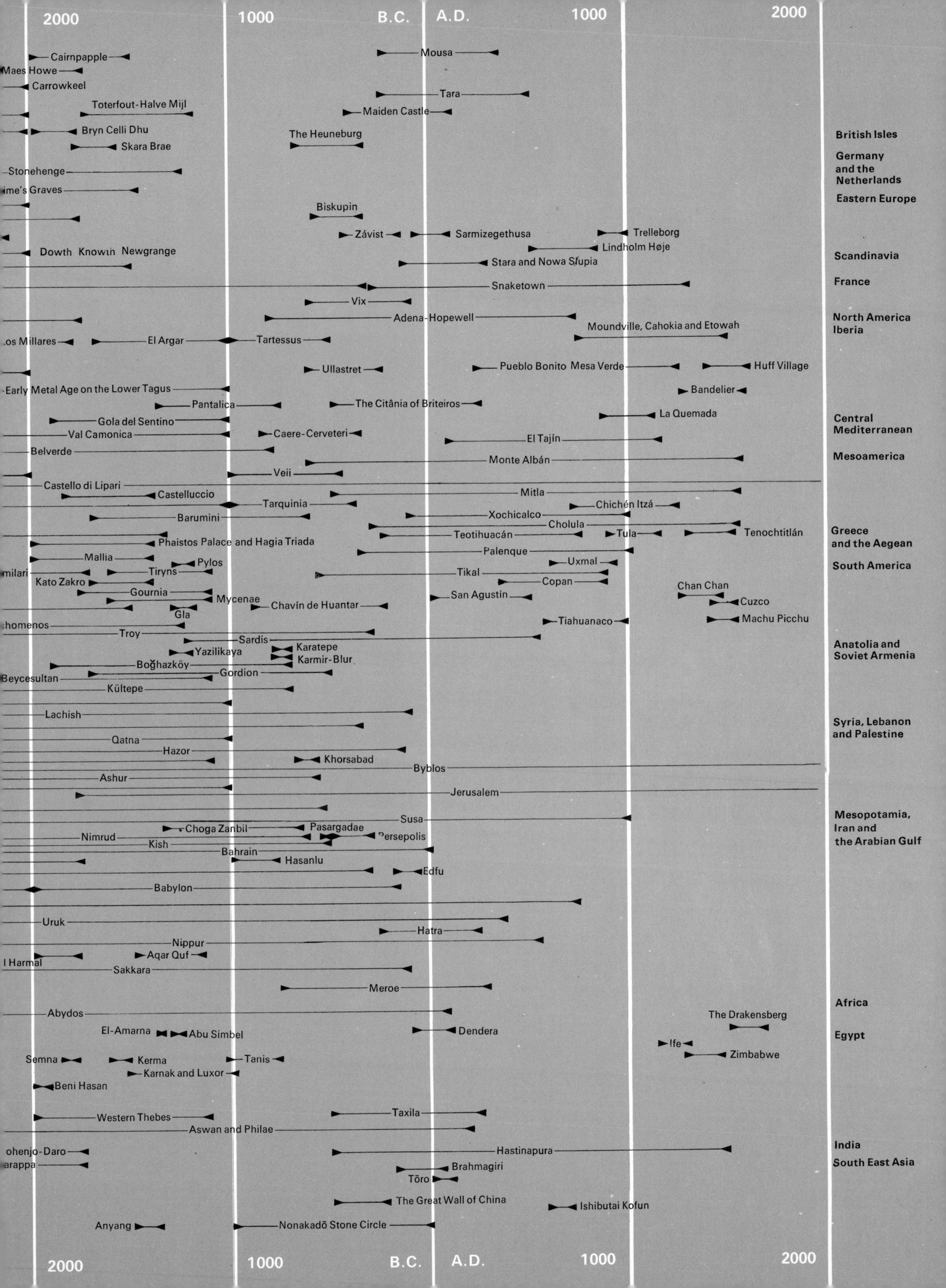

2000
1000
B.C.
A.D.
1000
2000
Cairnpapple
Mousa
Maes Howe
Carrowkeel
Tara
Toterfout-Halve Mijl
Maiden Castle
Bryn Celli Dhu
Skara Brae
The Heuneburg
British Isles
Germany and the Netherlands
Stonehenge
ime's Graves
Eastern Europe
Biskupin
Závist
Sarmizegethusa
Trelleborg
Lindholm Høje
Dowth
Knowth
Newgrange
Stara and Nowa Słupia
Scandinavia
Snaketown
France
Vix
Adena-Hopewell
North America
Iberia
Moundville, Cahokia and Etowah
os Millares
El Argar
Tartessus
Ullastret
Pueblo Bonito
Mesa Verde
Huff Village
Early Metal Age on the Lower Tagus
Bandelier
Pantalica
The Citânia of Briteiros
La Quemada
Gola del Sentino
Central Mediterranean
Val Camonica
Caere-Cerveteri
El Tajín
Belverde
Monte Albán
Mesoamerica
Veii
Castello di Lipari
Castelluccio
Mitla
Tarquinia
Chichén Itzá
Barumini
Xochicalco
Cholula
Teotihuacán
Tula
Tenochtitlán
Greece and the Aegean
Phaistos Palace and Hagia Triada
Palenque
Mallia
Uxmal
South America
Pylos
milari
Tiryns
Tikal
Kato Zakro
Copan
Gournia
Chan Chan
Mycenae
San Agustín
Chavín de Huantar
Cuzco
Gla
homenos
Tiahuanaco
Machu Picchu
Troy
Sardis
Anatolia and Soviet Armenia
Yazilikaya
Karatepe
Karmir-Blur
Boğhazköy
Gordion
Beycesultan
Kültepe
Lachish
Syria, Lebanon and Palestine
Qatna
Hazor
Khorsabad
Byblos
Ashur
Jerusalem
Susa
Mesopotamia, Iran and the Arabian Gulf
Choga Zanbil
Pasargadae
Nimrud
Persepolis
Kish
Bahrain
Hasanlu
Edfu
Babylon
Uruk
Hatra
Nippur
Aqar Quf
l Harmal
Sakkara
Meroe
Africa
Abydos
The Drakensberg
El-Amarna
Abu Simbel
Dendera
Egypt
Ife
Semna
Kerma
Tanis
Zimbabwe
Karnak and Luxor
Beni Hasan
Taxila
Western Thebes
Aswan and Philae
India
ohenjo-Daro
Hastinapura
South East Asia
arappa
Brahmagiri
Tōro
The Great Wall of China
Ishibutai Kofun
Anyang
Nonakadō Stone Circle
2000
1000
B.C.
A.D.
1000
2000

Glossary

acroterion: Stone pedestal set at the apex and sides of a pediment to support a statue.

apotroaic: Describes a charm or other object intended to avert misfortune and evil.

Archaic: An early stage in the evolution of high civilization. In Egypt the name is an alternative for the Early Dynastic, covering the first two dynasties (c. 3200–2800 BC); in Greece it is applied to the period c. 750–480 BC. See also under American Period Terminology below.

Australopithecines: The earliest genus of men, living in Lower and Middle Pleistocene times. It comprised a number of species and whether or not a particular fossil man should be assigned to the genus is often disputed. Typically they were short (about four feet – 1·2 m), with brains no larger than those of modern anthropoid apes and with many apelike cranial and facial characteristics. On the other hand the form and setting of their teeth were already approaching the human, and they walked upright. Nearly all the fossils have been found in southern and eastern Africa, but one has come to light in Israel. Some at least of the species of *Australopithecus* seem to have made the earliest pebble tools, and probably the most progressive were ancestral to the Pithecanthopines (*Homo erectus*).

barrow: An earthen mound covering a grave. In Britain a long form, usually with one end larger than the other, is characteristic of the Neolithic period. These were raised over multiple burials contained in some form of mortuary structure in perishable materials or over a megalithic chamber. Circular mounds were also often raised over megalithic chambers. Typical round barrows, however, often in the past called *tumuli*, are very much commoner and usually cover singly buried remains, either inhumed or cremated. In Britain and Europe the great majority date from the Bronze Age, but others, often of large size, may be Roman, Anglo-Saxon, Viking, Scythic Lydian etc.

Bronze Age: A period in which bronze, an alloy of copper and tin, was the economically significant material for tools and weapons. It can be said to have begun in the Middle East at the end of the 4th millennium BC and to have extended rapidly to Egypt, eastern Europe and eastward to the Indus Valley, more slowly further to the east and west. The term is not used in the Americas although bronze was used in Argentina and Peru from the first millennium BC until the Spanish conquest.

cairn: A burial mound or barrow built of stones rather than earth.

capstone: A stone used for roofing. The most distinctive are large blocks used to span the walls of dolmens, passage-graves and other megalithic tombs.

castro: Portuguese term for a hillfort or other ancient fortified site.

Carbon 14 dating: See Dating Systems below.

Chalcolithic: Applied to periods or cultures in which copper was in extensive use. In various parts of the Old World such a phase intervened between the Neolithic and Bronze Ages.

cist: In archaeology a term applied to a rectangular container made of stone slabs and used for burial – or, much more rarely, for storage.

Classic: Most commonly applied to fully mature Graeco-Roman civilization, but see also under American Period Terminology below.

Copper Age: See Chalcolithic.

corbelling: A method of roofing stone chambers. At the top of the wall each subsequent course of stones oversails the one below until the opening is small enough to be spanned by a capstone.

corvée: Forced labour for an overlord.

cuneiform: Writing by means of wedge-shaped impressions or incisions. It was first developed in Sumeria during the first half of the 3rd millennium BC when the earlier pictograms were stylized through the use of cut reeds impressed on soft clay. It was adapted to write Akkadian, Assyrian, Hittite etc., and at Ugarit even to an alphabetic script. For public inscriptions cuneiform could be carved on close-grained stone.

cyclopean: Masonry built with huge blocks; characteristically close-fitting but irregular.

dolmen: A name, probably derived from Cornish tolmen, much used by early antiquaries to describe megalithic tombs denuded of their covering mounds. Now generally applied to relatively small, closed megalithic chambers, such as the *dysser* of Scandinavia.

Early Horizon: See under American Period Terminology below.

Early Intermediate: See under American Period Terminology below.

Formative: See under American Period Terminology below.

gallery grave: A chamber tomb with parallel sides – as distinct from the separate passage and chamber of the passage grave. Typically megalithic, but sometimes cut in the rock. In some regions divided by septal slabs or with side chambers opening from the gallery. All belong to the Neolithic period, but probably cover a rather later range of dates than do the passage graves.

halberd: In archaeological usage a bronze weapon with a blade set at right-angles to the top of the shaft. Found in the European Early Bronze Age, most frequently in Ireland and central Europe.

Hallstatt: Name given to a period covering the Late Bronze and Early Iron Age of central Europe. In western Europe it is applied to the early Iron Age from 7th–5th centuries BC.

Homo erectus: See under Pithecanthropine.

intaglio: A design cut into the surface of a hard stone. Particularly used for seal stones in order to obtain impression standing in relief.

Iron Age: The third stage of the Three Age system (see Stone Age), in which iron superseded bronze as the dominant metal for tools and weapons. Iron was first worked in Asia Minor and was a monopoly of the Hittites until their collapse in c. 1200 BC allowed the blacksmith's secrets to spread. In parts of Africa an Iron Age followed immediately upon the Stone Age: in pre-Columbian America iron-working was unknown. (See also Hallstatt and La Tène)

karum: An Akkadian word originally meaning 'quay' then extended to the market place by the quay, and hence to a trading post and the corps of merchants of a city.

kiva: An underground chamber in the village of the Pueblo indians of the American south west. Used by the mens' societies for ceremonial meetings and other religious purposes. Commonly circular, though occasionally rectangular, they are entered by a projecting ladder through an opening in the flat roof.

lanceolate: Like a spearhead in shape, narrow and tapering towards each end. In archaeology usually applied to flaked stone blades of laurel-leaf form.

La Tène: The second period of the European Iron Age. It refers essentially to Celtic cultures, beginning in the mid 5th century BC and ending with the Roman conquest of their various regions.

Late Intermediate: See under American Period Terminology below.

lintel: A horizontal stone slab or wooden block forming the top of a door or window.

loess: Fine, wind-blown soil mainly carried from the edge of ice sheets and glaciers and deposited on surrounding land.

marl: A soil mainly composed of clay and carbonate of lime. Valuable as a fertilizer.

mastaba: Arabic name given to a type of tomb prevalent in Early Dynastic and Old Kingdom Egypt. The burial was usually at the bottom of a shaft, while the superstructure built of mudbrick or stone or a combination of the two contained a chapel, a statue of the deceased and sometimes large numbers of rooms. The outer walls sloped slightly inwards, and the form certainly contributed to the origin of the royal pyramid. At first kings as well as their nobles and officials were buried in mastabas, but from Dynasty III Pharaohs had their pyramids and the mastaba's of their eminent subjects were built round them.

megalithic: Built of large, natural or roughly dressed stones.

Characteristic are chambered tombs, including gallery graves, passage graves and dolmens, most of them dating from neolithic times. Circles of standing stones, commonest in Britain, tend to be rather later: Early to Middle Bronze Age. Alignments of standing stones are probably of much the same date as the circles.

megaron: A hall of a rather narrow rectangular plan; the side walls project at the entrance front to form a porch, sometimes pillared. The hall usually has a central hearth, and an inner doorway leading into one or more storerooms. Buildings of this type date far back into prehistoric times on both sides of the Aegean, but are best known as the great painted halls of Mycenaean princes; the name comes from Homer.

menhir: A single large standing stone.

mesa: A steep-sided, flat-topped hill or tableland. In the American south west used for settlements in pre-Columbian times. Some are still occupied by the Pueblo indians.

Mesolithic: The 'Middle Stone' Age, a term applied to the period of transition between the Palaeolithic and Neolithic periods when the old hunting and collecting way of life had to be adapted to new conditions at the close of the last glaciation, about 8000 BC. In south-west Asia farming came too soon for a clearly established Mesolithic, but round the Mediterranean and in Europe it lasted much longer: in the west and north until towards the end of the 4th millennium BC. The equipment was designed for fishing and fowling as well as hunting and often included many tiny flints, or microliths, that were set in wooden shafts and hafts.

microlith: See under Mesolithic.

midden: A rubbish heap, in prehistoric times usually consisting of heaps of bones and shells with a mingling of potsherds, tools and other discards. Some of the largest shell middens were accumulated by shore-dwellers in Mesolithic Denmark.

Middle Horizon: See under American Period Terminology

monolithic: Made from a single block of stone.

Neanderthal man: An extinct breed which, with Neanderthaloid variants, was dominant through much of the habitable regions of Europe, Asia and Africa during the last interglacial and the first half of the final (Würm) glaciation. These men were characterized in varying degrees by low foreheads and massive brow ridges, lack of chin and rather clumsy limbs. Although the vault of the skull was thick and low its breadth gave room for a large brain. Neanderthal men were makers of the Late Middle Palaeolithic Mousterian cultures. Their name comes from that of a valley near Dusseldorf where one of the first skulls was found.

necropolis: A city of the dead: applicable to any large cemetery.

Neolithic: The 'New Stone' Age, the latest phase of the Stone Age when agriculture and stock-breeding displaced hunting. Farming generally led to a more settled life in villages; the crafts of potting and weaving were invented; axes and other implements of polished stone were commonly used. The Neolithic Age began in the Near East before 7000 BC; it spread east and west and lasted for varying lengths of time according to the date for the introduction of metallurgy. In western and northern Europe it extended into the 2nd millennium BC. While the term is still often employed in this chronological sense (with dates varying from region to region) it is now more usually indicative of a stone-using, farming way of life. In this sense it can be said that the pre-Columbian farming cultures of the New World were Neolithic.

oculus: A decorative and religious motif symbolizing an eye. Often apotroaic.

oppidum: A Roman word for a town, usually an administrative centre, applied by Julius Caesar to large Celtic settlements in Gaul. It is now used for all such settlements, commonly of hill-fort type, in Celtic lands throughout Europe. These *oppida* were the first true towns north of the Alps.

orthostat: An upright block of stone, often part of megalithic walling.

268

Palaeolithic: The 'Old Stone' Age, an immensely long cultural period roughly corresponding to the Pleistocene Age of geology. It is divided into a Lower Palaeolithic beginning with the earliest pebble tools of nearly two million years ago and extending to include the whole of the Acheulian hand-axe cultures and contemporary flake cultures; a Middle Palaeolithic dominated by the Mousterian and related flake cultures; and an Upper Palaeolithic beginning about 35,000 BC. The Upper Palaeolithic saw the ascendancy of *Homo sapiens*, and a rapid advance to high hunting cultures, with the invention of the spearthrower and then the bow, and of flint industries based on narrow, parallel sided 'blades'. Hunter artists created engraving, sculpture and cave painting. The classic cultures of this era as first established in Europe are the Chatelperronian, Aurignacian; Gravettian; Solutrean and Magdalenian. Round 8000 BC the blade cultural traditions gave rise to those of the Mesolithic Age.

Palaeo-Indian: See under American Period Terminology below.

passage grave: Tomb chamber, usually megalithic, approached by a narrower passageway. Usually covered by a long or circular mound. See also under megalithic.

pithecanthropine: The type of early men who broadly succeeded the Australopithecines during the Lower Palaeolithic. Now more properly recognized as belonging to the genus *Homo* and referred to as *Homo erectus*.

pithecine: Related to the genus of apes.

Pleistocene: The geological period corresponding with what is sometimes called the Great Ice Age. It began more or less than 2,000,000 years ago when increasing cold led to changing species of many living forms, including elephants, horses and ox. The latter part of the period, perhaps after 700,000 years ago, was divided by a succession of glaciations divided by warmer or dryer interglacials. In the widely used alpine system there were the Gunz, Mindel, Riss and Würm (see table below). In North America the final glaciation, corresponding to the Würm, when man first entered the continent, is known as the Wisconsin. The Pleistocene ended about 10,000 years ago with the final retreat of the ice; it was succeeded by the Holocene or recent period.

podium: A solid platform or pedestal, often the base for a building.

pollen analysis: See Dating Systems below.

Post-classic: See under American Period Terminology below.

potassium-argon: See Dating Systems below.

Preclassic: See under American Period Terminology below.

quern: A handmill for grinding grain into flour. In the earlier form a smaller stone (muller) was pushed up and down on a much larger one; later a circular rotary mill was devised in which a concave upper stone with an attached handle was turned on a convex nether one.

radiocarbon: See Dating Systems below.

repoussé: Embossed metal work in which the relief has been pushed up from the back of the sheet.

revetment: A containing wall of stone, wood, turves etc. to support the vertical or steep face of an earthen rampart or ditch.

sarcophagus: A coffin or sepulchral chest of stone or terracotta, typically carved or inscribed and intended to be exposed to view. In Egypt it was the outermost container, with one or more wooden coffins and a mummy case within.

sarsen: Blocks of sandstone found on the surface of the chalk downs of Wiltshire, being the remnants of a Tertiary deposit. Best known for their use in Stonehenge.

scarcement: The set-back of a wall or embankment to form a ledge.

septal slab: A stone dividing a tomb chamber into separate compartments.

sherd: A broken fragment of pottery.

skeuomorph: An article which in its shape or decoration imitates an original made in a different material or by a different technique.

souterrain: A subterranean, stone-lined gallery common in Ireland and the west and north of Britain. They are usually associated with a house or settlement and seem to have been used for storage, or, on occasion as refuges. Most date from the last centuries BC or a little later. In Cornwall known as fogous.

stela: An upright slab bearing an inscription or design. Pl. stelae.

Stone Age: First in the Three Age System of Stone, Bronze and Iron. See also under Palaeolithic; Mesolithic; Neolithic.

stupa: Buddhist monument consisting of a circular mound with a dome-like casing of stone, often tiled. Intended to contain relics of holy men or of Buddha himself.

tell: A mound formed by the accumulation of city rubbish. Most consist very largely of the remains of mudbrick buildings that have collapsed and been levelled to make way for fresh building above them. Tells may be over a hundred feet high and span thousands of years from base to summit. Of Arabic origin.

tenoned: Joined by a knob or tenon fitting into a socket or mortise.

terramara: Local name for a mound of dark earth formed by the accumulated rubbish of a type of Bronze Age village found in the Po valley of northern Italy. Pl. terremare.

tholos: A beehive-shaped tomb chamber, the vault formed by corbelling. In the finest and most typical examples, such as the royal tombs at Mycenae, the corbelling is trimmed to form a smooth surface, and the ornamental doorway is approached by a masonry-lined, horizontal passage or *dromos*.

travertine: A water-deposited, hard, pale, limestone excellent for building.

tree-ring: See Dating Systems below.

trilithon: A megalithic construction of two upright stones spanned at the top by a third – the lintel stone.

tumulus: See barrow.

votive: An offering vowed to a divinity, generally with the intention of securing a favour or expressing gratitude for one received.

ziggurat: A temple tower, rectangular and sometimes square in plan, rising stage by smaller stage to support the temple building on its summit. The arrangement of the stairways leading from one stage to another varied greatly from one monument to another. The main mass was of mudbrick, the outer shell usually of fired brick. The ziggurat originated with the Sumerians, evolving out of the relatively simple, though lofty, temple platform of prehistoric times. It was adopted by the Elamites, Babylonians, Assyrians and other inheritors of Sumerian culture. The ziggurat at Ur was known as the Hill of Heaven and was planted with trees; one of the last and most famous was the 'Tower of Babel' in Nebuchadnezzar's Babylon. The tower was the high place of the god, the link between earth and heaven.

American period terminology:

In American archaeology the use of names for major cultural divisions, the equivalent of Palaeolithic, Mesolithic etc. in the Old World, is different for North, Central and South America and is variable even within those great regions. The only name which can confidently be used for all three is Palaeo-Indian (or sometimes Early Hunter) for the big-game hunting cultures prevalent from the first arrival of man down to about 7000 BC. In North America this is followed by the Archaic with cultures dependent on small game hunting and plant collecting, and lasting until about 1000 BC. The period following, when food production began, can be known as the Formative, although this term was coined for cultures leading up to high civilization – never achieved in North America. Sometimes, therefore, this period is named only after its regional cultures such as the Burial Mound, Temple Mound and Woodland in the east and the Hohokam, Anasazi etc. in the south west.

In Mesoamerica the system is clearly defined. The Palaeo-Indian period is followed down to about 2000 BC by a phase of Incipient Agriculture before the true Formative, or Preclassic, when the evolution of agriculture and the crafts was preparing for the civilizations of the Classic period. This began in about AD 300 and lasted until about AD 900, when the southern Mayan civilization collapsed. The succeeding Post-classic period ended with the Aztec imperialist age.

In South America the usage is very variable, but a nomenclature identical with that of Mesoamerica is sometimes applied. In addition the Formative may be divided into a Cultist and Experimenter; the Classic can be known as the Florescent or Mastercraftsman; the Post-classic subdivided into Expansionist, City Builder and finally, representing the Inca empire, Imperialist. Parallel with this runs a nomenclature for Peru based upon cultural styles; an Early Horizon beginning in 900 BC dominated by Chavín culture; an Early Intermediate beginning in about 200 BC with the establishment of regional styles and the earliest cities; a Middle Horizon beginning in AD 600 and dominated by the Tiahuanaco cultural style; beginning *c.* AD 1000, a Later Intermediate with the Chimu and other kingdoms which lasted until 1476 when the kingdoms were absorbed into the Inca Empire.

Dating Systems

pollen analysis: The estimation of the relative proportions of ancient pollen grains from various plants and trees present in peat, silts and other suitable deposits. This makes it possible to establish the sequence of vegetation change in each region, due to climate, human interference through forest clearance and the like. Once a vegetational-cum-climatic sequence has been established individual antiquities can be approximately dated according to the pollen content of the stratum in which they are found.

potassium-argon: Refers to a method of dating dependant on the fact that the isotope K^{40} of the potassium in the earth's crust decays at a known rate to argon A^{40}. It can be applied to certain volcanic minerals, for in these all argon will have been given off when they were molten so that any found therein will have formed since that time. The half life of K^{40} being 1,300 million years the amount of argon present is too small to be measured up to about a million years ago, but after that provides a rough dating. The method has been applied to early Pleistocene volcanic deposits, particularly to the lava flows in the Olduvai Gorge.

radiocarbon: A convenient shorthand term for a dating method also often referred to as Carbon 14. C^{14} is the radioactive isotope of the inert C^{12} and both are present in identical proportions in all living organisms. When the organism dies C^{14} begins to disintegrate at a fixed rate and is not replenished. Analysis of the proportion of C^{14} to C^{12} in the remains will therefore give an approximation to the date when the organism died. The method can be used back to about 50,000 years ago but becomes increasingly inaccurate through the latter part of the period. The range of probable inaccuracy is given as + or – so many years. Another type of inaccuracy appears to have been revealed by checking with tree-ring dates. It seems that before about 2000 years ago more C^{14} was occurring naturally so that carbon ^{14} analysis before that time gives dates that are too low. According to this check C^{14} dates of *c.* 1500 BC should be about 300 years earlier; those of *c.* 3000 BC as much as 500–1000 years earlier. The materials most successfully used for radiocarbon dating are bone, charcoal, shell and natural fibres (textiles).

tree-ring dating: This method of absolute dating, also known as dendrochronology, is based on the fact that the annual growth in the girth of tree trunks and branches, appearing as rings when sectioned, varies from year to year within given areas. A series covering several years, therefore, gives a recognizable pattern, and by matching a number of overlaps (the youth of one tree corresponding to the old age of another) it has proved possible to establish sequences covering thousands of years. A piece of timber found in an archaeological context can then be assigned to its place in the sequence. Dendrochronology has been greatly strengthened by the employment of the bristle pine of California. Individual trees of this species live to an immense age, and have made it possible to extend the system back to about 5000 BC.

Approximate Mean Dates of Glacial and Interglacial Periods

	European	North American	Dates
1st Glaciation	Günz	Nebraskan	600,000–550,000 years ago
1st Interglacial	Günz-Mindel	Aftonian	550,000–475,000 years ago
2nd Glaciation	Mindel	Kansan	475,000–425,000 years ago
2nd Interglacial	Mindel-Riss	Yarmouth	425,000–225,000 years ago
3rd Glaciation	Riss	Illinoian	225,000–180,000 years ago
3rd Interglacial	Riss-Würm	Sangamon	180,000–70,000 years ago
4th Glaciation	Würm	Wisconsin	70,000–10,000 years ago

Index

Where more than one reference to a site is given, the main one is in italics.